SECOND EDITION

ISLAMIC CAPITAL MARKETS

A Comparative Approach

SECOND EDITION

ISLAMIC CAPITAL MARKETS

A Comparative Approach

Obiyathulla Ismath Bacha
Abbas Mirakhor

INCEIF, The Global University of Islamic Finance, Malaysia

World Scientific

NEW JERSEY • LONDON • SINGAPORE • BEIJING • SHANGHAI • HONG KONG • TAIPEI • CHENNAI • TOKYO

Published by

World Scientific Publishing Co. Pte. Ltd.
5 Toh Tuck Link, Singapore 596224
USA office: 27 Warren Street, Suite 401-402, Hackensack, NJ 07601
UK office: 57 Shelton Street, Covent Garden, London WC2H 9HE

Library of Congress Cataloging-in-Publication Data
Names: Ismath Bacha, Obiyathulla, author. | Mirakhor, Abbas, author.
Title: Islamic capital markets : a comparative approach / Obiyathulla Ismath Bacha and Abbas Mirakhor, INCEIF - The Global University of Islamic Finance, Malaysia.
Description: Second edition. | New Jersey : World Scientific, 2018.
Identifiers: LCCN 2018041660 | ISBN 9789813274631 (hardcover) | ISBN 9789811204012 (softcover)
Subjects: LCSH: Capital market (Islamic law) | Capital market--Islamic countries. | Investments--Religious aspects--Islam.
Classification: LCC HG3368.A6 I87 2018 | DDC 332/.0415088297--dc23
LC record available at https://lccn.loc.gov/2018041660

British Library Cataloguing-in-Publication Data
A catalogue record for this book is available from the British Library.

First published 2018
Reprinted 2020

For any available supplementary material, please visit
https://www.worldscientific.com/worldscibooks/10.1142/11109#t=suppl

Desk Editor: Karimah Samsudin

Typeset by Stallion Press
Email: enquiries@stallionpress.com

Printed in Singapore

CONTENTS

LIST OF FIGURES

LIST OF TABLES

LIST OF BOXES

ABOUT THE AUTHORS

Professor Dr. Obiyathulla Ismath Bacha is currently Professor of Finance INCEIF. Prior to joining INCEIF, he has held several key positions at the International Islamic University Malaysia, including as Director of the university's Management Center. Professor Obiyathulla began his working career as a Credit Officer at Malayan Banking Berhad. On completing his doctoral studies, he was appointed an Assistant Professor of Finance at Boston University, where he taught at both the MBA and undergraduate levels. Professor Obiyathulla was President of the Malaysian Finance Association for five years, from 2013 to 2017. He has also been a trainer at several institutions in Malaysia, such as the Securities Commission and Bank Negara Malaysia. Internationally, he has conducted training programs in Islamic Capital Markets at the University of Luxembourg where he is an Adjunct Professor, The Chinese University of Hong Kong, Waseda University, Japan, Seoul National University, Korea, and several other institutions in Turkey. He has published scholarly articles in numerous local and international journals and has presented papers at several international and Islamic finance conferences. He is also author of a course textbook on Financial Derivatives, currently in its fourth edition. Professor Obiyathulla is Advisor to Great Eastern Life Assurance Malaysia for its Shari'ah compliant products, and Member of the Shariah Committee for SABANA, Singapore's first Islamic REIT. He had also been on HSBC Amanah's Shariah Committee as Finance expert for seven years. Professor Obiyathulla has undertaken Consulting Projects on Islamic Capital Markets for the World Bank, IDB/IFSB, and the UNESCAP. He received his Doctor of Business Administration (Finance), Master of Business Administration (High Honours), and Master of Arts (Economics) from Boston University, and Bachelor of Social Science from the Science University of Malaysia in Penang.

Dr Abbas Mirakhor is a graduate of the Kansas State University, U.S.A., where he received his Bachelor, Master, and PhD Degrees in Economics. In 1968, he started his academic career with University of Alabama, U.S.A. With the exception of a two-year stint at the AzZahara University in Tehran, Iran, throughout his academic career, Dr Abbas has worked as a Professor of Economics at the University of Alabama, Alabama A&M University, and the Florida Institute of Technology. In 1984, he joined the IMF in Washington DC as an economist. He spent 24 years with the IMF, serving as the organisation's Executive Director and Dean of the Executive Board, retiring in 2008.

Dr Abbas was conferred the "Order of Companion of Volta" for service to Ghana by the President of Ghana in 2005. In 2003, he received the Islamic Development Bank Annual Prize for Research in Islamic Economics, which he shared with Dr Mohsin Khan, another well-known economist at the IMF. The President of Pakistan conferred him the "Quaid-e Azam" star for service to Pakistan in 1997. He has published books, papers, and research articles on a wide range of areas including microeconomic theory, mathematical economics, and Islamic economics.

PREFACE

This second edition is the result of numerous additions and a substantive revision of the first edition published in 2013. While the rapid growth of the Islamic Capital Market (ICM) over the intervening years is reason enough for the needed changes, we have also included the many changes suggested by students and especially instructors using the text. The most obvious change is the addition of two new chapters. The first new chapter (Chapter 8) extends previous material on *sukuk*. Titled "Issues in Sukuk design and Trading", the chapter examines the more complex *sukuk* structures, describes the latest developments in *sukuk* design and explores potential new structures. The second new chapter (Chapter 15) examines the potential role of capital markets in addressing a key contemporary issue; that of rising inequality. In addition to these new chapters, every other chapter has had revisions, some more so than others. Additional problems have been added to the end-of-chapter questions and problems in all chapters. A final key change is the additional use of vignettes as illustrative boxes within the chapters.

This book is the result of my efforts in designing and teaching the Islamic Capital Markets (ICM) course at INCEIF. What began as class handouts and brief notes evolved first into the ICM course module for the Chartered Islamic Finance Professional (CIFP) at INCEIF. Subsequently, with input from my colleague and mentor, Dr. Abbas Mirakhor, that course module was developed into a full-blown textbook on Islamic capital markets.

The book covers the spectrum of capital market products, institutions, and markets, encompassing debt, equity, derivatives, and foreign exchange markets. Though we have tried to be global in orientation, by necessity, the book uses Malaysian examples, largely because Malaysia has been the pioneer in Islamic capital market development, and has put in place the full range of ICM products and institutions. Wherever possible, we have used examples from other countries such as Bahrain, the UAE, Turkey, Sudan, Saudi Arabia, and Pakistan.

Although the book is designed for a master's level course in capital markets, it can be used for similar courses in professional programs and at the advance undergraduate level. In ensuring the theoretical rigor necessary for a graduate level course, some amount of quantitative models and techniques are used. We have, however, tried to keep these to a minimum. As is evident from early on, we have tried to build the intuition behind the models and techniques. The material is written in an easy-to-read manner.

What is unique about this book is the combined coverage of both the conventional and Islamic version of instruments. For example, Chapter 4 discusses the conventional money markets while the subsequent chapter, Chapter 5, discusses the Islamic Interbank Money Market. In similar fashion, the bond market is covered in Chapter 6, while in Chapter 7, it is the market for *sukuk*. This arrangement not only enables easy comparison for readers but, more importantly, provides students with a complete picture of capital markets. This is important because ICM does not operate in isolation or exclusively. In most countries, ICM operates with or complements conventional capital markets. As teachers, we felt that the few ICM books currently available, by focusing solely on ICM products, miss the bigger picture. This handicaps students who might otherwise not get exposure to the larger and certainly more sophisticated conventional products. As these products have evolved over a long period, understanding them enables students to better understand and appreciate the design of their Islamic variant. This combined approach also enables the blending of the theoretical rigor behind conventional products with the *Shari'ah* compliance of Islamic finance products.

Overview of Contents

The book begins with an introductory chapter on founding thoughts of markets, asset prices, risk, uncertainty, and risk sharing. The risk sharing philosophy runs throughout the book. The first three chapters provide the foundation. Chapters 4 through Chapter 13 examine each ICM or conventional market and/or products. The final two chapters in the book examine macro issues such as the role of government in developing capital markets and how capital markets can be a means to address rising inequality.

Additional Materials

For instructors using the book, the following two supporting materials are available:

1. PowerPoint slides for each chapter.
2. Fully worked out solutions to all end-of-chapter questions and problems.

ACKNOWLEDGMENTS

In producing this book, we have benefited from many people. At least three batches of my students at INCEIF have had to go through the inconvenience of working with incomplete material and providing feedback, before the first edition was produced. Subsequent batches of students at INCEIF and elsewhere have provided feedback as users. Faculty who had used the first edition have also provided very useful feedback and suggestions. We are thankful to all of them.

Several of my graduate students have helped me directly as Research Assistants for this second edition. They are Mahmoud Mantai, Areef Ahmed, and Ndeye Djiba Ndiaye; our sincere thanks to each of them. Finally, we thank the editorial and production staff of World Scientific Publishing Co., especially Karimah Samsudin, of the Singapore headquarters.

Chapter 1

FOUNDING THOUGHTS: ADAM SMITH, CAPITALISM, AND ISLAMIC FINANCE

Topics in this Chapter

1.1 The Roots: The Economy, Real and Financial Sectors, Risk and Islamic Finance
1.2 Uncertainty and Risk
1.3 Why Do Uncertainty and Risk Exist?
1.4 Types of Risk
1.5 Risk in Real and Financial Sectors
1.6 Financial System of Capitalism: The Foundations
1.7 Smith and Arrow
1.8 Smith and Ethical Rules
1.9 An Arrow–Debreu Economy
1.10 What Happened to Smith–Arrow Risk-Sharing Ideal?
1.11 Can Economics Explain a Positive Predetermined Rate of Interest?
1.12 Islamic Finance: The Foundations
1.13 Islamic Rules Governing Exchange
1.14 Islamic Financial Market and Instruments
1.15 Islamic Finance Industry at the Present

Chapter Objective

This chapter is designed to introduce students to the conceptual basics of the linkage between the real and financial sectors. On completing this chapter, you should have a good understanding of the framework and theory of capitalism and a comparative understanding of the foundations of Islamic financial system

Key Terms		
Arrow-Debreu model	globalization	real sector
capitalism	intermediation	risk-sharing
complete contracts	invisible hand	Theory of Moral Sentiments
complete markets	markets and exchange	transparency
contracts and trusts	property rights	uncertainty and risks
financial sector	*Qur'an* and *Sunnah*	

1.1 The Roots: The Economy, Real and Financial Sectors, Risk and Islamic Finance

This book is about capital markets, a vital part of any economy. As Chapter 2 explains, an economy can be thought of as being composed of a real sector and a financial sector. The former is where goods and services are produced. The financial sector, on the other hand, facilitates real sector activities through provision of financing.

In any society, there are "surplus units", i.e., those who save surpluses remaining from their income after expenditures. There are also those who are "deficit units" in the sense that they are either spending more than the income they earn or are in need of funds to complete or initiate projects in the real sector of the economy. The important function of the financial sector of an economy is to act as an intermediate between these surplus and deficit units. It does so by providing short-term funds in the money market and medium-to-long-term funds through the capital market. In effect, the financial sector allows the surplus units to postpone their expenditure plans while making it possible for the deficit units to bring their expenditure plans forward. Both do so through the money and capital markets.

Up to the 1970s, the primary function of capital markets was to act as an intermediate for surplus funds by channeling them to investment, i.e., to create additional capital (capital formation) in the real sector of the economy. This, in turn, created additional employment and income. This is the economic understanding of the concept of investment. In day-to-day conversation, however, the word "investment" refers to purchases of any asset instrument that represents a flow of future income. For example, it may refer to purchases of already existing bonds or shares of stocks. This is not an investment in the economic sense but a transfer of ownership of existing assets, a process that does not necessarily lead to creating additional productive capacity and, thereby, additional employment and income.

Since the 1980s, much of the growth of capital markets has been attributed to a rapid increase in the latter types of transactions to the point that only a very small portion of the large volume of transactions in capital markets end up in new capital formation. In fact, a famous innovator and major market participant calls this type of ownership transfer "speculation", and considers that there is now a "clash of cultures" of investment and speculation in the market (Bogle, 2012). The difference between the two is that investment expands capital formation and increases employment and income, but speculation does not. Investment increases the income of the investor, jobholders, and households, while speculation increases the income of the asset holders (usually the rich).

What has become painfully clear during the post-2007/2008 financial crisis is that how well a financial sector performs its primary function of intermediation determines the stability of the financial sector and, consequently, that of the entire economy. Many economists believe that a major underlying cause of the crisis was that the relation between finance and real sector activities has become increasingly weakened in the last four decades.[1] Financial sector has grown much more rapidly than the real sector and has taken a life of its own; the sectors have decoupled. This phenomenon, driven by speculation, is referred to as financialization of the economy.[2] A crucial auxiliary function of the financial sector is to provide ways and means by which members of the society manage financial risks they face. Instruments developed in the financial sector are designed to perform this function. An understanding of risk is elemental to comprehending the role and functioning of the financial sector.

1.2 Uncertainty and Risk

Decision-making is one of the most fundamental capabilities of humans. Actions follow decisions. Individuals have to make decisions and take actions that affect their own as well as others' lives at some point in the future. However, the future is, for the most part, unknown, and therefore unpredictable and uncertain. Uncertainty is a fact of human existence as we all live on the brink of a future about which our information is dominated by ignorance. Facing an unknown and often unknowable future, individuals still have to make decisions and take actions. This they do by forming expectations about the payoffs to alternative courses of action.

Expectations can be formed by individuals objectively or subjectively. In the first case, the expected payoffs are based on known probability techniques, as in the insurance industry. Alternatively, individuals can base their expectations of payoffs to alternative decisions based on their own or others' personal experiences. Either way the expected outcomes will form expressions in terms of the probability of occurrences of the consequences of actions. Through this process, uncertainty is converted to risk. Therefore, risk is a consequence of choice under uncertainty. It is uncertainty about the future that makes human lives prone to risk.

Risk would arise because the decision-maker has little to no information regarding which state of affairs will materialize in the future. The individual nevertheless makes a decision and takes appropriate action based on expectations. Risk can also arise because the decision-maker does not or cannot consider all possible states or outcomes that may prevail in the future. There may be so much missing information that it is impossible to form expectations about payoffs to decisions and actions. This situation is referred to as ambiguity, which may lead to paralysis in decision-making. One way of dealing with ambiguity caused by missing information is patience; postponing decisions until more information becomes available.

1.3 Why Do Uncertainty and Risk Exist?

How can uncertainty and its overwhelming influence in human life be explained? Why is life subjected to so much uncertainty? These are particularly significant questions for those believing in "intelligent design" or in a Supreme Creator. Why is uncertainty created for humans? Bartholomeu (2008, p. 230) suggests that "risk is a necessary ingredient for full human development. It provides the richness and diversity of experience necessary to develop our skills and personalities". Moreover, he argues (2008, p. 200, p. 239) that the "development of human freedom requires that there be sufficient space for that freedom to be exercised. Chance seems to provide just the flexibility required and freedom; risk is the price we pay for freedom".

Similar reasoning is clearly discernible from the Qur'an. Freedom is a crucial characteristic of human dignity bestowed by the Supreme Creator. The right path, and the rules of traversing it, is prescribed and differentiated from the wrong path. It is then left to humans' freedom of choice to make decisions as part of their rights and responsibilities. Uncertainty and risk exist to allow humans to learn as they are confronted with choices. This process is termed "testing" in the Qur'an. Humans choose under uncertainty. Their choices determine the consequences. Confronted with a choice, they are tested as to the path they select. The test is whether or not they choose to act in accordance with rules prescribed by their Creator.

Clearly, individuals exercise their freedom in choosing to comply with these rules. In a number of verses, the Qur'an asserts that life on this earth is temporary. As such, it is a crucible of constant testing, trials, and tribulations (see, e.g., Verse 155, Chapter 2 and Verse 2, Chapter 76). Not even the believers are spared testing. In Verse 2 of Chapter 29 the Qur'an asks: "Do humans think that they will be left alone when they say: we believe, and they therefore will not be tested?" To every test, trial, and tribulation in their lives, humans respond, and in doing so, they demonstrate a measure self-awareness and consciousness of their Creator. If the response–action is in compliance with the rules prescribed by the Creator, then the test becomes an occasion for self-development and strengthens consciousness of the Creator. All actions are risky because the full spectrum of future consequences of actions, within the horizon of birth to eternity, is not known with certainty. As the Qur'an asserts "…at times you may dislike a thing when it is good for you and at times you like a thing and it is bad for you. Allah knows and you do not" (Verse 216, Chapter 2). In short, human life here is a time to be tested, and to learn and develop through the exercise of freedom of choice granted to humans by their Creator. Crucially, testing is not possible without risk and uncertainty.

1.4 Types of Risk

Individuals in any society face two types of risk. The first is systemic, the result of the exposure of the economy to uncertainty and risk due to external and internal economic circumstances of the society and its vulnerabilities to shocks. How well an economy will absorb shocks depends on its resilience, which depends on the institutional and policy infrastructure of risk management in the society. How flexibly the infrastructure will respond to shocks will determine how much this type of risk impacts individual lives when it materializes.

The second type of risk individuals face relates to the circumstances of their own lives. These include risk of injuries, illness, accidents, bankruptcies, or even change in tastes and preferences. This kind of risk is referred to as idiosyncratic, and when it materializes, they play havoc with people's livelihoods. This is because people's livelihoods, and therefore their consumption levels, often depend directly on their income. If income becomes volatile, so will their livelihoods and consumption levels. Participation in capital market activities can help mitigate idiosyncratic risk by diversifying the source of income. Capital market instruments, when purchased by individuals, reduce the correlation between income and consumption and strengthen the resilience of their lives to idiosyncratic shocks. Thus, when shocks reduce income, consumption levels of the individuals invested in capital market need not suffer.

1.5 Risk in Real and Financial Sectors

As mentioned earlier, there are two major sectors in the economy. The real sector is where goods and services are produced.[3] Until very recently, the major function of the financial sector was to facilitate the financing of projects. The decision to take risks to produce a product precedes the decision on what to do with the risk in financing the project. Once the decision to undertake a project in the real sector is made, a subsequent decision has to be made as to the mode of financing. The risk taken in the real sector has to consider risks associated with the business end of the project. The firm or the entrepreneur can finance the project from their own sources or seek external financing. The risk of financing can be transferred, shifted, or shared. Figure 1.1 shows how risks that originate in the real sector get transferred, shifted, or shared in the financial sector.

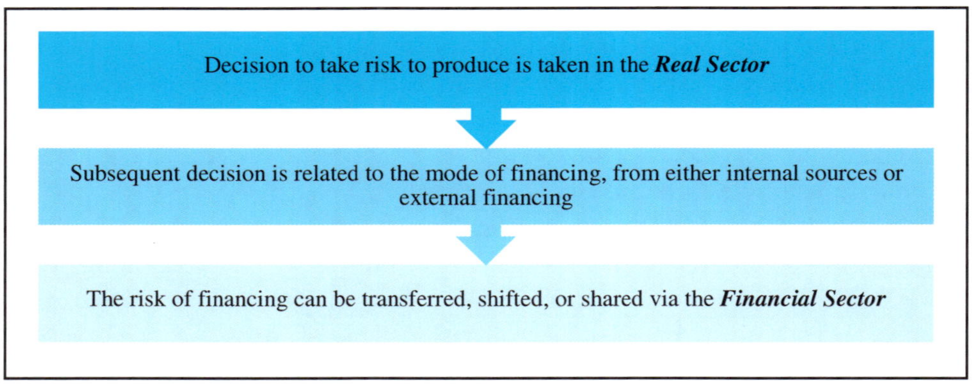

Figure 1.1. Risk in the Real Sector and in the Financial Sector.

Risk of financing is transferred when a trusted intermediary makes the surplus funds of savers available to the deficit units seeking funds for their project; the intermediary is trusted to know the borrowers well enough, by undertaking due diligence, to know that they could be trusted or obtain strong enough collateral to protect the funds. Finance risk is thus transferred from the surplus units to deficit units through the intermediation of the financial sector. Until the 1980s, the main function of commercial banks was risk transfer, where private sector's savings were channeled to finance real sector's activities. Risk of a financial (or real) transaction may be shifted to a third party that is not directly involved in the transaction without its knowledge or consent. An example of risk-shifting in the real sector is environmental pollution, whose costs are shifted to the society without its prior knowledge or consent. An example of risk-shifting in the financial sector is the financial trading prior to the crisis of 2007/2008 that shifted risk ultimately to the taxpayers who were unaware they were bearing the risk of the financial sector. Risk is shared when each party to a transaction carries business and finance risk in accordance to their ability to bear such risk.

1.6 Financial System of Capitalism: The Foundations

From the time of formal inception of contemporary capitalism until the second half of the 20th century, intermediation between surplus and deficit units in support of real sector activities was considered the most important function of the finance sector. As mentioned earlier, this is a framework for risk transfer. Virtually all supervisory and regulatory infrastructure of the financial sector was designed within the framework of risk transfer. The 2007/2008 crisis, however, demonstrated how easily and rapidly a system operating within a framework of risk transfer can switch into risk-shifting. Many scholars consider that the origin of systematic intellectual thinking about market capitalism began with Adam Smith's *The Wealth of Nations*. Much of the analytical efforts of economists from mid-19th to mid-20th centuries were devoted to proving Adam Smith's basic proposition that "a decentralized economy motivated by self-interest" would allocate resources more efficiently than other alternatives (Arrow and Hahn, 1971, pp. vi–vii). This conception envisioned the economy as a market system guided by the "invisible hand" toward smooth functioning, coordinating "autonomous individual choices in an interdependent world" (Evensky, 1993).

The process of developing a concrete and analytic vision of a capitalist market economy overlooked the fact that Smith's own vision of the economy, the subject of his book *The Wealth of Nations*, was embedded in his vision of a moral–ethical system. And that system was described well in Smith's book, *The Theory of Moral Sentiments*, written more than one and half decade earlier than *The Wealth of Nations*. Arguably, the first book established the institutional framework, or the rules of behavior for participants in the economy envisioned in *The Wealth of Nations* (Sen, 1982, 1987; Evensky, 1993, 2011; Mirakhor and Hamid, 2009; Askari *et al*., 2012).

Whereas conventional economics considered Smith's notion of "invisible hand" as a coordinator of independent decisions of market participants, in both *The Theory of Moral Sentiments* and in *The Wealth of Nations*, the metaphor refers to the design by the Supreme Creator, "who arranged the connecting principles such that the actions of all those seeking their own advantage could produce the most efficient allocation of resources, and thus the greatest possible wealth for the nation. This is indeed a benevolent designer" (Evensky, 1993, p. 9). Smith contended that the objective of the Divine Design must have been the happiness of humans "when he brought them into existence. No other end seems worthy of that supreme wisdom and divine benignity which we necessarily ascribe to him…" (Smith, 1976, pp. 186–189). Smith's major contribution in *The Theory of Moral Sentiments* is to envision a coherent moral-ethical social system consistent with the Supreme Creator's design and how each member of society would enforce ethical positions.

Recognition of human frailties led Smith to realize the need for an organic co-evolution of individual and society in a stage-wise process of accumulation of ethical system of values and its transfer from one generation to next. While it is possible for any given society to move forward or stagnate and even regress, the benevolence of the invisible hand of the "Author of nature" guides the totality of humanity in its movement toward the ideal human society. Compliance with and commitment to a set of values — virtues of prudence, concern for other people, justice, and benevolence — would ensure social order and cohesion.

1.7 Smith and Arrow

At the beginning of the second half of the 20th century, Kenneth Arrow, who was to win a Nobel Prize, and two of his co-authors Gerard Debreu and Frank Hahn, produced an elegant model that mathematically modeled Smith's conception of an economy. As this effort was primarily analytic, it abstracted from much of the well-spring of Smith's thought on the institutional scaffolding of the economy. Nevertheless, a crucial dimension of Smith's insight was not only preserved but also analytically demonstrated. In Smith's conception, the working of an economy relying on the market within the moral–ethical framework envisioned in *The Theory of Moral Sentiments*, where members of the society shared the risks of the economy. His insight into specialization and division of labor showed how efficiency and gains from trade are possible if the risks of economic activity are shared.

The work of Arrow and his colleagues (1954, 1971) led to the important result that in a decentralized market economy, the best allocation allows risk to be shared by the members of the society according to the ability of each participant to bear her/his share of risk. Two key assumptions of this work were complete contracts and complete markets. The first meant that it was possible to design transaction contracts that cover all contingencies. The second meant that there was a market available in which every conceivable risk could be traded or insured.

Crucially, in this optimal risk allocation (sharing) model, all future payoffs to transaction were contingent on the outcome of the project subject of the transactions. That is, there was no ex-ante determined rate of return; all returns were contingent on the outcome of the activity being financed. While not stated explicitly in his analytical work, Arrow subsequently made clear that it is "possible that the process of exchange requires or least is greatly facilitated by the presence of several…virtues (not only truth, but also trust, loyalty and justice) in future dealings... The virtue of truthfulness in fact contributes in a very significant way to the efficiency of the economic system… ethical behavior can be regarded as socially desirable institution which facilitates the achievement of economic efficiency in a broad sense" (Arrow, 1971, pp. 345–346). For example, if the institution of trust is strong in an economy, the universe of complete contracts can be replicated by simple contracts entered into by parties stipulating that terms and conditions of the contracts would be revised as contingencies arise. Arrow himself was to place emphasis on trust as the lubricant of the economy (Arrow, 1974).

Despite Arrow's attention to some important elements of the institutional structure that were integral to Smith's vision of an economy, the economics profession developed its own vision of that economy, focusing primarily on two concepts of "invisible hand" and "self-interest". The first was mentioned only once in *The Wealth of Nations* (see Smith, 1976: 456) and the manner in which the second was used by economists has been referred to by Walsh (2000) as a "vulgar…misunderstanding" of what Smith meant by "self-interest". This "narrowing" of Smith's view was subject of rather sharp criticism by Amartya Sen (1982, 1987) who suggested that: "Indeed, it is precisely the narrowing of the broad Smithian view of human beings in modern economics that can be seen as one of the major deficiencies of contemporary economic theory. This impoverishment is closely related to the distancing of economics from ethics" (Sen, 1987).

1.8 Smith and Ethical Rules

A careful reading of *Moral Sentiments* and *The Wealth of Nations* provides support for Sen's position. Even beyond Sen's spirited criticism of the misunderstanding of economists on Smith's (2006, pp. 186–189) self-interest motive is the latter's insistence on the need to comply with "general rules of conduct":

> "…[that] are the commands and laws of the Deity, who will finally reward the obedient, and punish the transgressor of their duty… When the general rules which determine the merit and demerit of actions comes thus to be regarded as the laws of an all-powerful being, who watches over our conduct, and who, in a life to come, will reward the observance and punish the breach of them — they necessarily acquire a new sacredness from this consideration. That our regard to the will of Deity ought to be the supreme rule of our conduct can be doubted of by nobody who believes his existence. The very thought of disobedience appears to involve in it the most shocking impropriety. How vain, how absurd would it be for man, either to oppose or to neglect the commands that were laid upon him by infinite wisdom and infinite power. How unnatural, how impiously ungrateful not to reverence the precepts that were prescribed to him by the infinite goodness of his Creator, even though no punishment was to follow their violation! The sense of propriety, too, is here well supported by the strongest motive of self-interest. The idea that, however, we may escape the observation of man, or be placed above the reach of human punishment, yet we are always acting under the eye and exposed to the punishment of God, the greatest avenger of injustice, is a motive capable of restraining the most headstrong passions, with those at least who, by constant reflection, have rendered it familiar to them."

Consideration of the above extract as well as the rest of *The Theory of Moral Sentiments* leads to at least three observations. First, this is the Smith that has been ignored by the economics profession. The Smith of economics is the author of the self-interest motive that is the basis of utility and profit maximization at any cost to the society, including the impoverishment and exploitation of fellow human beings as well as the destruction of the environment. Second, Smith makes clear in *The Theory of Moral Sentiments* that compliance with the rules prescribed by the Creator and with the rules of the market was essential to his vision. Third, it is also clear that Smith considers the internalization of rules — being consciously aware of the ever-presence of the Creator and acting accordingly — as crucial to all human conduct, including economics. A careful reading of *Moral Sentiments* shows that Smith shares some of the fundamental institutional scaffolding of Islam; belief in the One and Only Creator; belief in accountability of the Day of Judgement; belief in the necessity of compliance with the rules prescribed by the Creator; and belief that justice is achieved through full compliance with these rules.[4]

1.9 An Arrow–Debreu Economy

An economy in which there are contingent markets for all commodities — meaning that there are buyers and sellers who promise to buy or sell given commodities "if and only if" a specified state of the world occurs — is called an Arrow–Debreu economy. In such an economy, it is the budget constraints of the participants that determines the quantity bought of each contingent commodity at the price prevailing in the market. Since these commodities are contingent on future states, they are risky. Therefore, the budget constraints of individuals determine the risk-bearing ability of each market participant. Arrow (1971) recognized that requiring such a market is unrealistic, stating: "Clearly, the contingent commodities called for do not exist to extent required, but the variety of securities available on the modern markets serve as a partial substitute". Such securities, referred to as Arrow Securities, whose payoffs could be used to purchase commodities, would reduce the number of markets required while replicating the efficiency of risk allocation of complete contingent markets. Associated with complete markets are complete contracts. These are agreements contingent on all states of nature. In the real world, not all contracts can cover all future contingencies. Therefore, they are said to be incomplete contracts and may indicate inefficiencies in exchange. However, as suggested earlier, optimal contracts can be devised, provided there is mutual trust between the parties to the contract. That would be a simple contract with provisions for modification of terms and conditions should contingencies necessitate change.

A compelling case can be made that, in so far as the financial instruments are Arrow Securities, i.e., their payoff is contingent on the "state of nature" and depend on the outcome and not on fixed, predetermined interest rates and represent risk-sharing, this ideal system would have many characteristics of an ideal Islamic system (Mirakhor and Askari, 2017). However, not all Arrow Securities would satisfy *Shari'ah* requirements, as some may well represent contingent debt contracts to deliver a fixed predetermined amount of money if a given state of world occurs. These may not, therefore, represent ownership claim either. Shares of common stock of open corporations do meet these requirements. They are residual ownership claims and receive returns contingent on future outcomes; they are "proportionate claims on the pay offs of all future states" (Fama and Jensen, 1983). These payoffs are contingent on future outcomes. Stock markets that are well-organized, regulated, and supervised are efficient from an economic point of view because they allocate risks according to the risk-bearing ability of the participants. In essence, this is the contribution of the Arrow–Debreu model of competitive equilibrium (1954; see also Arrow, 1971), according to which efficient risk-sharing requires that the risks of the economy are allocated to market participants in accordance with their "respective degree of risk tolerance" (Hellwig, 1988).

1.10 What Happened to Smith–Arrow Risk-Sharing Ideal?

The economic/financial system envisioned by Smith and analytically modeled by Arrow and his colleagues did not materialize. By all counts, this was not because it was altogether unrealistic and not implementable, but because the whole project was derailed. Instead of optimally sharing the risk of the economy, the financial system ended up shifting it. The process began in the 1980s and culminated in the crisis of 2007/2008. As mentioned earlier, what the Arrow–Hahn and the Arrow–Debreu models set out to do was to analytically conduct a rigorous demonstration of the proposition that a decentralized economy motivated by self-interest would be compatible with a coherent disposition of economic resources that could be regarded, in a well-defined sense, as superior to a large class of possible alternative disposition ..." (Arrow and Hahn, 1971, pp. vi–vii). However, as Evensky (1989, p. 12) suggests, "the Smithian story told by Arrow and Hahn — and they are representative of modern economists — is an abridged edition. The spring that motivates action in Smith's story has been carried forward, but much of the rest of his tale has been forgotten".

It can be argued, as Arrow (1971) himself seems to imply, that the "rest of" Smith's "tale" would have been his vision of the institutional infrastructure (rules of behavior) that is envisioned in the *Theory of Moral Sentiments*, and, as such, it is unlikely that abstracting from them would be change the outcome of the mathematical analysis of Arrow–Debreu and/or Arrow–Hahn. Furthermore, had actual finance developed along the trajectory discernible from these works, i.e., steps taken toward completion of markets and of contracts, keeping in mind the overall institutional framework for the economy as envisioned by Adam Smith, the result might have been the emergence of conventional finance different from the contemporary system. That system would instead be dominated by contingent, equity, and risk-sharing financial instruments.

1.11 Can Economics Explain a Positive Predetermined Rate of Interest?

Perhaps the most influential factor in derailing that trajectory is the existence and the staying power of a fixed, predetermined rate of interest for which there has never been a rigorous theoretical explanation. All, so-called theories of interest from the classical economists to contemporary finance theories explain interest rate as the price that brings demand for and supply of finance into equilibrium. This clearly implies that interest rates emerge only after demand and supply forces have interacted in the market and are not ex-ante prices. In fact, in some theoretical models, there is no room for a fixed, ex-ante predetermined rate of interest. For example, introducing such a price into the Walrus or Arrow–Debreu–Hahn models of general equilibrium (GE) leads to the collapse of the models as they become overdetermined. As Cowen (1983, pp. 609–611) suggested:

> "Since the prices of all goods, whether present or future, are already specified by our set of Arrow-Hahn-Debreu equations, to now impose a discount rate on the economy (however derived) would overdetermine our system of equations. Hence, the interest rate is not the prices of capital goods or durable consumption goods. Instead, the own rates of return are given by the intertemporal price ratios we examine. Not only can there be no explanation of own interest rates that is not dependent upon our explanation of relative prices, but there can be no explanation of own interest rates which is not identical to our description of intertemporal relative price. However, if the goods are located in different time periods, then they must be considered different goods... The logical status of a theory of interest across different goods is rather dubious — how is it any different from a theory of "interest" which compares the price of apples to price of oranges? ...Once we define the interest rate as the set of intertemporal price ratio percentages, GE (general equilibrium) theory losses its ability to tell us anything specific about the magnitude of interest rates. These rates may be positive, negative, or even zero. Most likely, our system of equations will simultaneously contain all three possibilities as solutions."

Even though no satisfactory theory of a positive, ex-ante fixed rate of interest exists, all financial theory developed in the post-Arrow–Debreu–Hahn period assumed its existence in the form of a risk-free asset, usually Treasury Bills, as a benchmark against which the rates of return of all other assets, importantly equity returns, were measured. These include theories such as the Capital Asset Pricing Model (CAPM), Modern Portfolio Theory (MPT), and the Black–Scholes option pricing formula for valuing options contracts and assessing risk. For all practical purposes, the assumption of a risk-free interest rate introduced an artificial floor into the pricing structure of the real sector of the economy, and into all financial decisions. It can be argued that it is the existence of this exogenously imposed rate on the economy that transformed Arrow–Debreu vision of a risk-sharing economy and finance. The resulting system became one focused on transferring or shifting risk rather than sharing it. Such a system needed strong regulation to limit the extent of both.

Further developments in finance theory provided analytical rationale for strengthening interest rate-based debt financing as well as emergence of aggressive deregulation of finance in all economies. One was the Modigliani–Miller Theorem of neutrality of capital structure of firms. In essence, this theorem asserted that the value of a firm is independent of its capital structure. This implied that since firms want to maximize their value and since Modigliani–Miller showed that the value of the firm is indifferent as to its capital structure, firms would prefer to incur higher debt levels rather than issue additional equity, since the latter means erosion of ownership and, moreover, there is considerable incentive to opt for debt because of its tax advantages. However, the risk of additional debt would be shifted to other stakeholders (Jensen and Meckling, 1976).

Another development was the Efficient Market Hypothesis (EMH), which claimed that in an economy similar to that of Arrow–Debreu, prices prevailing in the market contained all relevant information such that there would be no opportunity for arbitrage. The implication was that if market efficiency is desirable, then the markets should be allowed to move toward completion, through innovation and financial engineering, in order to create financial instruments to allow insurance against all risks. For this to happen, it had to be demonstrated that it is possible to develop such a wide array of instruments and that regulation had to become passive or even regressive to allow an incentive structure to induce innovation. The latter was initiated in almost all industrial countries in the 1980s and continued with an accelerated pace until the 2007/2008 crisis. The former had already been demonstrated by the theory of spanning, showing that one basic financial instrument can be spanned potentially into an infinite number of instruments (see Askari *et al.*, 2010b, 2012). These developments, coupled with the high magnitude of leverage available from money–credit–debt–leverage creation process characteristic of a fractional reserve banking system represented an explosive mix that reduced the vision of Adam Smith to the rubble of post-2007/2008 crisis. The Arrow–Debreu vision of an economy in which risk was shared was first transformed into an economy in which the focus became risk transfer, but which quickly transformed into one in which risks were shifted, ultimately, to taxpayers (Mirakhor and Krichene, 2009; Sheng, 2009).

A question that arises is whether the risk-transferring, risk-shifting system is highly unstable and creates boom–bust bubble cycles and what explains its staying power. There are a number of reasons (see Askari *et al.*, 2012), but an important argument is that it is relatively inexpensive to borrow than either postpone consumption, in case of consumers, or issue equity shares, in case of business. However, the financial costs (aside from its human costs) to the society of establishing and administering a debt economy are, for the most part, hidden.[5] To explain the latter point, consider the findings of the contract theory.[6] The argument goes that, given the axioms of scarcity, self-interest, and rationality, there is a set of contracts referred to as "impossible contracts" because either both or at least one side have no incentive to enter into some contracts. To make "impossible contracts" possible, contracts have to be designed to become "incentive-compatible", meaning that the contract would have to include features that would incentivize parties to an impossible contract to agree to participate.

One such "impossible contract" is a debt contract. It is impossible because, again given the axioms of conventional economics, the borrower has no incentive to repay a loan. A debt-based economy therefore has to create a positive/negative incentive structure to make debt contracts possible. On the positive side, tax, policy, administrative, and legal incentives are created for parties to engage in debt contracts. On the negative side, an edifice of legal, administrative, and retributive institutions is established to enforce debt contracts. Seldom, if ever, are the costs to the society of establishing and then running this incentive structure necessary to make debt contracts possible mentioned. The only item in this incentive structure that is recognized is the tax incentive. However, even here, the opportunity costs of tax write-offs attributable to debt contracts to the society of forgone revenue to the governments that could otherwise be allocated to social investment programs are seldom acknowledged or mentioned.[7]

1.12 Islamic Finance: The Foundations

The fountainhead of all Islamic thought is the Qur'an. All knowledge Islamic, including that of finance, must find its roots in the Qur'an. The starting point of this discussion here is therefore Verse 275 of Chapter 2 of the Qur'an, particularly the part of the Verse that declares contract of *Al-Bay'* permissible and that of *Al-Riba* non-permissible. Arguably, these few words can be considered as constituting the organizing principle — the fundamental theorem as it were — of an Islamic economy. English translations of the Qur'an render *Al-Bay'* as "commerce" or "trade". They also translate *Al-Tijarah* as "commerce" or "trade". Consulting major lexicons of Arabic language (such as *Lisan Al-Arab*, *Mufradat Alfaz Al-Qur'an*, Lane's *Arabic Lexicon*, *Al-Tahquiq fi Kalamat Al-Qur'an Karim*, among others) reveals that there is a substantive difference between *Al-Bay'* and *Al-Tijarah*. Relying on various verses of the Qur'an (e.g., Verse 254: Chapter 2; 111: 2; 29–30: 35; 10–13: 61), these sources suggest that trade contracts (*Al-Tijarah*) are entered into in the expectation of profit (*ribh*). On the other hand, *Al-Bay'* contracts are defined as *Mubadilah Al-Maal Bi Al-Maal* — exchange of property with property. In contemporary economics, this phrase would be understood as the exchange of property rights claims. These sources also suggest a further difference in that those who enter into a contract of *Al-Bay'* (exchange) expect gains but are cognizant of probability of losses (*khisarah*).[8]

Given the above, a few points should be noted. First, all transactions, except spot exchange, involve time. From an economic point of view, time transactions involve a commitment to do something today in exchange for a promise of a commitment to do something in the future. All transactions involving time are subject to uncertainty, and uncertainty involves risk. Risk exists whenever there is more than one outcome possible. Consider, for example, a contract in which a seller commits to deliver a product in the future against payments today. There are a number of risks involved. There is a price risk for both side of the exchange; the price may be higher or lower in the future. In this case, the two sides are at risk which they share once they enter into the contract agreement. If the price in the future is higher, the buyer would be better off, and the price risk has been shed to the seller. The converse is true if the price is lower. Under uncertainty, the buyer and seller have, through the contract, shared the price risk. There are other risks that the buyer takes, including the risks of non-delivery and quality risk. The seller, on the other hand, also faces additional risks, including the risk that the price of raw materials, transportation, and delivery costs may be higher in the future. This risk may also be lower. Again, these risks have been shared through the contract. The same argument applies to deferred payment contracts.

Second, it may appear that spot exchange or cash sale involves no risk. However, price changes post-completion of spot exchange do occur often. The two sides of a spot exchange share this risk. Moreover, from the time of the classical economists, it is known that specialization through comparative advantage provides the basis for gains from trade. However, in specializing, a producer takes a risk of becoming dependent on other producers specialized in production of what he needs. Again, through exchange, the two sides to a transaction share the risk of specialization. Additionally, there are pre-exchange risks of production and transportation that are shared through the exchange. Therefore, it can be inferred that by mandating exchange (*Al-Bay'*), the Qur'an has ordained risk-sharing in all exchange activities.

Third, it appears that the reason for the prohibition of the contract of *Al-Riba* is that opportunities for risk-sharing are non-existent in this contract. It may be argued that the creditor does take risk — the risk of default. However, it is not risk taking *per se* that makes a transaction permissible. A gambler takes risks as well, but gambling is *haram*. Instead, what seems to matter is opportunity for risk-sharing. *Al-Riba* is a contract of risk transfer, at best, or of risk-shifting, at worst. As Keynes (1932, 1936) emphasized in his writings, if interest rates did not exist, the financier would have to share all the risks that the entrepreneur faces in producing, marketing, and selling a product (see Mirakhor and Krichene, 2009). However, by decoupling his future gains from the outcome of a project, by loaning money today for more money in the future, the financier transfers all risks to the entrepreneur. Fourth, it is clear that by declaring the contract of *Al-Riba* non-permissible, the Qur'an intends for humans to shift their focus to risk-sharing contracts of exchange.

It can be inferred from the above discussion that there are two types of contracts involving time:

(i) Contracts over time (or on spot) involving trade in which there is expectation of gain (*ribh*); and
(ii) Contracts over time involving an exchange in which there is expectation of gain (*ribh*) or loss (*khisarah*).

Here, a question arises. The Qur'an identifies three types of transactions: interest rate-based debt transactions (*Al-Riba*), trade transactions (*Al-Tijarah*), and exchange (*Al-Bay*). Verse 275 of Chapter 2 of the Qur'an defines the first type of transaction, while Verse 282 of Chapter 2 defines trade comprehensively. The question is about investment since it does not fall into the two categories of transactions. There are two possible answers. First, that it is ignored in the Qur'an; an answer no Muslim would accept since we believe nothing is ignored in the Qur'an. The second answer would be that the third type of transaction mentioned in Verse 275 of Chapter 2, *Al-Bay'* must refer also to contracts of investment with uncertain outcomes in terms of gain or loss. This, of course, does not mean that *mudarabah* and *musharakah* could not be used for longer-term trade in expectations of profits to be shared and for long-term investment, as was the case for centuries in the Muslim world as well as in Europe in the Middle Ages.

Borrowed from Muslims, and known as "commenda" in Western Europe,[9] *mudarabah* became quite popular as a means of financing long-term trade and investment (Mirakhor, 1983; Brouwer, 2005; Fischel, 1933; Udovitch, 1967, 1969, 1970; Goitein, 1955, 1964). Lopez (1976) suggests that there is a consensus among medieval historians that the commenda was of the highest importance and greatly contributed to the rapid growth of trade and investment, which led to economic change and growth in Europe. Commenda's contributions to the industrial development of the Ruhr Valley in Germany and in building railroads in Europe were particularly pronounced (see Mirakhor, 1983; Putri, 2017). Therefore, what needs emphasis is that *Al-Bay'* covers long-term investment contracts that allow the growth of employment and income and expansion of the economy (Bakkali, 2017). The focus of *Al-Tijarah* and all its financing instruments is the trade of commodities already produced. In effect, Islam meets the financing needs of trade as well as the requirements of resource allocation, investment, production, employment, income creation, and risk management.

1.13 Islamic Rules Governing Exchange

Given the above, major economic implications follow. First, as the definition of *Al-Bay'* indicates, it is a contract of exchange of property. This means that the parties to exchange must have property rights over the subjects of contract antecedent to the exchange. Second, parties must have the freedom not only to produce what they wish but also with whom they wish to exchange. Third, parties must have freedom to contract. Fourth, there must be means of enforcing contracts. Fifth, exchange requires a place for the parties to complete their transactions, meaning a market. Sixth, markets need rules of behavior to ensure an orderly and efficient operation. Seventh, the contract of exchange requires trust among the parties as to commitments to perform according to the terms and conditions of exchange. Eighth, there must be rules governing the distribution of proceeds. Lastly, there must be redistributive rules and mechanisms to correct for pattern of distribution emerging out of market performance. These are rules that govern the redemption of the rights of those who are not parties to the contract directly but who have acquired rights in the proceeds because, one way or another, they or their properties have contributed to the production of what is the subject of exchange. These implications are discussed below (see Askari *et al.*, 2012). Figure 1.2 outlines the ambit of Islamic rules governing exchange.

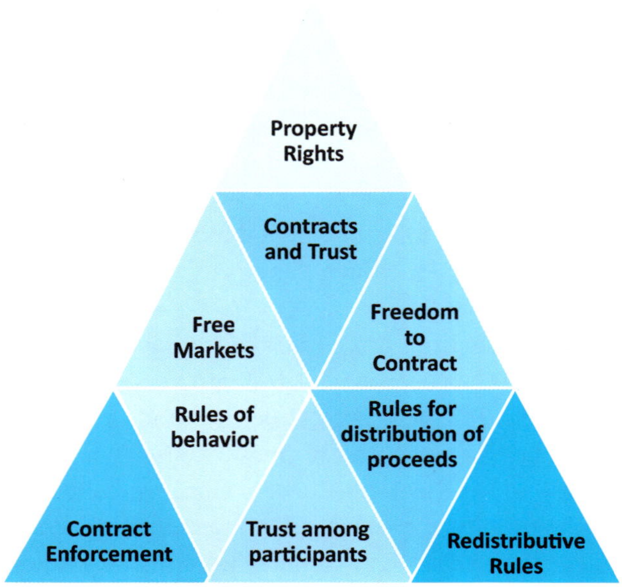

Figure 1.2. Islamic Rules Governing Exchange.

1.13.1 *Property Rights*

Briefly, the principles of property rights in Islam include the following:

(i) Allah (swt) has created all property and He is the ultimate owner;

(ii) Resources created by Allah (swt) are at the disposal of all humans to empower them to perform duties as prescribed by the Creator;

(iii) While the ultimate ownership is preserved for the Creator, humans are allowed to combine their physical and intellectual abilities with the created resources to produce means of sustenance for themselves and others;

(iv) The right of access to resources belongs to all of mankind universally;

(v) Humans can claim property rights over what is produced through their own labor or transfers through gift giving, exchange, contracts, inheritance, or redemption of rights in the produced property;

(vi) Since created resources belong to all humans, the inability of a person (physical, mental, or circumstances) to access these resources does not negate the individual's right to these resources;

(vii) These rights have to be redeemed — this establishes the rule of sharing with the less able;

(viii) Sharing is implemented through redistributive mechanisms, such as *zakah*, which refer to the redemption of rights and not charity;

(ix) Since work and transfers are the only sources of property rights claims, all sources of instantaneous property rights creation, such as theft, bribery, gambling, and *riba* are prohibited;

(x) Unlike the conventional system of property rights, Islam imposes strict limits on the freedom of disposing of property; there is no absolute freedom for the owner to dispose of property as there are rules against extravagance, waste, destruction of property, or its use in prohibited transactions;

(xi) Property rights must not lead to accumulation of wealth as the latter is considered the life blood of the society which must constantly circulate to create investment, employment, income, and economic growth opportunities; and

(xii) Once the principles governing property rights are observed, particularly the rule of sharing, the owner's right to the remaining property, cleansed of others' rights, is inviolate. For more detailed discussions, see Mirakhor, 2009; Mirakhor and Askari, 2017.

It is through its rules of property rights that Islam envisions economic growth and poverty alleviation in human societies (Al-Labban, 1967; Habachi, 1962; Khadduri, 1977). The latter is accomplished through the discharge of the obligation of sharing derived from the property rights principles which envision the economically less able as the silent partners of the more able. In effect, the more able are trustee-agents in using resources created by Allah (swt) on behalf of themselves and the less able.

In contrast to property rights principles of the conventional system, here, property rights are not means of exclusion but of inclusion of the less able in the income and wealth of the more able as a matter of rights that must be redeemed. In the conventional system, rich help the poor as a demonstration of sympathy, beneficence, benevolence, and charity. In Islam, the more able are required to share the consequences of the materialization of idiosyncratic risks — illness, bankruptcy, disability, accidents, and socioeconomic disadvantaged — for those who are unable to provide for themselves. Those who are more able diversify away a good portion of their own idiosyncratic risks using the risk sharing instruments of Islamic finance. The economically well-off are commanded to share risks of those who are economically unable to use the instruments of Islamic finance. It can be argued that unemployment, misery, poverty, and destitution in any society are *prima facie* evidence of violation of property right rules of Islam and/or non-implementation of Islamic instruments of risk-sharing. In Islamic teachings, the risks that would face the future generations are shared by the present generation through the rules of inheritance. These rules break up the accumulated wealth as it passes from one generation to another, to enable sharing risks of a larger number of people.

1.13.2 *Contracts and Trust*

Basically, a contract is an enforceable agreement. Its essence is commitment. Islam anchors all socio-political-economic relations on contracts. The fabric of the *Shari'ah* itself is contractual in its conceptualization, content, and application. Its very foundation is the primordial covenant between the Creator and humans (see Verses 172–173: Chapter 7). In an unambiguous verse (152: 6), the Qur'an urges the believers to fulfill the covenant of Allah (swt). This is extended to the terms and conditions of all contracts through another clear passage (Verse 1, Chapter 5) in which believers are ordered to be faithful to their contracts. They are ordered to protect faithfulness to their covenants and what has been placed in trust with them as a shepherd protects sheep (Verse 8: Chapter 32; also 34: 17; 172: 2; 91–92: 16). Thus, believers do not treat obligations of contracts lightly; they will take on contractual obligations only if they intend fully to fulfill them. Hence, their commitments are credible.

Contracts are means of coming to terms with future risks and uncertainty. They allocate risks by providing for future contingencies, and set obligations for each party and each state in the future as well as remedies for breach of contracts. Generally, there are four motives for entering into a contract: sharing of risk, transfer of risk, alignment of incentives, or to minimize transaction costs. Partnership contracts and the purchase of equity shares are examples of risk-sharing. Entering into an insurance contract is an example of transferring risks for a fee to those who can better bear them. Risk-shifting occurs when the risks of a transaction or a contract between two parties are shifted to a third party not directly involved in the transaction. This concept was discussed by Jensen and Meckling (1976) in the context of corporate managers resorting to debt finance instead of issuing additional equity, thus shifting the risk of debt burden to other stakeholders. To align incentives, one party (usually the principal) enters into a contract with another (an agent) through which incentives are created for the latter to take actions that serve their joint-surplus maximization objective (Hart and Holmstrom, 1987). Contracts that are designed to reduce transaction costs are usually aimed at establishing a stable, long-term relationship between parties in order to avoid ex-ante information, search and sorting costs, as well as ex post bargaining costs.

There is an organic relationship between contract and trust. Without the latter, contracts become difficult to negotiate and conclude, and costly to monitor and enforce. When and where trust is weak, complicated, and costly, administrative devices are needed to enforce contracts. Problems are exacerbated when, in addition to lack of trust, property rights are poorly defined and protected (Sheng, 2009). Under these circumstances, it becomes difficult to specify clearly the terms of contract, since transaction costs — that is, search and information costs, bargaining and decision costs, and contract negotiations and enforcement costs — are high. Consequently, there is less trade, fewer market participants, less long-term investment, lower productivity, and slower economic growth. Weakness of trust creates the problem of lack of credible commitment which arises when parties to an exchange cannot commit themselves or do not trust that others can commit themselves to performing contractual obligations. Empirical research has shown that where the problem of a lack of commitment exists and is significant, it leads to disruptions in economic, political and social interaction among people. Long-term contracting will not be possible, and parties to exchange opt for spot market or very short-term transactions (see, e.g., Halaissos and Bertaut, 1995; Knack and Keefer, 1997; Zak and Knack, 2001; Ng, 2015; Guiso *et al.*, 2004 and 2005).

Considering these issues, one can appreciate the strong emphasis the Qur'an has placed on trust, trustworthiness (see Verse 27: Chapter 8; 57: 4), and the need to fulfill terms and conditions of contracts, covenants, and promises one makes. These rules solve the problem of credible commitment and trust, thus facilitating long-term contracts. To illustrate the importance of trust, consider the role of complete contracts in the neoclassical theory of competitive equilibrium (Arrow, 1971). A complete contract fully specifies all future contingencies relevant to the exchange. In the real world, a vast majority of contracts are incomplete. This requirement, therefore, is considered too stringent and unrealistic. Not only does ignorance about all future contingencies make writing complete contracts impossible, even if all future contingencies are known, it would be nearly impossible to write a contract that can accommodate them all. However, if the parties to a contract trust each other, they can agree to enter into a simple contracts and commit to revising its terms and conditions as contingencies arise.

1.13.3 *Markets*

A major reason for a contract of exchange is that the parties to the contract wish to improve upon their own pre-contract welfare. For this to happen, parties must have the freedom to contract. This, in turn, implies freedom to produce, which calls for clear and well-protected property rights to permit production and sale. To freely and conveniently exchange, the parties need a place to do so, i.e., a market. To operate efficiently, markets need rules of behavior and clear, unambiguous rule-enforcement mechanisms to reduce uncertainty in transactions. Markets also need free flow of information. To reinforce the efficiency of market operations, trust has to be established among participants, transaction costs minimized, and rules established to internalize externalities of two-party transactions. Sheng (2009, p. 9) suggests that, "Successful markets all share three key attributes: the protection of property rights, the lowering of transaction costs and the high transparency".

To achieve these attributes, preconditions and infrastructures are needed, including:

(i) Freedom of market participants to enter and exit the market, to set their own objectives within the prescribed rules, to employ ways and means of their own choosing to achieve their goals, and to choose whomever they wish as their exchange partner;
(ii) An infrastructure for participants to access, organize, and use information;
(iii) Institutions that permit coordination of market activities;
(iv) Institutions to regulate and supervise the behavior of market participants; and
(v) Legal and administrative institution to enforce contracts at reasonable costs.[10]

Figure 1.3 summarizes the critical factors needed for the efficient functioning of markets.

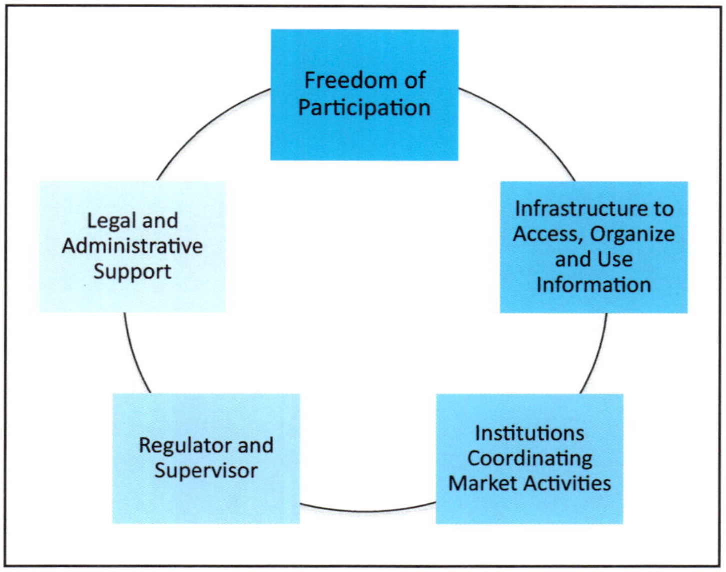

Figure 1.3. Critical Factors for Efficient Markets.

1.13.4 *Markets of the Prophet*

Both the Qur'an and the *Sunnah* place considerable emphasis on the rules of behavior. Once instated in Medina as the spiritual and temporal authority, the Messenger (saw) exerted considerable energy in operationalizing and implementing the property rights rules, the institutions of the market, the rules of exchange and contracts, as well as rules governing production, consumption, distribution, and redistribution. He also implemented rules regarding the fiscal operations of the newly formed state as well as governance rules. Specifically, regarding markets, before the advent of Islam, trade had been the most important economic activity in the Arabian Peninsula. A number of dynamic and thriving markets had developed throughout the area.

Upon arrival in Medina, the Messenger of Allah organized a market for Muslims structured and governed by rules prescribed by the Qur'an, and implemented a number of policies to encourage the expansion of trade and strengthen the market. Unlike the already existing market in Medina, and elsewhere in Arabia, the Prophet prohibited imposition of taxes on individual merchants as well as on transactions. He also implemented policies to encourage trade among Muslims and non-Muslims by creating incentives for non-Muslim merchants in and out of Medina. For example, traveling non-Muslim merchants were considered guests of the Muslims and their merchandise were guaranteed by the Prophet against (non-market) losses. The market was the only authorized place of trade. Its construction and maintenance were made a duty of State. As long as space was available in the existing one, no other markets were constructed. The Prophet designated a protective area around the market. No other construction or facility was allowed in the protective area. While trade was permitted in the area surrounding the market in case of overcrowding, the location of each merchant was assigned on a first-come, first-served basis, but only for the duration of the trading day (Mirakhor and Hamid, 2009; Sadr, 2016).

After the conquest of Mecca, rules governing the market and the behavior of participants were institutionalized and generalized to all markets in Arabia. These rules included, *inter alia*:

(i) No restriction on inter-regional or international trade, including no taxation on entering into or existing out of markets and on imports and exports;
(ii) Free movement of inputs and outputs between markets and regions;

(iii) No barrier on entry to or exit from the market;
(iv) Information regarding prices, quantities, and qualities were to be known with full transparency;
(v) Every contract had to fully specify the property being exchanged, the rights and obligations of each party to the contract, and all other terms and conditions;
(vi) The state and its legal apparatus guaranteed contract enforcement;
(vii) Hoarding of commodities were prohibited as were price controls;
(viii) No seller or buyer was permitted to harm the interests of other market participants, e.g., no third party could interrupt negotiations between two parties in order to influence the outcome in favor of one or the other party;
(ix) Short changing, i.e., not giving full weights and measure, was prohibited; and
(x) Sellers and buyers were given the right of annulment depending on circumstances.

These rights protected consumers against the moral hazards of incomplete, faulty, or fraudulent information. Interference with supply before market entrance was prohibited as they would harm the interests of the original seller and the final buyer. These and other rules — such as trust and trustworthiness as well as faithfulness to the terms and conditions of contracts — substantially reduced transaction costs and protected market participants against risks of transactions (Mirakhor and Hamid, 2009; Sadr, 2016).

1.14 Islamic Financial Market and Instruments

A financial market organized according to the Islamic precept would be embedded in an economy in which the institutional scaffolding, i.e., rules of behavior described, would be operational. Such a market would be served by a full spectrum menu of financial instruments (Chapra 2007; Mirakhor and Zaidi, 2007; Iqbal and Mirakhor, 2011; Haneef and Mirakhor, 2014; Maghrebi *et al*., 2016). The essential function of that spectrum would be spreading and allocating risk among participants rather than concentrating it among the borrowing class. In general, that spectrum will include instruments of risk-sharing for: (i) transactions (*mu'amalat*); (ii) redistributive instruments by which economically more able segment of the population shares the risk of the less able; and (iii) instruments that serve the inheritance rules specified in the Qur'an through which the wealth of a person at the time of passing is distributed among the present and future generations of inheritors.

The second set of instruments is used to redeem the rights of the less able in the income and wealth of the more able. These would not be instruments of charity, altruism, or beneficence, but instruments of redemption of rights of others as repayment of obligation of share. Figure 1.4 shows the broad objectives for Islamic financial markets and instruments.

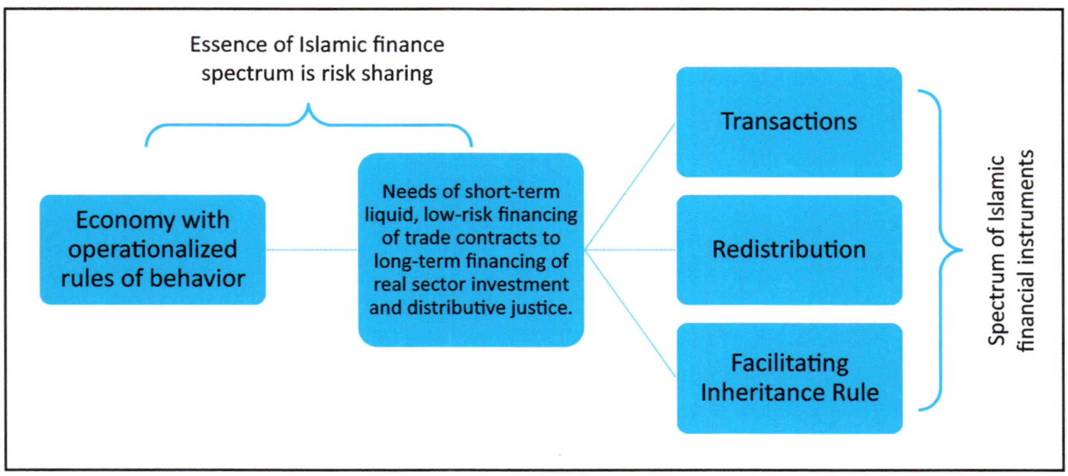

Figure 1.4. Islamic Financial Market and Instruments.

The spectrum of ideal Islamic finance instruments would run the gamut between short-term liquid, low-risk financing of trade contracts, to long-term financing of real sector investment. The essence of the spectrum is risk-sharing. At one end, the spectrum provides financing for purchase and sale of what has already been produced in order to allow further production. At the other end, it provides financing for what is intended or planned to be produced. In this spectrum, there does not seem to be room provided for making money out of pure finance where instruments are developed that use real sector activity only as virtual license to accommodate what amounts to pure financial transactions. There are *duyun* and *qardh hassan* that are non-interest-based debt, but only to facilitate real sector transactions in terms of consumption smoothing for those who have experienced liquidity shock. This is the case when a financier shares liquidity risk with the firms or consumers for whom the risk has materialized or for those who use non-interest borrowing as an insurance against liquidity shocks.

It may be argued that in a modern complex economy, there is need for a variety of ready-to-use means of liquidity, and so long as instruments being developed are, in the judgement of *Shari'ah* scholars, permissible, where is the harm? Usually, this argument starts with the reasoning that financial instruments that serve short-term, trade-oriented transaction contracts, such as *murabahah*, are permissible. From there, the argument goes that any instrument with connection, no matter how tenuous to the real sector transactions, is also permissible. It is worth noting that transaction contracts permissible in Islam and the financial instruments intended to facilitate them are not the same thing. Islamic real sector transactions contracts (*'uqud*) that have reached us are all permissible. However, it is possible that a financial instrument designed to facilitate a given permissible contract may itself be judged non-permissible. As the proliferation of derivative instruments in the period of run-up to the 2007/2008 financial crisis demonstrated that the number of financial instruments that have some relation, even if only nominal, to a real sector transaction is limited only by the imagination of financial engineers. It is possible that a financial instrument may have weaker risk-sharing characteristics than the Islamic transaction contract it intends to serve.

1.15 Islamic Finance Industry at the Present

This book is about the reality on the ground as it is. Hence, it describes the workings of the Islamic financial system and, in particular, focuses on a comparative presentation of conventional and Islamic capital and money market as they exist today. The present configuration of the Islamic finance industry has a short history of a little over three decades of operation at levels that could be considered significant. Over this period, it has had a remarkable growth. Despite this performance, there are anxieties that the industry is on a trajectory that does not assure its convergence to its ideal path described above. This is because the energies of financiers and financial engineers serving the Islamic financial industry (IFI) are focused on the design and development of instruments that accommodate the low end of time and risk-return spectrum described above. The concern is that without effort at developing long-term investment instruments of risk-sharing, there is the possibility that the future development of the industry will continue to see more — albeit in greater variety of the same. That is, more short-term, liquid, and safe instruments with risk transfer or risk-shifting characteristics (Alaabed *et al.*, 2016). In that case, IFI would have failed to achieve the hopes and aspirations embedded in the ideal vision of Islamic finance. That vision includes the emergence of a financial system with close links to the real sector of the economy, rather than a "paper economy" in which financial paper is traded without creating real sector added value.

Box 1.1. The Paper Economy

"Paper economy" is a term used by the Nobel Laureate economist, James Tobin, who suggested in 1984 that "we are throwing more and more of our resources into financial activities remote from the production of goods and services, into activities that generate high private rewards disproportionate to their social productivity, a 'paper economy' facilitating speculation which is short-sighted and inefficient" (Tobin, 1984).

A paper economy has several distinctive characteristics:

(i) Its finance is speculative rather than productive. In the latter, one buys a share of a business after thought and deliberation on its risk-return characteristics and then holds on to it for the long run; one buys and owns. In the paper economy, one speculates on a piece of paper that represents debt or its derivative, or a stock or its derivative, and turns it over quickly without taking interest in the underlying activity that the paper represents. This is rent-seeking instead of value-creating.

(ii) Its finance has a short-term focus: obsession with short-term results. This short-termism has no regard for the long-term implications or even short-term effects of the activity on third parties; "it involves buying pieces of paper and trading it back and forth in rapid turnover" (on short-termism, see Bogle, 2012, p. 47).

(iii) Its finance decouples from the real sector, gradually at first but then rapidly. A decade after James Tobin spoke the words quoted above, the brilliant President of Bundesbank, Hans Tietmeyer, was to warn that the financial sectors in advanced economies were decoupling from the real sector. The warnings were never heeded. The result was the 2007/2008 financial crisis.

(iv) Its finance is extractive of value from the real sector rather than adding value to the real economy.

(v) Its finance has no anchor in the real sector of the economy but crises that are triggered in the financial sector can be devastating to the real economy in terms of loss of jobs, and income (see also Power and Epstein, 2003; Epstein, 2005).

How does the 'paper economy' look like today, some five years after the crisis?

At the end of 2011, it was estimated that, in the US alone, the total nominal value of paper instruments (with no direct linkage to the real sector of the economy) "such interest rate swaps, collateralized debt obligations, derivatives such as commodity futures, stock indices, credit default swaps exceeded $700 trillion". This compares to the "total value of capitalization of world's stocks and bond markets of $150 trillion" at the same time. That is, the value of all the "paper" instruments in the US alone was five times larger than the total capitalization of all the stock and bond markets in the world (Bogle, 2012, p. 47).

To compare the relationship of the "paper" finance and real finance, consider that in the US over the past five years, "total equity IPO's (initial public offerings) provided fresh capital to young companies averaging $45 billion annually. Secondary offerings provided additional equity capital averaging $205 billion for a total of $250 billion per year. Total volume of stock trading over the same period averaged $33 trillion annually. Some 130 times the volume of equity capital". This implies that only 0.8% of finance went to equity and 99.2% to trading activity that does not add value to the real economy of the US. In other words, "speculation represented 99.2% of the activities" of the US market, and only 0.8% accounting for "capital formation" (see Bogle, 2012, pp. 1–10).

In fairness, it should be acknowledged that the IFI faces formidable challenges competing within the centuries old and well-entrenched system whose main fulcrum is the interest mechanism prohibited in Islamic finance. It should also be recalled that the non-availability of instruments in the conventional system to meet the demand of the Muslim investors for non-interest-based financial transactions represented a market failure. IFI, therefore, grew out of conventional finance to serve the here-to-fore unmet demand. In the process, it has had to compete with an industry in which interest reigns supreme. The first important challenge to and a constraint on the activities of IFI are the advantages and incentives granted for interest rate-based debt and credit contracts that are not granted risk-sharing and equity-based contracts.

The second challenge stems from the fact that the conventional system centered on a fractional reserve banking system created opportunities for leverage that can be highly profitable. Proper Islamic finance modes of operation are limited as to their capacity to use or create highly leveraged positions due to constraints on interest rate-based debt creation. The third challenge for IFI is that there is a lack of credible, competitive, liquid, long-term, widely used *Shari'ah*-compliant instruments for liquidity management and hedging. Conventional finance has recourse to risk-free assets in the form of government treasury bonds.

Fourth, in Muslim countries, fiscal and monetary policies are interest rate-based. Hence, in addition to the lack of *Shari'ah*-compliant instruments issued by governments that IFIs can use for liquidity and hedging management, the governments' macroeconomic policies strengthen interest rate-based debt financing against which the IFI has to compete. In effect, the governments in Muslim countries define exogenously competitive conditions for IFI without leveling the playing field. Fifth, IFI cannot operate in isolation from the international financial markets. There are, however, conflicts between *Shari'ah*-compliant IFI contracts and the legal system of major financial systems (see Mirakhor and Haneef, 2014). These challenges must be overcome to allow IFI to continue its growth and embark on a trajectory of convergence with its ideal path. The last chapter of this book will propose ways and means of meeting these challenges.

Questions and Problems

1. Explain the relationships between the real and financial sectors of an economy and the functions performed by each.
2. Explain the differences between risk and uncertainty. Where do they originate? What is their function according to the *Qur'an*?
3. Explain the function of rules as they relate to risk and uncertainty.
4. Explain the difference between risk taking and risk sharing. Define risk transfer, risk sharing, and risk shifting. What types of risk do people face?
5. What is the most important characteristic that Adam Smith's vision of an economy shares with the Qur'anic vision? Elaborate.
6. Explain the difference between contemporary economics and Adam Smith's vision.
7. What is the major characteristic of an Arrow–Debreu economy? Explain.
8. Explain the differences between an Arrow–Debreu vision and that of contemporary economics.
9. Can contemporary economics explain the existence of a fixed, pre-determined interest rate? Explain.
10. Use the arguments of the chapter to explain why interest-based debt contracts are prohibited by the Qur'an.
11. Explain the Islamic rules governing the operations of an economy and its financial sector. Elaborate on these rules that operate in the capital market.
12. Explain some of the most important characteristics of Islamic finance as it is.

Bibliography

Alaabed, A., M. Masih, and A. Mirakhor (2016). "Investigating Risk Shifting in Islamic Banks in the Dual Banking Systems of OIC Countries: Application of Two-step Dynamic GMM," *Risk Management*, Vol. 18, No. 4, pp. 236–263.

Al-Isfahani, Al-Raqib (1992). *Mufradat Alfaz Al Quran* (Damascus: Dar Al-Qalam), p. 155.

Al-Labban, I. (1967). "Islam is the First Religious System to Recognize the Right of the Poor to the Wealth of the Rich," *The Islamic Review*, August, pp. 14–19.

Al-Mustafaoui, S. H. (1995). *Al-Tahquiq Fi Kalamat Al-Quran Al-Karim* (Tehran: Ministry of Islamic Culture and Guidance). Vol. 1, pp. 363–365.

Arrow, K. J. (1971). *Essays in the Theory of Risk-Bearing* (Chicago: Markham Publishing Company) pp. 121–133, 143; 239–266.

Arrow, K. J. and G. Debreu (1954). "The Existence of an Equilibrium for a Competitive Economy," *Econometrica*, Vol. XXII, pp. 265–290.

Arrow, K. J. and F. Hahn (1971). *General Competitive Analysis* (San Francisco: Holden Day).

Arrow, K. J. (1974). *The Limits of Organizations* (New York: Norton).

Askari, H. *et al.* (2009). *New Issues in Islamic Finance and Economics* (Singapore: John Wiley and Sons).

Askari, H. *et al.* (2010a). *Globalization and Islamic Finance* (Singapore: John Wiley and Sons).

Askari, H. *et al.* (2010b). *The Stability of Islamic Finance* (Singapore: John Wiley and Sons).

Askari, H. *et al.* (2012). *Risk Sharing Finance: The Islamic Finance Alternative* (Singapore: John Wiley and Sons).

Bakkali, S. (2017). "Risk Sharing in Contemporary Finance: Fish Perspective." PhD Dissertation, INCEIF, Kuala Lumpur, Malaysia.

Bartholomeu, D. J. (2008). *God, Chance and Purpose* (Cambridge: Cambridge University Press).

Bogle, J. C. (2012). *The Clash of Cultures: Investment vs Speculation* (Hoboken, New Jersey: John Wiley).

Brouwer, M. (2005). "Managing Uncertainty through Profit Sharing Contracts from Medieval Italy to Silicon Valley," *Journal of Management and Governance*, Vol. 9, pp. 237–755.

Chapra, M. U. (2007). "Challenges facing the Islamic financial industry," in M. K. Hassan and M. K. Lewis (eds.) *Handbook of Islamic Banking* (Cheltenham, UK: Edward Elgar), pp. 325–360.

Cizakca, M. (2011). *Islamic Capitalism and Finance: Origins, Evolution and the Future* (London: Edward Elgar).

Cizakca, M. (ed.) (2014). *Islam and the Challenge of Western Capitalism* (London: Edward Elgar).

Cowen, T. (1983). "The Rate of Return in General Equilibrium: A Critique," *Journal of Post Keynesian Economics*, Summer 1983, Vol. 5, pp. 608–617.

Epstein, G. A. (2005). *Financializaton and the World Economy* (Cheltenham, UK: Edward Elgar).

Evensky, J. (1989). "The Evolution of Adam Smith's Views on Political Economy," *History of Political Economy*, Vol. 21, No. 1, pp. 123–145.

Evensky, J. (1993). "Ethics and the Invisible Hand," *Journal of Economic Perspectives*, Vol. 7, No. 2, pp. 197–205.

Evensky, J. (2011). "Adam Smith's Essentials: On Trust, Faith, and the Free Markets," *Journal of the History of Economic Thought*, Vol. 133, No. 2, pp. 249–268.

Fama, E. F. and M. C. Jensen (1983). "The Agency Problems and Residual Claims," *Journal of Law and Economics*, Vol. XXVI, pp. 327–349.

Fischel, W. (1933). "The Origin of Banking in Medieval Islam," *Journal of the Royal Asiatic Society*, pp. 339–352; 568–603. Also published in *Islamic Culture*, Vol. XIV. Cairo: Bureau of Compilation, Translation and Publication.

Graeber, D. (2011). *Debt: The First 5,000 Years* (London: Melville House).

Goitein, S. D. (1955). "The Cairo Ginza as a Source of the History of Muslim Civilization," *Studia Islamica*, Vol. 3, pp. 75–91.

Goitein, S. D. (1964). "Commercial and Family Partnerships in the Countries of Medieval Islam," *Islamic Studies*, Vol. 3, pp. 318–319.

Guiso, L. *et al.* (2005). "Trusting the stock market." NBER Working Paper No. 11648 (Cambridge: MA: National Bureau of Economic Research).

Guiso, L., P. Sapienza and L. Zingales (2004). "The Role of Social Capital in Financial Development," *The American Economic Review*, Vol, 94. No, 3. pp. 526–556.

Habachy, S. (1962). "Property, Right, and Contract in Muslim law," *Columbia Law Review*, Vol. 62, No 3.

Halaissos, M. and C. Bertaut (1995). "Why do so Few Hold Stocks?" *The Economic Journal*, Vol. 105, No. 432, pp. 1,110–1,129.

Haneef, R. and A. Mirakhor (2014). "Islamic Finance: Legal and Institutional Challenges," *ISRA International Journal of Islamic Finance*, Vol. 6, No. 1, pp. 115–151.

Hassan, M. K. and M. K. Lewis (eds.) (2007). *Handbook of Islamic Banking* (Cheltenham, UK: Edward Elgar).

Hart, O. and B. Holmstrom (1987). "The theory of contracts," in *Advances of Economic Theory, Fifth World Congress*, T. Bewley (ed.) (Cambridge: Cambridge University Press).

Hellwig, M. (1998). "Banks, Markets, and Allocation on Risks in an Economy," *Journal of Institutional and Theoretical Economics*, Vol. 154, No. 1, pp. 328–345.

Hixson, W. F. (1991). *A Matter of Interest* (Montgomery, Alabama: E-Book Time).

Ibn Mandhoor (1984). *Lisan Al-Arab* (Qum, Iran: Nashr Adab).

Iqbal, Z. and A. Mirakhor (2011). *An Introduction to Islamic Finance: Theory and Practice* (Singapore: John Wiley and Sons).

Jensen, M. C. and W. H. Meckling (1976). "Theory of the Firm: Managerial Behavior, Agency Costs and Ownership Structure," *Journal of Financial Economics*, Vol. 3, Issue 4, pp. 305–360.

Keynes, J. M. (1932). "Saving and Usury: A Symposium," *Economic Journal*, Vol. 42, No. 165, pp. 123–141. See also, *Economic Journal*, Vol. 41, No. 164.

Keynes, J. M. (1936). *The General Theory of Employment, Interest, and Money* (London: Macmillan; also St. Martin's Press, 1970).

Khadduri, M. (1977). "Property: Its relation to equality and freedom in accordance with Islamic law," in C. Wellman (ed.), *Equality and Freedom: Past, Present, and Future* (Franz Steiner, Verlag GmBH, Wiesbaden, Germany).

Kister, M. J. (1965). "The Market of the Prophet," *Journal of the Economic and Social History of the Orient*, Vol. 8, No. 3, pp. 272–276.

Knack, S. and P. Keefer (1997). "Does Social Capital have an Economic Payoff: A Cross-country Investigation," *The Quarterly Journal of Economics*, November, pp. 1,251–1,288.

Lane, E. W. (2003). *An Arabic-English Lexicon* (Lahore: Suhail Academy).

Lazzarato, M. (2011). *The Making of the Indebted Man* (Amsterdam: Agence litteraire Pierre Astier & Associes) (Trans. Semiotext (e), 2012).

Lopez, R. S. (1976). *The Commercial Revolution of the Middles Ages*, 9500–1350 (Cambridge: Cambridge University Press).

Maghrebi, N., A. Mirakhor and Z. Iqbal (2016). *Intermediate Islamic Finance* (Singapore: John Wiley).

Mirakhor, A. (2010). "Whither Islamic Finance? Risk Sharing in an Age of Crisis." MPRA Paper No. 56341.

Mirakhor, A. and I. Zaidi (2007). "Profit-and-loss sharing contracts in Islamic finance," in Hassan, M. K. and M. K. Lewis (eds.), *Handbook of Islamic Banking* (Cheltenham, UK: Edward Elgar), pp. 49–63.

Mirakhor, A. and N. Krichene (2009). "The recent crisis: Lessons for Islamic finance," *2nd Public Lecture on Financial Policy and Stability*, Islamic Financial Services Board, Kuala Lumpur, Malaysia.

Mirakhor, A. (1983). "Muslim contribution to economics," Paper presented at the *Annual Meeting of the South-Western Economic Association*, (London: Edward Elgar). March 1983, and reproduced in Murat Cizakca (ed.), 2014.

Mirakhor, A. (2009). "Islamic Economics and Finance: An Institutional Perspective," *Journal of Economics and Management*, Vol. 17, No. 1, pp. 31–37.

Mirakhor, A. and H. Askari (2010). *Islam and the Path to Human and Economic Development* (New York: Palgrave).

Mirakhor, A. and H. Askari (2017). *Ideal Islamic Economy: An Introduction* (New York: Palgrave Macmillan).

Mirakhor, A. and I. S. Hamid (2009). *Islam and Development: The Institutional Framework* (New York: Global Publications).

Ng, Adam *et al*. (2015). *Social Capital* (New York: Palgrave Macmillan).

Power, D. and G. Epstein (2003). "Rentier income and financial crises," Working Paper No. 57 (Amherst, MA: Political Economy Research Institute, University of Massachusetts).

Rayner, S. E. (1991). *The Theory of Contracts in Islamic Law* (London: Graham and Trotman).

Sadr, S. K. (2016). *The Economic System of The Early Islamic Period* (New York: Palgrave Macmillan).

Sen, A. K. (1982). "Rational fools," in A. K. Sen (ed.), *Choice, Welfare and Measurement* (Cambridge, MA: MIT Press).

Sen, A. K. (1987). *On Ethics and Economics* (Oxford: Blackwell).

Sheng, A. (2009). *From Asian to Global Financial Crisis* (Cambridge: Cambridge University Press).

Smith, A. (1776/1976). *An Inquiry into the Nature and Causes of the Wealth of Nations*. Edited in two volumes by W. B. Todd. See Vol. 2 of the Glasgow Edition of the Works and Correspondence of Adam Smith (Oxford: Clarendon Press).

Smith, A. (1976). *The Theory of Moral Sentiments*, D. D. Raphael and A. L. Manfie (eds.) (Oxford: Oxford University Press).

Putri, S. (2017). "The relevance of risk sharing for modern economies: The case of Germany, 1933–1935," PhD Dissertation, INCEIF, Kuala Lumpur.

Tobin, J. (1984). "On the Efficiency of the Financial System," *Lloyds Bank Review*, No. 153, 1–15.

Udovitch, A. L. (1967). "Credit and a Means of Investment in Medieval Islamic trade," *Journal of the American Oriental Society*, Vol. 87, No. 3, July–September, pp. 260–264.

Udovitch, A. L. (1969). *At the Origins of the Western Commenda: Islam, Israel, Byzantium?* (Princeton, NJ: Princeton University Press), pp. 198–207.

Udovitch, A. L. (1970a). "Commercial techniques in early medieval Islamic trade," in D. Richards (ed.), *Islam and the Trade of Asia*. Philadelphia: University of Pennsylvania Press, pp. 37–62.

Udovitch, A. L. (1970b). *Partnership and Profit in Medieval Islam* (Princeton, NJ: Princeton University Press).

Walsh, V. (2000). "Smith after Sen," *Review of Political Economy*, Vol. 12, No. 1, pp. 5–25.

Weiss, W. M. (1989). *The Bazaar: Markets and Merchants of the Islamic World* (London: Thames and Hudson).

Zak, P. and S. Knack (2001). "Trust and Growth," *The Economic Journal*, Vol. 111, April, pp. 295–321.

Endnotes

1. It should be noted that some scholars reject this real/financial dichotomy as artificial. In essence, they are two faces of the same coin: debt economy. See, e.g., Lazzarato (2011).
2. For a comprehensive discussion of financialization and its impact on the economy, see Abdulkarim, F. M. (2016). "Financialization of the Economy and Income Inequality in Selected OIC and OECD countries: The Role of Institutional Factors." PhD Dissertation, INCEIF, Kuala Lumpur, Malaysia.
3. It is worth noting that advances in information technology had expanded the traditional domain of commodities to a new commodity, data, which has become subject of exchange, trade and a major source of income for large corporation such as Google, Facebook, and other servers and social networks. They are making money off of a commodity that belongs to individuals. It could be expected at some point in the future, individuals may seek to benefit directly by claiming property rights of their own data which presently large corporations are explicitly using as a source of huge income.
4. For the ethical dimensions of Islamic finance, see Iqbal and Mirakhor (2017).
5. Some scholars have discussed the moral, emotional, and psychological costs of "debt slavery", or creditor–debtor relationship as "mechanism of exploitation and domination", or debt as a "capture", "predation", and "extraction" machine. See, e.g., Lazzarato (2011) and Hixson (1991). For a comprehensive coverage of the history of credit and debt, see Graeber (2011).
6. Contract theory developed in the 1980s. Two scholars who contributed to its development, Oliver Hart and Bengst Holmstrom, received the Nobel Prize for Economics in 2016.
7. It should also be noted that the debt system poses a serious threat to social solidarity in terms of its significant distributional impact stemming from the fact that it creates social conflict between the creditors (usually the rich) and the debtors (usually less economically able).
8. For an excellent and comprehensive discussion of the meaning and role of *Al Bay'* from a *Fiqhi* perspective, see Bakkali (2017).
9. For a review of this history, see Poitras, G. (2016). *Equity Capital: From Ancient Partnerships to Modern Exchange Trade Funds* Part I (New York: Routledge).
10. See Kister, 1965; Weiss, 1989; Cizakca, 2011, 2014.

Chapter 2

CAPITAL MARKETS: INTRODUCTION AND OVERVIEW

Topics in this Chapter

2.1. Introduction
2.2. Key Trends in Capital Market Development
2.3. Stock Exchanges in the Islamic World
2.4. The Debt Markets
2.5. The Money Markets
2.6. The Derivatives Market
2.7. Risks in Capital Markets

Chapter Objective

This chapter is designed to provide an overview of capital markets. It describes the many functions and roles played by the capital market in modern economies. The main components and instruments traded within capital markets are described. The link between capital market components and the overall economy is examined. On completing the chapter, you should have a good overview of capital markets, their components, and their function.

Key Terms		
bond market	inflation risk	real sector
capital market	liberalization	regulatory risk
credit risk	liquidity risk	*Shari'ah* risk
debt market	market risk	stock exchange
derivatives market	money market	*sukuk*
financial sector	moral hazard	transparency
globalization	political risk	

2.1 Introduction

The capital market plays a very important role in the development of a nation. In many ways, capital markets are at the heart of a nation's financial system. Economists often divide the overall economy into two sectors, the *real* sector and the *financial* sector. While the real sector of the economy produces the nation's output of goods and services, the financial sector plays the vital role of providing the financing needed to fund this productive capacity. It does so by mobilizing the savings of surplus chapters and channelling them to productive chapters that need the funds. Figure 2.1 shows the overall relationship between the financial and the real sectors and the position of the capital market *vis-à-vis* the other two.

While traditionally, the main role of the financial sector has been the mobilization and distribution of funds, modern financial systems have a much broader functional role within an economy. The financial sector also plays a key role in resource allocation, risk management through pooling of resources and diversification, price discovery, providing an efficient clearing and settlements system, and even in dealing with agency problems and informational asymmetries. Given the much broader functional role that the financial system now plays, governments pay greater attention to the well-being and development of the financial sector. Underlying all efforts to enhance financial sector growth would be basic requirements such as clarity of regulation, a simple but effective legal framework, enforceability of contracts, appropriate accounting/auditing supervision standards, and transparency.

As shown in Figure 2.1, capital markets are a sub-segment of the overall financial sector. Within the financial sector, there would also be entities such as banks and the banking system, money markets, insurance firms and pension funds, merchant banks, and other financial intermediaries. So, while the financial system encompasses all these entities, the term "capital market" refers to equity and debts markets, which undoubtedly are part of the financial system. While the capital market, like the rest of the financial system, plays the key role of providing "financing" to the real sector, a distinguishing feature would be the "direct access" that a business entity has in raising funds. Unlike bank financing where the bank lends from deposits it has received from surplus units, companies can access surplus units directly by issuing shares or bonds in the capital market.

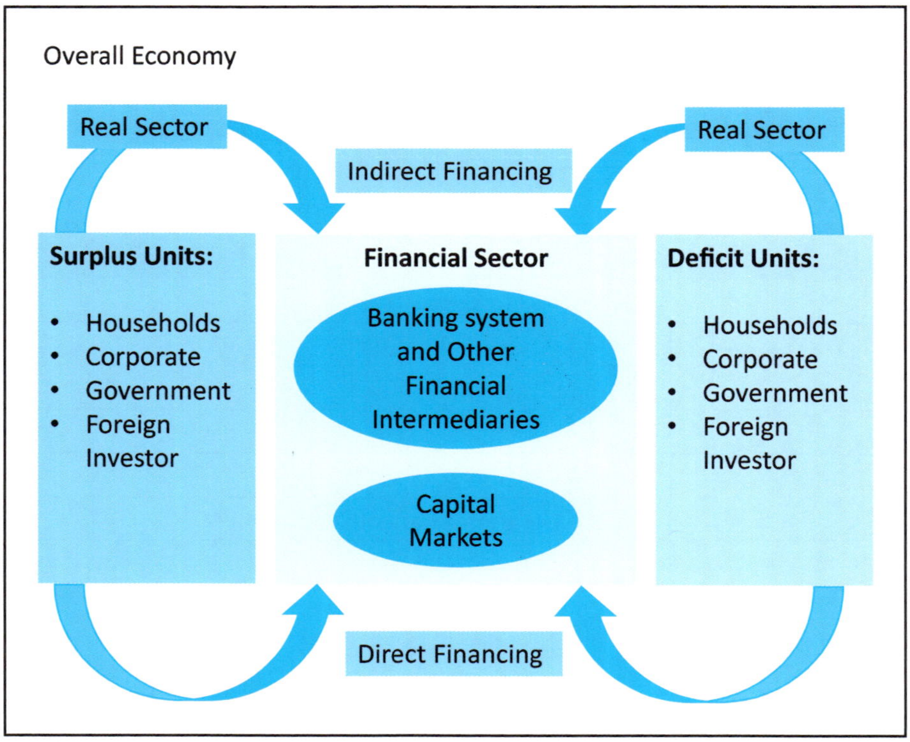

Figure 2.1. Capital Markets and the Financial and Real Sectors.

An important difference that arises as a result of this direct access is the risk transfer. In bank financing, the bank as an intermediary, takes on the risks associated with its lending. A bank's depositor is not directly exposed to the loans his bank has provided. The bank takes on the risks and is compensated for this by the interest spread (the difference between the interest the bank pays its depositors and the rate it charges its borrowers). In the case of capital markets, however, the investors in shares and/or bonds *(sukuks)* take on the risks associated with their investment. Thus, in the event of a fall in shares or *sukuks* price, a diminution of the original invested amount is possible.

In most countries, the "two legs" of the capital market would be the equity or stock market and the bond market. A third component, the derivatives market, is becoming increasingly important in many countries, including Malaysia. A final component is the foreign exchange market. The difference between these four markets has to do with the instruments traded. Stocks or common shares are an equity instrument whereas bonds are a debt instrument. Equity represents partial ownership, entitles the holder to a share in profits, and provides a residual claim on the assets of an issuing company; where maturity is concerned, it is perpetual since stocks have no maturity.

Debt, on the other hand, represents a fixed claim on the issuer, often restricted to a particular asset(s) and has a fixed maturity. Additionally, while the coupon/interest payments for a bond are compulsory, dividend payments for stocks are not. Thus, the risk profile of stocks and bonds would be very different. The third component of the capital market, the derivatives market, trades derivative instruments such as futures and options contracts. In Malaysia, derivatives such as call warrants, transferable subscription rights (TSRs), and irredeemable convertible unsecured loan stocks (ICULs) are also popularly traded. Since a derivative instrument must have an underlying asset from which it derives its value, the derivative market is linked to equity, debt, and commodities markets. Equity derivatives, which are derivatives with equity as an underlying asset, would obviously be linked to the stock market. Equity derivatives would be instruments such as call warrants, single stock futures, stock index futures, and index options, etc. Credit interest rate derivatives, on the other hand, would obviously be linked with the bond market. The foreign exchange market is related to foreign trade and capital transactions; it involves buying and selling foreign currencies for settling export and import operations and for capital transactions such as issuing or investing in stocks and bonds. Operators in foreign exchange markets are the central bank, banks, forex bureaus, multinational corporations, other businesses, and individuals who perform trade, transfer, and capital operations involving foreign currencies. As we will see in Chapter 11, besides trade and capital transactions, the foreign exchange market could be used for managing exchange rate risk and for speculation and arbitrage. Figure 2.2 shows the key components of a typical capital market.

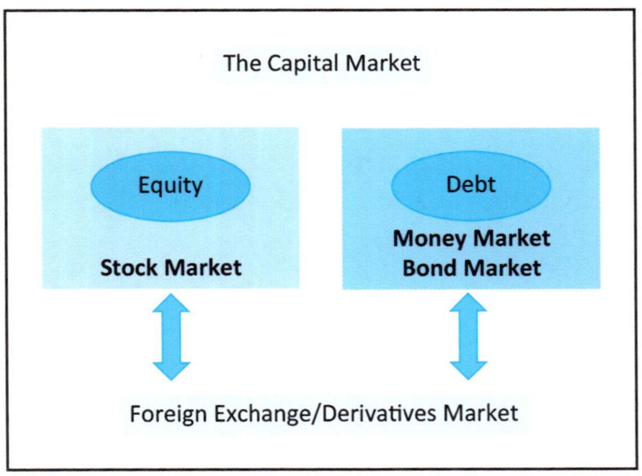

Figure 2.2. The Key Components of a Typical Capital Market.

Despite the rapid growth of Islamic capital market (ICM) components, as Figure 2.3 shows, capital markets of the Muslim countries are still small relative to the banking sector. The banking sector in these countries still

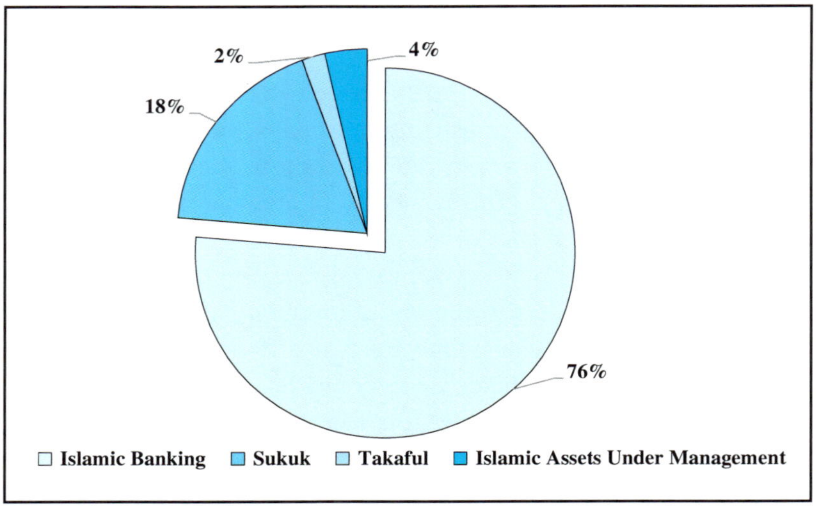

Figure 2.3. Global Breakdown of *Shari'ah*-Compliant Assets.

Source: Thomson Reuters 2016 Global Islamic Finance Development Indictors Report.

dominates the financial sector. ICMs are small relative to Islamic banking. There are a number of reasons for this scenario. First, Islamic banking has been around for a longer time. Second, relative to conventional markets, there is still a dearth of products/instruments within the ICMs. Third, the regulatory framework and trading infrastructure are only now being developed. Finally, it is a fact that countries at a lower level of development tend to have financial sectors that are very much bank-centric. The prominence of banks reduces as capital markets begin to grow.

2.1.1 *Key Functions of Capital Markets*

Traditionally, capital markets have four functions attributed to them. These are:

(i) Performing intermediation, between surplus and deficit units;
(ii) Providing the payments system;
(iii) Enabling inter-temporal transfers; and
(iv) Acting as a medium for monetary policy transmission.

In its first role as an intermediary, capital markets enable surplus units, savers, investors, and the like to place their funds by investing in stocks, bonds, and money instruments. These instruments are issued by the deficit units, i.e., the firms seeking funding through an equity issuance of shares or long-term debt by way of a bond issuance. Firms that require short-term financing would issue money market instruments. As the issuers of these instruments sell them through the different components of the capital market and savers/investors buy the instruments, intermediation happens. The provision of a payments system is not as important a role of capital markets as it is of the banking system. Nevertheless, capital markets can be a mode for payments. Since the payments system is essentially a means to transfer monetary value, a capital market instrument such as a stock or bond could be used at market value to settle one's obligations by transferring their ownership to the party to whom the obligation has to be met.

Inter-temporal transfers refer to the transfer of wealth across time. It is obvious that capital market instruments are well suited for this task. For example, an individual intending to transfer a portion of his wealth to his underaged son could simply buy shares or bonds today and register it in the beneficiary's name. When the son reaches the legal age, he can sell the shares and receive cash. Wealth has been transferred across time. As a medium for monetary policy transmission, capital markets, especially the money market, enables central banks to execute their intended policy actions. This role of money markets will be examined in depth in Chapter 4.

In addition to the four traditional functions of capital markets, modern capital markets have an expanded role. These additional roles are:

(v) Acting as a means and avenue for *risk management*
(vi) Contributing to *price discovery* — interest rates, cost of funds (cost of debt, equity); and
(vii) Assimilating the actions of participants and reflecting them as *market information.*

Capital markets today are a key avenue for risk management. As the economic environment gets increasingly complex, businesses are confronted with a myriad of risks. The typical modern firm faces interest rate risks, currency risks, commodity price risk, credit risk, and possibly also equity risk. Since these risks arise in the normal course of business, firms have little choice but to take the risks and then manage them off in their balance sheet. Companies turn to the capital market, in particular, the derivative markets, to manage these risks. In well-developed derivative markets, there are different products to manage different risks. Equity derivatives can be used to manage equity risk, credit derivatives for managing credit risks, currency derivatives for currency risk, and so on. Derivatives play such an important part in risk management today that it is hard to imagine a well-functioning economy without them. We will examine derivatives in depth in Chapter 11.

In market economies, prices act as signals for resource allocation. Thus, the discovery of prices is of critical importance. Price discovery happens when there is unhindered trading. In addition to the absence of hindrances to trade, players need to be well informed. A key function is to ensure that market players get the latest information cheaply and efficiently. Disseminating the information in a transparent way ensures efficient decision-making on the part of the participants. The ability of capital markets to disseminate information in a timely and cost-effective way is perhaps the most important function of markets these days.

As market-determined prices provide the price signals for resource allocation, the efficacy with which a capital market plays these roles ultimately determines the efficient allocation of resources within an economy. Where capital market functions are hindered, the result would be a misallocation of resources. Retarded capital markets lead to retarded national competitiveness. Inattention to the proper development of capital markets can prove very costly to nations.

2.2 Key Trends in Capital Market Development

Having examined the overall structure of capital markets, we now turn to a brief discussion of some of the key trends in the capital market development of Muslim countries. Over the last decade, there have been four main trends in capital markets: (i) Globalization; (ii) Liberalization; (iii) the increasing importance of Fintech; and (iv) the rise of Islamic finance. While most other regional capital markets have also experienced the first two, Islamic finance has played such an important role that it has changed the topography of the financial sector in many countries, most notably, in Malaysia. In these countries, Islamic finance has also been the main source of growth where capital market products/services are concerned.

2.2.1 *Globalization*

International capital markets have always existed historically, although it has been concentrated mainly among industrial countries for the past few centuries. *Globalization* refers to the integration of emerging capital markets with the international capital markets, and has led to capital markets becoming increasingly internationalized. The performance of most domestic capital markets is now increasingly linked with the performance of other markets. Improvements in communication technology and the trading infrastructure have meant that there is a rapid transmission of information on both positive and negative events across markets. Sentiments in developed markets have had an increasingly important role in the performances of most emerging markets. As a trading nation that has historically been closely linked with the international environment, the Malaysian capital markets, in particular, have always been integrated with the international capital markets. In fact, every stock market boom in Malaysia has typically been the result of foreign capital inflows. The stock market aside, these days, interest rate movements and bond market performance also depend on developments in other major markets — especially that of the US. As shocks are transmitted across markets very quickly and markets move in random fashion, policymakers, cognizant of these co-movements, invariably have to coordinate policies/regulations across boundaries. Such coordinated policies in turn serve to further synchronize markets.

Recent studies of trends in financial globalization appear to show three things. First, capital flows, which are at the heart of financial globalization, appear to have fallen quite substantially in size post-2007/2008 global financial crisis. Banks in the US and Europe, in particular, appear to have pulled back on their funding internationally, especially to developing countries. A second factor of note appears to be the change in the composition of the global capital flows. Where debt had previously dominated, it appears that foreign direct investment (FDI) and equity portfolio investments have become more important. In many ways, this is good as FDI is a lot more stable and more advantageous to recipient countries. The third factor that seems obvious with the recent international capital flows is the increased importance of China as a capital source and the substantially larger footprint of Chinese banks in global capital movements.

2.2.2 *Liberalization*

The second major trend within capital markets has been *liberalization*. Unlike in the 1960s and 1970s, when trade and capital account restrictions were the trend, and foreign capital was viewed with suspicion, today many countries appear to be in competition to liberalize and dismantle hurdles to foreign capital inflows, especially long-term inflows such as FDI. Where regulations are concerned, the thrust is to have a robust regulatory framework that aims at enhancing investors' protection and enlarging financial intermediation. In recent times, the overall policy stance in most emerging markets, including Muslim ones, appears to be one of *deregulation*, *streamlining*, and building *enforcement* capacity. Policymakers everywhere can see the huge benefit to nations in liberalizing capital. The experience of China over the last 30 years and India more recently show how effective capital market liberalization can be to economic development.

2.2.3 *The Rise of Fintech*

Fintech, which is short for financial technology, appears to be shaking up the world of finance. The financial sector most affected and probably bearing the brunt is banking. Ironically, Fintech began in banking as banks started to use technology for the backroom functions. Any standardized and repetitive process that does not require much skills can be undertaken much more efficiently and at vastly reduced operating costs through Fintech. Software developers who had helped banks automate their backroom operations saw a niche, and today, many Fintech firms have started to offer specific banking services like remittances, fund raising/credit provision, and even asset management. Being smaller and nimbler, the Fintech firms are able to serve large swathes of the population that are not served or are inadequately served by the banking system. The best example of this is crowdfunding. Crowdfunding, as the name suggests, refers to a crowd or large number of investors collectively funding a business undertaking or enterprise. Each investor makes a small investment. The system therefore has built-in risk management, in that the investment risk is dissipated across a large number of players. The potential downside to each investor is small. The medium by which all this happens is an electronic platform. The huge efficiency gains in information technology, communications, computing software, and hardware have made Fintech possible. It has become economically viable to monitor even small investments at short-time frequency and distribute the information to a large number of investors, something no banks with large overheads could do.

Box 2.1. Regulatory Framework: The Malaysian Example

Until the establishment of Securities Commission (SC) in March 1993, the Malaysian capital market came under the purview of several entities. Among these were the Registrar of Companies (ROC), the Capital Issues Committee (CIC), the Panel on Take-overs and Mergers (TOP), the Foreign Investment Committee (FIC), Bank Negara Malaysia (BNM, the Central bank), the Ministry of International Trade and Industry (MITI), and the Stock Exchange, Bursa Malaysia. It was obvious that this complicated regulatory framework was unsuited for a nation aspiring to be a regional financial center. The need for a single regulatory body for the capital market was first identified in the Sixth Malaysia Plan (1991–1995). This led to the promulgation in the Malaysian parliament of the Securities Commission Act (SCA). With the establishment of the SC, several entities such as the CIC, TOP, and the Commodities Trading Commission were dissolved, and their functions assumed by the SC.

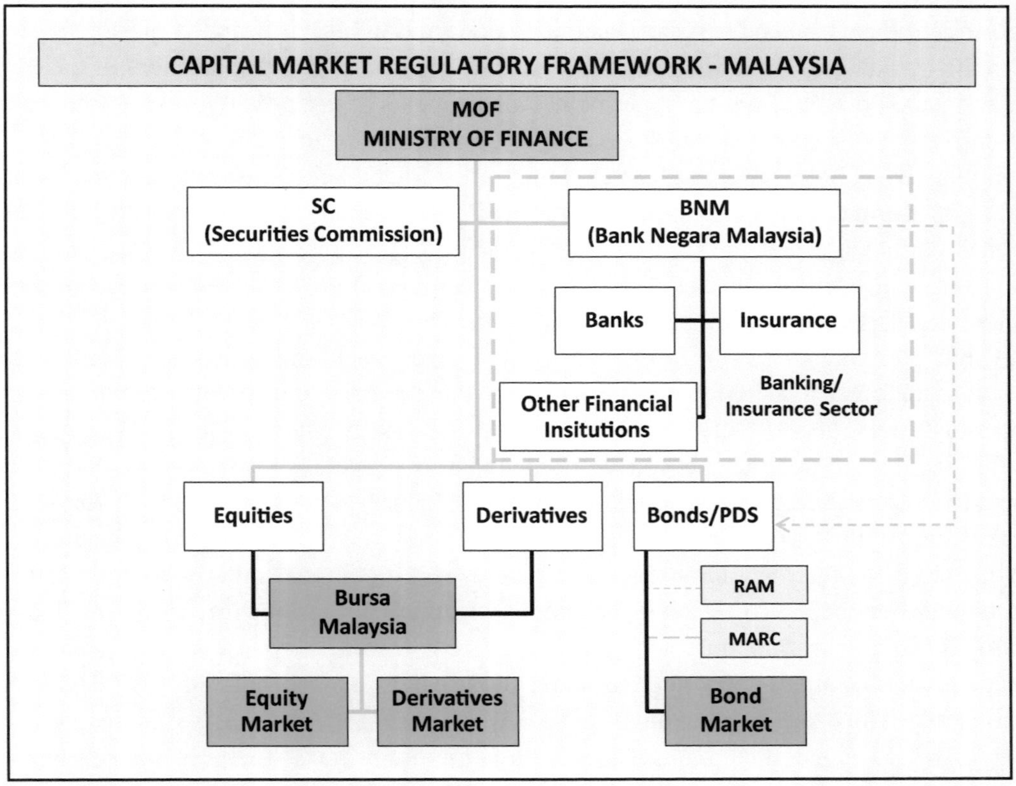

Source: Islamic Capital Markets, Obiyathulla Ismath Bacha, Abbas Mirakhor, Wiley, October 2013.

In addition, the regulatory functions of some of the other institutions that were related to capital markets were reformulated to come under the SC. A series of amendments to the SCA were undertaken over the 1995–2000 period. These amendments served to enhance the investigative powers of the SC and strengthen its enforcement programs. Effective July 2000, all regulation with regards to issuance of securities, including the power to approve prospectuses, have been centralized with the SC. Currently, the SC is the sole regulatory body for the Malaysian capital market. The exception being that, were a bank or financial institution established under BAFIA[1] want to raise funds in the capital market, the Central bank, BNM's approval may also be necessary. To enhance Malaysian international position, the Labuan offshore financial market has been founded. It is regulated by the Labuan Offshore Financial Services Authority, which falls directly under the purview of the SC.

Today, Fintech, which first started by serving the "unbankable", appears to be taking on banks head on. For example, mobile payment systems using mobile phones have eroded the monopoly banks once had on the payments system. Not all the developments in Fintech are bad for banks. Banks have benefited in many ways. The widespread acceptance of electronic banking has meant that banks now have to invest less in brick and mortar branch networks, a substantial saving to bank operating costs. In several countries, including Malaysia, banks have opted for fewer branches and increased emphasis on e-banking. Looking ahead, it appears that Fintech is likely to make the banking environment a lot more challenging. It seems possible that some parts of traditional banking products/services may be disintermediated away from banks. Fintech, which has already chipped away at the charter value of banks, has the potential to be even more disruptive.

2.2.4 *The Rise of Islamic Finance*

Of the three abovementioned trends, the rise of Islamic finance and ICMs has been the most pervasive. ICM, which broadly refers to the market in Islamic securities, has become the fastest growing segment of the capital market. In the case of Malaysia and possibly Bahrain, it permeates all segments of the capital market, equities, bonds, foreign, exchange, and derivatives. Islamic securities are simply capital market instruments that are *Shari'ah*-compliant. While such compliance has been fairly easy where equity instruments are concerned, the bond market has had to completely redesign the instruments in order to be *Shari'ah*-compliant. This has to do with the fact that the *Shari'ah* condones partnership and profit/loss-based financing but prohibits interest-based debt financing. Since equity financing is in congruence with the *Shari'ah*, listed equities and derivatives merely had to be screened in order to determine their acceptability as a *halal* stock. In the case of Malaysia, the *Shari'ah* Advisory Committee (SAC) of the SC has outlined a series of filters that a listed stock would have to pass in order to be designated a *halal* or *Shari'ah*-compliant stock. Globally, Dow Jones, the financial information provider, has worked with *Shari'ah* scholars to design *Shari'ah* screening filters for internationally listed stocks. Its Dow Jones Islamic World Markets (DJIWM) indices are popularly used (see Chapter 10).

Among the basic filters used in stock screening would be issues such as the nature of the issuing company's business and the form of its capital structure. For example, a company in a non-*halal* business like gambling, tobacco, or conventional banking, would obviously fail the most basic filter. Similarly, a company that has financed most of its assets with debt capital or earns a substantial portion of its earnings from interest income would also not be deemed to be *Shari'ah*-compliant.

Today, of the universe of about 950 listed stocks on Bursa Malaysia, approximately 65% have been deemed to be *Shari'ah*-compliant. Thus, the Muslim investor is never short of stocks that he could invest in. Where the Malaysian equity market is concerned, *halal* designation is important for a stock. Such a designation enables the stock to attract the huge pool of Islamic investible funds, both local and foreign. Empirical studies have shown that such designation leads to higher returns, higher traded volume, and increased liquidity for a stock. Unlike listed stock that can be screened for *Shari'ah* compatibility, bonds as debt instruments had to be totally redesigned in order to be *Shari'ah*-compliant. Islamic bonds, or *sukuks*, as they are known, are based on completely different underlying contractual arrangements. Despite their newness as an investible asset, Islamic bonds have been extremely popular. Most of the recent growth in the Malaysian bond market owes to this popularity. In fact, the majority of recent bond issues have been Islamic bonds. This trend toward Islamic finance is also evident in the area of derivative instruments, although at a slower pace. A number of Islamic structured products have been introduced recently that are essentially Islamic versions of conventional derivatives. The Islamic Profit Rate Swap is one well-known example. Before going into an in-depth discussion of individual components of capital markets, we examine briefly some of the key stock markets within Muslim countries.

Table 2.1 shows the top 10 stock markets in Muslim countries ranked by market capitalization. The first point to take note is that none of these markets fall within the top 20 or 30 stock markets of the world. The Taiwanese stock exchange, which was ranked number 20 as of 2009, had a market capitalization almost three times that of Saudi Arabia's *Tadawul*, which holds the top rank. Thus, going by world standards, these are small markets. Even though many of the markets in Table 2.1 have been established decades ago, for e.g., Pakistan's Karachi Stock Exchange, their size is miniscule. In many ways, stock markets of the Islamic world have remained infantile because, in many cases, governments have not provided the necessary ingredients for their full development. Some of the basic ingredients needed for the proper functioning and development of markets would be factors such as transparency, good governance, infrastructure, rule of law, enforceability of contracts, protection of property rights and corruption-free systems. Students of the *Shari'ah* would recognize that these are also requisites of the *Shari'ah* especially in the context of *mu'amalah* and not alien to the Islamic economic system.

2.3 Stock Exchanges of the Islamic World

As the stock market is typically the largest component of the capital market in most emerging markets, including Islamic countries, we shall briefly examine each of the stock markets listed in Table 2.1.

Table 2.1. Top 10 Stock Markets of the Islamic World by Market Capitalization (December 2015–2016).

Country	Stock Exchange Code	Market Capitalization (US$ Billion) 2015	Market Capitalization (US$ Billion) 2016	Name of Exchange	Year of Establishment
Saudi Arabia	*TASI*	US$421.06	US$448.83	Tadawul	1993
Indonesia	*JKSE*	US$353.27	**US$425.76**	Bura Efek Indonesia	1989
Malaysia	*KLCI*	US$382.98	US$359.79	Bursa Malaysia	1960
UAE	*ADX*	US$195.87	US$ 213.21	Abu Dhabi Securities Exchange	2000
Turkey	*XU100*	US$188.86	US$171.76	Istanbul Stock Exchange	1985
Qatar	*DSM*	US$142.56	US$154.82	Doha Securities Market	1997
Iran	*TSE*	US$89.42804	US$108.79	Teheran Stock Exchange	1967
Egypt	*EGX 30*	US$55.19187	US$33.3430	Egyptian Stock Exchange	1998
Oman	*MSI*	US$41.12317	US$23.2852	Muscat Stock Market	1988
Bahrain	*BSE*	US$19.25107	US$19.3941	Bahrain Stock Exchange	1987

Source: Based on World Development Indicators, World Bank.

2.3.1 *Tadawul (Saudi Arabia)*

Tadawul is the only stock exchange in Saudi Arabia. Until the early 1980s, when the Saudi government initiated efforts to formalize and install formal trading systems, the stock market existed in an informal manner. Though the stock exchange had been established in 1993, it went through a major revamp, which culminated in its current form in March 2003. The establishment of the Saudi Arabian Monetary Authority (SAMA) in 1984 was a critical milestone in the development of capital markets in Saudi Arabia.

The rapid growth of the financial sector required the establishment of a specialized regulatory body to monitor and develop the domestic market. The Saudi government responded to this need by establishing the Capital Market Authority (CMA) in 2003. The CMA initiated equity market reforms and helped restructure the existing stock exchange as the Tadawul in 2007. CMA supervises the exchange. The Tadawul All Share Index (TASI) consists of all 171 stocks traded in the Saudi stock market.

Currently, the Saudi bourse is the largest stock exchange in the region. Until December 2007, the Tadawul was open only to Saudi nationals. In December 2007, Gulf Cooperation Council (GCC) nationals were allowed to participate. Until 2008, non-residents could only participate through several mutual funds. In August 2008, the

Saudi CMA allowed foreigners to participate in share trading through swap arrangements with local CMA-designated intermediaries.

The first Islamic mutual fund in Saudi Arabia was launched in 1987. As of October 2016, there were 200 *Shari'ah*-compliant mutual funds listed on the Saudi Stock Exchange. With an estimated 18% of global Islamic banking assets and 14% of Islamic fund assets in end-2015, Saudi Arabia is considered to have one of the most developed Islamic financial markets. Today, the impending listing of ARAMCO (Arab-American Oil Company) which promises to be a blockbuster Initial Public Offer (IPO), will likely change the topography of the Saudi bourse. Given the market liberalization undertaken recently by the Saudi government, Saudi capital markets can look to a promising future.

2.3.2 *Bursa Malaysia*

As an emerging market, the Malaysian stock market has seen its share of ups and downs. The two decades from 1976 to 1996 appear to have been a period of very rapid growth. Stock market growth, measured by Total Market Capitalization, hit a peak of US$318.6 billion in 1996. This effectively placed the Malaysian market in the third spot among bourses in the Asia-Pacific region. Asia's star exchanges, Korea, Taiwan, and Singapore, were lagging behind the Malaysia market as at 1996. The onset of the Asia currency crisis in 1997 and the Malaysian government's imposition of capital controls had far reaching consequences for the stock market. Total Market Capitalization in 2002 stood at US$127 billion, essentially 40% of the capitalization in 1996. Though the real sector bounced back and recovered quickly, the financial sector, especially the stock market, had to work through a slower process before recovering from the currency-induced crisis. As of June 2006, total capitalization was approximately US$200 billion, placing the Malaysian market at 11th place among developing countries.[2] In 2010, a total of 1,025 companies were listed on the Bursa Malaysia. This represents an approximate fourfold increase from the 262 companies that were listed in 1973 when the single currency agreement with Singapore ended. Beginning with a Main Board of listed stocks, a Second Board was added in 1989. This was intended as a means by which smaller companies with less than RM20 million in capital could be listed.

Currently, in addition to two boards, Bursa Malaysia has introduced LEAP, which is an additional platform intended for Small and Medium Enterprises (SMEs) to raise funds. In addition to liberal listing requirements, listing and other costs have been reduced substantially for LEAP participants. Today, Malaysia's bourse is easily one of the most sophisticated in the Muslim world. In addition to equities and mutual funds, Bursa Malaysia offers Exchange Traded Funds (ETFs), Real Estate Investment Trusts (REITs), *Shari'ah*-compliant derivatives, and other products. Some of Bursa Malaysia's products like the Crude Palm Oil (CPO) futures contracts are traded on GLOBEX, an international trading platform which enables investors in other time zones to trade CPO even when Bursa is closed. Such globalized trading enhances price discovery by enlarging the participant base.

2.3.3 *Borsa Istanbul*

The predecessor to Borsa Istanbul, The Istanbul Stock Exchange (ISE), (Turkish: *İstanbul Menkul Kıymetler Borsası*, İMKB), established in December 1985, is the only securities exchange in Turkey. The ISE provides the platform for trading in equities, bonds, and bills; revenue-sharing certificates; private sector bonds; foreign securities and real estate certificates; as well as international securities. Trading began in early 1986. The ISE was founded as an autonomous, professional organization. Like most other exchanges, the ISE operates as a self-regulating entity. In 2012, following the adoption of a Capital Markets Law, the ISE became known as Borsa Istanbul. The new law effectively consolidated all Turkish exchanges under a single new entity known as Borsa Istanbul.

The exchanges' stock price indices are computed and published throughout the trading session, while the return indices are calculated and published at the close of the session only. Though there are several stock and other indices reported by the exchange, the main index is the Borsa Istanbul 100 index. This is a market capitalization weighted index of the 100 largest listed companies on Borsa Istanbul.

2.3.4 *The Indonesian Stock Exchange*

The Indonesian Stock Exchange (IDX), or Bursa Efek Indonesia (BEI), is a stock exchange based in Jakarta, Indonesia. It was previously known as The Jakarta Stock Exchange (JSX) before its name changed in 2007. The name change followed a merger of The Jakarta Stock Exchange with the Surabaya Stock Exchange (SSX).

First opened in 1912 under the Dutch colonial government, the IDX was reopened in 1977 after several closures during World War I and World War II. Following its reopening in 1977, the exchange was under the management of the newly created Capital Market Supervisory Agency (Badan Pengawas Pasar Modal, or Bapepam), which came under the Ministry of Finance. Trading activity and market capitalization grew alongside the development of Indonesia's financial markets and private sectors — highlighted by a major bull run in 1990. On July 13, 1992, the exchange was privatized under the ownership of Jakarta Exchange Inc. As a result, the functions of Bapepam changed to become the Capital Market Supervisory Agency. On March 22, 1995, JSX launched the Jakarta Automated Trading System (JATS). Despite a much larger economy than Malaysia, the Indonesian Stock Exchange (IDX) has a little more than 500 stocks listed. The potential for future growth by way of increased listing is obvious. The IDX has two main stock indices: the Jakarta Composite Index (JCI), which is a composite index of all listed stocks; and the Jakarta Islamic Index (JII), which is an index of *Shari'ah*-compliant stocks listed on the exchange.

2.3.5 *The Qatar Exchange*

The Qatar Exchange, which began as The Doha Securities Market (DSM), was established in 1995 and began trading in mid-1997. Though only about 50 Qatari companies are listed, the exchange has big hopes of becoming a regional player. Accordingly, in 2009, the Qatar Investment Authority, which is the owner of the exchange, entered into an agreement with NYSE Euronext, the world's leading exchange group, to establish a world class exchange in Qatar. As a result of this, the Doha Securities Market was renamed the Qatar Exchange. A fully electronic exchange, the Qatar Exchange has benefited from liberalization efforts by the Qatari government. Foreigners are now allowed to own up to 25% of shares listed for trading.

The DSM20 Index, which used to be the market barometer, was replaced in 2010 with the QE Index. The QE Index is a market capitalization weighted index of the 20 largest and most liquid companies. As in the case of other Gulf countries, Qatar too has seen market liberalization to some extent. Under the liberalized regime, foreigners can invest in any listed stock provided they do not own more than 25% of the total value.

2.3.6 *Kuwait Stock Exchange*

The Kuwait Stock Exchange (KSE) was established in March 1983 and trading began in September 1984. It is the country's only stock exchange. Although several shareholding companies existed in Kuwait prior to the creation of the KSE, it was not until October 1962 that a law was passed to organize the country's stock market. The Kuwait Stock Exchange is also among the first and largest stock exchanges in the Gulf region and is now gaining prominence as one of the most potentially important in the world.

The KSE has two indices: an equally weighted price index and a capitalization weighted index. The Kuwait stock exchange is also one of the few exchanges in the Middle East to have equity derivatives traded. The KSE trades index options and futures contracts on single stocks.

2.3.7 *The Egyptian Stock Exchange*

The Egyptian Stock Exchange (EGX), which is Egypt's main stock exchange, has a colorful history. It began operations in Alexandria in 1883. Though known as the Alexandria Stock Exchange, it was more of a commodity futures exchange trading futures/forward contracts in cotton. This was followed by the Cairo Stock Exchange, which was established in 1903. Despite a major crash in 1907, both the Cairo and Alexandria exchanges were among the most active in the world in the early 1900s. Following a series of financial mishaps, the two exchanges were merged as the Egyptian Stock Exchange in 1961. Though these were the oldest exchanges in the Middle East and the Islamic world, today, the Egyptian Stock Exchange has paled in significance. Egypt's experiment with socialism in the 1960s to 1970s dashed any hopes of rejuvenation that the exchanges may have had.

Since March 2009, the Egyptian Stock Exchange's main index is known as the EGX 30. The index's value is calculated in local currency terms and denominated in US dollars since 1998. EGX started publishing its dollar-denominated index on March 1, 2009. The EGX 30 index includes the top 30 companies in terms of liquidity and activity. It is weighted by market capitalization and adjusted by the free float. For a company to be included in the EGX 30 index, it must have at least 15% free float. This ensures that the index constituents truly represent actively traded companies and that the index is a good barometer for the Egyptian market.

As an emerging stock market, the EGX lists stocks, bonds, mutual funds, and some ETFs. A small number of structured products are also available. Of late, the Egyptian Stock Exchange has initiated a number of Memorandums of Understanding (MOUs) with exchanges in other countries such as Brazil's Bovespa, The Bombay Stock Exchange, and The Sydney Stock Exchange.

2.3.8 *Tehran Stock Exchange (Iran)*

The Tehran Stock Exchange (TSE), which is Iran's largest stock exchange, began in early 1967 with six companies listed for trading. Currently, there are about 420 companies listed with a total market capitalization of about US$72 billion.

The idea for a national stock exchange dates back to 1936, when Bank Melli, the largest bank in Iran, together with Belgian experts, examined the prospects of having an operational stock exchange in Iran. Despite the early start, it was not until 1967 that the Government ratified the Stock Exchange Act. With the ratification, a small exchange, TSE began its operations in 1967.

The oil-induced economic boom of the 1970s and the Iranian government's offer of stocks to employees of its commercial entities led to a boom in stock market participation. The exchange was trading Government bonds and "Land Reform Bills", in addition to common stocks.

Everything came to a standstill with the Islamic Revolution. Aside from the nationalization of banks and major corporations, the Islamic government introduced regulation prohibiting interest. The banking sector was restructured under "Usury Free Banking". The eight-year-long Iran–Iraq War proved to be another dampener on the stock market performance. With the end of the war in 1988, the government embraced economic reforms with a massive privatization initiative in 1989. All these brought life back to the exchange, and trading volume showed impressive gains and a period of growth began for the exchange. In 1992, the TSE became a member of the International federation of Stock Exchanges. In 2006, the TSE completed its demutualization. Demutualization refers to the process by which an exchange becomes a public listed entity, where previously it was privately owned by broker's affiliated to the exchange. In 2008, TSE introduced a new platform for SMEs known as *Iran Farabourse*. The year 2010 saw a series of deregulation measures for foreign investors on TSE. The same year saw TSE launching its online trading system and the introduction of Single Stock Futures (SSFs). Two years later, in 2012, TSE introduced an additional derivative product, an Embedded Put Option.

As with all exchanges, the TSE has a number of indices. The most popular are the TEPIX, which stands for TSE All share price index, and TEDPIX, which is a dividend and price index. The TEDPIX is essentially a total return index that includes dividend yields.

2.3.9 *The Pakistan Stock Exchange*

The Pakistan Stock Exchange (PSX), previously known as the Karachi Stock Exchange (KSE), is located in Karachi, Pakistan's largest city and commercial center. Founded in 1947, it is the country's largest and oldest stock exchange. The exchange lists both Pakistani and some foreign companies. Like other exchanges, the KSE has migrated from an open outcry system to a fully automated electronic system. The exchange has gone through major reforms. It now has risk management facilities, market making systems, and a globally accepted compliance system. The KSE underwent a demutualization exercise in 2012. Though there were other exchanges in Lahore and Islamabad, the KSE was far by the most prominent. The Pakistani government initiated efforts to consolidate all its three exchanges, the Karachi Stock Exchange, The Lahore Stock Exchange, and The Islamabad Stock Exchange, into a single entity. This consolidation resulted in the formation of the Pakistan Stock Exchange (PSX) in January 2016.

The PSX currently has about 560 companies listed. In addition to stocks, government bonds and REITS are the key listed products. The exchange plans to introduce ETFs, Derivatives, and other products in the future. The KSE 100 and the PSX KMI All Shares Index are two popular stock indices of the PSX. In June 2017, the PSX was included in MSCI's Emerging Markets Index.

2.3.10 *Muscat Stock Market (Oman)*

The Muscat Securities Market (MSM) was established in June 1988. All listed securities in Oman are traded on this exchange. Ten years later, in 1998, the Omani government established the Capital Market Authority (CMA) as the sole regulatory agency. The exchange is a government entity supervised by the CMA. In 1998, a centralized depository for shares, the Muscat Depository and Securities Registration Company, was established. The Omani MSM 30 index is composed of the 30 most highly capitalized, liquid, and profitable companies listed on the MSM. The exchange trades stocks of listed companies, government bonds, corporate bonds, and listed mutual funds.

2.3.11 *Abu Dhabi Securities Exchange (UAE)*

Abu Dhabi Securities Exchange (ADX) was established on November 15, 2000, to facilitate trade in shares of UAE companies. ADX has four trading locations in Abu Dhabi: Al Ain, Fujairah, Sharjah, and Ras Al Khaimah. ADX has seen a substantial rise in the number of companies listed and currently has more companies listed than the neighboring Dubai Financial Market (DFM) although the volume traded is substantially lower than that of the latter. Overall, the ADX is small, with approximately 60 listed companies. Though the ADX allows for the listing of mutual funds, bonds, and ETFs, there are few listings of these products. The stock market barometer is the ADX General Index, which is a market capitalization weighted index of all listed stocks.

2.3.12 *The Dubai Financial Market*

The Dubai Financial Market (DFM) was established in March 2000 as a regional exchange. Located in the Middle East's main financial hub of Dubai, DFM is itself a listed company. It is also designed to be a *Shari'ah*-compliant exchange. In an interesting development, DFM combined its operations with that of Nasdaq Dubai, which is another exchange. The consolidation enables investors of one exchange to seamlessly trade securities listed on the other exchange. While DFM is home to domestic companies, Nasdaq Dubai lists international stocks. As of early 2016, there were 178 companies listed on DFM. The Dubai Financial Market General Index is market's barometer.

In concluding our above discussion of the key equity markets of the Muslim world, it would be useful to ask which of the above markets is most comprehensive, has broad representation of the underlying economy, and has the range of products reflective of developed markets. Though Malaysia's stock market, Bursa Malaysia, is not the

Box 2.2. Islamic Finance Needs to Emphasize Capital Market Development

Development economists often divide the overall economy into two sectors: the *real* and *financial* sectors. The real sector constitutes the aggregate of productive capacity and accounts for the output of goods and services. The financial sector has the role of funding the real sector. Just as a computer's hardware and software have to work well together for optimal computing performance, so should the two sectors of the macroeconomy. When one sector is stunted or lags, economic growth would be handicapped. The composition of the financial sector matters as well. A nation's financial sector has two broad components: the banking system and capital markets. Whereas the banking system is typically monolithic in the type of funding it provides — debt financing — the capital market offers more variety through its bond, equity, derivative, and money markets. Capital market financing can vary from debt to equity and hybrids. The form and means by which funding is provided has consequences for systemic risk within an economy, so does the relative size of the banking sector *vis-à-vis* the capital markets.

A bank-dominant financial sector would invariably be riskier relative to one that is capital market centric. This has to do with differences in the nature of the intermediation process. First, funds flow between surplus units (investors) and deficit units (borrowers) indirectly in the case of banking but directly in capital markets. The depositor has no idea who the bank lends his money to, nor should he care since there is risk transfer. The bank takes on the credit risk, not the depositor. Second, banks perform maturity transformation, i.e., lend long term using short-term deposits/funds, thereby creating a mismatch. In capital markets, when an investor buys shares or bonds, he takes the risk directly. The capital market intermediary does not take on the risk. Furthermore, there is no inherent maturity mismatch as in banking.

The banking model also results in risk concentration, where a single imprudent bank can bring down the entire system. Banking does not have the inbuilt stabilizer that capital markets have. In capital markets, risks get dissipated across thousands, if not millions, of investors, making the system much more resilient to shocks, both internal and external.

With risks transferred on to banks and concentrated within the system, and due to the inherent maturity mismatches and other motivational inconsistencies, governments have little choice but to provide banks with a range of implicit and explicit guarantees. Though intended to make the banks more resilient, the guarantees have instead incentivized recklessness, moral hazards, and a host of other issues, including "too big to fail". The resulting contingent liability to governments is massive. Capital markets of course require no guarantees or bailouts, nor do they give rise to any contingent liability to governments. Smart policy-making should therefore be pushing for quicker development of capital markets.

This brings us to the state of affairs with Islamic finance. Though Islamic finance today transcends borders and operates in many countries, it has a similar impact within the domestic economy. In the majority of countries where it operates, the Islamic finance sector is, in many ways, a subset of the overall domestic financial sector. Given identical products and processes, governments face pretty much the same contingent liabilities with Islamic banks as they do with conventional ones. An ICD-Thomson Reuters report on Islamic Finance shows that, as at end of last year, the total assets were slightly above US$2 trillion. An Islamic Financial Services Board (IFSB) study forecasts that the total Islamic finance assets are expected to grow to US$3.5 trillion by 2021. These are indeed very impressive growth numbers, but they may be masking an underlying skewness. Some 73% or close to three-quarters of total Islamic finance assets are within Islamic banks. *Takaful* accounts for a mere 2% while the remainder 25% constitute assets within capital market instruments such as *sukuk*, mutual funds, and others. Thus, within the Islamic finance space, therefore, banking is at least three times the size of capital markets. Given our discussion above of the inadequacies of a bank-reliant financial sector, economic planners and policy-makers would be well advised to seek not just to grow Islamic finance but focus on the capital markets component. This is not just good from a systemic risk and macroeconomic vulnerability viewpoint, but is also more in keeping with the *Shari'ah* philosophy of risk-sharing.

Source: Author's op-ed column in *Derin Ekonomi*, September 2017.

largest Islamic country market, it is one of the oldest and most established. More so than the stock market, Malaysia has been the forerunner in developing an ICM. The Malaysian government has undertaken several initiatives to ensure the development of a well-functioning ICM that complements its already well-established conventional capital market. Malaysia is probably one of the few Islamic countries which come close to what economists would call "a complete market". A complete market, for an asset, is one in which trading, hedging, and arbitrage are all possible. It is for this reason that in this course, we will examine many issues in the context of the Malaysian capital market.

2.4 Debt Markets

Unlike developed markets, where the debt markets (bond and money markets) are huge in comparison to equity markets, the opposite is the case in emerging markets. The corporate markets are more likely to raise debt financing by borrowing from banks rather than issue bonds or debt instruments. Thus, in most emerging markets, including Islamic countries, there are no well-developed debt markets. The market for credit is highly bank-centric. The lack of good regulatory framework and trading infrastructure for debt papers are key reasons. Add to this the general reluctance of Muslim businesses to use interest-based financing, and we have a ready explanation for the infantile bond markets in Muslim countries.

Of late, a new development has brought new life to the otherwise moribund "debt markets" of the Muslim world. This has to do with the huge popularity of *sukuks*. Though *sukuks*, as we will see in Chapter 7, are a hybrid instrument and not "debt" in the conventional sense, the markets at least considered them as "Islamic bonds". The fact that issuing companies do not have to dilute ownership as an equity issuance would is probably a huge contributor to the immense popularity of *sukuks*. As Figures 2.4 and 2.5 show, *sukuk* issuance has seen a rapid growth.

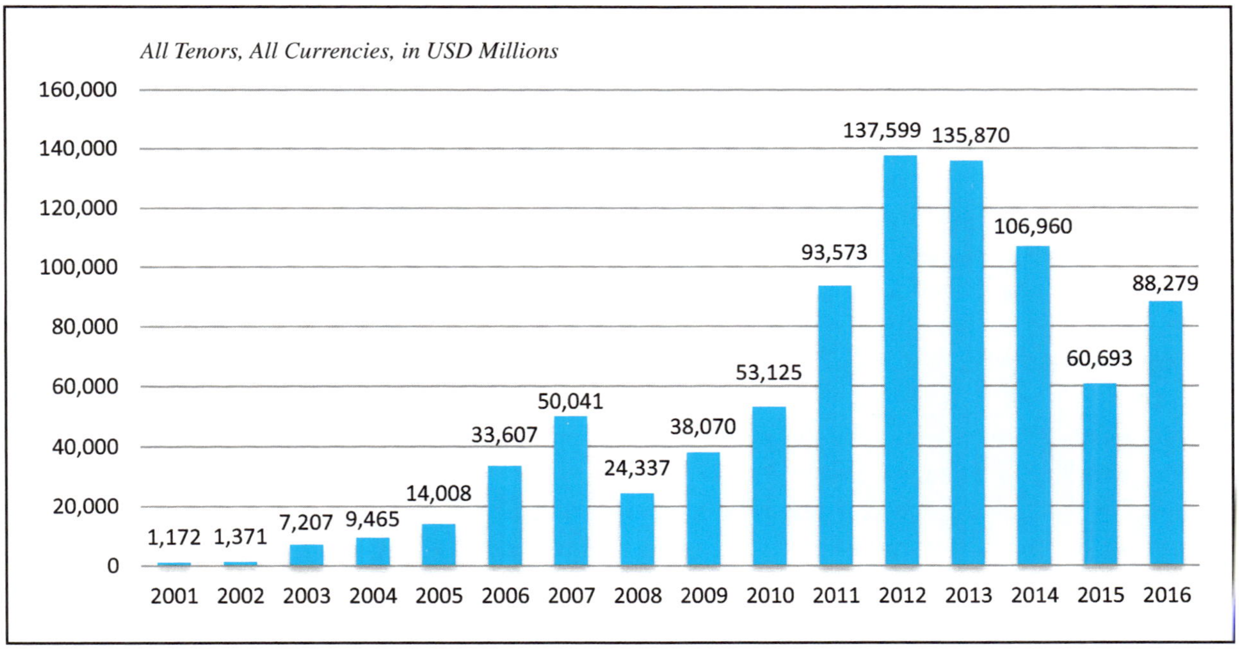

Figure 2.4. Total Global *Sukuk* Issuance (January 2001–December 2015).

Source: Based on the IIFM 2017 Sukuk Report. "A Comprehensive Study of the Global Sukuk Market", July 2017, 6th edition, International Islamic Financial Market (IIFM) http://www.iifm.net/system/files/private/en/IIFM%20Sukuk%20Report%20%286th%20Edition%29_2.pdf

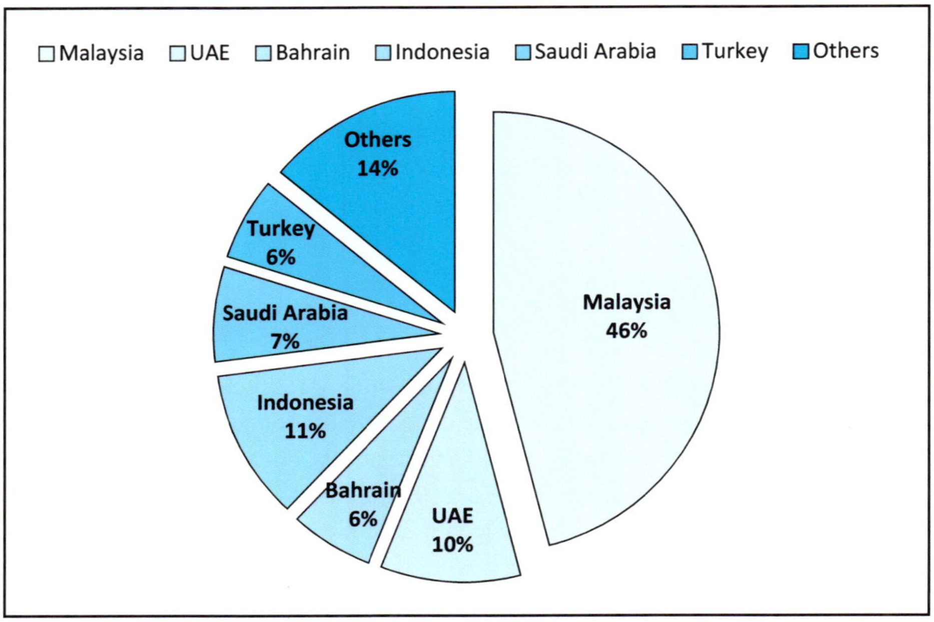

Figure 2.5. Total Global *Sukuk* Issuance by Country.

Source: MIFC — Global Sukuk Report 2016. 2016 Global Sukuk Market: A Record Year for Corporate Issuance http://www.mifc.com/index.php?rp=sukuk_report_270317.pdf Malaysia International Islamic Financial Centre (MIFC)

In a typical *sukuk* arrangement, funds raised from selling *sukuks* are used to purchase an asset. Ownership of this asset is "detached" from the other assets of the issuing company and placed within a bankruptcy-remote Special Purpose Vehicle (SPV). Profits derived from the asset are then divided between the issuing firm and *sukuk* holders according to a predetermined profit-sharing ratio. Of late, lease-based *sukuks*, or *sukuk-al-ijarah*, have become more popular. In this arrangement, proceeds from the sale of *sukuks* go to an SPV which uses the fund to purchase the needed asset/machinery. This asset is then "leased' to the *sukuk*-issuing company. The company makes periodic lease payments over a predetermined period. These lease payments would be an amount sufficient to amortize the original investment of the *sukuk* holders while also providing an agreed rate of return on the funds.

In addition to the fact that the popularity of *sukuk* may be due to pent up demand for a *Shari'ah*-compliant alternative to credit instruments, a number of Muslim countries have undertaken tax reforms to regularize their tax structures to at least neutralize the potential bias against Islamic finance-based transactions. Malaysia has gone a step further to provide tax incentives. Among these incentives have been:

(i) Exemption of stamp duty for all instruments relating to issue and transfer of private debt securities PDS (effective 2000);
(ii) Exemption of stamp duty and real property tax on all approved securitizations;
(iii) Tax deductibility of floatation costs;
(iv) Removal of withholding tax for foreigners repatriating income earned from bonds/*sukuks*; and
(v) Income tax deduction of earnings received from bond investments.

Though Malaysia is a leader in *sukuk* origination, the *sukuk* phenomenon is global. Increasingly, many non-Muslim entities, such as companies like General Electric in the US, and municipalities in Germany, etc., have issued *sukuk* to raise financing. Given its current popularity, it seems likely that *sukuk* will dominate and possibly change the nature of capital markets in Muslim countries. While *sukuk* appears to be developing unimpeded, the absence of an active secondary market remains a problem. Aside from liquidity, this also raises issues of pricing and valuation. Moving forward, these will be the challenges for the *sukuk* market.

2.5 Money Markets

The money market is a key component of a country's financial system. The money market was an essential component of the credit market in the 18th and 19th centuries. It enabled banks to grant short-term loans and companies to discount trade bills and finance short-term commercial operations. The money market is a part of debt markets, in that it trades short-term debt papers. Thus, the short-end of the yield curve[3] is derived from money market trading. It is not uncommon, therefore, to hear of the money market being characterized as the market for short-end debt. Besides companies, banks depend on the money market to manage their liquidity. Banks with tight liquidity borrow from banks that have ample liquidity at the inter-bank rate generally using repo-agreements. The London Inter-Bank Offered Rate (LIBOR) is an example of an inter-bank money rate. While liquidity management is not the only use of money markets for banks, it is by far the most important. As we will see in Chapters 4 and 5, there are several other key functions that the money market plays, including providing the platform for monetary policy execution and transmission.

As is the case with bonds and *sukuk*, the money market in Malaysia has both a conventional and *Shari'ah*-compliant version, the latter known as the Islamic Interbank Money Market (IIMM). One other country with a *Shari'ah*-compliant market for managing short-term liquidity requirements is Bahrain. The Bahraini Central Bank and the government have established the Liquidity Management Centre (LMC) to enable Islamic Banks and other Islamic financial institutions to buy or sell short-term papers from LMC in order to manage their liquidity.

2.6 Derivatives Market

A derivative is simply an asset that derives its value from its underlying asset. Forwards, futures, options, and swaps are common exchange-traded derivatives. The need to trade the derivative asset when the underlying asset itself is available for trading arises from the need to manage risk. In the complicated world of trade and commerce, risk arises from different sources and in myriad forms. In well-developed derivative markets, there would be different categories of derivatives available for managing different types of risks. For example, currency derivatives for managing currency risk, interest rate derivatives for managing interest rate risk, equity derivatives for equity risk, and commodity derivatives for managing price risk, and so on. Some of the common risks in financial/capital markets will be discussed later.

Though the rationale for derivatives is hedging or risk management, as we will see in Chapter 10, given their features, derivatives can be used just as easily for arbitrage or speculative purposes. It is this easy usage for speculative purposes that make derivatives anathema to a section of *Shari'ah* scholars. The issue of their acceptability is examined in-depth in Chapter 12.

As in the description of the various stock exchanges of the Islamic world, derivatives are indeed traded on at least three exchanges. In Kuwait, the KSE trades equity derivatives; the Egyptian exchange, which had its roots in the trading of cotton futures, trades commodity futures; and Bursa Malaysia trades equity, interest rate, and commodity derivatives.

Box 2.3. Malaysia's Experience with Derivatives

Malaysia's experience with exchange-traded derivative instruments has thus far been a mixed one. The most successful product in terms of traded volume and open interest is the Crude Palm Oil (CPO) futures contract. The contract's popularity owes to the fact that the Malaysian exchange, Bursa Malaysia, is the only exchange in the world that trades this product. As such, the daily settlement price of the CPO futures contract is often used as reference price in third-party trade of CPO. The CPO futures contract also happens to be the first derivative instrument to have been introduced in the

(*Continued*)

Box 2.3. (*Continued*)

country in 1980 following the establishment of Malaysia's first derivative exchange, The Kuala Lumpur Commodities Exchange (KLCE), in the same year. Given the huge success of the CPO contracts, the KLCE introduced a series of new commodity futures contracts based on Malaysia's other export commodities, rubber, tin, and cocoa. However, the trading performance of these latter commodity contracts has been disappointing. Given very illiquid trading, the exchange has discontinued their trading. Today, only two commodity futures contracts are traded: the CPO futures contract and a futures contract based on Crude Palm Kernel Oil.

The Malaysian derivatives market received a major boost in 1995 when the country's first financial derivative contract was launched. This was a Stock Index Futures contract based on Malaysia's most popular stock index, the Kuala Lumpur Stock Exchange Composite Index (KLSE CI). Based on the 100 constituent stocks within the index, the contract is cash settled. This new financial derivative, however, was traded on a newly established exchange known as KLOFFE (The Kuala Lumpur Options and Financial Futures Exchange). In 1996, the older derivative exchange (KLCE) established a wholly owned subsidiary, the Malaysian Monetary Exchange, to list and trade another financial derivative, the three-month KLIBOR futures contract. This is an interest rate derivative based on the three-month Kuala Lumpur Interbank Offer Rate.

The introduction of these new financial derivatives served to rejuvenate the otherwise sedate market in derivatives. With the introduction of the Stock Index Futures Contract in December 1995, Malaysia was among the pioneers in Asia to have introduced financial derivatives. At that point, only Japan and Hong Kong had futures contracts based on their own stock indices. The initial response, especially to the Stock Index Futures Contracts, was impressive. Kuala Lumpur's aspirations to be an Asian financial hub appeared to be on track. However, the outbreak of the currency crisis in late-1997 and the imposition of capital control in September 1998 put a brake on many of these developments. The trading volume and open interest for both financial derivatives, especially the Stock Index Futures Contracts, fell sharply. For the subsequent four years, the average daily volume was less than half the pre-crisis levels. This slump in activity began to turn with the de-pegging of the ringgit. From late 2003 onwards, both traded volume and open interest have recovered quite impressively.

Currently, three derivative contracts account for most of the traded volume and open interest. Depending on when the measurement is taken, a good approximation would be that 90% of volume and open interest comes from the three products, CPO futures, KLSE CI Index futures, and the three-month KLIBOR futures contracts. Among the three, the CPO futures are by far the most popular.

A number of additional products have been introduced. In December 2000, KLOFFE had introduced Stock Index Options based on the KLSE CI. Subsequently, three interest rate futures contracts were launched. These were the three-year, five-year, and 10-year Malaysian Government Securities (MGS) futures, the underlying asset being MGS of the respective maturity periods. Perhaps, due to their launch in the immediate period following the currency crisis, these contracts have not been popular. In April 2006, single stock futures (SSFs) were introduced. An SSF is a futures contract based on an individual listed stock. At the time of launch, a total of 10 SSF contracts were listed based on 10 individual blue chip stocks. Thus far, the trading performance of these SSF contracts has been mixed.

In addition to the above-mentioned exchange-traded derivatives, Malaysia has an active over-the-counter (OTC) market in derivatives. OTC products are customized products designed by financial institutions for their customers. Forwards and swaps are common OTC instruments. In Malaysia, there is a very active and highly liquid forward market in currencies. Given that the currency forward market is also very cost-competitive, there has been little need for a currency futures market. The interest rate swap market is also fairly active. Banks and other financial institutions use interest rate swaps to manage their interest rate exposure. Derivative-like structured products are an increasingly popular segment of the OTC derivatives market. Structuring products to be *Shari'ah*-compliant appears to be the focus of the more innovative Malaysian banks. Several Islamic structured products have been launched of late, usually to overwhelming response. This segment of *Shari'ah*-compliant products promises to be the hottest growth area within the OTC market.

Box 2.4. Malaysia Embarks on Capital Markets Masterplan 2 (CMP2)

The first decade of the millennium saw Malaysia recovering from the Asian crisis of 1997/1998, and embarking on mending investor confidence and strengthening regulatory framework to pursue growth. The equity markets and bond markets have increased three-fold since 2000. The ICM had shown a tremendous increase to a value of RM1,050 billion at the end of 2010 from RM294 billion in 2000.

Going further from 2010, the Malaysian capital market has already crossed RM2 trillion and is attracting interest and investments from large institutional investors, both local as well as regional players. As Malaysia embarks on an aggressive transformation of economy from a middle-income country to a high-income country by 2025, the capital market needs to further internationalize the opportunities it offers, and position itself as a global hub. Under the Capital Markets Masterplan 2 (CMP2), Malaysian capital markets target to attain international benchmarking by actively pursuing regulatory framework in line with global standards. The resilience shown by the capital market during the global financial crisis has attracted much attention, and risk management has emerged as a key challenge going forward.

CMP2 aims to support the New Economic Model by facilitating and acting as the support agent for the growth of the Malaysian economy.

- CMP2 focuses on enhanced capital formation by promoting private sector participation in private equity and venture capital. It aims to promote growth of small- and mid-cap companies, and to widen access to bond and *sukuk* financing and increase in asset classes.
- CMP2 aims to expand intermediation efficiency and deepen liquidity by addressing savings concentration via addition of new value-adding instruments and by promoting new business models to attract investments. In 2010, RM377.4 billion was recorded as assets under management by Malaysian Investment management companies. CMP2 is targeting an increase to RM1,610 billion by 2020.
- Malaysian Capital Markets, whose value stand at RM2 trillion in 2010, are expected to grow to RM4.5 trillion by 2020. CMP2 lists potential upside up to RM5.8 trillion through internationalization of listing opportunities and promoting Islamic fund management.

2.7 Risks in Capital Markets

Capital markets play a number of roles, such as intermediation; inter-temporal transfers, i.e., saving for the future (e.g., pension plan); risk transfer/management; and several other functions. In enabling these functions, capital markets provide the needed platforms and instruments for players to fulfil their needed objectives. ICMs are no different in this sense. In playing these roles, risk becomes an inevitable feature of capital markets. In this concluding section, we perform a quick overview of the different types of risks commonly found in today's markets. Risk in finance refers to the uncertainties associated with returns from an investment. Fluctuations in the prices of a traded instrument would mean volatility of returns. Thus, the common measure for risk is standard deviation of returns. Any asset that does not come with "guaranteed" fixed returns has some amount of uncertainty. In fact, even a "guaranteed" instrument has risks if the issuer's credibility is questionable. The following are some of the most common forms of risks found in modern capital markets, both conventional and Islamic.

2.7.1 *Market/Price Risk*

Price risk refers to changes in an asset's price due to changes in market conditions: either demand/supply conditions and/or sentiments. Any number of factors can cause changes in demand/supply and market sentiments. Thus, price risk is quite encompassing. All market-traded asset instruments have exposure to this risk. For instance, mortgage-backed securities fall in value when a housing boom becomes a bust. Foreign exchange rate fluctuation is also an example of price risk. A depreciation of the exchange rate benefits sellers of foreign exchange (e.g., exporters) and penalizes buyers (e.g., importers); inversely, for an appreciation of the exchange rate, it penalizes sellers and benefits buyers of foreign exchange.

2.7.2 *Interest Rate Risk*

Interest rate risk refers to the changes in asset values due to changes in nominal interest rates. This is a particularly important source of risk for fixed income securities. It is the result of discounting to find prices. In the case of fixed income securities, the numerator (coupon or interest) is unchanged while the denominator increases with an increase in nominal interest rates. The price of bonds varies inversely with the interest rate. An increase in interest rate causes a fall in bond value and therefore a capital loss. A decline in interest rate causes an increase in bond value and therefore a capital gain. Interest rate risk can also be in the form of funding or financing risk. Here, the risk is that a change in interest rates can change the cost of funds or financing.

2.7.3 *Default/Credit Risk*

This risk, which is also sometimes known as *counterparty risk*, refers to the changes in the financial integrity of the counterparty or the issuer of the asset. When an issuer of financial instruments, for e.g., bonds/stocks, gets closer to bankruptcy, there is increased default risk. On the other hand, there would be a resultant decrease in default risk if the issuer's financial position improves. Though investors can lose their entire investment when an issuer goes bankrupt, it is often the case that there would be huge *anticipatory losses* even before bankruptcy actually happens. As such, although outright bankruptcies are a rare occurrence, default risk is relevant because of the possible anticipatory losses. As a result, a financial instrument could go down very substantially in price (close to worthless) even though the issuer has not technically declared bankruptcy.

2.7.4 *Liquidity Risk*

A business entity may be solvent; however, it may have a liquidity risk due to a mismatch between assets and liabilities. Liquidity risk also refers to the risk that arises from thin or illiquid trading. When an asset is thinly traded, liquidity risk could arise. Thinly traded instruments have higher price volatility, i.e., price changes tend to be larger between trades as opposed to those of highly liquid, continuously traded assets. In thin, illiquid markets, one cannot dispose of an asset quickly. The only way to quickly sell the asset would be by taking a big discount on the price.

2.7.5 *Political Risk*

Political risk refers to the risk faced by international investors. Most political risks are of regulatory nature. It refers to risks such as expropriation/nationalization, imposition of exchange controls that disallow foreigners to withdraw their funds, the imposition of unfavorable tax or ownership requirements, etc. Political risk therefore refers to the diminution in the value of a foreign-held asset as a result of unfavorable regulatory change overseas.

2.7.6 *Regulatory/Moral Hazard/Inflation Risks*

Regulatory risk refers to risk arising from changes in regulation or government policy. While regulatory changes are generally infrequent, banking/financial sector regulations are often changed quickly. This will be especially true during times of financial crises. Regulations on statutory requirements for reserves and the eligibility of money market instruments which would qualify in meeting such requirements are changed quite frequently in some cases. Governments that have frequent policy changes or policy flip-flops are perceived to have a high degree of regulatory risk.

Often, governments encourage financial institutions to lend irrespective of risk, and force significant reduction in interest rates in order to create an economic boom and push asset prices upward. Booms are followed by downturns. Governments bailout falling financial firms and create a moral hazard. Namely, financial markets take higher risk on the assumption that governments will always rescue them.

Noticeable changes in the purchasing power of money pose a risk. A fall in prices penalizes borrowers and benefits creditors, while an increase in prices has the opposite effect. While in economies using *fiat* money, the risk of deflation has been rare, rapid inflation could become a threat and disrupt capital markets. Recognizing the fast depreciation of money, lenders will curtail lending and add an "inflation premium" to lending rates.

2.7.7 *Transparency and Misreporting Risks*

Misreporting accounting risks typically refers to the risk that may hide losses, overstate profits (swindlers), or understate profits, depending on the scheme sought by the company mangers. Rating agencies may mislead investors by rating high-risk assets as low-risk assets. A borrower in a profit-sharing relationship might understate profits. Capital market instruments based on *mudarabah*- and *musharakah*-type contracts would be susceptible to such risks. A good example of this risk would be the new policy that Bank Negara Malaysia had to introduce to overcome the problem of "understated" profits by borrowers issuing the Mudarabah Interbank Investments (MII), an instrument traded in Malaysia's Islamic Interbank Money Market (see Chapter 4).

2.7.8 *Shari'ah Risk*

Shari'ah risk is a counterpart of regulatory risk and specific to ICMs, it refers to the possibility that transactions/ instruments currently deemed acceptable could subsequently be prohibited. Some examples of this type of risk are: (i) the issue of mark-ups in Pakistan and (ii) the controversy surrounding *bay al-dayn*-based transactions. Such transactions certainly appear to be decreasing in Malaysia. Of late, even the contracts based on the highly popular *bay bi thaman ajil* (BBA, deferred payment sale) in Malaysia are being questioned. The fact that Green Banker's Acceptance (BAs), once popularly traded instrument on the Malaysian Islamic Interbank Money Market, has now completely stopped, is a good example of such risk.

In efficient and well-functioning capital markets, the management of these risks would also be possible. The derivative markets in particular are designed to enable the risk management function. As we will see later, different derivative instruments are intended for managing different types of risk. *Risk management* refers to the process/ techniques of reducing the risks faced in an investment. What makes risk management challenging is the fact that risks and returns are generally positively correlated. Thus, the *risk–return trade off*. The challenge of risk management is to protect the expected returns while simultaneously reducing or laying off the risks.

Risk management generally involves three broad steps: (i) identifying the source and type of risk; (ii) measuring the extent of the risk; and (iii) determining the appropriate response/methods. We will examine risk management through the use of hedging techniques in later chapters that cover derivatives and foreign exchange markets.

Box 2.5. Are Capital Markets Necessary?

Whether capital markets are necessary for growth and development have been debated for quite a while; to be precise, for at least a hundred years — from Bagehot (1873), who argues that an efficient financial system is needed for economies to grow, to Lucas (1988), who argues that economists "badly over-stress" the role finance plays in growth. In between these polar arguments is Schumpeter (1911), who argues that services offered by financial sector players are essential for technological innovation and overall economic development. Goldsmith (1969) and McKinnon (1973) empirically illustrate the close links between financial sector and economic growth. The one notable study that is in line with Lucas

(*Continued*)

Box 2.5. (*Continued*)

(1988) is Robinson (1952), who finds that rather than being a determinant of growth, financial sector development follows economic growth. A number of later studies by Pagano (1993), King *et al.* (1993), Bakaert and Harvey (1997), and Levine *et al.* (2007) all find financial and capital market development to be a key contributing factor to economic growth. In fact, Levine *et al.* (2007) show that financial development not only contributes to aggregate economic growth but also "disproportionately boosts incomes of the poorest quintile and reduces income inequality", a finding in direct contrast to the commonly held perception that financial development has little impact on the poorer segments of society. Using data of 80 countries over the 30-year period from 1960–1989, King and Levine (1993) show evidence consistent with Schumpeter's view that financial development promotes economic growth. They document strong correlation between financial sector growth and; (i) the real per capita GDP growth; (ii) the rate of physical capital accumulation; (iii) the efficiency of physical capital use and; (iv) that financial development is a good predictor of long-run growth over the next 10 to 30 years. They conclude therefore that "policies that alter the costliness and efficiency of financial intermediation exert a first-order influence on economic growth". In the light of such strong evidence, perhaps the answer to the malaise plaguing economic growth of Muslim countries is self-evident.

Source: Excerpt from *Islamic Capital Markets and Development*, Obiyathulla and Abbas (2012).

2.8 Economic Indicators and their Role in Capital Markets

Modern capital markets as we saw earlier are driven by information. Market participants are constantly on the lookout for new information that can impact financial markets. The large institutional market players often invest huge amounts of money in data analytics, data mining, and all sorts of methods to ferret out potentially advantageous information. While these are proprietary information, there is plenty of publicly available information that move markets. The most common of these are the economic indicators released by the central banks, Ministries of Finance, and government statistical departments. In most cases, governments or their entities release this information at scheduled intervals. Some information may be released monthly, quarterly, semi-annually, and so on. Table 2.2 provides a short list of common economic indicators reported in most countries.

Table 2.2. Key Economic Indicators.

No.	Name of Indicator	Method of Computation	Information Provided
1	Consumer Price Index (CPI)	Based on the change in prices of a basket of goods and services. $\{((CP_t - CP_{t-1})/CP_t) \times 100\}$	Indicates the rate of change in the general price level or rate of inflation. Aside from being a burden on consumers, high inflation rates impact corporate cash flows and the nominal interest rate. CPI is widely watched as inflation has a broad-based impact on the economy.
2	Unemployment Rate (%)	Computed as the number of unemployed as % of total labor force.	An increase in unemployment would signal that companies are not hiring but may even be shedding workers. A decrease would signal optimism among hirers, generally a lagging indicator.
3	Industrial Production Index (IPI)	Measures real production output in selected industries. Computed as a rate of change from a base year.	Increases in the IPI would indicate heightened activity and increased output in the manufacturing, mining, utilities, and the production sectors included. Decreases would imply the opposite. The IPI can be a leading indicator of GDP performance in the immediate future.

(*Continued*)

Table 2.2. *(Continued)*

No.	Name of Indicator	Method of Computation	Information Provided
4	Balance of Trade (BOT)	Total Exports minus Total Imports. (Imports and Exports of both goods and services)	BOT or simply trade balance is a first indicator of a country's health in terms of external trade. A negative BOT would mean a deficit trade balance, implying the country has to "borrow" the difference. A surplus BOT would mean the country in exporting more than its imports is effectively "lending" to its trade partners.
5	Current Account (CA) to GDP	{(Current Account deficit or surplus)/ GDP} ×100 (CA is BOT adjusted for net income from abroad and net current transfers)	Since CA is a broader measure of a nation's external activities, and typically the largest component of the Balance of Payments, whether it is in deficit or surplus is a key indicator of a nation's economic health and the direction of its currency. For relative comparisons between countries the percentage of the CA surplus or deficit to GDP is used.
6	Public/ Government Debt to GDP	{(Total Government Debt/GDP) × 100}	Indicates a government fiscal health. Government debt to GDP is used for relative comparison across countries. High and a rising trend would indicate vulnerability, especially if a substantial portion of the debt is in foreign currency.
7	Total Private Sector Debt to GDP	Aggregate of Non-Banking private sector debt as % of GDP.	A gradual increase indicates economic growth, but a rapid increase could indicate a credit boom and asset bubbles. Again, as in the case of government debt, can increase vulnerability to external shocks if a major portion is foreign-currency–denominated debt.
8	Consumer Sentiment Index	Usually through telephone surveys of consumers opinion of the state of the economy.	A statistical measure of the perceived overall health of the economy. It is an indicator of the level of consumer optimism. As consumption accounts for a large part of a nation's GDP, high levels of consumer confidence and optimism would indicate increased consumption and therefore higher GDP growth.
9	Business Confidence Index (BCI)	Like other sentiment indexes, BCI is measured through questionnaire surveys of businesses. While some BCI are numerical, others are qualitative. For example, a numerical reading above 50 indicates optimism, whereas a reading below 50 indicates negative assessment of business conditions.	In free market economies, businesses generate GDP growth. BCI as a measure of business sentiment is a good indicator of economic conditions.
10	Producer Price Index (PPI)	Measures price movements within three categories of products: finished goods, intermediate goods, and crude commodities or raw material. Price changes for a period are reported relative to a constant index level of 100. A 5% increase in prices would be reported as PPI of 105 whereas a PPI of 92 would indicate an 8% drop in prices.	Like CPI, PPI is a measure of price changes. PPI, however, is at the level of producers. Since PPI would inevitably pass through to CPI, market players trying to forecast future inflation would watch PPI closely.

(Continued)

Table 2.2. (*Continued*)

No.	Name of Indicator	Method of Computation	Information Provided
11	PMI (Purchasing Managers' Index)	Based on surveys of purchasing managers in manufacturing firms. The surveys are designed to capture several levels of the manufacturing process like inventories, production levels, new orders received, etc.	PMI indicates current manufacturing activity and implications for the immediate future. Since the manufacturing sector is a key driver of overall GDP growth, PMI is a leading indicator.
12	Money Supply (M2)	M2 is M1 + near money (time deposits + money market mutual fund shares + money market deposit accounts, etc.) *M1 refers to narrow money; notes, coins, and monetary equivalents.	M2 measures the amount of monetary assets available in an economy. It is a closely watched indicator as it provides information on the current state of liquidity and future movements in inflation and interest rates. As a money supply indicator, the currency markets closely watch the M2 for indications of potential exchange rate movements.

Summary

The capital markets play a very important role in the development of nations. Being part of a country's financial system, the capital markets help to finance the production and investment activities of players in the real sector. By way of intermediation, a well-functioning capital market provides businesses the opportunity to raise funds at a competitive cost and in a timely manner while minimizing risks. There appears to be four major trends where the capital markets of Muslim countries are concerned. These are: globalization, liberalization, Fintech, and the rise of Islamic finance. Developments in Fintech have serious implications for the financial sector. It has the potential to change the future topography of the financial sector, in particular, banking. The capital market has several components. The equity and debt markets are two of the largest. The debt market can be divided into the money market and the bond market. The money market is for short-term debt instruments, whereas the bond market trades medium- and long-term instruments. In a sense, the short end of the yield curve is determined by activities in the money market whereas the long end is derived from bond market activity. In Malaysia, both the money and bond markets have their *Shari'ah*-compliant alternatives. The Islamic interbank money market trades *Shari'ah-compliant* money market instruments while the *sukuk* market provides a means for *Shari'ah*-compliant non-equity financing. The foreign exchange and derivative markets are the other key components of the capital market. While equity and debt markets can be used to raise funds, businesses would use derivative and foreign exchange markets largely to manage the many risks that arise from doing business. A well-developed capital market would be one that is complete, in the sense that business entities can use it for a variety of purposes. Modern capital markets are information driven. Economic indicators that are released by the government or its agencies are closely monitored by market participants and have the potential to move markets.

Questions and Problems

1. What is a capital market and what are some of its functions?
2. Describe how a capital market can act as a link between the real and financial sectors of an economy.
3. What are some of the key components of a capital market? Which is typically the largest component in capital markets of Islamic countries?
4. What are the similarities and differences between a capital market and the banking system?
5. Discuss why a well-functioning capital market is essential for a nation's development.
6. How is the Islamic Capital Market (ICM) different from its conventional counterpart?
7. What accounts for the popularity of *sukuk*? What government initiatives may have helped?
8. In what way is the money market different from the bond/*sukuk* market?
9. What are derivatives? What are their key uses?
10. Identify and describe five common types of risks in modern day capital markets.
11. What is Fintech? Why is it a major trend in financial markets?
12. What are economic indicators? Why are they closely monitored?
13. How are economic indicators related to key functions of capital markets? In what way can they enhance the role played by capital markets?

Bibliography

Ayub, M. (2007). *Understanding Islamic Finance* (John Wiley & Sons Ltd). West Sussex, England

Bagehot, Walter. 1873. *Lombard Street: A Description of the Money Market*. London: Henry S. King and Co.

Bank Negara Malaysia, Annual Reports — several years.

Beck, T., A. Demirgüç-Kunt, and R. Levine. 2007. "Finance, Inequality and the Poor." *Journal of Economic Growth* 12: 27–49.

Bekaert, G., and C. R. Harvey. 1997. "Capital Markets: An Engine for Economic Growth." National Bureau of Economic Research, Cambridge, MA., (unpublished)

IOSCO (2005). "Islamic Capital Markets: Fact Finding Report." The International Organization of Securities Commission. Available at: www.sc.com.my/eng/html/icm/ICM-IOSCOFactfindingReport.pdf, July 2004.

King, R. G., and Levine R. 1993. "Finance and Growth: Schumpeter Might Be Right." *The Quarterly Journal of Economics* 108 (3, August): 717–37.

Lucas, Robert. 1988. "On the Mechanics of Economic Development." *Journal of Monetary Economics* 22 (February): 3–42.

Malaysia Financial Sector Master Plan, http://www.bnm.gov.my/files/publication/fsbp/en/BNM_FSBP_FULL_en.pdf.

Malaysia Capital Market Master Plan. https://www.sc.com.my/capital-market-masterplan-1/

McKinnon, Ronald. 1973. *Money & Capital in Economic Development*. Washington, DC: Brookings Institution Press.

Obiyathulla, I. B. (2017). *Financial Derivatives: Market and Applications in Malaysia*. 4th Edition (McGraw Hill Education, Malaysia).

Obiyathulla, I. B. and Abbas, M. (2012). *Islamic Capital Markets and Development* (INCEIF) (unpublished manuscript).

Obiyathulla, I. B. *Derin Ekonomi* (2017). September. They are published in a monthly magazine in Turkey.

Pagano, M. 1993. "Financial Markets and Growth: An Overview." *European Economic Review* 37: 613–622.

Securities Commission (2001). The Capital Market Master Plan–Malaysia.

Websites

http://www.bnm.gov.my — Bank Negara Malaysia

http://www.mifc.com/index.php?ch=menuhttp://www.sc.gov.my

Websites of respective Muslim Country Stock Exchanges

http://www.zawya.com/middle-east/financial-markets

http://www.bursamalaysia.com — Bursa Malaysia

Websites of the various Stock exchanges

http://data.oecd.org/gga/general-government-debt.htm

http://ec.europa.eu/eurostat/web/products-datasets/-/tipspd20

http://www.frbsf.org/economic-research/publications/economic-letter/2014/march/private-credit-public-debt-financial-crisis/

http://www.aimnet.org/publications-research/business-confidence-index.cfm

http://lexicon.ft.com/Term?term=business-confidence

Endnotes

1. Banking and Financial Industry Act (1989).
2 The Futurist; Stock Market Capitalization in Developing Countries.
3. The yield curve describes the term-structure of yields; it associates with each maturity its respective yield.

Chapter 3

ISLAMIC FINANCE: UNDERLYING PHILOSOPHY, CONTRACTS, INSTRUMENT DESIGN, AND REQUISITES

Topics in this Chapter

3.1. Introduction
3.2. Underlying Themes and Fundamentals of *Fiqh Mu'amalah*
3.3. Requirements for Islamic Capital Market Instruments/Transactions
3.4. *Shari'ah*-based contracts for Financial Transactions
3.5. International Regulatory Institutions for Islamic Finance

Chapter Objective

This chapter is designed to provide an overview of the underlying philosophy of Islamic finance, and the resulting requirements for financial instruments and contracts. Following a description of the key contracts, the chapter examines key issues such as the relevance of the commodity *murabahah* contract and issues regarding *tawarruq*. On completing the chapter, you should have a basic understanding of the philosophy and underlying fundamentals of Islamic finance, the key prohibitions, and the common contracts.

Key Terms		
bay' al-bithaman ajil	*maysir*	*riba nasi'ah*
commodity *murabahah*	*mudarabah*	*riba qurudh*
diminishing *musharakah*	*murabahah*	*rishwah*
financial crisis	*musawamah*	risk-sharing
fiqh mu'amalah	*musharakah*	*salam*

(*Continued*)

(*Continued*)

Key Terms		
gharar	parallel *salam*	*Sunnah*
ijarah muntahiya bittamleek	*qiyas*	*takaful*
ijma	Qur'an	*tauhid*
istisna'	*rahn*	*tawarruq*
jahl	*riba*	*wadi'ah*
mah kah	*riba buyu'*	*wakalah*
maslahah	*riba fadhl*	*zakah*

3.1 Introduction

In this chapter, we examine the underlying principles of Islamic finance, some of the key contracts, and *Shari'ah* requirements for capital market instruments. We also examine the source of rulings and Islamic ideology, and discuss current trends.

The *Shari'ah*, which teachers how to manage Islamic finance, translates into "the way" or "path", and is a set of rules designed to transform the faith of believers into the daily life of Muslims. The *Shari'ah* is based on *aqidah* by way of Islamic ideology. The *Shari'ah* emanates from *aqidah*, which is the core set of rules between man and his Creator, and is the basis of Islamic ideology. At a basic level, there are three key components of Islamic ideology: *tauhid, nubuuwa*, and *ma'ad*. *Tauhid* refers to the oneness of God, while *nubuuwa* refers to the concept of prophethood. The concept of *ma'ad* refers to one's inevitable return to Allah (swt) for the final judgment, the implication being that one is answerable for all his actions.

The primary sources of the *Shari'ah* are the Qur'an and *Sunnah*. The *Sunnah* refers to practices of the Prophet (saw). Both the Qur'an and *Sunnah* form the main body or thrust of the *Shari'ah*. Secondary sources of the *Shari'ah* are also allowed. The two common secondary sources are *ijma* and *qiyas*. *Ijma* refers to consensus among *Shari'ah* scholars. *Qiyas*, on the other hand, refers to analogical reasoning or drawing similarities/inferences from earlier situations, usually prophetic times. A third possible source is *maslahah* or public benefit; in other words, situations where ruling is needed for the general interest of the community.

While the secondary sources give the *Shari'ah* the dynamism and the adaptability needed to always remain relevant, they have also been the source for differences among *Shari'ah* scholars. Differences in opinion among *fuqaha* (jurists) about the acceptability of a practice, contract, or transaction emanate largely from differences in interpretation, in particular, on *qiyas*-based rulings. Furthermore, interpretation of the *Shari'ah* has evolved along the lines of *madhahib*. The *madhahib* being: (i) *Hanafi*, (ii) *Maliki*, (iii) *Shafi'i*, and (iv) *Hanbali*. Since each *madhab* had taken root in different geographic regions, cultural settings, and social systems, interpretations and inferences may be colored by local values.

The *Shari'ah* being comprehensive and all-encompassing relates to both the spiritual (*ibadah*) and socioeconomic aspects of Muslim life. Accordingly, *Shari'ah* is often categorized into two broad categories: matters relating to *ibadah* and matters relating to *mu'amalah* or transactions. While the former is sourced exclusively from the Qur'an and has no room for differences arising from scholastic interpretation, the latter, *fiqh mu'amalah*, is open for interpretation and therefore to differences in opinion. Much of Islamic finance, economics, and Islamic banking/capital markets are governed by the rules of *fiqh mu'amalah* (see Figure 3.1).

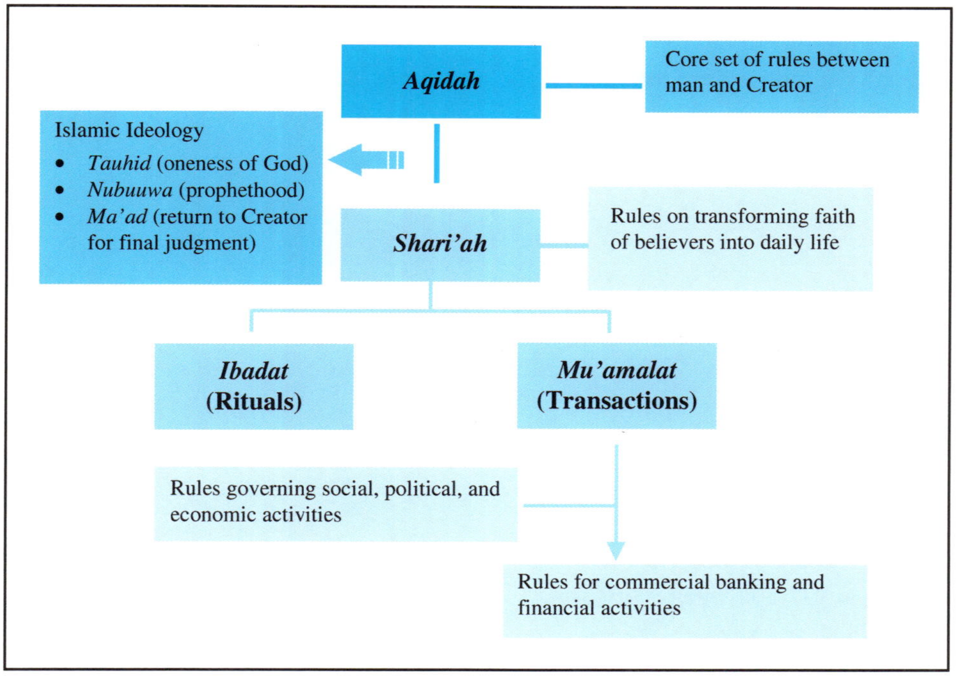

Figure 3.1. The Islamic Ideology and the *Shari'ah*.

3.2 Underlying Themes and Fundamentals of *Fiqh Mu'amalah*

Given Islamic ideology and the *Shari'ah*, there are important implications for economics and finance. First, Islam points to how economic systems should be organized with regards to individuals and institutions. Second, it lays out the rules for economic functions, such as production, trading/exchange, and distribution. Finally, the *Shari'ah* provides for the types of contracts that can enable the undertaking of real sector activities. We examine these contracts in Section 3.3.

From an overall viewpoint, there are certain common threads or underlying fundamentals that run through all *Shari'ah*-compliant business activities and contracts. These underlying fundamentals can be summarized as follows.

(i) Every activity of an economic agent must have roots in the *aqidah*, i.e., one is answerable for all his actions/transactions.

(ii) As opposed to the "Economic Man", the *Shari'ah* sees man as a subset of society with obligations to his fellow mankind and Creator. While the pursuit of profit and enterprise is not denied, societal needs are paramount; thus, the compulsion of *zakah*. Spiritual and moral values are just as important as material possessions.

(iii) Justice and equity must prevail in all circumstances. Transparency and mutual consent are compulsory. All contracts/transactions are required to have a "balance" or equivalence in the rights and obligations of the contracting parties.

(iv) Transactions should be real asset-based and must have a beneficial outcome (*maslahah*). Transactions that do not benefit the greater society or brings harm should be avoided, even if the transacting parties privately gain.

(v) Return to capital should be based on risk-sharing and ex-post, not fixed ex-ante.

While the *Shari'ah* recognizes and provides protection for property rights of individuals, it also emphasizes one's obligations to society at large and the economic environment. According to the *Shari'ah*, rights come with obligations.

3.3 Requirements for Islamic Capital Market Instruments/Transactions

Emanating from the above underlying fundamentals, there are certain features that financial instruments or transactions must have in order to be *Shari'ah* compliant. At a primary level, all financial instruments and transactions must be free from at least the following five items:

(i)	*Riba*	usury/interest
(ii)	*Rishwah*	corruption
(iii)	*Gharar*	unnecessary/excessive risk
(iv)	*Maisyir*	gambling/speculation
(v)	*Jahl*	profiting from others' ignorance

3.3.1 *Riba*

The avoidance of *riba* is the foundation *raison d'être* of Islamic banking and finance. There are many verses in the Holy Qur'an that clearly oppose *riba*, in particular, *Surah al-Baqarah* (Verse 278–279). In Arabic, *riba* means an increment or increase. There are several kinds of *riba*, and the prohibition applies to all forms of it. Broadly, *riba* can be divided into (i) *riba qurudh* and (ii) *riba buyu*. *Riba qurudh* is akin to conventional interest on lending. For example, *riba qurudh* applies when someone with an outstanding loan is required to pay a sum larger than the original principal in order to settle the loan. The rescheduling of a loan to a longer period but with a higher settlement amount would also constitute *riba qurudh*.

The second category, *riba buyu*, can in turn be divided into two categories, namely: *riba nasi'ah* and *riba fadhl*. *Riba buyu* generally arises from the trading of "*ribawi*" goods. *Ribawi* goods are generally commodities that can be a medium of exchange, such as gold and silver, or non-perishable staple food items like barley, wheat, dates, salt, and even rice. So, when gold is lent to be repaid in gold at a higher quantity, *riba buyu* would be present (debatable). The same would apply if a staple food like rice or wheat is lent today for repayment at a higher quantity of the same kind.

Riba can be in different forms and is prohibited in all its forms. Some *fuqaha* have argued that *riba* can also occur when one gets a positive return without taking any risk or putting in commensurate effort. When we evaluate *riba* in the light of the *Shari'ah's* underlying fundamentals, it is easy to see why *riba* is prohibited. First, it violates the equity (fairness) issue, which is fundamental to *Shari'ah*. The lender receives his fixed return regardless of how the borrower's business fares. Second, it also violates the requirement for risk-sharing. Recall that the return to capital should come from sharing in the risk of the underlying. In conventional, interest-based lending, the debt holders' returns are *independent* of the underlying businesses' returns and fixed ex-ante. A third violation would be a violation of the need to have a balance, or equivalence in the rights and obligations of the contracting parties. It is often the case that the borrower has little say in the drawing up of interest-based debt contracts.

Shari'ah scholars feel that the practice of interest has been the root cause of financial crises. In each financial crisis, banks fail, unemployment increases, and impoverishment aggravates. The economic recession could become an economic depression and can extend over many years before the economy recovers. The Asian financial crisis of 1997 and the recent global financial crisis of 2007 illustrate the instability of interest-based financial systems.

3.3.2 *Gharar*

Gharar can be defined as unnecessary risk, deception, or internationally induced uncertainty. In Arabic, related words would mean dangerous or cheating. In the context of financial transactions, *gharar* could be thought of as looseness of the underlying contract, such that one or both parties are uncertain about possible outcomes. *Gharar* could also have different connotations across *madhahib*. The *Hanafi* consider *gharar* to mean something with unknown outcomes or consequences. The *Maliki* takes it to mean suspicion, while the *Shafi'i* defines *gharar* to mean high risks.

While *gharar* is something to be avoided, *fuqaha* are of the opinion that the mere presence of *gharar* does not automatically invalidate a contract. The consensus is that where the *gharar* is small (*gharar yasir*), the transaction or contract is acceptable, particularly where there are other benefits and the *gharar* cannot be avoided. However, where there is *gharar fahisy* (plenty), the contract would be invalid. Where the *gharar* is deemed moderate (*gharar mutawassit*), there are differences in opinion about their acceptability.

3.3.3 *Maisyir*

Maisyir in Arabic refers to gambling or high speculation. *Maisyir*, from a financial instrument viewpoint, would be one where the outcome is purely dependent on chance alone, as in gambling.

3.3.4 *Jahl*

The term *jahl* refers to ignorance. From a financial transaction viewpoint, it would be unacceptable if one party to the transaction gains because of the other party's ignorance. Often, in financial contracts, informational asymmetry, rather than outright ignorance, could also be caused by *jahl*.

3.4 *Shari'ah*-Based Contracts for Financial Transactions

Table 3.1. Prohibition of *Riba* and Time Value of Money (Islamic Financial Contracts/Transactions).

Ijarah	An *ijarah* contract refers to an agreement made by an Islamic Financial Institution (IFI) to lease to a customer an asset specified by the customer for an agreed period against specified instalments of lease rental. An *ijarah* contract commences with a promise to lease that is binding on the part of the potential lessee prior to entering the *ijarah* contract.
Ijarah Muntahiya Bittamleek	An *ijarah muntahiya bittamleek*, or operational *ijarah*, is a contract coupled with a promise of ownership of the asset to lessee at the end of a lease period, if all its obligations are fulfilled. Often, the *ijarah* contract leads to a binding promised lease to the potential lessee after owning the potential asset which is leased by an IFS after the *ijarah* contract is established.
Istisna	An *istisna* contract refers to an agreement to sell to a customer a non-existent asset, which is to be manufactured or built according to the buyer's specifications and is to be delivered on a specified future date at a predetermined selling price.
Murabahah	A *murabahah* contract refers to a sale contract whereby the IFI sells to a customer a specified kind of asset that is already in their possession at an agreed profit margin plus cost (selling price). The IFI should disclose the cost and the profit.
Mudarabah	A *mudarabah* is a partnership contract in profit between the capital provider and a skilled entrepreneur through contribution, whereby the capital provider would contribute capital to an enterprise or activity which is to be managed by the entrepreneur as the *mudarib* (or labor provider). Profits generated by that enterprise or activity are shared in accordance with the percentage specified in the *mudarabah* agreement whilst losses are to be borne solely by the capital provider unless the losses are due to the *mudarib's* misconduct, negligence, or breach of contracted terms.
Musharakah	A *musharakah* is a contract between the IFI and a customer to contribute capital to an enterprise, whether existing or new, or to ownership of a real estate or moveable asset, either on a temporary or permanent basis. Profits generated by that enterprise or real estate/asset are shared in accordance with a percentage specified in the *musharakah* agreement whilst losses are shared in proportion to each partner's share of capital.

(*Continued*)

Table 3.1. (*Continued*)

Musharakah Mutanaqisah (*Diminishing Musharakah)*	Diminishing *musharakah* is a form of partnership in which one of the partner promises or agrees to buy the equity share of the other partner gradually until the title to the equity is completely transferred to the buying partner. The transaction starts with the formation of a partnership, after which buying and selling of the other partner's equity takes place at market value or the price agreed upon at the time of entering into the contract. The distribution of profits and the allocation of losses are done based on the respective shares of equity.
Musawamah	A sale of commodity with agreement on a selling price without reference by the seller to either costs or asking price.
Parallel *Istisna*	A parallel *istisna* is a contract where a third party will be manufacturing for the IFIs, a specified kind of asset, which corresponds to the specification of the *istisna'* contract.
Salam	A *salam* contract refers to an agreement to purchase, at a predetermined price, a specified kind of commodity not available with the seller, which is to be delivered on a specified future date in a specified quantity and quality. The IFIs as the buyers make full payment of the purchase price upon execution of a *salam* contract. The commodity may or may not be traded over the counter or on an exchange.
Parallel *Salam*	A parallel *salam* is a contract with a third party acquiring, from the IFI, a specified kind of commodity which corresponds to that of the commodity specified in the *salam* contract, and sets a specific date consistent with the schedule without a link between the contracts.
Rahn	*Rahn* is a pledge to ensure that the borrower pays the creditor. The creditor is entitled to sell or keep the commodity or property to meet its debt in the event of a default.
Bay Al-Bithaman Ajil	*Bay Al-Bithaman Ajil* is a deferred sale contract. The IFI purchases an asset at a spot price and resells to the customer at a price that includes a profit mark-up. The customer repays the IFIs in periodic instalments over an agreed future period.
Takaful	*Takaful* is derived from an Arabic word which means solidarity, whereby a group of participants agree among themselves to support one another jointly against a specified loss. In a *Takaful* arrangement, the participants contribute a sum of money as *tabarru'* (donation) into a common fund, which will be used for mutual assistance of the members against specified loss or damage.
Unrestricted Investment account holders (IAH) vs. Restricted IAH	Unrestricted IAH refers to an account where the account holders authorize the IFIs to invest their funds based on a *mudarabah* or *wakalah* investment without laying down any restrictions. The IFIs can commingle these funds with its own or other funds. However, restricted IAH refers to an account where the account holders authorize the IFIs to invest their funds based on the *mudarabah* or *wakalah* investment, with certain restrictions as to where, how, and for what purpose these funds are to be invested. *Wakalah* refers to an agency contract where the customer (*muwakkil*) appoints the IFIs as an agent (*wakil*) to carry out business on their behalf for a fee or without a fee.
Wadī'ah	An amount deposited whereby the depositor is guaranteeing the borrower or the institution to open its current account to restore his/her fund in full.
Wakalah	An agency contract where the *takaful* participants (as principal) appoint the *takaful* operator (as agent) to carry out the underwriting and investment activities on their behalf.

Source: Islamic Financial Standards Board (IFSB), *https://www.ifsb.org*.

The types of contracts used by the Islamic Financial Institutions (IFIs) have evolved over recent times. Let us take the case of Bank Islam Malaysia Berhad (BIMB), Malaysia's first IFI, which began its initial years using classical *mudarabah* based transactions. However, given the acute agency and moral hazard problems, the Malaysian IFIs quickly moved away from *mudarabah*-type contracts to *bay al-bithaman ajil* (BBA) and *murabahah* type contracts. These were essentially fixed rate contracts. There was a time when approximately 90% of an IFI's customer financing would be under such fixed rate financing. Given the increasing criticism of these contracts, especially the BBA contract, Malaysian banks have moved away from them. Today, there is a clear preference to use contracts such as modified *musharakah, musharakah mutanaqisah* (diminishing *musharakah*), *ijarah*, and other such contracts. In the case of *sukuk, ijarah* appears to be the contract of choice, even globally. In the case of home financing, it is *musharakah mutanaqisah*. Based on past experience, with the ongoing financial innovation, it is obvious that even this would change.

While Islam prohibits *riba,* it does not mean that the concept of Time Value of Money (TVM) has no relevance to Islamic finance. As a concept, TVM has many uses in conventional finance. The principles of TVM are used in evaluating cash flows, investment appraisals, and financial decision-making. The discount rate used in TVM computations is much more than merely an interest rate. It is typically the cost-of-capital which includes the cost of equity, premiums for different kinds of risk, the opportunity cost, etc.

Since all of these factors would still be relevant even in an interest-free Islamic system, TVM will not be irrelevant to Islamic finance. Furthermore, while the Qur'an prohibits the charging or paying of interests, it allows for trading on a deferred basis. There are several *Shari'ah*-compliant contracts that allow for a mark-up on deferred payment, e.g., *murabahah,* BBA, and *bay muajjal* contracts. Many *fuqaha* argue that the implication of Verse 275 of *Surah Al-Baqarah* is that, while interest-based lending/borrowing is prohibited, debt-creating financing is permissible and recognized in *Shari'ah.*

The mark-up or higher price for a deferred sale is justified on at least two grounds. As Islamic finance is real asset-based, a mark-up on a deferred sale would compensate the seller in the following instances: (i) benefits arising from usufruct or use of the underlying asset by the purchaser even though he has not fully paid for it; and (ii) real assets depreciating with use and over time. Thus, it is only fair that the purchaser, who is using the asset before full payment, compensate the seller for such depreciation through use. In line with this argument, some scholars call for the use of the term, Time Value of Asset, as opposed to Time Value of Money, in Islamic finance. Regardless of name, the fact remains that the techniques of TVM and the underlying mathematics are just as relevant to Islamic finance as it is to conventional finance.

3.4.1 *Other Commonly Used Capital Market Contracts*

3.4.1.1 *Al-Hewalah*

The *hewalah* contract is one that is used extensively in the transfer of obligations (debt) arising from trade. *Hewalah,* which means to transfer or move, is used in transmitting obligations from one party to another. For example, "A" may have an obligation of RM2 million to "B". If, due to trade, another entity, "C", has a RM2 million obligation to "A", entity "A" transfers its obligation of RM2 million of RM2 million to "B" on to "C". That is, C now takes on A's debt to B in exchange for extinguishing its earlier obligation to A. Diagrammatically, Figure 3.2 shows the mechanics of a *hewalah* contract.

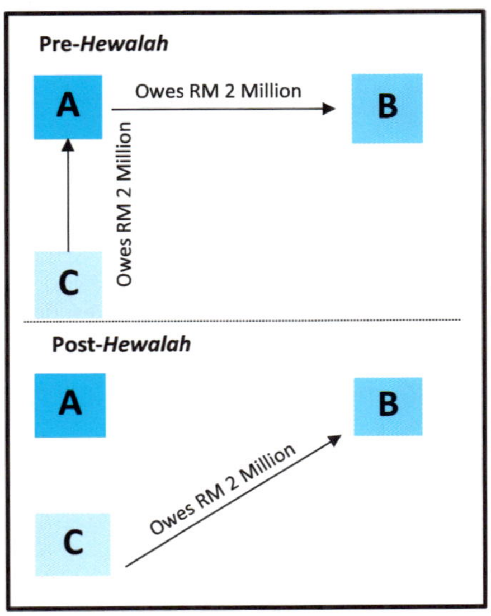

Figure 3.2. *Hewalah* Contract.

By way of *Al-Hewalah*, A has used its receivable from C to offset its obligation to B. B still has a RM2 million receivable, but it is now owed by C and not A as previously indicated. C, on the other hand, continues with its RM2 million obligations; however, that obligation has now changed from A to B. Notice that as a result of the *hewalah*, two things have happened: first, B's debtor has changed from A to C; second, C's creditor has changed from A to B. There are two key conditions to the *hewalah*: first, all parties to the contract must agree on the terms, and second, the total obligation transferred must be of equal amount.

3.4.1.2 *Tawarruq*

The *tawarruq* contract is typically the underlying contract in transactions involving liquidity management. *Tawarruq*, which means "seeking liquidity silver", is a *Shari'ah*-compliant way to obtain needed liquidity without using interest-based financing. It typically involves four parties as follows:

(i) The liquidity provider or *lender* purchases a tradable asset from

(ii) An *owner* of such asset for cash; the tradable asset is then sold to

(iii) The party requiring the liquidity (*borrower*) for payment on deferred terms, for example, in 90 days. The borrower who now has in his possession the tradable asset then sells the asset to an *unrelated party* for cash.

At the end of the transaction, the borrower would have received the liquidity he needed. Figure 3.3 shows the chronological order of the *tawarruq*.

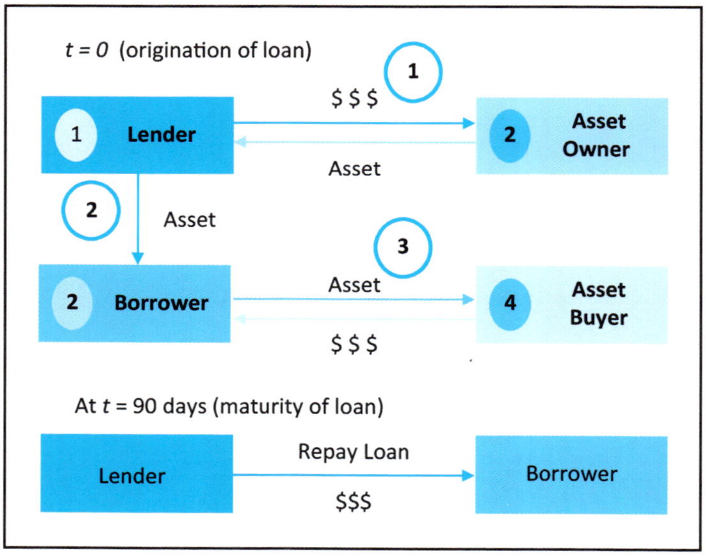

Figure 3.3. *Tawarruq.*

As a result of the *tawarruq* shown in Figure 3.3, the borrower has been able to source the liquidity he needed for 90 days. Since liquidity management is short term by definition, the *tawarruq* concept is well suited for *Shari'ah*-compliant liquidity management solutions. Indeed, based on the *tawarruq*, the commodity *murabahah*, which involves the use of an exchange traded commodity, has become very popular. While many Gulf Cooperation Council (GCC)-based commodity *murabahah* transactions have used commodities such as copper, and other metals are traded on the London Metals Exchange (LME), Malaysian Commodity *Murabahah* is almost exclusively based on Crude Palm Oil (CPO).

3.4.1.3 *Tawwahut*

The *tawwahut* is a means by which *Shari'ah*-compliant hedging is possible. *Tawwahut*, which means hedging, has become the umbrella concept under which a number of *Shari'ah*-compliant swaps and other means of hedging are possible. The Islamic Profit Rate Swap and Islamic Currency Hedging Techniques that are described in Chapter 12 are based on *tawwahut*. Transactions within the *tawwahut* framework would include other contracts like *Musawwamah* and *Wa`ad*. The *tawwahut* contract came to the forefront when the International Islamic Financial Market (IIFM), a Bahrain-based institution (described later in the chapter), launched the *Tawwahut* Master Agreement (TMA) in April 2010. The TMA, designed in collaboration with International Swaps and Derivatives Association Inc. (ISDA) is based on the 2002 ISDA Master Agreement. Though designed to be applicable in all jurisdictions where Islamic Finance is practiced, the TMA is voluntary and may need adaption to different legal processes.

3.4.1.4 *Bay al `Inah*

The *Bay al `Inah* is a variation of the *tawarruq*. Unlike the *tawarruq* where the parties to the purchase and sale of assets are different, in the *Bay al `Inah*, the seller is the re-purchaser. In a typical *Bay al `Inah* transaction, a borrower buys an asset from the lender on a deferred payment basis and resells the same asset to the lender for a lower cash price. The *Bay al `Inah* is essentially a sale and buyback contract. Though *Shari'ah*-compliant, over-reliance on the use of this contract is frowned upon by *Shari'ah* scholars, who see the *Bay al `Inah* as being misused to shroud interest-based financing.

3.4.1.5 *Bay al Dayn*

Bay al Dayn refers to the transaction of debt obligations or the secondary market trading of debt instruments. *Bay al Dayn* is allowed when the documents represent debt arising from the trade of *Shari'ah*-compliant products. In addition to being the result of actual trade, the originator or obligor must be of good standing; in other words, the debt must be of good quality. The acceptability of *Bay al Dayn* varies by *madhab*. The *Hanafi madhab* disallows *Bay al Dayn*, whereas the *Maliki madhab* allows it under certain conditions. The *Shafi madhab* allows *Bay al Dayn*, provided the debt is "guaranteed" and represents debt arising from transaction in goods that must be delivered immediately.

Given these, there is mixed reception for *Bay al Dayn*. Malaysia's Securities Commission has explicitly resolved to accept it and forms the basis for the trading of *Shari'ah*-compliant money market instruments in Malaysia.

3.4.1.6 *Sarf*

Sarf refers to the exchange of money. Though contemporary money is fiat currency, the *sarf* rules for the size; traditional monetary items, wheat, barley, salt, dates, gold, and silver applies. The basic rules in the exchange of these items are hand-to-hand — (i.e., without a time delay) and of equal weights/amounts (with any excess/ increase). Finally, both parties must make and take possession of their counter values before departing. The implication is that the spot trading of currencies is allowed. Though there is no provision for currency trading of a forward nature, many IFIs have resorted to using unilateral *wa`ad*-based contracts to enable the hedging of currency.

Box 3.1. An Islamic Capital Market

What is an Islamic Capital Market (ICM)? An ICM would simply be a capital market that meets the requisites of the *Shari'ah*. Both the instruments and trading processes would be in line with *Shari'ah* requirements for transactions. While *Shari'ah* requirements such as the avoidance of corruption, for e.g., bribe (*rishwah*), gambling (*maysir*), the use of poorly defined contracts (*gharar*), enforceability of contracts, and the like are common to all markets, what truly separates an ICM from others would be the reliance on risk-sharing contracts/transactions. Since no business has fixed returns, the avoidance of fixed returns as in interest-based debt is automatically avoided in risk-sharing contracts. As should be evident to even casual observers, most conventional capital markets, especially those of developed countries, would come close to fulfilling most of the basic requirements for an ICM. However, the two differentiating features of an ICM would be the use of risk-sharing contracts in lieu of debt and the avoidance of *riba* (interest). In fact, one could argue that risk-sharing and avoidance of *riba* are two sides of the same coin. One cannot coexist without the other. Risk-sharing, by definition, excludes fixed interest-based lending. Risk-sharing is such a differentiating feature that a true ICM will have topography vastly different from that of conventional capital markets.

The underlying principle or starting point for the requirement of risk-sharing is probably Verse 275 of *Surah Al-Baqarah*, which declares that while Allah (swt) has permitted *Al-Bai'*, he has prohibited *Al-Riba*. Broadly, *Al-Bai'* "is a contract covering all types of exchange except those prohibited by the Shariah". The Qur'an establishes all human relations firmly on the basis of contract (*'aqd*). These include the entire spectrum of relations from marriage to economic/financial transactions to legitimacy of political authority. The most fundamental contract underlying human transactions is the contract of *Al-Bai'*. *Al-Bai'* is defined as "the exchange of property with property". Contemporary economic language would render this definition as "exchange of one bundle of property rights for another". This means that permissible contracts are those that allow full transfer of property rights over the subjects of transactions. The same part of the verse declares contracts of *Al-Riba* as non-permissible. In contrast to contracts of exchange, *Al-Riba* contracts are those where property rights over the subject of contract are not exchanged fully. Such is the case of interest-based debt contracts. In these contracts, the property rights over the amount loaned are not transferred to the debtor. While the creditor maintains full property right over the amount loaned, the contract creates an instantaneous property right for the creditor over the property of the debtor to the amount of an ex ante-determined interest payment tied to the amount loaned. Such contracts are not considered legitimate bases for economic/financial transactions.

To base economic transactions on exchange means freedom of contract, freedom of production, and freedom of selecting one's partner to exchange. In turn, exchange promotes specialization, a concept which from the time of the classical economist has meant risk-sharing, coordination, cooperation, and trust, all leading to efficiency in resource allocation. Exchange needs markets and markets need rules governing the behavior of participants. These rules are prescribed in the Qur'an and in the Tradition of the Prophet.

The essence of Verse 275 has been inferred to mean that "by mandating Al-Bai, Allah (swt) has ordained risk-sharing in all exchange activities". *Riba*-based transactions, on the other hand, constitute risk transfer rather than risk-sharing. In interest-based financing, the financier takes no part in the risks of the business for which the money is being borrowed. All risks are transferred to the borrower.

One would be tempted to ask if indeed there is a true ICM anywhere in the world. The short answer is no. Not because an ICM would be detached from reality, for there are other risk-sharing markets and well-functioning ones. These are the equity markets. The problem is that, today, equity markets are heavily linked to debt markets. Thus, stock market bubbles can be created when debt is cheap and easily available. In other words, when debt coexists with risk-sharing, excesses can and do happen. An ICM would be one where risk-sharing is the predominant, if not the only, type of contract.

Source: Excerpt from *Islamic Capital Markets and Development*, Obiyathulla and Abbas (2012).

3.5 International Institutions for Islamic Finance

Given the global nature and growth of Islamic finance, there are a number of international institutions that play either a regulatory and/or supportive role. While some have official jurisdiction within their country of establishment, they often play a supporting role in developing Islamic banking and finance offshore. We see below a brief description of some of these institutions.

3.5.1 *The International Islamic Fiqh Academy*

The International Islamic Fiqh Academy (IIFA) is an offshoot of the Organization of Islamic Conference (OIC). Located in Jeddah, Saudi Arabia, the IIFA is host to a number of highly prominent jurists and *Shari'ah* scholars. Though its fatwas are not binding, given the influence of the IIFA, its seal of approval is much sought after. The IIFA was established with the objective of providing a uniform regulatory regime for the Islamic banking and finance industry. The IIFA, often criticized for being conservative, has a highly prominent *Shari'ah* board.

3.5.2 *The Islamic Financial Services Board*

The Islamic Financial Services Board (IFSB) was established at the initiative of Malaysia's Central Bank, Bank Negara Malaysia. Its objective is to be the international standard setting for Islamic banks, *takaful*, and Islamic finance related areas. As a standard setter for Islamic financial institutions, the IFSB complements the Basel Committee for Banking Supervision and the International Association of Insurance Supervisors. Under the IFSB Act of 2001, the Malaysian government has granted IFSB privileges and immunities usually granted to international organizations and diplomatic missions. Thus far, the IFSB has issued 12 standard Guiding Principles and Technical Notes for the industry. Its standards have been accepted by regulators for adoption in at least Malaysia and Bahrain, two of the most vibrant places for Islamic banking and finance.

3.5.3 *Accounting and Auditing Organization for Islamic Financial Institutions*

The Accounting and Auditing Organization for Islamic Financial Institutions (AAOIFI), which is a Bahrain-based organization, is the standard setter for accounting and auditing issues with the Islamic banking and finance industry. They essentially design *Shari'ah*-compliant standards based largely on International Financial Reporting Standards (IFRS). AAOIFI's work becomes highly relevant in areas where the IFRS either does not provide coverage or may be in conflict with *Shari'ah* requirements/compliance. In addition to standard setting, AAOIFI also provides specialized training for industry participants, AAOIFI is a non-profit organization funded by its institutional members. As an independent international organization, its standards and rulings have been adopted by regulators in a wide range of Muslim and non-Muslim nations.

3.5.4 *The International Islamic Financial Market*

The International Islamic Financial Market (IIFM) was established in Bahrain as a global standardization body for the Islamic capital market, money market, and the Islamic financial services industry. Established with the support of the central banks of Bahrain, Brunei, Sudan, and Indonesia, the IIFM has its primary focus in the standardization of Islamic products, processes, and underlying documentation. IIFM is currently working with International Swap Dealers Association (ISDA) and International Capital Markets Association (ICMA) on *Shari'ah*-compliant master agreements/documentations for capital and money market transactions.

3.5.5 *The Islamic International Rating Agency*

The Islamic International Rating Agency (IIRA) is a Bahrain-based credit rating agency for *sukuk* and other Islamic finance papers. In addition to credit rating, the IIRA also provides assessment of *Shari'ah*-compliant database of actual capital market activity. Its objective is to become the ultimate reference point for credit ratings in accordance with *Shari'ah* principles. The IIRA is established as an independent agency, sponsored by multilateral development institutions, Islamic banks, and other rating agencies. It began its operations mid-2005. The IIRA also publishes a series of analytical research reports for the Islamic financial services industry.

3.5.6 *The Malaysia International Islamic Financial Centre*

The Malaysia International Islamic Financial Centre (MIFC), established in 2006, is a Malaysian government initiative to promote the country as the international hub for Islamic finance. This is to be done through MIFC emphasis on *sukuk* origination, Islamic fund and wealth management, international Islamic banking, international *takaful*, and human capital development.

Rather than undertaking activities directly, the MIFC is designed to be a "one-stop" coordination centre for players in Islamic banking and finance, especially foreign players. Under MIFC, foreign and local players are allowed to undertake a full range of Islamic banking and *takaful* activities in foreign currency.

3.5.7 *The International Shariah Research Academy for Islamic Finance*

The International Shariah Research Academy for Islamic Finance (ISRA) is a Malaysian research academy established by the Malaysian Central Bank, Bank Negara Malaysia. The objective is for ISRA to act both as a repository of knowledge on *Shari'ah* views/*fatwas* and an initiator of applied *Shari'ah*-based research on contemporary issues affecting the Islamic banking and finance industry. ISRA is also to act as a platform for greater cooperation among practitioners, *Shari'ah* scholars, and academics.

3.5.8 *The International Islamic Liquidity Management Corporation*

The International Islamic Liquidity Management Corporation (IILM) is a Kuala Lumpur, Malaysia, based institution established to provide for a robust Islamic liquidity management platform. IILM does this by issuing short-term *sukuk* to facilitate cross-border liquidity management by IFIs. Established in 2010 by a group of Central banks and monetary authorities, IILM issued its first *sukuk* in 2013, amounting to about US$500 million. Since then, the *sukuk* has been reissued several times. The underlying asset for the *sukuk* constitutes sovereign assets pledged to the IILM by its founding members. In keeping with *Shari'ah* requirements, the underlying portfolio for the *sukuk* is made up of 51% tangible assets and 49% receivables. As Islamic finance becomes globalized with increasing cross-border flows, the need for a high-quality liquid asset is obvious. Though still small, the potential for IILM is large.

Summary

This chapter examined the underlying philosophy of Islamic finance. It also described the *Shari'ah* requirements for capital market instruments and some of the key contracts in Islamic finance. Islamic finance is apparent in the *Shari'ah*. The *Shari'ah* emanates from *aqidah*, which is the core set of rules between man and his Creator and is the basis of Islamic ideology. *Tauhid*, *nubuuwa*, and *ma'ad* are the three key components of Islamic ideology. The primary sources of the *Shari'ah* are the Qur'an and *Sunnah*. The secondary sources are *ijma* and *qiyas*. *Maslahah* or public need/benefit is a third possible source. The *Shari'ah*, which is very comprehensive, is often categorized into two parts: (i) matters relating to *ibadah*, and (ii) matters relating to economics and commerce or *mu'amalah*. Islamic finance, banking, and capital markets are governed by the rules of *fiqh mu'amalah*. For financial instruments, contracts, and transactions to be *Shari'ah*-compliant, they must be ethical and based on fairness and justice. In addition, they must be free from (i) *riba*, (ii) *rishwah*, (iii) *gharar*, (iv) *maisyir*, and (v) *jahl*. The chapter also described the various international governing bodies for Islamic banking and finance.

Questions and Problems

1. What is *Shari'ah* and how is it related to *aqidah*?
2. *Aqidah*, which is the basis of Islamic ideology, has three components. Describe each of these.
3. What are the primary and secondary sources of *Shari'ah?* Describe them.
4. What is meant by *fiqh mu'amalah*? Describe some of the underlying fundamentals of *fiqh mu'amalah.*
5. The *Shari'ah* has certain specific prohibitions for Islamic financial contracts/instruments. Describe each prohibition and its implication for Islamic capital market instruments.
6. Using any recent financial market crisis as example, show how *Shari'ah* prohibitions may have helped to avoid or minimize such crisis.
7. Differentiate between *riba buyu* and *riba qurudh.* Give examples for each.
8. Evaluate a proposal for a commodity *murabahah* program based on gold in the light of *riba buyu.*
9. Describe the differences between contracts within each pair;
   (a) *Mudarabah* and *musharakah*
   (b) *Istisna* and *ijarah*
   (c) *Bay al-bithaman ajil* and *salam*
   (d) *Murabahah* and *musawamah*
10. Though interest is prohibited, the time value of money concept is relevant to Islamic finance. Discuss why this is so.
11. Describe any two international Islamic finance institutions. Describe their role in the Islamic finance ecosystem and explain why their role is important.
12. Given the description of Islamic financial contracts, evaluate and classify them on a spectrum with debt at one end and equity at the other.

Bibliography

Capital Market Issues According to Islamic Jurisprudence. Resolutions of the Securities Commission *Shariah* Advisory Council–Securities Commission, Kuala Lumpur. *https://www.sc.com.my/en/resolutions-of-the-sc-shariah-advisory-council/*

Al-Suwailem, S. (2006). "Hedging in Islamic Finance," Occasional Paper No. 10, Islamic Development Bank, Jeddah.

Ayub, M. (2007). *Understanding Islamic Finance* (John Wiley & Sons Ltd).

IOSCO (2005). "Islamic Capital Markets: Fact Finding Report," The International Organization of Securities Commission.

Iqbal, Z. and A. Mirakhor (2006). *An Introduction to Islamic Finance: Theory and Practice* (John Wiley & Sons, Singapore).

Kahf, M. (1994). "Time Value of Money and Discounting in Islamic Perspective; Re-visited," *Review of Islamic Economics*, Vol. 3, No. 2, pp. 31–38.

Kahf, M. (2006). "Objectives of Shariah in the Prohibition of Riba — Implications for Modern Islamic Finance," Paper presented at *IIUM International Conference on Maqasid al-Shariah*, 8–10 August 2010. Kuala Lumpur.

Obiyathulla, I. B. and Abbas, M. (2012). *Islamic Capital Markets and Development*. INCEIF (unpublished manuscript).

Papazaian, A. V. (2010). "Space Value of Money," *Islamic Banking & Finance*, Vol. 8, No. 26, pp. 22–23.

Sardehi, N. (2008). *Islamic Capital Markets — Developments and Challenges* (VDM Verlag Publishers, Germany).

Vogel, E. F. and S. L. Hayes (1998), *Islamic Law and Finance. Religion, Risk and Return* (Kluwer Law International, Cambridge).

Websites

www.sc.com.my/eng/html/icm/ICM IOSCOFactfindingReport.pdf

http://www.islamonline.net/servlet/satellite

http://www.ifsb.org

http://www.iifm.net

http://www.iirating.com/about

http://www.lmcbahrain.com

http://www.mifc.com/index.php?ch=menu

http://www.telegraph.co.uk/finance

http://www.iilm.com

Chapter 4

THE INTERBANK MONEY MARKETS

Topics in this Chapter

4.1. Introduction
4.2. Money Market — Components
4.3. Instruments Traded in the Malaysian Money Market
4.4. The Pricing of Money Market Instruments
4.5. Determining the Yield of a Money Market Instrument
4.6. Interest Rates, Yields, and Price of Money Market Instruments
4.7. Malaysia Money Market — Trading Performance
4.8. The Central Bank, Money Market, and Monetary Policy Operations
4.9. Commercial Banks and the Money Markets

Chapter Objective

This chapter is designed to provide an in-depth understanding of the Interbank Money Market and the instruments traded therein. The rationale for money markets, its functions, key components, and trading mechanisms are explained. On completing the chapter, you should have a good understanding of the need for the money market, its role and links with the rest of the financial system, and the types of instruments traded.

Key Terms		
benchmark yield curve	financial system	money market
Cagamas	foreign exchange	money market instruments
Central Bank	government bonds	open market
cheque clearing system	interbank deposit system	REPOs
commercial banks	KLIBOR	risk-free rates
commercial papers	liquidity	trading efficiency
credit allocation	monetary policy	

4.1 Introduction

The money market is a key component of a country's financial system. If the banking system and the capital markets are the two wheels of a country's financial system, the money market can be thought of as the gear that moves both these wheels. The money market is connected to the capital market, in particular, the bond market, in that it trades short-term debt papers. The money market was the main credit market in the 18th and 19th centuries; most banking activities were concentrated in short-term commercial loans to finance trade operations. Money market operations used to be carried out through discounting commercial bills, issuance of banknotes, and short-term credit. Thus, the short-end of the yield curve is derived from money market trading. It is not uncommon therefore to hear of the money market being characterized as the market for short-end debt. If tenor links the money market to the capital markets, it is linked to the banking system in another critical way. Banks depend on the money market to manage their liquidity. While liquidity management is not the only use of money markets for banks, it is by far the most important. In fact, banks depend so much on the money markets that often they are known as the Interbank Money Market. The Interbank Money Market is no different from the money market, only that it is bank dominated. With the exception of the US, where the money market is *securities dominated*, with funds being channeled through use of short-term securities such as Treasury bills and Commercial papers, most money markets are bank dominated. In bank-dominated money markets, funds are moved through use of bank deposit instruments such as Bankers' Acceptances (BAs) and Certificates of Deposit (CDs).

Given the links that the money market has with both the capital market and the banking system, it has become the ideal avenue for central banks to conduct monetary operations. As such the first impact of a monetary policy change is always felt first in the money market. It is the short interest rate/yield, derived from money market trading, that first responds to central bank policy implementation. Adjustment in the bond, equity market, and banking system follow the money market reaction. Thus, a well-functioning money market properly transmits policy initiatives to the rest of the financial system. Occasionally, central banks may also use the money market for credit allocation purposes. Today, given the many functions that the money market plays, there is a wide range of players who use and depend on the money market for their activities (see Figure 4.1).

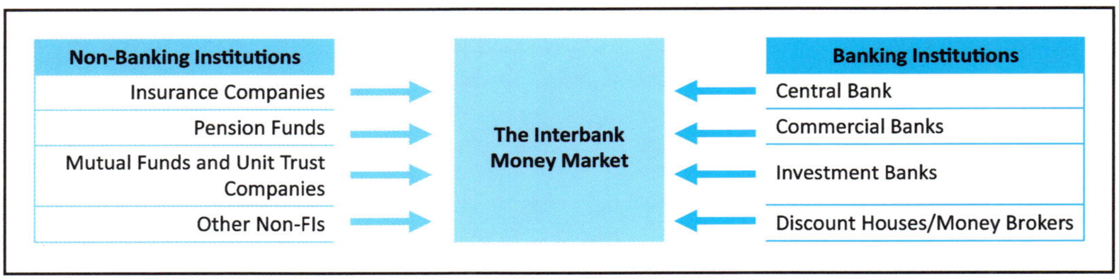

Figure 4.1. Key Players of the Money Market.

Source: Author.

Though money markets play many critical functions today, they had humble beginnings. Money markets began as a needed extension of the correspondent banking system. In the early days, with banking being largely a localized business, the need for economies of scale required banks to go into relationships with banks in other cities/regions in order to extend their reach. This gave rise to correspondent banking. Deposits that country banks placed with their correspondent banks in the money centers and regional imbalances, in deposit creation and credit demand, supported the development of national money markets. The need to minimize counterparty risk and have transactions on an arms' length basis, led to the creation of tradable debt papers or commercial bills as they were then known. A market to discount and trade these papers was the next logical extension. Figure 4.2 portrays these early beginnings.

While the above description was the typical evolution of money markets in the UK and US, Malaysia's money market as with its Islamic counterpart, the IIMM, were established by *fiat*, i.e., at the behest of Bank

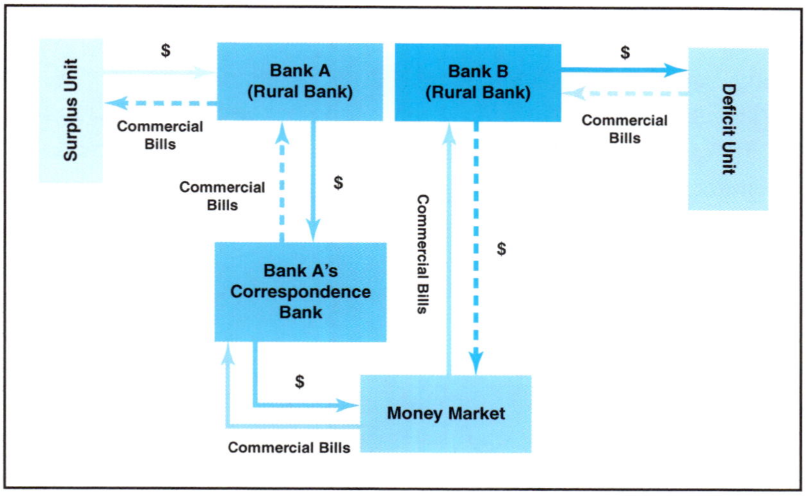

Figure 4.2. Money Markets and Correspondent Banking.

Note: C. Bills = Commercial Bills.

Negara Malaysia (BNM). Though established in the 1980s, the conventional money market was moribund for several years. Trading was tepid, with most players holding on to papers purchased until maturity. The market was characterized by very illiquid trading, ineffcient pricing, an inadequate market structure, and a very limited range of products/instruments. All these changed in 1989 when BNM undertook a series of measures to rejuvenate the money market. A total of five key initiatives were undertaken over the next several years. These were:

(i) Appointment of principal dealers to make markets;
(ii) Creation of a benchmark yield curve;
(iii) Interest rate deregulation (in February 1991);
(iv) Increased capital requirement for non-bank players in money market (in 1998); and
(v) Infrastructure development (1989–1997).

Under the principal dealership system, BNM appointed selected banks based on their equity capital and capability to handle large volume trading to be principal dealers (PDs). These institutions were obliged to: (a) bid for at least 10% of the instruments offered in a primary auction conducted by the central bank; (b) participate in money market tenders; and (c) stand ready to provide two-way price quotations. In exchange for taking on these obligations, they were granted certain cost-saving privileges, for e.g., on REPO agreements with BNM and other specific advantages. This market-making initiative led to a significant improvement in secondary market trading and substantially improved liquidity. For example, trading in government securities jumped more than 600% between 1995 and 1996.

Since the pricing of money market instruments was a serious handicap, the government undertook the issuance of a series of government bonds of different maturities in order to establish a "benchmark yield curve". These were the *Khazanah* bonds. Interest rate "deregulation" took place when banking institutions were freed from administrative controls. This partial deregulation was intended to help in the "price discovery" process. In addition, there was an increase in capital requirement of the non-bank money market players, this was intended to minimize counterparty risk in money market transactions. Finally, the last initiative aimed at improving the trading effciency was by developing new infrastructure for trading and information dissemination. A few series trading platforms were introduced; SPEEDs in 1989, and RENTAS, which replaced SPEEDs in 1999. In addition, other automated systems, such as FAST, were introduced to complement RENTAS and enhance the auction process of government securities.

4.2 Money Market: Components

The money market typically has two key components: (i) an interbank deposit system and (ii) a platform for transactions in money market instruments. A third common component is the interbank cheque clearing system. The need to clear cheques is really the result of bank customers writing/issuing cheques, where transactions are concerned, and the money market can be divided into two broad categories: (i) trading in interbank deposits and (ii) the trading of money market instruments.

4.2.1 *The Interbank Deposit System*

The interbank deposit system is a means by which banks borrow and lend among themselves. The need for a bank to borrow and lend arises from the mismatches in the daily cash flows of the bank. Cash-flow mismatch for a bank on any given day could arise from a number of sources. Imbalances between customers' deposits and withdrawals and the offsetting balance of the cheque clearing process would be two key sources of cash-flow mismatches on a daily basis. When the amount of withdrawals exceeds on a given day, the bank would have a cash shortfall; this shortfall may also occur when the banks have issued more loans than it should. Similarly, if the cheques are drawn upon a bank, i.e., cheque issued by its customers exceeds cheques deposited by its customers in their favor, again, a shortfall occurs. Alternatively, if cash deposits exceed withdrawals or cheques deposited exceed the amount of cheques drawn on the bank, a cash surplus will result. In addition to these two common sources of cash imbalances for banks, there is a third important source that can cause short-term cash-flow problems to a bank. When the items on a bank's balance sheet "mature", a cash-flow results. For example, when an asset or a loan given by the bank matures, the repayment results in a cash inflow; similarly, when an item on the liability side matures, e.g., a fixed deposit, there will be a cash outflow. As such, the size and timing of these maturing assets and liabilities would determine whether a bank will have a net cash inflow or outflow. If more assets than liability items mature over a given period, the bank will see its cash surplus increase by the amount of the net cash inflow. A cash deficit will result if the opposite happens.

It is obvious that a bank may have little influence on the above three determinants of cash imbalances. In managing these temporary imbalances, the interbank deposit system comes in handy. Until assets can be acquired, and loans are found, a bank has to invest the surplus cash it has. Money has a cost, and banks have to pay depositors for the surplus cash even if it has not been lent out. Similarly, when a cash outflows are larger than inflows, a source of funding to meet the shortfall has to be found. In allowing banks to borrow and lend among themselves, the interbank deposit system or interbank market allows banks to manage their liquidity.

Tenors for interbank deposits range from overnight to a maximum of one year. However, most transactions are at the short end, and seldom extend beyond six or nine months. The interest rate charged on such interbank borrowing and lending is the Kuala Lumpur Interbank Offer Rate (KLIBOR). Since the borrowing–lending transactions are of different tenors, there are different KLIBOR rates. For example, there is an overnight KLIBOR rate, a one-month KLIBOR, a three-month KLIBOR, and so on. Though BNM, the central bank, can have a big influence on the KLIBOR rates, the rates are mostly determined by market forces. Thus, at times of high liquidity, when most banks have cash surpluses, the KLIBOR rates ought to be low since few banks want to borrow. Alternatively, during times of tight liquidity, the rates could climb. As we will see later, movements in the interbank rate is heavily influenced by Bank Negara.

As an interbank market, the money market is essentially a "wholesale" market, i.e., transaction sizes are large given that it is an institutional market. Just as the wholesale price of an item determines its retail price, the KLIBOR rates that prevail in the interbank market dictate the interest charged by banks. The KLIBOR rates constitute a benchmark cost of funds to commercial banks. Even if a bank is not currently borrowing in the interbank market, the prevailing KLIBOR rate would constitute an opportunity cost since that is the rate it could earn by lending in the interbank market. Given the short-term nature of interbank deposits and the fact that the players are mainly the banks and the central bank, the KLIBOR rates are, in essence, risk-free rates. In emerging markets, where the treasury bills have illiquid markets, the interbank rates are often used as the risk-free rate.

Box 4.1. The Kuala Lumpur Interbank Offerred Rate (KLIBOR) — Illustration: A Typical Interbank Deposit Transaction

Suppose given temporary excess outflows, CIMB wants to borrow RM100 million for a one-month period. Assume that Maybank has a cash surplus which it wants to place out for a short period in the interbank market. Given CIMB's needs, Maybank would place RM100 million as a one-month deposit with CIMB. The interest rate that CIMB will pay for interbank deposit will be the prevailing one-month KLIBOR rate.

If the one-month KLIBOR rate is say, 6% annualized, the amount that CIMB would have to return to Maybank one month later would be determined as;

$$\text{RA} = \text{Principal} \times \left[1 + \frac{\text{KLIBOR}}{N}\right]^{t}$$

where;
RA = the redemption amount
KLIBOR = the appropriate annualized KLIBOR by tenor
N = number of tenor periods within a year
t = tenor period

In this case, the redemption amount would be;

$$\begin{aligned}\text{RA} &= \text{RM } 100{,}000{,}000 \times [1 + (0.06/12)]^{1} \\ &= \text{RM } 100{,}000{,}000 \times [1.005] \\ &= \text{RM } 100{,}500{,}000\end{aligned}$$

The redemption amount is simply the initial deposit plus accumulated interest. Note that these amounts are not physically moved but debited and credited into the respective bank's accounts.

4.2.1.1 *Interbank deposits: Trading activity*

When trading activity is measured by the ringgit amount, interbank deposits typically account for a large portion of total interbank market activity. Over the 10-year period of 1990–1999, interbank deposit activity accounted for an average percentage of the total money market activity. Trading in money market instruments accounts for the remainder. Over the years, money market instruments appear to have become increasingly popular. In 2005, for e.g., the approximate breakdown between the two types of money market transactions was 54% interbank deposits and 46% for money market instruments. Within interbank deposits, the short tenors, overnight, weekend, and one-week tenors were the most popular. Overnight deposits typically account for close to 70% of volume traded in ringgit terms. This popularity of overnight deposits is attributable to the overnight borrowing/lending needed to settle balances arising from the cheque clearing. An example of this is shown in Box 4.2.

Box 4.2. Illustration: Overnight Interbank Deposit from Cheque Clearance

Suppose on a given day, HSBC has RM250 million worth of cheques drawn on it from Maybank's customers, but only RM200 million drawn on Maybank by HSBC's customers. At the end of cheque clearing, HSBC has to pay Maybank the differential amount of RM50 million. If the amount is settled the following day by HSBC, it will be liable to Maybank for the interest accrued for the overnight period. In essence, at the end of the cheque clearing process, Maybank would be deemed to have "placed" an overnight interbank deposit of RM50 million with HSBC. Assuming the quoted overnight interest rate is 5.8% overnight KLIBOR (annualized), the amount HSBC will have to pay Maybank can be determined using our earlier equation as:

$$\begin{aligned} RA &= RM\ 50{,}000{,}000 \times 1.000159 \\ &= RM\ 50{,}007{,}945.21 \end{aligned}$$

The amount of RM7,945.21 would constitute the interest for the overnight period.

Thus, the huge popularity of the overnight tenor has to do with the need to settle differences that result from the interbank cheque clearing process.

4.2.2 *Money Market Instruments*

The second key component of the money market as mentioned earlier constitutes the trading of money market instruments. If the interbank deposit system enabled banks to borrow and lend directly among themselves, money market instruments achieve the same objective of borrowing and lending through the issuance/purchase of debt instruments. The advantage of using instruments is that it enables the debt to be transferred easily through secondary market trading. Thus, a bank that purchases money market instruments today could sell them off within the next few days and recoup their money without having to wait until the maturity date of the instruments. The highly liquid secondary market for money market instruments enables debt to be sold and resold before maturity. Aside from reducing liquidity risk, such trading enables rapid repricing and thereby effcient price discovery.

Relative to interbank deposits, money market instruments have a much larger constituent base. This is because, unlike interbank deposits which are largely restricted to banks, players in money market instruments are more diverse. Even non-financial corporations can raise short-term debt by issuing money market instruments such as commercial papers or bankers' acceptances. While the term money market instruments typically refer to short-term debt papers, it is quite common to see long-dated debt like government bonds being traded. Often these bonds are nearing maturity and are therefore really "short-term", even though they may have been issued several years before.

We now turn to a discussion of some of the common money market instruments traded in the Malaysian money market. Since there is a separate section on the Islamic interbank money markets where Islamic money market instruments will be discussed, we restrict our discussion here to conventional money market instruments.

4.2.3 *Malaysian Treasury Bills*

Malaysian Treasury Bills (MTBs) are short-term government securities traded on yield basis. The yield is specified as a rate of discount and the tenor of MTBs is expressed in actual number of days. The typical maturities are three, six, and 12 months. Since they are traded at a discount to face value, at maturity, the holder receives the face or nominal value. MTBs are often issued by means of weekly tenders.

4.2.4 *Bank Negara Malaysia Bills*

Bank Negara Malaysia Bills (BNBs) are short-term securities issued by BNM and are bid on yield basis. The maturity is always less than a year. The yield is specified as a rate of discount and the tenor of BNB is expressed in actual number of days. Like MTBs, they are issued on a discount basis, with holders receiving the nominal (face value) at maturity.

4.2.5 *Malaysian Government Securities*

Malaysian Government Securities (MGSs) are sovereign debt papers or bonds issued by the Malaysian government to raise funds in the domestic capital market. They typically have fixed coupon rates (interest rates) that are paid on a semi-annual basis. The coupon rate is determined by the weighted average of the successful yield. Like all bonds, they are traded in secondary markets based on prices determined by the required yield to maturity. MGSs that are close to maturity are often traded in the money market.

4.2.6 *Bankers' Acceptances*

Bankers' Acceptances (BAs) are short term, zero coupon debt papers issued by companies. They are guaranteed by a bank and are therefore known as BAs. The bank guarantee enhances credit rating and makes it transferable and therefore suited to secondary market trading. BAs are traded on a discount basis.

4.2.7 *Commercial Papers*

Commercial Papers (CPs) are short-term, unsecured (promissory notes) debt instruments issued by corporations. Typically issued by companies with good credit rating, they can be very liquid. Yields are higher than government paper of similar maturity, reflecting the risk spread. CPs are sold on a discount basis and are flexible in that issuers can easily roll over the debt by issuing new papers to redeem outstanding ones.

4.2.8 *Cagamas Notes*

Cagamas notes are short-term securities with a tenor of 12 months or less. The notes are similar to MTBs and normally issued at a discount. The issuer is the National Mortgage Corporation or Cagamas. At maturity, they are redeemable at nominal value.

4.2.9 *Cagamas Bonds*

Cagamas bonds are longer-term debt instruments issued by the National Mortgage Corporation. The bonds are often the result of securitization of housing loans of local commercial banks that have been purchased by Cagamas. The bonds have either a fixed coupon rate or a floating coupon rate. Floating rate bonds are medium/long-term bonds with an adjustable coupon rate. The coupon could be based on either the three-month or six-month KLIBOR rate. The fixed rate bonds are of fixed coupon, payable semi-annually.

4.2.10 *Khazanah Bonds*

Issued by Khazanah Nasional Berhard, a government agency charged with managing government-linked companies (GLCs), *Khazanah* bonds are essentially rated as government paper. They share many of the same features of MGS securities. Typically long-term bonds, the fact that they are essentially sovereign ensures a liquid market for these bonds.

4.2.11 *Negotiable Instrument of Deposits*

As the name suggests, these are instruments created as a result of bank deposits, the objective being to enable these deposits to be traded on the secondary market. Negotiable instrument of deposits (NIDs), being of private issuance, typically provide a higher yield than the treasury bills. They are traded on a discounted basis to their nominal value.

4.2.12 *Repurchase Agreements*

Repurchase Agreements (REPOs) are not an instrument but an extremely popular type of transaction in money markets. This is also true of the Malaysian money market. REPOs are bilateral transactions involving the purchase and resale of securities by agreement. The underlying asset is typically an MGS, a government bond, or other liquid instruments. One party buys the underlying instrument at an agreed price from a seller who promises to buy it back at a stipulated future date. The party that first purchases and then resells is effectively the lender of funds. The counterparty is the borrower. Since the resale price is always higher than the original price, the price difference is the implied interest for the loan.

4.3 The Pricing of Money Market Instruments

It should be evident from our above discussion that money market instruments have a variety of features. Some are long-term bonds with fixed or floating coupon rates, while others like Treasury bills, CPs, and BAs are money market specific. Bonds such as Cagamas and *Khazanah* bonds, would also be traded in the bond market which is a part of the long-term capital market. Since the pricing of bonds is examined in detail in Chapter 5, we will restrict our discussion here to the pricing of money market instruments.

You would have noticed from our above discussion that most money market instruments are traded at a discount to face or nominal value, and they are redeemable at face value on the maturity date. Since a discounted price is always smaller than the redeemable face value, the difference between the price paid and the redeemed amount at maturity is the "return" to the investor. Thus, to determine what an instrument's correct price should be, we would need to know the following four factors:

(i) Time left to maturity (in days);
(ii) The nominal or face value of the instrument (redeemable amount);
(iii) The required return or yield for the instruments (discount factor); and
(iv) The coupon/interest payment, if any

Since most money market instruments being short term pay no interim coupon or interest, the fourth item above is not applicable in most cases. The three factors needed to determine the price/value of a money market instrument are: time to maturity, face value, and required yield or discount factor. A generalized pricing model would be

$$P = FV \times \left[1 - \frac{(r \times t)}{36500}\right], \tag{4.1}$$

where
P = Price of instrument
FV = Face value or redeemable amount at maturity
r = Required yield (discount factor)
t = number of days left to maturity
(Note: the 36500 is essentially 365 × 100 to account for the fact that r goes in the numerator as a whole number and not with decimals.)

Box 4.3. Illustration: Determining the Price of a Money Market Instrument

(a) Suppose a banker acceptance with 48 days left to maturity and a face value of RM100,000 is available. What would be the correct price if the required yield is 7% annualized?

$$\text{P} = \text{RM } 100{,}000\left[1 - \frac{(7\times 48)}{36500}\right]$$

$= \text{RM } 100{,}000\ [1 - (0.009205)]$
$= \text{RM } 100{,}000\ (0.990795)$
$= \text{RM } 99{,}079.45$

(b) A Malaysian Treasury Bill with RM1 million face value and 60 days to maturity is being offered to you. Assuming the required yield is 4.5%, what would be the appropriate price of the T-bill?

$$\text{P} = \text{RM } 1{,}000{,}000\left[1 - \frac{4.5\times 60}{36500}\right]$$

$= \text{RM } 1{,}000{,}000\ [1 - (0.007397)]$
$= \text{RM } 1{,}000{,}000\ (0.992603)$
$= \text{RM } 992{,}603.74$

4.4 Determining the Yield of a Money Market Instrument

Often times, one would be interested in knowing what the yield on an instrument is, given its price. For example, we may be offered an instrument at a given price. Given the offer price, we may want to know whether the return earned, i.e., yield, justifies making the investment. The yield on an instrument can be determined as:

$$Y = \left[\left(\frac{FV - P}{FV}\right)\times(365/t)\right], \tag{4.2}$$

where
Y = yield on instrument
FV = face value of instrument
P = current price
t = days to maturity
(Note: The yield using Eq. (4.2) is often known as *yield on a bank discount basis.*)

Box 4.4. Illustration: Determining Yield

Suppose a commercial paper with a RM1 million face value and 30 days to maturity is being quoted RM992,000.00 what is the yield on the CP if held until maturity?

$$Y = \left[\left(\frac{RM1{,}000{,}000 - RM992{,}000}{RM1{,}000{,}000}\right)\times(365/30)\right]$$

$= [(0.0080)\times(12.17)]$
$Y = 0.097$, which is 9.7% annualized.

4.5 Interest Rates, Yields and Price of Money Market Instruments

As pricing of most money market instruments are based on discounting, they are very sensitive to changes in interest rates. The yields or discount rates used to value these instruments are directly related to the KLIBOR rates (with an addition of risk premiums according to the credit rating of the issuer). As such, when interest rates as reflected by KLIBOR rates change, the values of these instruments change. The relationship is obviously an inverse one (negative relationship). That is, when interest rates go up, the prices go down, and vice-versa. The pricing conventions in money markets are indeed designed to capture this inverse relationship.

Both the interbank deposit system and the market for money market instruments are intricately linked. Funds flow easily between the two and this ensures co-movement in their yields/rates of return. Banks with a surplus of short-term funds have a choice of either placing them as deposits with other banks that have a need for funds or investing in the money market instruments. Similarly, banks faced with a funding deficit can either borrow in the interbank market or sell money market instruments to raise the needed funds. Figure 4.3 shows the common access that banks and the banking system have to the two components of the money market. As shown in the figure, banks could either borrow/lend among themselves through interbank deposits or the purchase/sell or issuance of money market instruments. A bank with surplus funds could invest its surplus by purchasing money market instruments. On the other hand, a bank in deficit and in need of funds would either sell money market instruments it owns or issue new ones to raise the needed short-term funding.

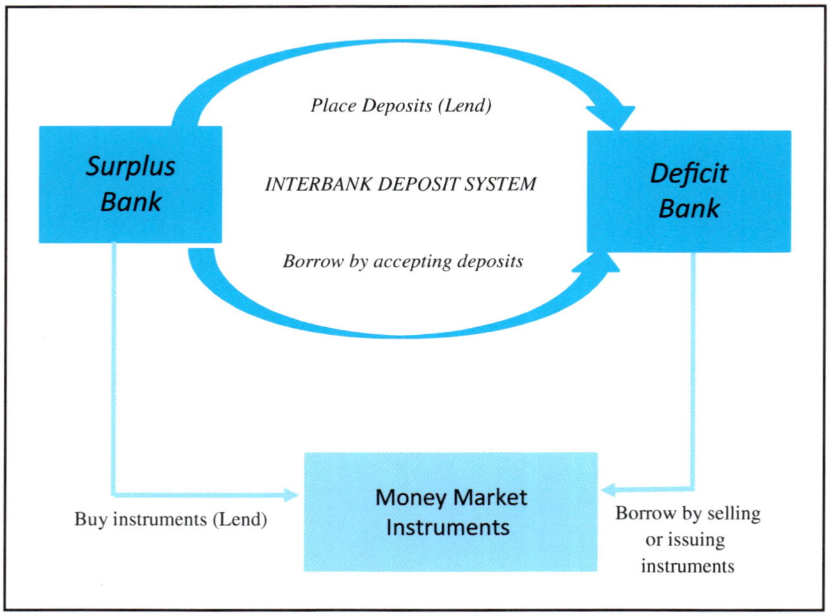

Figure 4.3. Funding Through Interbank Deposits and Money Market Instruments.

Box 4.5. Barclays Gets Fixed for "Fixing" the LIBOR

Barclays, the British banking giant, was fined £290 million by British and US regulators, following charges that the bank had submitted false readings for its LIBOR transactions. The LIBOR rate (London Interbank Offer Rate) is calculated daily by Thomson Reuters, the financial data provider on behalf of the British Banker's Association — the industry body. Thomson Reuters would provide daily LIBOR rates by getting participating banks (usually the top 14 or 15 banks) to submit their LIBOR rates at which they borrowed or lent on a given day. Most information providers use such submissions

(Continued)

Box 4.5. (*Continued*)

to work-out an "average" after eliminating extreme values. This reported rate is then used in pricing money market instruments for secondary market trading.

The charge on Barclays is that the bank systematically provided incorrect LIBOR rates. This, it appears, were particularly true in the tumultuous period following the collapse of Lehman Brothers in September 2008. As described in Box 4.7, the immediate aftermath of the Lehman Brothers collapse saw credit yield spreads widening and liquidity drying up in money markets in both New York and London. Much of this had to do with heightened counterparty risks. As rumors of banks and other institutions being in financial distress became rampant, market players were looking at an institution's cost of borrowing, i.e., its borrowing rate in LIBOR, for indications of desperation. An institution desperately trying to survive would have to borrow at any rate whereas one that is not desperate could choose not to borrow at that time. Showing high costs of borrowing would mark an entity as being "distressed" and potentially drive its yield spreads even higher.

Thus, it was in the interest of players to "under report" their borrowing costs, and this, it appears, was precisely what Barclays did. Though it is now apparent that a number of other banks could also have done the same, Barclays is the first to come under the hammer. While it is hard to tell how much such "rigging" would have profited Barclays, the bank has been hard hit by the scandal. Its chairman, Marcus Agius, and Chief Executive Officer, Bob Diamond, have had to resign. In addition to the fine of £290 million (US$430 million), Barclay's stock price fell 17% immediately following the news, thereby wiping out £3.2 billion from its market value. A very expensive lesson indeed for Barclays' shareholders.

4.6 Malaysia Money Market: Trading Performance

Figure 4.4 shows the total traded volume in billions of Ringgit for the money market over the 21-year period from 1995 to 2015.

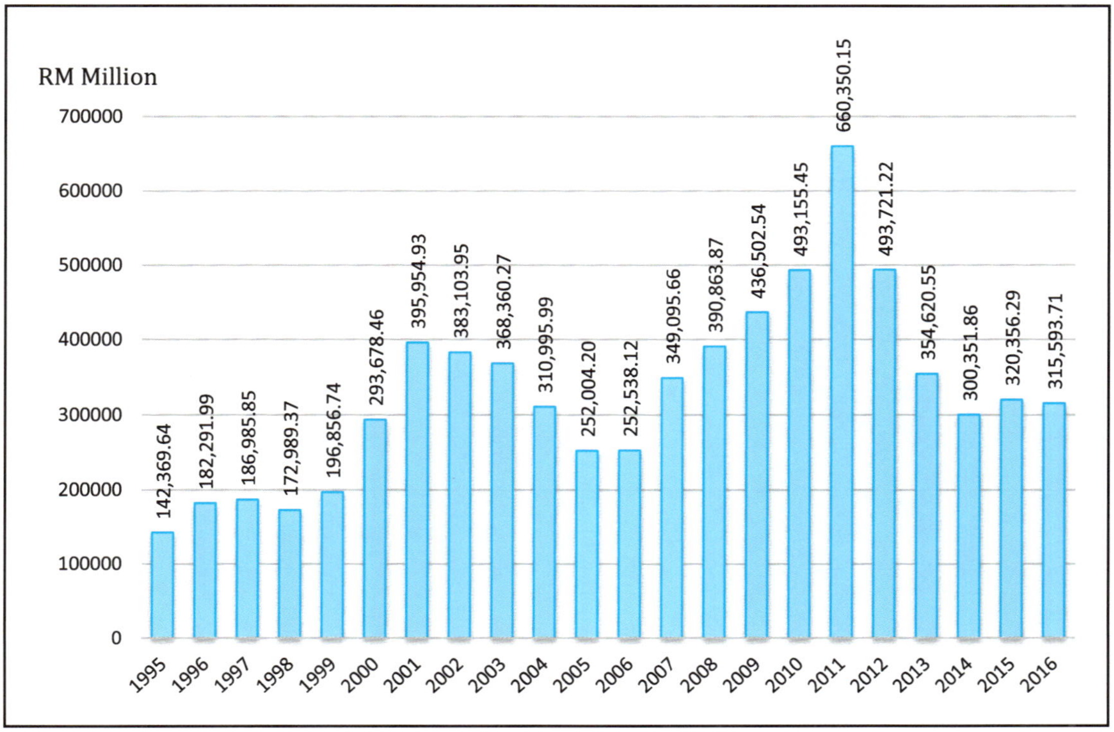

Figure 4.4. Total Traded Volume of Money Market Instruments (1995–2016) (RM Millions).

Source: Bank Negara Malaysia.

Trading performance over the 21-year period, from 1995 to 2016, appears to have had two peaks. Trading showed steady growth over a six-year period, from 1995 to 2001. This was really the continuation of a rising trend that began earlier in 1989. For example, over the 10-year period of 1989–1998, traded volume had increased from a total of approximately RM245 billion in 1989 to RM1,823 billion in 1998. Total volume reached RM1,860 billion in 1997 and remained there for the next two years before continuing the rising trend. Volume peaked in 2001 at close to RM400 billion. For the six-year period from 1995 to 2001, this would constitute a total growth of 167% or a compounded annual growth of about 17.8%. The second phase, from 2001 to 2009, shows an overall U-shaped pattern. The second peak was in 2011 when total annual traded volume reached approximately RM680 billion. Following that peak, volume appears to have fallen steadily until stabilizing at about RM300 billion in 2014 and 2015.

As for the proportion of traded volume between the two components of the money market, interbank deposits, and money market instruments, their respective shares appear to be fluctuating. Though the proportion of money market instruments has increased, its share of total volume fluctuates. For example, in 2005, approximately 45% of the total money market volume was accounted for by money market instruments and the remaining 55% by interbank deposits. Figures 4.5 to 4.8 show volume growth for the four key money market instruments: Bankers' Acceptances, Negotiable Instruments of Deposit, Malaysian Treasury Bills, and Bank Negara Bills.

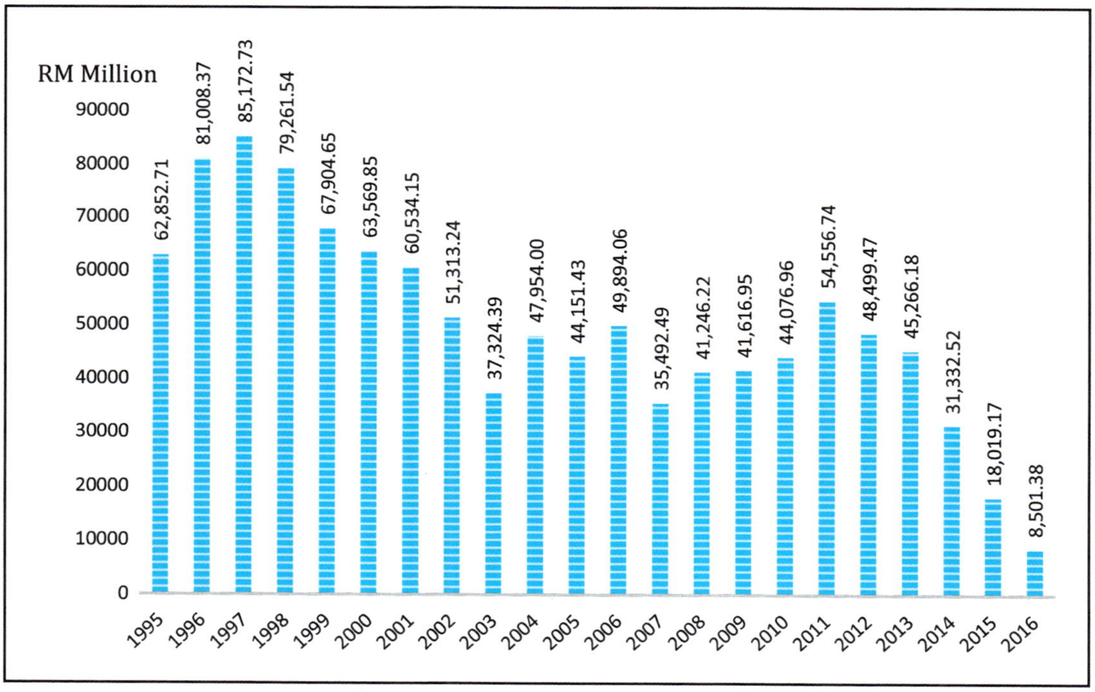

Figure 4.5. Bankers' Acceptances (1995–2016) (RM Millions).

Source: Bank Negara Malaysia.

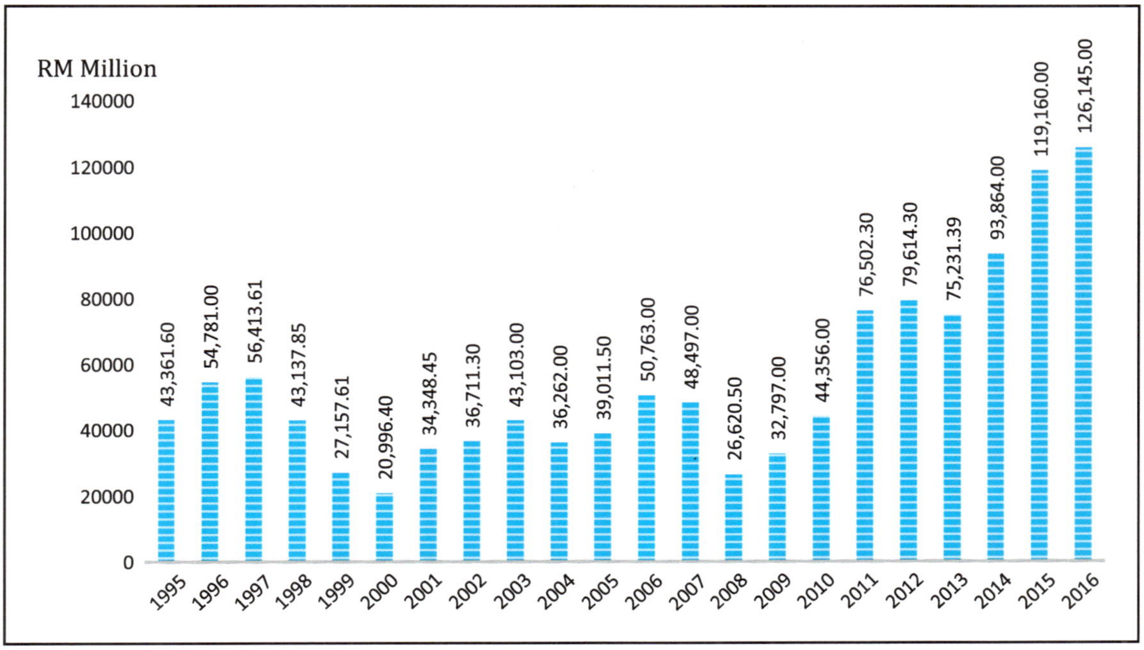

Figure 4.6. Negotiable Instruments of Deposit (1995–2016) (RM Millions).

Source: Bank Negara Malaysia.

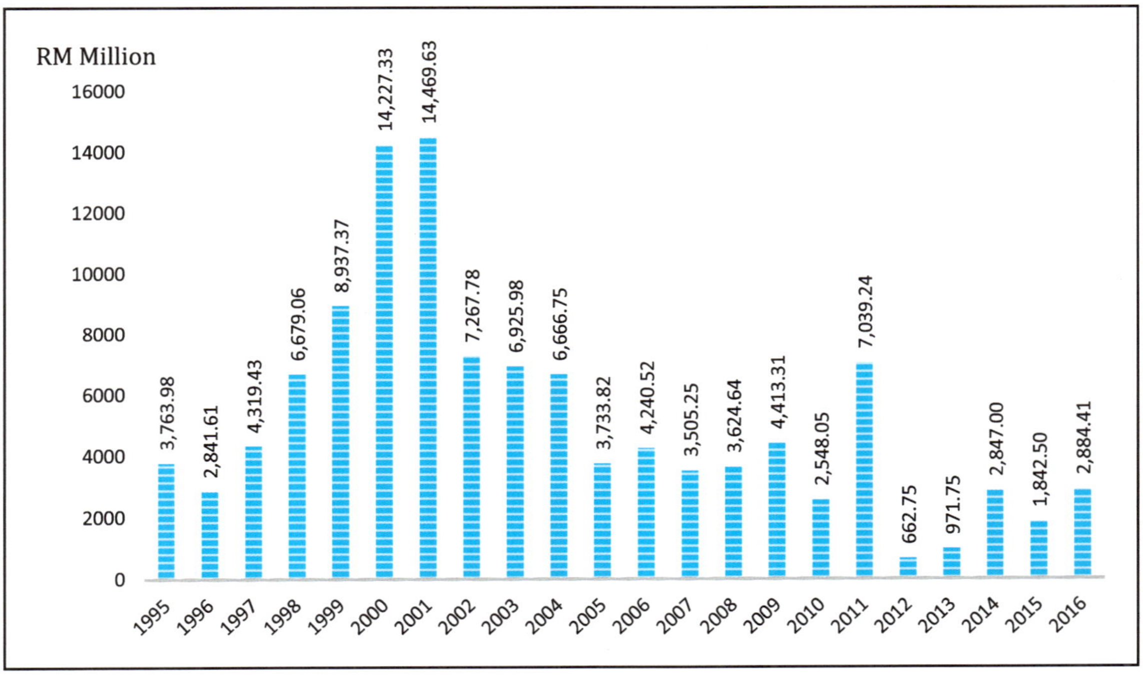

Figure 4.7. Malaysian T-Bills (1995–2016) (RM Millions).

Source: Bank Negara Malaysia.

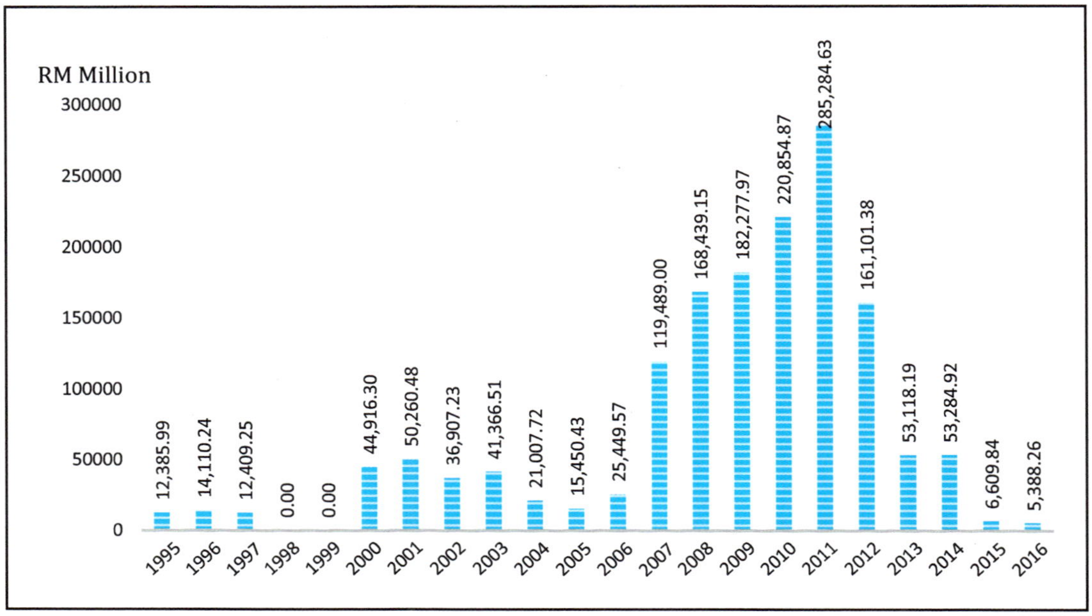

Figure 4.8. Bank Negara Bills (1995–2016) (RM Millions).

Source: Bank Negara Malaysia.

4.7 The Central Bank, Money Market, and Monetary Policy Operations

The central bank, as mentioned earlier, is a key player in the money markets. In modern financial systems, central banks see the money market as a key avenue for the implementation of monetary policy and other needed activities. Bank Negara's role in the domestic money markets in both conventional and Islamic banking is no different.

A central bank's activity in money markets typically has four broad policy objectives:

(i) Ensuring the smooth functioning of the banking system;
(ii) Implementation of monetary policy;
(iii) Offsetting imbalances resulting from the external sector; and
(iv) Sterilization of forex market operations.

4.7.1 *Ensuring Smooth Functioning of the Banking System*

In ensuring the smooth functioning of the banking system, the central bank uses the money market to ensure that there are no imbalances in liquidity. Recall from our earlier discussion that while some banks will have surplus funds and others a shortfall, there is nothing to ensure that the total of surpluses will equal the aggregate shortfall. Thus, at any given time, there could be either a net excess or shortage of liquidity. Small imbalances may not cause problems, but when the imbalance is large, problems associated with liquidity would arise. A huge net shortage could lead to a credit crunch if unchecked. Alternatively, a huge surplus can cause excess liquidity within the overall monetary system causing the interest rates to fall below desired levels. Since extremes on either side can cause problems for the banking sector, the central bank steps in frequently to smoothen out the imbalance.

Central bank intervention, in this case, would be to offset the liquidity imbalance. For example, if there is a net deficit, the central bank "creates" liquidity by either allowing banks to borrow from it or through open-market operations (OMOs).

An OMO is essentially an activity initiated by the central bank to influence liquidity. This is done through the sale or purchase of government securities and/or money market instruments. Since a sale of government securities, for e.g., Bank Negara Bills (BNBs), would enable the central bank to place-out government papers in exchange for cash, the sale drains cash or liquidity from the system. An OMO in which the central bank buys securities would have the opposite effect of increasing liquidity.

Box 4.6. Central Banks Seek New Reference Rates to Replace LIBOR

Following the LIBOR fixing scandal described in Box 4.5, central banks like the Federal Reserve (FED) of the US and the Bank of England (BOE) have initiated efforts to identify and use new benchmark reference rates to replace LIBOR. The US Government had set up the Alternative Reference Rates Committee (ARRC) to study and recommend a new gauge to replace LIBOR for US interbank transactions. ARRC has now recommended the use of a rate derived from the Treasuries Repo financing rate in lieu of LIBOR. The FED appears to have consented to using this Treasuries Repo financing rate for use in the settlement of interbank transactions and US dollar derivatives. ARRC's recommendation comes on the heels of BOE's announcement that its Working Group on Sterling Risk-Free Reference Rates has recommended that LIBOR be replaced with SONIA, which stands for Sterling Overnight Index Average, and is an average of the overfunding costs for banks in the unsecured Sterling market. The BOE is expected to begin using a finalized version of SONIA in April 2018.

4.7.2 *Implementation of Monetary Policy*

Given the above description of how the central bank can affect liquidity, it should be easy to visualize how the central bank can affect the monetary policy. Monetary policy has two legs: interest rates and money supply. Since the money market was described earlier as the link between the banking system and the capital market, it is often an ideal platform for the execution of a monetary policy. To raise interest rates and money supply via the money market, the central bank can undertake the sale of government securities. Sustained selling would drive down liquidity and thereby raise the yields and interest rates. In the interbank market, the central bank can achieve the objective by offering higher rates on deposits of commercial banks that are placed with it. Since all banks have to have an account with the central bank, adjusting the rate it offers can change liquidity in the money market and the banking system. Implementing an expansionary monetary policy would entail the opposite, i.e., the central bank cutting the interest rate it offers for deposits placed with it by banks, and/or buying government securities/money market papers.

4.7.3 *Offsetting Imbalances Resulting From the External Sector*

For open economies, especially a small open economy such as Malaysia, external imbalances can quickly translate into sudden imbalances within the domestic economy. For example, a sudden inflow of foreign funds whether in the form of portfolio investments or short-term inflows, can quickly cause excess liquidity within the money market. An outflow of funds due perhaps to higher interest rates elsewhere in the region would have the opposite effect. In these cases, the central bank will likely use open market operations to offset the liquidity imbalance.

4.7.4 *Sterilization of Forex Market Operations*

Central banks often intervene in foreign exchange markets to influence exchange rates. Such intervention often creates side effects. These side effects are typically changes in domestic liquidity as a result of the exchange rate intervention. Thus, central banks often complement a foreign exchange intervention with action in the money market to neutralize the effect. Such an intervention is referred to as a "sterilized intervention". A sterilized intervention is essentially a foreign exchange intervention that is complemented with an OMO. The objective of the OMO would be to neutralize the impact of the foreign exchange intervention. When forex market intervention leads to increased liquidity, the OMO would be the sale of bonds to bring money market liquidity back to normal. On the other hand, if the forex intervention leads to reduced liquidity because the forex intervention entailed the purchase of ringgit, then the OMO would require Bank Negara to purchase bonds and other money market instruments.

4.8 Commercial Banks and the Money Market

4.8.1 *Managing Asset: Liability Mismatches*

The maturing of existing items or the creation of new items on a bank's balance sheet has implications on the banks' cash flows. The maturing of an item on the asset-side, for e.g., the maturing of a loan given out, would constitute a cash inflow to the bank. The customer essentially repays the outstanding amount at maturity. On the other hand, the maturing of an item on the liability side would constitute a cash outflow for the bank. For example, when a fixed deposit placed with the bank by a customer matures, the customer redeems the amount resulting in a cash outflow for the bank. Unless the maturing items are of equal size, the bank would either have a cash surplus or deficit. For example, if the aggregate of asset items maturing at a given time is larger than the total of liability items, the cash inflows for the bank would be larger than the outflows, resulting in a cash surplus. A cash deficit would result if the liability maturing were larger than maturing assets.

It is easy to see where money markets come into these cash-flow mismatches. As mentioned earlier in the chapter, banks can use the money markets to adjust these imbalances. For example, as shown in Figure 4.3, a bank with surplus funds can lend by either placing deposits with other banks in the interbank deposit system or purchasing money market instruments. A bank with a cash deficit can borrow by either taking/accepting deposits in the interbank deposit system or selling money market instruments. Notice that, either way, the interbank money markets only allow for short-term borrowing or lending. Thus, when a bank's imbalances are temporary in nature, depending on the interbank, money market is perfectly acceptable.

There have been cases, however, where banks have used funding raised in the money market to fund their asset growth, i.e., use the short-term funding accorded by the interbank money market to lend long or medium term. While this may be a profitable strategy, it is a very risky one. Since the cost of funds raised from the money market is the short-term rate, the profit spread can be large if the yield curve is steep. It is at such times that banks may be tempted to grow their asset side using short-term funds raised in the money market. The reason this strategy is risky is because the money market rates/yields are highly sensitive to changing economic conditions. Since monetary policy implementation, exchange rate intervention, and other central bank policy initiatives are executed via the interbank money markets, rates can quickly change. A study by Arsudalli and Obiyathulla (2003) found that Malaysian banks that had relied on the money market funds to fund asset growth had suffered significantly more than banks that were less reliant on the money market. The moral of the story is that one should fund long-term needs with long-term financing and only short-term needs with short-term financing.

Box 4.7. Lehman Brothers Collapses and the US Money Market Seizes

Lehman Brothers, one of the world's oldest investment banks, went belly up in September 2008, resulting in a tightening of interbank credit markets never experienced before. During the early days of the financial crisis in 2007, Lehman Brothers had narrowly survived and kept itself afloat by utilizing its Federal funds Primary Dealer Credit facility. It was living on borrowed time. Though obvious that an equity injection was needed, Lehman decided against an equity issuance as it was deemed likely to be very costly. Lehman's outstanding shares declined steadily as its financial problems worsened. The stock's value dove substantially in late August 2008. By early September, it was clear that the firm's survival was at stake. Reacting to this dire situation, the Federal Reserve (the US Central Bank) convened a meeting of senior executives from the top US banks to find some ways to keep Lehman Brothers afloat. Despite intense negotiations from September 12 to 14, the meeting ended in a deadlock, no bank was willing to come to Lehman's rescue. With no bailout or guarantee from the government, Lehman was forced to declare bankruptcy on Monday, September 15, 2008. This initiated unparalleled financial market turmoil.

The interbank money markets that had taken a huge hit and experienced illiquidity in early 2008 were on the path to normalizing post Bear Sterns bailout in March 2008. The last thing the fragile market needed was another jolt, which was

(*Continued*)

Box 4.7. (*Continued*)

precisely what the Lehman Brother's bankruptcy was. Almost immediately, credit markets stalled. Counterparty risk suddenly became the most serious risk. Within two working days, the interbank borrowing rates represented by LIBOR spiked to 3.06%, an eight-month high. The commercial paper market, which acts as a key lending avenue for financial institutions, dried up with its monetary volume, reducing to $1.7 trillion in a week's time, a size less than what it had in early 2005. The TED spread, which measures the difference between the three-month US Treasury yields and the interbank three-month LIBOR rate, the rate at which U.S. banks and money market players borrowed and lent among themselves, broadened by unheard of levels. Clearly, a flight to quality had begun. Institutions with excess funds shunned the interbank market and rushed to place their funds in risk-free US treasuries, thereby reducing US treasury yields while simultaneously increasing the LIBOR rate. The following figure shows the spike in three-month LIBOR and the TED spread.

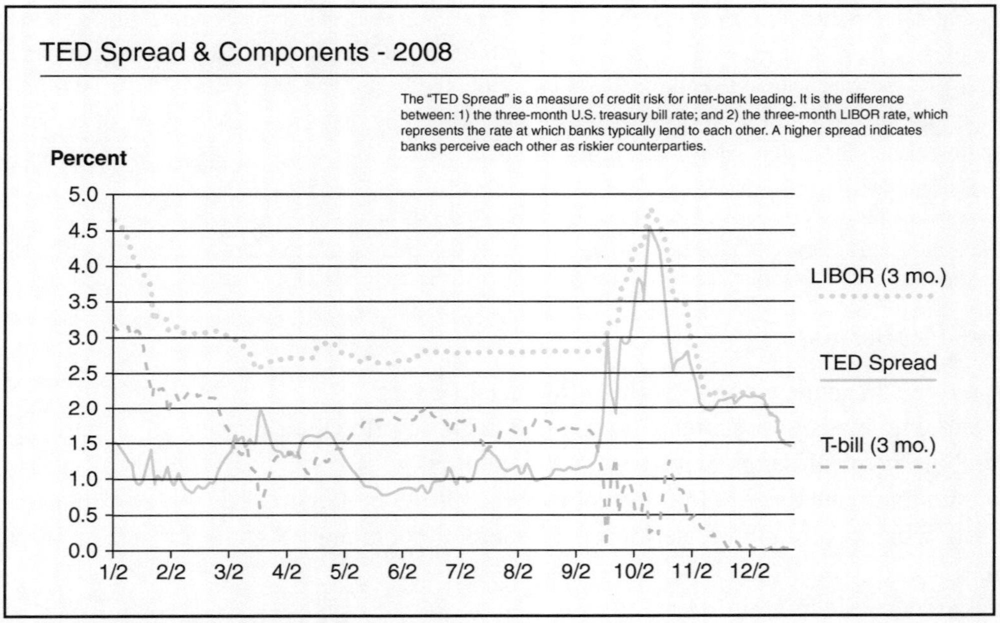

Source: TED Spread, https://en.wikipedia.org/wiki/TED_spread.

TED increased substantially in September and October of 2008, even in the face of constant easing of monetary policy by Federal Reserve since September 2007. It reached a high of 4.65% or 465 basis points on October 10, 2008. With financial markets clogging up and borrowing rates spiking, the fear of further collapses was real. With news of financial giants running into trouble, the money market mutual funds experienced a silent "bank run". Withdrawals of nearly $150 billion were made within a matter of two weeks. Money market mutual funds being major players in the commercial paper market meant that the reduction in their asset size reduced fund inflows into the money market. US investment banks and other corporations planning to rollover their commercial papers were simply left stranded.

The Government Responds: Within days of the Lehman Brother's collapse which sent financial ripples throughout the US, the government and the Federal Reserve initiated frantic efforts to save the seizure in the financial markets. By October, the government initiated new plans and bailout mechanisms to ease the credit crunch. The largest initiative was the $700 billion TARP or Troubled Asset Relief Program. Started in early October, this program authorized the US Department of Treasury to purchase or insure up to $700 billion of "troubled assets". The Federal Reserve, for its part, launched the Commercial Paper Funding Facility on October 20. This was meant to ease the illiquidity in the interbank money market by acting as a buyer for commercial papers. In the first month of this facility, over $250 billion worth of commercial papers were bought by the Fed. In the same month, the Federal Reserve also stepped up lending facilities already in place. The short-term lending facility against mortgaged backed securities was expanded to $300 billion a month. By November, the key numbers had started normalizing and pressure on both the government and Fed's emergency lending windows had reduced. LIBOR as shown in the figure, had reduced and some form of "normalcy" had returned to the money markets.

Summary

The interbank money market is a key component of the financial system. The money market is also a link between the banking sector and the capital markets. Given the dominance of banks, the money market is often known as the interbank money market. The money market, given its links to both the capital market and the banking sector, provides an ideal avenue for central banks to conduct monetary policy. Aside from the central bank, the key players in the money market are the banking institutions and non-bank institutions like pension funds, insurance companies, mutual funds, and others.

The money market typically has three big components: (i) the interbank deposit system, (ii) the platform for transactions in money market instruments, and (iii) the interbank cheque clearing system. The interbank deposit system is a means by which banks borrow and lend among themselves. The need for a bank to borrow and lend arises from the mismatches in the daily cash flows of the banks. Banks could also borrow by issuing and selling market instruments or lend by purchasing such instruments. The purchasing bank/institution is effectively lending funds to the issuing bank. Several short-term funding instruments like Treasury bills, Commercial Paper, and Negotiable Instrument of Deposits are traded. The pricing of these instruments is typically on a discounted basis. The required yield would reflect the tenor and riskiness of the issuer, in addition to the current cost of funds. The unit also examined the use of the money market by the central bank to execute monetary policy operations and how banks can use money market instruments to manage their asset–liability mismatches.

Questions and Problems

1. Describe the role of a money market within a financial system.
2. Who are the main players in the money markets? Briefly describe their purpose in using money markets.
3. What are the three typical components of a money market?
4. Describe the function and use of the three components of the money market.
5. Given the following information, determine the redemption amount (RA) as a result of an interbank deposit transaction.
   - Principal amount: RM50 million
   - Three-month KLIBOR: 4.8% (annualized)
   - Tenor of deposit: 60 days (two months)
6. Bank A has RM360 million drawn on it by Bank B's customers. Bank A's customers have RM270 million drawn on Bank B on the same day. The difference in amount will result in an overnight deposit. Assume the overnight rate is 4% annualized.
   (a) Which bank has lent and which bank has borrowed as a result of the above cheque clearance?
   (b) Determine the ringgit amount of interest payable by the borrowing bank.
7. State and describe some of the instruments traded in money markets.
8. A Malaysian T-bill has 34 days left to maturity. Its face value is RM5 million. What is the appropriate price of the T-bill if the required yield is 2.5% annualized?
9. A Banker's Acceptance with a face value of RM200,000 has 60 days to maturity. If the required yield for such an instrument is 4.8% annualized, determine its price.
10. If the Banker's Acceptance in Question 9 above is being offered to you at RM196,500, is it appropriately priced? What is the implied yield at this price?
11. Briefly explain why a banking system cannot really work in the absence of money markets.
12. Why is the money market often described as the interface between the banking system and capital markets?

Bibliography

Alvi, I. A. (2009). Interbank Money Market Operations Powerpoint slides, *AAOIFI — World Bank Annual Conference on Islamic Banking and Finance*, December 14–15, 2009, Bahrain

Arsudalli and Obiyathulla (2003) "*Bank Operating Strategies and Impact of Crisis: The Malaysian Case.*" In Global Financial Markets, Issues and Strategies, edited by D. K. Ghosh and M.Arief. Westport, CT. Praeger 2004.

Bank Negara Malaysia, Annual Reports — several years.

Derin Ekonomi — January 2016

Malaysian Islamic Capital Market, Quarterly Bulletin — several issues

Websites

http://www.bnm.gov.my — Bank Negara Malaysia
http://www.iimm.bnm.gov.my — Islamic Money Market

Chapter 5

THE ISLAMIC INTERBANK MONEY MARKET

Topics in this Chapter

5.1. Introduction
5.2. The Islamic Interbank Market
5.3. Pricing *Mudarabah* Interbank Investment Funds
5.4. The Islamic Interbank Cheque Clearing System (IICCS)
5.5. Key Islamic Money Market and Instruments
5.6. Pricing of Islamic Money Market Instruments
5.7. The Islamic Interbank Money Market (IIMM) and Issues of Risk
5.8. Trading Performance on IIMM
5.9. The Kuala Lumpur Islamic Reference Rate (KLIRR) and The Bursa Suq Al Sila (BSaS)
5.10. Commodity *Murabaha*
5.11. The Liquidity Management Centre (LMC)

Chapter Objective

This chapter is designed to introduce the Islamic Interbank Money Market (IIMM). In addition to describing the structure and trading mechanisms, the chapter also examines the instruments traded and their pricing. On completing this chapter, you should have a good understanding of the IIMM, its structure, trading mechanism, and instruments traded.

Key Terms		
accounting risk	Islamic Interbank Money Market (IIMM)	*qard al-hasan*
ar-rahn	Kuala Lumpur Islamic Ref-erence Rate (KLIRR)	regulatory risk
bay' al-dayn	Liquidity Management Centre (LMC)	*Shari'ah* risk
counterparty risk	liquidity risk	trade financing
hibah	*mudarabah*	*wadi'ah*
interest rate risk	*murabaha*	*wakalah*
Islamic Interbank Cheque Clearing System (IICCS)	*profit*	

5.1 Introduction

About a decade after the establishment of the first Islamic bank in the country, Bank Islam Malaysia Berhad in 1983, the creation of an Islamic Interbank Money Market (IIMM) was announced. The intervening 10 years had shown the need to have a *Shari'ah*-compliant money market. Until the establishment of the IIMM in January 1994, the Islamic banking sector had to rely on a single instrument, the Government Investment Certificate (GIC),[1] to manage liquidity. Aside from the fact that it was the only available *Shari'ah*-compliant instrument, there was another limitation: there was no secondary market for the instrument. The Islamic financial institutions could only deal with Bank Negara Malaysia (BNM), the central bank. They would buy the GICs from BNM when they had surplus liquidity and sell them to BNM when in need of liquidity. For a banking sector that was fast growing, this was an inadequate arrangement. Thus, a full-fledged IIMM was needed. In "designing" an Islamic monetary market, BNM had no existing workable model to follow. In creating its own design, the obvious choice was to structure a *Shari'ah*-compliant version of conventional money markets. Thus, the IIMM was created using the template of a conventional money market. While this was once again the path of least resistance and one that would be familiar to Malaysian bankers, as we will see later, it exposes the Islamic banks to certain risks which paradoxically should not exist for Islamic banks.

Following the structure of conventional money markets, the IIMM had three components. A *mudarabah*-based interbank market for deposits, a platform for issuing and trading short-term Islamic financial instruments, and an Islamic Cheque Clearing System (ICCS) (see Figure 5.1).

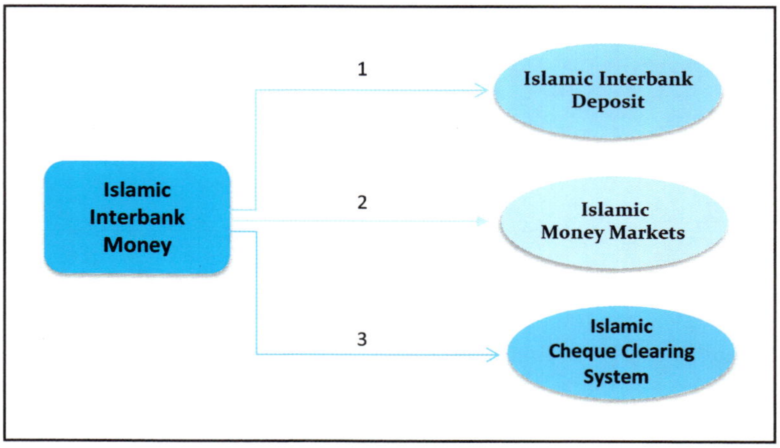

Figure 5.1. Overall Structure of IIMM.

When placed within the country's overall financial system, the IIMM's role and connection is depicted in Figure 5.2.

As Figure 5.2 shows, as a result of Malaysia's dual banking system, there is an interesting dimension to IIMM. Not only Islamic banks and other Islamic financial institutions but also conventional banks, insurance companies, and other conventional non-bank financial institutions (NBFIs) have access to IIMM. In particular, the second component of IIMM, which is Islamic money market instrument. While Islamic financial institutions, being *Shari'ah*-compliant, have no access to the conventional money market, the same cannot be said about the opposite. Conventional financial institutions have access to IIMM. There are no limits on the participation of conventional financial institutions in buying Islamic money market instruments or selling the ones they own. They can neither issue their own Islamic papers in IIMM nor bid for them in the primary market. In the secondary market, however, there is no differentiation. In fact, until the end of 2003, conventional banks were allowed to issue Green BAs, which were essentially Islamic bankers' acceptances. This effectively meant that conventional banks could raise funds in IIMM. The *Shari'ah* compatibility of Green BAs came

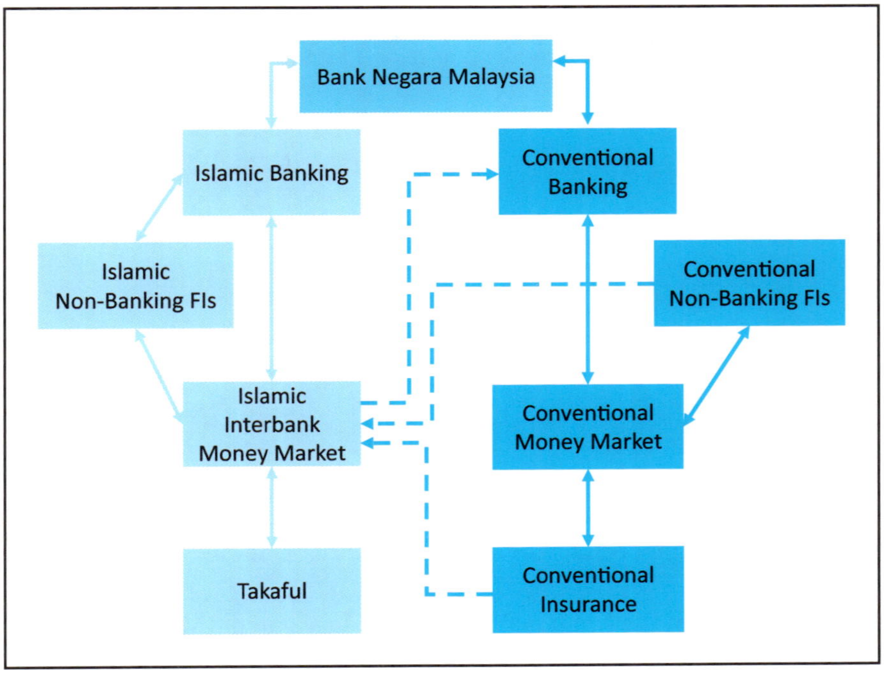

Figure 5.2. The IIMM within the Overall Banking/Insurance System.

from the fact that their underlying asset was *halal*. Since January 2004, the practice has been disallowed, and Green BAs have ceased to exist.

5.2 The Islamic Interbank Market

Before proceeding to discuss the instruments traded, we provide a quick overview of the other two components of IIMM, the Islamic Interbank Market and the cheque clearing system. Of the two, the interbank market is by far the more important. At the heart of the Islamic Interbank Market is a mechanism known as the *Mudarabah* Interbank Investment Scheme (MII). This is the mechanism by which the Islamic banks finance their deficits or invest surplus funds among themselves. Banks with surplus funds invest with those with liquidity deficits. As the name suggests, the financing is *mudarabah*-based, with a negotiated profit-sharing ratio. The minimum amount of investment in MII is RM50,000. The tenor of investment can vary from overnight to 12 months. In the early years of the Islamic Interbank Market, the rate of return on MII used to be based on the gross profit rate on one-year investments that the receiving (borrowing) bank was paying its depositors. It soon became evident that there was an incentive problem here. It was to the receiving bank's advantage to "declare" a lower profit rate. In a sense, the rates of return were dictated by the returns of the "inefficient" banks. To overcome this problem, BNM revised the rules by setting a minimum benchmark rate for the MII.[2] With this revision, the minimum rate of return for the MII was set to equal the prevailing rate of the GIC (Government Investment Certificate) plus a spread of 0.5%.

$$\text{Rate of return for MII} \geq \text{Return on GIC} + 0.5\%$$

5.3 Pricing the Mudarabah Interbank Investment Funds

Given the above description of the MII, the pricing or cost of funds for a given amount and tenor would depend on two unknowns: (i) the profit-sharing ratio (PSR), which is to be negotiated, and (ii) the gross profit rate before distribution of the receiving bank on one-year investments that it will declare. This declaration will be made by the receiving bank at the maturity date of the MII. This means that once the profit-sharing ratio is agreed upon, there is only one unknown, the profit rate, that will be declared by the receiving bank. However, part of this uncertainty is reduced in the sense that the investing bank knows that it will be the *higher* of the following;

- The prevailing rate on GIC of the same tenor + 0.5% (annualized), if the declared profit rate is lower than this or
- The declared profit rate adjusted for PSR, if it is higher than the GIC + 0.5% annualized.

The formula used in determining the (price) profit amount due to the provider of funds (investing bank) is as follows:[3]

$$X = \frac{P \times r \times t \times k}{365 \times 100}$$

where
X = Ringgit (RM) amount to be paid to the investing bank
P = Face value/principal amount of investment
t = Tenor in days of investment
r = Gross profit rate before distribution declared by the receiving bank on one year investments.
k = Profit sharing ratio.

The following is an illustration of the Mudarabah Interbank Investment (MII) mechanism and settlement.

Box 5.1. Illustration: Settlement of *Mudarabah* Interbank Investment at Maturity

To see how an MII transaction would be settled at maturity, let's work through a simple example. Suppose, Ambank Islamic has a surplus of RM5 million that it wishes to place out for three months in the Islamic Interbank Market. Bank Muamalat, on the other hand, is in need of liquidity, assuming it needs RM5 million dollars of funds for three months. Since the quantum and tenor of funds is dictated by their needs, the only thing that has to be negotiated is the profit-sharing ratio (PSR). Let us say they agree on a PSR of 75:25. That is, Ambank, which is the investing bank, will receive 75% of Bank Muamalat's declared gross profit before distribution on year investments (deposits) that it has had.

Based on this agreement, Ambank Islamic will place a RM5 million deposit with Bank Muamalat. After 90 days, the receiving bank, Bank Muamalat, will have to return the principal of RM5 million plus a profit amount. This profit amount will depend on the one remaining unknown, which is Bank Muamalat's declared gross profit on one-year investments. If this profit is higher than the prevailing GIC rate + 0.5%, then the declared profit percentage will be used in Equation 5.1 to determine the profit compensation to Ambank. On the other hand, if the declared gross profit of Bank Muamalat on one-year investments is lower than the GIC rate + 0.5% annualized, then Ambank profit amount will be determined by the latter percentage.

Let us say, Bank Muamalat declares a gross profit of 6% before distribution on its one-year investments. Assuming this is higher than the prevailing GIC rate + 0.5%, the profit amount to be paid by the receiving bank to the investing bank Ambank Islamic would be:

$$\begin{aligned} X &= \frac{[\text{RM}\,5{,}000{,}000\ (6\%)\ (90)\ [0.75]}{36{,}500} \\ &= \frac{2{,}700{,}000{,}000 \times [0.75]}{36{,}500} \\ &= \frac{2{,}025{,}000{,}000}{36{,}500} \\ &= \text{RM}55{,}479.45 \end{aligned}$$

So, on Day 91, Bank Muamalat would have to return an amount of RM5,055,479.45 to Ambank Islamic, being the principal plus profit due.

Source: Author.

5.4 The Islamic Interbank Cheque Clearing System

In addressing the need to establish a separate cheque clearing system for the Islamic banking sector, BNM undertook two initiatives. First, it required all Islamic banks to maintain an *Al Wadiah*-based (safe custody basis) current account with BNM. Second, it required the same Islamic banks to empower it to automatically offset the funding position between surplus and deficit banks, during the automatic cheque clearing process at midnight. The empowerment by the banks to BNM is based on the *Al Wakalah* concept. The surplus funds of an Islamic bank are placed with other Islamic banks that might have a deficit.[4] Once again the placement of funds from a surplus bank to a deficit one is done on the *mudarabah* concept, as in the case of MII. However, in this case, the profit-sharing ratio is fixed at 70:30. The same formula as in Equation 5.1 is used in determining the profit to be paid by the deficit units. The Islamic Interbank Cheque Clearing System (IICCS) is actually a subsegment of the overall cheque clearing system handled by KLACH (Kuala Lumpur Automated Clearing House).

5.5 Islamic Money Market Instruments

In developing the Islamic money market, BNM had introduced a series of *Shari'ah*-compliant money market instruments. In doing so, the basic strategy was also one of replication. Recall that replication was also the strategy used in introducing Islamic banking. Extending this strategy to money market instruments, common money market instruments were made Islamic by removing the interest-bearing feature and replacing it with either a profit rate or a mark-up feature. Thus, where there were Banker's Acceptances (BAs), we have Islamic BAs; Negotiable Instruments of Deposits (NIDs) were replicated as Negotiable Islamic Instruments of Deposit (NIIDs); Malaysian Treasury Bills became Malaysian Islamic Treasury Bills, and so on. Depending on when the observation is made, there could be eight to ten different types of instruments available for trading in the IIMM. The number of instruments varies since some instruments may only be issued intermittently. The following is a discussion of key Islamic Money Market Instruments and their underlying Islamic contracts.

5.6 Key Islamic Money Market Instruments

5.6.1 *Government Investment Issue*

To meet the need for a liquidity management instrument that is also *Shari'ah*-compliant, the Malaysian Parliament passed the Government Investment Act in 1983. This act enabled the Malaysian government to issue a non-interest-bearing money market instrument, known as Government Investment Certificates (GICs), (now replaced with Government Investment Issues (GII)). The GII was introduced in July 1983 under the concept of *qard al-hasan*.

Since a *qard al-hasan*-based instrument would not have a predetermined fixed "face value" at maturity, it would not be suited for secondary market trading. Thus, beginning with a June 15, 2001 issue, GIIs are now issued under a new concept of *bay al-inah*. This added depth and liquidity to the IIMM as the GII is now tradable in the secondary market via the concept of *bay' al-dayn* (debt trading).

Typically, BNM will identify a *Shari'ah*-compliant asset which then becomes the underlying asset for a GII transaction. BNM will then invite Islamic banks to bid for the said asset. The highest bidder wins and gets to buy the asset at its bid price. The asset is then sold back to BNM on either a deferred sale (BBA) basis if there are periodic coupons or cost plus, or a *murabaha* basis if there are no coupons (zero coupon). The debt incurred is securitized through the issuance of GII by BNM to the investing bank. Where the sale is BBA-based, the face value of the GII will equal the bid value paid by the Islamic bank. Where the GII is *murabaha*-based, the bidding bank will receive GII with a discounted value equal to its bid value. The face value of the GII which the investing bank will receive at maturity will include the profit that will be accreted.

The price of a GII at a given time would be the present value of its future cash flows. Since the GII has two cash flow components, coupon and face value, its price would be the sum of the present value of coupon payments and of the redeemable amount at maturity. The GII's value can thus be computed as:

$$\text{Price} = \left\{ \frac{RV}{\left[1+\frac{r/2}{100}\right]^{N-1+T/E}} \right\} + \left\{ \sum_{K=1}^{N} \frac{c/2}{\left[1+\frac{r/2}{100}\right]^{N-1+T/E}} \right\}$$

where

FV = Face value

RV = Redemption value (= FV, if redemption is at par)

c = Coupon rate

r = market yield for a similar maturity period

N = Number of semi-annual coupon payments between the value date and maturity date

T = Number of days from the value date to the next interest payment date

E = Number of days in the coupon period in which settlement takes place

Box 5.2. Illustration: Determining the Price of a Government Investment Issue (GII)

Suppose you are being offered a GII with the following features:

- Issuance date : 15 May 2009
- Maturity Date : 15 May 2012
- Transaction date : 23 November 2010
- Coupon : 8% per annum, paid semi-annually
- Maturity value : RM50,000
- Yield : 9% per annum

Determine the appropriate value of the GII.

$$\text{Price} = \left\{ \frac{50,000}{\left[1+\frac{4.5}{100}\right]^{[3-1+(173/181)]}} \right\} + \left\{ \sum_{K=1}^{n} \frac{2,000}{\left[1+\frac{4.5}{100}\right]^{[3-1+(173/181)]}} \right\}$$

= RM48,048

The correct value of the GII would be RM48,048. Investing in the GII at this price and holding it to maturity would provide a 9% annualized rate of return.

5.6.2 *Bank Negara Negotiable Notes*

Bank Negara Negotiable Notes (BNNN) are a short-term money market instrument issued by BNM. The underlying contract is that of *bay al-inah*. First introduced to the IIMM on November 29, 2000, it is now popularly traded in the secondary market. The price of the BNNN is determined on a discounted basis. Tenor is typically up to one year. The BNNN is designed as a liquidity management tool.

Given the features of the BNNN and its objective of use for short-term liquidity management, the instrument can be priced as follows:

$$P = FV \times \frac{[1-(\mathrm{r} \times t)]}{36500}, \tag{5.3}$$

where
P = Price of instrument
FV = Face value or redeemable amount at maturity
r = Required profit/return (discount factor)
t = Number of days left to maturity

Box 5.3. Illustration: Pricing a Bank Negara Negotiable Note (BNNN)

A BNNN with RM5 million face value and 74 days to maturity is being offered to your Bank. If your Bank's required profit rate is 10% per annum, what price would you be willing to pay for the note?

$$P = \text{RM5.0 mil. } \{1-(10 \times 74)/36{,}500\}$$
$$P = \text{RM4,898,630.14}$$

The correct price of the BNNN would be RM4,898,630.14. Since the note was priced using a 10% required profit, our return on the investment would be 10% annualized if held to maturity.

5.6.3 *Islamic Accepted Bills*

The Islamic Accepted Bill (IAB) was introduced in 1991. The objective was to provide a *Shari'ah*-compliant instrument to conventional BAs, particularly for trade financing. IAB is formulated on the Islamic principles of *al-murabaha* (deferred lump-sum sale or cost-plus). The secondary market trading of the instrument is based on *bay' al-dayn* (debt-trading).

Murabaha is based on a cost-plus profit margin or mark-up agreed to by both parties. *Bay' al-dayn* refers to the sale of a debt arising from a trade transaction in the form of a deferred payment sale. There are two types of financing under the IAB facility, namely:

(i) ***Trade Financing/Imports***: A *murabaha*-based, working capital financing mechanism. The Islamic bank appoints the customer as its purchasing agent for the underlying goods. As agent, the customer purchases the needed goods from the seller (foreign exporter) on behalf of the bank, which pays the seller/exporter and resells the goods to the customer at a marked-up price. The customer is typically allowed a deferred payment of up to 200 days. Since the sale of goods by the bank to the customer on deferred payment constitutes a debt, the debt is securitized in the form of a bill of exchange drawn by the bank on the customer for the full amount of the selling price. The bank can then decide to sell the IAB to a third party on a *bay' al-dayn* basis.

(ii) ***Trade Financing/Exports***: An exporter, with an approved IAB facility, prepares the export documentation as required under the sale contract or letter of credit. The export documents shall be sent to the importer's bank. The exporter then draws on the foreign commercial bank a new bill of exchange as a substitute bill and this will be the IAB. The bank shall purchase the IAB at a mutually agreed price using the concept of *bay' al-dayn* and the proceeds will be credited to the exporter's account.

5.6.4 *Islamic Negotiable Instruments*

Islamic Negotiable Instruments (INIs) come in two varieties: (i) as instruments of deposit and (ii) as negotiable Islamic debt certificates. The following is a brief description of each.

5.6.4.1 *Islamic Negotiable Instruments of Deposit*

Islamic Negotiable Instruments of Deposit (INID) is based on the concept of *al-mudarabah*. The underlying asset is usually a sum of money deposited with an Islamic banking institution and repayable to the bearer on a specified future date. Since the underlying contract is *mudarabah*, the return to the investor will obviously depend on the agreed PSR and the profit/earnings declared by the "borrowing" party.

5.6.4.2 *Negotiable Islamic Debt Certificate*

The concept of Negotiable Islamic Debt Certificate (NIDC) involves two steps: (i) the sale of an Islamic bank's assets to a customer at an agreed cash price; (ii) the customer resells the asset to the bank at an original sale price plus a profit. The bank will pay the customer this new amount at an agreed future date.

5.6.5 *Islamic Private Debt Securities/Islamic Bonds*

Islamic Private Debt Securities (IPDSs) are essentially *Shari'ah*-compliant corporate bonds. Introduced in 1990, they form the backbone of the Malaysian Islamic bond market. Most of the IPDSs currently outstanding were issued based on concepts of *bay al-bithaman ajil, murabaha, al-mudarabah*, and increasingly, *al-ijarah*. Many of these Islamic bonds are traded in the IIMM. In fact, these private debt securities or bonds are the second most popularly traded instrument after GIIs (see Figure 5.4).

5.6.6 *Sell and Buy Back Agreement*

Essentially a replication of the conventional Repurchase Agreement (REPO), the Sell and Buy Back Agreement (SBBA) is an Islamic money market transaction. It is a bilateral agreement in which an SBBA seller (*seller*) first sells an asset to the SBBA counterparty (*buyer*) at an agreed price. Subsequently, both parties enter into a separate agreement in which the buyer promises to sell back the asset to the seller at an agreed price.

In addition to the above, *ijarah*-based *sukuk* are also available. The *bay' al-dayn,* or debt trading concept, is applicable to instruments such as Islamic Accepted Bills (IABs). Given the controversy surrounding the acceptability of *bay' al-dayn*, it is not as popular as it once was. *Qard al-hasan*, which used to be the mode underlying the GICs and later the GIIs, appears to have fizzled out. Given the uncertainty of the redeemable face value under the *qard al-hasan* concept, it was not suited for a secondary market traded instrument. Thus, the GII is now issued under the *bay al-inah* concept, while secondary market trading of these papers is based on *al-dayn*. Perhaps in response to rising wariness and some unease about trading financial papers, BNM has recently launched the commodity *murabaha* contract described below. Based on crude palm oil (CPO), this commodity *murabaha* contract is intended to be a liquidity management tool. The only contract that continues to use the *qard al-hasan* concept is the *Rahnu* Agreement (RA-i). However, this is a collateralized facility which is only available with BNM.

Aside from replicating conventional instruments, a number of trading methods/processes have also been adopted from conventional money markets. The best example of this is the replication of the highly popular REPOs as SBBAs. Under the SBBA, following the initial sale at a negotiated price, the parties enter into a separate agreement to reverse the trade at a newly negotiated price.

5.7 Pricing of Islamic Money Market Instruments

As IIMM's instruments and processes have largely been structured using the conventional template, the pricing of these instruments by and large follows the conventional logic of discounting, the key difference being that, whereas the prevailing interest rate of appropriate tenor is used in conventional pricing, the profit-rate or mark-up rate is used in discounting Islamic papers. In fact, even the RA-i facility described earlier as being based on the *qard al-hasan* concept provides a *hibah* (gift) which is determined based on average Islamic interbank rates of return.

If product designs, trading processes, and pricing methods have all been synthesized from conventional forms, it raises the question of how different is the Islamic money market from its conventional counterpart. In so far as the objective of providing the Islamic banking sector with proper avenues for liquidity management is concerned, the IIMM has undoubtedly succeeded. However, such a replication also implies that the same risks that prevail in conventional money markets would also be present in IIMM.

5.8 IIMM and Issues of Risk

The money market, as is the case with any financial market or instrument, has a number of associated risks. Where the conventional money market is concerned, most previous literature identifies *four* key risk categories. These are: (i) *Counterparty risk,* (ii) *Liquidity risk,* (iii) *Interest rate risk*, and (iv) *Regulatory risk*. Of these, liquidity and interest rate risks are typically the more important ones. Where the Islamic money market is concerned, there may be *two additional* risks unique to them. These are *accounting risks* and *Shari'ah risk*. We now take a quick overview of each of the other risks.

Counterparty risk simply refers to the potential default/non-payment of the counterparty. Though counterparty risk is low, given the short-term nature of money market instruments, it is still a risk, especially where the instrument is non-sovereign. Commercial paper issued by private entities is an example. The experience of Penn Central, which collapsed with almost half a billion US dollars of commercial papers outstanding and the serious dislocation it caused to US money markets is a case in point. Additionally, in Malaysia's IIMM, a number of IPDSs and *sukuk* are traded. In at least one such case, a default has taken place. So, counterparty risk is applicable to IIMMs.

Liquidity risk refers to risk that arises from illiquid or inactive trading. Indeed, the traded volume of a number of IIMM instruments such as IABs and INIs have been patchy. There have been periods of low trading velocity. The problem with illiquidity is that illiquid trading often leads to increased price volatility, which in turn increases bid-ask spreads and transaction costs. While the presence of market makers helps for instruments such as GIIs and BNNNs, the lack of an active secondary market means liquidity can be a problem for other instruments.

Regulatory risk refers to risk that arises from changes in regulation or policy. While regulatory changes are generally infrequent, banking regulations can and often are changed quickly. Regulations on statutory requirements and the eligibility of money market instruments which would qualify in meeting such requirements are changed, in some cases quite frequently. Regulatory risk therefore is a feature of financial markets, including IIMM.

Shari'ah and *accounting risks* would be additional risks applicable to the Islamic financial sector. *Accounting risks* in this context refers to the risk that the borrower in a profit-sharing relationship might understate profits. Instruments based on *mudarabah*- and *musharakah*-type contracts would be susceptible to such risk. While one might think that such a risk would be substantially less for money market instruments, given their short-term nature, misreporting is highly relevant. A good example would be the new policy that BNM had to introduce precisely to overcome the problem of "understated" profits with the *Mudarabah* Interbank Investments (MIIs). In February 1994, about a year after the establishment of IIMM, BNM had to introduce a minimum required return on MII equivalent to prevailing GII + 0.5% (annualized). This move was necessitated by fact that "there was exploitation by the inefficient banks".[5] Though the PSR is dictated by the investing bank, the profit rate declared at maturity is determined by the receiving bank. The receiving banks were understating profits, leading to possible disintermediation of the process, thus the need to impose a minimum required rate of return.

Shari'ah risk, a counterpart of regulatory risk, refers to the possibility that transactions/instruments currently deemed acceptable could subsequently be prohibited. Some examples of this type of risk would be: (i) the issue of mark-ups in Pakistan and (ii) the controversy surrounding *bay' al-dayn*-based transactions. Such transactions certainly appear to be reducing in Malaysia. Of late, even the highly popular BBA-based contracts in Malaysia are being questioned. The fact that Green BAs, once a popularly traded instrument on IIMM, have now completely stopped is a good example of such risk.

Of the risks discussed thus far, *interest rate risk* is probably the most critical where money market instruments are concerned. From a conventional viewpoint, a key role of money markets is price discovery, i.e., essentially, the formation of short-term interest rates and thereby the short-end of the yield curve. Since money market trading is designed to be reflective of rate movements, Islamic trading, as with conventional money market instruments, are highly rate sensitive. Additionally, since central banks typically use the money market to execute monetary policy, the money market would usually be the first to react to rate or liquidity changes.

Interest rate risk manifests itself in several ways, the three key forms being:

(i) Prepayment risk;
(ii) Reinvestment risk; and
(iii) Repricing risk.

Given the short-term nature of money market instruments, prepayment risk is a non-issue. Reinvestment risk is relevant. Repricing risk is by far the most important for money market instruments. Given the discounted form of their pricing, rate movements would have a highly significant and direct impact.

5.9 Trading Performance on IIMM

Figure 5.3 shows the total annual traded volume in the IIMM over the 17-year period of January 2000 to 2016. In the initial years, traded volume shows a steady increase until 2006. The global financial crisis of 2007/2008 caused a relatively sharp drop in traded volume on IIMM in those two years. The year 2009 saw some recovery. From 2010 onward, volume growth was stable until 2012. There appears to have been a trough over the next three years. Traded volume was at its historic high in 2016.

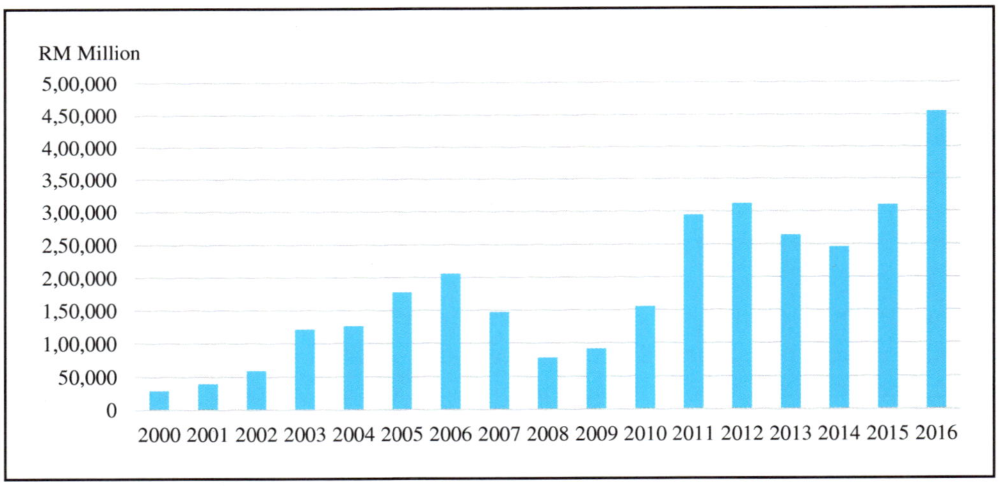

Figure 5.3. Total Annual Traded Volume of IIMM Instruments (RM Millions).

Source: IIMM Website (iimm.bnm.gov.my).

Figure 5.4 shows total traded volume for some the key IIMM instruments for the 16-year period from 2001 to 2016. GIIs are by far the most popularly traded instrument. This is followed by Islamic Medium Term Notes (IMTNs). Islamic bonds or IPDBs and BNNNs are the next most popular. Taking traded volume as a proxy for liquidity, it is obvious that GIIs are the most liquid instrument.

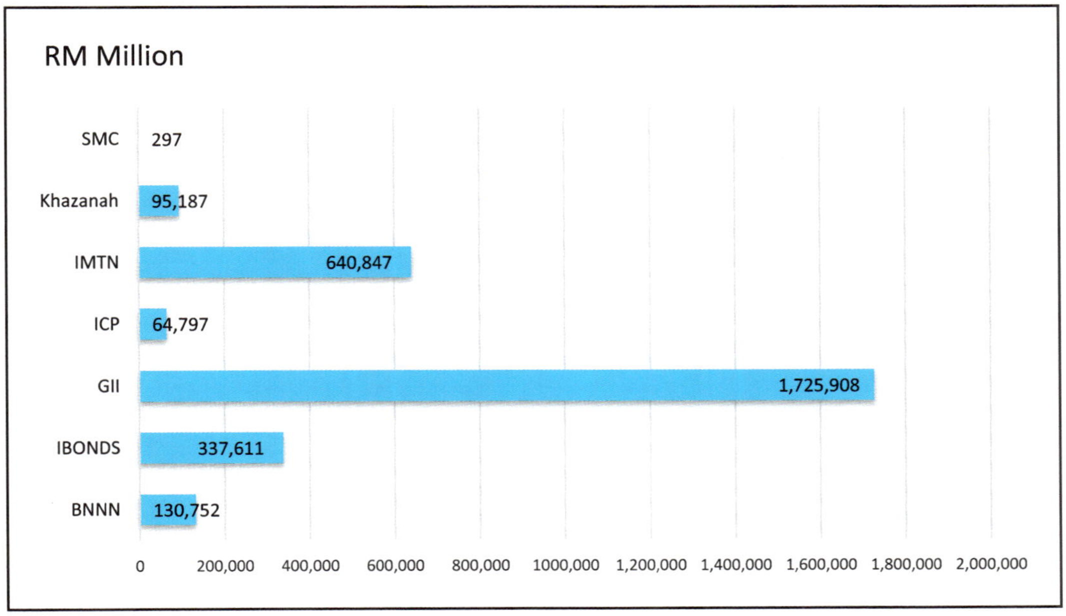

Figure 5.4. Total Traded Volume of key IIMM Instruments (RM Millions) (January to December 2016).

Source: IIMM Website (iimm.bnm.gov.my).

5.10 The Kuala Lumpur Islamic Reference Rate

As is the case with all money markets, price discovery in the form of reference interest rates is the key function. These references rate form the short end of the yield curve. Chapter 4 described the functions of Malaysia's conventional money market. The interest rate that gets priced in that market is the Kuala Lumpur Interbank Offer Rate (KLIBOR). In IIMM, there is an Islamic interbank rate. This is a daily weighted average rate of the *mudarabah* interbank investment rates offered by individual Islamic banks. The individual rates are weighted according to the volume transactions carried out at those rates. In addition to this Islamic interbank rate, there is a more popular rate, which is the Kuala Lumpur Islamic Reference Rate (KLIRR). While the interbank rate is for placements/transactions among banks alone, KLIRR is the adjusted average of rates quoted by individual Islamic banks for all players. Just as there are KLIBOR rates for several tenors, KLIRR too has rates ranging from overnight to a maximum one-year period. Figure 5.5 shows a plot of the KLIRR over several maturities for a given day (February 3, 2016).

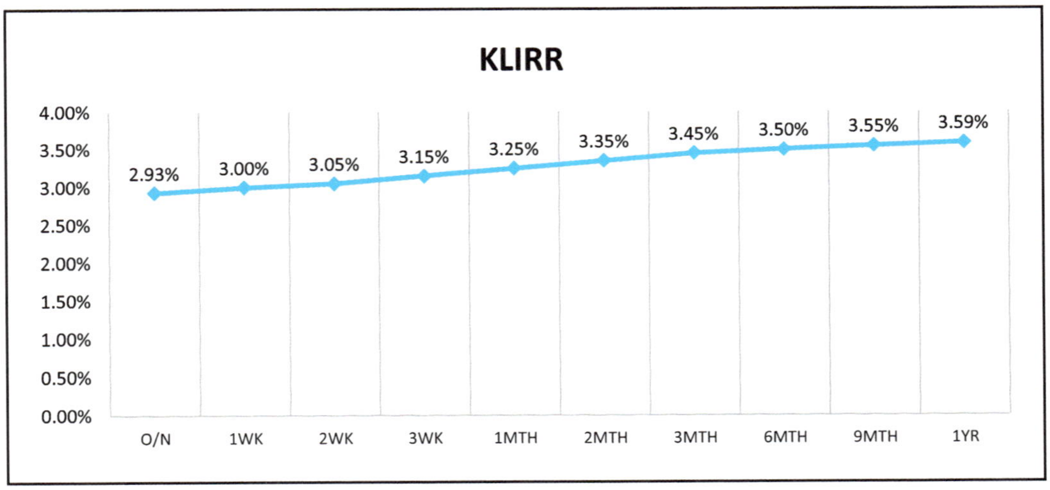

Figure 5.5. The Traded KLIRR by Maturity.

In Malaysia, aside from IIMM, there is one other facility by which Islamic Financial Institutions (IFIs) can manage their liquidity needs. This is the newly established Bursa Suq Al Sila (BSaS), which complements IIMM rather than competes with it. The following section will provide a brief description of the BSaS and the commodity *murabaha* contract that it trades.

Figure 5.6 shows a comparison of the IIBR rates with LIBOR rates of the same tenor. Four tenors are shown: (i) overnight, (ii) one month, (iii) three months, and (iv) six months; for the five-year period from November 2011 to November 2016. The close correlation between the IIBR and LIBOR is clearly evident.

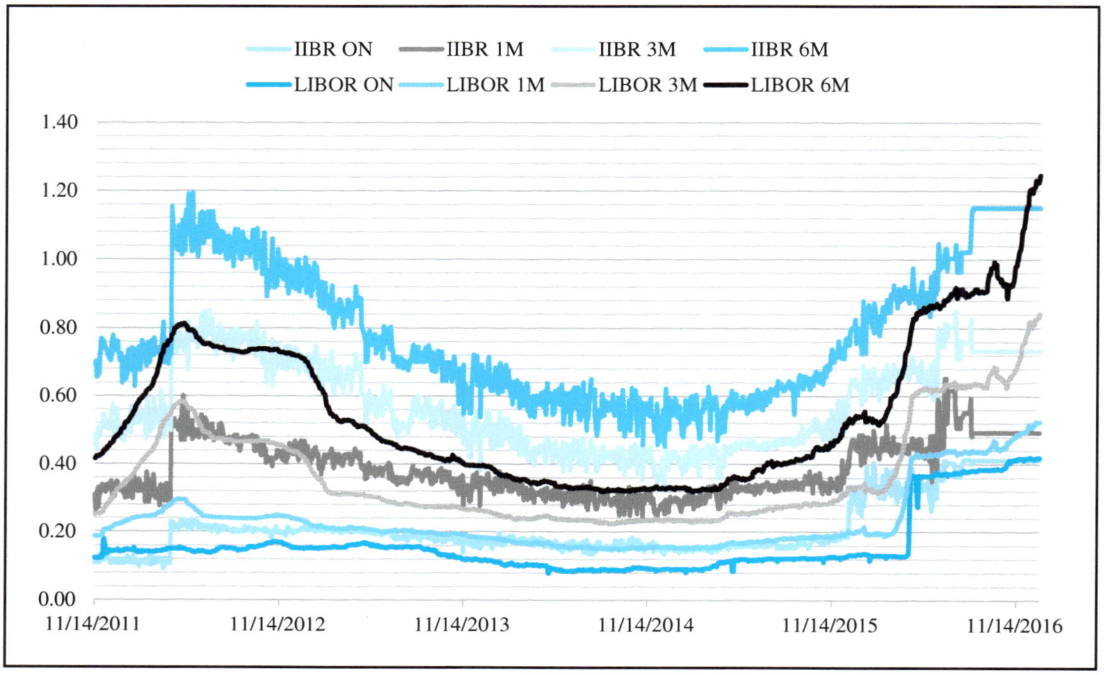

Figure 5.6. IIBR Rates Compared to LIBOR Rates.

Box 5.4. Islamic Finance Gets its Own Benchmark Rate

Thomson Reuters, in collaboration with industry stakeholders and leading Islamic institutions, launched in 2011 the first Islamic finance benchmark rate named the Islamic Interbank Benchmark Rate (IIBR) (Arabic: *Muashshir al Ribh bayn al Masarif al Islamiyah*). Since the inception of Islamic finance and rapid development in Islamic banking over the last three decades, the issue of a reliable benchmark for pricing of financial transactions and products has embroiled the scholars and practitioners. In absence of *Shari'ah*-compliant benchmarks, the industry has relied on the conventional counterparts such as LIBOR, KLIBOR, and KIBOR.

In this context, IIBR is an attempt to fill the void of an objective and *Shari'ah*-compliant indicator for the expected profit rate on *Shari'ah*-compliant funding. The scope of usage for IIBR is multifold, from pricing of interbank market transactions and retail and corporate Islamic financial products to the pricing of *sukuk* and other fixed income structures.

The IIBR calculation methodology is similar to the standard calculation methodology. A poll of 16 banks is taken at 10:45 am Makkah time, where the contributing banks are required to contribute rates in the following eight tenors:

- *Overnight* *3 months*
- *1 week* *6 months*
- *1 month* *9 months*
- *2 months* *12 months*

Automated and manual audit of the rates is conducted, eliminating the top and 12 bottom quartile on descending value basis to remove outliers' bias. The arithmetic mean of the mid-quartiles is the representative IIBR, rounded to five decimal places.

(*Continued*)

Box 5.4. (*Continued*)

The contributing banks for IIBR are positively skewed toward GCC, with only three Malaysian banks. None of the banks from Pakistan, Sudan, Europe, Indonesia, and Iran (which has the largest Islamic banking assets) were members of the contributing panel. This breeds doubts over IIBR as a true reflection of global Islamic finance industry, and utilization as the benchmark rate for cross-country Islamic funding.

The IIBR Rate Setting Process

IIBR is touted as the first step in decoupling of the Islamic financial markets from their conventional counterparts and a major step forward for the nascent Islamic finance industry. The acceptance of IIBR as the global standard for the industry and cross-country funding is yet to be seen by acceptance of IIBR as standard benchmark by IFIs.

5.11 *Bursa Suq Al-Sila*

The Bursa Suq Al-Sila (BSaS) is an interesting initiative under the Malaysia Islamic Finance Centre (MIFC). Operated by Bursa Malaysia's wholly owned subsidiary, Bursa Malaysia Islamic Services Sdn. Bhd; it is a fully electronic platform for end-to-end *Shari'ah*-compliant trading of commodities. Suq Al-Sila, which means commodities market in Arabic, is the world's first such facility. The Suq Al-Sila will provide a platform for commodities trading under *murabaha, tawarruq*, and *musasuwamah* contracts. As such, institutions can use the facility for managing liquidity and investing and financing purposes. The commodity *murabaha* (see below) is a very commonly used technique for liquidity management. In the case of the Suq Al-Sila, the underlying commodity will be Malaysia's crude palm oil (CPO). Other commodities are expected to be used in future. Internationally, commodity *murabaha* contracts typically use metals traded on the London Metals Exchange (LME). Though only Ringgit-denominated transactions take place currently, foreign currency denominated transactions are expected to be possible in the future on BSaS. In enabling Islamic institutions to manage their liquidity through the commodity *murabaha* program, the BSaS will complement Malaysia's IIMM (see Table 5.1).

Table 5.1. Contract Specification of *Bursa Suq Al-Sila*.

Specification	Parameters
CONTRACT CODE	CM-CPO
PRICE	Based on (benchmarked against) previous trading day settlement of the FCPO spot month contract. Price remains the same for the day.
SETTLEMENT	Delivery of CPO (with provision for cash settlement).
CONTRACT GRADE	Free Fatty Acid (FFA) of palm oil delivered into the tank must not exceed 4% and from the tank must not exceed 5%. Moisture and Impurities (M&I) must not exceed 0.25%. Deterioration of Bleachability Index (DOBI) value of palm oil delivered into the tank must be at a minimum of 2.5 and of palm oil delivered from the tank must be at a minimum of 2.31.
DELIVERY POINT	Crude palm oil of good merchantable quality, in bulk, unbleached, at the CSP storage location.

Specification	Parameters
CONTRACT CODE	CM-PE
PRICE	Polyethylene price will be benchmarked against the price provided by CSP (plastic supplier). Price remains the same for the day.
SETTLEMENT	Delivery of the Polyethylene (with provision for cash settlement).
CONTRACT GRADE	Density (kg/m^3): 0.92–2.0 Melt Index @ 2.16 kg (g/10 min): 0.8–3.0
DELIVERY POINT	CSP storage location.

BSaS has been a huge success. Traded volumes had increased manifold as Malaysian Islamic banks have started to use the commodity *murabaha* as a common means to finance most of their financing. As the available supply of CPO was not sufficient to support the huge volume of financing transactions, BSaS has added several underlying commodities. Plastic resin was first added, followed by palm olein and timbers. Thus, the underlying asset for commodity transactions on BSaS can be any one of these several available commodities. On any given trading day, a commodity's traded price on BSaS will be the previous day's close price of the commodity in the spot market. Since the trading price of a BSaS-listed commodity remains unchanged for a full day, there is no execution risk, i.e., there is no risk that the price would change during the course of a transaction. The absence of execution risk, the relative low transaction costs, and the ease and efficiency of the platform has meant the banks and other players have gravitated toward BSaS for short-term financing transactions.

5.12 Commodity *Murabaha*

A commodity *murabaha* is a *Shari'ah*-compliant transaction, designed to enable liquidity management through short-term financing. The institution in need of funds, i.e., "the borrower", buys a commodity (which is usually an exchange traded one and is highly liquid) from the bank at a price (i.e., Spot + Mark-up) to be paid on deferred terms. The borrower immediately sells the commodity to participating brokers of the commodity exchange at the spot price on cash basis. As a result of this transaction, the borrower has received cash/funds equivalent to the spot price of the commodity sold but has an obligation with the bank equal to the bank's sale price of the commodity.

Since the turnaround in the transactions is almost simultaneous, the borrower faces little price risk and its cost of funding is locked-in. The commodity *murabaha* transaction is arranged with simultaneity in mind precisely to minimize price or execution risk. The quick turnaround from the selling bank to buying broker is possible because of the presence of participating brokers who stand ready to offer immediate quotes for the commodity. In the case of the Bursa Suq Al-Sila, there were at least 26 commodity suppliers/brokers ready to participate in the commodity *murabaha* program at the time of its establishment. Figure 5.7 shows the mechanics of a typical commodity *murabaha* transaction. A customer in need of financing approaches an IFI, which funds the customer by way of commodity delivered for deferred payment. The customer simply sells that commodity for immediate funds. The flows in the diagram are numbered chronologically.

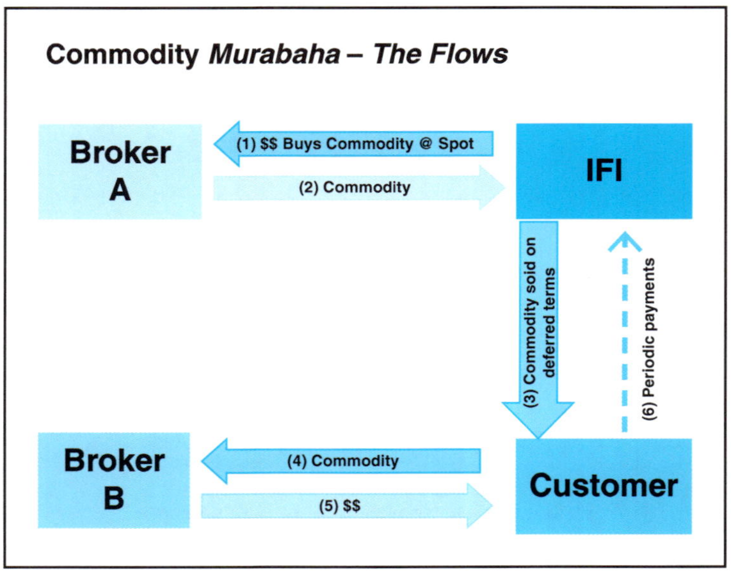

Figure 5.7. Mechanics of a Commodity *Murabaha* Transaction.

Box 5.5. *Tawarruq*, Commodity *Murabaha*, and the Surrounding Controversy

The commodity *murabaha* described above is based on the concept of *tawarruq*. *Tawarruq* loosely means "paper replacing monies" or silver. In other words, the objective of the transactions is the liquidity rather than the product or commodity. In a typical *tawarruq*, a customer buys a commodity at a deferred price (payable over a period in the future) and immediately sells the commodity to another party for a cash price. The objective is to get liquidity. The cash price is S_0, then he receives S_0 today in exchange for a payable in the future. The deferred price at which he bought the commodity could have been a marked-up price, or *murabaha* price. The commodity *murabaha* programme of Bursa Suq Al-Sila described above is based on the *tawarruq* concept. Just as one can buy a commodity from a bank on a deferred payment basis and sell it in the spot market to receive a cash in flow, the opposite could be done to place out excess liquidity known as the Reverse *Tawarruq*, an entity with surplus cash would buy a commodity at the spot price using its cash and sell the same commodity to a bank on a deferred payment basis. Again, the deferred price could be based on *murabaha*, spot price plus mark-up.

While *tawarruq* is obviously a *Shari'ah*-compliant contract, its rampant use has rattled and caused unease among several *Shari'ah* scholars. Several variants of the basic *tawarruq* appear to have evolved. In one variant, the customer sells the commodity for cash to the same entity he bought it from at the deferred price. Not surprisingly, scholars have rejected this type of *tawarruq*, arguing that it is really *inah* or debt trading, and there is avenue for *riba* to creep in. In general, *Shari'ah* scholars appear to frown upon organized *tawarruq*. An organized *tawarruq* is essentially one where everything is pre-arranged. Keep in mind that in classical *tawarruq*, the buying and selling of the commodity is with different parties and at independently negotiated prices. This obviously entails execution risks, which means that one will not be able to lock-in a cost of funds until all parts of the transaction are complete.

The commodity *murabaha* programme of the Suq Al-Sila as described above minimizes execution risk arising from delays in the transaction by having assigned parties standing ready to execute transactions very quickly. The fact that the underlying commodity is a standard one that has a deep and very liquid cash market makes it easier (lower risk) for brokers to stand ready to provide quotes. While such organized transactions reduce the risk to all parties (buyer, seller, and intermediary), *Shari'ah* scholars feel uneasy that the objectives are funding rather than the commodity. The fact that the parties of the *tawarruq* may never take delivery of the underlying commodity makes some argue that organized *tawarruq* may merely be a means to sidestep *Shari'ah* requirements for all financial transactions to be based on real physical assets.

As mentioned earlier, IIMM is one of a kind globally. Malaysia is the only country with a formally instituted Islamic money market. Others have informal arrangements or institutions specializing in providing liquidity management services to IFIs. The most popular institution of this type is Bahrain's Liquidity Management Centre.

5.13 Liquidity Management in Other Jurisdictions

5.13.1 *Bahrain*

The Liquidity Management Centre (LMC) is a Bahraini government initiative to help its burgeoning Islamic banking and finance sector with liquidity management. Cash flow mismatches are an inherent part of banking. Conventional banks use the interbank money market to manage this mismatch (see Chapter 3). Since the instruments traded in a conventional money market are obviously interest-based, Islamic banks would not be able to use them for their liquidity management. To address this shortcoming, Malaysia chose to establish its own IIMM with instruments and trading processes that, while similar to the conventional, are *Shari'ah*-compliant. Bahrain, on the other hand, chose to establish LMC, which provides liquidity management facilities to Islamic finance/banking institutions by providing a platform for easy and active secondary trading. This is done through the introduction of several *sukuk*-based instruments. Aside from enabling secondary *sukuk* market activities, the LMC also provides standardized facilities for primary *sukuk* issuance. In addition to providing coordination among parties to enable bilateral funding structures, LMC also provides services for Islamic Investment Fund issuance. For Islamic banks in the region, LMC's Open-ended Short Term *Sukuk* program (STS) is probably the most important facility. This program enables collateralized borrowing and lending facilities among institutions, thereby minimizing counterparty risk.

Of late, the Central Bank of Bahrain (CBB) introduced market instruments based on the principle of *sukuk ijarah* and *sukuk salam*. CBB acts as an agent of the Government of Bahrain in issuing and managing the periodic *sukuk* issuances.

The *sukuk* are backed by the government's properties as underlying assets. The issuance of *sukuk ijarah* is dependent on the debt profile and cash requirements of the government. *Sukuk salam* is an instrument which is issued in the money market by CBB to have a direct impact on level of current account balances of Bahraini Dinar held by CBB for commercial banks, thereby influencing the monetary conditions.

Sukuk salam is denominated in Bahraini Dinar and is issued with a maturity of 91 days, at a monthly interval. At any point in time, there are three outstanding issues of *sukuk salam* in the market. The return of *sukuk salam* is predetermined by the Monetary Authority, while the issuance size is determined by the Ministry of Finance on a yearly basis in advance. *Sukuk ijarah* issuances by CBB are of two classes: (i) a local currency issuance with a 182-day maturity period; (ii) of a longer maturity, between three and 10 years, and denominated both in local currency as well as USD.

Class A, the short-term maturity *sukuk ijarah* certificates are issued every month and do not have a secondary market. The long-term *sukuk ijarah* are issued on *ad hoc* basis with issue size variable. This class of *sukuk* is listed on the Bahrain Stock Exchange with the guarantee of CBB for buyback at maturity. The returns on this class may be fixed or floating, and is paid on a semi-annual basis. Figure 5.8 provides the structure of the *sukuk* certificates.

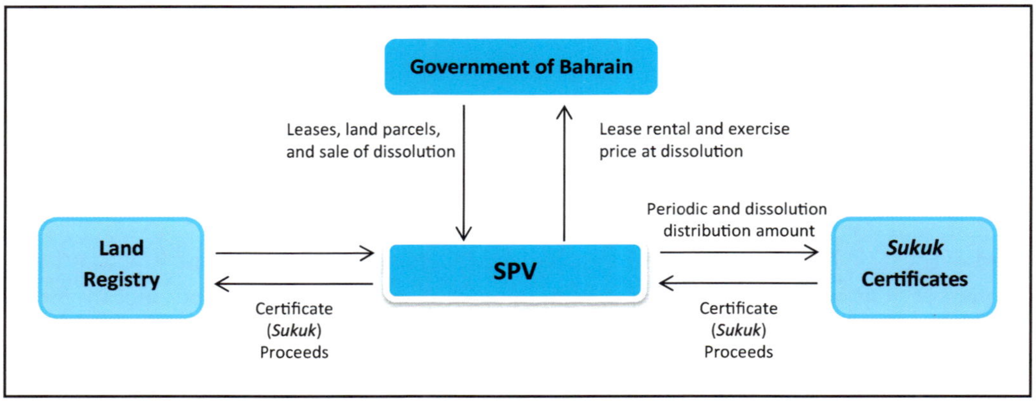

Figure 5.8. Structure of the *Sukuk* Certificates.

Source: Technical Note on Issues In Strengthening Liquidity Management Of Institutions Offering Islamic Financial Services by IFSB.

In 2015, CBB launched a new *Shari'ah*-compliant *wakalah* liquidity management instrument. This *wakalah* instrument is designed to provide an investment opportunity for retail Islamic banks that wish to deposit their excess liquidity with the central bank which acts as a *wakil*. Interestingly, the duration of the *wakalah* is one week and is available for Islamic retail banks every Tuesday.

Kuwait has taken a different approach to liquidity management and monetary operations. It uses *Tawarruq* to manage the system's liquidity as desired by the central bank. In this *Tawarruq* arrangement, the Islamic banks make payments to the central bank from their own treasury, an amount equal to the value of the spot sale of the commodity. This payment obviously constitutes a liquidity withdrawal, the cost to the Central bank of these arrangement is determined by the future installment payment over the spot payment (mark-up).

5.13.2 *Qatar*

The Qatar Central Bank issues a series of short-term Treasury Bills based on a calendar of issuance to Islamic banks. Secondary market trading has so far been negligible. Since December 2011, all Treasury Bills have to be listed at the Qatar Exchange and secondary trading has to take place on the Qatar Exchange, as over-the-counter trading is not allowed. Thus, the three-six-nine-month Treasury Bills issued to Islamic banks are not tradable, but can be used as collateral with the Qatar Central Bank for REPO transactions.

5.13.3 *The United Arab Emirates*

The Central Bank of UAE issues standardized instruments for collateralized *murabaha* transactions. However, according to a recent IMF report, money markets in the UAE are rather shallow but are complemented by the foreign exchange (FX) markets. The FX market is actively used to access liquidity. This is possible given the currency's peg to the US dollar and the significant dollarization of banks' assets and liabilities. The UAE also has an Islamic money market fund known as the Emirates Islamic Money Market Fund, which is a *Shari'ah*-compliant investment that aims to achieve a higher profit return than the traditional *Shari'ah*-compliant deposits of similar liquidity. The fund primarily invests in diversified portfolio of *Shari'ah*-compliant money market instruments including, but not limited to, Islamic deposits, *Shari'ah*-compliant synthetic instruments, *murabaha*, *sukuk*, and international trade contracts. The instruments are diversified across a range of durations and levels of liquidity. The fund is a subfund of the larger Emirates Fund.

5.13.4 *Saudi Arabia*

In conducting the monetary operations, the Saudi Arabian Monetary Authority (SAMA) permits Islamic banks to use *murabaha* as collateral for REPO transactions. Nevertheless, to help promote the development of domestic debt markets and conduct monetary policy, SAMA issued its own instruments, including those that are *Shari'ah*-compliant to cater to the needs of Islamic banks. The introduction of Islamic borrowing instruments has been relatively recent in Saudi Arabia as in the rest of the world. The first *Shari'ah*-compliant instruments were introduced in the early 2000s with short-term *murabaha* securities in 2002. Meanwhile, in January 2016, the Ministry of Finance issued long-term *murabaha* instruments with the tenors of five, seven, and 10 years to fund the government's budget deficit.

In addition to the above, Brunei and Pakistan have introduced *sukuk* issued by the government which can be bought and sold by domestic IFIs to manage their liquidity. In 2006, the Central Bank of Brunei issued *sukuk*-based on the *ijarah* concept for liquidity management purpose of local IFIs and *takaful* operators. In both these countries, there appear to be plans to introduce a variant of Bahrain's successful rolling monthly programs of short-term *sukuk al-salam* that has been in place since 2001 through LMC.

5.13.5 *Sudan*

Sudan has been one of the pioneers in developing Islamic banking and financial institutions. The Central Bank of Sudan was one of the first to introduce *Shari'ah*-compliant market-based instruments for monetary operation by introducing Central bank Musharakah Certificates (CMCs) in 1998.

CMCs were issued by the Sudan's Central Bank and represented claims on a portion of Government's and Central Bank's equity stake in the commercial banks. The stake for CMCs was separated and held by a special purpose vehicle named Sudanese Financial Services Company. The return of these instruments was linked to the expected underlying securities returns.

In 1999, the second wave of instruments were introduced in the Islamic money market instruments, titled Government *Musharakah* Certificates (GMCs). These certificates were on similar lines as CMCs, with the underlying asset being government's stake in profitable state-owned enterprises and ventures. GMCs were introduced with a one-year maturity period, at the end of which they were redeemable at market value.

In 2003, as a step toward phasing out of CMCs and GMCs, the Sudanese government introduced Government Investment Certificates (GICs) representing securities for fiscal financing using *ijarah*, *istisna'*, *murabaha*, *salam*, and other contracts, with the majority (51%) being *ijarah* contracts.

In the GIC structure, The Sudanese Financial Services Company acts as the *Mudarib*, investing funds from security issuance in multiple government finance contracts. The return of these contracts generates profits which are shared between the *Mudarib* and the *Rab ul Mal* in the ratio of 5% to 95%, respectively. The GICs are readily tradable on the Khartoum Stock Exchange. Figure 5.9 shows the structure of the GIC.

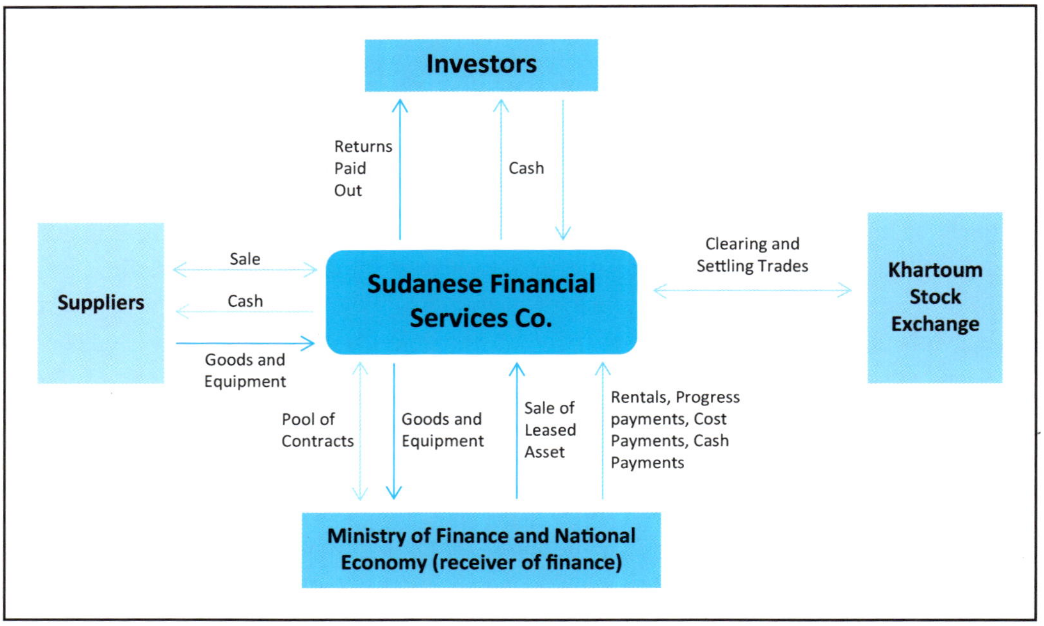

Figure 5.9. Structure of GICs.

Box 5.6. Liquidity Management and Islamic Banks: The Need for Markets

A recent IMF study which compared Islamic and conventional banks in the Gulf Cooperation Council (GCC) countries made several interesting observations. Of these, two key points were as follows: first, Islamic banks have much more liquidity (liquid assets) on their balance sheets relative to conventional banks. Second, Islamic banks are on average less profitable than conventional banks over the six-year period of study, when measured by Return on Assets (ROA) or Return on Equity (ROE). Holding liquid assets earns a bank nothing, the fund has to be put to use as customer financing. Not only are potential returns foregone but depositors whose funds it manages, will be expecting returns. Thus, the lower ROA and ROE of Islamic banks in the GCC is the direct result of carrying too much liquidity.

That Islamic banks hold too much liquid assets appears to be a global phenomenon. The question that arises is, why is this the case? Banking, whether conventional of Islamic, has an inherent mismatch. Banks take in money as deposits, which can be withdrawn at any time and give out the money as loans with fixed future maturities. This maturity transformation has inbuilt liquidity mismatch. Conventional banking, rather than hold huge amounts of cash to meet liquidity mismatches, has over time evolved ancillary systems to help in the liquidity management. This is the interbank money market. The money market evolved to meet the liquidity challenges of the banking system, but more than merely being a platform for players to borrow and lend among themselves, it has now become a source of price discovery. That is, the determination of short-term rates. The short end of the yield curve is derived from activity in the money market. The money market acts as a sponge, contracting and expanding in tandem with banking sector liquidity needs. Well-developed money markets enable banks to minimize the liquid assets they need to hold, thereby enabling them to put to

(*Continued*)

Box 5.6. (*Continued*)

use and earn from funds that otherwise would be kept idle, even for short periods. In addition to helping banks with outplacement and enhancing returns, efficient money markets can reduce the cost of funds to banks. In developed capital markets, money market funds are usually the cheapest source of funds for banks. Such reduced costs enable banks to price their loans competitively.

As money markets evolved, their price discovery function became more important than the liquidity management ability. Taking a macro viewpoint, it is easy to see how important money markets can be to both banking and overall macro-economic efficiency. It is also easy to see how their absence can be a huge drag on macro-economic efficiency. With the exception of Sudan and Iran, Islamic banks operate within dual banking systems. Islamic banks have products and processes that mimic conventional banks and are expected to be cost competitive with them, yet, with the exception of Malaysia, Islamic banks have no access to money markets. The result is the above IMF finding that Islamic banks have excessive liquid assets and lower profitability. There is more to this than reduced operational efficiency of banks.

In all countries other than Malaysia, Islamic banks have to manage their liquidity mismatches by way of bilateral arrangements usually with their Central banks or an affiliated agency of the Central bank. Borrowing and lending takes place by buying and selling papers/*sukuk*. For example, the Islamic bank with surplus funds will buy *sukuk* from the central bank and resell it to the Central bank when it needs liquidity. The Islamic bank is a price taker; how the Central bank determines the required yield is unknown, but, there appears to be a high correlation with prevailing interest rates in the conventional banking sector. While such bilateral arrangements solve the liquidity problem of banks, there is no means for price discovery. So, how are loans priced by Islamic banks? Answer, in most cases by using rates similar to those charged in the conventional banking system. It is no surprise therefore that after more than 30 years of Islamic banking, there is no Islamic benchmark rate. This obvious absence is due to a lack of market trading. Without market trading to determine required returns, Islamic banks and Islamic finance more broadly, cannot shake off its reliance on interest rates. Thus, today, we have several large global sovereign *sukuk* outstanding that have their returns benchmarked on LIBOR (London Interbank Offer Rate), which is an interbank money market rate arrived at through trading in London. *Shari'ah* scholars have conveniently accepted this practice as "mere benchmarking" or the use of a proxy, but it points to a much larger issue, the superficiality of Islamic banking even after a 30- to 40-year presence. The fact that it has not been able to put down the roots needed to create its own pricing mechanism is testimony to misplaced emphasis, that being on form rather than substance. Continuing on this path is likely to lead to a convergence with conventional banking and the irrelevance of an Islamic banking system built to mimic.

Source: Author's op-ed column in *Derin Ekonomi*, January 2015.

Summary

IIMM is the *Shari'ah*-compliant version of Malaysia's conventional money market. Islamic financial institutions, like conventional counterparts, are subject to inherent mismatches in cash flows. The management of liquidity is a key purpose of its use by IFIs. As the world's first Islamic money market, Malaysia designed it on the conventional template. Thus, IIMM can perform all the functions and provide the facilities that a conventional money market can. Its three main components are the interbank deposit facility, the trading platform for Islamic money market instruments, and Islamic cheque clearing system. Many of the conventional instruments have been replicated into *Shari'ah*-compliant ones. Though structurally the same, IIMM has had its own set of issues. The fact that non-IFIs can have access to IIMM has meant that funds can flow between the two money markets. This enables easy arbitrage and the implication is that the yields prevailing in IIMM have to be in line with that of the conventional money market. Aside from the normal risks that apply to instruments traded in the conventional market, IIMM traded instruments also face accounting and *Shari'ah* risks. The Bursa Suq Al Sila is a commodity *murabaha* facility offered by Bursa Malaysia. It complements IIMM in that Malaysian and international IFIs can use it to manage their liquidity. This chapter also provides a description of Bahrain's LMC, which was established for the same objective as that of IIMM, providing a facility for the management of liquidity by IFIs.

Questions and Problems

1. Compare and contrast the Islamic Interbank Money Market (IIMM) with its conventional counterpart.
2. Describe the three components of the IIMM and explain the role of each.
3. Islamic Bank A (IBA) takes a 90-day *Mudarabah* Interbank Investment deposit from Islamic Bank B (IBB). The face value of the deposit is RM10 million. The PSR is 70:30. Assuming the gross profit declared by IBA on a one-year deposit is 4.5% annualized, determine the total amount that IBA is obliged to pay IBB on Day 91. The Government Investment Certificate rate (GIC) is 3.0%.
4. Islamic Bank A (IBA) has placed a 30-day *Mudarabah* Interbank Investment deposit with Islamic Bank X (IBX). The details are as follows:

   - Principal = RM45 million
   - Tenor = 30 days
   - PSR = 70/30

   Determine the amount IBA will receive on Day 31 if IBX's declared profit rate on one-year deposit is 5.8% (annualized).
5. Your bank, an IFI, has approximately RM60 million of surplus funds available in a little more than 90 days from now. Suppose the current return on Bank Negara Negotiable Notes is 6% and you are acceptable to that rate of return, what amount you would have to invest today in BNNN of 90-day maturity, if you want to receive RM60 million on Day 91?
6. Describe the features and application of any three IIMM instruments.
7. Describe some of the risks in money markets and explain in what way would they differ where the IIMM is concerned.
8. Best Electronics, a distributor of consumer electronic items, is seeking short-term working capital financing to finance shipment of products. Mr. Tan, the Treasurer of Best Electronics, believes he needs financing of RM20million for a 90-day period. He is open to using commodity *murabaha* to raise the funding. Structure a commodity *murabaha* transaction by which Best Electronics can fulfil its requirements.
9. Compare and contrast the following institutions:

   (a) IIMM versus LMC (Liquidity Management Centre Bahrain)
   (b) Bursa Suq Al-Sila versus LMC

10. Malaysia has both conventional and Islamic money markets operating in tandem and the latter is accessible to non-Islamic institutions, whereby funds can flow from one to the other. What is the implication of this to yields/profit rates in the two markets?
11. Syarikat ABC wants a RM10 million loan repayable annually over the next 12 years.

    (a) Structure a commodity-*murabaha*-based loan that will facilitate Syarikat ABC's requirements. (Show the diagram and direction of flows, number the flows, etc.)
    (b) If the repayment amount is RM1 million paid to the bank at the end of each year for twelve years, what is the effective annual cost (in percentage) of the RM10 million loan?

12. An Islamic bank (IB) wants to aggressively grow its profits by growing its assets. Given competition for customer deposits, the bank chooses to issue huge tranches of securities in the Islamic Interbank Money Market (IIMM). It uses the funds thus raised to give out term loans, such as car financing, SME loans, etc. Evaluate the bank's strategy from a cost and risk viewpoint.
13. Your company raises RM20 million from an Islamic bank through a commodity *murabaha* arrangement. The amount is payable monthly over three years. Is there rate risk in this type of arrangement? Explain.

14. (a) An Islamic interbank instrument with 60 days to maturity and RM500,000 face value is being offered to you. Assuming your required return is 5%, what price would you be willing to pay for the instrument.
    (b) If the above instrument is being sold at RM493,000, what is the implied yield?
15. A. Three *Murabaha*-based IIMM instruments each with a face value of RM1 million and 90 days to maturity are trading at the following prices;

    (i) RM987,000
    (ii) RM978,000
    (iii) RM991,000

    (a) If an investor buys each and holds it to maturity, what is his return?
    (b) What accounts for the difference in returns between the instruments?

    B. Several studies have shown very high correlation between the KLIRR rates of IIMM and the KLIBOR rates of the conventional money market. Briefly explain why this is the case.

Bibliography

Alvi, I. A. (2009). Interbank Money Market Operations, Powerpoint slides, AAOIFI — World Bank Annual Conference on Islamic Banking and Finance, 14–15 December 2009, Bahrain.

Ayub, M. (2007). *Understanding Islamic Finance* (John Wiley & Sons Ltd).

Bank Negara Malaysia, Annual Reports — several years.

Capital Market Issues According to Islamic Jurisprudence. Resolutions of the Securities Commission Shariah Advisory Council. — Securities Commission, Kuala Lumpur.

Basu, R. *et al.* (2015). *Monetary Operations and Islamic Banking in the (GCC): Challenges and Options*, IMF Working Paper WP/15/234, pp. 1–27.

Qatar, IMF Country Report No.17/89, Selected Issues, April 2017, pp. 1–33.

Derin Ekonomi, January 2015.

Websites

http://www.ifsb.org

http://www.iifm.net

http://www.iimm.bnm.gov.my — Islamic Money Market

http://www.iirating.com/about

http://www.lmcbahrain.com

http://www.bursamalaysia.com — Bursa Malaysia

http://gulfnews.com/business/sectors/banking/gcc-islamic-banks-funding-expected-to-weaken-but-liquidity-to-remain-sound-1.2015779

Endnotes

1. The GIC has now been replaced by the GII (Government Investment Issues).
2. This revision became effective February 1995.
3. *Note*: the 36,500 in the denominator is 365 days × 100. Thus, in the numerator the percent r will be entered as a whole number and not as decimal.
4. When the total surplus and deficits are not equal, a weighted average method is used in allocating funds.
5. See: The Central Bank and the Financial System in Malaysia, A decade of change BNM (40th Anniversary Issue), p. 248.

Chapter 6

BONDS AND BOND MARKETS

Topics in this Chapter

6.1. Introduction
6.2. Bank Borrowing versus Bond Issuance; Debt versus Equity; and Bond Features Debt versus Equity
6.3. The Pricing of Bonds
6.4. Bond Yields and Yield; Curves Yield Curves and Credit Spreads; What Constitutes a Yield?
6.5. Interest Rate Change, Bond Yields, and Duration
6.6. Risk Associated with Bonds
6.7. Types of Bonds
6.8. Ratings and Yields/Credit Spread

Chapter Objective

This chapter provides an in-depth analysis of bonds. The pricing/valuation of bonds, bond trading mechanics, and related issues like the yield-to-maturity, the yield curve, nominal and real interest rates, and duration are examined. On completing this chapter, you should have a good understanding of bonds, their valuation techniques, impact of inflation on interest rates, determination of yields to maturity, interest rate risk, and bond duration.

	Key Terms	
basis point	discounted cash flow (DCF)	nominal interest rate
bond capital gain	duration	present value
bond pricing agency	equity	public debt securities
callable bond	fixed coupon rate	putable bond
collaterized bond	floating coupon rate	rating agency
commercial papers	immunization	tenor
convertible bond	indexed bond	treasury bill
corporate bond	inflation indexed bond	yield curve
coupon rate	inflation risk	yield-to-maturity (YTM)
credit risk	interest rate	zero-coupon bond
credit spread	interest rate risk	
creditworthiness	KLIBOR	

6.1 Introduction

Bonds are probably the most commonly traded debt instruments. As a debt instrument, they represent a claim on the issuing company. In a sense, they are nothing but IOUs or promissory notes. Bonds are typically issued by business or government entities when they want to raise debt financing. In Malaysia, as in most countries, government bonds are collectively known as Public Debt Securities, whereas bonds issued by business or corporate bonds are known as Private Debt Securities. One could also differentiate debt instruments by their maturity or tenor. Short-term debt instruments usually have a maturity less than one year and are traded in money markets (see Chapter 3). Bonds, on the other hand, typically have longer maturities and are therefore considered long-term debt instruments. Being long term, they are traded in bond markets which are a part of the capital markets. Thus, depending on the tenor of debt financing that an issuer wants, they would float (introduce) the issue in either the money market or capital market. For example, when a company wants to raise short-term debt, they would issue short-term debt instruments known as Commercial Papers in the money market. Alternatively, when a company wants to raise long-term debt financing, they would issue Corporate Bonds in the bond markets. The bond market is a part of the capital market. Recall that the capital market is where long-term financing is raised. As is the case with Commercial Paper and Corporate Bonds, when the government wants to raise short-term debt financing, it issues Treasury Bills in the money market. On the other hand, to raise long-term debt, the government would issue Government Bonds in the capital market (see Figure 6.1).

Tenor	**Issuing entity**		**Traded-In (Secondary market)**
	Government	Business	
Short-term (< 1 year)	Treasury Bills	Commercial Papers	Money Market
Long-term (> 1 year)	Government Bonds	Corporate Bonds	Bond Market

Figure 6.1. Debt Instrument, Issuer, and Secondary Market.

In raising debt financing, one is essentially borrowing. In Malaysia, as in most other countries, an entity that wants to borrow can do so in two common ways: (i) borrow from a bank or (ii) borrow by issuing debt papers, commercial paper, or bonds, depending on whether one needs a short-term or long-term loan.

6.2 Bank Borrowing vs Bond Issuance

It is obvious that there will be a huge difference between borrowing from a bank versus borrowing through a bond issuance. There are advantages and disadvantages in each method. Bank borrowing would be much faster, requires less documentation, and would need little if any regulatory approval. The borrowing entity would only have to satisfy the lending bank of its creditworthiness. The drawdown of funds and repayment schedules can be flexible. In other words, with bank debt, customization is possible. While these are the benefits, there are disadvantages. Bank debt is not liquid, cannot be traded, and can be costlier. The cost disadvantage comes from the fact that bank debt is indirect financing. The bank being the intermediary has to earn a profit to justify the credit risk it takes on.

With bonds, however, the issuing company accesses "lenders" directly. Since there is no intermediary, it would imply lower funding cost. Additionally, as bonds are tradable, there are lower liquidity risks, which in turn mean lower required liquidity risk premiums. Yet another key advantage of debt raised through bond issuance is the fact that, given active trading of its bond, the borrowing firm can tell the "true cost" of its funds at any given point in time. As we will see later, when a company's risk profile changes, its cost of debt will change. This change in cost of debt will show up as a change in the market price of the outstanding bond. Thus, with market traded bonds, a firm can see the impact of changes in its fundamentals (e.g., increase in sales, profits, new innovations, etc.) on its

Table 6.1. Raising Debt Financing: Bank Borrowing versus Bond Issuance.

Bank Borrowing	Bond Issuance
• Time: Short, fast • Few pre-conditions • Few regulatory requirements • Satisfy bank of creditworthiness • Not tradable (illiquid) • Cost may not be reflective of company's fundamentals — especially after loan is taken • Company may not be able to tell what its cost on a new loan is likely to be • Funds raised may be limited	• Time: Lengthy • Extensive preconditions to be met, both financial and legal • Several regulations have to be complied with both pre- and post-issuance • Mandatory rating required • Tradable: Can be very liquid • Cost can be reflective of company fundamentals • Issuer can tell from its current bond yields, what its cost on new debt is likely to be • Large amount of funds can be accessed from bond market

Source: Author.

cost funds. For example, when a firm's fundamentals improve, the traded price of its bonds would increase, implying a lower cost of debt. This means that if the firm were to issue new debt, it can do so at the current lower cost. This "price signal" is an important feedback mechanism for the firm.

While bond issuance as a form of raising debt has several advantages over bank borrowing, it does have some disadvantages relative to bank debt. As an instrument publicly traded on the secondary bond market, a bond issue would have to meet several regulatory requirements. In Malaysia, until 2016, all bond issues were subject to mandatory rating requirement. This means that a company intending to issue bonds must get the bonds rated by one of Malaysia's two bond rating agencies: Rating Agency of Malaysia (RAM) or Malaysian Rating Corporation (MARC). Since 2016, however, in keeping with the practice of developed markets, bond ratings are no more mandatory in Malaysia. The bond issuer must also fulfill the requirements of the Securities Commissions' Guidelines on the Offering of Private Debt securities. To enable a company to chart through all these, the issuing company would typically appoint a "principal adviser", which is a merchant bank. Given all these requirements, a bond issuance would be a more time consuming and much more expensive affair than bank borrowing. Aside from paying the rating agency and merchant bank, other floatation costs like issuance of prospectus and trustee fee would have to be incurred. In addition, during the tenor of the bond, compliance is necessary, both in terms of the issuer's financial condition and legal issues.

As with most economic choices, there are several trade-offs between bank borrowing and bond issuance. An entity intending to raise debt financing must balance these trade-offs. In Malaysia, between two sources of debt financing, bond issuance has certainly become much more popular, especially following the Asian Currency Crisis of 1997/1998. Policymakers, having witnessed the dangers of a bank-centric financial system, appear determined to expand bond issuance and develop the bond market while reducing reliance of the Malaysian corporate sector on bank loans.

6.3 Debt versus Equity and Bond Features

As a financial instrument that has secondary market trading, there are some common features that all bonds have. These features are driven by the characteristic of debt financing. Recall that there are two common ways by which a business entity could raise the funding needed to finance itself. These would be debt financing and equity financing. While bonds are the most common debt financing instrument, shares or stock would be the most common equity instrument. Equity represents ownership, entitles the holder to a share in profits, and provides a residual claim on the issuing company's assets. By residual claim, we mean that shareholders would be the last to be "paid" in the event that the company is liquidated; we also mean that they have a claim on all unencumbered assets of the firm. Where tenor or maturity is concerned, equity is perpetual. Stocks have no fixed maturity. As long as one has not sold off the stock, and the issuing company is in business, all rights of stock ownership apply. Debt, on the other hand, represents a fixed claim on the issuing company and has a fixed maturity or tenor.

Table 6.2. Key Differences between Debt and Equity.

	Debt	Equity
Instruments	Bond	Share
Claim	Fixed	Residual
Tenor	(principal + interest) Fixed	(all "free" assets) Perpetual
Priority of claim	Prior to equity	Residual
Repayment	Compulsory Interest / principal	Principal never repaid Dividends not compulsory
Collateral	May have specific asset as collateral	No collateral
Profit participation	No	Yes

Source: Author.

A debt-holder's claim on a company would equal the fixed amount due him (principal plus accrued interest). While the amount due may vary with time since interest accumulates, his claim on the firm is fixed at that amount. Thus, the two key factors that differentiate debt from equity are the fixed claim and fixed tenor.

The features of a bond therefore are driven by the characteristics of debt.

6.4 Face Value and Par Value

Being a promissory note signifying a debt, the face value or par value is an important feature of a bond. The face value of the bond is essentially the amount the buyer of the bond would receive when redeeming the bond at maturity. The face value of the bond is therefore the amount owed by the bond-issuer to the bond-holder. In Malaysia, the typical face value for bonds is RM5 million. In most other countries, the face value is much smaller. In the US, a bond with face value as small as US$1,000 is available. A bond is selling at par if the market value is at a price equal to the face value. If the market price is less than the face value, the bond is traded at a discount; if the market price is higher than the face value, the bond is traded at a premium.

Since debt represents a fixed claim on the issuer, par value is critical for bonds. In the event of liquidation, when the proceeds from sale of the company's assets have to be distributed, a bond-holder's "claim" on these funds will be determined by the face value of each bond and the number of bonds that he holds. His claim will be limited to, or fixed at, the par value and accumulated coupons on each bond and the number of bonds he holds. Since equity-holders have no such "fixed" claim but are residual claimants, the par value of a stock is irrelevant. Thus, some stocks in the US have no par or face value.

6.4.1 *Tenor*

The tenor of a bond is the period to maturity of the bond. A 10-year bond issued in 2000 would "mature" or be redeemable in 2010. A 20-year bond issued in 2000 would mature in 2020. Since all claims of a bond-holder is settled at maturity, the tenor of a bond determines the period over which the bond-holder enjoys the returns on the bond. As an instrument with secondary market trading, the bond-holder can of course sell the bond before maturity. As we will see later, the bond-holder may or may not earn a capital gain in the process of selling. So, while bonds have a fixed maturity, there is no compulsion for an investor to hold it to maturity.

6.4.2 *Coupon Rate*

The coupon rate of a bond is essentially the interest paid for the bond. The coupon rate refers to the interest rate. A 10% coupon rate would mean that the bond would pay an interest rate of 10%. The ringgit amount of interest would equal 10% of the bond's face value, a 10% coupon rate would mean an interest amount of RM100 (RM1,000 × 10%).

There are variations on the coupon feature. For example, a zero-coupon bond is a bond that pays no coupon. This simply means that one does not earn an interest income from the bond. Why would anyone invest in a zero-coupon bond? While investing in a zero-coupon bond would provide no interest income, investors in zeros, as zero-coupon bonds are commonly referred to, have to earn a return to justify their investment. Their returns come from capital gains or the change in the value/price of the bond. As we will see later, the returns from investing in a bond comes from two potential sources: coupon return or coupon yield and capital gains yield. As a traded financial instrument with a secondary market, bond prices change continuously. Increase in the price of a bond held would mean positive capital gains. So, while a coupon bond may provide a total return that comes partly from coupon yield and partly from capital gains yield, the returns from investing in a zero-coupon bond would come entirely from capital gains. In this section, we will examine the pricing of bonds and discuss what determines the capital gains or losses for a bond.

A second variation on the coupon is whether it is fixed or floating. A fixed coupon rate implies that the coupon will be unchanged over the life/tenor of the bond. A floating coupon rate would mean that the rate and amount of coupon paid would vary over the life of the bond. Typically, a floating coupon rate would be linked to a reference interest rate. The reference interest rate would be a "traded" rate such as the three-month or six-month KLIBOR (Kuala Lumpur Inter Bank Offer Rate). As an example, a floating rate bond might state its coupon rate as; six-month KLIBOR + 2% or 3-month KLIBOR + 1% and so on. The three- or six-month KLIBOR rate is the reference interest rate. The +2% or +1% is the premium over the reference rate. Thus, the coupon paid on the bond at any given time would depend on what the reference interest rate is and the premium. For example, suppose a bond with a RM1,000 face value has a stated coupon rate of six-month KLIBOR + 1.50%. If at the time the coupon payment is due, the six-month KLIBOR is say at 8%, then the bond should pay 8% + 1.5% = 9.5% of the face value. Thus, the coupon payment due on the bond would be RM95.00 (RM1,000 × 9.5%). If at the next period when coupon is due, the six-month KLIBOR is at 6.5%, then a coupon of 8% (6.5% + 1.5%) or RM80 is due on the bond.

Aside from the type and size of coupon rate, the frequency of coupon payment could also differ across bonds. Coupon payments could be on an annual or a semi-annual basis. Occasionally, bonds with quarterly coupon payments may also be available. A bond with a 10% annual coupon would pay 10% face value once a year. On the other hand, a bond with a 10% coupon paid semi-annual, would pay half the coupon in each half-year period, i.e., 5% of face value in the first six months and 5% in the second half of the year. Assuming a RM1,000 face value, a 10% annual coupon bond would pay a single coupon of RM100 at year end. However, a 10% semi-annual coupon bond, would pay RM50 (5% of RM1,000) on June 30 and RM50 at the end of December.

While the above three features, face/par value, tenor, and coupon, are the most common, there are other features that bonds may have. We will discuss some of these in later sections. To recap our discussion, as a market-traded debt instrument, a bond must have the following basic features:

- Issuer name
- Face value
- Coupon rate
- Coupon frequency
- Tenor

Box 6.1. The Malaysian Bond Market

Unlike the stock market, the Malaysian bond market has been a late bloomer. Until the 1990s, the bond market was insignificant and a secondary market in bonds almost non-existent. Over the 1970s and 1980s, the only bonds outstanding were government bonds or Malaysian Government Securities (MGSs). These were government papers, issued to finance the occasional fiscal deficits. What made the situation more tepid was that statutory requirements resulted in financial institutions, mainly banks, simply holding the papers until maturity. All these changed in 1989 when the government undertook a series of initiatives aimed at promoting a secondary market in bonds. Among these initiatives were:

(*Continued*)

Box 6.1. ***(Continued)***

(i) The establishment of a system of principal dealers who would underwrite issues and stand ready to provide two-way quotes for secondary trading. As of 2000, there were a total of 15 principal dealers for MGS

(ii) The setting up of a scriptless computerized trading system known as SPEEDS. In 1999, SPEEDS was replaced by an upgraded real-time system, RENTAS.

(iii) The establishment of credit rating agencies (CRAs), which play a critical role in the development of bond markets. By subjecting bond-issuers to professional scrutiny, the system's integrity and transparency is enhanced. In addition to making it mandatory for all issuers to get their bonds rated, the government established two bond rating agencies, the first, Rating Agency of Malaysia (RAM) in 1990 and a second, The Malaysian Rating Corporation (MARC), in 1995.

Government initiatives asides, a number of factors have converged to rejuvenate the bond market. The privatization program that the government undertook from the mid-1980s led to the issuance of Private Debt Securities (PDS) — essentially corporate bonds. In addition to the privatization of government entities, the privatization of large infrastructure projects to the corporate sector on a build-operate-transfer (BOT) mode, made it necessary for the awarded company to issue PDS to finance the project. As a result, corporate bonds which were almost non-existent in the 1970s and 1980s and a miniscule RM3 billion in 1990s exploded to more than RM100 billion, or 21% of GDP in 2000. The graph below plots the growth in total outstanding local currency (MYR) bonds in Malaysia from 2000 to June 2017.[1] The combined total of Corporate and Government bonds went from MYR 262 billion at end-2000 to MYR1,246 billion in June 2017. As a percent of GDP, total bonds outstanding were 96.3 % of GDP in mid-2017. This is obviously an impressive growth by any measure.

Ironically, the currency crisis of 1997/1998 has been an eye-opener and a catalyst for bond market development. What started off as a speculative currency attack led to a banking crisis, in the true form of what economists call a "twin crisis". The dangers of a bank-centric financial system became apparent. Total bank loans as a percent of GDP had averaged approximately 20% and 30%, respectively, over the 1970s and 1980s. These had ballooned to nearly 100% of GDP[2] over the 1990s. During the post-crisis period, the government pushed its efforts at bond market development in order to reduce the nation's reliance on bank financing. One of the main post-crisis initiatives was the setting up of a National Bond Market Committee (NBMC), to rationalize the regulatory framework. Based on the recommendation on this committee, the SC became the sole regulatory authority for the corporate bond market.

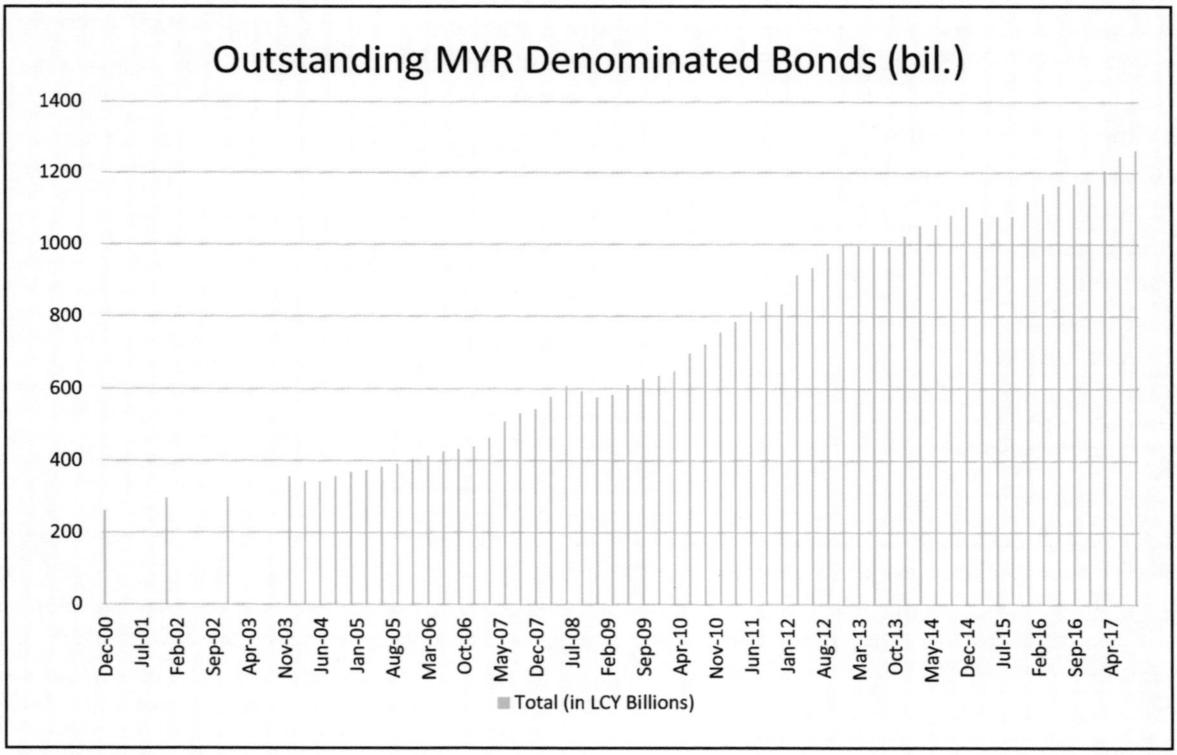

6.5 The Pricing of Bonds

The value of financial assets like bonds can be determined using the discounted cash-flow (DCF) technique. The logic is to find the present value of future cash flows that can be derived from the bond. Generally speaking, the value of an asset from a finance viewpoint is equivalent to the present value of all future cash flows that can be derived from the asset. In arriving at present values, we discount future cash flows using an "appropriate" discount rate. The appropriate discount rate may be the cost of funds, the required return based on market forces, the opportunity cost, etc. As we will see later, for market-traded instruments, the market price of the asset at any given point provide us the market's implied required return for the instrument. The present value of an asset's discounted cash flows can be computed as:

$$PV = \sum \frac{CF_1}{(1+k)} + \frac{CF_2}{(1+k)^2} + \frac{CF_3}{(1+k)^3} + \cdots + \frac{CF_n}{(1+k)^n} \quad (6.1)$$

where PV is the present value of future cash flows; CF_t is cash flow in future period; and n is the number of future periods over which cash flows will accrue. A bond, being a fixed income security/asset, has known future cash flows for a fixed period of time. For example, suppose a 10-year corporate bond has an 8% annual coupon and a RM1,000 face value, its cash flows would be:

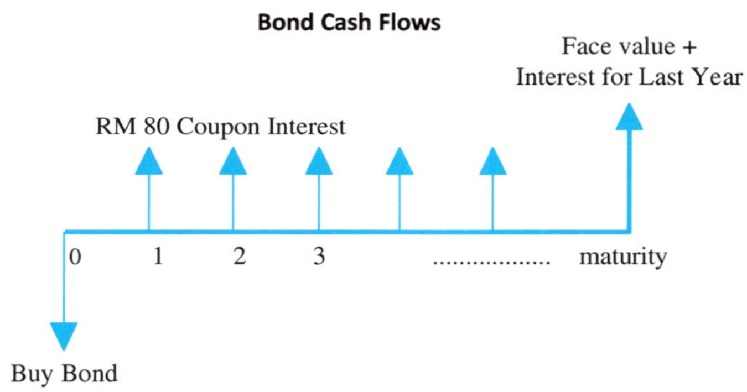

$$\text{Price} = \sum_{t=1}^{n} \frac{Coupon_t}{(1+k)^t} + \frac{Face\,Value_n}{(1+k)^n} \quad (6.2)$$

where k is the appropriate discount rate.

Notice that in Equation 6.2, we find the present value of each of the two cash flows and add them. The sum total represents the bond's current value.

Box 6.2. Illustration: Bond Pricing

The bond described above has a 10-year maturity, an 8% annual coupon, and a RM1,000 face value. To determine the bond's price, we need to know the appropriate discount rate that should be used. Let us say the correct required return on the bond should be 10%. Using Equation 6.2, the bond's price is:

$$\text{Price} = \sum_{t=1}^{n} \frac{RM80}{(1.10)_t} + \frac{RM1{,}000}{(1.10)_n}$$

(*Continued*)

Box 6.2. (*Continued*)

Using the present value formula in EXCEL; the present value of the coupon payments is:

PV of coupon payments (annuity)

RM80 (PVAF, 10%, 10*n*)
RM80 (6.145) = RM 491.60

The present value of the second cash flows for the single face-value payment in year 10 can be determined by multiplying the RM1,000 amount with the Present Value Interest Factor.

RM1,000 (PVIF, 10%, 10n)
RM1,000 (0.386) = RM386

Adding the PV of both cash flows:

PV of Coupon Payments = RM491.60
PV of Face Value = RM386
Bond Value = RM877.60

The value of the bond is **RM877.60**

Using a financial calculator, we would have to input four variables in order to determine the PV/price of bond. The four input variables and keys would be: (i) Face value (*FV*); (ii) Maturity of bond (*n*); (iii) Coupon amount (*PMT*); and (iv) Required return (*i*). Having entered these four variables, we press the [Comp] key followed by the [PV] key. To price the above bond;

$$\left.\begin{array}{l} n = 10 \\ PMT = 80\,\text{Coupon} \\ FV = \$1{,}000 \\ i = 10\% \end{array}\right\} \textbf{COMP PV = 877.10}$$

Thus, the value of the bond is **RM877.10**.

Notice the small difference in value between the two methods, the RM0.50 or 50 cents difference has to do with round error. The table values are to three decimal places whereas the calculator programmed to eight decimal places.

6.6 Bond Yields and Yield Curves

Notice from Eq. (6.2) above that in solving for a bond's price, one needs to define four variables as inputs. The four inputs being: (i) face value; (ii) time to maturity (*t*); (iii) the coupon amount; and (iv) the required yield as discount rate. The first three variables are straight forward and can be easily determined. Face value, time to maturity, and coupon amount would be stated as part of a bond's features. The fourth variable, required yield, would have to be determined. However, how does one determine this? The answer is that one derives the required yield for a bond from the *yield curve*, also called the *term-structure of interest rates*. The yield curve is essentially a locus of points relating the required yield to the time to maturity for a given risk class of bonds. As bonds differ in risk quality and belong to different risk classes, there is typically a "family" of yield curves. Each yield curve represents a certain risk class. The yield curve applicable for a given bond would depend on the bond's rating. The higher the bond's rating, the lower the yield curve and the lower the required yield. Figure 6.2 depicts a typical set of yield curves.

The symbol *rf* stands for risk-free interest rate. For any given maturity, the required yield will be higher for lower-quality instruments. Thus, the required yield or discount rate on a bond is inversely related to its rating. The

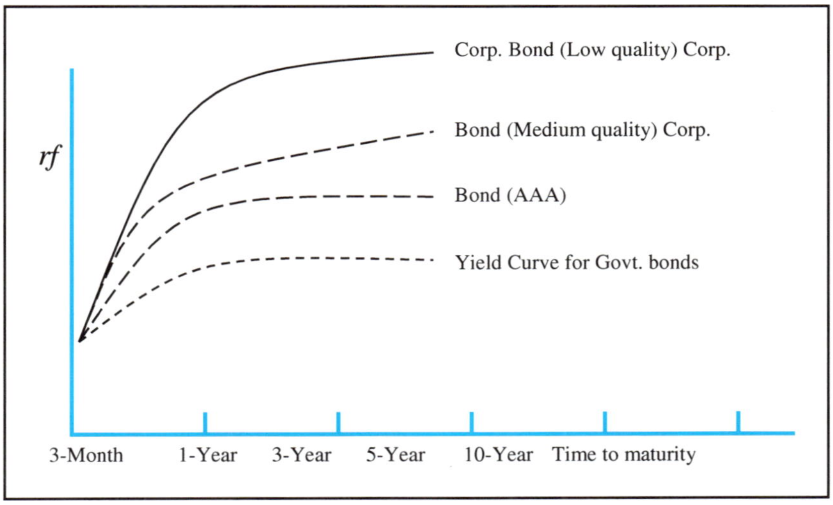

Figure 6.2. Bond Quality, Yield Curve, and Required Yields.

higher the bond's quality, as determined by its rating, the lower the relevant yield curve and so, the lower the required return. The higher yield curve for lower-quality bonds simply reflects the higher risk associated with investing in them. And in efficient markets, riskier investments will require higher returns/yield.

6.7 Yield Curve and Credit Spreads

As we saw above, different yield curves are applicable for bonds of different credit quality. The difference in the required yield between two bonds is often referred to as the *credit spread*. The size of the credit spread is a reflection of a bond's quality relative to another. For example, one might often hear that a bond has a credit spread of 300 basis points over MGS. What this means is that the bond has a yield which is 3% higher than a government bond. MGS refers to *Malaysian Government Securities* which are essentially government-issued bonds. A *basis point* is a hundredth of one percent. Though credit spreads between bonds tend to be stable, they could change substantially during "bad times" or periods of market crises, during which there is a flight to safety or flight to quality.

6.8 What Constitutes a Yield?

To understand what yield is and how it differs from the coupon rate, consider a bond with the following features:

Par Value = \$1,000
Maturity = 3 years
Coupon = 10% (annual)

Suppose the market price of this bond is now = \$951.96.
What is the yield on this bond?
Solving, we obtain i =12%

$$\left.\begin{array}{l} 1{,}000\ \text{FV} \\ -951.96 \\ 3\,\text{n} \\ 100\,\text{Pmt} \end{array}\right\}\quad \text{comp}\, i = 12\%$$

Entering the above variables and solving for return would provide a return of 12%. What this means is that, if we bought the bond today and held it to maturity, our annual yield would equal 12% per year. One would be tempted to ask, how can the annual return be 12% when the coupon rate is only 10%? This is precisely the difference between coupon return and yield on the bond. The 12% annual return is known as the *yield-to-maturity* (YTM), which can be thought of as the *net total return* that one receives from investing in a bond. Since a bond's return comes from two sources, coupon yield and capital gains, YTM is the sum total of the two returns.

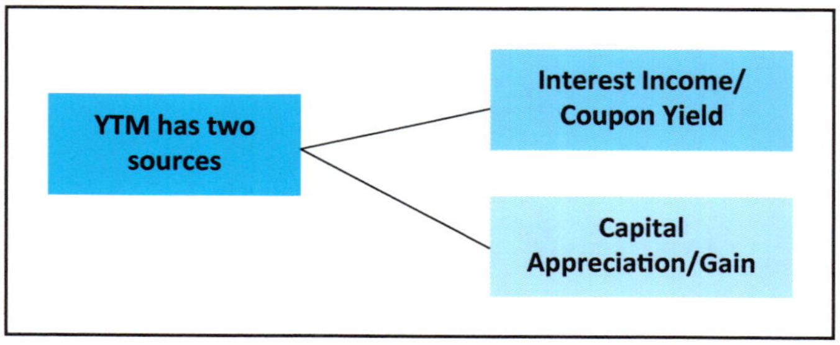

YTM is therefore the Holding Period Return (HPR). Given the above bond's price today of RM951.96, YTM is now 12%. The fact that the total return from holding the bond will be 12% per year when the coupon is yielding only 10% per year implies that the remaining 2% must come from capital gains yield. This will be in the form of a price appreciation of the bond by about 2%. It is quite easy to see why one can be "assured" of a positive capital gain when a bond's current price is at a discount to face value. Since a bond must be worth its face value on its maturity day, we can be sure that the above bond's price must increase from the current RM951.96 to RM1,000, three years from today when it matures. If interest rates are unchanged, there would be a gradual increase in the bond's value due to accretion, but if interest rates fluctuate then, value increase would not be gradual but fluctuating. In any case, the bond's value must equal RM1,000 at maturity since the bond will pay off that amount as redemption value.

To extend the logic, if a bond that is selling at a discount now will *ceterus paribus* appreciate in value as it approaches maturity, it follows that a bond that is currently selling at a premium to face value must depreciate in value as it approaches maturity. In other words, holding interest rates constant, a bond which is at a premium now will experience *negative* capital gains as maturity approaches. The figure below shows the value/ price trajectory for three bonds. Bond A, which is the above bond, selling at a discount to face value, Bond B which is selling at Par (price = face value) and Bond C which is selling at a premium to face value. All three bonds have the same features, three years to maturity, 10% annual coupon, RM1,000 face value. However, the required return or YTM for each bond is different due to differences in risk/rating. Bond A, which has the highest risk, has a required YTM of 12%, whereas Bond B, 10%, and Bond C, which is the least risky of the three bonds, has a required YTM of only 8%. It is this difference in required YTM that gives rise to the difference in the current prices.

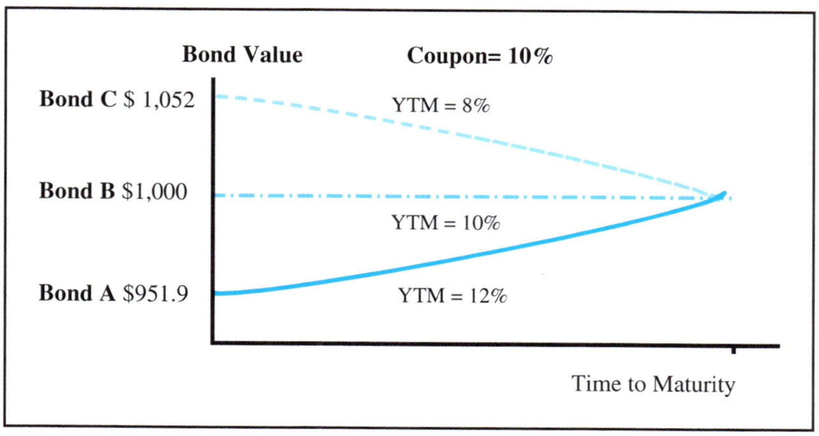

Assuming the market interest rate is unchanged, the bonds' prices' will adjust to equal RM1,000, which is the face value at maturity. At maturity, a bond's value must equal its face or par value. Thus, the following relationships hold:

> **At Maturity**
>
> Bond Price = Face Value
>
> **Before Maturity**
>
> 1. If C (coupon rate) = YTM, Bond Price = Face value.
> 2. If C < YTM, Bond Price < Face Value (discount)
> 3. If C > YTM, Bond Price > Face Value (premium)

Recall that a bond's YTM could change if market interest rates change. We now turn to a discussion about how changes in interest rates can cause a change in YTM by way of a change in the bond's value/price.

6.9 Interest Rate Change, Bond Yields, and Duration

It is obvious that a change in interest rate would cause a change in bond prices. The transmission of a change in interest rates to changes in bond prices works through the yield curves. Suppose the government, given macro conditions, wants to move to a more restrictive monetary policy.[3] One obvious way to do this would be by raising interest rates. Central banks would typically do this by "intervening" in the interbank money market. The interbank money market is the wholesale market for loans. As such, causing a change in the cost of funds in the wholesale market inevitably causes a change in interest rates throughout the financial system. Suppose the Malaysian Central Bank, Bank Negara Malaysia (BNM), wants to move up interest rates, it would usually do this interest rate "intervention" through the interbank money market. In effect, BNM will stand ready to borrow at a higher rate than that currently prevailing. For example, suppose the current rate is 2.5% for three-month borrowing. If BNM offers to borrow at 3% for the same tenor, it will attract all available funds, thereby causing all potential borrowers to pay at least 3% for three-month money, in effect causing a jump in three-month borrowing from 2.5% yesterday to 3% today. In the interbank money market, the three-month KLIBOR rate goes up by 0.5%. With an increase in this base rate, one can visualize an upward shift of all the yield curves. The required yields would increase, and given the higher discount rates, cause bond and other asset prices to fall.

We have thus far established that changes in interest rates are inversely related to bond and asset prices.

Interest Rate	Required Yield	Bond/Asset Values
↑	↑	↓
↓	↓	↑

However, one might want to ask whether the impact is uniform. That is, when interest rates rise, bond prices fall, but would all bonds fall equally in value? The answer is no. The extent to which a bond falls in value for a given increase in interest rates will depend on its duration. Duration can be thought of as a measure of a bond's sensitivity to interest rate changes. The higher the bond or an asset's duration, the more sensitive it is to interest changes. The duration of a bond is calculated as follows;

Where;[4]

$$\text{Duration} = \sum t\left[\left(\frac{CF_t}{(1+y)_t}\right) / P_0\right] \tag{6.3}$$

where
CFt = Coupon and Face Value received from the bond
y = required yield
P_0 = current market price of the bond

Duration is defined as the *weighted average* of the maturities of each of the security's component cash flows. Going by this definition, the more interim cash flows there are for a bond, the *shorter* its duration will be. Thus, a three-year zero-coupon bond, for e.g., would have a duration equal to three years. This is because there are no interim cash flows, and therefore there is a single cash flow that occurs at the end of the third year. On the other hand, a three-year coupon bond would have a duration of less than three years because there are interim cash flow of coupon payments. While the duration of a zero-coupon bond will simply equal its maturity, duration of a coupon bond will always be less than maturity. To understand this better, we compute the duration of the above three-year 10% annual coupon bond using Equation 6.2.

Notice that Equation 6.3 essentially involves five steps as follows;

(i) Take coupon face value payments.
(ii) Discount them at the respective YTM.
(iii) Divide by the current price of the bond to determine the weight of each cash flow.
(iv) Multiply by t (time in years) and
(v) Sum it all up to arrive at the duration.

The duration of the three-year 10% coupon bond is 2.74236 years. This means that if the interest rate increases from 8% to 9%, by one percentage point, the bond price will fall by 2.74%. Inversely, if the interest rate declines from 8% to 7%, the bond price will increase by 2.74%. Notice that although the maturity of the bond is three years, the duration is only 2.74 years. The size of the duration determines an asset's interest rate sensitivity. The larger a bond's duration, *ceterus paribus*, the more sensitive its value will be to changes in interest rates. The following generalizations seen in Table 6.3 can be drawn:

Table 6.3. Calculating the Duration of a Three-Year 10% Coupon Bond, Discounted at 8% Per Year.

(1) Time Until Payment (in years)	(2) Payment	(3) PV of Payment Discounted at 8%	(4) Weight = Column (3) divided by bond price	(5) Column (1) × Column (4)
1	$100	$92.5926	.088054	.088054
2	100	85.7339	.081532	.163064
3	1,100	873.2155	.830414	2.49124
Totals		1,051.542	1.00000	2.74236

Box 6.3. Key Duration Relationships

- Duration of a zero-coupon bond = maturity.
- Duration of a perpetuity $= \dfrac{1+YTM}{YTM}$

For example, if YTM for the perpetuity is 9% then, $D = \dfrac{1.09}{0.09} = 12.11\,\text{years}$

Given the same coupon rate, the bond with the **longer maturity** has a longer duration.

For example, let us take two bonds of the same risk class, face value, and coupon rates, but different maturities at prevailing *YTM* of say 10%; both are priced at RM1,000.

Two-Year Bond A		**Three-Year Bond B**	
$1{,}000\,FV$	$PV = 1{,}000$	$1{,}000\,FV$	$PV = 1{,}000$
$101\,PMT$		$100\,PMT$	
$2n$		$10n$	
$10i$		$10i$	

However, suppose interest rates rise and *YTM* now increases to 12% tomorrow, then:

B COMP		**A** COMP	
$1{,}000\,FV$	$PV = \mathbf{966.20}$	$1{,}000\,FV$	$PV = \mathbf{966.20}$
$101\,PMT$		$101\,PMT$	
$2n$		$10n$ or **887.00**	
$12i$		$12i$	

$$\%Price \downarrow = \frac{1{,}000 - 966.20}{1{,}000} \times 100 = \mathbf{-3.38\%}$$

$$\%Price \downarrow = \times 100 = \mathbf{-11.3\%}$$

$$\frac{1{,}000 - 887}{1{,}000}$$

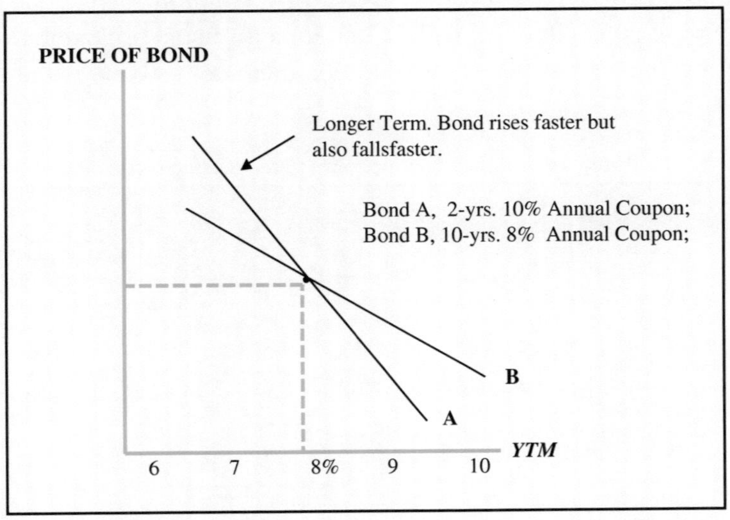

(*Continued*)

Box 6.3. (*Continued*)

- Alternatively, given the same maturity, the bond with a lower coupon has a higher duration.

10%Coupon	**5%Coupon**
A	**B**
COMP	COMP
$\left.\begin{matrix}1{,}000\,FV\\100\,PMT\end{matrix}\right\}PV = \mathbf{1{,}000}$	$\left.\begin{matrix}1{,}000\,FV\\50\,PMT\end{matrix}\right\}PV = \mathbf{913.22}$
$2n$	$2n$
$10i$	$10i$

- Now if YTM ↑ to 12%.

Bond A	**Bond B**
COMP	COMP
$\left.\begin{matrix}1{,}000\,FV\\100\,PMT\end{matrix}\right\}PV = \mathbf{966.20}$	$\left.\begin{matrix}1{,}000\,FV\\50\,PMT\end{matrix}\right\}PV = \mathbf{881.70}$
$2n$	$2n$
$12i$	$12i$

Bond A

$$\textbf{\%Price } \Delta = \frac{1{,}000 - 966.20}{1{,}000} \times 100 = \mathbf{-3.38\%}$$

Bond B

$$\textbf{\%Price } \Delta = \frac{913.11 - 881.7}{913.22} \times 100 = \mathbf{-3.45\%}$$

Table 6.4 summarizes the relationship between bond maturity, duration and coupon rates. As illustrated above, there are two key relationships to note within the table. First, for a given maturity, duration *decreases* as the coupon rate *increases*. Second, for a given coupon rate, bond duration increases as bond maturity lengthens.

Table 6.4. Bond Duration for Different Coupon Rates.

	Coupon Rates (% Per Year)			
Maturity in Years	**2%**	**4%**	**6%**	**8%**
1	0.995	0.990	0.985	0.981
5	4.742	4.533	4.361	4.218
10	8.762	7.986	7.454	7.067
20	14.026	11.966	10.922	10.292

6.9.1 *Estimating Bond/Asset Value Change Using Duration Analysis*

Since duration is a measure of rate sensitivity, there is a more interesting use for duration. By knowing the duration of a bond or asset, we can estimate the likely change in the value of the asset for an expected change in interest rates. For example, having calculated the duration, we can estimate the likely impact of a given interest rate increase on the assets value. Equation 6.4 can be used to estimate this expected change in value/price;

$$\%\Delta \text{ in Price} = -D \times \left[\frac{\Delta i}{(1+i)}\right] \tag{6.4}$$

where
D = duration of the asset
i = interest rate
Δ = change in variable

This potential change in the value of a bond as a result of a change in interest rates is referred to as interest rate risk. We will discuss this in the context of interest rate risk in the next section.

6.9.2. *Immunizing a Portfolio of Bonds From Interest Rate Risk*

Suppose a manager of a bond portfolio wants to protect or hedge his portfolio from interest rate risk. The process of hedging or eliminating the interest rate risk from a bond portfolio is known as Portfolio Immunization. There are two commonly used immunization techniques. These are: (i) a *maturity matching* strategy and (ii) a *duration matching* strategy. Immunization is intended to protect the total value of a bond portfolio such that its value is the same at some future date as it was at the time of its purchase.

An immunized portfolio would therefore have a return equal to the expected return on the portfolio. In other words, you try to lock-in the current yield of the bond portfolio. Recall that interest rate risk really has two dimensions: (i) *price risk* (capital gain/loss) and (ii) *reinvestment risk.*

It should be noted that these two risks act in the opposite direction. For example, while an interest rate reduction will see capital gains on the bonds held, it also means having to reinvest the coupons from the bond at lower interest rates. Thus, the gain from higher bond value will be offset by reduced returns earned from the reinvestment of coupons received. An immunized bond portfolio is one where the two above effects offset each other and thereby neutralize any impact on bond portfolio value.

6.9.2.1 *Maturity matching*

Here, we begin with an examination of the first technique, i.e., maturity matching.

Immunizing a zero-coupon bond through maturity matching

The basic idea in maturity matching is to immunize a portfolio by matching cash flows of exactly the same maturity on both the asset and liability side.

As an example, suppose a company had issued a 10-year zero-coupon bond with face value of RM10 million five years ago (so there are five more years left to maturity). The company had been setting aside some amount of money each year in a trust account to redeem the bond at maturity. It now has RM5,674,268.56 in the trust account. Assume that in the current interest rate environment, the company can earn a 12% interest on the available money.

If the trust bank that manages the trust account is willing to pay a 12% fixed rate for the next five years, then there is no risk, since the current amount in the trust will grow at 12% per year over the next five years to equal RM10 million in Year 10, An amount sufficient to enable the company to redeem the zero-coupon bonds at face value. However, if the trust bank pays floating interest rates, then falling interest rates could hurt the company. It may not have sufficient amount at redemption to fully redeem all outstanding bonds. How can the company hedge or immunize itself from the interest rate risk?

Answer: Since the company has a liability, it can immunize itself by creating an asset with an exactly matched cash flow and maturity.

For example, assume there is a default free zero-coupon bond of five-year maturity with a 12% YTM. The company can immunize itself by going long (buying) this bonds for RM10 million face value. (Note: its current price will equal the amount it has available.)

If the maturity of these bonds exactly matches the maturity of the company's outstanding bonds, then the company is immunized since the inflow from the asset will exactly match the outflow on the liability and it has "locked-in" a 12% return!

Immunizing a coupon bond with maturity matching

The above was a somewhat simplistic example of an outstanding zero-coupon bond, which was easily matched with yet another five-year zero. What if the outstanding bond to be immunized is a three-year, 10% coupon bond with FV of RM1,000?

Though a little more tedious, the underlying logic is still the same. Here, the coupon bond will have to be immunized by going long (buying) *today*, the following three default free zeros:

(i) a one-year zero with FV = RM100
(ii) a two-year zero with FV = RM100
(iii) a three-year zero with FV = RM1,100

By so doing, the three-year 10% coupon bond portfolio is immunized by matching the cash flows and locking in an interest rate equal to the YTM at which the three zeros were bought today.

6.9.2.2 *The duration matching strategy*

The duration matching strategy essentially revolves around matching the duration of an asset with an equal duration liability or vice-versa. The duration matching strategy is more realistic since finding zeros with exactly matching cash flows and maturities is not easy. Thus, in hedging a bond portfolio with a duration matching strategy, you first determine the duration of your portfolio of bonds.

Duration of a Portfolio of Bonds

The duration of a portfolio of bonds is quite simply the value weighted average of the duration of individual bonds that make up the portfolio. For example, suppose a portfolio is made up of two bonds, Bond *A* and Bond *B*. The duration of the portfolio is determined as:

$$D_p = \frac{V_A(D_A) + V_B(D_B)}{V_A + V_B}$$

where $V_A + V_B$ are the Ringgit values of the two bonds and
D_A and D_B are the durations of Bond *A* and Bond *B*.

Suppose the total value of the above portfolio is RM10 million and its duration is say 2.5 years. Then, in immunizing the bond portfolio to interest rate risk, the manager has to create a liability equivalent to RM10 million and with duration of 2.5 years. Once such a liability is created, the bond portfolio is protected because declines in the value of the portfolio due to rising interest rates will be exactly offset by the reduced value of the liability (obligation). Since the bond portfolio (asset) and the liability created both equaled RM10 million and had the same duration, going by Equation 6.3 earlier, both will experience the same diminution in value.

Box 6.4. Cagamas: Malaysia's National Mortgage Corporation

Cagamas Berhad, which is essentially the National Mortgage Corporation, is an important player in Malaysia's bond and *sukuk* markets. Cagamas issues debt securities, known as Cagamas bonds for conventional and *sukuk* for Islamic, to fund its purchase of housing loans from commercial banks. Established in 1986 at the initiative of Bank Negara Malaysia, Cagasmas is tasked with promoting the secondary market in mortgages. It does this by purchasing housing loans from domestic banks and other government entities and securitizing these loans as collateral for the bonds it issues. Cagamas therefore plays the very essential role of providing liquidity to the banks, creating and sustaining a secondary market for mortgages and stimulating growth of the bond market by its issuance of credit-enhanced papers. Since its establishment, Cagamas has been a resounding success. Its papers are very popular among investors while providing a means of liquefying long-term loans at low cost for banks. Cagamas began issuing *sukuk* in 1994, its maiden *sukuk* being the *Senadat Mudarabah*. In 2004, its *sukuk* were based on *bay al-bithaman ajil* (BBA). The fact that funds received from Cagamas are not subject to the statutory reserve and liquidity requirements of banks makes it a popular funding alternative for banks. Society benefits by way of increased availability of housing loans. In later years, Cagamas has innovated new *sukuk* structures such as ALIm, a structure combining *ijarah* and commodity *murabahah* and 51% tangible assets qualifying the *sukuk* for secondary market trading.

6.10 Risk Associated with Bonds

Like other financial assets, bonds are subject to risks. We know from the above discussion that bonds with higher risk will have a lower rating, which implies a higher required yield. However, where do bond risks come from? While there are numerous potential sources of risk, the four key sources are: (i) *credit/default risk,* (ii) *liquidity risk,* (iii) *inflation risk*, and (iv) *interest rate risk*. Since we have already discussed interest rate risk, we will discuss the other three risks.

Credit or default risk refers to the risk of non-repayment. Credit risk is a key criterion in the credit rating process (see box on Bond Ratings). As a bond is essentially an IOU, the ability of the bond-issuer to repay principal and coupons is key to valuation. When a default has happened on a bond, the subsequent cash flows are lost. Capital loss, however, can happen even without a default or bankruptcy. Mere news that an issuer is in financial distress would be sufficient to cause big reductions in the bond's value. Periods of crisis can heighten risk aversion. Companies perceived to be in difficulty would see a big sell-off in its papers. A heightened sense of risk aversion could mean that institutions with short-term debt paper may not be able to "roll them over". This is exactly what happened to Bear Stearns and other financial institutions during the recent subprime-induced financial crisis.

Liquidity risk refers to risk that arises from thin or illiquid trading. When an asset is thinly traded, getting in and out of such an asset may be difficult. If one wishes to quickly convert such asset to cash, one would have to give a discount on the price. This price cut is a capital loss and therefore liquidity risk. Another way by which liquidity can contribute to risk is by way of increased volatility. There is ample empirical evidence to show that assets that are thinly traded tend to have higher volatility of prices. This higher volatility translates into higher required risk premium.

Inflation risk refers to risk arising from the loss in purchasing power as a result of inflation. When inflation is factored in, the present value of future cash flows would be lower. This effect can be very substantial on long-dated fixed rate instruments. When there is inflation, the nominal discount rate (or required return) would have to rise by the rate of inflation. Since the numerators which constitute the coupon and face value is unchanged, the present value falls. This reduction in value would be larger for longer-dated instruments. In highly inflationary macro-environments or sovereign bonds issued by countries experiencing high inflation rates, the required increase in premium to compensate for the inflation risk can be substantial.

In addition to the above four common sources of risk for bonds, there are other potential sources of risk. For example, when investing in foreign-issued bonds, risks such as political risk, regulatory risk, and especially exchange rate risk, would be considerations. We examine exchange rate risk in detail in Chapter 13.

6.11 Types of Bonds

Bonds, like other financial assets, come in several varieties. We examine below some of the main types of bonds.

Convertible Bonds are bonds that can be converted to a predetermined number of the issuing company's common stock at maturity. The conversion ratio stated in the bond would determine the number of stocks that could be redeemed in exchange for the bond. At maturity, the holder of the convertible bond can choose to either get back the face value of the bond or convert it to shares. Since conversion to shares will only occur if the value of the shares is higher than the redemption (face) value, the convertible bond effectively provides an additional avenue for profit, i.e., an embedded call option. Given this advantage, relative to an ordinary (straight) bond, convertible bonds would command a higher price relative to straight bonds. This implies that the required return (YTM) on a convertible bond would be lower than that of an equivalent straight bond.

Callable Bonds are bonds that can be called for redemption prior to maturity. In this case, the issuer gets the option to recall the bond earlier. An issuer would want to redeem a bond early if interest rates have fallen. For example, suppose a company had issued a bond two years ago at 10% annual coupon in order to be able to sell at par. Currently, given lower interest rates, the company could issue the same bonds at say 8% annual coupon. However, unless the earlier bonds were callable bonds, the company cannot do anything to take advantage of lower interest rates. Had the earlier bonds been callable ones, the company could now issue eight-year, 8% annual coupon bonds, and use the proceeds to redeem the 10% coupon bonds issued earlier. By doing so, the issuer is effectively *refinancing* a 10% loan into an 8% one.

As the benefit of the "call option" in the callable bond is to the issuer and not the investor, the required YTM for a callable is usually higher than that of a similar straight bond.

Of late, there has been a new variant known as the "Putable" bond. Here, the option to redeem earlier is given to the bond-holder. Like the callable bond, the Putable bond would have a schedule of Face Values that one could get for early redemption on predetermined dates/years before maturity.

Indexed Bonds are bonds with coupon rates linked to an index. The most common indexed bond is the Indexed Inflation Bond. The inflation indexed bond provides a coupon rate that varies with the rate of inflation. The coupon rate rises by the percent of inflation as measured by the agreed upon inflation index. The basic idea behind the inflation indexed bond is to provide a guaranteed real return. Since the inflation indexed bond provides inflation protection, it is an advantage to the stakeholder. Thus, relative to similar straight bond, inflation indexed bonds provide an advantage to bondholders. Given this, the required YTM for an indexed bond would obviously be lower than that of a straight bond with the same maturity and risk class.

Collaterized Bonds are bonds with underlying collateral. For example, the issuer of a collateralized bond pledges an asset and/or a building as collateral for the bond. These bonds are also often known as mortgage bonds or secured bonds. They allow bond-holders to foreclose on the collateralized asset in the event of a default. Given this added protection to bond-holders, the required YTM for a collateralized bond would be *lower* than that of a straight bond with no collateral.

Floating Rate Bonds are bonds with coupon rates that are not fixed but floating according to a reference interest rate. For example, a 10-year bond with semi-annual coupon rates referenced on three-month LIBOR (the three-month LIBOR is the interbank money market rate in London). The three-month LIBOR rate that prevails at the time of coupon payment would be used to determine the coupon amount. As interest rates as measured by the three-month LIBOR rise, the coupon paid by the bond rises.

The floating rate bond would have a coupon quoted as follows, assuming the reference interest rate is the three-month LIBOR:

Coupon = three-month LIBOR + 2%

The floating rate bond is particularly useful to investors who want to hedge interest rate risk. Since the coupon rate is reflective of prevailing interest rates, there is minimal interest rate risk associated with the bond. The duration of such bond would essentially be six months (as the reset period is the semi-annual period between coupon payments). Though the interest rate risk for such bonds is low, the required YTM relative to a straight bond with fixed coupon would depend on expected future interest rates. If interest rates are expected to rise, the required YTM would be lower, vice versa if rates are expected to fall.

In addition to floating rate bonds, there are *inverse floaters*. An inverse floater is a bond whose coupon payment varies inversely with reference interest rates. That is, for example, when the LIBOR increases, the inverse floater pays a lower coupon. On the other hand, when LIBOR reduces, the inverse floater pays higher coupon. The inverse floater can be means by which an investor with floating rate exposure can hedge himself. Assuming the three-month LIBOR is the reference rate, an inverse floater would have coupon quoted as follows;

Coupon = 10% – three-month LIBOR

Given such a quotation, the percentage coupon rate will increase as the three-month LIBOR decreases and vice versa.

Zero-Coupon Bonds are essentially bonds that do not pay any coupon. Investment in a zero-coupon bond or zeros, provides a single payoff at maturity — the face value. Since there are no interim cash flows (coupons), the present value of the zero-coupon bond is simply the present value of the face value to be received at maturity. Thus, the zero-coupon bond will always sell at a discount to face value. It is for this reason that the zero is often known as Original Issue Discount (OID). The cash-flow diagram for a 10-year zero-coupon bond with RM1,000 face value would be as follows:

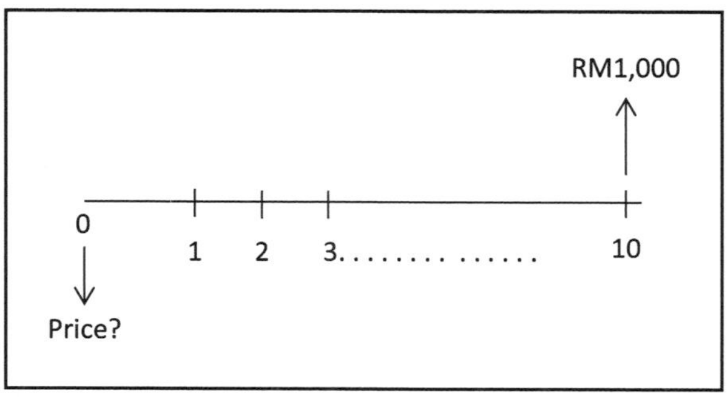

To determine the correct price of the bond, we simply find the present value of the RM1,000 due in Year 10 using the appropriate required yield given the risk class of the bond.

The holder of a zero-coupon bond would, by definition, receive no coupon yield. His returns would come entirely from capital gains, i.e., the increase in the price of the bond over time as it approaches maturity. As such, changes in the interest rate environment would affect the zero-coupon bond just as it does coupon bonds. And, as in the case of coupon bonds, the investor who buys the zero and holds it to maturity would lock in the YTM as annual return.

Given our discussion earlier about duration, it should be obvious that since the zero-coupon bond has no interim cash flows, its duration will simply equal its maturity. Relative to a coupon bond of the same maturity and risk class, the zero-coupon bond would have longer maturity.

The popularity of the zero-coupon bond in the US and other developed markets lies in the tax advantage it provides. Since zero-coupon bonds only have capital gains and no coupon yield, the tax applicable would only be the tax on capital gains, which is a much lower and flat rate relative to coupons which would be taxed at the bond-holders' tax bracket. Because the overall tax incidence is lower, zero-coupon bonds provide higher after tax yields. This has been a major contributory factor to the popularity of zero-coupon bonds in the US.

***Coupon stripping and zero-coupon bonds*:** In view of the huge popularity of zero-coupon bonds and its insufficient issuance by the US government, a number of US investment banks do what is known as coupon stripping to meet demand. The investment banks buy large amounts of coupon bonds issued by the US government and use them as the "collateral" for issuing new bonds. The basic idea is to strip the coupon portion of the coupon — effectively rendering it a zero-coupon bond. The coupon portion becomes an annuity that pays an amount every year equal to the coupon. Thus, two new bonds are issued using the original coupon bond as underlying asset.

Box 6.5. Replication and Arbitrage

The replication principle is often used to value an asset. Following its first use in the pricing of Options, it has been used extensively in financial engineering. The replication principle is based on the fact that, *the value of an asset is equal to the sum of its parts.* Thus, to value a *"big" complicated asset*; we could value it *by valuing smaller* assets which when put together would provide the same cash-flow as the *"big"* complicated asset. Valuation of an asset by way of replication can be thought of as yet another way to value an asset in addition to computing the present value of the asset's future cash flows. Since an asset's value is dependent on the value of its cash flows, the replication principal is based on the logic that if it will cost $*X*, to replicate the cash flows of an asset, then the correct value of the asset is equal to $*X*. Aside from enabling one to value an asset, the replication principal has a huge implication. It implies that if two different assets with the same risk profile and cash flows have different market prices, there is mispricing and arbitrage is possible. In efficient markets with knowledgeable participants, the possibility of arbitrage would ensure that "correct prices" prevail. We see below a simple example of how the replication principal could be used to value a coupon bond.

Suppose we want to value a three-year 10% coupon bond, using a replication strategy.

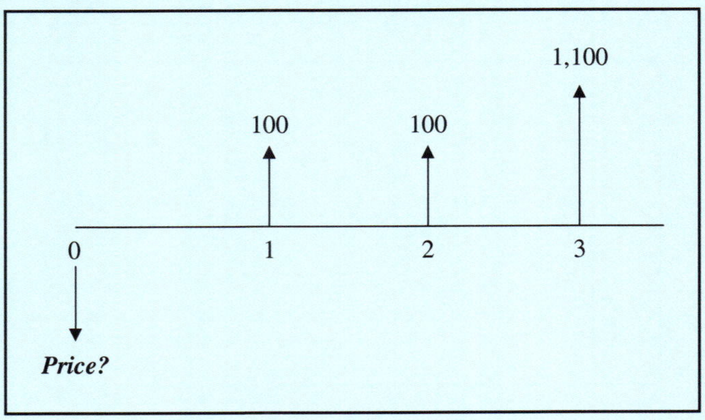

One way to find the correct present value (PV) of the above bond is to get the *market prices* of "smaller" assets *of equal risk* which when put together would provide the exact replica of cash flows. Suppose there are zero-coupon bonds of the

(*Continued*)

Box 6.5. (*Continued*)

same risk class but of different maturities being traded, then to replicate the above bond's cash flow, we would need three zeros with one-, two-, and three-year maturities.

(i) A zero-coupon bond with FV of RM100 maturing one year from now.
(ii) A zero-coupon bond with FV of RM100 maturing two years from now.
(iii) A zero-coupon bond with FV of RM100 maturing three years from now.

(1)

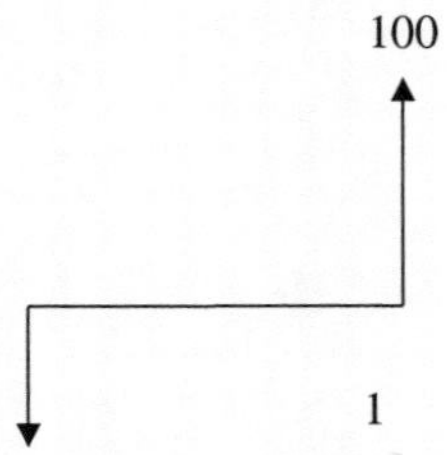

Find PV of the zero-coupon bond

(2)

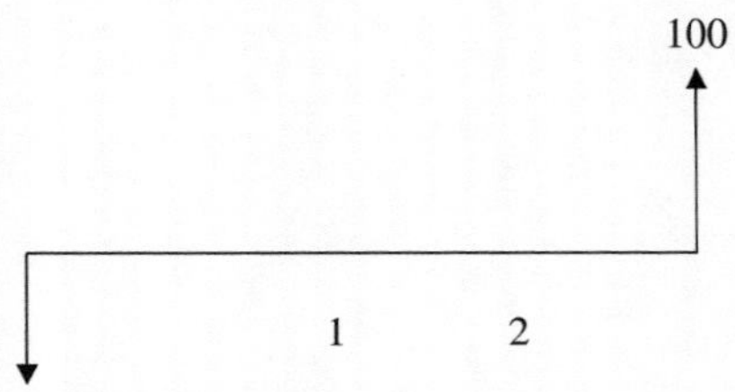

Again find PV of this zero.

(3)

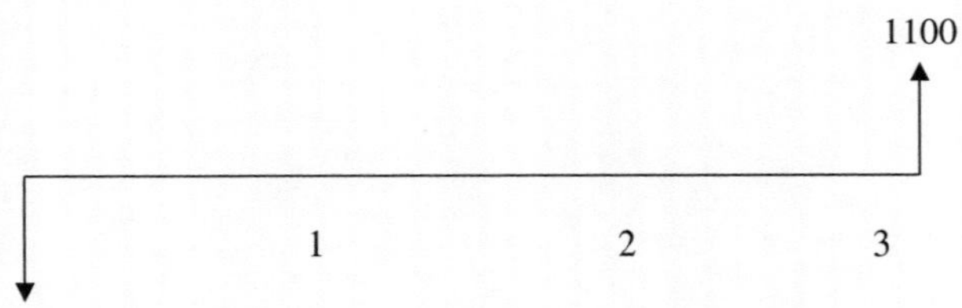

PV of this Zero

Since the first three-year 10% bond could be replicated by the three zero-value bonds, it must follow, that the ***total*** price of the three zeros must be the "correct" price of the three-year 10% bond.

Arbitrage

What if the prevailing market price of the three-year 10% bond is *not equal* to the total price of three zeros? Then, we have an arbitrage opportunity. To see how the mispricing can be arbitraged, we work through the following example.

Suppose the prevailing price of the three-year 10% bond is RM1,050.00 but the total market price of the three zeros computed above is $1,070.00. Clearly, there is mispricing. Either the coupon bond is *undervalued* relative to the zeros or the zeros are *overvalued* relative to the coupon bond. To the arbitrageur, what matters is relative mispricing. Once there is mispricing, and the amount of mispricing is larger than the transaction costs involved, it is worthwhile for the arbitrageur to undertake the arbitrage. The arbitrage strategy is straightforward. One should always buy (long) the undervalued asset while simultaneously sell (short) the overvalued asset. By doing so, the arbitrageur locks-in the mispriced amount as his profit. The simultaneity of the transaction also ensures that the arbitrage will be riskless. The riskless nature of the arbitrage and the locked-in profit can be seen from the computation below.

(*Continued*)

Box 6.5. (*Continued*)
Cash flows of the Arbitrage Transaction

Action/ Strategy	Now	1 year from now	2 years	3 years
Buy three-year 10% bond	**–1,050**	**+100**	**+100**	**+1,100**
Short				
1 yr. $100 FV Zero		**–100**		
2 yr. $100 FV Zero			**–100**	
3 yr. $100 FV Zero				**–100**
Total Short Proceeds	**+1,070**			
Net CF	**20**	**0**	**0**	**0**

The offsetting cash flows of the arbitrage.

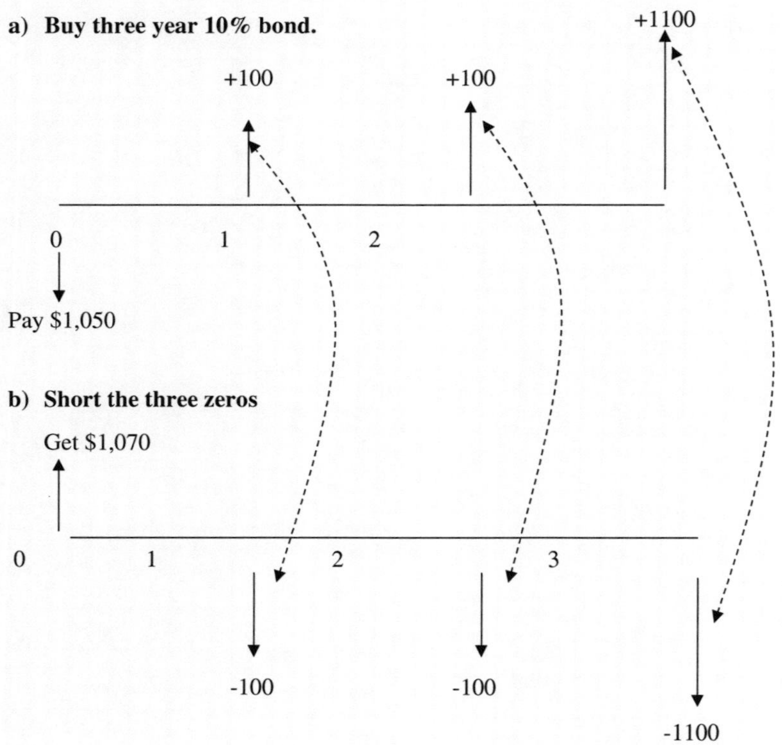

Notice from the table and the diagram the exact offsetting nature of all future cash flows. For example, the arbitrageur uses RM100 received from the first coupon to pay for the redemption of the one-year zero-coupon bond. Thus, by putting in place the transactions today, the arbitrageur makes an immediate profit of RM20 but has no other outlays in the future. He simply meets the obligation on the zeros from the proceeds of the coupon bond that he has gone long (bought).

6.12 Bond Ratings

A bond's rating can be thought of as a credit rating agency's (CRA) opinion about an issuer's ability to repay/ service the bond as scheduled. Since creditworthiness is the key criterion being examined, CRAs emphasize financial analysis. A wide-ranging set of financial ratios are analyzed to determine the issuing company's credit

Table 6.5. Moody's versus Standard & Poor's Bond Ratings.

Bond Rating			
Moody's	Standard and Poor's	Grade	Risks
Aaa	AAA	Investment, Highest Quality	Lowest Risk
Aa	AA	Investment, Very High Quality	Low Risk
A	A	Investment, High Quality	Low Risk
Baa	BBB	Minimum Investment Grade	Medium Risk
Ba	BB	Junk, Speculative	High Risk
B	B	Junk, Very Speculative	Higher Risk
Caa	CCC	Junk, Default Possible	Higher Risk
Ca	CC	Junk, Default Probable	Extreme Risk
C	D	Junk, in Actual or Imminent Default	Highest Risk

Source: www.investopedia.com.

rating. Most important would be the company's leverage (gearing), profitability, and turnover ratios. This analysis is then translated to a predetermined rating scale. Companies with the best fundamentals receive the highest rating. As the business environment is dynamic, a company's fundamentals could change over time.

As such, credit rating analysis is not a one-off affair; rather, it is a continuous process with periodic reviews. Credit raters typically review the companies they have rated at least once a year, often semi-annually or quarterly. An initial rating on a bond can subsequently be revised upwards or downwards. The downgrading of a bond's rating is often unpleasant. The issuer will undoubtedly be upset with the downgrade since it effectively means that the company's cost of funds will rise. Given this unpleasantness, CRAs have been slow to downgrade bonds. This slowness has in turn been the source of criticism against CRAs. Following the US financial crisis, CRAs like Moodys and Standard & Poor's have come under heavy criticism for having been slow in downgrading the bonds and structured products that they had rated. Aside from slowness, the CRAs have been accused of lacking transparency.

Some of the criticisms may be valid, given the fact there could be extensive conflict of interests in the relationship between the rater and the rated. While a CRA is supposed to be independent and provide its evaluation based strictly on its analysis, the fact remains that it receives payment from the rate for the rating. Rates therefore can "shop" around for a favorable evaluation. CRAs, given the competitive environment in which they operate, may not be as detached and clinical as they are supposed to be.

In Malaysia, there are two CRAs: (i) Rating Agency of Malaysia (RAM) and (ii) Malaysia Rating Corporation (MARC). Globally, the largest raters are Moody's and Standard & Poor's. A summary of the ratings is shown below.

6.13 Ratings and Yield/Credit Spreads

Figure 6.3 shows what credit rating differences mean in terms of required yields. It shows the indicative credit spreads of Malaysian corporate bonds against the benchmark five-year MGS (Malaysian government Security). There are two important issues to note: (i) the (1) The spread is larger the lower the quality of the paper; and (ii) the. (2) The size of the spread changes during times of turbulence, induced by interest rate changes. The period between August 2008 and 2009 is one such period. This has to do with flight to quality. When times are bad, investors get out of riskier instruments and move into safer ones, thereby driving the yield difference further apart.

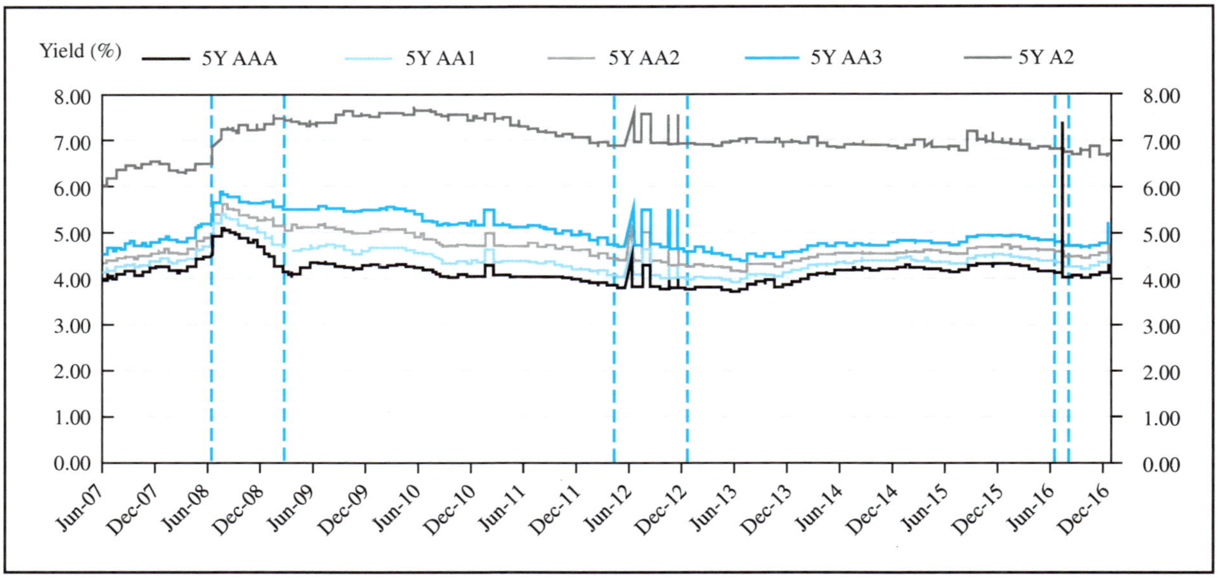

Figure 6.3. Indicative Credit Spread Year 2007–2019

Source: Thomson Reuters Eikon.

Summary

Bonds are the most commonly traded debt instruments and are typically issued to raise long-term debt financing. They are traded in secondary markets. As debt instruments, bonds have face value, fixed maturity, and coupon payments. Given a required return, bonds can be priced using discounted cash flow techniques. The return from investing in a bond come from two sources: coupon yield and capital gains. Given a bond's market price and its other features, the bond's yield to maturity (YTM) can be determined. YTM is the percentage annual return that one can get from buying and holding the bond to maturity. The required return for a bond can be determined from the yield curve. The yield curve varies by risk class. A bond's rating would determine the yield curve applicable to price the bond.

Interest rates and bond prices are negatively correlated. As interest rates rise, bond prices reduce and vice versa. The sensitivity of a bond's price to interest rate changes depends on its duration; the longer a bond's duration, the more sensitive it would be to interest rate changes. Aside from interest rate risk, bonds can be subject to other risks like default risk, liquidity risk, inflation risk, etc. The more risks associated with a bond, the higher the required risk premium will be. This will imply a higher required return for the bond and *ceterus paribus*, a lower bond value. The types and magnitude of a bond's risk are reflected in its credit rating.

Questions and Problems

1. Identify some of the key differences between bank borrowing and bond issuance.
2. Explain some of the basic features of a bond. Why is there a necessity for a face value?
3. A zero-coupon bond with seven years to maturity has a face value of RM1,000 and a required yield of 8.5%, what would be its appropriate price today?
4. If the bond in Question 3 above has a 10% coupon paid annually, what would its price be if all other features and yield are the same? Is the bond selling at a premium or discount to face value? Why is this so? (Hint: Relate coupon to YTM).
5. Illustrate how an increase in the risk of an issuing company would translate into a lower bond price.
6. Using a yield curve, show how an increase in interest rates could cause a decline in a bond's price.
7. A bond with two years to maturity is selling at RM1056.40. Its face value is RM1,000 and the coupon is 10% annualized.

   (a) Determine the bond's YTM assuming interest rates are unchanged.
   (b) Plot the likely price trajectory until maturity.
   (c) Why would a rationale investor want to invest in a bond that is likely to have negative capital gains?

8. Calculate the duration of 8% coupon bond with two years to maturity, a RM1,000 face value, and a required YTM of 10%.
9. Calculate the duration of the following bonds:

   (a) A zero-coupon bond with RM1,000 face value, six years left to maturity and required YTM of 8%
   (b) Perpetuity with a required YTM of 6%

10. Identify the four key risks associated with bonds. Describe each risk and differentiate among them.
11. A 10-year corporate issue zero-coupon bond with RM1,000 face value is selling for RM590. Assuming the required yield for the bond is 7.5%, determine whether the bond is mispriced.
12. Suppose another zero-coupon bond with the same features and risk class is selling for RM540:

   (a) Determine if there is mispricing.
   (b) Briefly outline the arbitrage strategy using the two zeros.

13. You are provided the following information about three bonds, A, B, and C.

	A	B	C
Maturity	3 years	10 years	7 years
Coupon (Annual)	6 %	10%	8%
Face Value (RM)	1,000	1,000	1,000
YTM	8%	12%	10%

   (a) Given the information above, determine their correct prices.
   (b) If the actual market prices for the bonds were as follows:

   A = RM976.40
   B = RM887
   C = RM884
   Derive the actual yield for each bond.

   (c) Assuming all three bonds belong to the same risk class, plot the relative position of each bond on the yield curve.

14. Bond X is a 8% coupon bond with 15-year maturity that is selling at par. Bond Y also has 8% coupon and 15 years to maturity but is selling below par. Which of the bonds above has a higher duration? Explain.
15. A bond fund manager has to decide between two alternative bond portfolios. Portfolio X has duration of 6.25 years. Portfolio Y has duration of 3.5 years. Given the current outlook for interest rates, which portfolio would you recommend for him? Explain why.

Bibliography

Bodie, Z., A. Kane and A. Marcus (2014). *Investments*, 10th Edn. (McGraw Hill Education, New York).
Cecchetti, S. G. (2014). *Money, Banking and Financial Markets*, 4th Edn. (McGraw Hill/Irwin, New York).
Mishkin, F. S. (2015). *The Economics of Money, Banking and Financial Markets*, 11th Edn. (Pearson Education, Boston, MA).
Obiyathulla, I. B. (2017). *Financial Derivatives: Markets & Applications in Malaysia* (McGraw Hill Education, Malaysia).
Thomson Reuters Eikon

Websites

www.investopedia.com
www.bnm.gov.my
www.secom.gov.my
https://asianbondsonline.adb.org/malaysia/data/bondmarket.php?code=LCY_Bond_Market

Endnotes

1. Source: Asian Bonds Online ADB. https://asianbondsonline.adb.org/malaysia/data/bondmarket.php?code=LCY_Bond_Market
2. In economies where interest rates are not influenced by the central banks, interest rates are determined according to the supply and demand for loanable funds. They are also determined by the supply of savings and demand for investment. An increase in demand for loanable funds or for investment would raise interest rates. An increase in supply of loanable funds or savings would reduce interest rates. In an open economy, interest rates could be influenced by interest rates abroad.
3. The above duration is called Macaulay duration, to be distinguished from modified duration. The latter is defined as: Modified duration = Macaulay duration/(1+ y).

Chapter 7

SUKUK AND *SUKUK* MARKETS

Topics in this Chapter

7.1. What are *Sukuk*?
7.2. *Sukuk* Fundamentals
7.3. Underlying Islamic Contracts for *Sukuk*
7.4. *Sukuk* Structures
7.5. *Sukuk* Players
7.6. Risk Associated with Investing in *Sukuk*
7.7. *Sukuk* in Malaysia *Sukuk* in Malaysia: Growth and Evolution
7.8. Underlying Asset and the Structuring and Pricing of *Sukuk*

Chapter Objective

This chapter is designed to introduce students to *sukuk* and expose them to the many issues related to the design and trading of *sukuk*. On completing this chapter, you should have a good understanding of *sukuk*, their structures, and underlying contracts. You should also have a good appreciation of the issues surrounding the design and trading of *sukuk*.

Key Terms		
asset-backed security (ABS)	*maslahah*	*salam*
Black Scholes Option Pricing Model (BSOPM)	micro-risk	sale-purchase agreement
Contingent Claims Analysis (CCA)	MTFCS	securitization
embedded call option	*mudarabah*	*Shari'ah* compliance risk
exotic *sukuk* structure	*murabaha*	special purpose vehicle (SPV)
foreign exchange risk	opportunity cost	*sukuk* structure
ibra (rebate)	originator	*sukuk*-holder
investment certificate	present value	trustee
macro-risk	put option	

7.1 What are *Sukuk*?

Sukuk, which is plural for *sakk*, refers to an investment certificate. It could also mean a trustee certificate. *Sukuk*, it appears, have been used extensively by Muslims in the Middle Ages as papers denoting financial obligations from commercial activities. Some have argued that the contemporary term "cheque" has its origins in the word *sakk*. In his famous treatise, *al-Muwatta*, Imam Malik ibn Anas describes the use of *sakk* by the Ummayad government. *Sakk* was used as partial payment to soldiers and government servants. The *sakk*, which came to be known as "grain permits", entitled holders to receive a predetermined amount of commodities from the state treasury on the maturity date. Since the *sakk* represented a state obligation, they were often traded/exchanged among *sukuk* holders.[1] *Sukuk* have therefore been a tradable instrument in Muslim societies in times past. Bahrain-based Accounting and Auditing Organisation for Islamic Financial Institutions (AAOIFI) defines *sukuk* as "certificates of equal value representing undivided shares in ownership of tangible assets, usufruct and services or (in the ownership of) the assets of particular projects or special investment activity".

Being a fund-raising product, *sukuk* have often been referred to as "Islamic bonds" and subjected to comparison with conventional bonds. While the objective of a *sukuk* issuance may be the same as that of a bond, i.e., to raise financing, there are many differences between the two instruments. To begin with, one has to keep in mind that a bond is an instrument that evidences debt of the issuer to bond-holders. *Sukuk*, on the other hand, represent an undivided ownership right of the underlying asset of the *sukuk*. An undivided ownership right is very much like equity, however, *sukuk* being terminal, whereas equity is perpetual, places it as a hybrid instrument. Furthermore, while *Shari'ah* allows trade financing, there is little room for "debt" financing in Islamic finance. The only acceptable debt there is in Islam, is *qard al-hasan*, which is a benevolent loan, i.e., one which does not have a compulsion on repayment. Given this, while *sukuk* are intended to raise external financing just like bonds, their operational, legal, and regulatory frameworks are vastly different. We will address some of these differences later.

Sukuk are perhaps the most successful and most visible Islamic finance product today. Given the range and international diversity of *sukuk* issuers, it is obvious that *sukuk* have become an internationally accepted Islamic finance product. Malaysia, which used to be the world's largest originator of *sukuk*, has now been overtaken by Saudi Arabia and the Gulf states. Figure 7.1 shows the growth in global *sukuk* issuance over the 16-year period

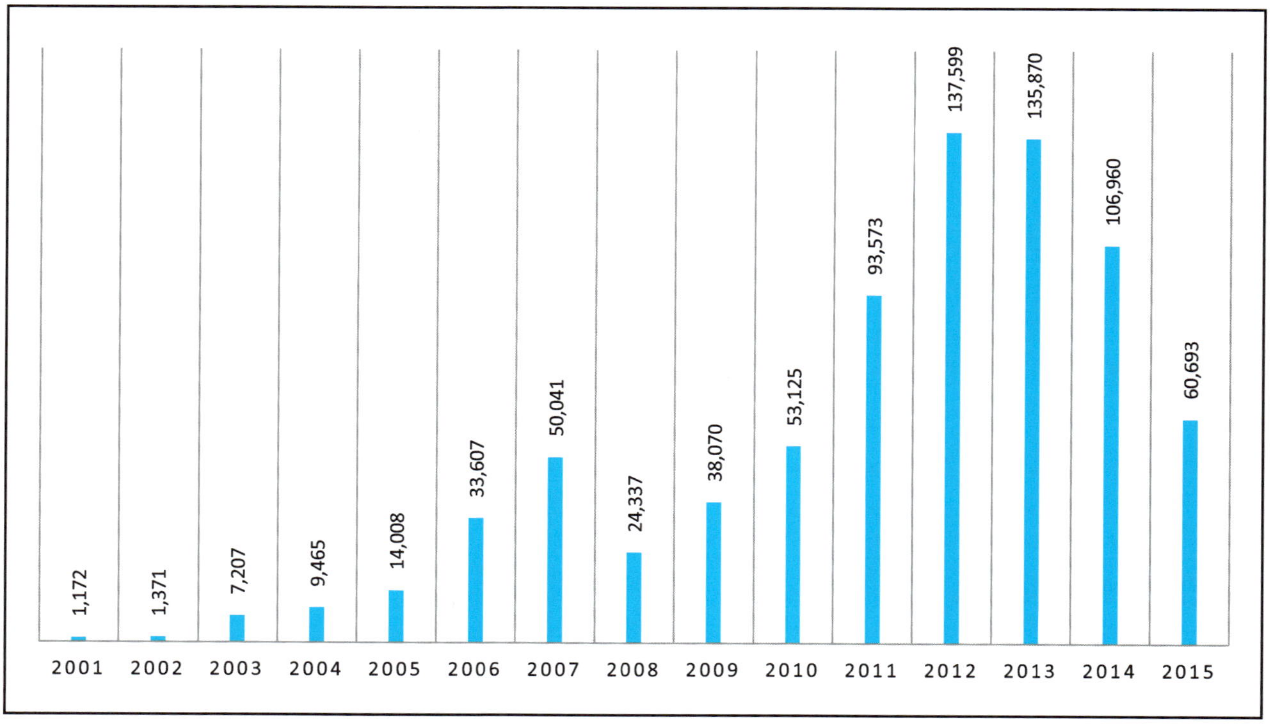

Figure 7.1. Global *Sukuk* Issuances from 2001 to 2015 (US$ Billions).

Source: IIFM 2016 *Sukuk* Report.

from 2001–2015. The exponential growth seen in *sukuk* issuance from 2001 was first interrupted in 2008 with the onset of the US subprime-induced Global Financial Crisis (GFC). Following recovery, growth in *sukuk* issuance was again strong until 2012 and 2013. The poorer showing in the last two years is attributable, to the massive decline in oil prices. Figure 7.2 shows *sukuk* issuance by currency over the same period.

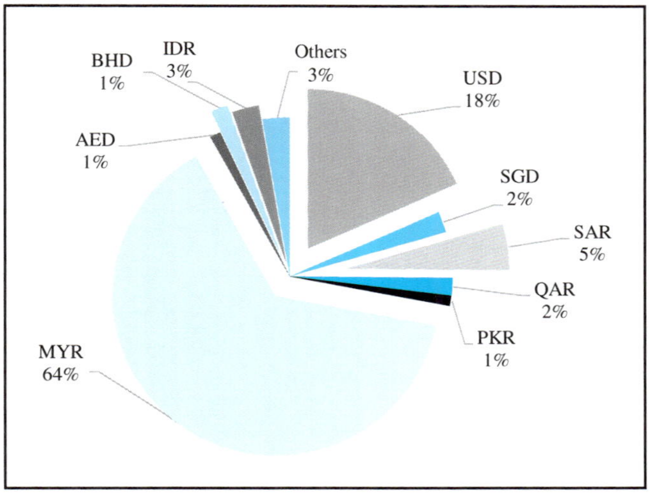

Figure 7.2. Global *sukuk* Issuance by Currency, All Tenors (2001–2015).

Source: IIFM 2016 Report and Author's Compilation.

As Figure 7.2 shows, Malaysia's dominance until recently in *sukuk* issuance is evidenced by the 64% of *sukuk* outstanding that is denominated in the Malaysian Ringgit (MYR). The next closest currency of issuance is the US Dollar (US$). Most sovereign issuance of *sukuk* tend to be denominated in US$ as they are often listed in exchanges in London, Luxembourg, Dublin, and the like. US$ denomination obviously reduces the currency risk to international investors.

7.2 *Sukuk* Fundamentals

As an Islamic finance product, there are certain underlying *Shari'ah* principles that *sukuk* must comply with. These are in addition to the basic requirement that all Islamic finance products and transactions must be free of *riba, gharar, rishwah, masyir*, and *jahl*. Where *sukuk* are concerned, the additional requirements are as follows:

(i) All funds raised through the *sukuk* issuance must only be used for *halal* or *Shari'ah*-compliant activities.
(ii) Where the funds raised are used to finance needed tangible assets, specificity of assets is important. That is, the asset(s) being financed should be clearly identified.
(iii) Income received by *sukuk*-holders (investors) must be derived from the cash flows generated by the underlying asset, not from other sources external to the asset.
(iv) *Sukuk*-holders have a right to the ownership of the underlying asset and its cash flows (viewed from this perspective, a *sukuk* is essentially hybrid equity).
(v) There should be clear and transparent specification of rights and obligations of all parties to the transaction, in particular the originator (*mudarib*) and *sukuk*-holders.
(vi) As with all other Islamic finance instruments, there should be no fixity of returns.

Given the above ground rules, it is easy to see why *sukuk* would have a risk-return profile very different from that of conventional bonds. First, unlike bonds, there will be no fixed coupon payments. Second, the redemption amount at maturity need not be fixed but may be made contingent upon the asset's performance. Third, unlike conventional debt, which is detached from the earnings performance of the issuer, a *sukuk*-holder's returns are derived from cash flows/earnings generated by the asset underlying the *sukuk*. Whereas a bond provides the same coupon rate, regardless of the issuer's earnings over the period, and bond-holders can foreclose on the issuing entity if it fails to pay the predetermined coupons on time, *sukuk*-holders' returns will depend on underlying asset's returns. Even if the *sukuk*-issuing firm performs well, if the underlying asset performs poorly, *sukuk*-holders will receive low or no returns. Given these differences, while the risk profile of a conventional bond is dependent on the issuer, a *sukuk's* risk profile would be dependent on its underlying asset/project rather than the issuer. Table 7.1 outlines some of the key differences between conventional bonds and *sukuk*.

Table 7.1. Key Differences Between Conventional Bonds and *Sukuk*.

Item	Conventional Bond	*Sukuk*
Tenor	Short-, Medium- and Long-Term	Short- and Medium-Term (usually ≤ 5 years)
Financing Category	Debt	Not debt but ownership of specific asset and its cash flows
Underlying	Not necessary, unless collateralized	Necessary underlying asset, usually tangible asset
Claim	Fixed in time and amount	Ownership claim on specific asset and its cash flows
Pricing	Depends on rating, yield environment, and demand (book building)	Use of indicative yields — benchmarked on reference rates
Total returns	Fixed Income (known/predetermined cash flows)	No guarantee in returns
Funding purpose	Unrestricted	Restricted for use only in *Shari'ah*-compliant assets and in a predetermined manner.

7.2.1 *Underlying Assets and Other Requirements for Sukuk*

All *sukuk* by definition must have an asset that is tangible. Although some *fuqaha* allow for a portion of the asset to be in intangible form, all jurists require that there be an underlying asset. This is an important differentiating feature of Islamic finance and one that can be considered a source of strength since the requirement for an underlying asset precludes the possibility of excessive leverage. While an underlying asset is indeed necessary for a *sukuk*, not all assets qualify to be the underlying. According to the *Fiqh* Academy (Jeddah) in its ruling No. 5, 1998, on *sukuk* underlying, any *halal* asset or collection of assets can be the underlying for a note or *sukuk*. Such *sukuk* can also be sold (traded) provided that the underlying asset(s) consists mainly of tangible physical assets with a minimal if any part of it being cash and/or interpersonal debts.

Though the *Fiqh* Academy's rulings are not binding but advisory, the above ruling would inhibit the securitization of receivables as the underlying asset for a *sukuk* issuance. Securitization is the process of pooling assets (usually debt instruments) and then issuing a new asset which is backed by the pooled assets. All assets that have a cash flow can be securitized. The resulting instrument from a securitization process is often referred to as an Asset-Backed Security (ABS). In Malaysia, however, the SAC of the Securities Commission accepts the principle of *bay' al-dayn*, which is the trading of debt. This acceptance is based on the principle of *maslahah*, or public interest. The acceptance of *bay al-dayn* has meant that, in Malaysia, it is possible to securitize a *sukuk* based on receivables. Such *sukuk* are essentially ABSs. We thus see in Malaysia, *mudarabah*-based *sukuk*, whose underlying is a pool of Islamic hire purchase financing. In addition to the acceptance of *bay al-dayn*, SAC has a set of guiding principles for Malaysian *sukuk* issuance/acceptability. These are:

(i) Enabling a buyer/seller to make a prior agreement on sale or purchase. That is, one or more principals of the *sukuk* transaction may make a prior agreement to sell and repurchase/buy back the asset (*Ittifaqdhimni*).

(ii) Allowing a creditor to forfeit a part of the debt when the debtor pre-pays. That is, an *ibra* (rebate) can be a *syart* (condition) of a *sukuk*. However, the *ibra* must be independent and not be factored into the pricing of the *sukuk*.

(iii) *Sukuk* originators can arrange for third-party guarantee on the capital. For example, an issuer/originator can get a bank to provide a guarantee of the face value of the *sukuk* amount. This would be particularly relevant to *musharakah/mudarabah*-type bonds.

(iv) Contracts awarded by the government or its agencies can be the underlying asset for a *sukuk*. Here, the underlying asset is obviously not a physical or tangible asset but a contractual undertaking awarded by the government to the entity originating the *sukuk*.
(v) *Sukuk* can be based on a "when-issued" basis, i.e., some form of self-registration is possible.
(vi) A floating rate mechanism can be used when determining profit rates for *sukuk* based on *bay al-bithaman ajil* (BBA), *murabaha*, and *istisna'* contracts. The *ibra* (rebate) to be used in determining profit rate.
(vii) For *sukuk* involving the sale/purchase of assets as in *ijarah*, BBA, *murabahah*, and the like, the SAC has determined that if the sale price involves a premium over market price/value, the price must not exceed 1.33 times the market price. An asset sold at a discount should not be at a price lower than 67% (0.67) of the market price. Where the market price is indeterminate, pricing can be on a "willing buyer-willing seller" basis.

7.3 Underlying Islamic Contracts for *Sukuk*

As all Islamic finance products and transactions must be based on a *Shari'ah*-compliant contract, *sukuk* are typically designed on one or more such *Shariah*-based contracts. We know from Chapter 3 that there are differences between these Islamic contracts, and it is these differences that determine their suitability for different transactions. Theoretically, a *sukuk* can be based on any *Shari'ah*-based contract. Aside from the 14 commonly used *Shari'ah* contracts, several *sukuk* are issued based on combined contracts. For example, *sukuk* structured on the *istisna–ijarah* combination is used extensively to finance infrastructure and construction projects, the *istisna* contract being in force during construction and the *ijarah* triggered once revenue is generated. The following are the commonly used underlying contracts for *sukuk*:

- *Ijarah* (lease-based transaction);
- *Murabahah* (profit mark-up sale);
- *Wakalah* (agency contract);
- *Istisna'* (progress-based arrangement — manufacturing);
- *Bay Salam* (forward sale);
- *Musharakah* (partnership, with both partners providing labor and capital); and
- *Mudarabah* (profit and loss sharing arrangement).

Of these contracts, *sukuk* based on the *musharakah* principle appear to be the most popular in Malaysia. This is followed by *ijarah*- and *mudarabah*-based *sukuk*. BBA-based *sukuk*, which were popular in the early years, have paled given the controversy surrounding its acceptance. Globally, it appears that *ijarah*-based *sukuk* are now the most popular. This global acceptance of the *ijarah sukuk* may be due to the fact that it fits the requirements for a tangible underlying asset which is clearly identifiable and has "fixed" timely payments and cash flows that are binding on the issuer. *Ijarah* with lease payments based on a floating reference rate is also possible. The popularity of *ijarah sukuk* is reflected in the fact that just about all sovereign *ijarah sukuk* have been oversubscribed. In many cases, the oversubscription has been several folds. A sovereign *sukuk*, like a sovereign bond, is one that is issued by a government. Figures 7.3(a) and 7.3(b) show global *sukuk* issuance by underlying contract for two different periods, 2001–2007 and 2013–2014. Comparing Figures 7.3(a) and 7.3(b), the evolution in contract type is evident. Three noticeable changes are evident. First, *ijarah*-based *sukuk* have increased in proportion from 27% in the first period to 42% in the latter period. Second, *salam*-based *sukuk*, which accounted for nearly half of all *sukuk* types in the 2001–2007 period have all but disappeared in 2013–2014. The third obvious feature is the huge increase in the issuance of *Wakala*-based contracts in the latter period. As will be discussed later, there are several considerations that go into the choice of underlying contract. Factors like legal requirements within a jurisdiction, tax incidence, the availability and type of underlying asset, investor preference, and market acceptance are some of the considerations.

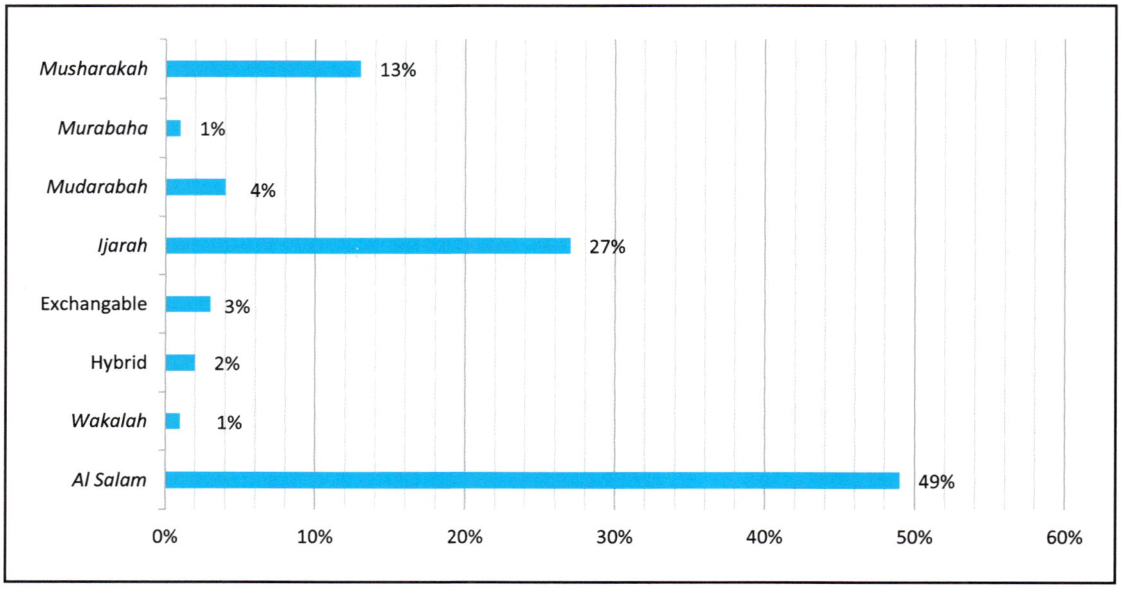

Figure 7.3 (a) International *Sukuk* Issuance by Type of Contract (2001–2007).

Source: IIFM Sukuk Report.

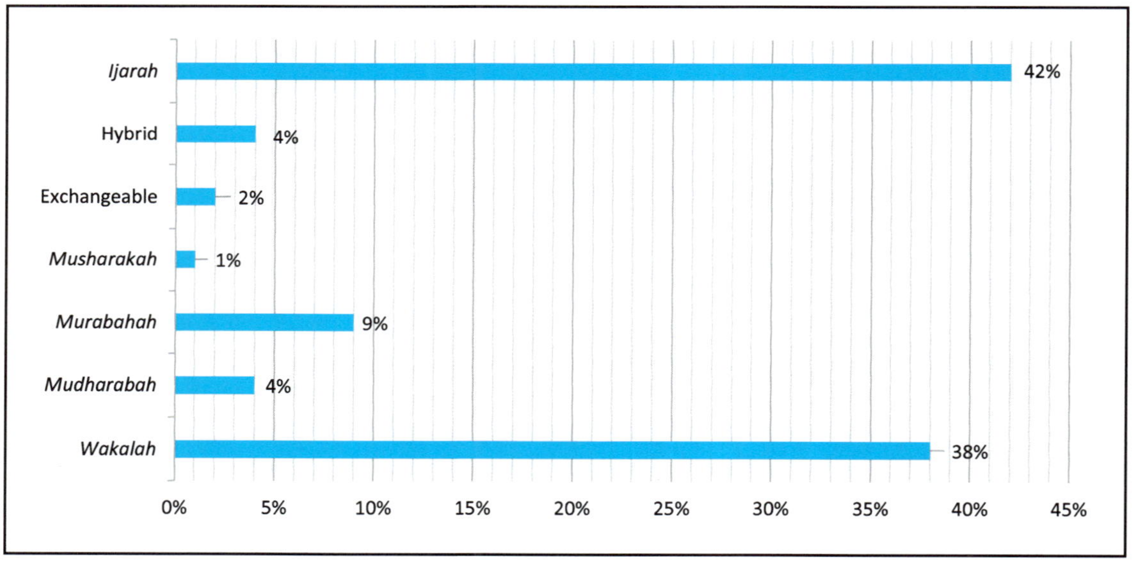

Figure 7.3 (b) International *Sukuk* Issuance by Type of Contract (2013–2014).

Source: IIFM Sukuk Report.

Figure 7.4 shows *sukuk* issuance in 2016 by sector. Where previously, the government sector (sovereign) accounted for the bulk of *sukuk* issuance, today there are a diversified range of issuers. *Sukuk*-issuers range from infrastructure companies, utilities, transportation, manufacturing and a range of other industries. Aside from evidence of the acceptance of *sukuk* as a fundraising instrument by a diverse set of players, the wide range of originators imply that diversification across industries becomes easier for *sukuk* investors. This is obviously a positive trend for *sukuk*.

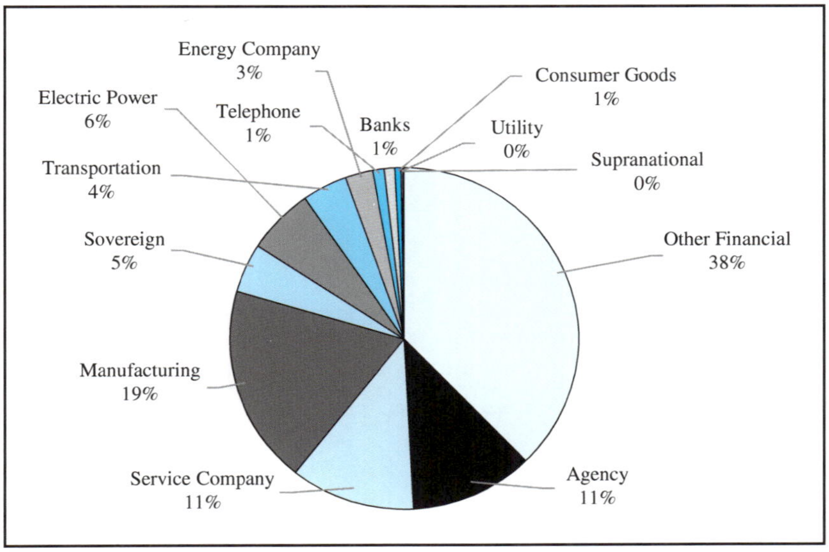

Figure 7.4. *Sukuk* Issuance by Sector, 2016.

Source: *DataStream Eikon* and Author's Compilation.

As mentioned earlier, *sukuk* could be based on more than one Islamic contract. *Sukuk* are often structured on multiple contracts in order to have a needed risk profile and/or a desired cash flow stream. For example, a real estate developer intending to build and rent condominiums could finance the development by way of an *istisna/ijarah sukuk*. The combined structure allows for flexibility within a single *sukuk*. The *istisna* contract would be in force during the period of construction. Investors in such a *sukuk* will receive little, if any, dividends during the *istisna* period. Once construction is complete and the condominiums begin to be rented out, the *istisna* contract lapses and the *ijarah* is triggered. The developer begins paying out *ijarah* payments from the rental income received. Table 7.2(a) outlines some of the key features of *sukuk* based on their underlying contracts and the resulting cash flows. Table 7.2(b) shows categorization of *sukuk* by their underlying contracts.

Table 7.2(a). *Sukuk* — Features and Cash Flow Variation by Contract.

Underlying contract	Originator (*Mudarib*)	Investor (*Sukuk*-Holder)	Interim Cash Flows (to *Sukuk*-Holders)	Cash Flow at Maturity
Ijarah (lease)	Lessee of asset; Pays lease payments	Lessor	Periodic Lease Payments	At maturity from sale of asset
***Wakalah* (Principal–agent relationship)**	Agent undertaking investment in underlying asset	Principal Owner of invested asset	Cash Flows generated by investment	Dependent on type of invested asset and/or economic life of project; No fixed return
***Bay Al-Bithaman Ajil* (sale based on deferred payments)**	Purchaser of underlying asset	Owner/seller of underlying asset	Payment of purchase price in instalments	May and may not have a final balloon payment
Mudarabah	*Mudarib* (entrepreneur in need of financing)	*Rab-ul-Mal* (provide capital)	Periodic cash flows from asset as determined by PSR	Unlikely; Final payment could simply be the last periodic payment given tenor of *mudarabah* contract

(*Continued*)

Table 7.2(a). (*Continued*)

Underlying contract	Originator (*Mudarib*)	Investor (*Sukuk*-Holder)	Interim Cash Flows (to *Sukuk*-Holders)	Cash Flow at Maturity
Salam **(Contract for goods to be delivered later — forward)**	Seller of commodity/ goods which will be delivered later	Purchaser of commodity/ goods which will be delivered later	Proceeds from sale of goods received — if there will be delivering in the interim	Usually the largest cash flows occur at maturity when delivery occurs. Cash flow is from sale proceeds
Istisna'	Purchaser of asset under construction	Financier for asset under construction	Payments from *mudarib* if any	Profit from sale of completed asset
Murabaha	Purchaser of asset	Financier of asset	Periodic payments received from *Mudarib* representing price of asset *plus* mark up	Unlikely; Final payment could simply be the last periodic payment of contract

Table 7.2(b). Categorization of *Sukuk* by their Underlying Contract.

***Sukuk* Categorization By Contracts**
Sales-Based Contracts
Salam
Murabaha
Istisna
Bay Al-Bithaman Ajil
Agency-Based Contracts
Wakalah Bi Istimar
Lease-Based Contracts
Ijarah Muntahiya Bi Tamlik (Sales-Leaseback)
Ijarah Mawsufah fi Dhimmah (Forward Lease)
Partnership-Based Contracts
Musyarakah
Mudarabah

7.4 *Sukuk* Structures

Being a structured product, a *sukuk's* design would depend on several factors. Key among these would be: (i) compliance with underlying *Shari'ah* contract(s); (ii) the needed risk profile; (iii) the desired cash flow profile (for both the originator and investor); and (iv) potential market acceptance of the *sukuk*. As a result of this multitude of factors, *sukuk* structures can vary from simple structures to very complicated ones. Generically speaking, while the underlying contractual framework may be different, most *sukuk* appear to have the following structural framework.

7.4.1 *A Generic Asset-backed Sukuk Structure*

In the generic asset-backed structure (see Figure 7.5), the *mudarib*, who is the originator (borrower), first establishes a special purpose vehicle (SPV), which is a legal entity. The SPV is legally separate and is bankruptcy remote, in that it has no part in the originator's liabilities. The originator then pledges or transfers the asset which will become the underlying asset of the *sukuk*, to the newly established SPV. The SPV, which is technically administered by external trustees, is the issuer of the *sukuk*. Since the "collateral" for the *sukuk* is the SPV's asset, the *sukuk* is an ABS. The servicing of the needed *sukuk* payments to the investors is made by the SPV from payments it receives from the *mudarib* (originator) for use of the asset (usufruct). If there is a final redemption amount on the *sukuk*, the cash flow would come from the "sale" of the underlying asset to the *mudarib*.

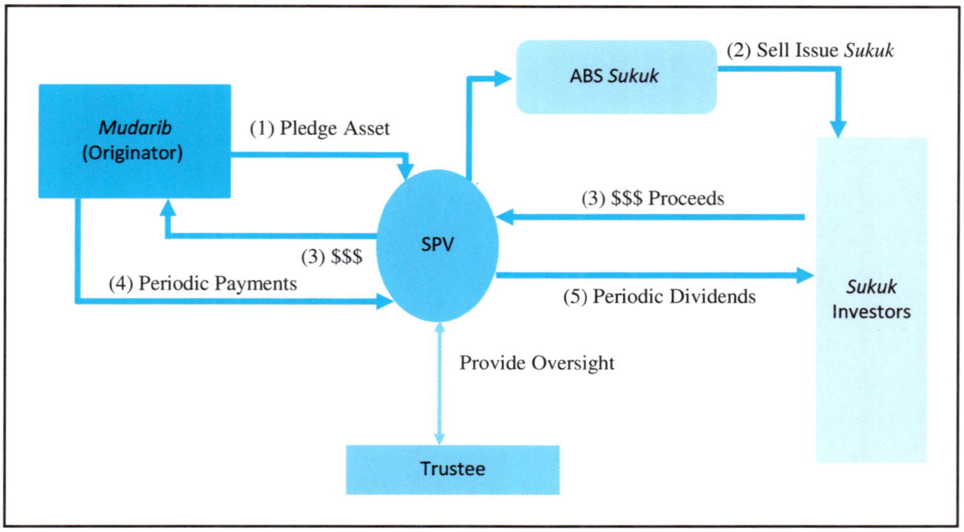

Figure 7.5. A Generic Asset-Backed *Sukuk* Structure.

Having discussed the generic ABS, we now turn to a discussion of other *sukuk* structures. Since there can be any number of *sukuk* structures, with different permutations of the features, we look at three different structures. Two of these three are common while the third is somewhat unique with embedded options. The first common structure is the *sukuk al ijarah* or a lease-based *sukuk*. Figure 7.6 shows the typical structure of an *ijarah sukuk*.

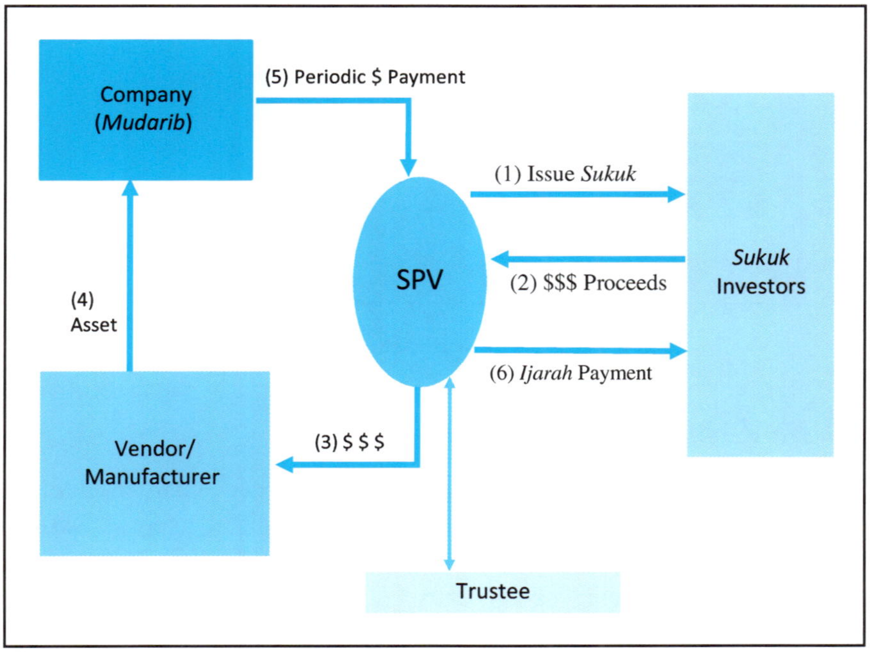

Figure 7.6. A Typical *Ijarah*-Based *Sukuk* Structure.

7.4.2 *Sukuk Al-Ijarah*

In the *ijarah* structure, the *mudarib* begins with the establishment of the SPV. The SPV issues the *sukuk* to investors and uses the proceeds to buy the asset from the vendor/manufacturer. The SPV, which is now the owner of the asset, "leases" the asset to the *mudarib's* company in return for periodic lease payments. The lease payments received from the company are passed through to investors as their returns on the *sukuk*. The *ijarah* structure typically has an embedded sale contract enabling the *mudarib* to purchase the asset from the SPV at the end of the lease period. From a *Shari'ah* viewpoint, the sale price should not be predetermined/fixed upfront, but determined at the end of the lease period and dependent on market conditions then.

7.4.3 *Bay Al-Bithaman Ajil Sukuk*

In a *Bay Al-Bithaman Ajil Sukuk* (BBA)-based *sukuk*, a *mudarib*, who is the originator, seeks funding for the purchase of a needed asset through the issuance of a *sukuk*. Again, the issuer will be the SPV, which will be the legal owner of the asset. The SPV uses the proceeds from *sukuk* issuance to pay the vendor/manufacturer for the asset needed by the *mudarib*. On receiving payment from the SPV, the vendor/manufacturer delivers the asset to the *mudarib*. The *mudarib* will be obliged to pay the SPV the purchase price plus a profit mark-up. The sum will be paid as an annuity of instalments. These periodic payments are passed through the SPV to the *sukuk* investors as *sukuk* cash flows. Though the structure is straightforward and has been popular in Malaysia, many *fuqaha* have been uneasy with the BBA structure. The fixity of payments and the predetermined cash flows are a concern from the *Shari'ah* viewpoint. Following much criticism from Middle Eastern scholars and investors, the BBA structure is not as popular as it once was. As will be discussed later, Malaysian *sukuk* issuers have moved away from BBA-type structures to *sukuk* structures based on other more globally accepted contracts. Figure 7.7 shows the BBA-based *sukuk* structure.

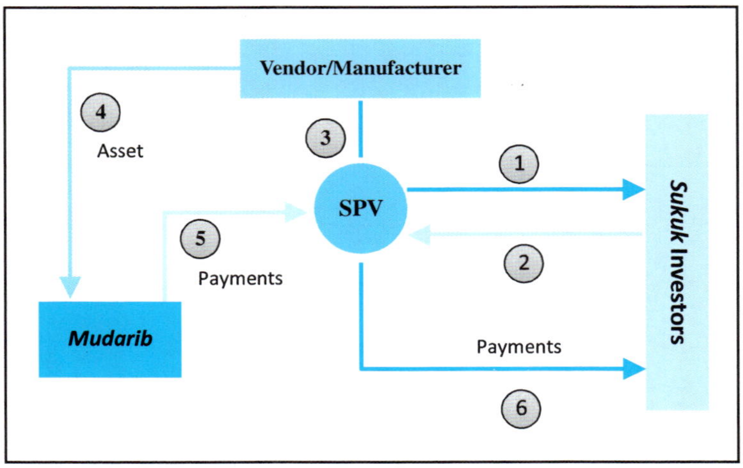

Figure 7.7. A BBA-Based *Sukuk*.

7.4.4 *Sukuk Wakalah Bi Al-Isthimar*

Figure 7.8 shows the structure of a *sukuk wakalah*. The *wakalah* is an agency contract. In the typical *sukuk wakalah* structure, the obligor or issuer is a *wakil* or agent of the *sukuk*-holders. The agent is tasked with using the *sukuk* proceeds to invest in a specific project or business, manage it, and provide a return to *sukuk*-holders based on the returns of investment. The *wakalah* or agency agreement specifies the arrangement. The obligor would be entitled to either a fixed or variable fee from the profits of the investment. The obligor is entitled to enter into other contracts like *mudarabah*, *ijarah*, etc., with other parties in the course of undertaking and managing the investment.

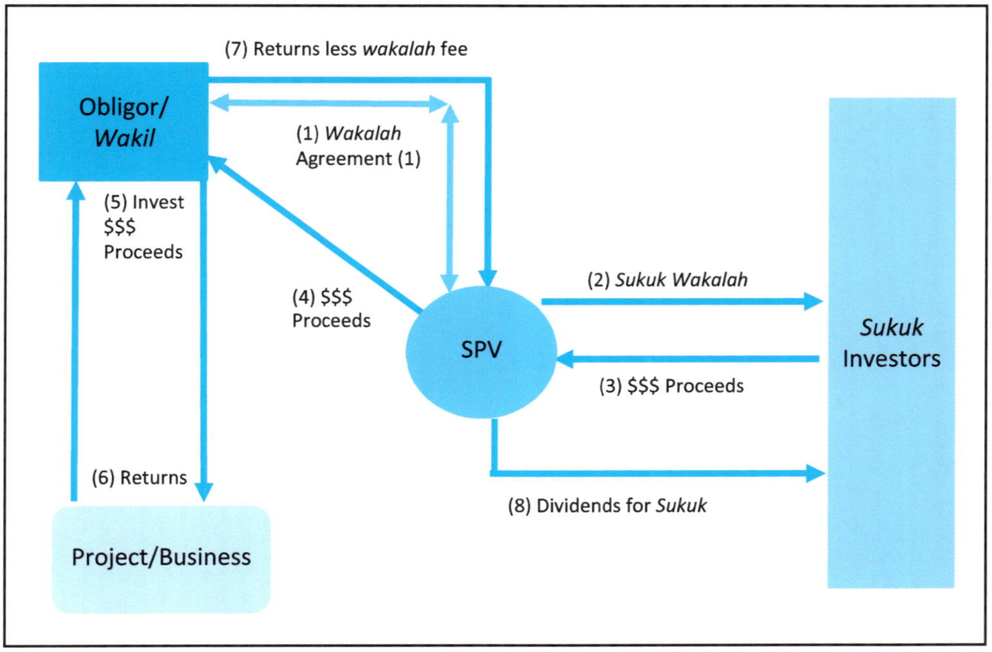

Figure 7.8. The Structure of a *Sukuk Wakalah* (*bi al-istimar*).

The *wakalah* contract has of late become very popular given its flexibility. Several *wakalah sukuk* are designed to provide "fixed" dividends to *sukuk*-holders regardless of the subject investment's performance. The popularity of such a structure stems from the fact that *sukuk*-holders get exposure to underlying investment without bearing the full brunt of the inherent volatility.

The obligor, in such an arrangement, takes on the risk associated with cash flow variability in exchange for the fee and leftover or residual portion of the profits, if any.

7.4.5 *A Commodity Murabahah Sukuk*

The commodity murabahah (CM) transaction that we saw in Chapters 3 and 4, is being increasingly used in the issuance of *sukuk*. A commodity like crude palm oil (CPO) is often used as the underlying asset to the transaction. Other commodities like copper, tin, and other metals, especially those traded on the London Metals Exchange (LME), have also been used in cross-border CM transactions. To understand how a *sukuk* issuance can be based onCM, we examine a hypothetical CM-based *sukuk* issued by Cagamas, the National Home Mortgage Corporation of Malaysia. Figure 7.9 shows the structure of the *sukuk*. The first usual step is to set up the SPV. The SPV then purchases RM10 million worth of commodity, usually CPO that is traded on the *Bursa Suq Al-Sila* trading platform (see Chapter 4). Using CPO as underlying, the *sukuk* is issued. The proceeds from the *sukuk* issuance are used to pay the broker for the CPO purchased. The CPO is then sold to the obligor, Cagamas, for deferred payment at a marked-up *murabahah* price. In this case, the deferred price is RM12 million, to be repaid in monthly installments of RM1 million each for 12 months. On receiving the CPO, Cagamas turns around and sells the CPO to another broker on the platform. Since all of these are done within the same day, the CPO price is unchanged (see Chapter 4 for an explanation of the mechanics). Cagamas receives RM10 million for the CPO. At this point (Step 7 in the diagram), Cagamas has received the RM10 million it intended to raise as financing. The repayment happens over the next 12 months as monthly repayments of RM1 million per month. The *sukuk* in this case may be a private placement. The details of the deal would have been worked out earlier. The commodity, CPO, is used merely to execute the transaction.

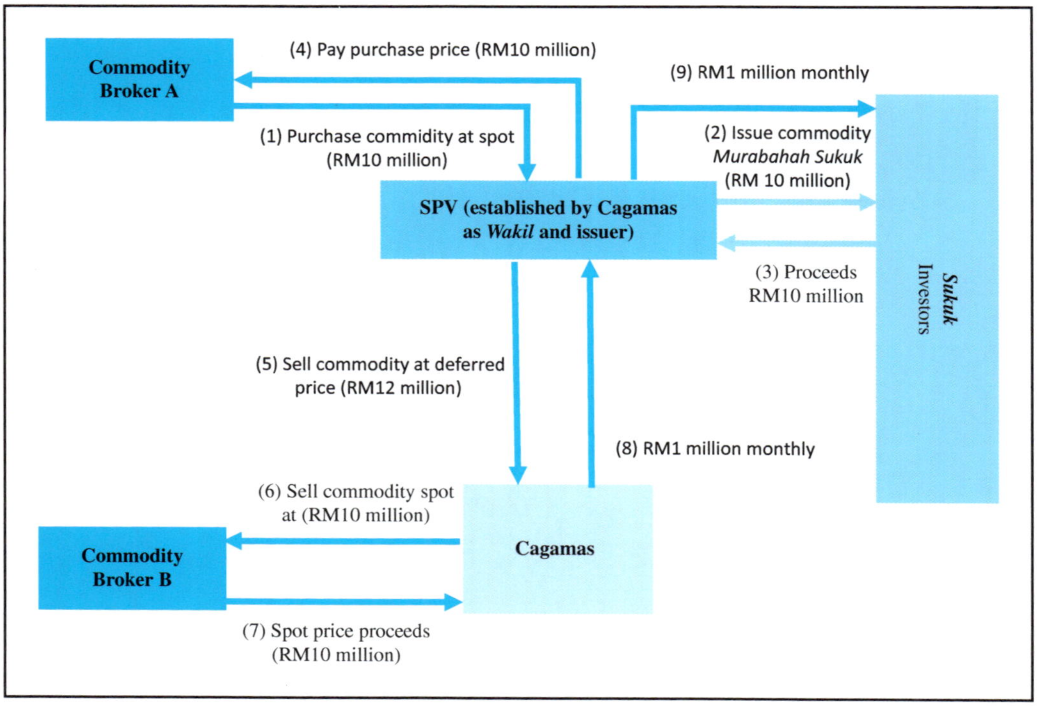

Figure 7.9. A CM *Sukuk* — Cagamas.

Notice that unlike the other structures where there is a physical underlying asset, there is no physical underlying asset here. The commodity is used only for trade execution. Thus, CM-based *sukuk* are like debentures or uncollateralized bonds. The CM structure therefore is riskier from a credit risk viewpoint. Unlike the *ijarah*, where there is usually a physical underlying asset that collateralizes the *sukuk*, there really is no collateral in a CM *sukuk*. Critics of CM have pointed to this and argued that the commodity is used to merely to enable money to change hands and that ownership of the commodity is never the intended objective. CM, however, is quite different from a goods *murabahah*. In a goods *murabahah*, ownership of the underlying product is indeed the objective. The financier purchases the good on behalf of the customer from its producer and the resells the goods to the customer at a marked-up *murabahah* price that would be paid on a deferred basis. The customer may be using the goods as raw material for his own production. While *Shari'ah* scholars have no problems with goods *murabahah*, CM transactions are the ones that make some of them uneasy, and they often accuse the latter as organized *tawarruq*.

7.5 *Sukuk* — Players

As an instrument for raising long-term funds, *sukuk*, like bonds, go through an often elaborate issuance process. Given the long-term nature and the substantial amount of funds raised, there are a number of key players in the market for *sukuk*. In between the issuer or originator, who is often known as the *mudarib*, and the final *sukuk*-holder/investor, there are a number of other entities, each with a role in the proper functioning of the *sukuk* market.

The key players would be as follows:

- *Originator/Mudarib* (could be government-sovereign or corporate);
- *Regulator* (SC in Malaysia);
- *Credit Enhancer* (Government for GLCs, third party for others);
- *Trustee* (to manage and administer the SPV);
- *Vendor/Manufacturer* (of asset/machinery that is the object of financing);
- *Rating Agency* (to rate and monitor the *sukuk*);
- *Investment Bank* (for structures, *sukuk*, compliance, prospectus, and to bring to market);

- *Shari'ah Advisors* (at the investment bank level and at the regulators); and
- *Sukuk Investor.*

The *mudarib*, who would be the ultimate beneficiary of the funding raised, is usually the originator. In initiating the *sukuk* issuance, the originator would typically first hire an investment bank. The investment bank would do all the necessary groundwork, including filings with regulators and other paperwork. The investment bank would also design and structure the *sukuk* as per the needs of the originator and market requirements. In doing this, the investment bank would work with at least three other parties: (i) the *Shari'ah* advisors (either in-house or external), (ii) the lawyers who will draft the documentation, and (iii) the trustees who will have to manage the SPV and protect the interests of the *sukuk*-holders. The trustees are often bank-related entities that offer custodial and trustee services. Once the design and terms of the issue are complete, it goes to the rating agency for a rating evaluation. It is usually just prior to this point that the credit enhancer, if there is one, would have provided the needed undertaking for the issue. In the case of sovereign issues or originators who are government-linked entities, the government would stand guarantee, thereby enhancing the credit risk of the issue. In the case of private originators, a bank might stand guarantee in return for a fee from the originator. As in all cases of providing a guarantee, the bank is taking on contingent liability. When all processes are complete and the needed requirements met, the issue is submitted to the regulators for approval. When regulatory approval is received, the issuance can be brought to market. Where the issue size is large, the investment bank may organize "road shows" during which institutional investors are invited and provided the details of the issue. A book-building exercise may also be undertaken.

7.6 Risks Associated with Investing in *Sukuk*

As a long-dated financial instrument that is subject to secondary market trading, *sukuk* have a range of potential risks. Much of these risks are the same ones afficting conventional financial instruments that are market traded. Table 7.3 shows a list of some of the most common types of risks faced by an investor in *sukuk*.

Table 7.3. *Sukuk* — Risks.

Macro-risk	Risk in the macro-environment
Credit/Counterparty Risk	Risk of non-repayment
Liquidity Risk	Risk arising from thin trading
Market/Price Risk	Risk due to fluctuating prices
Inflation Risk	Risk from loss of purchasing power
Foreign Exchange Risk	Risk arising from changes in exchange rate
Interest Rate Risk	Risk arising from change in asset value
Shari'ah compliance Risk	Risk arising from non-compliance

Given the types of risk above, we now turn to a brief discussion of each of these.

(i) ***Macro-risk*** refers to risk in the macro-environment. Changes in macro-economic conditions, especially that of a systemic nature, can have substantial influence on the values of financial assets traded within an economy or originating from one. Macro-risk is especially relevant where sovereign *sukuk* issuances are concerned.

(ii) ***Credit/Counterparty risk*** refers to risk arising from the potential inability of the originator to honor its obligations. For example, the inability of the originator to meet the periodic *ijarah* payments or the inability to honor the required repurchase of the underlying asset from the SPV would constitute credit risk. Where the underlying asset does not produce "profits" but provides usufruct to the originator, the *sukuk*-holders will have depended on cash flow generated by the originator's line of business to meet *sukuk* obligations.

(iii) ***Liquidity risk*** refers to risk arising from the thinness of trading in an asset. There are two ways in which this risk can occur: first, when an asset's trading is illiquid, its prices tend to be more volatile. Second, one cannot liquidate such an asset quickly. Urgency may require the offering of a discount from current values, implying lower proceeds from the sale. To compensate themselves from such risk, dealers/intermediaries require larger bid-ask spreads. This in turn increases the transaction costs in such assets. Most *sukuk* markets have thin trading. Additionally, given captive markets, often with a surplus of investible funds, the bid-ask spreads tend to be wider.

(iv) ***Market/Price risk*** refers to risk arising from changes in the market price of an asset due to changes in the demand or supply of the asset. Changes in an asset's demand and supply can arise from any number of factors. Generally, assets that have unstable demand or are subject to supply shocks would have high price risk. In the case of *sukuk*, as with other long-dated financial instruments, changes in the interest rate environment can affect *sukuk* values. Thus, interest rate volatility can be a key determinant of price risk for *sukuk*. The fact that there are no hedging instruments accentuates this.

(v) ***Interest rate risk*** refers to changes in an asset's value due to changes in the interest rate. Recall that we discussed these at length in the case of bonds in Chapter 7. In the case of *sukuk*, since most are issued and traded in countries with dual systems, changes in the interest rate regime would invariably affect *sukuk* prices. This can happen through changes in the opportunity cost or cost of capital, which would require the *sukuk* to be re-priced for market trading. As in the case of bonds, there is a negative correlation between *sukuk* prices and interest rates. And as with bonds, this risk will be minimal for *sukuk* with floating rates of return, but higher for fixed rate ones.

(vi) ***Inflation Risk*** refers to risk arising from the loss of purchasing power due to inflation. The extent of this risk will depend on the tenor (maturity) of an instrument and the economic environment within which it is traded. Generally, the longer the maturity of the asset and the higher the inflation rate, the higher the inflation risk. Where a sovereign *sukuk* is denominated in a currency experiencing a high rate of inflation, the inflation risk premium would be high.

(vii) ***Foreign Exchange Risk*** refers to currency exposure arising from investing in a *sukuk* denominated in a foreign currency. Changes in the value of the foreign currency against one's home currency would mean changes in the expected return. For example, if the foreign currency depreciates against home currency, exchange adjusted returns from investing in the *sukuk* would be lower. Alternatively, a foreign currency appreciation would be favorable since one would receive both an exchange gain in addition to the returns from the *sukuk*.

(viii) ***Shari'ah compliance risk*** arises mainly from differences in interpretation by jurisdiction — for example, *bay' al-dayn*-based *sukuk* are acceptable in Malaysia, but not in the Middle East. Furthermore, differences in interpretation can also be time-variant. A *sukuk's* prospectus often defines events that can cause a *sukuk* to be null and void from a *Shari'ah* viewpoint, such as when the cash portion of the underlying asset becomes larger than the tangible portion, or in cases where a *sukuk* involves more than one contract, for example, a combination of *istisna'* and *ijarah*. The *sukuk* could be null and void if the *istisna* portion is higher. Where sale/purchase price of the underlying asset exceeds the acceptable bounds, for e.g., in Malaysia, the SAC has set an upper limit of 1.3 times market price and a lower limit of 0.67 times.

7.6.1 *Other Risks Affecting Sukuk*

In addition to the above, other possible risks for *sukuk* could be operational risks (arising from management of *sukuk* payments or the SPV), and regulatory risks (risk arising from changes in the regulatory framework). Each *sukuk* prospectus has provisions for the termination of the certificate in the event of a default by the obligor. In case the obligor fails to pay the rentals on the *ijarah* agreements that form the coupon payments, the certificate-holder can exercise the right to nullify the contract and force the obligor to buy back the assets. Furthermore, in the event that the obligor fails to reimburse the principal amount, the certificate-holder can exercise the right to take legal action and force the obligor to enter into debt payment proceedings. Coupon payment risk may arise when the obligor fails to pay the required coupons on time. The originator has to buy back the underlying assets from the certificate-holder. Asset redemption risk arises when the principal amount paid is less than the *sukuk* issue amount and, as a result, there is the risk that the assets may not be fully redeemed. Risks related to the asset may arise. The underlying assets of the *sukuk* certificates are subject to numerous risks as well. Primarily, there is the risk of loss of the assets. These are minimal with regards to *ijarah* assets of land parcels. However, in the case of equipment and large-scale construction, the risk of loss may not be so negligible. Nevertheless, Islamic finance has *Shari'ah*-compliant provisions for insurance claims in the form of *Takaful*, and these arrangements will have to be utilized to mitigate the risks of asset losses. Also related to the asset risk is the need to maintain the structures of the assets. Proper maintenance will ensure adequate returns to the certificate-holder. According to *Shari'ah* principles, the SPV will usually be required to bear the responsibilities on ensuring asset structure maintenance.

7.6.2 *Managing Sukuk Risks*

Sukuk perform the functions of conventional bonds and tradable securities in resource mobilization. In order to attract investors and expand *sukuk* as a mode of Islamic financing, instruments of risk management need to be innovated and traded. The commonly used instruments of risk managements are derivatives such as futures, options, and swaps. Securitization of assets has also played a major role in managing risk, namely banks were able to sell their loans such as mortgage loans and reduce interest rate mismatch. The risk of mortgage loans was transferred to investors who bought ABSs and was also insured via credit default swaps (CDSs). Some risk management instruments for enhancing the competitiveness of *sukuk* structures can be suggested to overcome some of the undesirable underlying risks. These instruments emphasize the liquidity aspect of *sukuk*, the use of derivatives for hedging interest rate risk, and the use of embedded options for redeeming *sukuk*, converting or exchanging them into equities.

7.6.2.1 *Liquid secondary market*

The efficacy of any primary market depends heavily on the development of a sustainable and robust secondary market that provides liquidity to investors. *Sukuk* certificates are unique in that the investor becomes an asset-holder and is directly tied to the nature and functioning of the underlying asset pools. *Sukuk* certificate holders carry the burden of these unique risks. The primary concern of an Islamic secondary market is liquidity of assets. A certificate-holder would rather participate in a well-regulated secondary market instead of trading in a poorly run market. By doing so, the investor's chances of liquidating his investments as efficiently as possible are enhanced.

7.6.2.2 *Sukuk and the challenge of derivatives*

Derivatives in conventional markets have been developed to provide hedge instruments for traders against adverse price movement and to manage risk. Many derivatives are traded to manage interest rate risk. Fixed and floating rate swaps have been very effective in reducing the funding costs and have very effectively been used to manage credit and market risks. Futures contracts on bonds can be employed to transfer interest risks. The hedger of the cash position must decide what the effect of changes in interest rates will be on the open position. A depreciation of spot value with an increase in interest rates will necessitate a short position in interest rate futures contracts. If interest rates do subsequently rise, profits will be achieved on the fall in futures prices. Conversely, an expected decrease in interest rates will necessitate a long position in futures contracts. The value of these contracts will appreciate and their prices will increase. Subsequently, the hedger will benefit from a profit. The futures contracts come in a variety of standards such as T-notes with maturities ranging between two and 10 years as well as T-bonds, T-bills, and Eurodollars. The challenge for the hedger then becomes to identify the nature of future contracts to invest in as well the amount of contracts to buy.

7.6.2.3 *Embedded options as a risk management tool*

Conventional investors have a wide range of financial instruments to select from through which to construct different investment strategies. Bonds with embedded options are one of many such instruments. *Shari'ah* guidelines do not allow the sale of debts but it allows the exchange of debts for real assets, goods, and services. Thus, the opportunity of an exchange of debts against real assets and usufructs can be added to the debt certificates as an embedded option for the settlement of debts. Practically, the enterprise that would invest the funds would write the embedded option. Such an option would not be binding on the financier, but if utilized, the user of funds is bound by the promise. Convertible *sukuk* are those that may be converted into equity shares of the issuing company. Exchangeable *sukuk* are those that may be converted by the issuing company, not into its own equity shares, but into equity shares of other companies.

Box 7.1. Goldman Sachs Announces a *Sukuk* Issuance and Courts Controversy

Goldman Sachs International (GSI) the top American investment bank announced at end 2011 that it intends to issue a series of CM-based *sukuk*. The *murabahah*-based *sukuk* program was to be multicurrency with denomination in US$, Singapore $, Saudi Riyal, and UAE Dirhams, and issued by Global Sukuk Company Limited (GSCL), a Cayman Islands-based SPV established by GSI. While the stated objective of the issuance was to diversify Goldman Sach's investor base, the company was really "testing the waters" to see the extent to which *Shari'ah*-compliant investors would be receptive to the issue. Market response, however, was far from positive. The proposal came under heavy criticism. Broadly, the criticism revolved around three issues. The first that the proposed structure involves GSI and its own subsidiaries, and not the three or four different parties that are typically involved in a *tawarruq* arrangement. While a CM arrangement (within the *tawarruq*) would typically lead to *sukuk*-holders "owning" the commodity, in the proposed GSI structure, it was argued that the issuer would also be owning the asset — a form of reverse *tawarruq*. The second and perhaps more important point of contention was that GSI did not show how the proceeds of the *sukuk* issuance would be used in a *Shari'ah*-compliant way. It was argued that, given the lack of clarity on usage of funds, GSI might use the funds in its conventional investment banking business. The third criticism relates to the proposed listing of the *sukuk* on the Irish Stock Exchange. It was feared that the *sukuk* might be traded together with other conventional fixed income securities, in which case it may appear to be no different from other listed conventional bonds. The issue of guarantee provided by the holding company, the Goldman Sachs Group (GSG) on the principal plus deferred profits, was yet another point of contention.

Source: The Goldman Sachs Sukuk — What is the Issue? *RAM Ratings Newsletter*, 2012.

7.7 *Sukuk* in Malaysia

As mentioned earlier, Malaysia has been a pioneer in many Islamic finance products, including *sukuk*. Malaysia's first *sukuk*-issuers were private entities. Shell MDS Sdn. Bhd. was the first Malaysian *sukuk*-issuer in the year 1990. Based on the BBA contract, it consisted of two tranches: a five-year maturity for RM75 million and a RM50 million tranche with an eight-year maturity. This first issuance was followed in 1991 with a *musharakah*-based *sukuk* by Sarawak Shell Berhad. This was a RM600 million "guaranteed" *musharakah* with participating certificates. The third ringgit-denominated *sukuk* was issued in 1993 by Petronas Dagangan. This consisted of RM300 million of unsecured redeemable paper with RM120 million worth of detachable warrants. In a sense, this *sukuk* was a variant of the convertible bond in that the warrants could be converted into shares of the listed Petronas Dagangan. The warrants simply delay the issuance of equity.

Following the first three issues, a series of subsequent issues have taken place. What started as tentative steps has snowballed to make Malaysia the largest issuer of *sukuk*. Malaysia has been a pioneer in several innovative *sukuk* structures. While we examine the more exotic structures in the next chapter, the sections below describe some of the innovative structures used in the earlier days.

7.7.1 *KFC Holdings — Sukuk with Warrants*

One of the earliest *sukuk* innovations was the issuance in 1997 of *sukuk* with warrants attached. Kentucky Fried Chicken (KFC), Malaysia, issued what were known as redeemable *sukuk* with warrants. This was in essence a variant of the convertible bond. Warrants which were attached to the *sukuk* provided the *sukuk*-holder the right to purchase (buy) KFC Holdings stock at a predetermined exercise price. So, the *sukuk* had two parts: the *sukuk* portion which constituted an obligation to repay the *sukuk*-holder the face value at maturity; and the warrants, which are long-dated call options that provide *sukuk*-holders the right to buy KFC Holdings stock at a predetermined price. As the warrants provide a potential profit opportunity, they are intended to make the underlying security, *sukuk* in this case, more attractive to investors. As we will see in the Chapter 8, this increased attractiveness can translate into a lower required return (yield) by investors, which in turn means lower funding costs to the issuer.

7.7.2 *Gutherie Global Sukuk*

This was the first issue of a global *sukuk*. A global *sukuk* is one that is designed to be traded globally. As such, the *sukuk* was US$ denominated. It consisted of two tranches: the first for US$50 million due in 2004, and the second for US$100 million due in 2006. An *ijarah*-based *sukuk*, the two tranches had two different pieces of land as underlying asset. The first tranch offered a 1% undivided ownership in the underlying land, whereas the second a 0.5% ownership in the second asset. *Ijarah* payments for both tranches were due semi-annually based on LIBOR + 1.5% per annum and LIBOR + 2.0% per annum, respectively. Thus, the *sukuk*-holder in Tranche A will receive LIBOR + 1.5% multiplied by his investment amount as the semi-annual *ijarah* payment.

7.7.3 *Government of Malaysia Sukuk*

This was the first sovereign *sukuk* by the Malaysian government. Known as the Malaysian Global *Sukuk*, it was issued for a sum of US$600 million with maturity in 2007. Based on the *ijarah* contract, the *sukuk* provided undivided beneficial ownership of four land parcels that had been placed in a trust. The land parcels were sold by the government to an SPV, which then leases it back to the government in return for semi-annual lease payments. The lease payments were determined based on LIBOR as the reference rate. The payments were six-month LIBOR + 0.95%. This implies that if the six-month LIBOR is 5% at the time a lease payment is due, the *sukuk* will pay:

$$[(5\% + 0.95\%)/2]\ \$600 \text{ million} = \$17.85 \text{ million}$$

The payment of $17.85 million will constitute *ijarah* or lease payment for the prior six months period.

Listed for trading on the Luxembourg Stock Exchange, this *sukuk* was the first to comply with all the needed regulations to be tradable internationally. In essence, it complied with the needed regulation for a conventional bond to be listed and traded internationally. This *sukuk* was also the first "asset-based" rather than asset-backed *sukuk*. This had to do with the fact that an asset-backed *sukuk* would violate the standard negative pledge of Malaysia's other outstanding international bonds. In effect, the asset-backed *sukuk* would not rank *pari-pasu* with the Malaysian government's other conventional bonds that were outstanding. (see the following discussion on asset-backed versus asset-based *sukuk*).

7.8 *Sukuk* in Malaysia: Growth and Evolution

Figure 7.10 shows the growth of *sukuk* issuance in Malaysia over the 16 years from 2000 to 2016. It is obvious that the growth in Malaysian *sukuk* issuance has been phenomenal. Total *sukuk* issuance in 2000, which was approximately RM11.5 billion, grew to nearly RM340 billion in 2012. This constitutes a near 30-fold increase in issuance value. Since reaching a peak in 2012, issuance volume shows steady reduction. This is similar to what was seen in Figure 7.1

earlier, which showed global *sukuk* issuance. There are probably two key reasons: the reduced GDP growth and the sharp reduction seen in oil prices in the latter years. Malaysia, as with the Gulf countries, is a net exporter of oil. The reduction seen in *sukuk* issuance is more cyclical than structural. If anything, as discussed below, Malaysia has continued to make huge strides in making the *sukuk* issuance and trading ecosystem much more efficient.

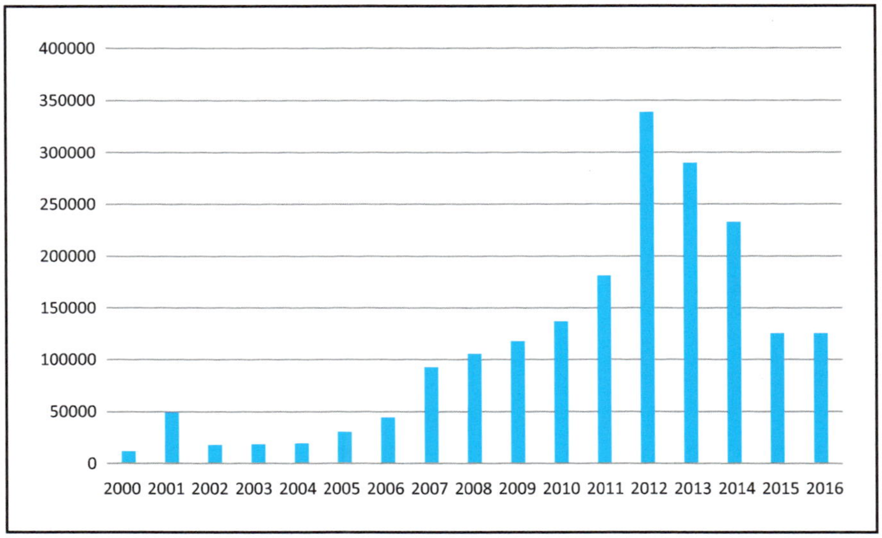

Figure 7.10. *Sukuk* Issuance in Malaysia (2000–2016) (RM Millions).

Source: *Thomson Reuters Eikon.*

Though the growth patterns in Malaysia match that of global *sukuk* issuance, as seen in Figure 7.1, there has been a fundamental change taking place within the Malaysian *sukuk* market. This has to do with the type of *sukuk* issued. Recall that in the early days, most Malaysian *sukuk* issues were structured on BBA and *murabahah* contracts. Given the unease with such fixed rate instruments in the Middle East, there was a clear attempt by Malaysian issuers to move away from the heavy reliance on BBA-type *sukuk*. Figures 7.11(a) and 7.11(b) show this evolution. In 2004, the BBA structure was by far the most popular, with some 57% of all *sukuk* issued, while *Murabahah*-based issues accounted for 38%. Thus, these two structures accounted for 95% of the total *sukuk* issued. By 2016, as shown in Figure 7.11(b), BBA-based issues had shrunk to a mere 4%. *Murabaha*-based *sukuk* have become dominant, with 43%. There has also been a big growth in *ijarah*, and especially *musharakah*-based issues. It is clear that a major evolution had taken place in the Malaysian market for *sukuk* issuance. Whereas in the early years, the BBA contract had dominated, today it is totally absent.

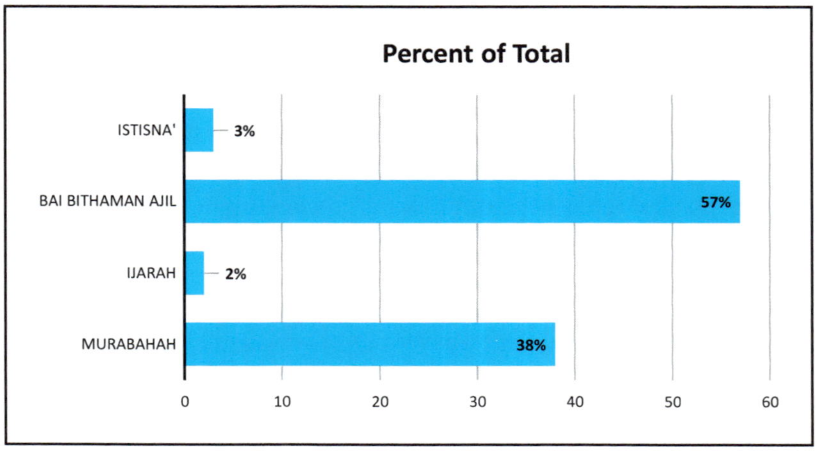

Figure 7.11. (a) Malaysian *Sukuk* Issuance by Contract (2004)

Source: Securities Commission, Malaysia; *Thomson Reuters Eikon*.

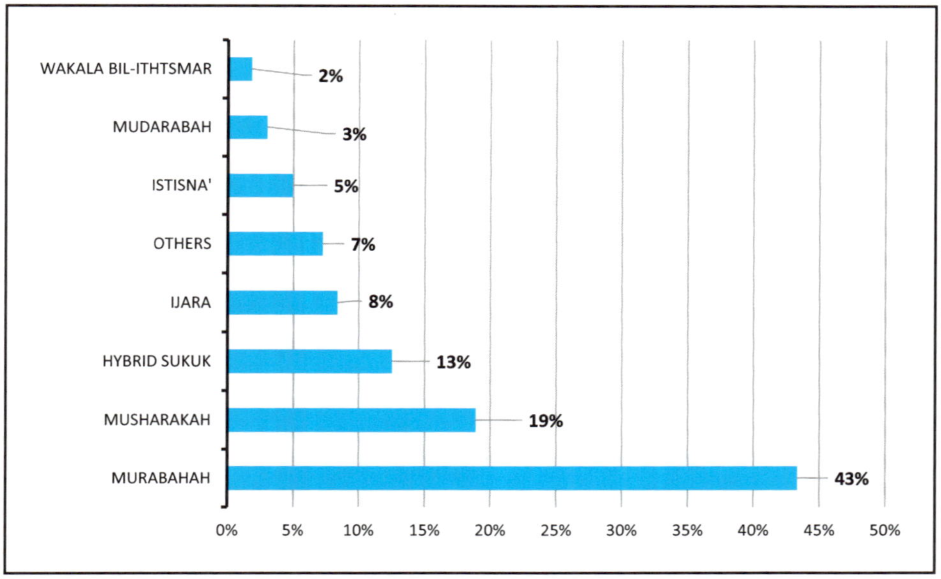

Figure 7.11. (b) Malaysian *Sukuk* Issuance by Contract (2016).

Source: Securities Commission, Malaysia; *Thomson Reuters Eikon*.

7.9 Underlying Asset and the Structuring of *Sukuk*

The need for the underlying asset is an obvious requirement in all Islamic financial transactions. *Sukuk*, as mentioned earlier, are no different in this regard. Despite the clear requirement for an underlying asset, many contemporary *sukuk*-issuers appear to have moved away from ensuring compliance with this requirement. This has been the source of controversy surrounding some recent *sukuk*. There are two basic issues: (i) whether the underlying asset should constitute only tangible assets, or could a portion of the underlying assets also include intangible assets such as receivables, and (ii) should the underlying asset provide backing for the *sukuk* or merely provide the basis for *sukuk* issuance.

Beginning from an asset-backed *sukuk*, which provides "collateral" to *sukuk* investors in the form of underlying tangible assets, there appears to be a trend towards asset-based structures. In an asset-based *sukuk*, while there may be a "sale" of the asset by the originators to the SPV (which is the *sukuk*-issuer), from a legal viewpoint, *sukuk*-holders may not have recourse or any stake in the underlying asset. The only assurance that *sukuk* investors have is the purchase undertaking that the originator gives to the issuer (SPV). This undertaking is usually in the form of a *wa'ad*. A *wa'ad* is a unilateral "promise" that one party provides to another in a transaction. The price at which the asset will be purchased at maturity is usually set equal the redemption value outstanding on the *sukuk*. In addition, sale of the underlying asset at *sukuk* maturity can only be to the originator and not to any other third-party.

The *asset-based sukuk* is therefore a very different animal from the classic *asset-backed sukuk*. In an asset-backed *sukuk*, the sale of an asset by the originator to the SPV (issuer) is executed by means of an S&P (Sale-Purchase) Agreement. The asset is legally transferred to the SPV which will be bankruptcy remote. The originator often gets a call-option to buy back the asset from the SPV at *sukuk* maturity. The purchase price may be the prevailing market price, or an exercise price deemed to be in-the-money (see Chapter 9). If the originator is unable to repurchase the asset at maturity or experiences financial distress rendering it unable to repurchase the asset, the *sukuk* holders could sell the asset to a third-party. So, clearly there is a very big difference in the risk profile to *sukuk*-holders, whether the *sukuk* is structured as asset-backed or asset-based. The holder of an asset-based *sukuk* is equivalent to the holder of an unsecured bond. To an originator, an asset-based structure may be preferable first for the convenience and lower transaction costs, but more importantly, since the asset-based structure will ensure that the originators do not "lose control" of the asset. This is an important consideration, especially in cases where the sale of the asset in issuing an asset-backed *sukuk* could trigger the negative pledges which are a standard feature of most loan/bond issues.

A sovereign issuer, such as the Malaysian government which already has several previously issued bonds outstanding, cannot issue asset-backed *sukuk* without triggering the negative pledges of the outstanding bonds. It is no surprise therefore that the Malaysian government's first sovereign *sukuk* of 2002 was the first asset-based *sukuk*.

While the asset-based *sukuk* does provide convenience to originators and avoids the complications arising from asset transfer, etc., *sukuk*-holders would be at the losing end. This is particularly true in cases where the underlying asset may consist substantially of intangible assets like receivables. As many of these assets may not have a secondary market, much less a market price, even a legal recourse may not mean much in terms of cost recovery. Yet, despite this obvious disadvantage to *sukuk*-holders, the market appears to be moving in the direction of asset-based and away from asset-backed *sukuk*.

Where a *sukuk* is asset-backed, the risk profile is dependent on the underlying asset, whereas for asset-based *sukuk*, since *sukuk*-holders have no recourse to the underlying asset but are dependent on the purchase undertaking, the risk profile is very much dependent on the financial ability of the originator. Table 7.4 provides some of the key differences between asset-backed and asset-based *sukuk*.

Table 7.4. Asset-Backed *Sukuk* versus Asset-Based *Sukuk*.

Asset-Backed Sukuk	***Asset-Based Sukuk***
Sale: True sale of asset to SPV	"Sale" of asset to SPV
Recourse: *Sukuk*-holders have recourse to underlying asset	*Sukuk*-holders have no recourse or stake in underlying asset
Potential Purchaser: Can sell asset to third-party	Originator is the only possible purchaser
Purchase Price: Market value of asset at maturity	Redemption/outstanding value of *sukuk*
Profile: *Sukuk*-holders get upside potential from rising asset value	*Sukuk*-holders do not benefit from rising underlying asset value
Risk Category: Collateralized (based on type and value of underlying asset)	Unsecured (*sukuk* will be rated as unsecured debt of originator)

Box 7.2 provides an illustration of the different types of *sukuk* structures. Like bond issues, *sukuk* too have term sheets. A term sheet is essentially a summary of the key features of an instrument to be issued to the public. The *sukuk* term sheets below were chosen to highlight the "unique" features of some *sukuk*. The National Bank of Abu Dhabi (NBAD) *sukuk* illustrates a fixed rate *sukuk* whereas the Sukuk Bahrain shows the use of floating rates referenced on LIBOR. The Saudi Hollandi Bank *sukuk* uses a dual profit rate structure. The Prolintas *sukuk* illustrates a sale-leaseback arrangement. Finally, the Khazanah Exchangeable *sukuk* shows the use of an embedded call option.

Box 7.2. Illustration: Term Sheets of Select *Sukuk* Issues

NBAD Ringgit-Denominated *Sukuk* (Fixed Return)

NBAD Ringgit-Denominated *Sukuk* under NBAD RM3 billion (US$937 million) program **RM500 million (US$156 million)** **National Bank of — Abu Dhabi** **June 29, 2010**	Obligor/Issuer	National Bank of Abu Dhabi (NBAD)
	Tenor	Five Years
	Return	4.75% per annum fixed profit rate
	Payment	Semi-annually (profit)
	Maturity Date	June 29, 2015
	Governing Law	Malaysian Law
	Purpose of Issuance	Finance of *Shari'ah*-compliant (Islamic) assets/activities. The proceeds raised from the issuance of the *sukuk* under the NBAD Ringgit-dominated program will be utilized by NBAD for the purpose of financing existing and future *Shari'ah*-compliant investment and/or in connection with Islamic finance activities which includes, without limitation, covering the acquisition cost of the existing and future *Shari'ah*-compliant assets of NBAD.
	Principal Activities	Diversified Financial Services Group
	Rating	AAA — RAM Rating Services Group
	Shari'ah Advisor	HSBC Amanah Malaysia The Royal Bank of Scotland Maybank Investment Bank

Source: *Islamic Finance News*, Vol. 7, Iss. 28.

***Sukuk* — Bahrain: Returns Based on Floating Reference Rate**

Instruments	*Sukuk Al Manfa'a*
Issuer	Golden Belt 1 *Sukuk* company, a special purpose vehicle established in Bahrain
Principal Activities	Saad Trading, Contracting and Financial Services Company (Saad) is the principal trading company in the Saad Group, with its principal activities being investment in real estate and equity securities (mainly in the banking sector and construction and contracting-related activities.
Dates of Listings	
Issue Size	Pending — the application is currently with the Bahrain Stock Exchange
Coupon	US$650 million Based on a calculation of "periodic distribution amounts" as follows: (LIBOR for six-month period + 0.85%) × 650,000,000 × number of days in the period/360.
Payment Schedule	
Authorized Paid-up	Six-monthly returns, capital repaid by bullet at maturity
Capital	100%
Identified Assets	Land parcels in the Kingdom of Saudi Arabia
Shariah Advisor	The *Shari'ah* board of BNP Paribas

(*Continued*)

Box 7.2. (*Continued*)

Method of Issue	The issue price was set at 100% of the *sukuk*'s principal amount, and the conditions provide that the *sukuk* will be redeemed at par on May 15, 2012. The issuer of the delegates has the option, for the benefit of the holders of the certificate, to terminate the underlying leasing arrangements; to require Saad to make payment of the termination sum; and to redeem the certificates. Following the occurrence of a dissolution event. Saad's obligation to make payment of the termination sum is backed by a promissory note in the full amount of the *sukuk*.
Purpose of Issue	General corporate purposes, including funding the development of Saad's core business of real estate investment and development and for making other investments.
Ratings	Baal from Moody's and BBB + from Standard and Poor's and Baal from

Source: *Islamic Finance News,* Vol. 4, Iss. 25.

Saudi Hollandi Bank (*Mudarabah sukuk* with Dual Fixed Rates of Return)

Saudi Hollandi Bank (SHB) *Mudarabah Sukuk*	Tenor	Due in 10 years (December 2019), callable after Year Five (December 2014) and each year-end thereafter.
	Return	190 basis points from Years One to Five, 550 bps from Years Six to Ten.
SAR725 million (US$193 million)	Payment	Every six months (June and December).
	Profit/Coupon Rate	Six monthly SIBOR (Saudi Interbank Offered Rate) plus Margin (up to year Five)/Step-up Margin (Year Six onwards).
	Listing	The Saudi Stock Exchange (*Tadawul*)
December 2009	Minimum Investment	SAR 500,000 (US$133,000)
	Purpose of Issuance	• The *Mudarabah* Certificates' proceeds will be invested by the issuer (*Mudarib*) in its Islamic banking and finance business. • Profit generated by the *mudarabah* will be distributed between the issuer and certificate-holders as per pre-agreed proportions with a cap on certificate-holders' profit.

Source: *Islamic Finance News* Vol. 7, Iss. 02.

Prolintas Expressway (Lease with Sell Back Provision)

Prolintas Expressway Syndicated Islamic Financing Facility	Obligor	Prolintas Expressway (PEX)
	Tenor	13 years from date of initial drawdown
	Maturity Date	November 20, 2022
	Lead Arranger	Bank Islam Malaysia
	Trustee	MIMB Investment
RM327 million (US$96 million)	Legal Counsel	Albar & Partners
	Governing Law	Malaysia
	Purpose of Issuance	To fully refinance PEX's existing facility amounting to RM327 million (US$96 million)

(*Continued*)

Box 7.2. (*Continued*)

	Principal Activities	To manage and maintain the expressway as per the concession agreement.
20th November 2009	Facility Type	Syndicated Islamic Financing facility based on Ijarah Muntahiya Bittamleek.

Source: *Islamic Finance News*, Vol. 7, Iss. 05.

Khazanah Exchangeable *Sukuk* (A Call Option on Underlying Asset/ Stocks)

Instrument	US Dollar Periodic Payment Exchangeable *Sukuk*
Issuer	Cherating Capital
Obligor	Khazanah Nasional
Securities Offered	US dollar denominated Periodic Payment Exchangeable Trust Certificates due 2012, exchangeable into ordinary shares of PLUS Expressway (PLUS) offered and sold in reliance on Regulation $ only.
Date of Listing	June 27, 2007
Issue Size	US$850 million
Issue Price	100%
Maturity	5 years
Scheduled Dissolution Amount	114. 14%
Payment Schedule	The payment will be 2% per year, payable on an annual basis in arrears. Periodic payments will be funded by the dividend income received in respect of the exchange property and payable up to the maximum periodic payment of 2% per year. Periodic payments will not be guaranteed by the issuer or the obligor. Periodic payments are cumulative (but if the dividend) income received in respect of the exchange property is insuffcient to fund the periodic payments in full; this will not constitute a dissolution event. Any excess dividend income received in respect of the exchange property will be accumulated in a sinking fund (subject to the order of priority set out in the offering circular) up to the total maximum periodic payment and the aggregate shortfall amounts if any, and shall be applied by the issuer to pay the periodic payments.
Denomination	US100,000 and integral multiples thereof
Exchange Property	Ordinary shares RM0.25 (US$0.07) par each of PLUS listed on Bursa Malaysia securities
Governing Law	English Law
Shariah Advisor	CIMB Bank's *Shari'ah* Advisory Board
Listing	Application has been made to list on the Hong Kong Stock Exchange, the Labuan International Financial Exchange, and the Dubai International Financial Exchange.
Exchange Right	Exchangeable into shares at the election of the certificate-holders at any time on or after the 40th day after the closing date, until the close of business on the date which falls 10 business days prior to the schedule dissolution date, unless previously called for dissolution prior to the scheduled dissolution date, and then up to close of business on the 10th business day prior to the data fixed for dissolution.
Purpose of Issue	Khazanah Nasional intends to use the proceeds as additional working capital and other general corporate purposes relating to its principal business activities.
Ratings	The certificates will not be rated as the issuer is not rated.

Source: *Islamic Finance News*, Vol. 4. Iss. 26.

Summary

Sukuk are investment certificates that are tradable. From a conventional finance viewpoint, *sukuk* are a hybrid instrument. Though *sukuk* are often referred to as Islamic bonds and have been compared to conventional bonds, they can be very different. While the typical bond is a fixed income security, a *sukuk*, depending on its underlying contract, may have no fixed cash flows. Despite their newness, *sukuk* have become a very successful Islamic finance product. Global issuance of *sukuk* has increased several folds in the last few years. The *ijarah* and *musharakah* mode of *sukuk* have become the most popular. Like all Islamic finance products, *sukuk* need to fulfil several requirements in order to be *Shari'ah*-compliant. For example, all funds raised through a *sukuk* issuance can only be used to fund *halal* activities. Income derived by *sukuk*-holders must come from the *sukuk's* underlying assets, which must be a *halal* asset. A *sukuk* could be based on any *Shari'ah* contract. In some cases, they may be based on more than one contract. The typical *sukuk* structure would have a SPV which would be the legal owner of the *sukuk's* underlying assets. A trustee will manage the SPV and be responsible for ensuring compliance. The trustee would also be tasked to ensure that *sukuk*-holders receive their dues in a timely fashion.

These days, there are a number of exotic *sukuk* structures. The need for these complex structures has been the result of wanting altered risk profiles, different cash flows or contingent based payoffs, and the need to avoid fixed returns. These have also meant the use of embedded options within *sukuk*. As is the way with other market-traded financial assets, *sukuk* face a number of risks. Many of these risks are common to conventional bonds. The pricing and valuation of *sukuk* can be more diffcult than that of conventional bonds. Aside from cash flows that may not be fixed, different underlying contracts can result in very different cash flow and risk profiles. Despite the differences, the underlying logic and techniques of valuation in the conventional can be used to value *sukuk*.

Questions and Problems

1. Compare and contrast a *sukuk* with a conventional bond.
2. Compare the cash flows of an *ijarah sukuk* with fixed semi-annual *ijarah* payments and a pre-determined redemption value with a semi-annual coupon bond.
3. Explain why a *mudarabah*- or *musharakah*-based *sukuk* might be considered riskier than an *ijarah sukuk*.
4. There are certain restrictions on the use of funds raised through a *sukuk* issuance. State some of these restrictions.
5. Briefly describe how a *sukuk* based on *ijarah* may be different in terms of cash flows from one based on *mudarabah* and one based on *murabahah*.
6. What is the role of the following within a *sukuk* structure?
   (a) SPV
   (b) The trustee
7. Compare the duration of a 10-year *ijarah sukuk* with fixed semi-annual payments with that of a 10-year *ijarah sukuk* with semi-annual payments referenced on six-month LIBOR. Which *sukuk* is likely to have a shorter duration? Why?
8. Describe some risks that are common to both *sukuk* and conventional bonds. Identify a risk that would be unique to *sukuk* alone.
9. A developer is considering a *sukuk* instead of a conventional bond to finance an apartment complex in downtown Kuala Lumpur. Construction will take three years. The developer intends to lease (not sell) the units. Given the location, there should be no difficulty in getting tenants.
   (a) Outline an appropriate *sukuk* structure for this project (with an accompanying diagram).
   (b) What underlying Islamic contract(s) would you propose? Justify.
   (c) In what way(s) would the financing you propose in (a) and (b) above, be better than conventional bonds?
10. Suppose a 10-year *murabahah sukuk* has a convertible feature included in its structure, the conversion being to underlying stocks of the issuer;
    (a) Would this *sukuk* be any less *Shari'ah*-compliant than a *murabahah sukuk* that does not have such conversion?
    (b) Would this *sukuk* be less or more risky than a *murabahah sukuk* that does not have such conversion?
    (c) In what way would the required return for an investor be different for this *sukuk* relative to a *murabahah sukuk* that does not have such conversion?
    (d) What are the advantages and disadvantages of issuing such a convertible *sukuk* to the issuer?
11. (a) A bond fund manager is seeking to increase portfolio returns by selling the short-term bonds in his portfolio and using the proceeds to invest in longer-term bonds. He argues that since the new bonds would have the same rating as the ones sold, such a strategy would enable higher return without increased risk. Evaluate the strategy.
    (b) What is the likely impact on duration of including a *mudarabah/musharakah*-based risk-sharing *sukuk* into a portfolio of *murabahah* and fixed rate *ijarah sukuk*?
12. What is the difference between an asset-backed versus an asset-based *sukuk*? Which way is the market trending? Why? What is the implication for required yields under the two different structures? Explain why the required yields cannot be equal.
13. Examining the underlying contracts of outstanding *sukuk*, there appears to be a clear bias in favor of certain types of contracts. *Ijarah* appears popular internationally while the *murabahah* contract appears to be the favorite of Malaysian issuers. Why is this so? What are the implications of this for the future growth of Islamic finance?

Bibliography

Nathif, A. J. and A. Thomas (2004). *Islamic Bonds — Your Guide to Issuing, Structuring and Investing in Sukuk* (Euromoney Books, London).

Bank Negara Malaysia, Annual Reports — several years.

Capital Market Issues According to Islamic Jurisprudence. Resolutions of the Securities Commission Shariah Advisory Council. Securities Commission, Kuala Lumpur.

Dabu, I. F. *Tawarruq, Sukuks, Its Reality and Types* [Unpublished Manuscript] Bahrain.

Diaw, A. (2011). "Performance/Commodity-Linked Sukūk for Private and Public Sector Funding: Some Proposed Models." (Unpublished PhD Thesis, INCEIF).

Haneef, R. (2009). "From asset-backed to asset-light structures: The intricate history of Sukuk," *ISRA International Journal of Islamic Finance*, Vol. 1, No. 1, December 2009, pp. 103–126.

Hijazi, F. (2009). International Structured Finance, Special Report, Moody's Investors Service, 10 November.

IOSCO (2005). Islamic Capital Markets: Fact Finding Report, The International Organization of Securities Commissions.

Memon, N. A. (2009). "Sukuk Structures and Markets," *Journal of Islamic Banking and Finance*, July–September 2009, pp. 64–76.

RAM Ratings Newsletters, various issues.

Shabnam, M. (2009). "Function of Wa'ad in Asset Backed Sukuk," *ISRA Bulletin*, Vol. 04, December 2009, pp. 7–10.

Standard & Poors (2009) *Islamic Finance Outlook — 2009*. Standard & Poors Rating Services.

Websites

http://www.bnm.gov.my — Bank Negara Malaysia
http://www.sc.com.my
Thomson Reuters, Eikon

Endnote

1. See Rafe Haneef (2009).

Chapter 8

ISSUES IN *SUKUK* DESIGN AND TRADING

Topics in this Chapter

8.1. *Sukuk* Contracts and Risk Profile
8.2. Exotic *Sukuk* Structures
8.3. Innovations in *Sukuk* Design
8.4. Risk-Sharing *Sukuk*, Perpetual *Sukuk*
8.5. *Sukuk* Pricing, Valuing *Sukuk* with Embedded Options
8.6. Valuing Risk-Sharing *Sukuk*
8.7. *Sukuk* Yields versus Bond Yields
8.8. Managing *Sukuk* Risks, *Sukuk* Defaults

Chapter Objective

This chapter examines issues related to *sukuk*, their design, trading, and pricing. The variance in risk profile according to the underlying contract is described. Exotic *sukuk* structures and the innovations in their design are evaluated. The need and rationale for risk-sharing and perpetual *sukuk* is described. The underlying logic of *sukuk* pricing and the variance in pricing formulation according to the *sukuk's* underlying contracted is discussed. The chapter ends with a discussion of *sukuk* defaults. On completing the chapter, you should have a good understanding of how *sukuk* design affects risk, required returns, and the formulation of pricing. You should also appreciate the need for continuous innovation in *sukuk* structure.

Key Terms		
air time *sukuk*	embedded *sukuk*	multi-currency issuance
Black Scholes Option Pricing Model (BSOPM)	exchangeable *sukuk*	perpetual *sukuk*
bond yields	exotic *sukuk* structure	pricing embedded options
commodity-linked sukuk	foreign exchange risk	risk-sharing structures
convertible *istisna'*	GDP-linked risk	*sukuk* defaults
convertible *mudarabah*	hybrid equity	*sukuk* yields
embedded call option	*ijarah* with embedded options	
embedded put	initial public offer (IPO)	

8.1 Underlying *Sukuk* Contracts and Risk Profile

As is the case with all Islamic finance products, *sukuk* must have an underlying *Shari'ah*-based contract. As discussed in the earlier chapters, there are 14 commonly used underlying contracts. Since each contract specifies different types of obligations, cash flow commitments and the like, the risk profile and payoff characteristics of a *sukuk* is dependent on its underlying *Shari'ah* contract. Since *sukuk* are a fund-raising instrument, much like bonds and stocks are, evaluating *sukuk* in terms of debt and equity raises interesting results. If one were to categorise the 14 *Shari'ah* contracts on a continuum ranging from debt to equity, it would be obvious that some contracts such as *murabahah* are, in essence, debt contracts.

A *murabahah*-based *sukuk*, given the fixed nature of the obligation and cash flows, would resemble the cash flow of a bond. Similarly, an *ijarah sukuk* with fixed interim *ijarah* payments would closely resemble the cash flows of a coupon bond. Both the *murabahah* and *ijarah* contracts can result in cash flows that resemble conventional bonds. While the *murabahah sukuk*, which has no underlying asset since the commodity is bought and sold only to transfer funds from "financier" to "borrower", would resemble a debenture or an uncollateralized bond, the *ijarah sukuk*, with its underlying asset, resembles a collateralized bond. By and large, the cash flows and risk profile of the *murabahah* and *ijarah sukuk* mimic that of a debt instrument.

Ironically, it appears that it is this resemblance to debt that makes these two contracts highly popular. The majority of global sovereign *sukuk* are based on *ijarah* contracts, largely because of demand- and supply-side considerations that favor debt-like structures. On the supply side, fixed *ijarah* payments and predetermined maturity cash flows reduce uncertainty to investors and so reduce the required return. This translates directly into reduced cost of funds to issuers. In addition, ratings, which are often mandatory, become a lot easier if cash flows are fixed and predetermined. Such fixed structures would receive more favorable ratings, which again leads to lower required yields and lower costs. On the demand side, as most investment banks that do *sukuk* placement would attest, structures that mimic debt instruments are much easier to be placed out. Large portions of sovereign *sukuk* are often sold to conventional fund/bond managers in the developed markets of the West. These fund managers are interested in *sukuk* for their diversity and not *Shari'ah* compliance. Thus, their interest is in the fixed debt like cash flows and the ratings that go with it.

While the *murabahah* and *ijarah* contracts mimic debt instruments, risk-sharing *Shari'ah* contracts like *mudarabah* and *musharakah* would be at the other end of the continuum that is closer to equity. In fact, what differentiates a *mudarabah* from pure equity is the terminality of *mudarabah*. A perpetual *mudarabah sukuk*, therefore, is essentially a pure equity product. Evaluating *sukuk* from the viewpoint of debt and equity would mean that, depending on the underlying contract, the *sukuk* can be either debt-like, equity-like, or in between. As alluded to in the earlier paragraph, the reality is that the majority of outstanding *sukuk* today belong to the debt-like category, as depicted in Figure 7.3(b) in Chapter 7. While the risk-sharing contracts like *mudarabah* and *musharakah*, being quasi equity, truly provide differentiation and bring value-added of an Islamic product, the debt-like contracts do not. A *murabaha* and *ijarah sukuk* would have the interest rate sensitivity and the leverage-inducing feature of conventional debt.

8.2 *Sukuk* versus Bond Yields

To understand how much convergence there has been between debt-like *sukuk* structures and conventional bonds, one needs to merely examine the correlation in their yields. Figure 8.1 shows the plot of yields for Malaysian, Indonesian, and Turkish government bonds and *sukuk*. Since, the issuer is the same and features similar, if markets were to treat both the bond and *sukuk* as identical instruments, then there should be high correlation between the yields of the two instruments.

Figures 8.1a, 8.1b, and 8.1c prove the point about the convergence between *sukuk* and bond yields. In efficient markets, any two instruments that are alike must have similar returns/yields. Each figure shows three plots, the topmost plot (green) is the yield for government bonds that are denominated in domestic currency. These would be

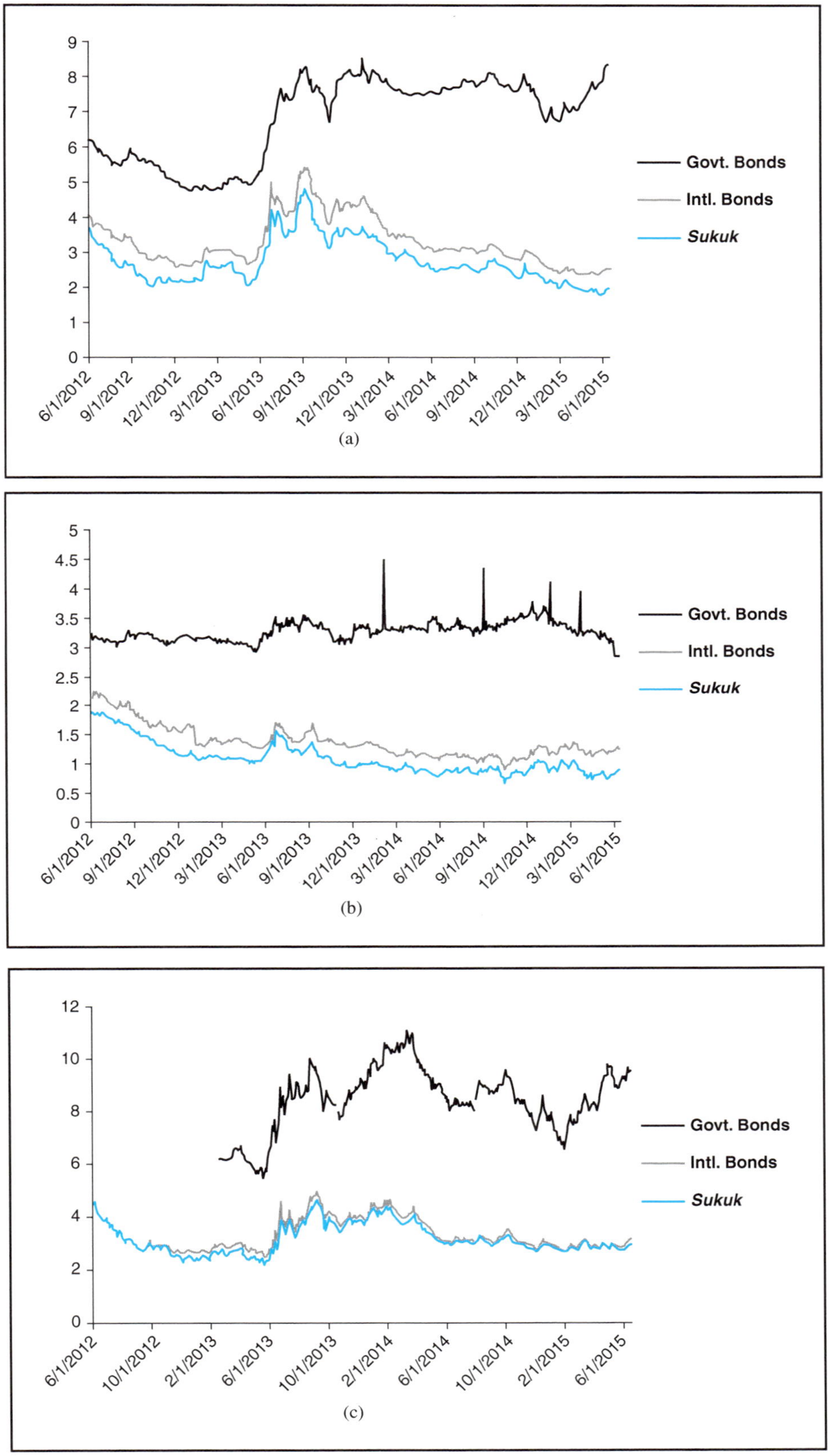

Figure 8.1. Comparison of *Sukuk* and Bonds Yields. (a) Correlation of *Sukuk* and Bond Yields — Indonesia (*Sukuk* 2018). (b) Correlation of *Sukuk* and Bond Yields — Malaysia (*Sukuk* 2016). (c) Correlation of *Sukuk* and Bond Yields — Turkey (*Sukuk* 2018).

Source: Karatas (2018).

the Indonesian Rupiah (Figure 8.1a), Malaysian Ringgit (Figure 8.1b), and Turkish Lira (Figure 8.1c). The other two plots (in blue and red) are the yields for sovereign international bonds and *sukuk* issued by the respective governments.

Both these instruments are denominated in US dollars and have maturities that are close. There are two key points to note from the above figures. First, there is very high correlation between the yields of the *sukuk* and international bond. They move closely together. Though the yields are comparable, the Indonesian and Malaysian *sukuk* appear to have marginally higher yields; this is perhaps a reflection of the lower liquidity of *sukuk* and so, a small liquidity risk premium for the *sukuk*. The second point to note is the marked difference in yields between the domestic currency bond and the US dollar-denominated international bonds. The yield spread here is an obvious risk premium for the currency risk associated with the domestic currency.

8.3 Exotic *Sukuk* Structures

While the *murabahah*, *ijarah*, and *wakalah* structures examined in Chapter 7 are the most common *sukuk* structures, there has been a trend toward more complex structures. These have been the result of wanting to have altered risk profiles, dfferent cash flows profiles, or cash flow profiles dependent on outcomes (contingent payoffs). The need to avoid fixed cash flows is yet another key reason. Exotic structures could also be used to overcome limitations such as the availability of unencumbered physical assets to place as underlying, etc. Thus, we have seen of late, *sukuk* that would have payoffs attached to commodity prices, *sukuk* that are exchangeable at maturity to equity of the *mudarib* (KFC, Malaysia), or groups of stock of other companies held by the *mudarib* (Khazanah, Malaysia). There has also been several *sukuk* with embedded options. The embedded options could be "Call" options on the underlying asset made available to the *mudarib* or "Put" options on the asset made available to the SPV (trustees).

8.3.1. *Sukuk with Embedded Options*

Figure 8.2 shows the structure of a *sukuk* with embedded options. The *mudarib* first executes the sale-leaseback agreement and transfers the asset to the SPV. Using the asset as underlying, the SPV issues *ijarah sukuk* which will be sold to investors. The proceeds of the *sukuk* are then passed on to the *mudarib* as payment for the asset. Simultaneously, the asset which is now owned by the SPV on behalf of *sukuk*-holders is leased to the *mudarib*, who

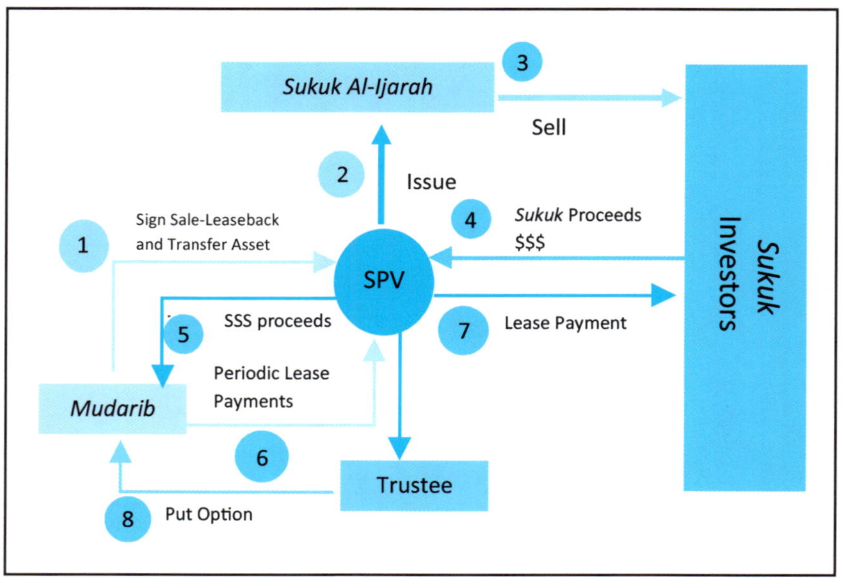

Figure 8.2. A *Sukuk Ijarah* to Finance a Sale-Lease Arrangement with an Embedded Put Option.

makes periodic lease payments. The Put option granted by the *mudarib* to the trustees provides the investors (*sukuk*-holders) with the "assurance" that the *mudarib* will buy back the asset at maturity at a pre-determined exercise price. If the Put option has a European-style exercise, the sale price is pre-determined. However, given the option, there is no guarantee that it will be exercised. What the Put option does is to give investors the assurance that they can enforce the sale on the obligor. Theoretically, the Put option sets a floor price on the underlying asset since, *sukuk*-holders can choose not to exercise the Put option if they can find a third-party willing to pay more.

While the embedded put option serves to protect the interests of *sukuk*-holders, a worried obligor/issuer who fears that he may not be able to purchase the underlying asset at maturity can insist on an embedded call option to protect his interest. An embedded call option would enable the obligor to exercise the right to purchase the underlying asset at a predetermined price. The Call option would effectively set a ceiling price of the underlying asset to the obligor. For example, if the obligor can find the same underlying asset available at a lower price, he can choose not to exercise the embedded call, but purchase the asset outside. This would obviously mean that *sukuk*-holders will now have to find a buyer for the asset.

The use of an embedded Straddle, which constitutes a Long Call and Long Put at the same exercise price, would simultaneously protect the interests of both sides. However, such a straddle effectively fixes the price at which the underlying asset would be bought or sold. If not fixing the price of the underlying is intended, then the use of a long Strangle instead of a Straddle would be logical. In a long Strangle, the long Put option has an exercise price that is lower than the exercise price of the Long Call option. In such a case, the price at which the underlying asset is transacted is not fixed but will be at or within the range of the two exercise prices.

The need to avoid a fixed return in the interim cash flows has meant that many *sukuk* have moved away from having pre-determined fixed rates of return to fluctuating ones. There are many problems in making the interim returns payable to the *sukuk*-holders dependent solely on the underlying asset's returns. For example, some assets may be a cost center and valuing their contribution to overall profits is inaccurate at best. In addition, such a dependence can cause serious "agency problems" or incentive problems. Where the interim payments on a *sukuk* would depend solely on earnings derived from the asset, it will be in the interest of the *mudarib* to under-report the asset's earnings. This is a common problem in conventional venture capital financing and joint ventures. The inherent asymmetry in information makes this agency problem possible. How do we avoid fixing returns while also minimizing the agency problem? The answer, it appears, is in using a transparent external measure over which none of the parties to transaction have an influence. One such measure is LIBOR or the London Interbank Offer Rate. It should not be surprising therefore that several global *sukuk* have payoffs referenced on LIBOR. In allowing reference to the LIBOR, *fuqaha* are of the opinion that this may be the most transparent externally derived measure until an equally liquid and market-derived Islamic alternative is found. Table 8.1 shows some examples of *sukuk* with embedded options. It is obvious from the table that the use of embedded options within *sukuk* is widespread. *Sukuk* originators from many different countries have resorted to the use of embedded options.

Table 8.1. Examples of *Sukuk* with Embedded Options.

No	Issuing Firm / Institution Name	Sukuk Structure	Embedded Option/s	Issuance Date	Maturity Date	Issue Size
1	Alam Maritin Resources Berhad (AMRB)	*Sukuk Ijarah* MTN	Call and Put	July 20, 2006	15 Years	RM600 Mil.
2	Saudi Electricity Company	*Ijarah*	Change of Control Put	April 3, 2012	2017 & 2022	US$0.5 & US$1.25 Bil
3	Dar Al-Arkan	*Ijarah* + *Murabahah*	Certificate holder Put	March 24, 2017		US$1.8 Bil
4	Equate Petrochemical	*Murabaha*	Change of Control Put right	Feb 21, 2017	Feb 21, 2024	US$500 Bil
5	MAF Sukuk Ltd	*Wakala*	Change of Control Put	Feb 7, 2012	Feb 7, 2017	US$ 400Mil.

(*Continued*)

Table 8.1. *(Continued)*

No	Issuing Firm / Institution Name	Sukuk Structure	Embedded Option/s	Issuance Date	Maturity Date	Issue Size
6	TF Varlik Kiralama A.S.	Lease + *Murabaha*	Change of Control Put	April 30, 2013	May 2, 2018	US$ 500 Mil.
7	TNB Global Ventures Capital Berhad	*Wakalah* + *Murabaha* + Lease	*Sukuk*-holders Put right	October 19, 2016	—	US$ 2.5 Bil. (Multi-currency)
8	SIB Sukuk		*Sukuk*-holders Put Option	May 24, 2015	—	US$ 3.0 Bil.
9	Saudi Electricity Global Sukuk Company	*Ijarah sukuk*	Change of Control Put Option	April 8, 2014	April 8, 2024 April 8, 2044	US$1.5 Bil. US$1.0 Bil.
10	MB Holding Company LLC	*Ijarah sukuk*	Change of Control Put option + call option	June 29, 2016	2021	Max US$1.5 Mil.
11	MAF Sukuk Ltd	—	Change of control Put option	November 3, 2015	Nov 3, 2025	US$ 5.0 Bil.
12	Saudi Electricity Global Sukuk Company	*Ijarah*	Change of control Put	April 3, 2012	April 3, 2017 April 3, 2022	US$ 0.5 Bil. US$1.25 Bil.
13	Equate Sukuk PC	*Murabahah*	Change of Control Put Right	February 21, 2017	Feb 21, 2024	US$500 Mil.
14	Golgohar Company's	Standard *Salam*	Put and Call Options	July 2014	March 2015	IRR820 Bil.
15	MAF Sukuk Ltd	Global Certificate Exchangeable (*Wakalah*)	Change of Control Put Option	February 7, 2012	Feb 7, 2017	US$400 Mil.
16	Fatima Fertalizer Company Limited	*Ijarah sukuk*	Call Option	November 28, 2016	Nov 28, 2021	PKR 10,500 Mil.
17	Maybank Islamic Berhad	*Murabahah* (via *Tawarruq*)	Call Option	November 22, 2016	—	RM10.0 Bil.
18	GEMS Education	*Mudarabah* (Perpetual)	Call Option	November 21, 2013	Perpetual	US$200 Mil.
19	NOOR Bank	*Mudarabah* (Perpetual)	Call Option	June 1, 2016	Perpetual	US$500 Mil.
20	ADIB	*Mudarabah* (Perpetual)	Call Option	November 19, 2012	Perpetual	US$1.0 Bil.
21	DIB	*Mudarabah* (Perpetual)	Call Option	March 20, 2013	Perpetual	US$1.0 Bil.

Aside from the need to secure cash flows at maturity, embedded options may also be used in other instances. For example, DP World, a Dubai-based, government-linked entity that operates ports, issued a *wakalah*-based *sukuk* in 2016, which had an embedded put option, giving *sukuk*-holders the right to redeem the *sukuk* if a "change of control event" occurs. A change of control event was deemed to have occurred if the Government of Dubai ceases to own, either directly or indirectly, 50% of issued share capital of DP World. Here, the embedded put option is designed to protect *sukuk*-holders in the event of an ownership change of the company. FlyDubai, a low-cost airline operating out of Dubai and also owned by the government of Dubai, had a similar Put option that could be triggered by a change of control event. The use of such an option helps to reduce the funding costs as *sukuk*-holders know they are protected from any potential change in ownership.

In another example of embedded option that had little to do with ensuring cash flow at redemption, the Al Bilad Bank of Saudi Arabia issued a 10-year *sukuk* in 2016 that had an embedded call option exercisable from the end of the fifth year. The *sukuk*, which was based on the *wakalah* structure, had a floating coupon rate referenced on three-month SIBOR (Saudi Interbank Offer Rate). The call option enabled *sukuk*-holders to convert their *sukuk* into equity shares of the bank at predetermined conversion ratios. In effect, the *wakalah*-based *sukuk* is, in some ways, similar to a convertible bond. Convertible bonds can be thought as delayed equity issuance. If the *sukuk* requires conversion and does not have the alternative of cash settlement, then it is purely a delayed equity issuance. The Al Bilad *sukuk* was deemed to be in compliance with Basel III requirements for bank equity. Companies typically issue convertible bonds for two key reasons: first, to delay the issuance of equity (in order to delay the dilution that results with equity issuance); and second, to reduce funding costs. The required yield on a convertible bond will *ceterus paribus* be lower than that of a similar bond without conversion. This has to do with the fact that with a convertible bond, the bond-holder has the choice of either receiving the face value amount or converting to shares. It would only make sense for the bond-holder to exercise the right to convert if it would be profitable for him to do so. This potential for additional profit gets priced-in as reduced required return of bond-holders, and so, reduced cost of funds to issuers.

8.4 Innovations in *Sukuk* Structure/Design

In addition to the use of embedded options, innovations in *sukuk* design have also moved in the direction of underlying physical assets. The presence of an underlying asset, usually a tangible asset, has been a differentiating feature of *sukuk*. While the presence of a physical underlying asset for a *sukuk* reduces its credit risk and therefore the required yields, the need for an issuer to pledge such unencumbered assets has been a limitation. New high-tech industries and firms like Microsoft, Amazon, Facebook, Alibaba and the like, that began with highly valuable ideas but had little physical assets would not have been able to engage in *sukuk*. They would not have had physical assets to pledge for *sukuk* issuance in the first place. Yet, in today's world, ideas and technologies are the real currency, not physical assets. Enlightened policymakers and organizations can see this reality. For example, Malaysia's Securities Commission has, since 2016, allowed for Intellectual Property Rights (IPR) to be pledged as underlying asset for *sukuk*. We examine other examples of such innovation in the following subsections.

8.4.1. *The Etisalat Airtime Sukuk*

Etisalat, a UAE-based telecommunication firm with operations in several countries in the region, pioneered the use of airtime as the underlying asset for a *sukuk*. The US$1 billion *sukuk* issued in 2010 used airtime for the purpose of securitization. In buying the *sukuk*, the investors were essentially buying airtime vouchers, which were then resold gradually to Etisalat for onward sale to its mobile phone customers. The value of airtime pledged as underlying equaled the issue size. The sale of airtime by Etisalat to its phone customers provides the cash flow for the periodic payments to *sukuk*-holders. A purchase undertaking required Etisalat to purchase and pay *sukuk*-holders for any unsold airtime. Thus, *sukuk*-holders did not have to carry the business risk of unsold airtime. This innovative use of airtime, which effectively enabled Etisalat to securitize its future sales/revenue, was followed by a number of other telecom service providers. Ooredoo, the Qatari telecommunications firm, imitated this structure in its 2013 issue of a five-year *sukuk* for US$1.25 billion. Though the Ooredoo *sukuk* was based on *murabahah*, the pledged underlying asset was airtime. Similarly, Axiata, the Malaysian telecom firm, had issued airtime *sukuk* denominated in Chinese Yuan in 2012. The CNY 1 billion issue was based on a *wakalah* structure. The underlying asset was airtime vouchers. In 2014, Pakistan Mobile Communication Limited (PMLC) also issued *sukuk* with the pledged underlying asset being airtime vouchers. The PMLC *sukuk* was based on a *musharakah* structure. Figure 8.3 shows a simplified version of the Etisalat Airtime *Sukuk* structure.

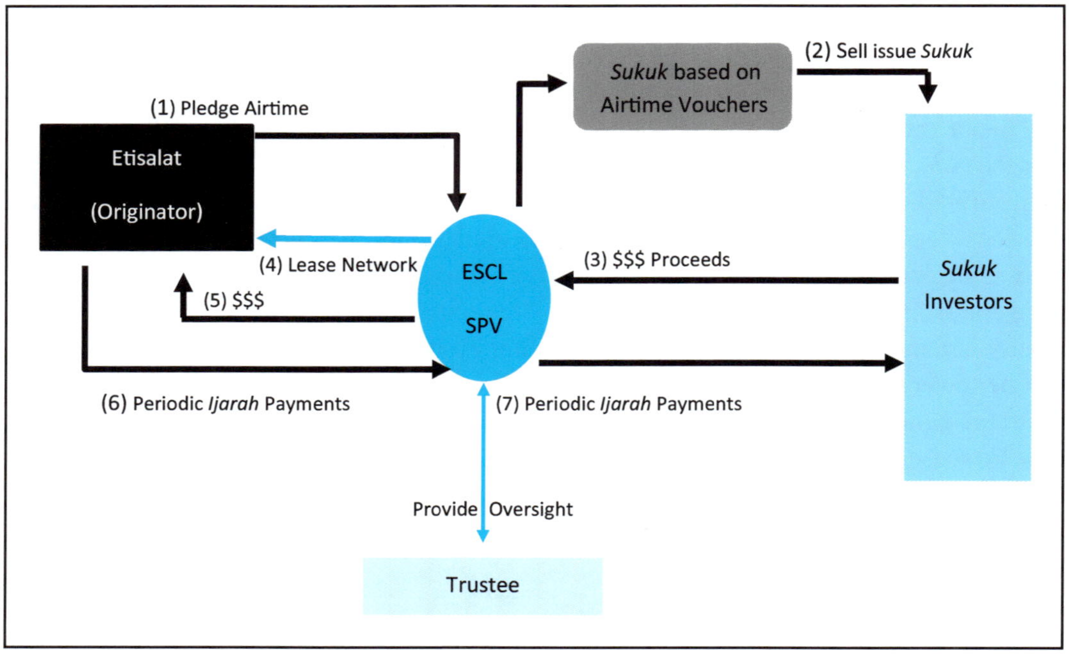

Figure 8.3. The Etisalat *Sukuk* using Airtime Vouchers.

8.4.2 *The Emirates Airline Sukuk Based On Passenger Seat Miles*

If telecom companies such as Etisalat, Ooredoo, and Axiata have used airtime to securitize their *sukuk*, airlines have started to use air passenger miles or Available Tonne Kilometers (ATKM) as the underlying asset for *sukuk* issuance. In a first of its kind, Emirates Airlines issued such a *sukuk* for US$1 billion to finance the purchase of four Airbus A380 aircraft. The innovation was that there were no tangible assets as underlying for the *sukuk*; instead, future revenue from the funded aircraft was being securitized. This ability to issue *sukuk* based on future revenue has important implications. Aside from removing a persistent bottleneck to *sukuk* financing, the need for a physical tangible asset to be used as underlying, such an innovation opens up the possibility of using *sukuk* to fund Greenfield projects. The higher risk associated with reliance on future sales for *sukuk* repayment was reduced in this instance, through a purchase undertaking by Emirates Airlines to make good any shortfall in needed revenue. In addition, a reserve account was used to smoothen periodic repayments. Figure 8.4 shows a simplified version of the structure.

In the simplified version shown in Figure 8.4, Emirates Airlines, as obligor, pledges Rights to Travel (ROT) or ATKM worth the issuance amount to the SPV (Mejdool), which is managed by the trustee. Using the pledged "asset" as underlying, the SPV issued a 10-year *sukuk wakalah bil-isthimar*, set to mature in 2023. Proceeds from *sukuk* issuance are passed on to Emirates Airlines as payment for the ROT. The *sukuk* provides its holders undivided ownership rights over the ROT. The trustee acting on behalf of the *sukuk*-holders appoints Emirates Airlines as *wakeel* to sell the ROT to its airline customers. Revenue from the sale of airline services as represented by the ROT are passed on to the trustee as periodic payments for the *sukuk*. The Emirates Airline *sukuk*, in its innovative form, appears to have been a profitable proposition. The airline was raising US$1.175 billion in total, comprising US$1 billion in *sukuk* and US$750 million of conventional bonds. Interestingly, the *sukuk* were priced to yield approximately 50 basis points *lower* than the conventional bonds, a reflection of the high demand for *Shari'ah*-compliant papers in UAE at the time. The lower yield on the *sukuk* meant that the financing cost to the airline was lower.

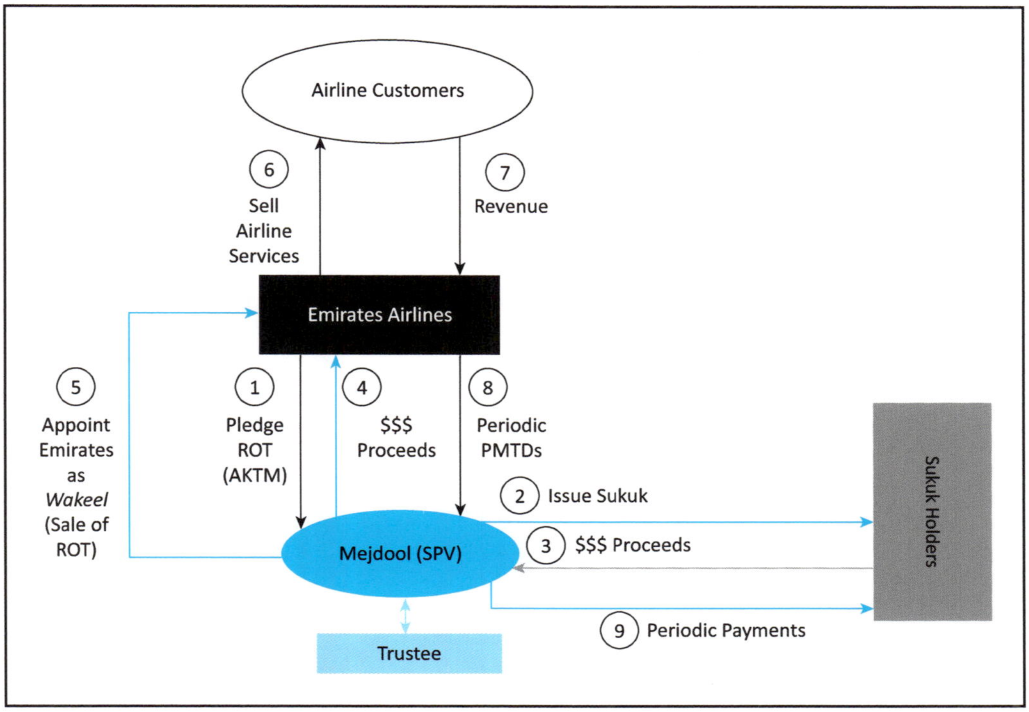

Figure 8.4. The Emirates Airline *Sukuk* Based on Passenger Seat Miles (2013).

Both the Etisalat and Emirates Airlines *sukuk* are examples of innovation aimed at overcoming the limitations imposed by the need for physical tangible assets as underlying asset for *sukuk* issuance. Aside from encumbering a valuable asset, the need to transfer assets to the SPV and then back to the originator at maturity increases complexity, transaction costs, and tax/stamp duties. Furthermore, such an asset requirement biases in favor of large companies with huge asset portfolios. Start-ups will not be able to use *sukuk* to raise financing since they may not have the needed unencumbered asset.

If the pioneering initiatives of Etisalat and Emirates Airlines helped to overcome the limitations of underlying asset requirements, the innovation surrounding Perpetual *sukuk* by the likes of the Abu Dhabi Islamic Bank (ADIB) and the Dubai Islamic Bank (DIB) in 2012 and 2013 respectively, allowed the issuers to overcome a regulatory barrier.

8.4.3 *The Khazanah Exchangeable Sukuk*

In September 2006, Khazanah Nasional Berhad issued the world's first *"Shari'ah* compliant exchangeable trust certificates". These were, in essence, *sukuk* that were convertible into shares at maturity. The underlying asset for the issuance was Telekom Bhd. shares which were owned by Khazanah. The coupon payments for the *sukuk* are to be derived from the dividends paid on the underlying Telekom stock. Since, there is no certainty to the dividends to be paid by Telekom, the coupons would be uncertain. However, coupon fluctuations have been minimized by the establishment of a sinking fund using dividends received to smoothen the coupon payments. The exchangeable *sukuk*, in this case, has a payoff profile similar to that of a convertible bond. In the case of convertible bonds, however, the bonds would typically be convertible into stocks of the issuer, not that of a third-party as is the case here. Still, the exchangeable *sukuk* provides the same upside profit potential from conversion that convertible stocks do.

In the transaction, Khazanah first established an SPV (Orchid) to which the Telekom shares were transferred. Another entity, Rafflesia was established to be the issuer of the *sukuk*. Based on trust undertaking, Raffesia issued *sukuk* to be sold to the investors. Proceeds were then channelled to Khazanah in exchange for the Telekom stocks placed with the SPV. *Sukuk*-holders who wish to convert their *sukuk* to Telekom shares could do so over the period from November 2006 to October 2011. The conversion price was set at RM10.85 per Telekom stock. At maturity of the *sukuk* in October 2011, all remaining Telekom shares (that have not been converted) are to be sold back to Khazanah. Proceeds to Rafflesia from this sale would be used to redeem the unconverted *sukuk*. To ensure this, Khazanah had entered into a Purchase Undertaking with Rafflesia, the issuer. Figure 8.5 shows the structure of the exchangeable *sukuk*.

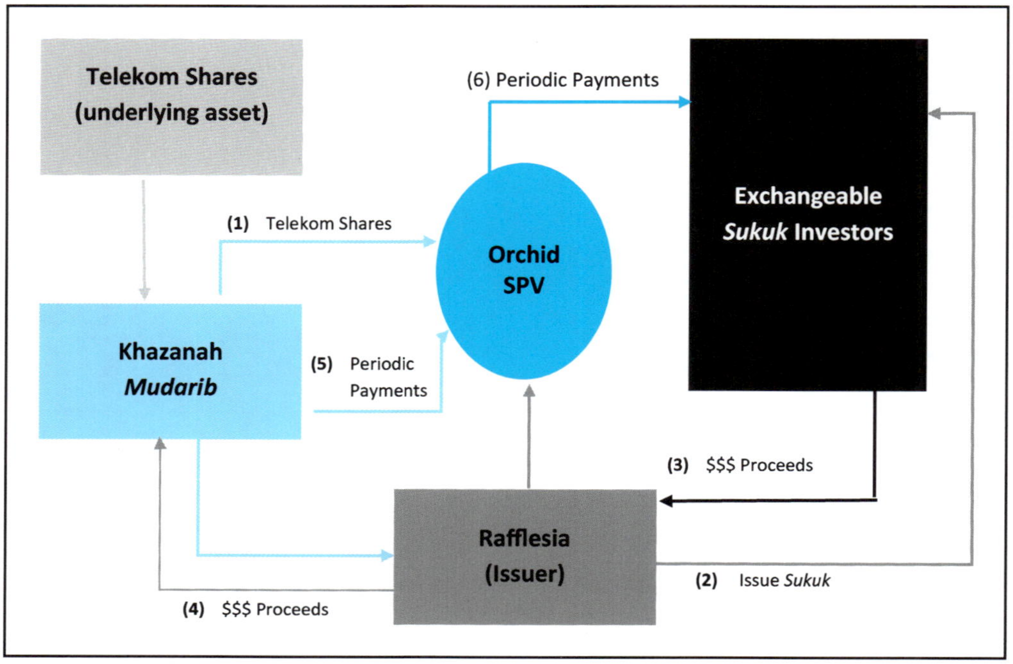

Figure 8.5. Structure of the Khazanah Exchangeable *Sukuk*.

The RM10.85 conversion price constituted a 19% premium over Telekom stock's reference price (traded price on a particular day just prior to *sukuk* issuance). To Khazanah, the exchangeable *sukuk* was similar to a *Covered Call Write*, which is a strategy to sell a call on a stock that is owned. The call sold or shorted has an exercise price higher than the prevailing price of the stock. The call sold or shorted by Khazanah is the embedded call option (long call) the *sukuk*-holder receives (the ability to choose whether to convert to stocks or redeem for cash). Recall that the *sukuk*-holder has the right but not the obligation to covert to stock. That right is the call option received by the *sukuk*-holder. The pricing of the *sukuk* would be such that Khazanah gets compensated for the call it sells/shorts. The covered call position is a fairly common strategy used by fund managers to earn extra returns from their holdings of stocks, by selling call options at higher exercise prices. If the buyer of the call exercises the option, the fund manager sells the stock at the exercise price. Since the exercise price was higher, he makes a capital gain. Alternatively, if the buyer of the call does not exercise, because it is unfavorable for him, then the fund manager gets to profit from the call premium received. The covered call strategy is usually done on low-beta or defensive stocks.

As a *Shari'ah*-compliant instrument, the exchangeable *sukuk* had to be always in line with *Shari'ah* requirements. Here, the issue of *Shari'ah* compliance depends on the underlying Telekom stock being always deemed *Shari'ah*-compliant over the five-year tenor of the *sukuk*. To remain continuously on the Shariah Advisory Council's (SAC) list of *Shari'ah*-compliant stocks, Telekom must not breach any of the requirements. To ensure that *sukuk*-holders are always protected in the event Telkom stocks exceed certain thresholds, for e.g., the 33%

threshold on debt, there was also an embedded put option. This embedded Put option allowed *sukuk*-holders to redeem their *sukuk* immediately if Telekom stock was removed from the *Shari'ah*-compliant list (see Chapter 10).

Following the successful launch of the first exchangeable *sukuk* in 2006, Khazanah has followed up with several other equity-linked issues. Its second exchangeable *sukuk* was on PLUS Expressways, another Malaysian listed stock. In 2008, it issued its third *Shari'ah*-compliant exchangeable *sukuk*. A *musharakah*-based *sukuk*, this time the underlying assets were Khazanah-owned shares of Parkson Retail Group Limited, a company listed on the Hong Kong Stock Exchange. Khazanah has also issued exchangeable *sukuk* on Malaysia's Tenaga Nasional, and even more recently on the stocks of Beijing Enterprises Water Group (BEWG), a China-based water and sewerage treatment service provider.

8.4.4 *The Perpetual Sukuk*

The perpetual *sukuk*, which has now been issued by several Islamic banks, was in response to tighter capital adequacy requirements. Following the Global Financial Crisis of 2008/2009, the Bank for International Settlements (BIS) came out with revised requirements for capital adequacy of banks. Known as Basel III Framework, it was designed to address the deficiencies of Basel II, which were laid bare by the financial crisis. In essence, Basel III required banks to have much higher equity capital. Basel III removed an existing Tier 3 capital and streamlined capital into two tiers: Tier 1, which consisted of Common Equity Tier 1 (CET1) and Additional Tier 1 (AT1), and Tier 2 (T2). So, banks, in meeting the new requirements for Tier 1 capital, could either issue new common equity or quasi-equity instruments that were subordinated, had no maturity, were loss-absorbing, and had fully discretionary non-cumulative dividends/repayment. Abu Dhabi Islamic Bank (ADIB) was the first to see the potential to use a *mudarabah*-based perpetual *sukuk* to raise funds under the AT1 category. Recall that the *mudarabah* contract is essentially a quasi-equity, risk-sharing contract. The one key difference between the *mudarabah* contract and equity is the terminality of *mudarabah*. A perpetual *mudarabah* would therefore mimic equity. BIS appears to have accepted this parallel between *mudarabah* and equity. Accordingly, in November 2012, ADIB issued the first ever perpetual *sukuk*. The issuance was for US$1.0 billion. The *mudarabah*-based *sukuk* came with an embedded call option. The call option enabled the issuer to call back predefined portions of the outstanding *sukuk* after a non-call protection period of five years.

ADIB's issuance of the perpetual *sukuk* in late 2012 was quickly followed by the Dubai Islamic Bank (DIB) in early 2013. The structure was also based on *mudarabah*. Several other Middle Eastern banks have followed suit with similar *mudarabah*-based perpetual *sukuk* to meet their capital adequacy requirements. Several Saudi banks, such as NCB, Saudi Investment Bank, and Banque Saudi-Fransi, have issued perpetual *sukuk* to meet either Tier 1 or Tier 2 categories of their capital requirement. Several Malaysian banks, such as Public Bank Islamic, RHB, Hong Leong, Ambank, and Maybank, have had similar perpetual *sukuk* issuance. The Malaysian banks, however, in meeting their Tier 2 requirements, have structured their *sukuk* under a *murabahah* or *ijarah* contracts. Of late, Kuwait-based Ahli Bank issued a perpetual *sukuk* for US$ 200 million in 2016 while another Kuwaiti institution, Warba Bank, issued a similar *sukuk* in 2017 for US$250 million.

The perpetual *sukuk*, which has thus far been issued only by banks, has had geographical diversity. Though the initial ones were *mudarabah*-based and appropriate for AT1 requirements, the latter issuances, especially those of Malaysian banks, have used debt-based structures to meet their Tier 2 requirements.

8.4.5 *The Islamic Development Bank Sukuk Program: Multi-currency Issuance*

The Jeddah-based Islamic Development Bank (IDB) has been a major catalyst and pioneer in the development of *sukuk* structures and issuances. The IDB first started using *sukuk* to mobilize funds in 2003. In 2005, the IDB established a US$1 billion, Medium Term Note (MTN) Program, which was subsequently increased to US$ 3.5 billion in September 2010. Under this MTN Program, the IDB has issued a series of *sukuk* in alternative currencies as follows:

- Series 1, US$500 million issued in 2005 (matured in June 2010)
- Series 2, SG$200 million private placement issued in 2009 (maturity in September 2012)
- Series 3, US$850 million issued in 2009 (maturity in September 2014)
- Series 4 and 5, two tranches of SAR 1.875 billion private placement issued in 2010 (maturity in September 2020)
- Series 6, US$500 million issued in 2010 (maturity in October 2015)

The funds raised from the *sukuk* issuances are utilized mainly for financing the development projects in IDB member countries. The latest, Series 6 *sukuk*, utilizes a *wakalah* structure, where IDB acts as a *wakeel* of the SPV named IDB Trust Services Ltd., which acts as the issuer and trustee for the *sukuk*. The SPV utilizes the funds raised to purchase assets from IDB's portfolio. The restrictions on the purchase are:

- 51% minimum should be tangible assets, shares or *sukuk*
- Intangible assets comprising receivables from *murabahah* or *istisna* cannot exceed 49%.

The SPV, IDB Trust Services, appoints IDB under the *wakalah* agreement to manage the portfolio. Profits from the portfolio, after deducting the expenses of the Trust, are passed on to the *Sukuk*-holders. IDB also commits to purchasing the portfolio at maturity from the SPV. The purchase price is to be determined as the sum of aggregate nominal amount of trust certificate and accrued unpaid periodic distribution. Figure 8.6 shows the structure of the *sukuk*.

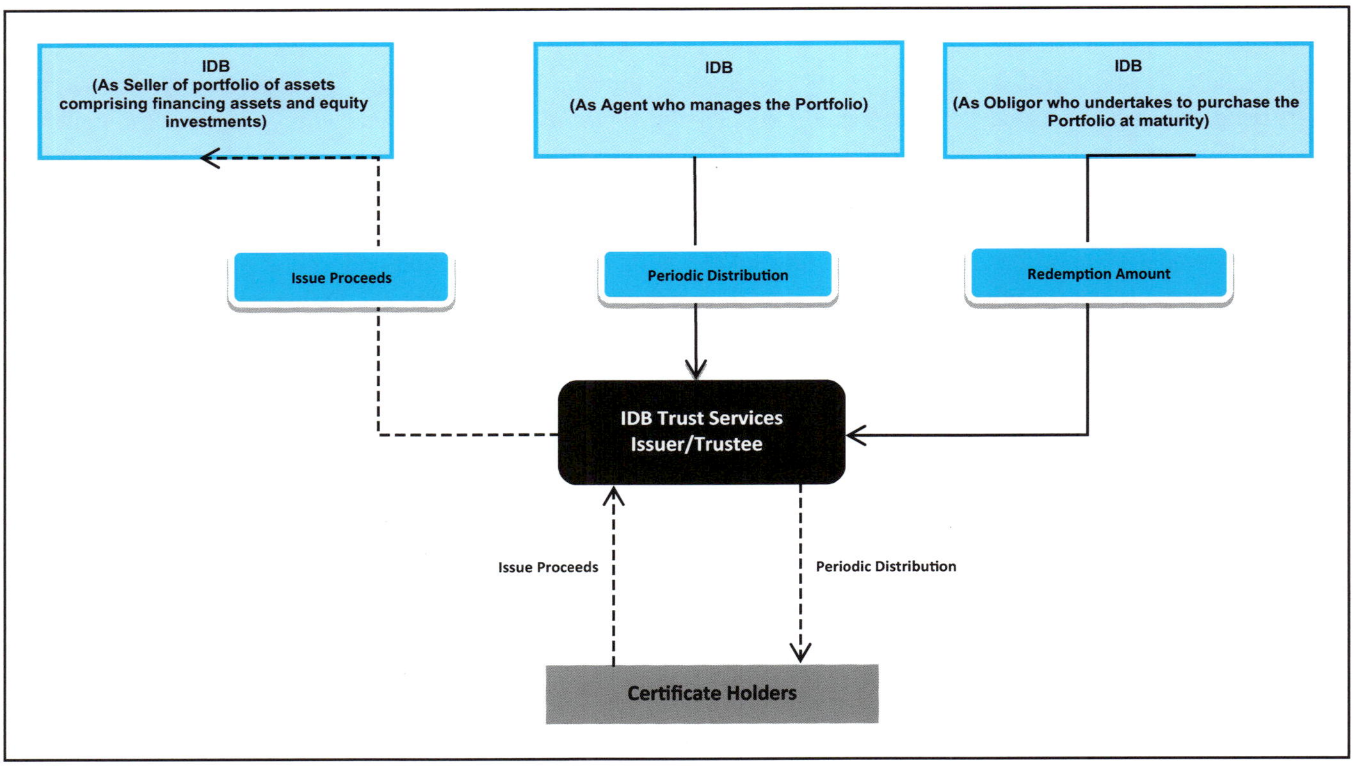

Figure 8.6. The IDB Medium Term Note Program (*Wakalah*).

Source: IDB and IIFM.

8.4.6 *The General Electric Capital Sukuk*

General Electric (GE) Capital, which is the financing subsidiary of General Electric Corporation, was the first American company to have issued a *sukuk* (see Figure 8.7). The *sukuk* was novel as it was the first *sukuk* issuance based on beneficial ownership interest in aircraft assets and revenue tied to lease income generated by those assets. The issuer in this arrangement was GE Capital Sukuk (Bermuda), which acquired beneficial interests in aircraft assets from Sukuk Aviation Leasing (SAL), another subsidiary of General Electric Capital Corporation, and appointed SAL as the servicing agent. SAL also furnished an undertaking to repurchase the underlying asset at maturity. A total of 90% of the *sukuk* proceeds are to be used to purchase a beneficial interest in aircraft assets via SAL. The remainder is to be kept with SAL in a Funded Reserve Account (FRA). The FRA is executed through a Commodity *murabahah*. As servicing agent, SAL collects the lease payments (rentals) which will then form the basis for periodic payments to *sukuk*-holders.

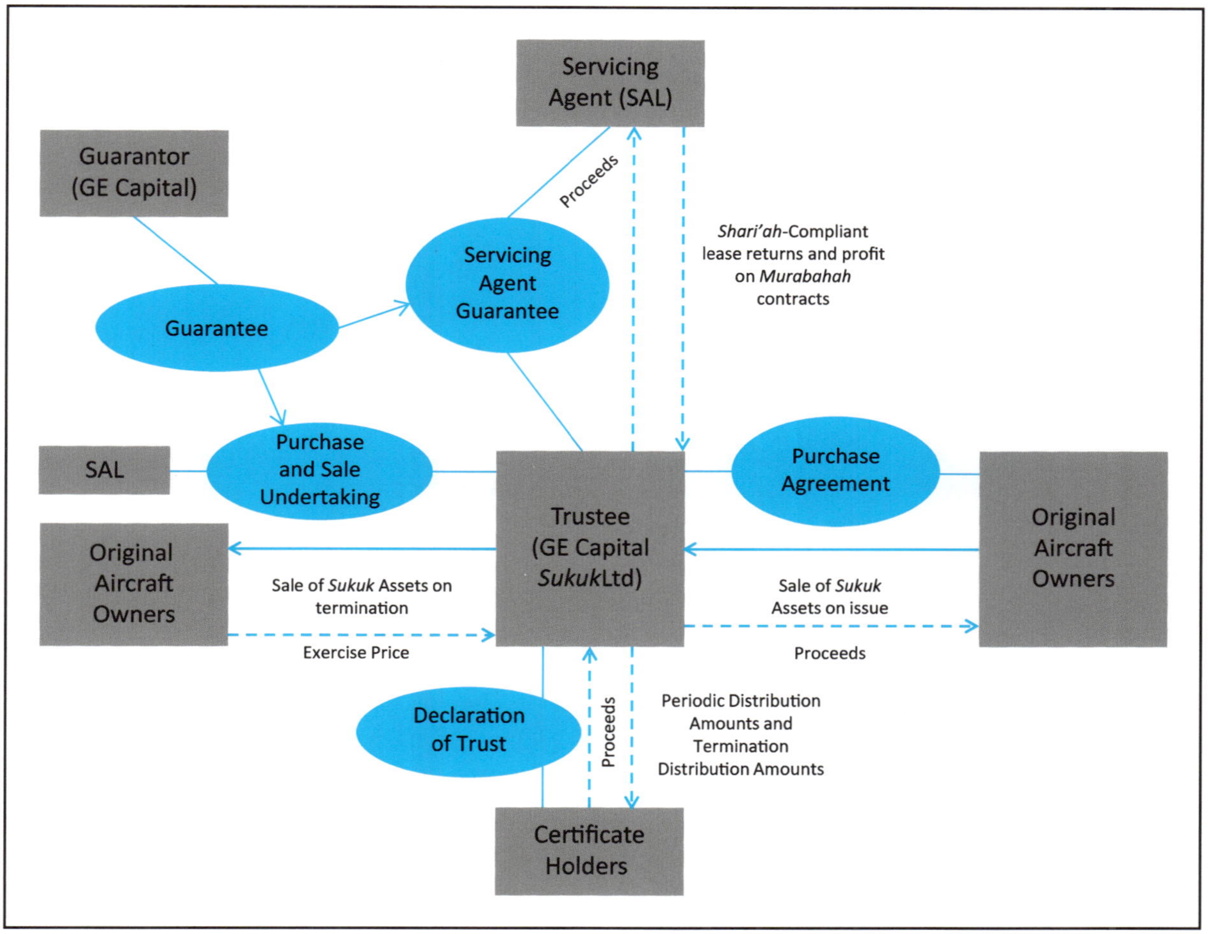

Figure 8.7. The GE Capital *Sukuk*.

Source: GE Capital Sukuk Offering Document.

Collections in excess of the required periodical rental are retained in an Unfunded Reserve Account (URA) for the issuer's benefit. Part of URA may be paid as an advance incentive fee to SAL. These funded accounts are essentially means by which to "smoothen" returns to *sukuk*-holders. For example, when the rental amount is less than the needed periodical distribution to *sukuk*-holders, the difference could be covered in three different ways:

(i) SAL credits back from the advance incentive fee to the URA and utilizes the money to meet the shortfall.
(ii) However, if the URA funds are insufficient, SAL will withdraw from the FRA.
(iii) If both the FRA and URA do not have sufficient funds to cover the shortfall, SAL can extend an interest free loan to the issuer.

8.5 What the Future Holds: New *Sukuk* Structures

In this section, we examine some of the new *sukuk* structures being researched and proposed. In particular we examine three new proposed designs. These proposed designs seek to avoid some of the criticisms against current *sukuk* structures. Most of the criticism have been in the following four areas:

(i) The violation of some *Shari'ah* principles in the area of transaction through recourse to legal "tricks" (*hiyal*) and the combination of controversial contracts.
(ii) The lack of a risk-sharing element in many current *sukuk* structures due to the detachment of the cash flows from the performance of the underlying asset and the real sector of the economy.
(iii) The complexity of some *sukuk* structures that induces additional costs and legal uncertainty.
(iv) The replication mode has meant that the majority of outstanding are based on debt contracts like *murabahah*, *ijarah*, and the like. Even where *wakalah* and other contracts are used, the clauses of the *sukuk* effectively replicate fixed rate debt contracts. As a result, Islamic financing leads to the same problems of debt, leverage, and vulnerability.

In view of these criticisms, new research has focused on risk-sharing *sukuk* structures based on modified *mudarabah*/*musharakah* contracts. Box 8.1 makes a case for why modification to these contracts are needed and describes the key modification.

Box 8.1. Modifying the *Mudarabah* for contemporary needs.

The *mudarabah* and *musyarakah* contracts are at the heart of the risk-sharing philosophy of Islamic finance. Yet, one would be hard pressed find them used in Islamic banking or capital market products. Even in cases where sukuk are structured on these contracts, the risk-sharing spirit may be missing. Thus, a *sukuk* may be labeled as *Mudarabah*, but have fixed returns/coupon. This is often achieved through clauses that provide for waivers. This is unfortunate as the risk-sharing contracts of Islamic finance can offer an alternative to the debt/equity tradeoff in finance. Further, given the huge build up in debt/leverage globally and as the world seeks alternatives to debt financing, these risk-sharing contracts could be a solution. The *mudarabah* contract in particular is well suited as a risk-sharing financing contract. Interestingly, it had once been successfully adapted in the Middle Ages, by the Italian city states and renamed as commenda. The commenda appears to have contributed to the financing of the Italian and European renaissance. Commenda later resurfaced as the venture capital financing technique that made Silicon Valley what it is today. Yet, the Muslim world appears to have missed the opportunity to use risk-sharing contracts effectively. To understand this irony, one has to separate the philosophy from the operational features of the contract. The early Italians and contemporary venture capitalists kept the philosophy but tweaked the operational mechanics. And that may be what we would need today within Islamic finance.

In classical *Mudarabah*, one party, the Rab-Ul-Mal or financier, provides the capital, while the other party, the *Mudarib*, provides the entrepreneurship and effort to run the business. The underlying contractual relationship is that of a partnership, with the Rab-Ul-Mal as the silent or sleeping partner. Profits derived from the business or investment are shared by the two parties according to a predetermined profit-sharing ratio (PSR). This could be, say, 70:30, with the larger portion accruing to the *Mudarib*. In the event of losses, the Shariah stipulates that all losses must be borne by the financier. Yet, the financier is not allowed to interfere in the running of the business. Thus, a *Mudarabah* arrangement looks very much like an equity investment by a shareholder in a public listed company. In fact, Islamic banks consider *Mudarabah* financing to be the equivalent of equity financing.

However, *Mudarabah* financing is really a hybrid. It is neither equity nor debt because to a *Mudarib*, the financing is like conventional equity for the following reasons: (i) there are no "fixed" annual payments that are due (unlike

(*Continued*)

Box 8.1. (*Continued*)

interest); (ii) payments made to the Islamic banks come from profits, much like dividends, they need be paid only if there are profits; (iii) the Islamic bank cannot foreclose or take legal action if there are no profits and therefore nothing to be shared; and (iv) like equity, using *Mudarabah* financing does not increase a firm's risk the way debt financing does through increased financial leverage.

On the other hand, *Mudarabah* has features of debt such as: (i) it represents a "fixed" claim by the Islamic bank, this being the initial amount plus whatever accrued profits (or losses) that are due to the bank; (ii) like debt, *Mudarabah* financing is terminal, the *Mudarib* can end the relationship by repaying the principal and accrued profits to the Islamic bank.

Thus, unlike equity which represents an unlimited and perpetual claim on the company, *Mudarabah*, despite the features that make it seem like equity, represents an asset specific and terminable claim. The terminality makes *Mudarabah* seem like debt, hence the earlier, argument that *Mudarabah* is really a hybrid in the conventional sense.

Unfortunately, as *Mudarabah* has the features of both debt and equity and the Shariah prohibits the Rab-Ul-Mal from interfering in the business but requires him to absorb all losses, the agency problems (conflicts of interests) of *Mudarabah* are higher than that of debt or equity. While profits will be shared and profits are revenues less costs, the *Mudarib* has the incentive to increase those costs that accrue to him as benefits. The allocation of overheads and other costs to the project, the use of transfer pricing, etc., are ways by which the profits to be shared can be minimized. As the Rab-Ul-Mal cannot interfere in the business, he cannot put in place the internal controls that conventional equity holders can. Given the fixed and terminal claim of *Mudarabah*, adverse selection and moral hazard problems of debt can also exist within *mudarabah* relationships. Classical *mudarabah* therefore is an entirely trust based contract. Trustworthy behavior is essential for its proper functioning. This explains the dearth of *mudarabah* financing among Islamic banks today. Yet, as proven in the case of Silicon Valley and medieval Europe, it can work if its operational features can be modified.

Modifications on how costs are to be enumerated, which costs are to be allowed, the use of industry benchmarks and best practices, and the use of equity kickers to hold the *mudarib* responsible would all bring in the type of controls now lacking. With good internal controls and transparency, development infrastructure could be funded using such modified *mudarabah* contracts. With almost all OIC countries running budget deficits, the financing of development infrastructure is a critical issue. The continued use of debt to fund development is not sustainable. The consequences of debt reliant growth is obvious. Too many countries have been brought to their knees as a result of debt. Modified *mudarabah sukuk* can be the means to fund development without leverage. Given their hybrid features they can be a new asset class and one not easily susceptible to contagion.

Source: Adapted from author's Op-Ed piece in *The Malaysian Reserve*, 10 July 2017.

8.5.1 *Risk-Sharing Sukuk for Corporations to Fund Revenue-Generating Projects*

Where a *sukuk* based on a risk-sharing contract is used to fund a revenue-generating asset, risk-sharing should be based on the revenue generated by the asset. In other words, the returns to the financier (sukuk holder) will be linked directly to the earnings of the project. In this sense, it is like an equity instrument. However, unlike a new issue of common stock, which would have a claim on all existing assets including the new project, this *sukuk* would have a claim only on the earnings of the new project. Given the asset specificity and the complex nature of the cost allocation in accounting, there will have to be agreement on revenue recognition and on identifying and measuring the relevant/allowable costs attributable to determining the earnings to be shared. Aside from avoiding *gharar*, such clarity will also help with estimating cash flows.

The underlying contract can be a modified *mudarabah* or *musharakah* combined with a *wakalah*.[1] The instrument will be terminal and have fixed term. The tenor will depend on a number of factors: (i) the economic life of

[1] *mudarabah* (contract between capital owner and investment manager), *musharakah* (partnership with both parters as maagers), *wakalah* (contract of agency).

the project or underlying asset; (ii) the cash flows/earnings generated; (iii) the profit-sharing ratio (PSR); and (iv) the required return given the riskiness of the project. The term should be set such that for a given PSR and required return, the sukuk holder can expect to get back his initial investment plus his required profit. This funding instrument is intended to be listed and traded on secondary markets. Secondary trading brings numerous benefits, including enhanced liquidity, which would attract a wider range of investors. Small denominations would attract small retail players and their attraction would be furthered if the buying and selling of these instruments could also be handled through banks and institutions such as the post office. This would enable rural investors to participate with their small savings. A rural investor who wants to buy can do so at current prices and sell through his local bank or post office with the sale being affected at the day's closing price much like mutual funds. In Section 8.6 below, we examine the pricing of such a corporate instrument.

8.5.2 *Modified Mudarabah Sukuk for Infrastructure Projects — Illustration*

To see how risk-sharing finance using *Mudarabah* can be used in an infrastructure project, we work through a simple example. Assume that a developing country is in need of a new power generation plant to serve a region that has been suffering brownouts. The government has negotiated with a foreign contractor who has the expertise to design and build the plant. The expected output from the plant will not only overcome current shortages but provide extra capacity to attract industries to the region. The total investment needed for the project is $750 million. The government will provide land and other basic infrastructure including all rights to connect the plant's output to the national grid. The government will also provide seed funding of $20 million. The total value of the government's investment is $75 million or 10% of needed total investment. Construction will take three years with production beginning in early Year 4. Based on a PPA (power purchase agreement), all the output will be sold to the National Electricity distributor at a predetermined unit price. Assume that the net profit in Year 4 will be $50 million and will increase to $60 million in Year 5 before stabilizing at $70 million from Year 6 onwards. Since electricity has a regulated price, net profits are expected to remain at around $70 million in subsequent year.

The government now needs to determine how to fund the needed $675 million. To raise these funds, the government could issue 10-year convertible *Istisna-Mudarabah* sukuk. In essence it is a convertible "Islamic bond" with a construction and profit/loss sharing contract. An *Istisna*-embedded sukuk is commonly used in infrastructure sukuk. The Istisna is a contract that will be in force during the period of construction. Once construction is complete the Istisna is fufilled and automatically lapses.

Given the three stages of the project; construction, revenue sharing and IPO, Figures 8.9 (a), (b) and (c) show the structure of the sukuk arrangement in each stage while figure 8.8(d) shows the post IPO situation.

In Stage 1, the government works with its investment bankers to establish an SPV which will be administered by a Trustee. The underlying land, seed fund and other government inputs are pledged to the SPV. As is the case with all sukuk issues, the SPV is bankruptcy remote, ring-fences the project and is designed to be self-liquidating at the end of year 10 upon completion of the IPO process. The sukuk issued should preferably be traded in secondary markets.

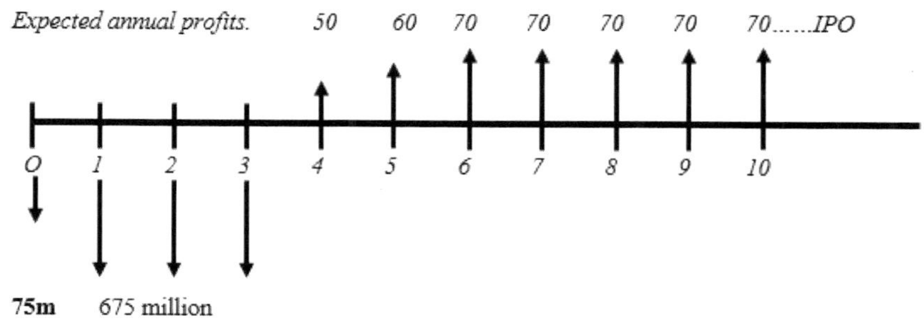

Figure 8.8 Expected Cash Flows/Net Profit of Project.

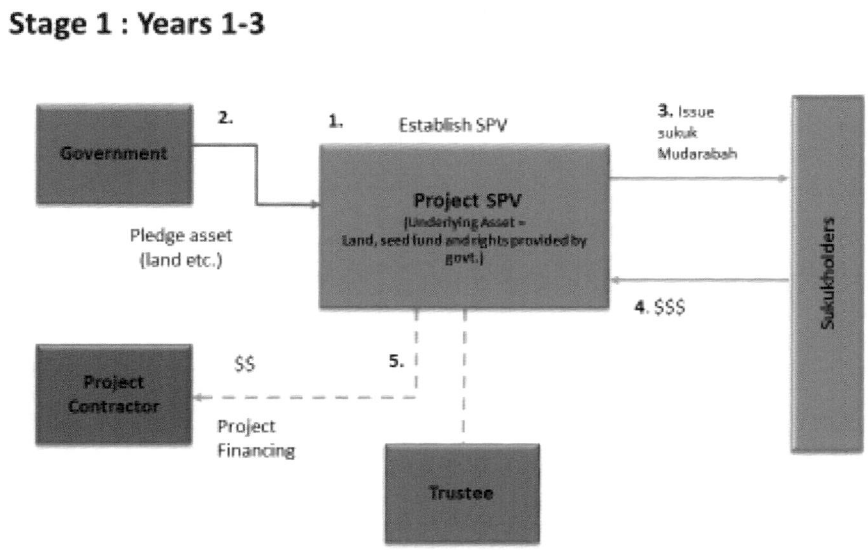

Figure 8.9(a) The Sukuk Issuance Process.

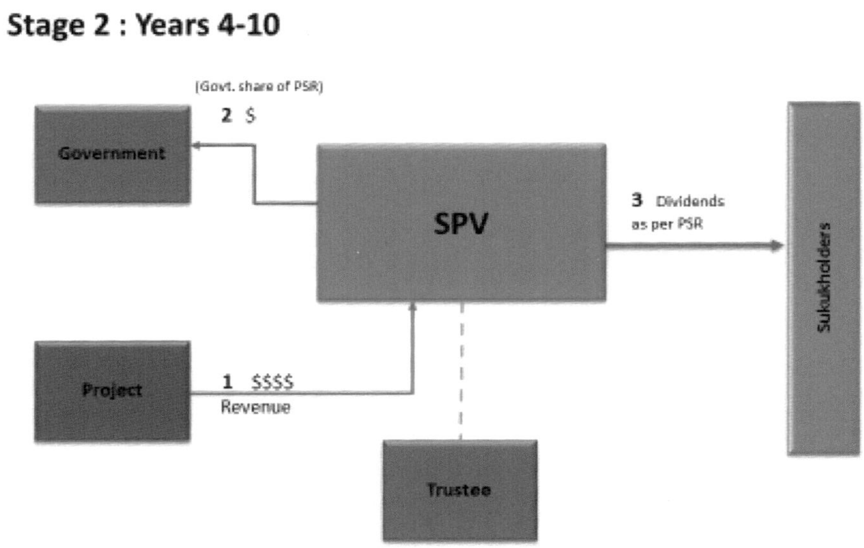

Figure 8.9(b) Revenue Generation and Distribution.

In Stage 2, as the revenue begins, the project pays out dividends to both the government and sukuk holders as per the predetermined profit-sharing ratio (PSR). The PSR can be based either on capital contribution, 10% to government and 90% to sukuk holders, or some negotiated ratio, for example 80/20, where 20% goes to the government even though its capital contribution was only 10%. Much depends on the riskiness and desirability of the project. Where a development project is low risk and desirable, the government can keep a larger portion of the ownership to itself. The nature of the project determines how much bargaining power the government has.

In Stage 3, at the end of Year 10, with the project and its ancillary infrastructure all up and running and a seven-year track-record of profits, the IPO process should be executed. The process of identifying the stock exchange or exchanges should be initiated earlier, perhaps in the latter part of Year 9. Where a project is very large, listing on multiple exchanges should be considered. The domestic stock market should be the focus. The development of local capital markets ought to be an indirect objective of development financing. Given expected Year 10 revenue/

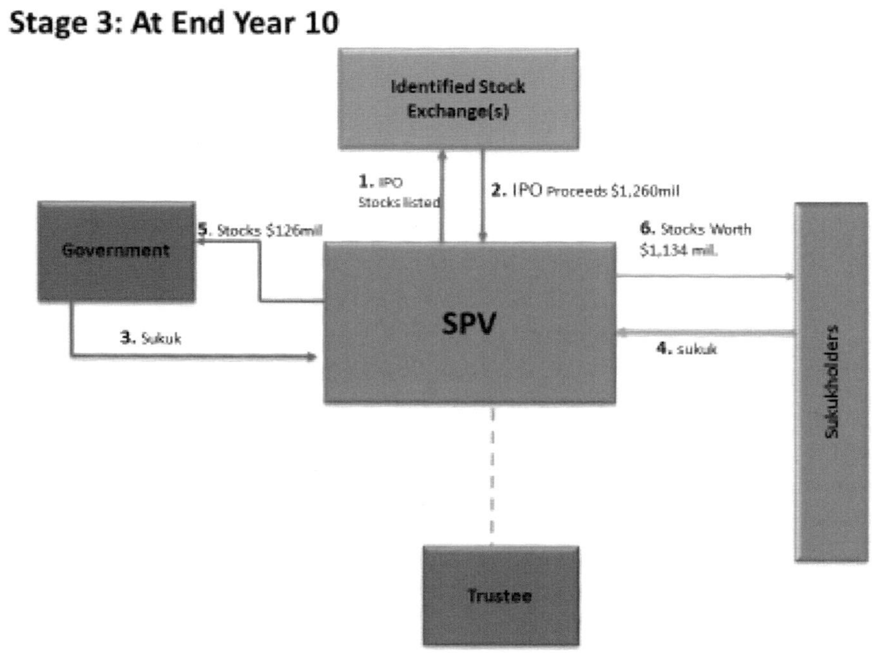

Figure 8.9(c) The IPO Process.

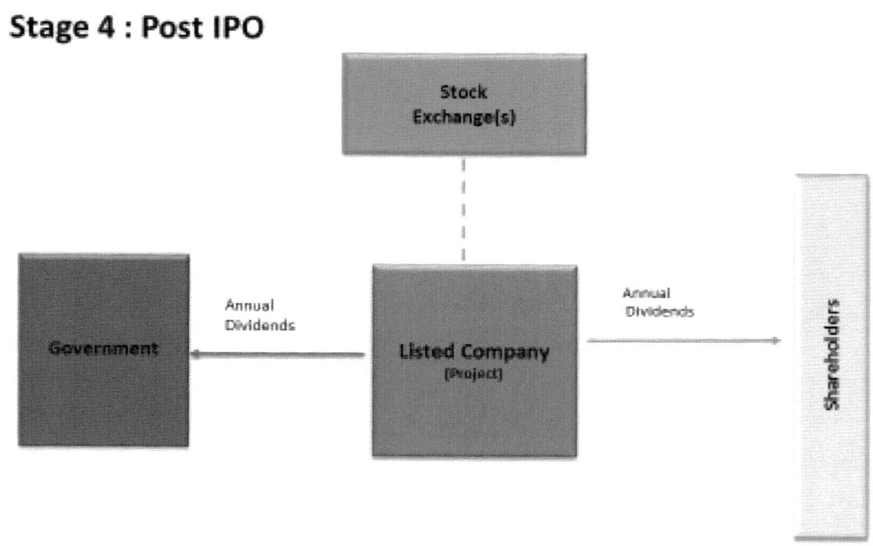

Fig. 8.9(d) Post-IPO — Listed Company.

profits, the IPO valuation of the project is fairly straightforward. The price-earnings multiple (P/E ratio) is a commonly used guide to estimate IPO valuation. Investment banking practice is to use industry average P/E ratio multiples to estimate IPO valuation. For example, if the average P/E multiple for listed power generation plants is 16 to 20 times globally, then the IPO valuation for this power plant would be \$70 million × 18 times P/E [2] = \$1,260 million or \$1.26 billion. Figure 8.8 earlier shows the cash flows.

[2] 18 times P/E ratio is the mid-point.

The proceeds of $1,260 million is split between the government which receives $126 million worth of stocks, for its 10% portion of initial investment, and *sukuk* holders who in exchange for their sukuk receive stocks worth $1,134 million. Notice that the IPO process enables both the government and private *sukuk* holders to recognize a capital gain of approximately 68% on the initial investment.[3] By making the IPO a part of the original sukuk structure, markets will factor in this upside potential and accordingly price the *sukuk* at issuance. The IPO in effect is an embedded call option in the sukuk. In raising the original value of the sukuk at issuance in Year 0, the call option effectively lowers the required return by investors or the cost of capital.

Figure 8.9(d) shows the entity post-IPO. The SPV has been dissolved, the trustee has no further role. The power generation project is now a publicly-listed company. *Sukuk* holders who are now shareholders receive dividends as would the government.

There are a number of factors to note. First, unlike the use of debt financing, there is no financial obligation for the government beyond its initial investment. The government initiates and coordinates the funding and project execution. Development projects get going without any stress on the government budget yet the government stands to benefit during and post IPO. The government can either sell off its stake or continue to hold the listed shares and earn dividends. In addition, with the listing of such large and stable cash-flow projects on the domestic stock exchange, local equity markets grow and develop. Well-developed domestic capital markets can reduce the cost of domestic fund raising and minimize the need to seek funding overseas. By keeping the face value of at least a portion of the *sukuk Mudarabah* small, financial inclusion can be enhanced. The project becomes inclusive with even small investors participating in the largest of projects. Egypt's recent issuance of *Suez Canal Certificates* to fund the construction of a second channel of the Suez Canal is one example of mass mobilization of domestic funds by way of small denomination securities. We examine the pricing of such modified *mudarabah sukuk* in Section 8.6 below on *sukuk* pricing.

8.5.3 *Funding Non-Revenue Generating Infrastructure Projects*

The risk-sharing principle is applicable even in cases of funding non-revenue generating infrastructure. However as there is no revenue to be shared, the risk-sharing occurs by linking the repayments to the earnings capacity of the obligor. Linking repayments to the earnings capacity of the government brings in an "automatic stabilizer". The government has to pay more when it earns more and has the capacity to and pays less when its capacity reduces. The problem with debt funding is that repayments are fixed and independent of the obligor's capacity. When debt servicing exceeds a government's capacity, a crisis is triggered. The risk-sharing model proposed here shares the financing burden with the government and avoids the problems associated with debt. There are two ways of doing this. In both cases, the idea is to link the returns of the funding instrument to the earnings capacity of the government or some indicator of that ability. Accordingly, one could have a *sukuk* that provides returns linked to the export earnings of a country or alternatively a *sukuk* with returns linked to nominal GDP growth.

8.5.3.1 *Sukuk with returns linked to nominal GDP*

Nominal GDP is a measure of a country's output of goods and services. It is therefore a good indicator of a government's income/revenue. With many developing countries adopting the GST (Goods and Services Tax) framework, nominal GDP becomes even more closely linked to government revenue. That GDP growth can be linked to returns of a government's debt papers is not something new. GDP warrants have been issued by countries such as Argentina, Bosnia, Costa Rica, and Ukraine. In fact, the origins may be traced to the Brady Plan of the 1980s which issued 'Brady Bonds' that promised additional payments if certain GDP or macroeconomic benchmarks were met.

[3]For government = [(126 – 75)/75] × 100 = 68%, For *sukuk* holders = [(1134 – 675)/675] × 100 = 68%.

Very recently, Blanchard, Mauro and Acalin (2016) argue that given unsustainable debt ratios, countries, even advanced ones ought to now consider growth-indexed bonds.

The seminal work in GDP-linked bonds has been by Borenstein and Mauro (2004). Aside from making the case that GDP-linked bonds can improve debt sustainability for governments during downturns, they point out several advantages over conventional fixed rate bonds. The first advantage is that debt servicing requirements reduce during downturns thereby reducing stress on government budgets and avoiding defaults and financial crises. Furthermore, GDP-linked bonds enable governments to avoid the pro-cyclical policies that conventional debt forces on governments. During downturns when government revenue is low, the fixed servicing requirement of debt forces government to cut development and other social welfare spending. Such a cutback is the exact opposite of what a government should be doing, and the result of such pro-cyclical action is to worsen the downturn. Since GDP-linked bonds would require lower servicing outlay during downturns, governments may not have to cut back much on spending if at all. Aside from worsening downturns, pro-cyclical spending cuts tend to have the most impact on the poorest segments of society.

Borenstein and Mauro (2004) also cite the case of Mexico which following the Peso Crisis in 1994, experienced high unemployment and a reduction in real tax revenues of about 8%. This revenue reduction forced among other cuts, a cut in healthcare spending of 17%. These cuts led to street protests and subsequent political crises. They cite, simulation which shows that if Mexico's public debt had been GDP indexed, the country would have saved the equivalent of 1.6% of its GDP. Such a substantial saving could have avoided the drastic spending cuts and the resultant political problems.

1. *Determining returns to GDP-linked Sukuk*

Borenstein and Mauro (2002), outline at least five different methods used to determine the returns to a GDP-linked bond. The method they propose is given as;

$$\text{if } g_r > b_r \qquad r = Max\,[(b_r + 0.5\,(g_r - b_r), 0] \tag{6}$$

$$\text{if } g_r < b_r \qquad r = Max\,[(b_r + 0.25\,(g_r - b_r), 0] \tag{7}$$

where;

r = *% of return in year*

g_r = *% of growth of real GDP in that year*

b_r = *base rate (average growth rate of last five years).*

It is obvious that depending on whether the country is rapidly growing or otherwise, the co-efficient 0.5 and 0.25 could be varied. Based on the above equations and co-efficient, the expected return on a GDP-linked bond or *sukuk* can be estimated given expected GDP growth over the tenor of the instruments. The above equations (6) and (7) can be used in the context of a risk-sharing *sukuk*. To understand how a risk-sharing *sukuk* could be used in a GDP-linked context, we work through an example.

2. *Illustration: Using a GDP-linked sukuk to fund a non-revenue generating project*

Suppose a developing nation wants to build a large public hospital in its capital city. The estimated total cost is US$300 million equivalent in local currency and construction will take three years. There are several *sukuk* structures or combinations that could be used. The most straightforward would probably be the *Ijarah* (sale-leaseback) structure. The *Ijarah* is a commonly used structure in global sovereign *sukuk*, several of which are listed on exchanges in Luxembourg, Dublin, etc. The structure would be as follows. First, an SPV is established which will be managed by an independent third-party trustee. Next, the government identifies a group of its assets, for example its office buildings which cumulatively have an estimated value of US$300million. These office buildings are then "sold" to the SPV for US$300 million equivalent in local currency. Based on these assets as underlying, the SPV issues GDP-linked *sukuk* to investors. The proceeds are passed on to the government which uses the funds to undertake the hospital project. At the end of every year, the government makes *Ijarah* payments linked to GDP to the SPV which then passes on the payments as dividends to *sukuk* holders. The annual payments are essentially lease payments that the government pays for the usufruct or benefit of continuing to use an asset it has already sold. The annual dividends received by a *sukuk* holder will be determined as follows.

Assume the face value of each sukuk is $1,000. The tenor is 20 years. Suppose the country's average growth rate over the last five years is 5% ($b_r = 5\%$). If in a given year the actual GDP growth rate is 7.5 %, since g_r is > then b_r; the return to *sukuk* holders given the Eq. (6) above will be;

$$r = 5\% + 0.5\ (7.5\% - 5\%) = \mathbf{6.25\%}.$$

In dollar terms, the total amount in dividends would be $18,750,000, being 6.25% of the $300 million. Since the face value of the *sukuk* is $1,000, *sukuk* holders receive a dividend of $62.50 equivalent in local currency for every *sukuk* held. Alternatively, if the economy had slower growth of only 4% then the payoff given $g_r < b_r$; would be $r = 5\% + 0.25\ (4\% - 5\%) = \mathbf{4.75\%}$ or **$47.50** of dividends per *sukuk*. Under this scenario, the total amount of dividends paid to *sukuk* holders would be $14,250,000 which is 4.75% of $300 million. The "debt" servicing obligation to the government reduces as GDP growth reduces. In this case, the reduction in payment to *sukuk* holders is $4,500,000 when GDP growth reduces from 7.5% to 4%. It is this in-built stabilizer that reduces financial stress and reduces macroeconomic vulnerability.

At the end of Year 20, the underlying assets, in this case the group of office buildings will be resold to the government for an agreed amount. Assuming the agreed resale price is US$300 million equivalent in local currency, the government pays this amount to the SPV which passes on the amount as final "bullet" payment to *sukuk* holders. The SPV is dissolved and the arrangement complete. Figure 8.10 shows the structure of the *Sukuk Ijarah*.

The narrative in the GDP-linked bond literature has always been about the periodic coupon or interest payments. In structures where the principal is amortized annually, the principal portion is often as large if not larger than the interest portion. However, the principal payment is usually not included in the discussion, implying a full repayment of principal portion regardless of economic condition. In a risk-sharing *sukuk Ijarah*, it would be possible to also link the annual principal payments to GDP growth for more flexibility. For example, in an alternative to the *sukuk* structure above which has a single lump sum payment of principal by way of selling the underlying asset back to the government at maturity, one could structure a *sukuk ijarah* which has amortization of principal. Here,

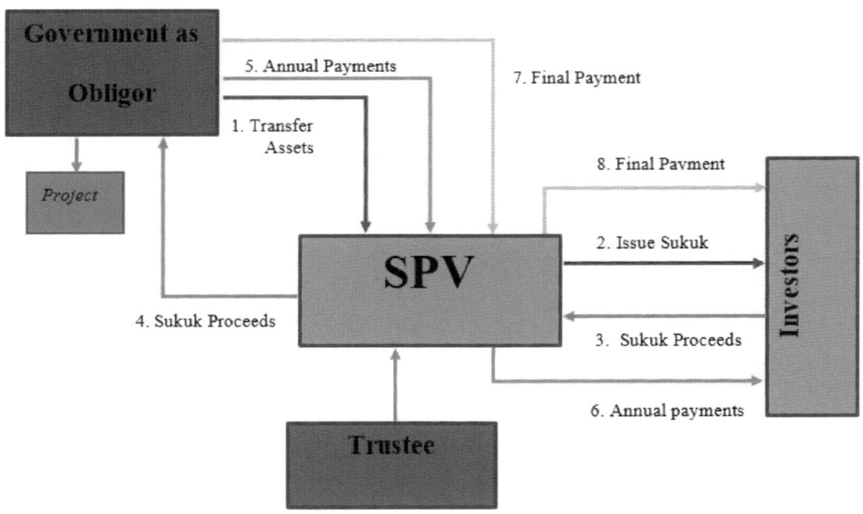

Figure 8.10 GDP-linked *Sukuk Ijarah*.

instead of buying back the asset in one lump sum at maturity, the government buys back portions of the underlying asset annually by making principal payments. At maturity, the government simply pays the final remaining portion of the $300 million original principal and gets full ownership of the underlying asset. The key difference here with conventional amortization is that, in conventional arrangements an equal amount of principal is due every year regardless of ability. In this proposed *sukuk ijarah*, the total principal to be repaid remains the same ($300 million) but the annual amounts vary according to GDP growth, just as the annual dividends.

For example, using the numbers for the above hospital project, the annual repayment of principal (by way of repurchasing portions of the underlying asset), would be;

$300 million / 20 years = $15 million per year.

To see how linking principal to GDP growth would work, we work through the two GDP growth scenarios used earlier.

3. *Illustration: Sukuk ijarah with both principal and returns linked to GDP growth*
In the hospital project above, we had used two alternative GDP growth scenarios, 7.5% and 4% to illustrate how returns/dividends to the *sukuk* would vary. We use the same GDP growth scenarios to examine how total repayments for a given year would vary as GDP growth changes.

Scenario 1: GDP growth is 7.5%

Principal portion due	$= \$\ 15{,}000{,}000 \times (1 + (g_r - b_r))$
	$= \$15{,}000{,}000 \times (1 + (7.5\% - 5\%))$
	$= \$15{,}000{,}000 \times (1.025)$
	= $15,375,000
Lease amount due	= $18,750,000 (*from earlier*)
Total annual repayment	= $15,375,000 + $18,750,000 = ***$34,125,000***

Scenario 2: GDP growth is 4%

Principal portion due	$= \$\ 15{,}000{,}000 \times (1 + (g_r - b_r))$
	$= \$15{,}000{,}000 \times (1 + (4\% - 5\%))$
	$= \$15{,}000{,}000 \times (0.99)$
	= $14,850,000
Lease amount due	= $14,250,000 (*from earlier*)
Total annual payment	= $14,850,000 + $14,250,000 = ***$29,100,000***

In a good year when GDP growth is high, the government pays a higher amount to amortize outstanding principal. In a poor growth year, it pays less. Notice that between the two scenarios explained earlier, the obligation on the government is lower by $5.025 million.

As mentioned earlier, the total principal that has to be repaid remains unchanged at $300 million. Thus, at maturity in Year 20, the government pays the outstanding balance of principal. A nation that has had above average growth over several years over the 20-year period, would have paid "extra" towards principal such that at maturity in Year 20, the outstanding balance is much less than $15 million. The opposite would be the case for countries that have had below average growth in GDP.

8.5.3.2 *Sukuk with returns linked to commodity exports*

Many emerging developing nations are commodity exporters. Their main source of revenue is the export of a few commodities. For such countries, the movement in the international price of these commodities is the key to foreign exchange earnings and government revenue. For such countries, the ability to repay will depend on commodity prices. As these countries are price takers and their commodity's prices are determined in international markets, the risk-sharing *sukuk* should have repayment obligations reflecting these price changes. To see how this could work we examine the case of a hypothetical developing country, whose main exports are four primary commodities.

4. *Illustration: Sukuk linked to Commodity Prices*

Commasia is a developing country in Asia whose main exports are four commodities; cocoa, coffee, sisal, and sugar cane. Together, these four commodities accounts for 90% of its exports. The breakdown of exports is as follows:

Percentage of Commodities as Exports

Commodity	% of Exports
1. Cocoa	40%
2. Coffee	20%
3. Sugar Cane	20%
4. Sisal	10%

Since a large portion of the government's revenue is based on direct and indirect taxes on these commodities, government revenue fluctuates with their international prices. The risk-sharing *sukuk* will have to be linked to changes in these commodity prices. The simplest way would be to compute a price weighted index based on the average prevailing price to determine the rate of change in price. This can be done as follows:

$$\text{Index} = \Sigma\ w_1 \cdot P_1 + w_2 \cdot P_2 + w_3 \cdot P_3 + w_4 \cdot P_4 \tag{8}$$

where P_i is the average annual price for Year t.

$$\%\ \Delta\ \text{Index} = [(\text{Index}_t - \text{Index}_{t-1})/\text{Index}_{t-1}) \times 100 \tag{9}$$

One could simply use the % Δ in Index to equal the percentage returns on the *sukuk*. However, while simple, given the typical volatility in commodity prices, returns would be volatile. Such volatile returns would necessitate higher required returns for the *sukuk* holders. To stabilize returns while still linking it to changes in commodity prices, one could determine *sukuk* returns as;

$$\%\ \text{Return to } sukuk = \alpha + \beta.\ \%\ \Delta\ \text{Index} \tag{10}$$

α is a constant and β, the coefficient that links changes in index to *sukuk* returns. There are several possible combinations of values that could be used for α and β. At the time of flotation, α and β should be values that given the expected one-year price for the commodities, provides a % return on the *sukuk* equal to "required" returns.[4] By setting expected returns equal to required returns at floatation, the *sukuk* could be sold at par. α and β should vary by country and commodity. For countries with higher country risk profile, α would need to be higher. Where a country's commodities have large price fluctuations year to year, the β would have to be lower. While the lower β reduces *sukuk* return volatility, the lower β may require a higher α to compensate, given expected required returns.

To avoid negative returns on the *sukuk*, in cases where the commodity price volatility is excessive and % Δ Index takes a negative value, such that Eq. (10) gives a negative return, a trigger clause could be embedded that provides for a minimal return, for example two percent. Alternatively, the β could be set to zero in cases where large

[4] Required returns can be estimated using the country's outstanding debt plus a premium for the novelty and additional risks

price falls could lead to negative *sukuk* returns. The following is an illustration of the return computation given changes in global prices for the four commodities above.

5. *Illustration: determining returns of sukuk linked to export commodity prices*

Average Price of Commodity per ton.

	Average Price	**US$ per ton.**
Commodity	**Year t – 1**	**Year t**
1. Cocoa	$2,950	$3,205
2. Coffee	$1,740	$1,890
3. Sugar Cane	$308	$270
4. Sisal	$1,700	$1,640

Using Eq. (8), the index value in year t – 1 and t would be;

Index value Year t – 1

0.40(2950) + 0.20(1740) + 0.10(1700) + 0.20(308) = ***$1,760***

Index value Year t

0.40(3205) + 0.20(1890) + 0.10(1640) + 0.20(270) = ***$1,878***

The percentage change in index using Eq. (9) is;

[((1878 – 1760)/1760) × 100] = ***6.70%***

Since the commodity price index has increased by 6.70%, assuming an α of 5% and β of 0.5 the return payable by the government for the *sukuk* would be, based on Eq. (10);

% Return to *sukuk* = 5% + 0.3 (6.70%) = 7.01%

It is obvious that the parameter values of α and β must be carefully determined and calibrated. This would be particularly important for commodities that have highly fluctuating prices. It may be the case that a range of values for β may have to be predetermined for different threshold levels of commodity prices effectively having an upper/lower constraint.

Box 8.2. Funding Growth Without Debt

A number of contradictions appear to be plaguing the Muslim world. *Sukuk*, the most popular fundraising instrument of Islamic finance, has seen declining issuance in 2015 relative to previous years. That this is happening at a time of increased need for infrastructure funding is a contradiction. The OECD estimates that approximately US$71 trillion will be needed globally by 2030 for investments in roads, rail, electricity, water, and other basic infrastructure. Much of these needs are within the Muslim world. Ironically, of all *sukuk* issued thus far, less than 10% has gone into the funding of infrastructure. This is indeed surprising since the *Shari'ah* requires investments to be in real assets, be long-term in orientation, have returns anchored in real sector returns, and bring benefits to society. Development infrastructure has all these features. They are tangible, can provide revenue over their long economic lives, and bring both economic and social benefits to the *ummah*.

(*Continued*)

Box 8.2. (*Continued*)

So, why hasn't more *sukuk* gone into the financing of development infrastructure? There are both demand- and supply-side reasons to this. If, as argued, supply creates its own demand, the structure of *sukuk* currently being brought to market (supplied), can explain its insignificance. The majority of outstanding *sukuk* are *ijarah* (lease), *murabahah* (trade credit), *salam*, and the like, all of which are essentially fixed rate contracts. Like conventional debt, these debt-based contracts require fixed servicing and thereby increase leverage and macro-economic vulnerability. Furthermore, most of these *sukuk* are short to medium term, with maturities mostly within five years. If *sukuk* look and behave like bonds, there is no value-added to Muslim nations that issue them in lieu of debt. In fact, there may be distinct disadvantages relative to a bond issuance. The most obvious being the higher issuance costs from the need for an underlying asset, an SPV and ownership transfers, etc. Thus, from the demand side, it is no surprise that countries looking to raise infrastructure funding, look elsewhere but at *sukuk*.

These nations need growth without leverage. Ironically, the solution to growth without leverage lies within Islamic finance. The risk-sharing contracts, *mudarabah* and *musharakah*, being hybrid equity, avoid the fixity of debt while providing the flexibility of equity. Governments that typically issue bonds to raise the debt to fund infrastructure can instead use innovative *sukuk*, such as a convertible *mudarabah sukuk*, to raise equity like funding. For example, suppose a government intends to build a power generation plant whose output will be distributed and sold through the national grid. Since the project will generate revenue and profits, risk-sharing structures that involve profit/loss sharing can provide the same funding at much lower risks. Revenue-generating development infrastructure typically require heavy upfront investments but provide very stable cash flows for extended future periods, the next 50 to 100 years. Instead of issuing bonds in Western financial markets and incurring currency exposure, reduced financial flexibility, increased debt service ratios, and the many constraints that come with increased debt, governments could issue convertible *mudarabah sukuk*. Much of these could be sold locally, with a needed portion overseas. Financial inclusion can be enhanced through issuance of a portion in small denomination. The recent experience of Egypt in raising funds domestically for the second Suez Canal is a case in point.

Since the power plant project involves construction during which no revenue is produced, the *sukuk* should be a convertible *istisna–mudarabah* structure. Assuming it takes three years to build the plant, the *sukuk* pays nothing in the three years during which the *istisna* contract is in force. On completion, as revenue begins to be generated, the *mudarabah* kicks in, with profits being shared with *sukuk*-holders. This could go on for perhaps the next seven years, i.e., Years 4 to 10 of the project. At end of Year 10, when all ancillary and supporting infrastructure has been built and power generation has achieved expected full capacity, the entire project could get listed through an initial public offer (IPO). *Sukuk*-holders can either choose to convert their *sukuk* to listed shares and become shareholders or sell their shares and redeem their investment at market value. The IPO process is important as it enables *sukuk*-holders to capture the upside of their investment. Such upside potential also makes it palatable to go through the first three years (construction period) without any returns.

If all the needed funds for the project are raised through the proposed *sukuk*, there is no pressure whatsoever on government budgets. Governments merely provide the land and facilitate the project and for this get a portion of the stake and receive their share of *sukuk*. At IPO, the government too becomes a shareholder and continues to share in future project revenue. Since none of the constraints of debt are applicable here, the government technically faces no limits in the number of projects that can be undertaken. As long as there are economically viable projects, the government can initiate such investments. The key to success would be good governance. The reason the world shies away from equity and is biased toward debt has to do with information asymmetry. Risk-sharing must necessarily mean the sharing of only the project's risk and no other risks like political risk, or risks arising from corruption, mismanagement, and the like.

Source: Author's op-ed article in *Derrin Ekonomi*, February 2016.

8.6 The Pricing of *Sukuk*

Islamic Financial Institutions (IFIs) that originate *sukuk* often consider the technique used in pricing the *sukuk* to be proprietary. Add to this the customized nature of these products and we can see that it is diffcult to have a generalized model for pricing *sukuk* as we do for conventional bonds. As it now stands, the industry practice appears to be to price a *sukuk* based on outstanding debt instruments of the issuer. That is, if a *sukuk* to be issued has to be priced, the IFI determines the initial offer price by examining the yields of the issuer's outstanding bonds. The yields of the outstanding bond(s) are used as a guide in estimating the required yield for the new *sukuk*. The bond's yield is adjusted for differences between the *sukuk* and bond, if any. For example, a *murabahah sukuk* may have the same required yield as that of a straight bond, especially if there is no substantial increase in the firm's overall leverage (debt to equity ratio, D/E level). If the issuance of the *murabahah sukuk* is large such that the overall D/E level deteriorates, then the required yield for the *sukuk* would be increased to reflect the higher resulting leverage and risk. Differences in the yields of bonds for different debt levels of firms from the same or similar industry can indicate the cost effect of different D/E levels. Using the same logic of adjusting the yield for risk would imply that *ceterus paribus*, an asset-backed *ijarah sukuk* would have lower required yield than a *murabahah sukuk* simply because in the case of the *ijarah sukuk*, there is a tangible underlying asset. The availability of a tangible underlying asset, especially one that is standard and can easily be disposed of in the event of a foreclosure, provides an added safety to the *sukuk*-holder.

If a *sukuk*-issuer has no outstanding bonds, then yields of proxy bonds are often used. For example, the bond of a company in a similar industry as the issuer is often used as guide. The yield of the proxy bond is then adjusted for differences in the leverage ratios, and other differences in the underlying business or clauses/indentures of the *sukuk*. This dependence on bond yields as benchmarks for *sukuk* pricing has had two key consequences. First, as seen in Figure 8.1(a), (b), and (c), the result has been the near convergence in yields of the sovereign *sukuk* and bond. The market appears to treat the *sukuk* as just another debt instrument, to be priced and traded as one. The second and probably bigger consequence of this practice of pricing *sukuk* based on bond yields has meant that the majority of *sukuk* issued tend to be based on debt contracts, especially *murabahah* and *ijarah*. The risk-sharing contracts like *mudarabah* and *musharakah* are avoided, largely because of the complication in their pricing.

Given the reliance on bond-based pricing, thus far there are no generalized theoretical models for *sukuk* valuation. Still, there is no reason why we cannot use the underlying logic and valuation principles used in conventional finance for valuing assets. Accordingly, in the discussion that follows, we describe common valuation techniques and show how they could be applied in pricing *sukuk*.

The basic logic of pricing an asset in finance can be described as follows:

(i) The value of a financial asset/instrument is equal to the present value of cash flows generated from the asset.
(ii) Where they are offsetting cash flows, value will depend on the net cash flow (i.e., all positive cash flows add to value whereas negative ones reduce value).
(iii) Where they are multiple cash flows, each cash flow should be valued individually and aggregated to arrive at the overall value of the asset/instrument.
(iv) Where a component cash flow is based on a Contingent Claims Analysis (CCA) which uses probabilities, we could use probabilities to determine "expected" cash flows.
(v) Where an asset has one or more embedded options, the options must be identified and valued individually.
(vi) Where an asset is based on another underlying asset, value is derived by valuing cash flows generated by the underlying asset.

To see how some of the above principles would be applied, we discuss three different Islamic *sukuk*. First, a *sukuk* with "fixed" cash flows, a Senadat *Mudarabah* Cagamas (SMC) *sukuk*; second, a *sukuk ijarah*; and third, a *sukuk ijarah* with warrants/options attached.

8.6.1 *Valuing a Sukuk with Fixed Cash Flows*

A good example of a *sukuk* with fixed cash flows would be the SMC *sukuk*. The SMC *sukuk* have maturities of up to 10 years, however, given the fixed nature of the coupon, the "government guarantee", and the relatively larger liquidity, they are popular in the Islamic interbank market. Pricing of the SMC bonds are done on a RM100 face value basis.

$$P = \left[\frac{100\left(100 + \left(\frac{C \times E}{365}\right)\right)}{100 + \left(\frac{r \times T}{365}\right)} \right] - FV\left(\frac{C \times t}{36500}\right)$$

where
P = Price per RM100 face value
C = Indicative coupon for current coupon period
E = No. of days in current coupon period
T = No. of days from transaction date to next coupon pmt. day
r = Yield to maturity
t = No. of days from last coupon payment date to the value date
NV = Nominal value of SMC transaction

8.6.2 *Valuing a Basic Sukuk Al-ijarah*

In a typical *sukuk ijarah*, an investor would receive two types of inflows in exchange for an initial outlay. The value or price of such a basic *sukuk* would be the present value of cash flows that one can receive from investing in the *sukuk*. The present value is simply the aggregate discounted value of each future cash flow. The discount rate would not be the interest rate commonly used in conventional finance, but an opportunity cost applicable to the investor. This opportunity cost could be risk-adjusted, in the sense that a higher opportunity cost of funds would be applied to *sukuk* issued by entities perceived to have higher risk.

Using the appropriate discount rate, one would first find the present value of the periodic lease payments. The aggregate of this is then added to the present value of the single proceed from the sale of the underlying asset to the *mudarib*. If the sale price is pre-determined, then one merely finds the present value of the amount given the opportunity cost and the time (in years) when the cash flow will occur. However, if the sale price is not pre-determined, then an estimate of the expected sale price has to be made. There are several ways to handle this estimate. One way would be to assign several possible sale prices and then assign probabilities to each potential price. The weighted average of this value is then taken to be the "expected" sale price. For example, suppose there are five possible sale prices with the following probabilities:

Scenario	Potential Sale Price	Probability
1	RM 120 million	0.10
2	RM 110 million	0.20
3	RM 100 million	0.40
4	RM 85 million	0.20
5	RM 60 million	0.10

The certainly equivalent value or expected sale price would be: Exp. Sale Price = Σ (*Pt SPi*)
Where
Pi = probability of the event/scenario happening
SPi = Sale price of asset under the scenario
Exp. Sale Price = Σ (0.10 × RM120 milllion) + (0.20 × RM110 million) + (0.40 × RM100 million) + (0.20 × RM 85 million) + (0.10 × RM 60 million) = RM97 million.

Illustration: Pricing a SMC

You are being offered a SMC with a face value of RM30 million. The details of the SMC are as follows:

- Issuance date : July 9, 2010
- Maturity : July 9, 2012
- Transaction Date : November 22, 2010
- Next Coupon Date : July 9, 2011
- Indicative Coupon : 6% (annual coupon)
- Yield to Maturity : 8%
- What is the appropriate value of this SMC?

$$P=\left[\frac{100\left(100+\left(\frac{6\times 365}{365}\right)\right)}{100+\left(\frac{8\times 228}{365}\right)}\right]-100\left(\frac{6\times 135}{36500}\right)$$

$$= 100.95 - 2.22 = 98.73$$

So, RM98.73 per RM100 of face value.

Thus, you would need to pay RM 29,619,000 in order to purchase the RM30 mil. SMC (0.9873 × RM30,000,000).

Note: In return for this investment, you will receive two coupon payments of RM1.8 million each and the RM30 million face value at maturity. The annual yield will be 8%. T = 135 days, excluding the day of the transaction. T = 228 days, excluding the day of coupon payment.

In this case, the probability weighted average of RM97 mil is the expected sale price. The price of the basic *sukuk al-ijarah* will be the sum total of the following two items:

(i) Total PV of periodic payments received

+

(ii) PV of Expected Sale Price of underlying asset at maturity.

8.6.3 *Pricing a Sukuk Ijarah with Warrants/embedded Options*

Of late, we have seen the issuance of several "exotic" *sukuk* that have embedded options within them. The Khazanah Exchangeable *Sukuk* and the 1997 KFC (Kentucky Fried Chicken Malaysia) Holdings *sukuk* which had warrants attached. Both these *sukuk* were akin to convertible "bonds" in that *sukuk*-holders could convert or exchange the *sukuk* to equities. In the case of Khazanah's 2006 issuance, it was Telekom Shares owned by Khazanah.

As for the 1997, KFC Holdings issuance, the *sukuk* came with warrants attached. These warrants were exercisable at maturity into stocks KFC Holdings at predetermined prices.

The attachment of a warrant to the *sukuk*, as in the KFC Holdings issuance, increased the value of the *sukuk* by the amount of the value of the warrant. A warrant is nothing but a long-dated call option. In determining the price of such a *sukuk*, one would have to determine the value of the call and add the call's value to that of the basic *sukuk*. The value of the call can be determined by way of the Black Scholes Option Pricing Model (BSOPM).

8.6.3.1 *Valuing the Embedded Call Option*

The warrant is a call option since it provides a right, but not the obligation, to buy the stock at a pre-determined price. The BSOPM is essentially an equation that provides a closed-form solution for the price of an option. It is used to value European-style calls (or Puts). See Chapter 11 for a detailed discussion of Option pricing using the BSOPM. A European-style option is one where the option can only be exercised at maturity and not before. In valuing a call using BSOPM, one needs to input the following five parameters:

i. The current stock price = S_0
ii. Estimated volatility of the underlying asset = σ
iii. Time to maturity of the call (warrant) as a percentage of a year = t
iv. The risk-free interest rate = rf
v. The exercise price of the call = k

BSOPM can be written as:

$$C = S_0.N\,(d_1) - Ke^{-rt}.\,N\,(d_1)$$

$$d_1 = \frac{In(S/K) + [r + (\sigma^2/2)]T}{\sigma\sqrt{T}}$$

$$d_2 = d_1 - \sigma\sqrt{T}$$

where

T = time to expiration (as % of year)
e^{rt} = exponential function of rf and T
$N(.)$ = cumulative standard normal distribution function
$In\ (S/K)$ = natural logarithm of S/K

$N\,(d_1)$ and $N\,(d_2)$ are probability values derived from a cumulative density function. $(1 - N\,(d_1) = Nd_2)$
In using the BSOPM to value the warrant attached to a *sukuk*, we do the following two modifications:

(i) We can replace the risk-free interest rate with the three-month KLIRR (Kuala Lumpur Interbank Rate of Return).
(ii) If exercise of the warrant will result in new shares being issued, then an adjustment has to be made for the dilution factor.

Finally, as the BSOPM equation above shows, the call is valued on a per share basis. Since warrants typically can be exercised into more than shares, one of the underlying stock, an additional adjustment has to be made. For example, if the warrant can be converted into 1,000 shares, then the call value arrived at using BSOPM should be multiplied by 1,000 to arrive at the value of the warrant. Suppose by using BSOPM we get a call value of RM0.34. This is value on a per share basis. If the warrant has a conversion ratio of say, 1,000 shares, then the value of the embedded option represented by the warrant will be worth RM340.00 (RM0.34 × 1,000).

Since the presence of the embedded options enables the *sukuk*-holder to potentially profit from the appreciation of the underlying shares, and since the ringgit value of that profit potentially has been valued at RM340 using BSOPM, we need to add the RM340 to the PV of the other cash flows derived from the *sukuk*. For example, if the *ijarah sukuk* has periodic *ijarah* payments, then the total value of the *sukuk* equals:

(i) PV of Periodic *ijarah* Payments, +
(ii) RM 340 (value of embedded option)

Illustration

You are being offered an Exchangeable *sukuk* with RM 10,000 face value and six months left to maturity. There will be no dividends for the *sukuk* over the next six months. The Exchangeable *sukuk* comes with an embedded option that gives the *sukuk*-holder the choice of either receiving the face value or converting to shares of large publicly listed stock at RM 4.00 per stock. You have gathered the following information;

(i) the stock is currently selling at RM4.30
(ii) the 3-month KLIRR is at 4.0% currently.
(iii) the stock's price volatility is estimated at 20%

(a) What is the value of the embedded option?

Since the embedded option is a right to buy, it is a call option. Using the BSOPM as described in Chapter 11, the value of the call is:

$$d_1 = \frac{\text{In}(4.30/4) + \{0.04 + (0.20^2/2)\}0.5}{0.20\sqrt{0.5}}$$

$d_2 = d_1 - 0.20\sqrt{0.5}$
$d_1 = 0.1023/\ 0.1414 = 0.7235$
$d_2 = 0.7235 - 0.1414 = 0.5821$

From table values (cumulative Normal distribution)

$N(d_1) = 0.7642$, $N(d_2) = 0.7191$
$C = 4.30\ (0.7642) - 4\ e^{-0.04(0.5)}\ (0.7191)$
$= 3.2861 - 2.8194$
$= 0.46$ or 46 cents per stock.

Since the exercise price is RM4 while the Face value is RM10,000, a total of 2,500 stocks could be bought.
Thus, value of embedded option = 2,500 × RM 0.46 = **RM1,150**
This value should be added to the PV of Cash flows.

(b) Assuming your required return is 8%, what is the correct price of the sukuk?

Total value of *sukuk* = PV of Cash Flows + Value of Embedded Option
PV of Cash Flow for the *sukuk* is only the face value receivable at end of month 6.
PV of CF = RM10,000 / $(1.08)^{0.5}$ = ***RM 9,615.38***
So, total value of *sukuk* = RM 9615.38 + RM 1150 = ***RM10,765.38***

8.6.4 *Pricing Risk-sharing Sukuk for Corporations to Fund Revenue-generating Projects*

A *mudarabah*-based risk-sharing *sukuk* is one in which earnings are shared according to an agreed profit-sharing ratio (PSR). The valuation or pricing of such an instrument should follow the logic of valuation in finance. That is, value should equal the present value of future expected cash flows from the investment. Generically:

$$\text{Price/Value} = \sum_{t=1}^{n} \frac{\hat{e}t \bullet PSR}{(1+k)^t}$$

where
$\hat{e}_t$ = Expected net earnings in year t

PSR = Profit-sharing ratio
k = Required return/profit rate

The expected net earnings can be determined given the parameters agreed to and the forecasted revenue/earnings. Alternatively, one could also use after-tax net cash flows in place of $\hat{e}_t$. After-tax net cash flows begin with net profit and adjust for non-cash expenses such as depreciation, amortizations, provisions, etc., and changes in net working capital, capital outlays, and other cash flows. The adjustment for non-cash expenses effectively neutralizes accounting-related biases.

PSR should be set such that the initial investment (I) is recoverable given the required profit rate and term. PSR, therefore, is a function of the term, average expected earnings, initial investment, and the required profit rate:

$$\text{PSR} = f\ (I, t, \bar{e}, k)$$

where
$\bar{e}$ = average of expected annual earnings

The appropriate term should differ according to the project being financed. Generically, the term can be determined as:

$$\text{Term} = \left[\frac{I(1+k)}{\overline{e}t \bullet PSR}\right] \leq Econ.Life$$

The required profit rate k is the other unknown. With trading, k should be a market-derived rate, much like the required return for stocks or the YTM[1] of bonds. Given the profit/risk sharing but terminal nature of this instrument, its "cost" or required return should be lower than the costs of the issuing firm's equity but higher than cost of debt. Since the claims of the instrument are directly on the earnings of the specific asset/or project, uncluttered by the firm's other obligations, the required return will be largely dependent on the volatility of the asset's earnings. Furthermore, as a market-traded instrument, the required return is essentially market-determined. For a given set of expected future earnings, term, and PSR, the required return will be implied in its market price:

$$\%k = \left[\frac{(\hat{e} \bullet PSR)}{Price}\right] \times 100$$

The percentage k, or holding period return, would constitute both the returns from profits received and capital gains; k therefore would be dependent on the volatility of expected earnings ($\hat{e}$), PSR, and market factors. Indicative k can be derived from the ROA (return on assets) of similar projects/industry. In fact, the returns of a firm in the same industry as that of the project can be unlevered to estimate k.

8.6.5 *Pricing of Infrastructure Sukuk Mudarabah and Determining Returns to Sukuk-holders*

In Section 8.5.2, we saw how *sukuk* based on risk-sharing contracts like *mudarabah* or *musharakah* could be used in financing development infrastructure. The key advantage of such *sukuk* is that they enable governments, especially of developing countries, to fund infrastructure without resorting to debt or leverage. If such *sukuk* are to be traded on secondary markets as proposed, then their pricing should be transparent and easily determined. In order to understand how secondary market prices would be determined for these infrastructure *sukuk*, we would first have to estimate the expected returns to the *sukuk*-holders and the government. We use the information of the above power generation project to work these out. Note that the government is investing a total of \$75 million or 10% of total initial investment. In addition, the government is entitled to 10% of profits from the *sukuk*-financed portion. Thus, the government will get the following sources of returns from the project when *sukuk mudarabah* is used:

(i) All the returns earned in the new project from its portion of financing (the $75 million that the government provided for new project).
(ii) 10% of the returns from the *mudarabah*-financed portion of the new project (since assumed PSR is 10/90).

The *sukuk*-holders, on the other hand, get 90% of the profits earned from the *mudarabah*-financed portion of the new project. Given these differences in claims on the projects' profits, to arrive at a generalized model of returns, we need to make one more notation. V_N, which is the value of the new project, denoted as:

$$\boldsymbol{V_N = \Delta + \lambda}$$

where

Δ = government's investment in the new project ($75 million at time of initial investment).
λ = the amount of *mudarabah* financing in the new project ($675 million)
Thus, the percentage returns to the government from using *mudarabah* financing for the new project would be determined as:

$$\boldsymbol{R_{Gi} = [(\Delta \times (R_{NI})) + \{(\lambda \times (1 + R_{NI}) - \lambda) \times \pi\}]} \tag{8.1}$$

$$\boldsymbol{\%\ R_{Gi} = [(\Delta \times (R_{NI})) + \{(\lambda \times (1 + R_{NI}) - \lambda) \times \pi\} \times 1/\Delta]} \tag{8.2}$$

s. t. = $V_N >$ \$ 75 milllion and $R_{NI} > 0$ where
$\boldsymbol{R_{Gi}}$ = total \$ return to government with *mudarabah* financing for given year
$\boldsymbol{R_{NI}}$ = % returns provided by the project for the period
π = % of profits to be received by the government given by PSR (10% this case)
Using the same notations, the returns to *sukuk*-holders could be determined as:

$$\boldsymbol{R_{SH} = \{[(\lambda \times (1 + R_{NI}) - \lambda) \times (1 - \pi)]\}} \tag{8.3}$$

$$\boldsymbol{\%\ R_{SH} = \{[(\lambda \times (1 + R_{NI}) - \lambda) \times (1 - \pi)] \times 1/\lambda\}} \tag{8.4}$$

where

$\boldsymbol{R_{SH}}$ = total \$ returns to *sukuk*-holders for a given year
$\boldsymbol{(1 - \pi)}$ = *sukuk*-holders' share of PSR

Box 8.3. Illustration: Computing Returns to Stakeholders

To see how the above equations can be used to determine returns to each stakeholder and the market price of the sukuk, we use the numbers from the above project. Suppose, the net profit after all costs in a certain year is $70 million, what amount would the government and sukuk-holders receive? The $70 million net profit for the year will constitute a percentage return of 9.33% (70/750). Using the numbers of the example and Equation 8.1, the government's return would be:

$R_{Gi} = [(\Delta \times (R_{NI})) + \{(\lambda \times (1 + R_{NI}) - \lambda) \times \pi\}]$
$R_{Gi} = [(\$75 \times 0.0933) + \{(\$675 \times (1.0933) - \$675) \times 0.10]$
$R_{Gi} = [7 + 6.3] = \$\ 13.3$ million

(Continued)

Box 8.3. (*Continued*)

The return to the *sukuk*-holders will be determined as in Eq. (8.3)

$$R_{SH} = \{[(\lambda \times (R_{NI}) - \lambda) \times (1 - \pi)]\}$$
$$R_{SH} = \{ [(\$675 \times 1.0933) - 675) \times 0.90]\}$$
$$R_{SH} = \$56.7 \text{ million.}$$

The \$70 million of net profit is shared amongst the government and *sukuk*-holders. The government receives \$13.3 million while the *sukuk*-holders get the remainder \$56.7 million. Suppose each *sukuk* had a face value of \$1,000, the share of profit received for each *sukuk* would be \$56,700,000 / 675,000 *sukuk*[2] = \$84, for a return of 8.4% for the year. Notice that this is marginally lower than the 9.33% earned from the project. This has to do with the fact that the[3] government, given the PSR of 10/90, gets a 10% share from the portion "owned" by the *sukuk*-holders. As the *sukuk mudarabah* is available for market trading, the market value or pricing will be determined by the expected annual net profits from the project and profit accruable to the *sukuk* using Eq. (8.3). A general pricing model can be written as;

$$P_i = \Sigma [\hat{E} (R_{SHi})/(1 + y)^i] + CV_n / (1 = Y)^n \tag{8.5}$$

where

$\hat{E} (R_{SHi})$ = expected return to *sukuk*-holder in year i
CV_n = value of conversion feature (call option) at maturity
Y = required yield for *sukuk*.

Notice that Equation 8.5 is the combined value of the cash flow stream or dividends received by the *sukuk*-holder and the conversion value when IPO occurs. As the projects gets completed and cash flow builds over the years, the *sukuk* will begin to rise in market value. This value increase will be driven by three factors: (i) increase in cash flows and profits; (ii) reduction in required yield as the project's riskiness gets lower with completion and stabilization; and (iii) expected gains from IPO. Thus, a well-executed and well-managed infrastructure project can be highly profitable to both the government and the *sukuk*-holders.

8.7 *Sukuk* Defaults

Being long-term financial instruments, *sukuk* have had their share of failures. A number of *sukuk* have defaulted. These defaults have been across several countries and have involved *sukuk* of different underlying contracts. Table 8.2 shows a sample of *sukuk* that have defaulted. The first four, East Cameron, Saad Group, The Investment Dar Company, and Nakheel World, were probably the largest defaults. The lower panel of the table shows some of Malaysia's largest *sukuk* defaults. With the exception of the East Cameron *sukuk*, which was a *musharakah*-based *sukuk*, all the defaulted *sukuk* in the sample were based on debt contracts such as *bay al-bithaman ajil* (BBA), *murabahah*, or *ijarah*. The Investment Dar *Sukuk*, though officially labeled as a *musharakah* had fixed dividends referenced on LIBOR. Again with the exception of East Cameron, which was hit first by falling oil and gas prices and then by a hurricane, rendering the obligor unable to meet its obligations, all the other cases involved liquidity problems arising from excessive leverage. It appears that the underlying cause of default is the same regardless of whether *sukuk* or conventional bonds are used. When cash flows generated from operations is insufficient to service the debt obligations, the issuer invariably defaults.

Table 8.2. Sample of *Sukuk* Defaults.

Issuer /SPV/ Country	Face Value/Year of Issue	Year of Default	Underlying Contract
East Cameron Gas (United States)	13-year, $165.6 mil, 2006	2008	*Musharakah and ijarah*
Saad Group's Golden Belt. (Saudi Arabia)	5-Year $650 mil., Issued in 2007	2009	*Ijarah*
The Investment Dar Company (Kuwait)	5-Year $100 mil., Issued in 2006	2009	*Musharakah* but with "fixed" dividends based on LIBOR +1.25%
Nakheel World (Dubai, UAE)	3-Year, $3.5 bil., issued in 2006	2009	*Ijarah manfaa*
Johor Corporation (Malaysia)	MYR 500 mil., 1999	2002	*Murabahah*
Europlus Corporation (Malaysia)	MYR 250 mil., 2000	2006	BBA (BAIDs)
Maxisegar Sdn Bhd (Malaysia)	MYR 300 mil., 2001	2006	BBA (BAIDs)
Memory Tech Sdn Bhd (Malaysia)	MYR 320 mil., 2005	2007	BBA (BAIDs)
Nam Fatt Corporation (Malaysia)	MYR 250 mil., 2006	2010	*Murabaha*

A debt-based *sukuk* based on *murabahah* is no different from a conventional bond in terms of the obligations imposed on the issuer. Theoretically, a risk-sharing *sukuk* based on *mudarabah* or *musharakah* cannot default because, like equity, repayment is dependent on cash flows generated by the project or ability to pay. When earnings are low, the returns to the financier is low, and if there are no profits, the financier receives nothing. The risk is much like equity risk. In the case of a debt contract like *murabahah* or *ijarah*, the servicing requirements of the *sukuk* would be independent of cash flows generated by the funded project. The debt servicing requirements are fixed and obligatory, regardless of project performance. Even so, as the East Cameron case cited above, and the Dana Gas case described in the Box 8.3 show, there have been cases of risk-sharing *sukuk* going into default. Careful examination of each case, however, would show that the defaults were due to externalities. In the East Cameron case, there was an *ijarah* obligation within the contract that required fixed repayments. The fall in oil and gas prices and the losses due to the hurricane impaired the obligor's ability to meet the *ijarah*-based payments, causing the *sukuk* to go into default. In the Dana Gas case, as described in the Box 8.3, it was an issue of governance rather than *sukuk* structure. The obligor appeared to be wanting to take the easy route of claiming *Shari'ah* noncompliance to unilaterally revise the repayment terms.

There are two key points to be mindful of: first, one should look beyond the labels to determine the true structure of the *sukuk*. Second, basic fundamentals like the need to avoid excessive leverage, the need for good governance, enforceability of contracts, and prudent/effective management must not be overlooked. These fundamentals apply equally to Islamic finance as they do in conventional finance.

Box 8.4. Dana Gas *Sukuk*: The Need for Improved *Shari'ah* Governance

Dana Gas, a Sharjah-based company listed on the Abu Dhabi Stock Exchange, has caused an upheaval in the US$100 billion *sukuk* market. The company recently announced that its *mudarabah sukuk*, issued in 2007, restructured in 2013, and which matures in October 2017 has been declared non-*Shari'ah*-compliant by its *Shari'ah* committee and therefore unlawful for repayment as per terms. Dana Gas was therefore proposing the exchange of that *sukuk* with another that had half the previous dividends and without a conversion feature. In effect, the *sukuk*-holders would be short-changed. Adding insult to injury, the company blamed *Shari'ah* evolution as the reason for its inability to play by agreed rules. According to a news report, the company had issued a statement that: "Due to the evolution and continual development of Islamic

(*Continued*)

Box 8.4. (*Continued*)

Financial instruments and their interpretation, the company has recently received legal advice that the sukuk in its present form is not Shariah compliant and is therefore unlawful under UAE law. As a result, a restructuring of the current *sukuk* is necessary to ensure that it conforms to the relevant laws for the benefit of all shareholders". In essence, Dana Gas was blaming changes in *Shari'ah* interpretation for its woes. The fact that a basic requirement of the *Shari'ah* is to uphold the terms of a contract agreed to, appears to have been lost. Furthermore, even where *Shari'ah* interpretation changes, the fact that applying a change retrospectively to an agreed contract goes against natural justice appears to also have been missed. This is not the first time *Shari'ah* interpretation has jolted *sukuk* markets. In 2009, Investment Dar, a Kuwaiti company, had tried to rescind its obligations to a bank using *Shari'ah* arguments. In this case, however, Investment Dar's *Shari'ah* committee had barred the company from using *Shari'ah* principles to argue its case. Earlier in 2007, Taqi Usmani had made his pronouncement that, based on *Shari'ah* principles, a majority of the outstanding *sukuk* were non-compliant.

For a *sukuk* market that, in many ways, is still in its infancy, these are unnecessary problems. More than anything, it points to the need for improved *Shari'ah* governance. Many would agree that the Dana Gas issue could not have happened in the Malaysian *sukuk* market, which has a tight and well-functioning *Shari'ah* governance framework. In Malaysia, a national body puts out resolutions, justified and clearly articulated in written form, which become the guideposts for *Shari'ah* committees at the firm/bank level. Under the country's Islamic Financial Services Act (IFSA), individual *Shari'ah* committee members are held personally liable to ensure compliance with the national resolutions. This assures synchronicity in interpretation and execution of *Shari'ah* rules. Such a governance framework, however, is sorely lacking elsewhere.

This has huge implications not just for future growth of *sukuk* but of Islamic finance in general. *Shari'ah* scholars are not the only ones required to interpret and make judgement calls. Many spheres of business, accounting, law, engineering, and others require its practitioners to make judgements, but they are guided by well-codified rules/regulations. Accountants, for example, have clear accounting standards like GAAP and IFRS that are accepted internationally. Similarly, lawyers and judges are guided by statutes. The professions are also guided by professional bodies that require accreditation and ensure that their members behave in ways intended to serve society as they are supposed to. The *Shari'ah* fraternity, however, appears to have neither of these. There are neither internationally accepted *Shari'ah* standards nor institutions that can chastise or hold scholars accountable for their decision, Malaysia being the exception here. As long as such standardization and governance mechanisms are missing, Islamic finance is likely to witness Dana Gas type issues from time to time.

Even if they are infrequent, such upheavals impose huge impediments to future growth. Markets are oiled by faith and confidence. Integrity of the processes and system are key to maintaining that faith and confidence. In markets where integrity is suspect, risk premiums or required returns increase. Islamic finance is already burdened by the higher transaction costs arising from the need to have and transfer underlying assets. Higher risk premiums to account for idiosyncratic risks arising from *Shari'ah* judgements add another layer of costs and pose the real danger of stunting future growth. There is an urgent need for clarity and justification of resolutions. Scholars must understand the consequences of their judgements not just on the *sukuk* or product being evaluated but on the broader market and society.

Source: Author's op-ed article in *Derrin Ekonomi*, August 2017.

Summary

This chapter continues from the previous chapter on *sukuk* fundamentals. Several issues related to *sukuk* are examined. A *sukuk*'s risk profile is dependent on its underlying *Shari'ah* contract. *Sukuk* based on debt-based contracts like *ijarah* and *murabahah* have fixed cash flows that mimic conventional bonds. Issuers who have both debt-based *sukuk* and bonds would see very high correlation in their yields. This is to be expected, as the cash flows of both instruments would be alike. Increasingly, the market is moving toward exotic *sukuk* structures. These have been the result of wanting to alter risk profiles, avoid fixed cash flows, and overcome the limitation of available physical assets to pledge as underlying. Aside from embedded options, there has been *sukuk* structured on future cash flows such as passenger seat miles and telephone airtime. *Sukuk* have also been issued that enable their conversion at maturity to be listed as *Shari'ah*-compliant stock. Several Islamic banks have issued perpetual *sukuk* to meet their Basel III capital adequacy requirements. These *sukuk* are *mudarabah*-based, with embedded call options exercisable after predetermined periods.

The chapter also proposes *sukuk* structures based on risk-sharing contracts like *mudarabah* and *musharakah*. The design of risk-sharing *sukuk* for corporates to fund revenue generating projects and for governments to finance development infrastructure is discussed. These risk-sharing *sukuk* structures enable governments of developing countries to avoid the leverage and macroeconomic vulnerability that comes with debt financing. The pricing of *sukuk* of various structures is discussed. *Sukuk* with fixed cash flows, embedded options, and risk-sharing structures were valued. The pricing models were based on the logic of valuation in conventional finance. The chapter concludes with a discussion of *sukuk* defaults. Several *sukuk*, some that were high-profile international ones, have defaulted. The majority of the defaulted *sukuk* were based on debt structures like *murabahah* and *ijarah*. As in the case of conventional debt instruments, *sukuk* default has been mainly due to excessive leverage or high debt burden of the issuing entity. Thus, it appears that the underlying fundamentals leading to default are the same, even if Islamic finance is being used.

Questions and Problems

1. How does a *sukuk*'s underlying contract determine its risk profile? Briefly explain why an *ijarah sukuk* may be considered safer than a *mudarabah sukuk.*
2. Refer to Question 1 above, how does risk differ from the viewpoint of the *sukuk*-holder versus the issuer?
3. What explains the convergence seen in the yields of sovereign *sukuk* and bonds?
4. Based on some of the innovative *sukuk* structures described in the chapter, explain the benefits of such structures. What limitations do they overcome?
5. What are the key advantages of the risk-sharing *sukuk* proposed in the chapter? Identify some potential problems/handicaps to their execution.
6. SELGLOVE, a Selangor-based manufacturer of rubber gloves, is looking to expand its production facilities in order to meet rapidly increasing foreign demand. The company requires RM300 million for a new factory, warehouse, and logistics center near Port Klang. The company is planning a 12-year *sukuk istisna/ijarah* using, as underlying, its three-acre land in Port Klang where the facilities will be built. The *istisna* will be over the first two years of construction while the *ijarah* payments equivalent to 8% of face value will be from Years 3 to 12. The *sukuk* has a repurchase agreement requiring the issuer to repurchase the factory, warehouse and logistics center for RM300 million at end of Year 12. A total of 30,000 *sukuk* will issued to raise the RM300 million. All *sukuk* have the same face value.
   (a) Draw the structure of the *sukuk*. Chronologically number the events/activity/cash flow.
   (b) Show the cash flow diagram and determine the correct value of the *sukuk* if the required return given its rating is 12%.
7. This question uses facts from Question 6 above.
   To make the *sukuk* attractive to investors, the issuer wants to embed a call option that will allow *sukuk*-holders to convert their *sukuk* to 2,000 shares of SELGLOVE in lieu of the face value. They will receive a 30-day period following maturity to decide if they want to convert or receive face value. Assume that at maturity:
   - SELGLOVE stocks are expected to sell at RM6.00 per stock around maturity and the month following.
   - The volatility of the stock is 25% annualized.
   - The risk-free rate is 4%.
   - Determine the value of the embedded option.

   Assuming you exercised the option, what is your average annual return assuming you paid the price calculated in 7b above.
8. A listed company, Asian Paper Inc., wants to raise RM300 million to buy land to plant its pulp-producing plants/trees. Its only unencumbered asset is its head office building. The company's CFO is considering the issuance of *sukuk al-ijarah* to fund the RM300million of needed funds. You have the following additional information:
   - Current market value of head office building = RM302 million
   - Intended tenor of *sukuk* = 10 years.
   - Estimated required return for *sukuk*-holders = 9% per year.
   - Face Value per *sukuk* = RM 10,000
   - Outline the structure of this *sukuk ijarah*. Number the events chronologically.

   Assuming Asian Paper Inc. is open to either a final repurchase of the asset (building) at RM300 million or an equal amortization of the principal amount over the 10 years, draw the cash flow diagram to *sukuk*-holders under each alternative. Determine the annual amounts that will be received by the *sukuk*-holders under each alternative.

   To make its *ijarah sukuk* more attractive to investors, Asian Paper Inc., is willing to attach a warrant to the *sukuk*. Each warrant will allow *sukuk*-holders to buy 100 shares of Asian Paper Inc. at an exercise price of RM6.00 per share. *Sukuk*-holders will have 30 days from the maturity date of the *sukuk* to decide if they want to exercise the *sukuk*. Using the additional information below, determine the value of the warrant. Also, show the payoff profile of the *sukuk* with the warrant.

- Tenor = 30 days
- Exercise Price per stock = RM6.00
- Expected volatility over 30 days post maturity of *sukuk* = 40%
- Expected average stock price over 30 days = RM6.70
- The 30-day IIMM yield = 3%

9. A large public-listed Malaysian conglomerate with businesses in a diverse range of industries is seeking to grow by investing in a wind farm. It has identified a hilly terrain in its palm oil plantation as being very suitable. Power generated by the wind farm will be sold to TNB (the national electricity corporation). Given the large tract of land and the numerous wind turbines that could be built on it, the company estimates a total investment need of RM 100 million. It plans to raise the funds by way of a *sukuk* issuance. It is considering one of two structures. An *ijarah sukuk* with the land pledged as underlying asset, with fixed semi-annual *ijarah* payments and the repurchase of the assets (turbines) at maturity at end year 10. The repurchase price will equal the initial investment of RM 100 million. The returns to *sukuk*-holders will be 8% per year.

   The alternative is a *mudarabah*-based *sukuk* with 80% of net profits paid out as annual dividends over a 15-year period. The returns to *sukuk*-holders under this structure is expected to be 12% per year.

   (a) Plot/draw the structure of the *ijarah sukuk*. Show the direction and chronologically number the flows.
   (b) How different is the cash flow impact of the *ijarah sukuk* from that of an 8% semi-annual coupon bond? Explain
   (c) Evaluate the impact of each *sukuk* structure on (i) ROE, (ii) the firm's leverage, (iii) riskiness of the firm, and (iv) beta of the stock.

10. An *ijarah sukuk* is being offered to you. It has following features:
    Offer price RM10,000 per *sukuk*
    - Number of *sukuk* issued = 1,000
    - Tenor = 8 years.
    - *Ijarah* payments totaling RM800,000 will be paid annually at end of each year.
      (*Note*: this is a total amount for all outstanding *sukuk*).

    The underlying asset will sold to the originator/issuer at maturity for a price to be determined then.
    Assuming your required profit rate for this *sukuk*'s rating class is 12%, what price must the underlying asset be sold for you to earn 12% on the *sukuk*?
    What would the percentage return be if the underlying asset is sold at maturity for RM12 million?
    What is the consequence of not predetermining the underlying asset's final resale value to the (i) *sukuk*-holders and (ii) the originator?

11. The Federal government has decided on building a Light Rapid Transit System (LRT) for Johor Bahru and intends to use *sukuk* to finance the project. The government has approached you on how best to structure the *sukuk*. You have been provided the following information:
    - Total construction cost = RM5 billion
    - Construction period = 2 years
    - Revenue begins from Year 3 onwards.
    - *Sukuk* funding to be raised in one lump sum for the entire RM5 billion.

    Wary of its rising debt to GDP ratio, the government intends to get it "off-the-books" at the end of Year 5. So, while no payments will be made to *sukuk*-holders during the two years of construction, payments will be made in Years 3, 4, and 5. At the end of Year 5, the government intends to list the project on the stock exchange by way of converting the *sukuk* to listed shares. All *sukuk*-holders will be required to convert their *sukuk* to shares at a ratio of 1:1,000 (each *sukuk* converts to 1,000 shares of the public-listed LRT company).

    Determine the appropriate *sukuk* structure. What contract(s) would you use? Draw the schematic diagram. (Number the flows chronologically). Justify your choice of contract(s).

12. Use the information provided in Question 11 above. Assume the listing price of the stock at the end of Year 5 is RM8.00 and the stock is expected to hit RM10.00 immediately following listing.
    In what way is this *sukuk* different from a convertible bond? Is it safer or riskier? Explain.
    Assuming a risk-free rate of 4% and stock price volatility of 25%; what is the value today of the conversion feature to each *sukuk*?

Bibliography

Derrin Ekonomi, August 2017.

Derrin Ekonomi, February 2016.

Hafizi, S., and A. Hafizuddin, (2011) "Sukuk Defaults and Its Implication: A Case Study of Malaysian Capital Market," Presented at the *8th International Conference on Islamic Economics and Finance*, Center for Islamic Economics and Finance, Qatar Faculty of Islamic Studies, Qatar Foundation.

Karatas, A. (2018). "High Quality Liquid Sukūk for a Megabank MDB's Lab Portfolio: Relevance, Practice, Empirical Research, And Prospects in a Challenging Global Environment." [Unpublished PhD Dissertation] The International Centre for Education in Islamic Finance (INCEIF)

Obiyathulla I. B., M. Abbas and A. Hossein (2015). "Risk Sharing in Corporate and Public Finance: The Contribution of Islamic Finance," *PSL Quarterly Review*, Vol. 68, No. 274 (September), pp. 187–213.

Sweder, v W. and Z. Sajjad, (2013), "Sukuk Defaults: On Distress Resolution in Islamic Finance," Duisenberg School of Finance, Tinbergen Institute Discussion Paper TI 13-087 / VI / DSF 57.

The Malaysian Reserve, July 10, 2017.

Websites

https://www.researchgate.net/publication/265085046_Sukuk_Defaults_and_Its_Implication_A_Case_Study_of_Malaysian_Capital_Market

http://papers.tinbergen.nl/13087.pdf

http://www.kantakji.com/fiqh/Files/Markets/m135.pdf

https://islamicbanker.com/ke/are-there-any-cases-of-the-asset-backed-sukuk-default-besides

Endnotes

1. Free cash flow refers to cash flow that is unencumbered.
2. ($ 675,000,000/ $ 1,000 per sukuk) = 675,000 sukuk issued.

Chapter 9

COMMON STOCKS AND EQUITY MARKETS

Topics in this Chapter

Chapter Objective

This chapter is designed to provide readers with an in-depth introduction to common stocks, their evolution, valuation, and pricing models. Beginning with an explanation of how equity differs from debt, the function of stock markets and the terminologies used are explained. The different schools of thought on stock price behavior are also explained. On completing the unit, the reader should have a good understanding of stocks, why companies choose to list and issue stocks, what returns investors get from holding stocks, how to value stocks, and finally, the alternative explanations of stock price behavior.

Key Terms			
Accelerated Growth Model	efficient market hypothesis (EMH)	model diversification	share ownership
authorized capital	Employee Stock Option Scheme (ESOS)	Modern Portfolio Theory	shelf registration
bonus stock	equity multiple	*mudarabah*	stock beta
book value per share	Free Cash Flow Model (FCFM)	net tangible asset (NTA)	stock market behavior
Capital Asset Pricing Model (CAPM)	fundamental analysis	outstanding shares	stock market index

(*Continued*)

(Continued)

Key Terms			
capital gain	Gordon Growth Model	paid-up capital	stock price dynamics
common stock	Gross Domestic Product (GDP)	par value	stock split
constant growth	holding period return (HPR)	premium	technical analysis (Chartism)
dividend	Initial Public Offering (IPO)	Price-Earnings (P/E) Ratio	transferability
Dividend Discount Model (DDM)	issued capital	private placement	Treasury stock
divisibility	liquidity listing	random walk	zero-growth model
Dow theory	market capitalization	required rate of return	
earnings per share (EPS)	market intermediation	rights issue	

9.1 Introduction

Investment in the form of equity is very different from investment in debt instruments. As explained in Chapter 5 on bonds, debt financing is fixed in claim and time. Equity, on the other hand, represents ownership and is therefore residual in claim and has no fixed time (maturity) — i.e., equity is perpetual. By residual in claim, we mean that an equity-holder has a claim on *all* assets that have not been mortgaged or pledged in any way. Whereas collateralized debt would constitute a claim on a specific asset(s), equity represents a claim on all assets of the firm and not specific ones. To understand what all these means, let us look at an example in Box 9.1.

Box 9.1. Illustration: A Common Stock Purchase

Suppose Ali buys stocks in Malaysia Airlines (MAS) at RM5.00 each for a total investment of RM5,000 (1,000 shares), Ali now becomes a shareholder in MAS. As a shareholder, Ali is essentially a co-owner of MAS. Ali co-owns MAS together with the thousands of other shareholders who have also invested in MAS shares. The size or proportion of Ali's ownership of MAS will depend on the size of Ali's holding relative to the total number of outstanding stocks. If, for example, MAS has a total of 100,000 shares outstanding, then Ali's stake is 1% of MAS. If, on the other hand, MAS has one million shares outstanding, then Ali's stake is 0.01% or a tenth of 1%. To understand why equity is a perpetual claim, unlike a bond which has no maturity, Ali's stake in MAS remains for as long as he holds the shares in the company.

Like other assets, an equity investment as represented by the stock can also be passed on to one's children as inheritance. To see why a stock is residual in claim, imagine if the company whose stock Ali owns gets into financial distress and has to be liquidated, eventually going bankrupt. As a stockholder, Ali's claim on the assets would come last. That is, other claimants such as the bond-holder, the firm's workers, etc., will first have to be paid off from the liquidated assets. If by following this, some assets still remain, the shareholders get their due. The proportion that Ali would get from the sale of the residual assets would depend on the proportion of Ali's ownership, which is the relative size of Ali's stockholding.

A stock, or share as it is often referred to, is the most common equity instrument. Thus, a firm that wants to raise equity from the public would do so by issuing stocks. In Malaysia and some other countries, a company wanting to raise equity financing by selling its stock to the public can only do so if it is first listed on a stock exchange. The very first time that a company sells its shares to the public is known as an Initial Public Offering (IPO). We will examine the IPO and listing process later in this chapter.

9.2 The Evolution of Stocks

Today, the stock market is often the largest component of the capital market in many countries, yet stocks have had humble beginnings. The idea behind modern-day stocks began more than a hundred years ago with the need for risk management, essentially, the need to pool risks arising from business undertakings. Some researchers trace the origin of the modern-day common stock to the establishment of the Joint Stock company. These were companies formed in Europe, especially the UK, in the days when these European nations were exploring the new world to acquire spices. Building, staffing, and equipping the ships that needed to go out to the Far East to trade and source the much-needed spices was lucrative but highly risky.

Given the lack of technology, especially navigation, meteorology, and communication, wealthy merchants financing these expeditions were taking a gamble. If after many months their ships returned safely, they would earn lucrative profits; otherwise, they would potentially face financial ruins. It occurred to these merchants that the logical way to manage the high risk was to pool resources to finance only one ship. Rather than each merchant financing their own ship, pooling resources among say 50 merchants to fund a ship meant that the potential for big losses were minimized. It also meant that an individual merchant could invest his wealth into several ships instead of just one, thereby diversifying and reducing risk.

An additional advantage was that, whereas previously the size of the expedition was limited to the wealth of a merchant, now with pooling of funds and joint investment, individual wealth was no longer a limiting factor. In order to apportion ownership in joint ventures, shares or stocks were issued. Purchase of these shares meant ownership in the expedition and the number of shares owned would determine the proportion of ownership. In time, companies organizing expeditions through stock issuance came to be known as Joint Stock Companies.

Therefore, the advent of the common stock brought many advantages. By enabling the pooling of investments, it was made possible to diversify and manage risk. Owning shares representing the underlying assets also meant that divisibility of ownership became possible. This enabled the formation of large corporations and conglomerates since capital was no more limited to the wealth of individual owners.

The next step in the evolutionary change was the need to enhance the liquidity of stock investment. Liquidity refers to the ability to convert an asset into cash. A highly liquid asset can be converted to cash quickly and cheaply while an illiquid asset can only be converted to cash with a time delay, or with incurring a large transaction cost, which may include selling the asset at a discount, or both. An asset such as government treasury bills would be highly liquid whereas assets such as real estate could be highly illiquid. Illiquidity depends on the degree of liquidity risk. The way to reduce an asset's liquidity risk would be by enabling it to be traded. An asset with a high traded volume would have little or no liquidity risk. Active trading enhances liquidity and thereby reduces liquidity risk. For an asset to be tradable, it must first be transferable.

Transferability refers to the ability to change ownership. While transferability enables trading, a good platform for trading is needed. This is where stock exchanges come in. A stock exchange is quite simply an entity that provides a service, the service being the provision of a platform where smooth and orderly trading of stocks can take place. Today, stock markets play a key role in capital market intermediation. Companies that wish to raise equity capital can do so by getting themselves listed on the stock exchange and then selling their shares or stocks to the investing public. Thus, stock exchanges are, in a sense, financial intermediaries because they help deficit units (companies that need funding) to access surplus units (equity investors).

As the preceding discussion shows, stocks have gone through a long evolutionary process. They have taken on features that will allow for easy, cheap trading, and enable issuers to have easy access to capital. Every one of their features has value-added and contributes to the omnipresence that stocks now have within modern economies. In many countries, including Muslim countries like Malaysia, the total market capitalisation, which is the total number of stocks multiplied by the market price, is often higher than the nation's Gross Domestic Product (GDP).

Table 9.1. Key Terms in Stocks and Equity Markets

Authorized Capital	A limit on the maximum amount of equity capital that a company can raise. This limit is usually set by the regulating authority such as the Securities Commission (SC) in Malaysia.
Issued Capital	The actual amount of funds raised by issuing shares which is usually less than the authorized capital. The difference between authorized and issued capital represents a slack that the company can utilize in the future.
Shelf Registration	Refers to a listed company getting approval for its stock issuance to be issued at future dates.
Par Value	Refers to the face value of a stock. While the par or face value of a bond represents the claim that a bond-holder has on the firm, par value is meaningless for stocks since equity is residual.
Paid-Up Capital	Par value of stock multiplied by number of stocks issued.
Premium on Paid-Up Capital	While a stock may have a par value of say RM1, it may have been offered for sale at a higher price. The difference in proceeds is accounted for as premium on paid-up capital.
Treasury Stock	Refers to stock that has been repurchased by the company or set aside by the company for the purpose of rewarding or compensating employees with stock rather than cash. This has the added advantage of making employees into stockholders.
Stock Dividends	Refers to dividends paid in the form of additional stock rather than cash. Though a stock dividend saves the company's cash outflow, it increases the number of stocks outstanding and therefore depresses the market price.
Stock Split	A company can "split" its stock by issuing additional stocks to existing shareholders for free. For example, a one-for-one split will result in a doubling of the outstanding stock. Companies undertake a stock split when their stock's price has risen to levels that jeopardize its liquidity. An example is IBM, the U.S.-based mainframe producer.
Bonus Stock	The free issuance of additional new shares to existing shareholders. Theoretically, a bonus issue should be a non-event and is similar to a stock split. An increase in the number of shares outstanding, without any in firm value, ought to simply reduce the market price per share. For example, a 3-for-1 bonus issue means a shareholder will receive three new shares for every share he currently owns. Since the issuance of the bonus would quadruple the number of shares, the share price should decline to a quarter of its previous price. However, it often does not. Instead, the price falls to perhaps 35% of its previous price, thereby inflating shareholder wealth. It is because of this that shareholders often look forward to bonus stock issues.
Market Capitalization	Also known as market value of the firm is determined as: {Market Price Per Share × Number of Shares Outstanding} A firm's market capitalization therefore varies as its stock price varies.
Book Value Per Share	Refers to a stock's value based on the balance sheet value of total equity which is computed as: {Common Stockholders Equity / Number of Shares Outstanding}
Net Tangible Asset (NTA)	Another balance sheet-based indicator of a stock's value. NTA is computed as follows: {Total Assets – Intangible Assets – Liabilities}
Price–Earnings (P/E) Ratio	Perhaps the most commonly used indicator of value, it is computed as: {Market Price Per Share / Earnings Per Share} Earnings Per Share is computed as: {Net Income / Number of Shares Outstanding}

Source: Author.

9.2.1 *Stock Options and Employee Stock Option Schemes*

Companies often adopt what is known as Employee Stock Option Schemes (ESOs). Under an ESO, employees are rewarded by way of granting stock options. The options allow the employee to buy a pre-determined number of stocks at an exercise price that is usually at a huge discount to current market values. Employees can choose to exercise these options over a stated period, for e.g., over the next five years. The stocks that the employee buys could be provided from the Treasury Stock that the firm is holding. Lately, ESOs and its variant ESOPs (Employee Stock Option Plans) under which funds from an employee's pension fund are invested in the firm's stock, by purchase at discounted prices, have become increasingly popular. By making employees shareholders, there will be better congruence between the interest of employees and the firm. This, in effect helps to reduce "agency problems" or conflicts of interest between shareholders and managers or employees of the firm.

9.2.2 *Rights Issue*

When a listed firm needs to raise additional equity financing, it is usually done through a rights issue. Existing shareholders are given the "right" to buy the newly offered shares at a pre-determined price which is usually at a discount to current market value. The rights offer will dictate how many new shares a shareholder would be eligible to purchase. For example, a one-for-two rights offer allows a shareholder to buy one new stock at the offer price for every two stocks that he currently owns. A rights offer typically comes with a time period within which the offer has to be exercised. A shareholder who is not interested in buying the stocks offered has the right to refuse the offer. The new shares that remain unsold, due to the offer refusal of some shareholders, would then be sold to other investors. The need to grant this "right" of first refusal to current shareholders is caused by the dilution of ownership as a result of issuing new shares. If the new shares are sold directly to new investors, existing shareholders would be unhappy since their ownership would automatically dilute.

9.3 Why Companies Choose to List

Companies choose to list on a stock exchange and sell their stocks to the investing public because of the many benefits that a listing brings. Companies get listed and sell their stocks for the first time through a process known as an Initial Public Offering (IPO). To be able to undertake an IPO and get its stock listed for trading on a stock exchange, a company would have to meet several pre-conditions, or listing requirements. Bursa Malaysia, like national exchanges elsewhere, has its own listing requirements. However, the elaborated key listing requirements would revolve around the need for: (i) sufficient paid-up capital, (ii) good earnings track record, and (iii) the ability of the aspiring company to meet all necessary regulatory obligations depending on whether the company wants to be listed on the main or second board, the requirements would be different. Main board requirements on capital and earnings track record would certainly be more stringent than that of the second board.

Given these pre-conditions, the typical company that wants to be publicly listed, would have been in business for several years. It may have been established as a family concern or a private partnership. In fact, most listed companies in Malaysia and other Islamic countries began as family-owned businesses. Many have also been around for generations. Not all companies that meet the listing criteria would want to be listed. This is because, as with all other factors in economic life, public listing has its advantages and disadvantages. A company's management would therefore have to balance the trade-offs. We examine some of these trade-offs later. If management decides to proceed with the listing, regulation in Malaysia and in other countries requires that the company first appoint an "advisor". This advisor is usually an investment bank. It is the task of the advisor to prepare the client for listing and file all the necessary documents needed by the several regulatory bodies. In Malaysia, aside from meeting Bursa Malaysia's requirements, a company wanting to list must meet the requirements of the Securities Commission and, if it is in the finance industry, also the requirements of Bank Negara Malaysia.

Table 9.2. Advantages and Disadvantages of Listing

Advantages	Disadvantages
• Access to equity capital	• Increased disclosure requirements. • More monitoring of firm's activities by external stakeholders.
• Lower cost of funds	• Need to meet additional regulatory requirements.
• Increases liquidity of shares owned by pre-listing owners/shareholders.	• Potential for hostile takeover and loss of control.
• Makes diversification possible for owners.	• Incur listing and other periodic costs.
	• Market myopia — shares may at times be "under- valued".

Source: Author.

Following an IPO, if a firm needs to raise additional equity capital, it can only do so through a rights issue. As mentioned earlier, the need to do it through a rights issue arises from the need to avoid ownership dilution of existing shareholders. Occasionally, a public-listed firm may sell additional new stock by means of a *private placement* rather than through an issuance of rights. A private placement is one where a tranche of stocks, e.g., 10 million new shares, are issued and sold directly to one or a few institutions. These institutions could be insurance firms, asset management companies, pension funds, etc. Their objective is to buy and hold the stocks for investment. The price at which the stocks are to be placed is negotiated. Since a private placement increases the number of stocks outstanding and inevitably causes a dilution in ownership of existing shareholders, the firm is required by law to first get the approval of existing shareholders before undertaking the private placement. Permission of the shareholders can be obtained through either an Annual General Meeting (AGM) or an Extraordinary General Meeting (EGM) as the case may be.

9.4 Rights of Share Ownership

Share ownership represents partial ownership of the firm that issued the owned shares. While a share or stock represents a "claim" of the stockholder on the firm, the firm is a separate legal entity. Thus, unlike a sole proprietorship or a private partnership where the shareholder or owner can exert direct control, a stockholder of a public-listed firm can only exercise influence indirectly, through the voting rights provided by his stock ownership. The lack of direct control is the flipside of the limited-liability feature of all listed companies. The limited-liability feature ensures that the maximum loss for a shareholder is limited to his stock investment.

Aside from voting rights, stock ownership entitles one to gain the profits of the firm through dividends that the firm declares. Stockholders are also entitled to attend and participate in the firm's AGM and are entitled to rights, stock bonuses, etc., when declared and receipt of the firm's audited financial statements. The voting right allows a shareholder not only to vote-in his or her preferred candidate for board membership, but also to vote on major issues related to the firm's operations and future performance. Important strategic issues involving the firm, matters such as mergers and acquisition, large investments, etc., require the shareholders' approval. A shareholder is entitled to either vote directly on these issues or he can pass on his vote to a proxy to vote on his behalf.

Box 9.2. Stock Ownership Entitlements

- ✓ Right to receive dividends
- ✓ Right to new shares, bonus issuance, etc.
- ✓ Right to attend and participate in AGMs/EGMs.
- ✓ Right to vote on or grant proxy to vote on issues of importance to the firm

Source: Author.

9.5 Equity Ownership and *Shari'ah* Compliance

Having discussed the features of and the entitlements from its ownership, it should be evident that equity investment through stock ownership is essentially a *mudarabah*-type arrangement. In a *mudarabah* contract, the *rab al-mal* provides the capital while the *mudarib* undertakes and operates the business. The underlying arrangement is a profit-and-loss contract. The modern-day common stock is essentially a profit–loss instrument. One receives dividends when the firm is profitable and experiences capital gains when the stock's market price appreciates. On the other hand, he would receive no dividends when the firm suffers a loss and may suffer from loss in value of the stock as its market price falls. So, with stock investment, one is taking on the price-risk and uncertainties that come with equity ownership. It is this risk-taking that justifies the returns that one receives. Seen from this risk-return viewpoint, there is no fixity of return and therefore no *riba* in earnings from stock investment. The only other consideration that needs to be fulfilled for a stock investment to be completely *Shari'ah* compliant is the underlying line of business that the stock-issuing firm is involved in. As long as the firm is not involved in an area of business that goes against the tenets of *Shari'ah*, investing in common stocks is largely a *mudarabah*-type arrangement, completely in consonance with *Shari'ah*. We address this issue in greater depth in Chapter 10.

Box 9.3. Cross-Listing of Stocks on Foreign Exchanges

Cross-listing is an increasingly popular phenomenon in the global equity markets. Cross listing happens when a financial asset is listed on one or more external stock markets, in addition to the home country exchange. For example, a company listed in one exchange may want to list its shares on the exchange of a foreign country. Such cross listing could be beneficial to both the stock-issuing and the host exchange overseas. The company benefits in a number of ways. First, it gains access to large foreign capital markets, an important consideration for companies from emerging markets. Second, such foreign listing raises a company's profile. Third, given larger traded volumes, foreign listing can increase the liquidity of a firm's shares. Finally, foreign listing can allow for better pricing of a firm's shares, implying a lower cost of equity capital. For companies, especially those from emerging markets, these are tremendous advantages. To the host exchanges, allowing foreign companies to list attracts new players interested in these stocks, allows for diversity in offering, and provides domestic investors with an easy means to diversify equity exposure. Though increasingly popular of late, cross listing on developed country stock markets is not a new phenomenon.

Introduced in the early 1920s, when American exchanges introduced regulations to attract foreign companies to tap into the US stock markets, American Depositary Receipts (ADRs) is the standard nomenclature for these secondary listings on American exchanges. As they spread out to other exchanges, primarily in Europe (Luxembourg) and the London Stock Markets, they have come to be known as Global Depositary Receipts (GDRs). Collectively known as Depository Receipts (DRs), these instruments provide cross-listing companies the opportunity to tap into liquidity beyond the geographical confines of their parent country.

As the following figure shows, in 2015, the total global value of outstanding DRs was close to $2.4 trillion. The cross-listing market is not restricted to any sector but well-diversified, as evident from the chart inset. In view of the benefits, efforts have been undertaken by regional economic alliances to promote cross listing. One of the prominent efforts has been by the ASEAN Capital Markets forum in bringing in regulations for expedited review and processing of cross listing among Singapore, Malaysia, and Thailand. Companies from several Islamic nations, such as Malaysia, Indonesia, Bahrain, and Egypt, and others have cross-listed their shares on the New York Stock Exchange as ADRs, and in Luxembourg or London as GDRs.

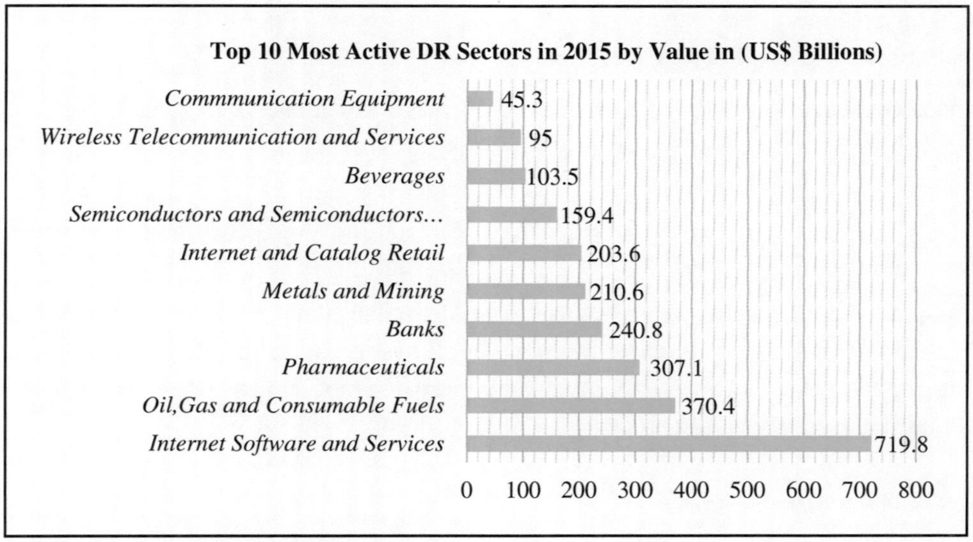

Source: BNY Mellon DR Market Review (2016).

9.6 The Valuation of Common Stocks

In Chapter 5, we saw the valuation of bonds. Bonds are valued by simply computing the present value of all future coupon payments and face value. The basic principle in valuation is that an asset's value should be the present value of all future cash flows derived from the asset. Applying this principle to the case of bonds is easy, since both the coupons and face value are fixed, pre-determined amounts. In the case of stocks, dividends are not compulsory and though stocks may have a par value, it does not mean that you will receive the par value at a time in the future. In fact, even at liquidation, there is no telling what a shareholder will receive since he is a residual claimant. In addition to this, keep in mind that stocks have no maturity. Given these complications, while the underlying logic that value should equal present value of future cash flows is the same, the pricing models are different. In this section, we examine three alternative stock valuation models. The most important of the three is the Dividend Discount Model (DDM), which we will examine in-depth, and the other two models are the Free Cash Flow (FCF) model and Equity Multiples.

9.6.1 *Common Stock Valuation — An Introduction*

Suppose you wish to buy a certain share which gives a dividend of RM2 each year. You plan to hold it for three years and expect the price at the end of Year 3 to be RM60. You intend to sell the stock at the end of Year 3. Assuming your cost of funds (or required return for the stock) is 10%, the correct price of the stock would be RM50.50, derived as follows:

$$P_0 = \frac{RM2}{(1.10)^1} + \frac{RM2}{(1+10)^2} + \frac{RM2}{(1+10)^3} + \frac{RM60}{(1+10)^3}$$

$$P_0 = RM4.97 + RM45.08$$

$$P_0 = RM50.05$$

The above computation can be written algebraically as:

$$P_0 = \sum_{t=1}^{n} \frac{d_t}{(1+k)^t} + \frac{P_n}{(1+k)^n}$$

where
d_1 = expected next dividend
P_n = expected stock price at period n
k = required discount rate or cost of capital

Notice that the above equation is very similar to the one used in Chapter 8 to value a bond. As in the case of bonds, there are two sources of returns:

(i) Dividends
(ii) Capital Gains (price appreciation)

While stock dividends are fairly stable, the above example makes a major assumption about the expected stock price in Year 3. It is this knowledge of the future price that allows us to use the above equation to value the stock. In reality, the future market price of the stock cannot be known. Thus, the above model, which was so handy in valuing bonds, cannot be used in valuing stocks.

9.6.2 *The Dividend Discount Model*

The Dividend Discount Model (DDM) is built on the standard underlying philosophy that an asset's value should equal the present value of its future cash flows. Since the only cash flows from holding a stock come from dividends, DDM values a stock by finding the present value of dividends expected from the stock. The DDM comes in three variants: (i) *the zero-growth model*, (ii) *the constant growth model*, and (iii) *the accelerated or multi-stage growth model*. The term "growth" refers to the growth in dividends. We now examine how each of these models work.

9.6.2.1 *The zero-growth model*

The simplest of the three variants of DDM, the zero-growth model, assumes no growth in the dividends paid from a stock. In other words, dividends are the same every year. The stock is a zero-growth stock. The cash flow stream from owning such a stock would be as follows:

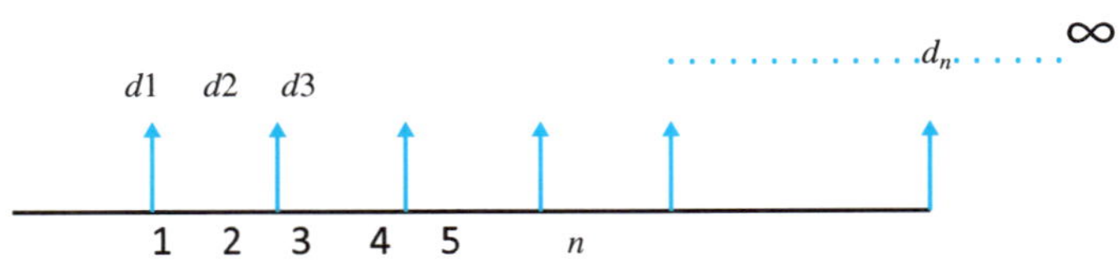

Students familiar with time value of money (TVM) should be able to recognize that the above cash flow is essentially a perpetuity. Perpetuity represents equal cash flows received or paid over an infinite period into the future. The value of a perpetuity can be determined as:

$$PV \text{ of Perpetuity} = CF/k$$

Thus, the zero-growth model values a stock as:

$$P_0 = \sum_{t=1}^{\alpha} \frac{d_t}{(k)^t}$$

where
P_0 = stock price
d_t = expected dividend at time t (or next dividend)
k = discount rate or cost of capital

Box 9.4. Illustration: Valuing Stock Using the Zero-Growth Model

Syarikat ABC, a food processing company, has been paying a dividend of RM2.00 per share for the last several years. Dividends are expected to be the same amount indefinitely. Assuming the appropriate discount rate for the stock is 8%, what should be the fair price of the stock?

Answer:

$$P_0 = d_1 / k$$

$$P_0 = \frac{\text{RM2.0}}{0.08} = \text{RM25.00 per stock.}$$

The correct current price of Syarikat ABC's stock is RM25. Since, the stock has zero growth in dividends and dividends are unchanged, this would imply that the stock's price will always be RM25 as long as the required return or discount rate remains at 8%. For example, what is the correct price of the stock six years from now?

(*Continued*)

Box 9.4. (*Continued*)

Answer:

$P_6 = d_7 / k$

Since d_7, which is the expected dividend for Year 7, is RM2.00, the stock would still be RM25.00.

$$P_6 = \frac{\text{RM2.00}}{0.08} = \text{RM25.00 per stock.}$$

Given unchanged future prices, the implication is that there will be no capital gains realized from investing in the stock.

9.6.2.2 *The constant growth model*

This model takes into consideration only dividends, but allows a constant dividend growth. The growth rate of dividends is assumed constant at g percent. So, dividend growth can be shown as follows:

$$d_1\ d_0(1+g)^1$$
$$= d_0 = d_0\ (1+g)^2$$
$$d_{10} = d_0\ (1+g)^{10}$$

The cash flow stream for investment in a stock with a constant growth in dividends would be:

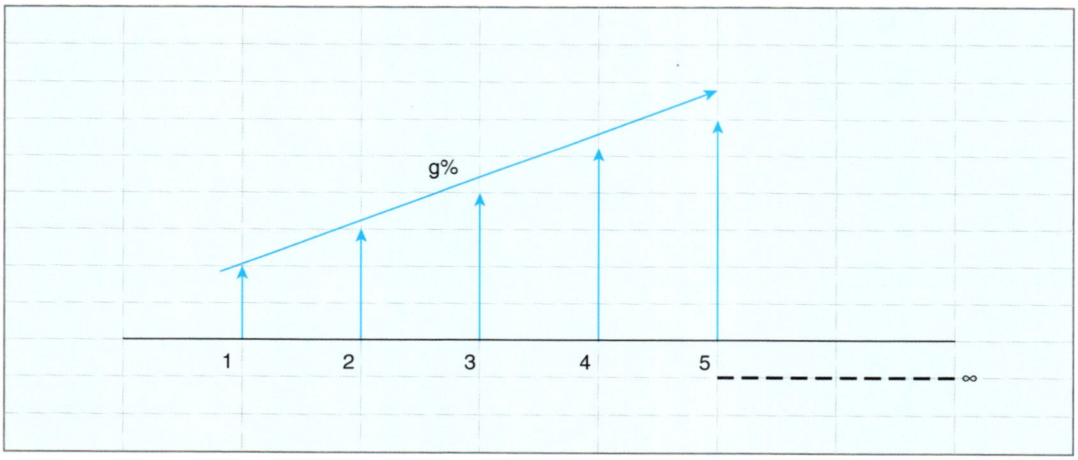

Pricing a stock with the above cash flow would algebraically be;

$$P_0 = \frac{d_0(1+g)^1}{(1+K)^1} + \frac{d_0(1+g)^2}{(1+k)^2} + \frac{d_0(1+g)^3}{(1+k)^3}$$

compounded

discounted

The above equation can be simplified as:

$$P_0 \frac{d_1}{k-g}$$ ==> This version is also known as the *Gordon Model*.

Where

d_1 = next year's expected dividend

k = discount rate/required return

g = annual growth rate in dividends

Box 9.5. Illustration: Valuing a Stock Using the Constant Growth Model

A company, Syarikat DEF, has a policy of constantly increasing its dividend over time. Its dividend for next year is expected to be RM2.00. Assuming a dividend growth rate g of 5% and a required return of 10%, determine the correct value of the stock.

$$P_0 = \frac{RM2}{10\% - 5\%} = \frac{RM2}{0.05} = RM40$$

The fair price for the stock currently is RM40.00. Here, since dividends are growing and would be higher in the future, the stock's price would not be static as in the zero-growth model earlier. The implication of stock price is discussed below.

If one were to purchase Syarikat DEF's stock at RM40 and hold it for a year, the total Holding Period Return (HPR) should be 10%, because the person had 10% as the discount rate in valuing the stock. In other words, if the use of a 10% discount rate priced the stock at RM40, then the purchase of the stock at RM40 should provide a 10% return. This raises the question of how or where the 10% return will come from when the dividend yield is only 5% {(RM2/ RM40) × 100}. The answer is, the remainder 5% will come from capital gains. In the constant growth model, since dividends are growing at 5% per year, it can be shown that the stock price will also increase at the same rate of 5%. Thus, the total expected HPR of 10% will come from dividend yield and capital gains yield, as follows:

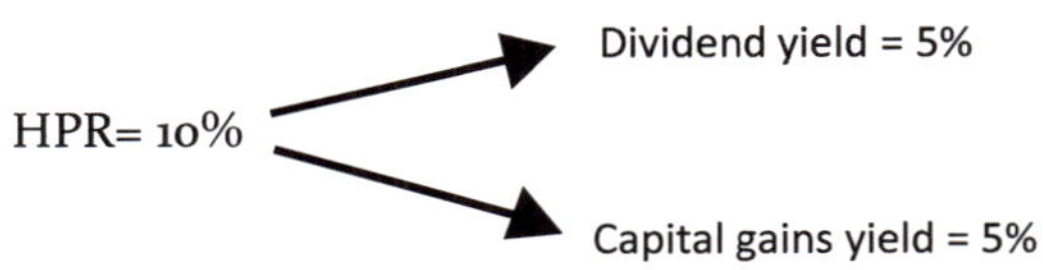

- Dividend Yield is computed as: $\{(d_1 / P_0) \times 100\}$
- Capital Gains Yield is computed as: $\{[(P_1 - P_0) / P_0)] \times 100\}$

To prove that the capital gains yield resulting from price appreciation will be 5% per year, let us examine what the equilibrium stock price will be a year from now (P_1) and two years from now (P_2).

$$P_0 = \frac{d_1}{k-g} = \frac{\$2}{0.10-0.05} = \$40$$

5%

$$P_1 = \frac{d_2}{k-g} = \frac{\$2.10}{0.10-0.05} = \$42$$

5%

$$P_2 = \frac{d_3}{k-g} = \frac{\$2.2050}{0.10-0.05} = \$44.10$$

Notice from the above calculations that P_1 is 5% higher than P_o while P_2 is higher than P_1, also by 5%. The implication is that, as long as k, the discount rate, is unchanged, the stock's price will increase at the rate of g. Since the capital gain is a direct consequence of the growth in dividends, it also implies that in the zero-growth models, where dividends are unchanged, a stock will not experience any capital gain. Since dividend is unchanged, stock price will also remain unchanged.

Stock price and investment horizon

We previously saw that, in the constant growth model, stock price increases every year at a constant rate g. This raises the question whether relative valuation would differ across investors with different investment horizons. In other words, would an investor with a three-year horizon be willing to pay more for the stock than an investor with a one-year horizon? This is a relevant question since the price at which the latter investor will sell the stock at the end of his one-year holding will be *lower* than the exit price for the three-year investor. The answer is, *stock price is independent of investment horizon*. Thus, regardless of investment horizon, the value should be the same to all investors. This is why we have an "equilibrium" price. If stock value were to change by investment horizon, there would not be a market-clearing price. The reason stock price is independent of investment horizon is because time value evens out the higher future price. To prove this, notice that stock price today will be the same, irrespective of whether the investment horizon is one, two, or even three years.

Current value of stock: One-year investment horizon

$$P_0 = \frac{d_1 + P_1}{1+k} = \frac{\$2 + \$42}{1.10} = \$40$$

Current value of stock: Two-year investment horizon

$$P_0 = \frac{d_1}{(1+k)^1} + \frac{d_2 + P_2}{(1+k)^2} = \frac{\$2}{1.10} + \frac{\$2.10}{1.21} = \$40$$

Current value of stock: Three-year investment horizon

$$P_0 = \frac{d_1}{(1+k)^1} + \frac{d_2}{(1+k)^2} + \frac{d_3 + P_3}{(1+k)^3} = \$40$$

Thus, regardless of how long we want to hold the stock, its present value, which is the price today, is always RM40. Figure 9.1 presents the diagrammatic proof.

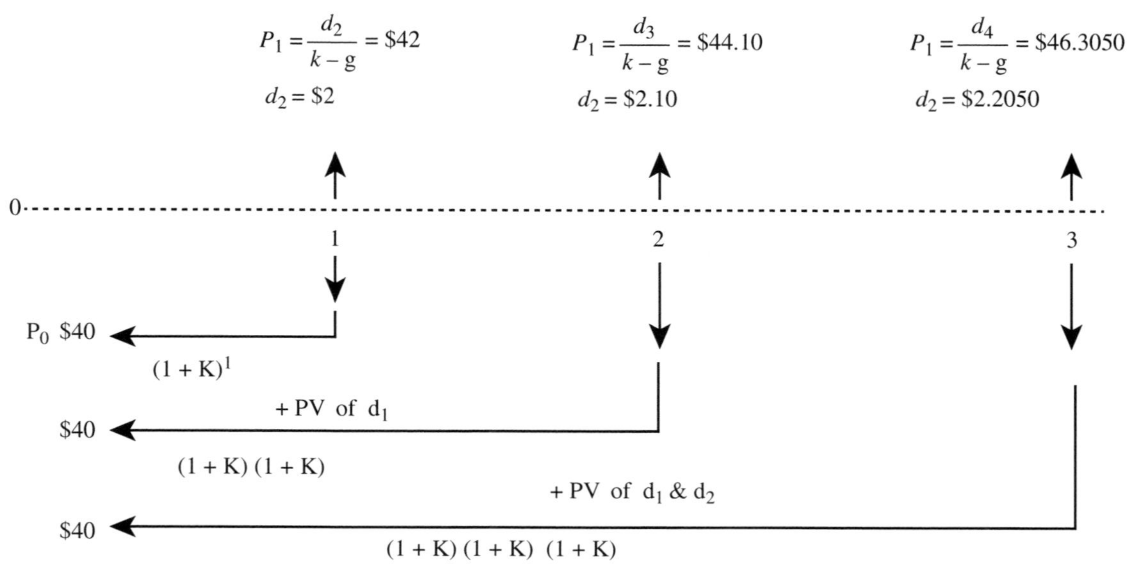

Figure 9.1. Diagrammatic Proof

The constant growth model is useful when valuing stocks of companies which have a steady growth rate. Utilities like water companies, telephone service providers, and gas and electricity providers would be good examples. In most countries, such utilities will see their revenue growth dependent on population growth. A final caveat about the constant growth model is that k must always be greater than g, otherwise the results would not be meaningful.

9.6.2.3 *Accelerated growth model*

While the constant growth model is useful in valuing stocks of companies with stable growth rates, it cannot handle situations where the growth rate varies. Firms, as we know, do not grow at steady constant rates but at different rates in different cycles of their lives. The Product Life Cycle theory argues that products (and firms that produce them) go through four typical stages: introduction, growth, maturity, and decline. It is logical that firms would have different growth rates at different times. It is in valuing stocks of firms with different growth rates that the accelerated growth model comes handy. The model comes in two forms: a basic two-stage growth model and an extended multi-stage growth model. Since the logic is the same and the multi-stage is a mere extension, we will focus our discussion here on the two-stage variant. The two-stage model assumes that a firm has a faster (accelerated) growth rate in the early years followed by a steady, slower growth rate as the firm matures. The dividend stream for a stock based on the accelerated growth model would be as follows:

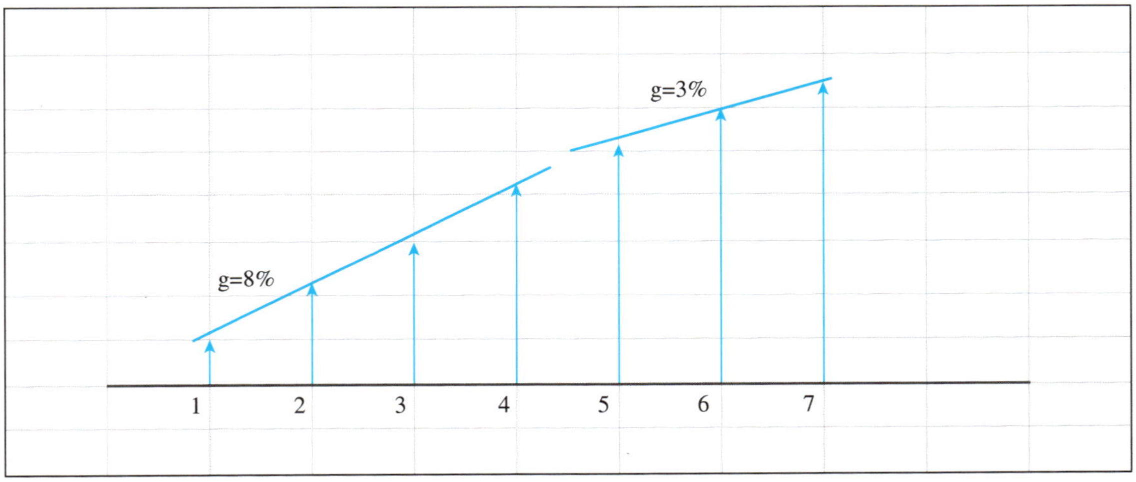

Box 9.6. Illustration: Valuing a Stock Using the Accelerated Growth Model

Anbar Holdings, a plastics manufacturer, paid a dividend of RM1.50 per stock last year. Given rapid expansion in revenue, its dividends are expected to grow 20% per year for the next four years. Following this, dividends are expected to grow at a constant 6% per year from Year 5 onward. If the required return for the stock is 16%, what should the correct price of Anbar Holding's stock be?

Answer: Since the growth rates of dividends are different, we first compute the expected dividends for each year until Year 5 when growth settles to a constant rate. Next, we plug the amounts into the equation and solve for PV.

$$d_1 = RM1.50 \times 1.20 = RM1.80 ==> RM1.50 \times 1.20_1$$
$$d_2 = RM1.80 \times 1.20 = RM2.16 ==> RM1.50 \times 1.20_2$$
$$d_3 = RM2.16 \times 1.20 = RM2.5920 ==> RM1.50 \times 1.20_3$$
$$d_4 = RM2.5920 \times 1.20 = RM3.1104 ==> RM1.50 \times 1.20_4$$
$$d_5 = RM3.1104 \times 1.06 = RM3.2970$$

(Continued)

Box 9.6. (*Continued*)

Since the growth rate from the fifth year onward is constant, we can use the constant growth model to determine what the stock price will be in Year 4 (P_4).

Thus, the correct price today for Anbar Holdings' stock is RM24.74, which is essentially the present value of future dividends from the stock.

$$P_4 = \frac{RM3.2970}{0.16 - 0.06} = \textbf{RM32}$$

$$\frac{d_1}{(1+k)^1} + \frac{d_2}{(1+k)^2} + \frac{d_3}{(1+k)^3} + \frac{d_4}{(1+k)^4} = \frac{RM32.97}{(1+k)^4}$$

P_0 = 1.5517 + 1.6052 + 1.6606 + 1.7178 + 18.2090

P_0= RM 24.74

9.7 The Market Required Rate of Return

The dividend discount models, particularly the constant growth model, can also help us determine the market's required return for a stock. That is, given a stock's market price, we can determine the required return, k, implied in the price. This can be done by simply rewriting the constant growth model as follows:

Since $$P_0 = \frac{d_1}{k-g}$$

$$k = \frac{d_1}{P_0} + g$$

Box 9.7. Illustration: Estimating the Required Return from the Stock Price

Suppose Syarikat ABC's stock is currently trading at RM12.00. The company's next dividend is expected to be RM0.80 per share. Assuming dividend growth is 4% per year, determine the market's required return implied in the price.

k = {(RM 0.80 / RM 12.00) + 0.04}
= (0.067) + 0.04
= 0.1067 or 10.67%

So, the required return, k, implied by the price of RM12.00 is 10.67%.

9.8 Required Return and Stock Price Dynamics

The required return or discount rate is a critical ingredient in the pricing of stocks. The required return is inversely related to a stock's value. Holding dividends (d) and growth rate (g) constant, a higher required return will mean a lower stock price and vice versa. There are extensive literatures, theories, and hypotheses about the determinants of the required return. An in-depth discussion of these theories is beyond the scope of this chapter. However, the common factor in all these postulations is that the required return is dependent on the asset's riskiness. That is, the higher the risk, the higher the required return. The most commonly used model in determining the appropriate required return for an asset is the Capital Asset Pricing Model (CAPM). This model, which is built on Harry Markowitz's Modern Portfolio Theory, argues that an asset's required return is a function of the risk-free return and the asset's systematic risk. The risk-free return (R_f), is generally taken to be the yield on short term (three-month) treasury bills or the three-month money market rate (three-month KLIBOR or LIBOR). An asset's systematic risk is the risk that remains after diversification. It can also be thought of as an asset's market risk. Systematic risk is denoted using the Greek term beta. Formally, the CAPM is written as:

$$Er = Rf + \beta\,(Rm - Rf),$$

where
Er = expected rate of return
Rm = return on market portfolio (or index)
Rf = risk-free rate of return
β = estimated beta of the stock

The expected return (Er) can also be read as the required return (k) in our examples. A stock's beta can be determined as:

$$Bi = \frac{Cov\,(Ri - Rm)}{Var\,(Rm)}$$

Since the beta is essentially the variance-covariance between a stock's return and that of the overall market portfolio, beta can be thought of as a measurement of the sensitivity of a stock's return to market returns. Thus, a stock with a beta of 2.0 will see its returns rise 20% when the market portfolio (or simply the stock index, like EMAS or S&P 500) rises 10%. Alternatively, if the market falls 12% in a given period, the stock's price would have fallen 24%. A beta of 2.0 implies returns twice as volatile as the market portfolio. Thus, by definition, the beta of the market portfolio must be 1.0. An asset with a beta of zero is simply uncorrelated with market returns. A negative beta (though infrequent), implies negative correlation with the market portfolio. For example, a stock with a beta –0.5 would *rise* 5% when the market falls 10% but would *fall* 5% if the market rises 10%.

Box 9.8. Illustration: Determining Required Returns and Stock Price Using CAPM

Hafzal Berhad's stock has a beta of 1.25. Its last dividend was RM0.80 per share. Dividends have been growing at 4% per year and can be expected to continue growing at that rate. Assuming a risk-free rate of 3.5% and a return on the market portfolio of 8.5%, determine the required return for Hafzal Berhad's stock and its appropriate price.

Answer:

Step 1: Determine the required return using CAPM

$k = Er = Rf + \beta\,(Rm - Rf)$
$k = 3.5\% + 1.25\,(8.5\% - 3.5\%)$
$k = 3.5\% + 1.25\,(5\%)$
$k = 9.75\%$

Step 2: Using the computed k, determine the stock price using the constant growth model.

$P_0 = \{d_1 / (k - g)\}$

$$P_0 = \frac{\text{RM}0.80\,(1+g)}{0.0975 - 0.04} \qquad P_0 = \frac{\text{RM}0.80\,(1.04)}{0.0975 - 0.04}$$

$$P_0 = \frac{\text{RM}0.832}{0.0575}$$

P_0 = RM14.47

So, the correct price of Hafzal Berhad's stock is RM14.47.

9.9 Dividend Growth and the Trade-Off with Capital Gains

As discussed earlier, the returns from investing in a stock come from two sources: dividend yield and capital gains or price appreciation of the stock. The proportion of returns from dividends or capital gains varies. Some stocks give high dividends while others little or no dividends. For stocks that give out little or no dividends, the return comes mostly from capital gains. Modigliani and Miller (M&M), two famous financial economists and Nobel Laureates, have argued that dividends may not really matter. They show that there is a trade-off between dividends and capital gains.

A company that pays out most of its net profits as dividends would have high dividend yields; however, since most of the earnings have been paid out as dividends, it will have little earnings to reinvest in the business. Given low reinvestment in the business, subsequent earnings, growth, and increase in firm value will be low. When a firm's value is unchanged or increases only marginally, stock price which reflects the firm's value would also increase only marginally. Alternatively, a firm that pays little dividends but reinvests most of its earnings will experience higher growth in firm value and therefore stock price.

Since higher dividend yields imply lower capital gains and vice versa, M&M argue that, from a theoretical viewpoint, given this trade-off, dividends are irrelevant. Investors would only care about the total returns they earn, not the components of the return. Despite the theoretical arguments, M&M conceded that dividends may have some non-pecuniary benefits. For example, investors feel good when receiving dividend cheques. Furthermore, M&M argue that there may be a signalling effect of dividends, especially when dividend pay-outs are changed. Since companies tend to be consistent with their dividend payments, a higher dividend would imply that management expects earnings to be higher in the future. In this sense, an increased dividend signals to investors that management is bullish about future earnings. The opposite signal would be sent if dividends are cut.

9.9.1 *Where Does the 'g' Come From?*

The growth in dividends or earnings is determined as follows:

$$g = b \times \text{ROI}$$

$$\text{where } b = 1 - [\text{div. pay-out ratio}]$$

Dividend growth is therefore determined by the plowback ratio, denoted by b and the firms return on investment (ROI). The trade-off mentioned earlier should be evident from the equation for 'g'. A higher dividend pay-out ratio will mean a lower 'b', plowback ratio and so a lower 'g'. A low dividend pay-out will have the impact of increasing growth if ROI is constant.

Frequently used Equations

(1) $==> k = \frac{d1}{P_0} + g$

(2) $==> P_0 = \frac{d_1}{k - g}$

(3) $==> g = k - \frac{d_1}{P_0}$

(4) $d_1 = d_0(1 + g)^1$
$d_2 = d_1\ (1 + g)^1$
$d_1 \Rightarrow P_0 \cdot (k - g)$
$d_2 = P_1 \cdot (k - g)$

or

(5) CAPM $==> k = rf + beta\ (rm - rf)$

Box 9.9. Growth and Development of the Malaysian Stock Market

The Malaysian stock market has had a colorful history, much of it tied to the political winds blowing between Malaysia and Singapore. Today, Malaysia has a single stock exchange, Bursa Malaysia Berhad, which itself is a public-listed company. The country's first formal stock exchange began in 1960 as The Malayan Stock Exchange. This exchange had its roots in the Singapore Stock Broker's Association, which was set up in 1931. A Malayan wing of this association, the Malayan Stock Broker's Association, was formed in 1937. Public trading of shares began in May 1960 with the establishment of the Malayan Stock Exchange. With the formation of the Federation of Malaysia in 1963, the exchange was renamed The Stock Exchange of Malaysia. However, when Singapore left the Federation of Malaysia in 1965, the exchange was renamed the Stock Exchange of Malaysia and Singapore. It was essentially a joint stock exchange for both countries.

In 1973, the Malaysian government decided to leave the currency board arrangement that had been placed among the three countries: Malaysia, Singapore, and Brunei. This effectively ended the single currency arrangement. In June 1973, the joint exchange was split into two national exchanges, the Kuala Lumpur Stock Exchange Bhd (KLSE Bhd) for Malaysia and the Singapore Stock Exchange. KLSE Bhd. was incorporated as The Kuala Lumpur Stock Exchange in December 1976 as a company limited by guarantee. Despite the separation, the Malaysian and Singapore Exchanges were linked by a dual-listing arrangement that enabled companies domiciled in either country to list their stocks on both exchanges.

In late 1989, the Malaysian government decided that Malaysian companies should only be listed on the KLSE and not both. The dual-listing arrangement came to an end in 1990. Singapore was the one at loss in this, since 196 Malaysian firms were delisted from its exchange whereas only 53 Singapore firms were delisted from the Malaysian Exchange. Since Malaysian firms accounted for the majority of the listed stocks and traded volume on the Singapore exchange, they created CLOB International, which was a means to continue trading Malaysian shares owned by Singaporean investors. The curtain finally came down on such offshore trading of Malaysian stocks when the KLSE went scriptless at end 1996. The process was further hastened by the onset of the Asian Currency Crisis of 1997 and the imposition of capital controls.

A critical milestone in the history of the Malaysian stock exchange was reached in April 2004 when the exchange became a public-listed company, following the demutualization of the KLSE. It was at this point that the exchange was renamed Bursa Malaysia Bhd. Shares of Bursa Malaysia began trading in March 2005. Bursa Malaysia Bhd., the holding company, has three business units: (i) the Exchanges Business Unit, (ii) the Clearing Settlement and Depository Business Unit, and (iii) the Information Services Business Unit. The main revenue generator is obviously the Exchange Business Unit.

A total of three exchanges come under this business unit: Securities Exchange, Derivatives Exchange, and the Offshore Exchange. The Securities Exchange, or Bursa Securities, is by far the most important since the three key markets, the Main Board, Second Board, and Mesdaq, are components of the Securities Exchange. The Derivatives Exchange, Bursa Malaysia Derivatives, offers seven financial and two commodity derivative contracts. The offshore exchange is a Labuan-based international offshore financial exchange. Known as the Labuan International Financial Exchange (LFX), it provides services that facilitate the listing and trading of offshore financial instruments. These instruments may be either Islamic-based or conventional. As an offshore exchange, transactions could be in multi-currency and duty-free. The following figure shows the structure of Bursa Malaysia.

(*Continued*)

Box 9.9. (Continued)

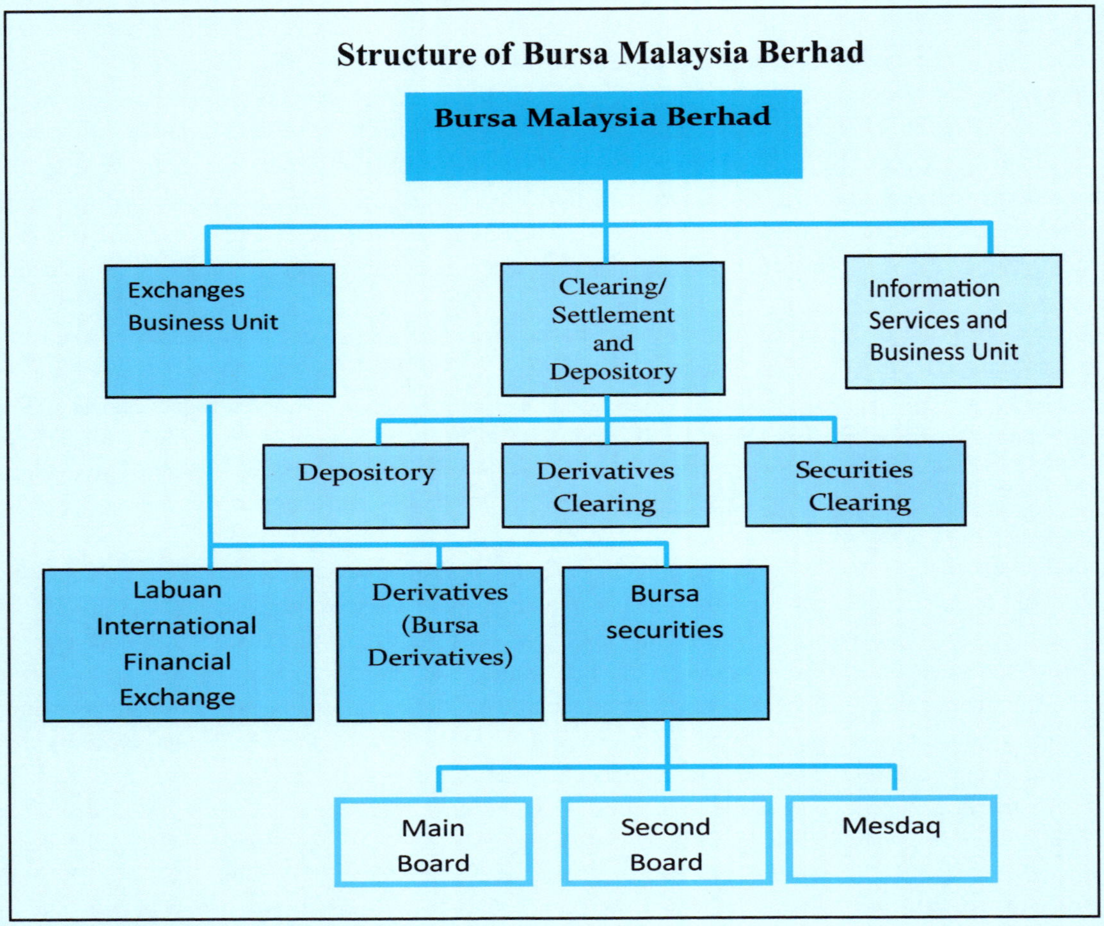

With the exception of the Labuan International Financial Services Authority (LOFSA), all other units of Bursa Malaysia including the holding company come under the regulatory domain of the Securities Commission.

9.10 Stock Market Indices

A stock index, like other indices, is essentially a statistical measuring tool. Just like the Consumer Price Index (CPI) measures inflation, a stock index measures stock market performance. And just as the CPI uses a select sample of goods and services to measure changes in the general price level, a stock market index uses a sample basket of stocks traded in an exchange to gauge overall market performance. The basket of common stocks would together make up an index. The stocks within an index are not selected randomly but through a technique known as structured sampling. Structured sampling ensures that the index will represent the overall market, in terms of the industry sectors. A stock market typically has several indices where some are designed to measure broad market movements. For example, the Dow Jones is an index of 30 stocks traded on the New York Stock Exchange (NYSE), designed to measure the overall movement of the NYSE. The FBMKLCI is an index of 30 stocks traded on Bursa Malaysia, while the Nikkei is an index of 225 stocks listed on the first board of the Tokyo Stock Exchange. These indices measure overall market movement. In addition, there are indices that measure the performance of subsectors within the stock exchange. For example, Bursa Malaysia's Small Cap Index measures the performance of smaller companies. The Dow Jones Transportation Index measures the performance of NYSE-listed companies from the transportation sector. Table 9.3 shows a list of some of the indices available on Bursa Malaysia.

Table 9.3. FTSE Bursa Malaysia Index

Series Index/Sector Name	No. of Constituents	Market Cap (RM 000's)
FTSE Bursa Malaysia Top 100 Index	100	1,314,385
FTSE Bursa Malaysia mid 70 Index	70	303,849
FTSE Bursa Malaysia EMAS Index	255	1,402,848
FTSE Bursa Malaysia Fledgling Index	380	41,758
FTSE Bursa Malaysia KLCI	30	1,010,536
FTSE Bursa Malaysia Hijrah Shariah Index	30	652,049
FTSE Bursa Malaysia Small Cap Index	155	88,464
FTSE Bursa Malaysia Palm Oil Plantation Index	9	132,729

Source: FTSE Monthly Report, January 2017.

9.10.1 *Index Construction and Types of Indices*

A stock index is essentially a barometer of stock market performance. As mentioned earlier, an index is made up of a basket of stocks. This basket of stocks that make up the index is usually carefully chosen to represent the market it is measuring. Indices are basically statistical sampling. There are three types of stock indices:

(i) An equally weighted (price weighted) index;
(ii) A value weighted (capitalisation weighted) index;
(iii) A geometrically weighted index.

Though the objective of measurement is the same, each of the above type of index varies in the way it is computed. Such a difference in computation can lead to small differences in market performance. Each method of computation has its own advantages and disadvantages.

9.11 Schools of Thought on Stock Price Behavior

Given the potential for profits and losses as a result of stock price movements, investors have looked, for a long time, at ways and means to predict and explain these price movements. Overtime, three main schools of thought evolved to explain the behaviour of stock prices. These three schools are *Fundamental Analysis*, *Technical Analysis*, and the *Efficient Market Hypothesis* (EMH). Recently, a fourth school, *Behavioural Finance*, has surfaced. We now briefly discuss each of these schools.

9.11.1 *Fundamental Analysis*

According to Fundamental Analysis (FA), a stock's price behavior is rooted in its fundamentals, such as the underlying firm's performance. Thus, the fundamentalists, as the adherents of this school of thought, would examine the issuing firm's growth in revenue, profitability, market share, and factors like quality of management, in trying to predict future performance of the stock. Fundamentalists can therefore be thought of as *rationalists* since they attribute stock price changes to changes in a stock's underlying fundamentals. Much of what is taught in finance courses in universities really belong to fundamentals analysis.

9.11.2 *Technical Analysis (Chartism)*

Technical Analysis, or Chartism as it is often known, is based on the philosophy that history repeats itself. Technical analysts or "chartists", as its practitioners are known, attempt to predict future stock price movements by analyzing a stock's price pattern history. The idea is to look for *buy* and *sell* signals from graphical analysis of price plots, thus the name Chartism. Chartists depend on price patterns, volume patterns, charts, and numerous graphical indicators to look for identifiable signals. For example, a *head and shoulders* pattern would signal the end of a bull market and the beginning of a bear market (down market). Alternatively, the formation of a "W" pattern, or a *reverse head and shoulders*, would signal the end of a bear market and the beginning of a bullish trend. This would arguably be a very strong buy signal. Technical analysis literally has tens of such patterns and indicators. Some technical analysts appear to prefer certain patterns (buy–sell signals) over others. While it is hard to rationalize the use of these graphical analyses, the underlying logic is that investor's psychology rather than fundamentals is what drives stock prices. And since humans are a creature of habit, they behave in certain predictable ways. So, to tell whether investors will chase up or pull down a stock's price, the underlying psychology portrayed in the price should be looked at.

Much of Chartism owes to the work of Charles Dow. Charles Dow, a founder-editor of *The Wall Street Journal*, had propounded what came to be known as the *Dow Theory*. A key tenet of the Dow Theory is that the stock market has three types of movements or cycles; firstly, a *primary cycle*, which is typically spread over several years. This primary cycle can be bullish or bearish. Within this primary cycle are then the *medium cycle* and *short cycle*. The medium movement can be over several weeks or months, whereas the short cycle or minor movement is usually over a few days. Thus, within a long-term primary bull cycle, short- and medium-term bearish cycles are possible. Where primary cycles are concerned, fundamental analysts would have little objection. The phenomenon of economies going through boom economic cycles is an accepted fact in macroeconomic thinking. However, where the chartists would diverge from the fundamentalist is in their ability to time stock investments according to the medium and short cycles.

9.11.3 *Efficient Market Hypothesis*

The Efficient Market Hypothesis (EMH) came out of the work of Eugene Fama in the 1960s. Fama's work had its roots in the work of Louis Bachelier, a French mathematician, whose *Theory of Speculation* first showed the unpredictability of stock prices. In the initial version, Fama argued that stock prices moved in a random fashion and that most financial series followed a "random walk model". The underlying philosophy of EMH is that the key causal factor for stock price change is the arrival of new information or "news". Since the arrival of new information itself is random, prices move randomly. An efficient market is one in which information is available cheaply, publicly, and in a timely fashion.

Later, in the 1970s, Fama refined the theory and showed that different markets may have different levels of efficiency. He put forth three versions or levels of market efficiency: (i) *weak form EMH,* (ii) *semi-strong form EMH*, and (iii) *strong form EMH*. The *weak form EMH* argues that future stock price movements are independent of past price changes. This effectively precludes the use of Technical Analysis or Chartism. *Semi-strong form EMH* postulates that all available public information is reflected in a stock's price. Since a stock's current price already reflects all known information, researching a stock's fundamentals or analyzing its past price behavior is irrelevant and will not yield excess returns, effectively implying that in a semi-strong form efficient market, both Fundamental and Technical Analysis is useless. *Strong form EMH* argues that a stock's price reflects not only all public but also private information about the stock. Thus, in a market that is strong-form efficient, even insider information will not lead to excess returns.

Though there has been much empirical support for weak and semi-strong form efficiency, *strong form EMH* appears to be a difficult proposition to accept. There has also been consistent evidence of systematic patterns in stock returns. The presence of systematic patterns obviously flies in the face of EMH since a systematic pattern is by definition non-random. Systematic patterns in stock returns have been documented in several areas, notably day-of-week returns, a January effect, a small-firm effect, and the consistent outperformance of value versus growth firms. The presence of these inconsistencies has given rise to a new school of thought, the Behavioral Finance School.

9.11.4 *The Behavioral Finance School*

Behavioral finance uses psychology-based arguments to explain investor behavior. Since other theories in finance assume rational investors, they are unable to explain the many stock market anomalies. Behavioral finance makes no such assumption but accepts the reality of human emotion and psychology in decision-making. Irrational financial decision-making that lead to market bubbles and panics are explained using cognitive theories from psychology in combination with conventional finance theories. Behavioral finance has its origins in the work of Kahneman and Tversky, two cognitive psychologists who began examining the role of rationality in economics. It was Richard Thaler, an economist, who saw the value in Kahneman and Tversky's work to explain the many phenomena that conventional finance and economic theories could not explain. Together, they laid the foundations of behavioral finance; though still new, behavioral finance has made much headway in conventional finance and much promise for Islamic finance where spiritual values and religion play a key role.

Box 9.10. High-Frequency Trading

High-frequency trading (HFT), a relatively new phenomenon, involves the use of specialized algorithmic trading to enable very quick turnover of relatively small positions in financial assets. Though there is no formal definition of HFT, the US Securities and Exchanges Commission (SEC) outlines the following characteristics of HFT:

- Usage of sophisticated computer programs for generating, routing, and executing orders — essentially, "program trading";
- Short holding period between establishing and liquidating positions;
- Submission of numerous orders that are cancelled shortly after submission; and
- Not carrying a significant amount of un-hedged overnight positions.

Despite its recent beginnings, HFT has quickly garnered popularity and usage. The rate of growth in HFT has been astounding to say the least. Though, the actual volume of HFT transactions is still unknown, the SEC estimates HFT to account for over 50% of the total equity volumes. It is also estimated that high-frequency traders, as a group, scooped up US$ 12.9 billion in profits in 2009 and 2010. Proponents of HFT argue that it has garnered this kind of interest and support precisely due to its positive impact of enhancing liquidity, reducing of trading spreads, and improving overall market efficiency.

However, HFT has been blamed for the flash crash of May 6, 2010, when the Dow Jones Industrial Average plunged about 9% and then recovered within minutes. It was the second largest point swing of the DJIA, a total of 1,010.14 points. The subsequent joint investigation by the SEC and the Commodity Futures Trading Commission (CFTC) attributed the exacerbation of the crash to HFT algorithms. This crisis highlighted the higher volatility risk but enhanced liquidity and market volumes that HFT brings to capital markets.

Continued criticism and the underlying risk of sudden spikes in traded volumes leading to sudden price changes, has led regulators to consider a crackdown on HFT. The European Commission in September 2011 unveiled a proposal for taxing speculators which would hit HFT. In the US, regulators have proposed a "large trader" rule which would require firms having high market participation, including high-speed traders, to disclose more about their activities.

9.12 Regulatory Restrictions on Trading

Equity exchanges in all countries are subject to various trading restrictions. In fact, other exchanges, like commodity or derivative exchanges, are also subject to such regulations. Since equity and other exchanges are nothing but platforms on which trading takes place, regulatory stance has always been that exchanges should be "level playing fields" in which every player, big or small, is treated fairly. In addition to ensuring fairness, regulation is also aimed at preventing trading excesses. Such excesses maybe the result of investor panic or "excessive" speculation, both of which could lead to extreme volatility in asset prices.

Aside from hurting genuine investors, high volatility in asset prices would require higher returns to compensate for the higher risk. Heightened risk premium translates into higher required costs of capital for firms whose shares are listed. This in turn retards the competitiveness of listed companies, in particular, companies that are competing internationally. Unchecked trading excesses can therefore have huge social costs, thus the need for regulation. Across countries, there is a very wide array of trading restrictions. We examine here some of the key regulations, found in most countries. For ease of elucidation, we categorize this under three subholdings:

(i) Rules to check price manipulation
(ii) Rules against speculative excess
(iii) Rules to prevent investor panic

9.12.1. *Rules Against Price Manipulation*

Price manipulation is probably the most abhorrent of violations against fair trading and so attracts the most severe penalties. Market regulators typically have broad powers to act against manipulators. The main instruments of regulators are insider-trading rules. In just about all countries, there are strict regulations against insider trading. Insider trading refers to the trading in stocks of a company by individuals who are either employees (insiders) of a firm or those with intimate knowledge of transactions undertaken by a company. While the former are usually top management or individuals sitting as directors in the firm's Board of Directors, the latter could be consultants, investment bankers, external auditors, and the like, who have access to a company's details. Where employees and directors of a firm are concerned, regulation requires that they disclose all their trading of the company's stock. They are required to report to the exchange, usually through the company's compliance department, of any purchase of sale of company stock. In some countries, this requirement would extend to include spouses and other close relatives of insiders.

The basic idea of insider trading regulation is to check against the unfair use of inside information. For example, if, just prior to the release of very favorable information, a member of the company's top management purchases the stock, that would constitute insider trading. Similarly, if a manager sells his stock holding in the company just prior to the release of bad news by the company, that too would be deemed insider trading. In either case, the company executive is making unfair use of his insider knowledge to profit from the expected stock price reaction. Often, to hide their manipulation, individuals with inside knowledge may pass on or "sell" the information to outsiders unrelated to the company. Such information leakages are also illegal. Though insider trading is always difficult to prove in a court of law, securities regulators everywhere are highly sensitive and always on guard against insider trading.

Aside from insider trading, the other common form of price manipulation in markets is "front-loading". Front-loading happens when brokers who receive a large customer buy order, purchase the stock/asset for their accounts before executing the customer's order. Since the customer's large order when executed will likely cause an increase in the stock or asset's price, the broker is likely to make easy profits from his earlier purchase. The opposite is done in the case of a large sell order received from a client. The broker short-sells the underlying stock or asset before executing the customer's sell order. The common means by which regulators and exchanges check front-loading activity is by way of required time-stamps. That is, requiring all customer orders to be time-stamped. Since all trade executions on an exchange are time-stamped, one could check the time-stamps for evidence of front-loading. Though time-stamps can also be circumvented, at least there is an audit trail.

A third form of price manipulation of exchange-traded assets is by way of syndicated price ramping. Here, a group of individuals acting in cohort either ramp up or ramp down the price of a stock or asset. The hope of such syndicates is that their coordinated action would cause substantial movement in prices that way may attract other investors to also buy or sell. Once an asset's price has been ramped up sufficiently, the syndicate unloads the asset quickly, thereby leaving other investors who bought in later with overpriced stocks. Often, these syndicates may even short-sell in order to profit from an impending crash in prices.

9.12.2. *Regulation to Check Speculative Activity*

Speculative activity provides liquidity to markets and can reduce transaction costs and liquidity risk. In addition, speculators, being risk-takers, stand ready to take on the risk passed to them by hedgers. Thus, speculative activity does have benefits, though when excessive, it can seriously hurt markets and the price discovery process. Exchanges and regulators have a number of tools available to check speculative excesses. Among these are:

(i) Changes to margin requirements;
(ii) Up-tick rules and
(iii) Position limits.

The use of margins enables speculators to leverage their position. With margins, a speculator gets to "borrow" to enlarge his exposure. Thus, when margins are small, a speculator can take a large position for a given amount of funds. However, when the required margin is increased, the ability to leverage is automatically reduced since he has to tie-up a larger amount of his investible capital in margins. This has two effects on a speculators intended position. First, by having to pay more for margins, his ability to leverage reduces as the cost of funds increases. The size of the position he can take is reduced. The second effect is that, with reduced leverage, the potential profit he can make for a given move in the asset or stock's price is reduced. Thus, the overall impact of a margin increase is that it makes speculation much less attractive. *Uptick rules* are simply rules that dictate that a sell order cannot be placed at or a price lower than current price. A tick refers to predetermined rates at which an asset's price quote can move. For example, a stock's tick-size may be 50 cents, which means that its price must move in 50 cent increments. Thus, when an uptick rule is in place, a seller has to quote a price at least 50 cents *higher* than last done price. Such a requirement obviously makes it difficult to sell and thereby depresses prices.

The objective is essentially to prevent short-selling and attempts to artificially depress prices. *Position limits* are used to check the build-up of very large positions by speculators. The position limit dictates the maximum size that an individual account can hold at any given time. Any holding larger than the position limit will be deemed to be a violation of trading rules. Nick Leeson, the rogue trader who bankrupted Barings PLC of Britain, was jailed in Singapore for having defrauded the Singapore Exchange (known as SIMEX then) by setting up fictitious accounts that enabled him to exceed his position limits on the Nikkei Stock Index futures contracts.

9.12.3. *Rules to Prevent Investor Panic*

Markets, especially the stock market, are often driven by greed and fear. Exuberance and greed cause asset price bubbles, and when prices have risen beyond what is justified by their fundamentals, fear creeps in. It is this fear and the desire to sell ahead of others at the first sign of trouble that leads to panic selling or panic buying (to cover short positions). Such panic reaction can seriously damage market trading, cause unnecessary losses, and tarnish an exchange's reputation. Price discovery would obviously be distorted. Given such consequences and in the interest of having orderly markets, regulators have devised a number of rules to ensure orderly conduct. The most commonly known rule against panic selling is the "circuit-breaker". Recommended by the Brady Commission, established to investigate the Black Monday crash of October 1987 in the US, circuit-breakers have become a staple of most exchanges worldwide. In essence, the circuit-breakers halt trading once prices move out of a predetermined band. For example, an exchange might set the band at +/– 10% for a given trading session. What it means is that, trading of a stock/asset will be halted once its traded price moves 10% higher or lower than its closing price of the previous session. Depending on exchange rules, the halt may last for the remaining part of the trading day or for a given time period, for e.g., for the subsequent 30 minutes. The basic idea behind circuit-breakers is to stop trading in order to enable market participants to take "time-off" to think through and rationalize events. Often times, the panic buying/selling may have been set-off by the arrival of new information. The time break provided by the circuit-breaker enables participants to think through their actions and evaluate whether the price reaction is proportionate or rational given the new information. In the absence of circuit-breakers, panic trading could lead to precipitous declines in prices, way beyond what is warranted. It is also for this reason that exchanges often require listed companies to make major announcements after hours, that is after trading hours. Similarly, major policy announcements by the government are often timed to be after trading hours, usually late afternoon on Fridays.

Box 9.11. Knight Capital Brought to Its Knees by an Algorithm Gone Awry

Global capital markets were shocked once again in early August 2012 by news of humongous losses caused by an algorithm gone awry. Knight Capital Group, a market maker, had built a new trading software which apparently had not been properly tested. As a market maker, Knight Capital would be an intermediary between buyers and sellers, especially at times of order imbalances. While trading software is fairly bland and straightforward, big players such as Knight Capital would invest huge amounts of money into building software or algorithms that could give them an edge. Built with artificial intelligence, fuzzy logic, neural networks, and the like, the algorithms seek to find patterns that they then seek to take advantage of. Going by the amount of money invested in such software, it is obvious that their use must be profitable. For capital markets, the upside of such computerized trading is increased liquidity; speedy execution, implying lower execution risks; and the lowering of transaction costs. Yet, the speed with which program trading happens and the immense sizes of the trades have meant massive blow-ups. With the dependence of all Wall Street firms on computerized systems and program trading, the blow-ups have happened every so often. In the case of Knight Capital, the algorithm apparently went berserk and set off rapid fire buy and sell orders of its own. By the time the algorithm was brought under control, the losses were enough to potentially sink the company. Knight Capital's total losses due to computer malfunction was US$440 million, an amount more than four times its reported profits in 2011. The losses more than wiped out the company's cash holdings, estimated at US$350 million. This is not the first time a Wall Street firm has been mortally wounded by bad algorithms. Several hedge funds, most notably Long Term Capital Management (LTCM), have been blown to bits. The "flash crash" in 2011 of NYSE Trading is another example in the ultra-high speed, high-stakes world of modern capital markets, where the tiniest glitches can cause gigantic losses.

Source: *The New York Times* and *NST,* August 5, 2012.

Summary

An investment in a company's stock represents partial ownership of the company's equity or assets. An equity-holder is a residual claimant. Unlike debt, which provides a fixed stream of cash flows to the investor, equity provides no "fixity" in returns. Equity investments therefore resemble *mudarabah*-type financing. Stocks began as an instrument to enable equity investors to divide ownership, diversify, provide liquidity, and thereby reduce their risk. Stocks and stock markets play an extremely important role within capital markets. Aside from deriving investment income, stocks can also be the means by which one can save and enable inter-temporal transfers. As stocks have no maturity or a redemption value, stock valuation models price the stock by valuing the expected dividends from the stock. There are three variants of the Dividend Discount Model (DDM). These are the zero-growth, constant growth, and accelerated growth models. The *zero-growth models* assume dividends would be unchanged and values the stock as perpetuity. As dividends have no growth in this model, a stock's price will remain unchanged as long as the required return for the stock is the same. The *constant growth model* assumes that dividends will grow at a steady constant rate into perpetuity. The growth in dividends implies that stock values would be higher as the dividend grows. Thus, under the constant growth model, the returns to an equity-holder come from both dividend yields and capital gains. The *accelerated growth model* takes into consideration higher growth rates in the early years of a company's life. The model assumes differential growth rates in dividends.

Under all three models, stock price is independent of an investor's investments horizon. The required return for a stock is dependent on the stock's perceived riskiness. Riskier stocks would require a higher return and vice versa. The most common way to determine the required return for a stock would be by way of the Capital Asset Pricing Model (CAPM). According to CAPM, the required return for a stock is dependent on the stock's beta and the market risk premium. The higher a stock's beta, the higher the required return.

The growth rate of a firm or its dividends depends on how much a firm plows back into the business and on the return from its investments. The higher the plow back ratio and the return on its investments, the higher the growth rate of the firm and its dividends. Stock market indices act as a barometer or measure of stock market performance. There are alternative schools of thought on stock price behavior, which are the fundamentalist, the chartist, or technical analyst, the Random Walk or Efficient Market Hypothesis (EMH), and the Behavioral School. Each school provides an alternative view of stock price behavior.

Questions and Problems

1. Describe some of the advantages to the firm of listing on a stock exchange.
2. What benefits, other than investment return, can shareholders get from investing in listed shares?
3. Differentiate between a stock-dividend and a stock split. What is the impact of each on the number of shares outstanding and their market value?
4. How important is the par value of a stock relative to that of a bond? Why is it so?
5. Between a stock and a bond, which is likely to have a higher required rate of return? Why?
6. A company has a reported net income of RM12 million and 60 million shares outstanding.
   (a) Estimate the stock's market price if the price earning (P/E) ratio is 14.0.
   (b) What is the company's value by market capitalization?
7. (a) Given the following information, determine the correct price of the stock.

Last dividend	=	RM2.00
Required return	=	14%
Expected grow rate of dividend	=	4% for the foreseeable future.

   (b) Suppose you purchased a stock at the price you computed in (a) above. If the firm subsequently faces financial distress causing the required return to increase by an additional 3%, what is the stock's new price likely to be?
   (c) Assuming you bought a stock at its value in (a), held it for a year and sold it at year end for the price computed in (b), compute your total returns, dividend yield, and capital gains.
8. You have the following information about Bantam Inc.

No. stocks outstanding	=	140 million
Last dividend	=	RM1.80
Return on Investments	=	15%
Dividend payout ratio	=	60%
Risk free rate	=	4%
Return of market portfolio	=	10%
Bantam Inc. stock beta	=	1.45

Determine:
   (a) Using CAPM, the required return for Bantam Inc. stock.
   (b) Using constant growth DDSLI, the correct price of the stock.
   (c) The value of the firm by market capitalization.
9. A stock is expected to have a dividend growth rate of 8% per year for the next two years and then 3% per year thereafter. If its last dividend was RM2.40 and the required return is 12%, determine its correct value.
10. Compare and contrast Efficient Market Hypothesis (EMH) with Chartism. What is the implication of EMH's message on the validity of Chartism?
11. Anza Corp. Stock paid dividends last year of RM1.60. Dividends are expected to grow at 4% per year. The stock's beta is 1.40. Assuming the return on the FBMKLCI (market) is 11% and the risk-free rate is 3%:
   (a) Determine the correct price of ANZA Corporation Stock.
   (b) Suppose in the near future (a month from now), conditions change to cause ANZA's business to become riskier, what will happen to the stock's price? Using the variables of the pricing model, explain what variables would change and how these changes would lead to stock price changes.
   (c) How relevant is the Dividend Discount Model (DDM) to valuation of a *Shari'ah*-compliant stock? Discuss.

12. Assume that the required return for computer chip manufacturers is 15%. MPI, a large Malaysian chip manufacturer, will pay a year-end dividend of RM0.40 per share.
    (a) If MPI's current stock price is RM5.00, what is the market's expectation of its dividend growth rate?
    (b) If as a result of technological change, MPI's ROI increases to 16%, its EPS is RM1.00 and dividends remain at RM 0.40 sen per share, what would the expected growth rate be?
    (c) Briefly describe how an increase in riskiness of the firm's business will alter the stock's price.
13. Can two stocks of companies in the same industry have different betas? Explain.
14. Safire Inc. has 180 million shares outstanding. Its last dividend was RM2.00 per share. The industry it is in has a return on investment (ROI) of 12%. Assuming a dividend payout ratio of 65%, a risk-free return of 3% and return on the market portfolio of 8%, determine the following if the stock's beta is 2.0:
    (a) The expected dividend growth rate
    (b) The company's cost of equity
    (c) The correct stock price and market capitalization

Bibliography

Ariff, M., S. Mohamad and A.M. Nassir (1998). *Stock Pricing in Malaysia* (UPM Press).

Bodie, Z., A. Kane, and J. Marcus (2009). *Investments*, 8th Edition (McGraw Hill, NY, US).

Brealey, R.A., S.C. Myers, and F. Allen (2011). *Principles of Corporate Finance*, 10th Edition (McGraw Hill, NY, USA).

Capital Market Issues According to Islamic Jurisprudence.

https://ribh.files.wordpress.com/2007/08/capital-markets-products-according-to-islamic-jurisprudence.pdf

Iqbal, Z. and A. Mirakhor (2006). *An Introduction to Islamic Finance: Theory and Practice* (John Wiley & Sons, Singapore).

Malaysian Islamic Capital Market, *Quarterly Bulletin* – several issues.

New Straits Times (2012). August 5.

Resolutions of the Securities Commission Shariah Advisory Council. – Securities Commission, Kuala Lumpur.

Chapter 10

THE ISLAMIC EQUITIES MARKET

Topics in this Chapter

10.1. Introduction
10.2. Components of an Islamic Equities Market
10.3. The Screening of Stocks for *Shari'ah* Compliance
10.4. Components/Products of an Islamic Equities Market
10.5. Islamic Equity Indices
10.6. The Stock Exchanges of the Islamic World

Chapter Objective

This chapter is designed to provide an in-depth understanding of *Shari'ah*-compliant equities and Islamic equities markets. Beginning with an explanation of alternative *Shari'ah* screening techniques, the components of an Islamic equities market are analyzed. The differences between these components and their conventional counterparts are pointed out. On completing this chapter, you should have a good understanding of the philosophy underlying *Shari'ah* screening techniques for stocks, the different components of the Islamic equities market, and how they differ from conventional ones.

Key Terms		
equity financing	islamic unit trust	Shari'ah advisory council (SAC)
equity REIT	liquidity risk	*Shari'ah* audit
hybrid REIT	market capitalization	*Shari'ah* screening
Islamic equities market	*maslahah*	*takaful*
Islamic equity index	net asset value (NAV)	transparency
Islamic ETFs	private equity fund (PEF)	*'umum balwa* (common plight)
Islamic mutual fund	qualitative method	*'urf* (custom)
Islamic REITs	*Shari'ah* advisors	

10.1 Introduction

Going by the *Shari'ah*, equity financing would be the preferred financing or investing technique. Equity financing has no fixity of return but has returns that are tied to the earnings of the underlying business and a risk profile not detached from that of the business. Thus, equity financing is very much profit and loss sharing, with all the business risks thrown in. As we saw in Chapter 9, the most common means by which a company raises equity financing is through the issuance of common stocks or shares. In many ways, investment in a stock resembles the provision of *mudarabah* financing. Given this congruence, *fuqaha* have little objection with the underlying philosophy of stock market investment. However, since some companies may be involved in businesses that are *haram* or involved in activities that may be prohibited, not all stocks listed in an exchange may be acceptable from a *Shari'ah* viewpoint. The need for a *Shari'ah* evaluation of stocks and the identification of *Shari'ah*-compliant stock has led to the development of *Shari'ah* filters, *Shari'ah* indices, *Shari'ah-compliant* Exchange Traded Funds (ETFs), and an entire industry of Islamic mutual funds. These mean that there is an Islamic Equities Market operating in parallel with the conventional equity market. Many of the products, services, and institutions that make up the broad conventional equity market have been replicated in *Shari'ah*-compliant ways to be part of the Islamic Equities Market.

10.2 Components of an Islamic Equities Market

What would constitute an Islamic Equities Market? Since stocks are the basic equity instruments, *Shari'ah*-compliant stocks would be the basic component. Based on these *Shari'ah*-compliant stocks, there would be other instruments or investment vehicles like Islamic ETFs, Islamic Real Estate Investment Trusts (REITs), Islamic Mutual Funds, and others like Islamic Private Equity Funds, Islamic Structured Products, etc. Figure 10.1 shows the typical structure of an Islamic Equity Market. An investor can participate in the Islamic Equities Market, either through the direct purchase of individual *Shari'ah*-compliant stocks that are listed and traded like any other stock or through investment vehicles like Islamic Mutual Funds, ETFs, and so on. As to which alternative would be most appropriate, it would obviously depend on the investor's risk profile, investment objective, investment horizon, and so on. We now turn to a discussion of each of the key components in detail. Since *Shari'ah*-compliant stocks form the basis, we begin with a discussion of the filtering techniques used in determining the *Shari'ah* compliance of a stock.

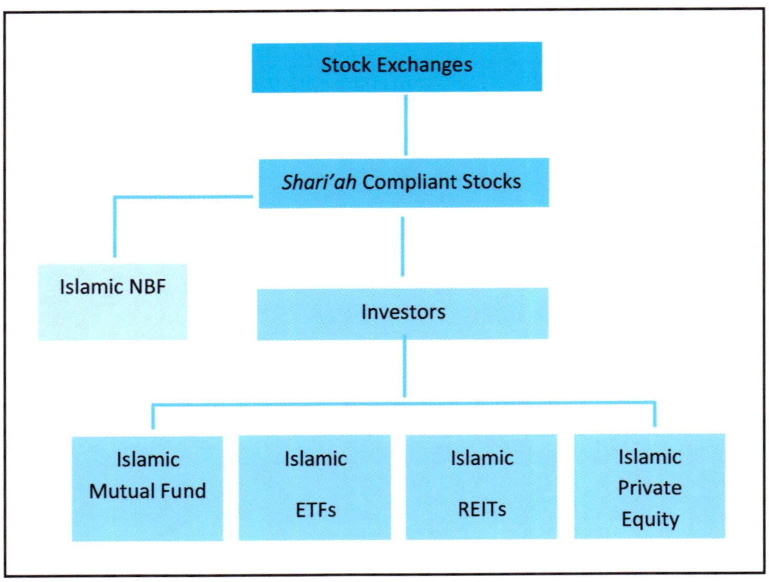

Figure 10.1. An Islamic Equities Market.

10.3 Screening of Stocks for *Shari'ah* Compliance

Malaysia was the first Muslim country with a conventional stock market to have come up with a formal evaluation for *Shari'ah*-compliant stocks and a *Shari'ah* stock index. Following this, in 1999, Dow Jones, the US-based publisher of *The Wall Street Journal* and financial information provider, designed the Dow Jones Islamic World Market Index (DJIWM). The DJIWM is a global index of *Shari'ah*-compliant stocks. In determining whether a stock is a *Shari'ah* compliant, a screening procedure is used. As we will see below, there is some variance in the filters used to determine *Shari'ah* compliance. We now discuss the screening procedure used in Malaysia as opposed to that used by Dow Jones.

10.3.1 *Shari'ah Screening of Stocks in Malaysia*

Shari'ah screening of listed stocks in Malaysia are based on parameters established by the Securities Commissions' Shari'ah Advisory Council (SAC). The SAC was established by the Securities Commission (SC) in 1996. The SAC's screening process, as with the DJIWM, begins with an examination of two broad criteria: (i) the line of business or core business of the underlying company and (ii) the company's finances. Essentially, the scrutiny is on how much interest-based borrowing there is in the capital structure and/or how much interest-based earnings the company makes.

In examining the line of business, a stock will be deemed ineligible for further filtering if the company's main line of business is a prohibited activity (see Figure 10.2). For example:

- If its operations are based on *riba* (interest), such as activities of conventional finance institutions like commercial banks, merchant banks, etc.
- Operations involving gambling.
- Activities involving the manufacture and/or sale of *haram* (forbidden) products such as liquor, pork, or meat not slaughtered according to Islam.
- Activities containing an element of *gharar* (uncertainty), such as conventional insurance.

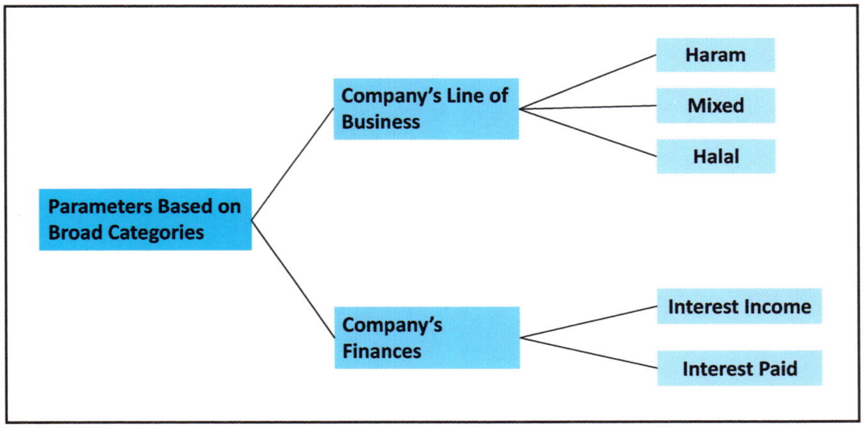

Figure 10.2. The *Shari'ah* Stock Screening Template.

Source: Author.

While it is easy to identify and eliminate companies involved in obviously *haram* activities, the challenge lies in evaluating companies that have "mixed" activities. These are companies that have some portion of their business in forbidden activities. It used to be that *fuqaha* would automatically disallow investment in such stock. However, given contemporary realities, *Shari'ah* scholars agree that such companies should be considered. As such, the SAC applies several additional criteria for such companies, these being:

- The core activity must not be one that is forbidden (i.e., the four criteria mentioned above). In addition, the *haram* element must be very small relative to the main line of business.
- The core activities of the company have importance and *maslahah* (benefit in general); the *haram* element, besides being small, involves matters such as '*umum balwa* (common plight) or '*urf* (custom) and involves the rights of the non-Muslim community which is accepted in Islam.

While the above criteria are all subjective, in order to translate these subjective criteria into actionable filters, the SAC uses two business activity benchmarks. These are a 5% benchmark and a 20% benchmark.

For businesses that are mainly in a *Shari'ah*-compliant business but include a minor portion in a non-compliant activity, the 5% benchmark applies. This is clearly a "mixed" category as defined above. For such a business, in order for its stock to be considered *Shari'ah* compliant, the non-compliant portion should not be greater than 5% based on the measures described below. The SAC lists the following activities as non-compliant and therefore subject to the 5% benchmark:

- Conventional banking/insurance
- Gambling
- Liquor and pork-related activities
- Non-*halal* food and beverages
- Tobacco and tobacco-related activities
- Entertainment that is non-*Shari'ah*-compliant in nature
- Interest income earned/received
- Dividends received from non-*Shari'ah*-compliant stocks
- Other activities deemed non-*Shari'ah*-compliant

10.3.1.1 *Screening process — Phase 1: Business activity*

The objective here is to compute the percentage contribution of the identified non-permissible activity to the company's overall income and profit before tax. The income and profit before tax would be that of the latest fiscal year, as shown in the company's Profit and Loss or Income Statement. The computation of percentage is carried out as follows:

Step 1: Determine the earnings (Total Income/Revenue) and profit before tax of the company.
Step 2: Identify and measure the income or earnings and profit before tax from the non-permissible activities.
Step 3: Determine the percentages as follows:

(i) $$\left[\frac{\text{Earnings from nor-}\textit{halal}\text{ activities}}{\text{Total Earnings of Firm}}\right]\times 100$$

(ii) $$\left[\frac{\text{Profit Before Tax (PBT) from nor-}\textit{halal}\text{ activities}}{\text{PBT all activities of firm}}\right]\times 100$$

Step 4: Decision rule: If both the above ratios are below 5%, accept stock as *Shari'ah* compliant. If the 5% benchmark is exceeded in either ratio, the stock is designated non-*Shari'ah*-compliant.

Companies whose earnings and/or profit before tax from non-permissible activities is more than 5% will have their stocks *excluded* from the list of *Shari'ah*-compliant stocks.

One should take note that this 5% threshold is only valid where non-*halal* earnings are clearly identifiable and measurable. For example, if a manufacturer of jewellery has more than 5% interest earnings from its conventional bank deposits, it will be excluded. Similarly, if an airline has more than 5% of its earnings from duty-free sale of liquor, its stocks will also be excluded. In both these cases, the non-*halal* activities are easily identifiable and measurable. But what do we do in cases where the non-compliance may be indirect? For example, a stock broker with both Muslim and non-Muslim clients would have to transact in both *Shari'ah*-compliant and non-compliant stocks on behalf of his clients. Similarly, a property firm may have, within its portfolio, properties rented out to restaurants that may also have non-*halal* offerings. In such cases, the SAC uses a 20% benchmark. The two ratios earlier are computed, and in each case, they have to be below 20% in order for the stock to be deemed *Shari'ah*-compliant.

10.3.1.2 *Screening Phase 2: How is the firm financed?*

Having determined the extent of non-compliant activity within a business, the second phase of the screening examines how the firm is financed and the profile of its assets. In evaluating how a firm has financed itself, the extent of conventional interest-bearing debt is examined. Next, in evaluating the profile of assets, the portion of interest-bearing cash deposits to total assets is examined. Accordingly, two ratios are computed. These are: (i) *Debt to Total Assets* and (ii) *Cash to Total assets.*

Debt to Total Assets

$$\text{Computed as:} = \left[\frac{\text{Interest Bearing Debt}}{\text{Total Assets}}\right] \times 100$$

Cash to Total Assets

$$\text{Computed as:} = \left[\frac{\text{Cash in interest earning instruments}}{\text{Total Assets}}\right] \times 100$$

Both the ratios must be below 33% in order for the stock to be accepted as *Shari'ah*-compliant. The underlying logic is that a firm with debt to total assets exceeding 33% is too reliant on interest-based debt financing. Similarly, a firm with cash to total assets in excess of 33% has too much assets invested in interest-earning assets. If the earlier ratio is an indication of excessive reliance of debt within the capital structure, the latter indicates too much assets invested in interest-earning activities.

Since businesses are dynamic and conditions change rapidly, a company that passes the threshold at a point in time may exceed it at a future date. For example, a manufacturer of home appliances may have interest earnings below 5% currently but could exceed it at a later point. The opposite situation may also be possible. Thus, the SAC reviews the list periodically. An updated list is issued every six months. Currently, about 70% of the listed stocks in Malaysia are deemed *Shari'ah* compliant, based on the SAC criteria. The percentage of *Shari'ah*-compliant listed stocks used to be higher at around 85% but had fallen following the SAC's inclusion of the two-phase two ratios.

10.3.2 *Stock Screening for the Dow Jones Islamic Index*

In some ways, the stock-screening procedures used by Dow Jones for its Islamic stocks index is tighter than that of Malaysia's SAC. As is the case with the Malaysian criteria, the Dow Jones screening procedure evaluates the nature of the business and the firm's financial aspects.

Dow Jones begins with an initial step that involves eliminating stocks of all companies involved in an exhaustive list of activities. These are industries related to alcohol, liquor, pork, conventional financial services (banking, insurance, merchant banking, etc.), hotels, entertainment (including cinema, music, etc.), tobacco, defence, weapons manufacturing, etc. Note that unlike the Malaysian screening procedure which takes into consideration firms with a minor portion of activities in non-compliant activities, the Dow Jones criteria do not.

Following the first step of determining the nature of a firm's business which is *qualitative*, the second step involves the *quantitative* analysis of the firm's financial statements. This numerical analysis has two aims: (i) identifying firms with "excessive" leverage in the capital structure and (ii) identifying firms with unacceptable levels of interest income. This is generally done by applying the following three key ratios:

(i) Debt to Trailing 12-Month Average Market Capitalization (TTMAMC)

Debt to TTMAMC

$$\text{Computed as:} = \left[\frac{\text{Total Interest Bearing Debt}}{\text{12 months Average Market Cap}}\right] \times 100$$

Threshold: 33%

Thus, any firm with a debt to TTMAMC exceeding 33% will be excluded. The rationale being that such a firm is paying a substantial portion of its earnings as interest on its debts.

(ii) Liquid Assets to TTMAMC

$$\text{Computed as:} = \left[\frac{\text{Cash deposits} + \text{Marketable Securities} + \text{Interest Bearing Instruments}}{\text{TTMAMC}}\right] \times 100$$

Threshold: 33%

(iii) Receivables to TTMAMC

$$\text{Computed as:} = \left[\frac{\text{Accounts Receivable} + \text{Trade Notes and Other Receivables}}{\text{TTMAMC}}\right] \times 100$$

Threshold: 33%

10.3.3 *Comparison of Stock-screening Techniques*

Though the philosophy and intended objective is the same, a comparison of the stock-screening techniques of the Dow Jones Islamic Index (DJII) with that of the Malaysian SAC points to an obvious difference, i.e., the tolerance for mixed businesses by the SAC. Recall that Malaysia's SAC allows for the inclusion of non-*halal* business as long as the contribution to earnings and profit before tax is no larger than 5%. In the case of DJII, there is no such allowance. If any part of a firm's business is in a prohibited industry, the firm is automatically dropped.

It is obvious that relative to Dow Jones, the Malaysian criteria are a little more liberal. This difference has more to do with economic realities than anything else. While the Malaysian criteria are intended to be country-specific, with Malaysian-listed stocks as the main target, there is no such restriction where the DJII is concerned. Any listed stock in a tradeable market anywhere is a potential stock where Dow Jones is concerned. Thus, for Dow Jones, it is a global universe of potential stocks. Given a much larger investible set of stocks, one can be stringent and still be able to identify a sufficiently large number of *Shari'ah*-compliant stocks. Since the SAC's criteria are

Malaysia-specific, using a stringent filter will undoubtedly result in a smaller group of eligible stocks and therefore a much narrower investible spectrum for Muslim investors in Malaysia. One might ask, what is wrong with having a smaller but "purer" group of investible stocks?

There are several problems with this. First, from a portfolio theory viewpoint, a smaller investible group of stocks restricts diversification and limits the benefits of diversification. Second, one cannot form efficient portfolios or superior risk-return portfolios if the group of investible stocks is restricted. Finally, by implication, one cannot be on the 'optimal' efficient frontier or get close to such a frontier. The net result would be portfolios that may be 'purer' but not necessarily efficient from a risk-return viewpoint. Thus, stringency in stock screening is not "costless". As with everything else in economics, there is a trade-off. The cost may be less efficient portfolios.

10.4 Components/Products of an Islamic Equities Market

Having discussed *Shari'ah*-compliant equities and their filtering criteria, we now discuss the key components of an Islamic Equities Market. As shown in Figure 10.1, among the key components are Islamic Mutual Funds, Islamic ETFs, Islamic REITs, and other *Shari'ah*-compliant structured products. We begin with the typically largest component, the Islamic Mutual Fund.

10.4.1 *Islamic Mutual Funds*

A mutual fund or unit trust is simply an investment scheme that pools funds from numerous individual or institutional investors. The pooled funds are managed by professional fund managers. The fund managers manage the pool of funds by investing it typically in stocks, bonds, and cash/money market instruments. An investor wishing to participate with a mutual fund would do so by purchasing units offered by the mutual fund. The price or value of these units varies daily according to the value of the assets held by the fund. Thus, a unit's price will depend on the fund's Net Asset Value (NAV). The NAV is the current market value of the fund's assets less its liabilities divided by the number of shares outstanding. In many countries, a fund's NAV would be quoted as a pair of bid-and-ask quotes, the ask quote being the price at which an investor *buys* into the fund, and the bid quote being the price at which he *redeems* his investments. In Malaysia, as with most developed markets, a single pricing mechanism is used. The quoted NAV therefore reflects both the fund's net assets and other built-in charges. There are many reasons why investing in a mutual fund is more advantageous than a direct investment by investors. Among these advantages are:

- Instant diversification;
- Professional management of funds;
- Low liquidity risk;
- Transparency in pricing; and
- Range of products to match needed risk profile.

There are different types of mutual funds based on the investment objective and risk profile of the fund. The generic types are:

- Growth fund;
- Value fund;
- Balanced fund; and
- Income/yield fund.

Yield/income and balanced funds have lower risks than growth funds, but they also have lower expected returns.

10.4.2 *Types of Funds*

A *growth fund* tries to invest in stocks that have high potential growth; these are typically high beta stocks, thus, having higher risks. A *value fund* seeks to identify and invest in "undervalued stocks"; again, making the risk and returns high. A *balanced fund* tries to allocate its available funds in a balanced way among stocks, bonds, and marketable securities. Since risk is relatively lower, returns too are lower relative to growth funds. An income or yield fund invests in low-risk bonds, high-dividend-yielding stocks, and/or money market instruments. An income fund would therefore have the lowest risk.

In addition to categorizing mutual funds by mandate of investment philosophy, value, growth, etc., mutual funds may also be categorized by subscription format. They are of two kinds: a *Close End Fund* and *Open End Fund*. An Open End Fund is one where the size of the fund can vary according to subscriber (investor) activity. For example, if for some reason, many investors buy into an Open End Fund, the inflow of money would be used by the fund manager to invest in more stocks. The NAV increases as the portfolio value increases. Alternatively, if investors withdraw from the Open End fund, the fund manager simply sells some of the stocks held in the fund's portfolio and uses the sale proceeds to meet the investor redemption. Thus, the NAV of the Open End Fund and the quoted/traded price should not differ. The NAV is simply the total value of stocks in portfolio divided by number of the funds units in circulation. Changes in investor demand for units of the funds simply changes the total portfolio of stocks held by the fund.

A Close End Fund, on the other hand, is very different. It has a fixed predetermined size of investments and units, and therefore, changes in investor demand changes the listed price of the fund not the NAV. For example, if there is increased investor demand, the Close End Funds asset portfolio is unchanged but the traded price increases, reflecting the increased demand. Thus, the funds' exchange traded price will be at a premium to its NAV. The opposite would be the case if demand for the fund falls. The traded price can be higher (premium) or lower (discount) than the NAV. This is very much like the value of a listed company's stock. At any one time, a company would have a fixed number of outstanding stocks. If more investors want the company's stocks, the market value or price of the stock goes up since the number of stocks available for trading is fixed. For example, most country funds listed on the New York Stock Exchange are Close End Funds. Similarly, ETFs, which are discussed below, are in some ways a Close End Fund.

A final category of mutual funds is the *Fund of Funds* (FOF). An FOF is simply a mutual fund that invests in other mutual funds, the benefit being mainly diversification. Investing in an FOF enables one to gain exposure to all the funds (and fund management styles) held by the FOF. An Islamic FOF would, by definition, invest only in *Shari'ah*-compliant mutual funds. While FOFs provide the additional benefit of wider diversification compared to a typical mutual fund, the management fees that the investor has to pay would also be higher. The higher fee reflects the fees due to managers of the underlying mutual funds.

An Islamic Mutual Fund or Islamic Unit Trust is built on the same template as a conventional mutual fund. The operational mechanisms are the same, but the investment philosophy differs. Whereas a conventional mutual fund would allocate its funds among stocks, bonds, and money market instruments, the latter two being interest-accreting instruments, an Islamic mutual fund would invest only in non-*riba* and *Shari'ah*-compliant investments. These investments are:

- *Shari'ah*-compliant stocks;
- *Sukuk; and*
- Islamic money market instruments.

Operationally, while a conventional mutual fund would allocate its funds between stocks, bonds, and money market instruments according to market outlook, an Islamic fund manager would do the same but across the *halal* asset components above. To ensure that only *Shari'ah*-compliant assets are being invested in, each fund management company would have a *Shari'ah* committee that provides oversight and conducts periodic *Shari'ah* audits.

10.4.2.1 *Contracts underlying Islamic Mutual Funds/Unit Trusts*

Every Islamic financial transaction or instrument must be guided by an underlying *Shari'ah*-based contract. Thus, Islamic Mutual Funds use one of the following three contractual arrangements:

(i) ***Mudarabah***
The investor is the *rab al-mal* while the mutual fund manager is the *mudarib*. The *mudarib* uses the invested funds to invest according to the agreed mandate and to the best of his efforts. He is entitled to a share of the profits but the *rab al-mal* bears the losses if any.

(ii) ***Musharakah***
All investors are participants or partners. However, only some partners (the fund management company) will be entitled to manage the investment. The managers, in addition to a predetermined share of profits earned, are also eligible to a portion of the revenue as compensation for their efforts.

(iii) ***Wakalah***
In this contract, the fund manager is the "agent" of the investor, who is the principal. The agent acts on behalf of the principal to invest the funds to the best of his efforts. In exchange for his efforts and expertise, the fund manager receives a fixed fee. To minimize the agency problems that could arise in this principal–agent relationship, an additional performance-based fee for the agent is a common feature.

10.4.2.2 *Typical structure of an Islamic Mutual Fund*

As the operational aspects of the Islamic Mutual Fund are similar to that of the conventional, much of the administrative and organizational frameworks are the same. The key difference from a structural viewpoint is the presence of *Shari'ah* advisors. These *Shari'ah* advisors may be internal, part of the Governing Board or Investment Committee, or external. External *Shari'ah* advisors, for example, could come from a firm specializing in *Shari'ah* advisory for Islamic funds. Some Islamic Mutual Funds may have a combination of internal advisors and an external *Shari'ah* advisor. In such a case the external *Shari'ah* advisors provide oversight and *Shari'ah* audit services (see Figure 10.3).

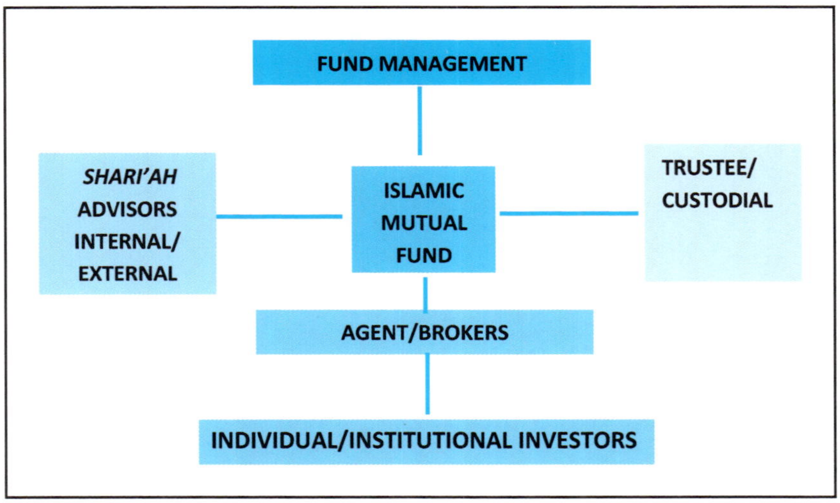

Figure 10.3. Typical Structure of an Islamic Mutual Fund.

Box 10.1 shows the potential volatility in returns associated with mutual fund investments. Keep in mind that equity mutual funds are essentially indirect means to invest in equity markets. Thus, the underlying stock market performance dictates mutual fund performance. Despite the best abilities of a fund manager, it is the underlying stock market's performance that would be the key determinant of an investor's return from investing in a mutual fund.

Box 10.1. Illustration: Investing in an Islamic Mutual Fund

Suppose you have RM10,000 which you wish to invest in an Islamic Mutual Fund. Your investment horizon is one year. Your bank, which is an Islamic bank, has its own mutual fund in addition to others which it also markets. After doing some research on past performances and fund rankings by Lipper and Morningstar (two international fund rating institution), you decide that Dana Al-Mu'min, an Islamic Mutual Fund offered by your bank, is best suited for you. You have the following information:

Fund name: Dana Al-Mu'min
Type: Growth
NAV: RM0.53 per unit

Given the fund's current NAV of RM0.53 per unit, your RM10,000 will enable you to purchase 18,867 units.

RM10,000/RM0.53 = 18,867.92
Purchasing 18,867 units means, your initial investment would be 18,867 × RM0.53 = RM9,999.51

In a year's time when you redeem your investment, the profit or loss you make will depend on the fund's performance over the year. We look at two scenarios, one where the fund performs well over the year resulting in a substantial increase in NAV, and a second scenario where the fund performs poorly.

Scenario 1: Fund performs well

NAV:	= RM0.67 per unit
Redemption Value:	= RM0.67 × 18,867 units
	= RM12,640.89
Profit in RM:	= RM12,640.89 – RM9,999.51
	= RM2,641.38
Holding Period Return:	= [RM2,641.38/RM9,999.51] × 100
	= 26.42%

Scenario 2: Fund performs poorly

NAV:	= RM0.44 per unit
Redemption Value:	= RM0.44 × 18,867 units
	= RM8,301.48
Loss in RM:	= RM8,301.48 – RM9,999.51
	= (RM1,698.03)
Holding Period Return:	= [(RM1,698.03) / RM9,999.51] × 100
	= –16.98%

10.4.2.3 *Growth of the Islamic Mutual Fund industry*

Figure 10.4 shows the growth and evolution of the global Islamic Mutual Fund industry. The graph plots the total asset value within the industry over the period 2005 to 2016. Growth appears to have been impressive from 2005 until 2008, when asset under management (AUM) had more than doubled, after which there was a fall, together with the stock markets, following the global financial crisis of 2007/2008. Post crisis, AUM appears to be cyclical. Ironically, total AUM at end 2016 appears to be lower than it was in 2005. This, as pointed out in Box 10.2, may have to do with several factors, including the inherent characteristics of *Shari'ah*-compliant portfolios and their performance in bull/bear markets.

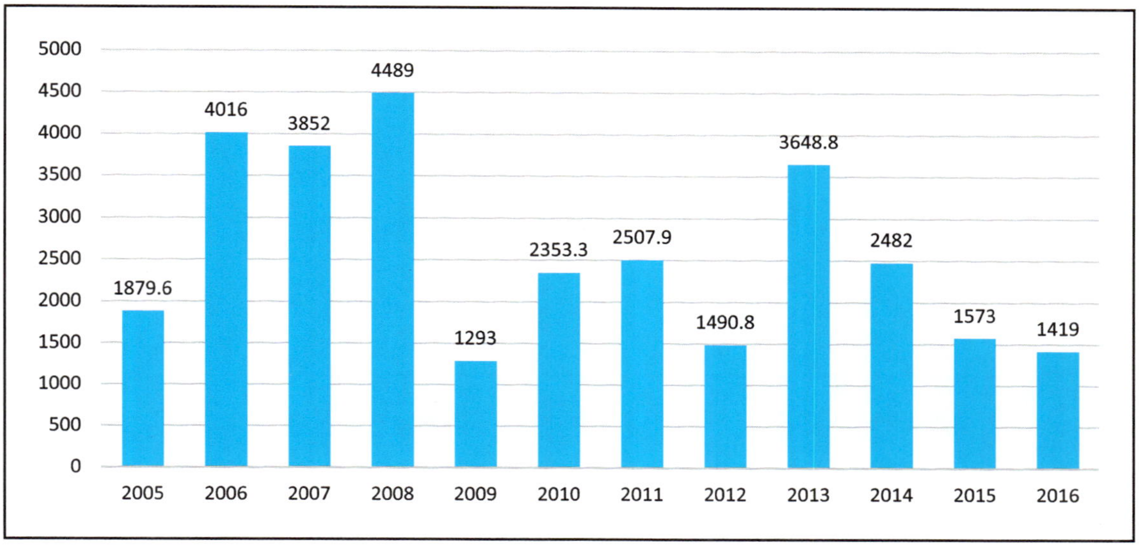

Figure. 10.4. Total Asset Value of Islamic Mutual Funds in US$ (Mils) (2005–2016).

Source: Bloomberg.

Globally, as of end 2016, there were approximately 1,345 funds; this was double the 650 funds that were available at end 2010. Thus, even though total AUM had fallen at end 2016, the number of Islamic Mutual Funds has grown. Figure 10.5 shows the geographical distribution of these funds.

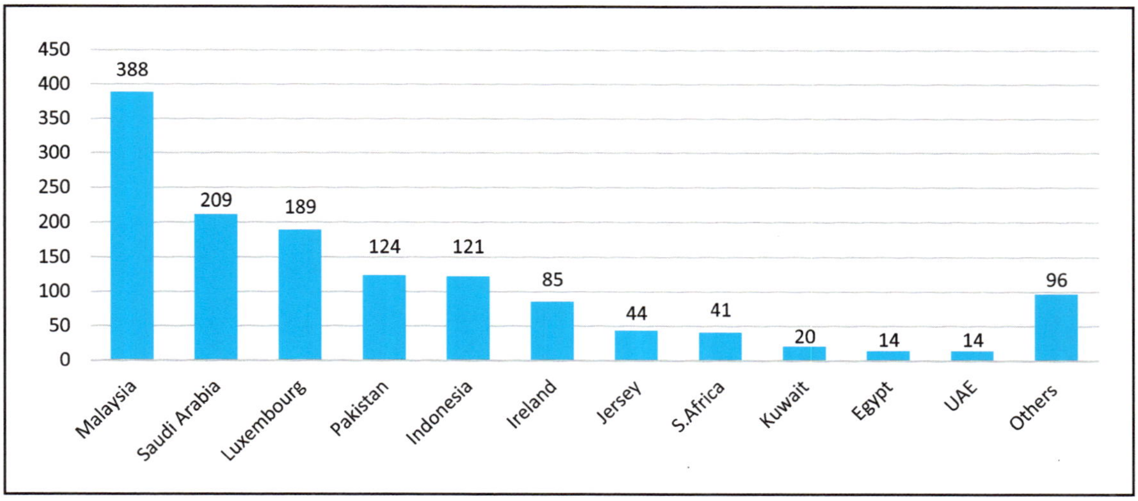

Figure 10.5. Number of Islamic Mutual Funds by Country — Q1, 2017.

Source: ISRA Islamic Finance SPACE — August 2017.

As is to be expected, Malaysia and Saudi Arabia lead with most number of funds. Interestingly, it is Luxembourg that is in third place, with 189 Islamic Mutual Funds domiciled. When we examine the relative size of AUM by country (see Figure 10.6), there are some changes. Saudi Arabia accounts for 35.6%, the largest percentage of AUM by country. Jersey, which is another international financial center like Luxembourg, comes in third place with about 12% of total Islamic AUMs.

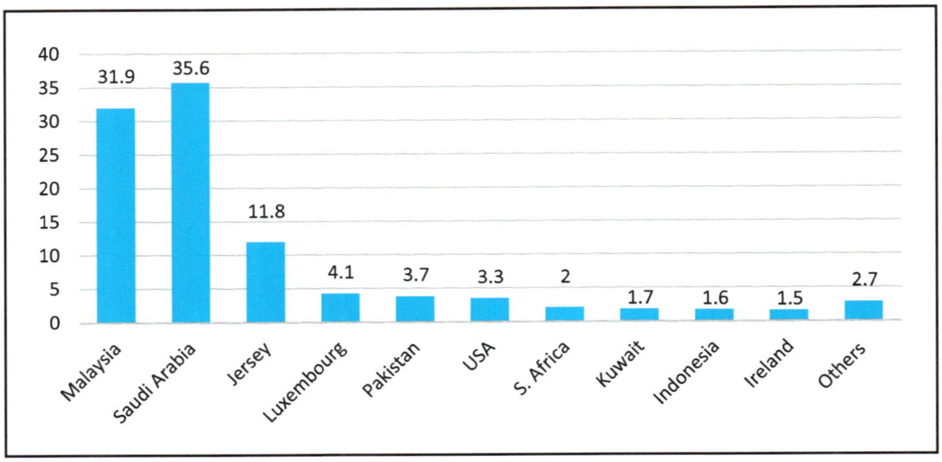

Figure 10.6. Islamic AUM, Percentage by Country — Q1, 2017.

Source: ISRA Islamic Finance SPACE — August 2017.

Figure 10.7 shows the category of assets that Islamic Mutual Funds invest in. Some 33% of funds are invested in equities, about 39% in short-term money market instruments, and about 12% in commodities. About 6% is invested in *sukuk* while a similar percentage is invested in real estate. Overall, the breakdown of assets appears to be fairly well distributed across several categories of assets. That the largest proportion was in money market assets is quite a surprise, but it probably also includes *sukuk* of short-term maturity, or long-dated ones nearing maturity.

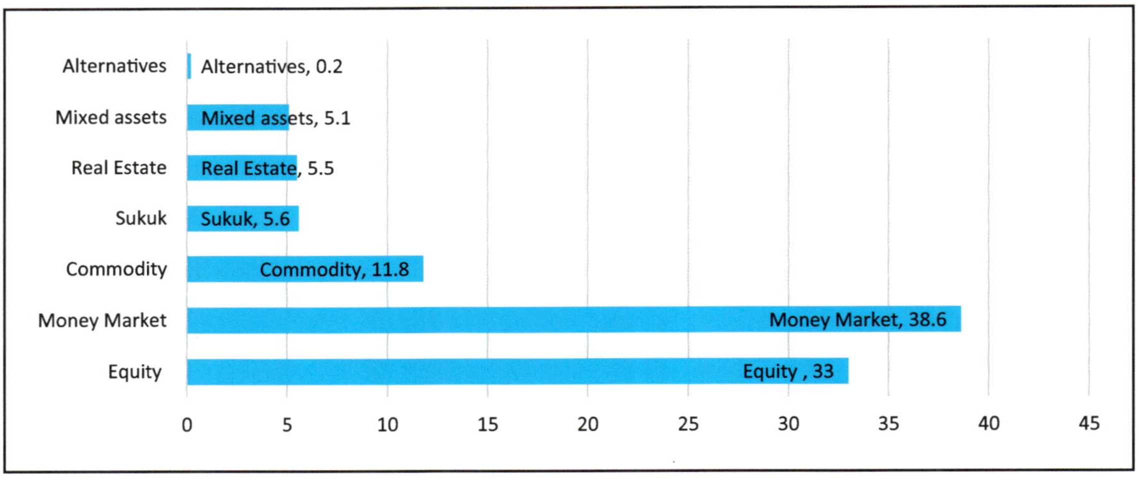

Figure 10.7. Type of Islamic Funds by Asset Category (%) — Q1, 2017.

Source: ISRA Islamic Finance SPACE — August 2017.

In Malaysia, the first Islamic unit trust was established in 1993. As of end Q1/2017, there were a total of 388 Islamic funds with a total NAV of US$22.6 billion (or approximately RM95 billion). Malaysia accounts for about 32% of the global Islamic funds industry. Islamic Mutual Funds, despite their explosive growth, account for less than half the aggregate funds under management in Malaysia. This should not be a surprise, given the fact that there are a number of government-linked institutions that have been established to gather and manage the savings of the majority Malay-Muslim population, the key institution being Permodalan Nasional Berhad (PNB). Others such as Tabung Haji and Lembaga Tabungan Angkatan Tentera (LTAT) are also key institutions.

Box 10.2. Are *Shari'ah*-compliant Portfolios Superior?

Islamic mutual funds and other *Shari'ah*-compliant investors are restricted to investing only in *Shari'ah*-compliant instruments. Thus, while the conventional fund manager allocates between stocks, bonds, and cash or money market instruments, the Islamic mutual funds would be restricted to *Shari'ah*-compliant equities, *sukuk*, and Islamic interbank money market (IIMM) instruments. Where Islamic money market instruments are unavailable, Islamic bank deposits would hold the cash. Of interest to all investors and fund managers, in particular, is the question of the performance of *Shari'ah*-compliant or Islamic equity portfolios relative to conventional ones.

The emerging consensus from numerous academic studies appears to be that *Shari'ah*-compliant portfolios have lower risk relative to conventional equity portfolios. That is, Islamic portfolios tend to have lower portfolio betas. Beta, being the measure of systematic risk, is the relevant risk measure. This has several implications, the most obvious being that a lower risk portfolio must necessarily also give lower returns. However, when evaluating portfolios, one needs to think in terms of both risk and returns, not just returns. For example, if a portfolio has 30% lower risk than another but only 10% lower returns, then it is obviously the superior portfolio in risk-return terms. A second implication of lower betas is the inherent defensive nature of low-beta portfolios. Portfolios with low betas would underperform in relative terms during up cycles but would outperform during downturns. Beta being a measure of the correlation between a stock or portfolio's return and overall market returns means that a low beta portfolio will rise less than the market during a bull run but will also fall less than the market during a downturn. Thus, in comparing Islamic portfolios with conventional ones, timing or the period of comparison matters.

The question that arises here is: why do Islamic equity portfolios have lower betas? When two identical equity portfolios, e.g., of the same sector are compared, the Islamic equity portfolio has been shown to have lower beta. The reason for this well-documented evidence is really the result of the process by which stocks are screened for *Shari'ah* compliance. While Malaysia's Securities Commission was the first to come up with a methodology for screening stocks to evaluate for *Shari'ah* compliance, today, there are several alternative stock-screening methodologies available. Though they differ in the details, they are broadly similar. All *Shari'ah* screening methodologies share a two-phase process. In the first phase, the nature of the business is examined. Stocks of companies in non-compliant businesses, like conventional banking/finance which is interest-based, breweries, casinos, non-*halal* food processors, etc., are dropped. Stocks that have passed the first phase are then subjected to numerical analyses of their financials in the second phase. Among others, a key variable in this phase is the level of debt within the firm's capital structure. The Malaysian screening filter uses a 33% threshold of interest-bearing debt to total assets. The Dow Jones filter, which is more universal, uses the same 33% debt, but to average market capitalization. Debt or financial leverage within a firm's capital structure is therefore a key hurdle. Thus, even if a firm is in a *Shari'ah*-compliant business but has debt exceeding 33%, it will be deemed non-compliant and its stock ineligible. Such a stock-screening process avoids not only the highly sensitive (volatile) sectors like the financial sector but also firms with high gearing or leverage. It is this elimination of firms with high levels of debt that acts to minimize an Islamic portfolio's beta. A stock's beta is really an aggregate of both its underlying business risk and financial risk, the latter being determined purely by financial leverage. The 33% cutoff for debt automatically eliminates highly geared firms from being included into *Shari'ah*-complaint portfolios. The result is that when comparing the *Shari'ah*-compliant equity portfolio with conventional ones, they tend to have lower betas or risk. Since a lower beta stock and portfolio simply moves less than the overall market, they are deemed to be defensive.

While Islamic equity portfolios have been established to have lower risk than comparable conventional ones, whether they are indeed superior in risk-return terms is an empirical question. One study that examined a paired comparison of a series of Dow Jones Islamic equity indexes with their conventional counterpart found the Islamic indices to have lower risk but returns that were statistically the same. This would imply that Islamic portfolios that mimicked the index would indeed be superior. Yet, other studies have found otherwise. As with most rule-based investment criteria, there is no systematic outperformance. Performance, it appears, is really time-variant. The empirical evidence, therefore, is truly mixed. This is a logical outcome, for if any rule-based investment criteria can consistently outperform, it will give rise to arbitrage. And arbitrage, as we know it, is the great leveler.

Source: Author's op-ed piece in *The Malaysian Reserve*, September 25, 2017.

10.4.3 *Islamic ETFs*

Exchange Traded Funds (ETFs) are a recent innovation. Some would consider ETFs to be an outgrowth of the index fund, which is a mutual fund that passively manages a portfolio mimicking a stock index. Like an index fund, it is passively managed and invests in a portfolio that tracks closely an underlying stock index. Of late, there are ETFs that are based on narrow categories like gold, real estate, or particular sectors of the economy. Gold ETF is one that invests only in stocks of firms involved in the gold business. On the other hand, the DJ Wilshire International Real Estate ETF offers exposure to stocks of real estate firms across a spectrum of countries.

The world's best-known ETF is probably the SPDR (also known as spider), which tracks the S&P 500 Stock Index of the US. Similarly, the Tracker Fund of Hong Kong tracks the Hang Seng Index. In Malaysia, there are two ETFs currently available. These are the FBM 30 ETF, which is a conventional ETF that tracks the FBM 30 Index. The FBM 30 is an index of the 30 largest companies listed on Bursa Malaysia. The second available ETF is an Islamic ETF known as *MyETF-DJIM Titan 25* (or simply MyETF). This is an ETF whose underlying is an index of 25 *Shari'ah*-compliant Malaysian companies listed within the Dow Jones Islamic Markets Index (DJIM). Introduced in January 2008, it is not only Malaysia's but also Asia's first Islamic ETF.

What makes ETFs an interesting proposition to investors is the exposure they provide to an index or basket of stocks in the form of a single unit or share of the ETF. That is, buying a single share of an ETF is similar to taking a small position in each of the underlying index of stocks. This is made possible by the fact that an ETF is listed on an exchange and its shares traded like any other shares. Besides the trading flexibility that it allows, ETFs offer instant diversification, access to diverse market segments, transparent pricing, and above all, lower transaction costs. The lower transaction costs result from the fact that ETFs are passively managed. Like other listed shares, the value of an ETF share gets a price quote which is dependent on the ETF's NAV. Table 10.1a provides a list of Islamic ETFs covered by *Bloomberg*. Ireland appears to have the largest number of Islamic ETFs. With a total of 53 ETFs, Ireland has a disproportionate number of ETFs. Most of these are ETFs sold in Muslim countries but listed in Ireland. It is interesting to note that, with the exception of the Malaysia and Saudi Arabia, the majority Islamic ETFs shown in the table are listed in non-Muslim countries. Table 10.1b shows a sample of Islamic ETFs by country and provider.

Table 10.1(a). Islamic ETFs by Country.

Country	ETF
France	2
Ireland	53
Malaysia	4
Nigeria	1
Saudi Arabia	3
Singapore	1
South Africa	1
Total	65

Source: *Bloomberg*, and author's compilation.

Table 10.1(b). A Sample of Key Islamic ETFs.

Islamic ETFs	Underlying Index	Country Listed	Provider
Db X-Trackers DJ Islamic Market Titans	DJ Islamic Market Titans 100 Index	Germany	Db X-Trackers
Db X-Trackers S&P Europe 350 *Shari'ah*	S&P Europe 350 *Shari'ah* Index	Germany	Db X-Trackers
Db X-Trackers S&P Japan 500 *Shari'ah*	S&P Japan 500 *Shari'ah* Index.	Germany	Db X-Trackers
iShares MSCI World Islamic	MSCI World Islamic Index	UK	iShares
iShares MSCI EM Markets Islamic	MSCI EM Markets Islamic Index	UK	iShares
MYETF DJ Islamic Market Malaysia	DJ Market Malaysia Titans 25 Index	Malaysia	i-VCAP
Bizim Securities DJ Islamic Market Turkey	DJ Islamic Market Turkey Index	Turkey	BMD Securities

Source: Aftab Khan — unpublished PhD manuscript, INCEIF (2016).

10.4.4 *Islamic REITS*

A Real Estate Investment Trust (REIT) is a listed entity which invests mainly in real estate or property-related investments. Its shares are listed and traded like any other listed stock. The value of the share depends on the REIT's NAV. So, in some ways, it is like an ETF, the exception being that a REIT can only invest in properties and other real estate. Some REITs specialize in certain types of properties, e.g., shopping complexes, hotels, office towers, or even residential units like condominiums. From a corporate taxation viewpoint, a REIT is a very different entity from other businesses. For example, REITs receive preferential tax treatments in many countries, where they are taxed at just 10% rather than the corporate tax rate, which would be substantially higher. In Malaysia, investors receiving dividends from REITs have a withholding tax of only 15% as opposed to 28%, which is the corporate tax rate. Malaysian REITs get a tax waiver on retained earnings, provided they distribute at least 90% of their income as dividends. Such a tax regime for REITs is fairly common among many countries. As a result of the high dividend pay-out, investors who need to receive regular income would gravitate to REITs. The basic idea in REITs, as in the case of stocks, is to provide divisibility in ownership. Just as stocks enable a multitude of investors to jointly own a company, REITs enable such ownership of large properties or a collection of properties. For the original owners of such properties, undertaking and listing a REIT enables them to liquefy a significant portion of their investment. This in turn enables them to take on new investment.

Box 10.3. Exchange Traded Funds (ETFs): A Multi-country Study of Relative Performance

A study titled "Performance and Trading Characteristics of Exchange Traded Funds: Developed versus Emerging Markets" examined the risk-adjusted performance, tracking error, and trading characteristics of 43 passively managed equity ETFs traded in emerging (EM) and developed markets (DM) over the eight-year period from January 2007 to December 2014. In the case of risk and returns, the study found that the average return of the Emerging Market (EM) ETFs was higher than the Developed Markets (DMs) ETFs during all periods. In analyzing performance based on risk-adjusted Sharpe ratios, it is found that the average Sharpe ratios of EM ETFs are higher than DM ETFs. The EM ETFs were also found to track the underlying indices much more closely in relative to DM ETFs. In terms of returns, the finding was that ETF returns reflect their underlying benchmark index returns. In other words, there were no "alphas" or excess returns. These findings are to be expected, as ETFs adhere to a passive management investing strategy and do not seek to beat the benchmark indices. As described in the text, ETFs are essentially standardized and exchange-traded mutual funds. They do not offer the active management that mutual funds do. However, as stated earlier, empirical evidence of the value of active management over longer periods is questionable. Still, using a Markov Switching model, the study finds DM ETF managers to have a more active replication strategy than those of EM ETFs. Accordingly, the DM ETFs had lower tracking error. The tracking error examines how far the returns of an ETF deviates from that of its underlying index. The fact that EM ETFs deviate more is indicative of reduced efficiency from the viewpoint of replication. Not surprisingly, the average tracking error of all the ETFs is higher during crisis periods, which implies that ETF pricing is more volatile during market downturns.

When different ETF characteristics were examined, it was found that asset size positively impacts performance, whereas the expense ratio and tracking error negatively influence ETF performance. Risk was found to have a positive correlation with tracking error. So, ETFs that had larger tracking errors were also more volatile. Finally, the liquidity of ETFs is influenced positively by turnover and negatively by the bid-ask premium.

Source: Khan, Obiyathulla and Masih (2015), *Capital Markets Review*, Vol. 23, pp. 40–64.

10.4.4.1 *Types of REITs*

In developed countries, there are typically three types of REITs:

(i) **Equity REIT**: This is the standard type of REIT, as described above. It invests in properties and provides a return to its shareholders from the rental and lease payments it receives.

(ii) **Mortgage Finance REIT**: This type of REIT does not necessarily hold properties; rather, it invests in financial instruments such as Collateralized Mortgage Obligations (CMOs) or debt instruments, where the collateral is real estate.
(iii) **Hybrid REIT**: This REIT takes on the features of the above two, i.e., Equity REITs and Mortgage REITs. Hybrid REITs may invest in both properties and mortgage instruments.

In the case of Malaysia and most Muslim countries, the listed REITs are generally of the first type, i.e., equity REITs.

10.4.4.2 *Why invest in REITS?*

REITs have been popular in many countries, including Muslim countries. In Malaysia, as of September 2018, there are a total of 18 listed REITs on Bursa Malaysia. There are also several listed REITs in Saudi Arabia and the Gulf States. Their popularity stems from the many advantages of investing in REITs. Among the key advantages are:
(i) A relativity steady income stream from dividends.
(ii) Preferential tax treatment of dividends paid out by REITs (smaller withholding tax).
(iii) Ability to participate in real estate and property investment even with a small amount of funds.
(iv) Being tradeable like any listed share, investment in REITs have low liquidity risk.
(v) Capital gains in addition to dividend income is possible.

10.4.4.3 *Islamic REITS*

An Islamic REIT is simply a Real Estate Investment Trust that is governed by *Shari'ah* principles. Like an Islamic Mutual Fund, an Islamic REIT has to have its own *Shari'ah* Advisory Committee whose job will be to ensure that the REITs' activities are in line with *Shari'ah* requirements. There are three main areas within which REITs activities would fall: (a) investing and managing property, (b) ensuring the assets are appropriately insured, and (c) investing and managing the rental and other received income. It is easy to see how *Shari'ah* requirements will affect these activities.

When it comes to investment in new properties, the Islamic REIT must ensure that the activities of tenants currently renting the property are *Shari'ah* compliant. In Malaysia, if a proportion of the rental is from existing tenants involved in non-*Shari'ah*-compliant activities, the REIT must ensure that it does not exceed 20% of total rentals received from the property. In addition, the *Shari'ah* advisors of the fund must ensure that no new tenants, whose business activities may be non-*Shari'ah*-compliant, are allowed. This applies even if the inclusion of the new tenants' rentals results in a proportion below the 20% threshold.

In the case of appropriate insurance for the assets of the REIT, an Islamic REIT is only allowed to insure its properties using *takaful* and not conventional insurance. Only if *takaful* schemes are unable to provide coverage can the REIT use conventional insurance. A REIT receives rental income throughout the year, yet dividends are paid once or twice a year. Thus, at any point in time, a REIT would have surplus funds. Income from investing such funds is typically an important source of income for REITs. Where Islamic REITs are concerned, they can only invest surplus funds in *Shari'ah*-compliant investments.

From an operational viewpoint, an Islamic REIT is very similar to that of conventional ones. Malaysia's first Islamic REIT was the Al-Agar KPJ REIT, which was listed on Bursa Malaysia in August 2006. It was the result of KPJ, a healthcare provider, placing six of its hospitals into the REIT. Following this, a number of other Islamic REITs have also been listed, the most notable of which is the Al-Hadharah Boustead REIT. This is the world's first Islamic plantation REIT. A summary term sheet of the Al-Hadharah Boustead REIT is shown in the following table (see Table 10.X).

Table 10.2. Al-Hadharah Boustead REIT.

Instruments	Initial Public Offering exercise of the units of the *Shari'ah*-compliant real estate investment trust, known as the Al-Hadharah Boustead REIT, constituted by a trust deed between Boustead REIT Manager and CIMB Trustee acting as trustee of the fund formed to own and invest primarily in plantation assets and assets as permitted under the Guidelines on Real Estate Investment Trusts and the Guidelines on Islamic Real Estate Investment Trusts issued by the Malaysian Securities Commission to generate investment income based on the Islamic principles of *ijarah*.
Issuer	Al-Hadharah Boustead REIT acting through CIMB Trustee & Boustead REIT Manager
Principal Activities	The issuer, a *Shari'ah*-compliant REIT, was formed to own and invest primarily in plantation assets and assets as permitted under the REIT Guidelines to generate investment income based on Islamic principles. The issuer issued units through the manager. The principal activity of the manager is to manage and administer Al-Hadharah Boustead REIT.
Board of Directors	Lt. Gen. (R) Dato' Mohd Yusof Din Datuk Azzat Kamaludin Dato' (Dr) Megat Abdul Rahman Megat Ahmad Tuan Hj. Johari Muhammad Abbas Gen. (R) Tan Sri Dato' Mohd Ghazali Hj. Che Mat Tan Sri Dato' Lodin Wok Kamaruddin.
Date of listing	February 8, 2007
Issue Size	US$138 million
Date of issue	January 15, 2007
Lead Arrangers	Affin Bank Berhad, MIMB Investment Bank, Pacific Alliance Capital, Affin Securities
Legal Counsel	Albar & Partners
Financial Adviser	Affin Bank, Pacific Alliance Capital
Underwrites	Affin Bank, MIMB Investment Bank
Trustee	CIMB Trustee
Shari'ah Adviser	Islamic Banking and Finance Institute Malaysia
Methods of Issues	Public offerings and 220 million comprising: (i) Retail offering of 22 million (ii) Institutional offering of 198 million 252 million units of the Al-Hadharah Boustead REIT issued to the vendors as consideration for the purchase of the plantation assets by the fund from the vendors. 1,000 units issued to the promoters (i.e. managers) prior to the listing of the Al-Hadharah Boustead REIT.
Purpose of issue	The Al-Hadharah Boustead REIT was undertaken by Boustead Group to realize the fair value of the plantation assets while retaining their productive use. The REIT will also allow Boustead Group to participate in the local real estate investment market through its proposed holding in the units of the Al-Hadharah Boustead REIT as well as its involvement together with LTAT in the management of the AL-Hadharah Boustead REIT. Al-Hadharah Boustead will use the units to be issued, proceeds from the proposed public offering, and Islamic financing facility to finance the purchase of the plantation asset and the listing expenses and working capital of the fund. The purchase of the plantation assets is primarily to facilitate the REIT exercise involving the arrangement to lease the plantation assets back to the vendors pursuant to the *ijarah* arrangements. Under the *ijarah*, the plantation assets are leased back to the vendors as tenants for a cumulative tenure of up to 30 years.
Rating	N/A

Source: Islamic Finance News.

Currently, there are 18 REITs listed in Malaysia, four of which are Islamic REITs: (i) Al Aqar KPJ, (ii) Boustead, and (iii) KLCC Real Estate Investment Trust. Given the relative size of the three Islamic REITs, they accounted for approximately 42% of total REIT capitalization as at end 2015. Regionally, Singapore's only Islamic REIT, SABANA, may be the largest in terms of size. An industrial REIT, SABANA, which is listed on the Singapore Stock Exchange (SGX), owns several industrial properties (factories, warehouses, etc.) across the island nation. The typical structure of an Islamic REIT can be seen in Figure 10.8.

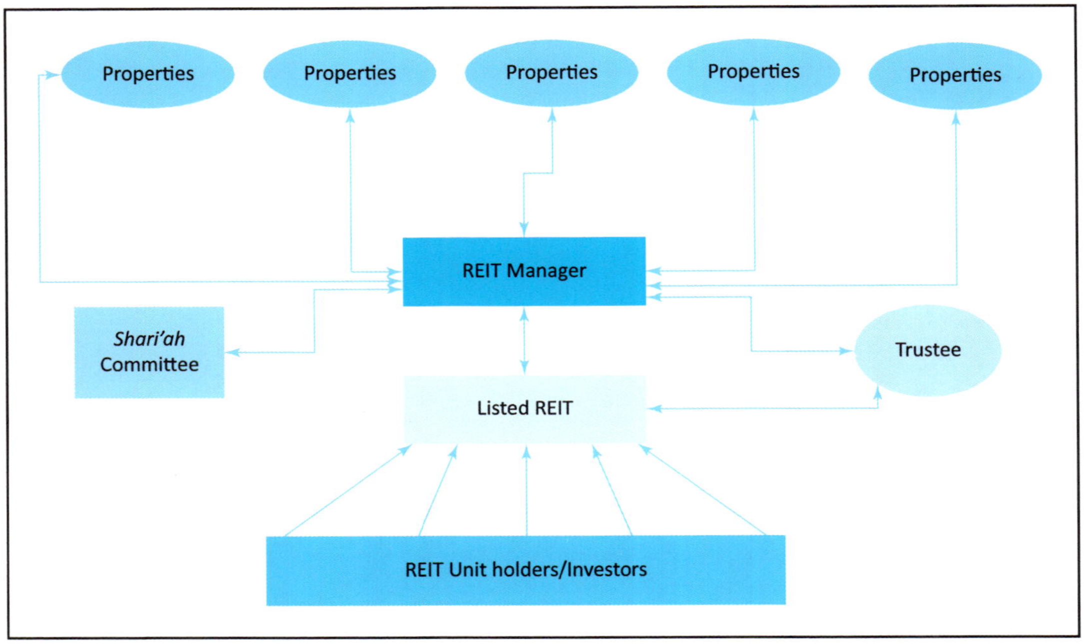

Figure 10.8. The Typical Structure of an Islamic REIT.

As Figure 10.8 shows, structurally, the Islamic REIT has one key difference with conventional REITS, that being the presence of the *Shari'ah* committee. The *Shari'ah* committee provides guidance, oversight, and has to approve acquisitions and other key decisions of the REIT manager. The committee also sets the parameters by which the REIT manager operates the REIT. The three key operational issues being: acquisitions, fund/cash management, and insurance.

10.4.5 *Islamic Private Equity Funds*

Private equity funds (PEFs) are private investment pools established to attract and manage funds from high net-worth individuals and institutions. One can think of them as private versions of a mutual fund. Being private, they have much flexibility that are not available to public mutual funds or listed ETFs. PEFs typically have a small pool of investors who make large investments. Though most PEFs have a mandate to invest in a broad category of investments, some specialize as Venture Capital funds, Leveraged Buy-out specialists, Vulture funds, etc. Unlike mutual funds, PEFs have the flexibility to take on leverage and to invest in exotic derivatives or structured products. Some PEFs also specialize in risky spread trading and arbitrage activities. As a result of the generally riskier profile of PEFs, some of them such as Long Term Capital Management (LTCM), Amaranth, etc., have been at the center of serious financial failures. However, other PEFs have had such stellar track records that even Sovereign Wealth Funds (SWFs) have been known to invest with them. Among these would be private equity firms such as The Carlyle Group, Kolberg Kravis Roberts, and The Blackstone Group.

Usually, a PEF would be established by a private equity firm which is the general partner. On establishing a new PEF, the firm or general partner will invite investors to participate in the new fund. Investors wishing to participate would come in as limited partners. The entire set-up is one of a terminal partnership. The limited partnership typically has a fixed term of say 10 years. At any given time, a private equity firm may have under its management several PEFs. A typical PEF structure would be as shown in the Figure 10.9.

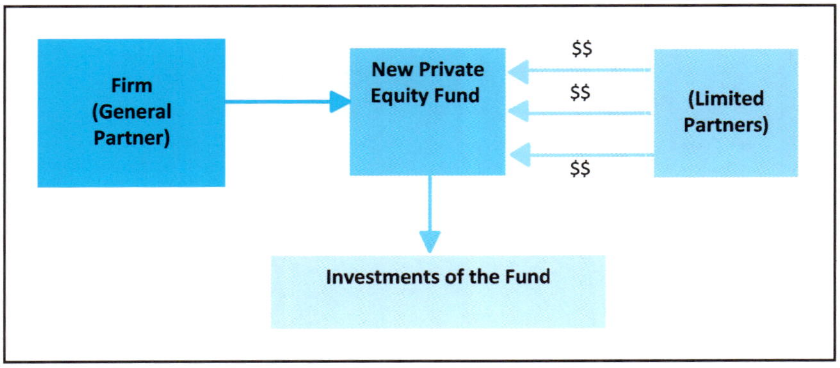

Figure 10.9. Structure of a PEF.

Like a mutual fund, investors in a PEF are passive investors who rely on the professional management of the general partner. However, there are a number of differences. First, unlike a mutual fund, a PEF would require a very significant amount of investment. For example, most would require investments in excess of a million ringgit. In addition, the investments usually have a lock-in feature of several years. For example, a five-year lock-in feature would mean that you cannot withdraw your investments for at least five years. Third, in a PEF, the investor or limited partner does not immediately inject his funds but makes a commitment. The funding of this commitment takes place gradually as the PEF identifies and makes new investments. Finally, the generally higher risk profile of a PEF implies greater volatility in returns and so, higher expected returns.

The Islamic PEF is designed in a similar format but would have a *Shari'ah* committee that will oversee and approve all investments. Though structurally, the Islamic PEF may resemble its conventional counterpart, *Shari'ah* compliance implies a huge difference in risk profile. Whereas conventional PEFs thrive on financial leverage, an Islamic PEF cannot take on interest-bearing debt. This lack of financial leverage not only limits the total exposure but avoids the volatility in returns which results from leveraging. In addition, *Shari'ah* compliance also means no speculative positions, risk arbitrage, or net short positions. Thus, an Islamic PEF would be required to avoid excessive risk and take only long (buy) positions. In addition, the need to avoid products that may have elements of *gharar* would mean that Islamic PEFs cannot use derivatives and most structured products. Thus, from an operational viewpoint, an Islamic PEF would be very different from its conventional counterpart even though the structures may look similar.

10.5 Islamic Equity Indices

As we saw in Chapter 10, an equity index serves as a barometer of overall market performance. Equity indices can be broad based, like the Wilshire 5000, Nikkei 225, S&P 500, or even Bursa Malaysia's EMAS Index, or can be narrow sector-specific ones. Either way, equity indices play three important roles:

(i) Measure of the market or sector's performance;
(ii) Benchmark to evaluate performance of funds and fund managers; and
(iii) Underlying asset for derivatives and structured products, for example, as the underlying asset for Stock Index Futures and/or Index Options.

With the advent of Islamic Mutual Funds, the need for Islamic equity indices is obvious. Accordingly, a number of Islamic indices have been introduced. The world's largest index providers, institutions such as Dow Jones, *Financial Times*, Standard & Poor's (S&P), and Morgan Stanley, have all introduced indices based on Islamic equities. Of these, Dow Jones is by far the largest provider. It has the most number of Islamic indices by virtue of having created Islamic versions of its many conventional equity indices. Table 10.2 provides a sample of the indices.

Table 10.3. Dow Jones Islamic and Conventional Equity Indices.

Islamic Index	Conventional
• DJIM Asia/Pacific	• DJ Asia/Pacific
• DJIM China Offshore	• DJ China Offshore 50
• DJIM Hong Kong	• DJ Hong Kong
• DJIM India	• DJ India Total Market
• DJIM Indonesia	• DJ Indonesia
• DJIM Malaysia	• DJ Malaysia
• DJIM South Korea	• DJ South Korea

Source: *Islamic Finance News*, September 25, 2009.

In the case of Malaysia, aside from Dow Jones, which computes the DJIM Malaysia index, Bursa Malaysia has two Islamic indices. These are the *FTSE Bursa Malaysia EMAS Shari'ah Index* and the *FTSE Bursa Malaysia Hijrah Shari'ah Index*. Though both indices are based on the universe of listed stocks on Bursa Malaysia, the evaluation or *Shari'ah* filtering criteria is different. The first index, the FTSE Bursa Malaysia EMAS *Shari'ah* Index uses the *Shari'ah* filter or evaluation process of the Malaysian Securities Commission's *Shari'ah* Advisory Council (SAC). Recall our discussion earlier in the chapter about the SAC's evaluation criteria. The latter stock index, the FTSE Bursa Malaysia Hijrah *Shari'ah Index*, is intended for an international investor base and therefore uses additional filters. Component stocks for this index are determined first, by applying the SAC screening filter and then using additional criteria developed by Yassar Ltd., an international *Shari'ah* advisory firm. These additional criteria are as follows: (i) the use of debt and debt service ratios and (ii) the use of cash and cash equivalents as percent of total assets and receivables to assets. If any of these ratios exceed pre-determined cut-off points, the stock will be excluded from the index. For both indices, a periodic review of component stocks is carried out in June and December of each year to ensure eligibility. Both these Islamic indices have a base date of March 31, 2006, and an initial index value of 6,000 points. Both indices are reported in real time. Calculation of the EMAS *Shari'ah* index takes place every minute during the trading day whereas the *Hijrah* Index is computed every 15 seconds.

10.5.1 *Islamic vs. Conventional Indices: Comparative Performance*

As pointed out in Box. 10.2, numerous studies have evaluated the relative performance of Islamic equity portfolios to conventional ones. As pointed out in the article, the results are time-variant. Islamic portfolios appear to outperform during down cycles (bearish markets) while conventional ones outperform during up-market cycles (bullish markets). Among the many reasons given for this is the near absence or under-representation of the financial sector within Islamic portfolios. Banks and finance sector stocks do indeed lead in up-market cycles and perform poorly during economic downturns. In this section, we undertake a comparative analysis of Islamic and conventional equities based on index returns and risk. Figure 10.10 shows the performance plots of four pairs of indices. Each pair constitutes a conventional equity index and its Islamic variant. Note from our discussion on indices that the Islamic index is typically a subset of a broader conventional index. The Islamic index is made up of stocks that have gone through the *Shari'ah* screening process used by the index provider. The figures below show

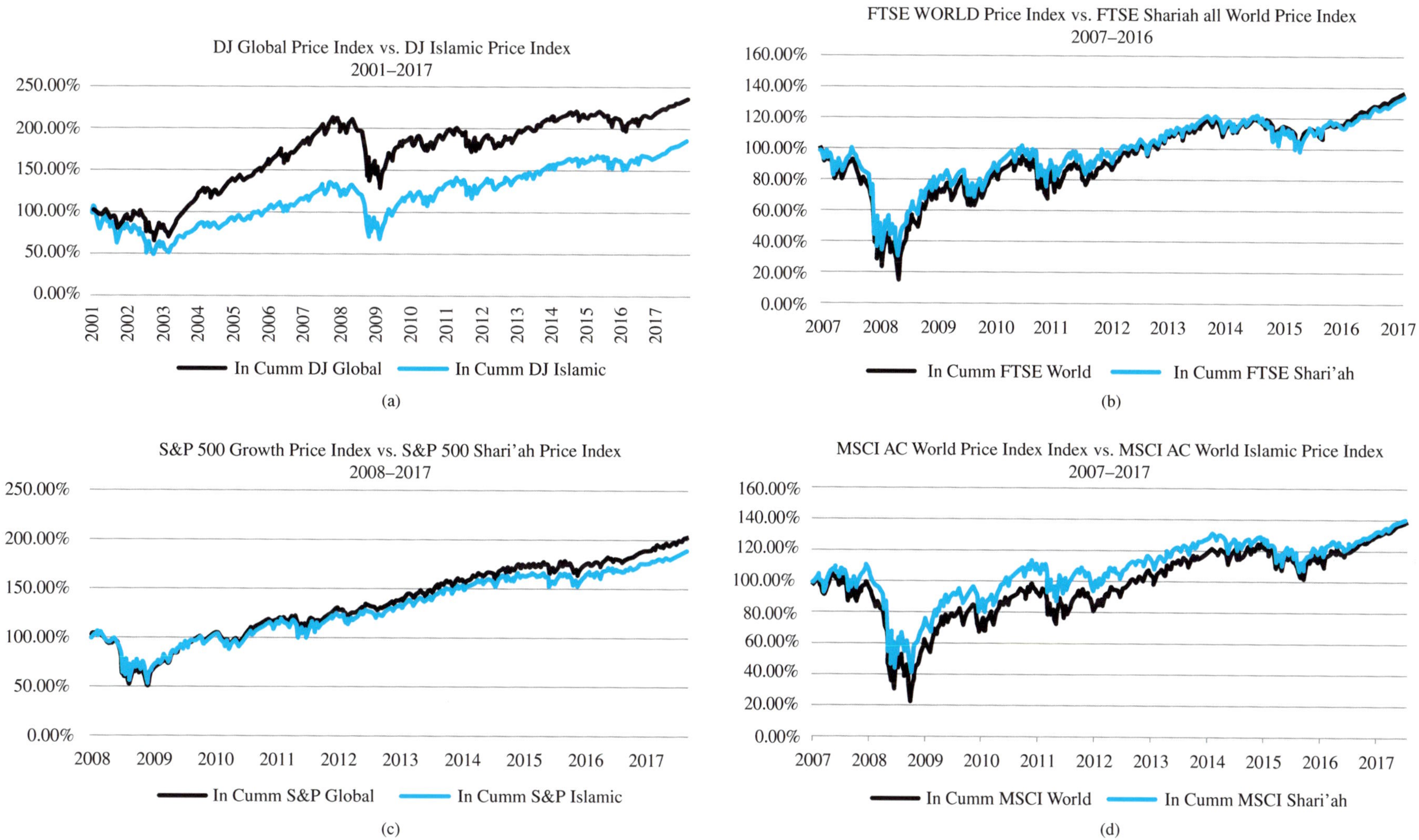

Figure 10.10. Comparative Performance of Islamic versus Conventional Index Pairs.

Source: DataStream.

the performance of four pairs of indices from four different index providers. These are: Dow Jones, *Financial Times* (FTSE), Standard & Poor's (S&P), and Morgan Stanley Composite Index (MSCI). The figures are based on cumulative daily returns computed as In Log (R_t/R_{t-1}). The index has been scaled to begin at a common point. The period covered in each case begins with the launch of the provider's Islamic index and ends in the third quarter of 2017. There are two key takeaways from the graphs. First, the pairs of indices move together and obviously have high correlation. This should not be surprising as the Islamic index is a subset of the conventional. The second point to note is that there is no conclusive evidence of one index consistently outperforming the other and vice-versa. Looking at the four pairs, the Islamic Index appears to have underperformed in the case of the Dow Jones pair, however, the opposite is the case where the MSCI pair is concerned. As for the FTSE and S&P 500 pairs, the co-movement appears to be much closer. Figure 10.11 shows the distribution of the difference in daily returns between the pairs. Notice that there is no skewness in the distribution. The spread appears to be evenly spread implying that neither the Islamic nor conventional index out or underperforms its pair consistently.

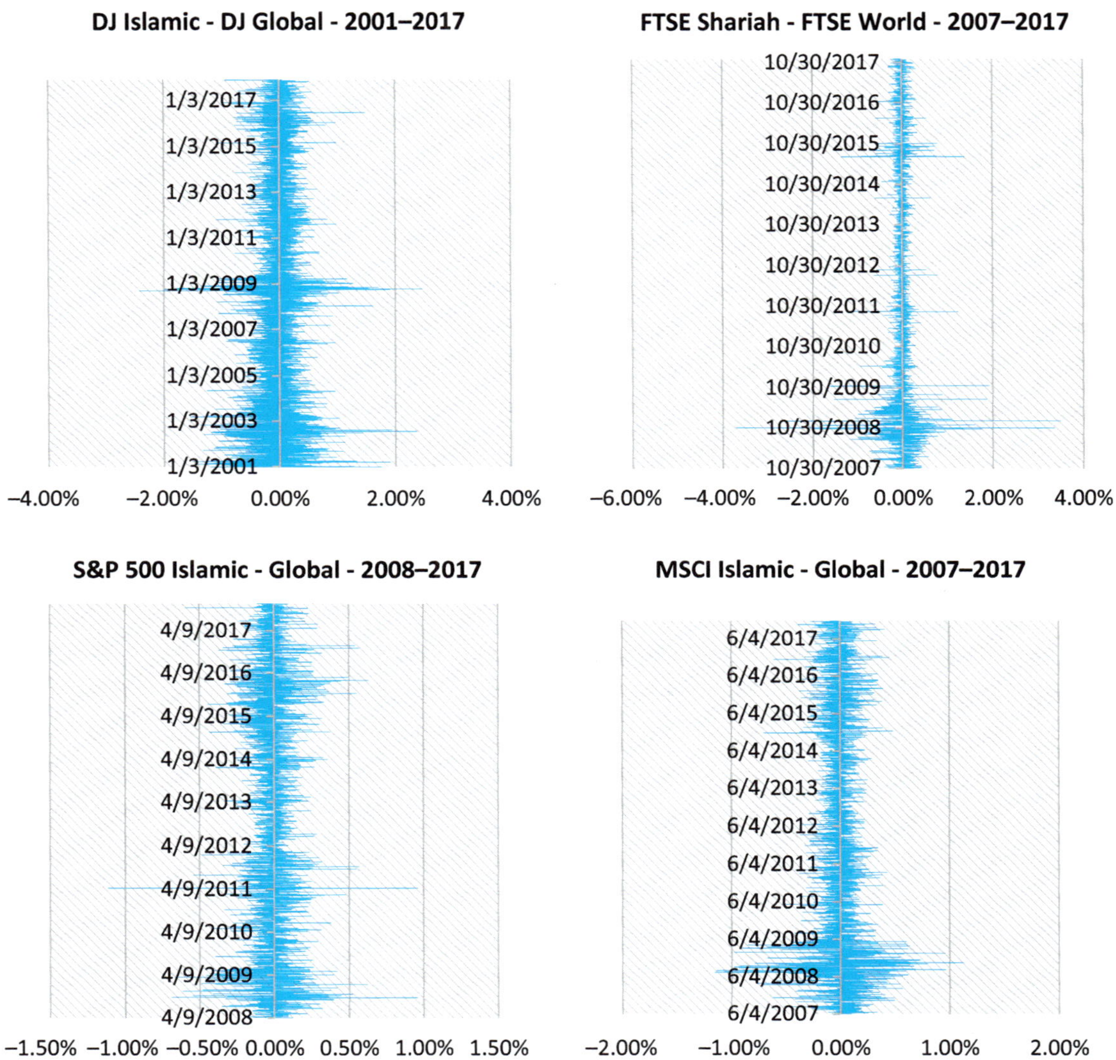

Figure 10.11. Distribution of Difference in Daily Returns.

Source: Computed based on data from *DataStream*.

Table 10.3 shows the summary statistics for the four pairs of indices. The mean daily returns and standard deviation (volatility) of the returns are shown in percentage. For three of the four pairs, Dow Jones, FTSE, and S&P 500, the mean daily returns and standard deviation is lower for the Islamic index relative to its conventional pair. Since both the mean returns and standard deviations are lower, it is hard to tell which index (portfolio), is superior from a risk-return viewpoint. On would have to compute Sharpe ratios for such evaluation. The MSCI pairs, however, show a different result. The mean daily return for the Islamic index is higher while the standard deviation is marginally lower. This would imply that the Islamic index/portfolio is superior in risk-return terms. The differences seen across the pairs obviously have to do with the different lengths of observation and the differences in index construction.

Table 10.4. Islamic vs. Conventional Index: Mean Daily Returns and Standard Deviation

Index	No of Daily Obs.	Mean Daily Returns (%)	Mean daily Std. Dev. (%)
DJ Global	4413	0.0308	0.0105899
DJ Islamic	4413	0.01956	0.0100077
FTSE World	2634	0.01356	0.0108397
FTSE *Shari'ah*	2634	0.0127	0.0105664
SP500 Global	2518	0.04106	0.0121951
SP500 Islamic	2518	0.03523	0.0118217
MSCI Global	2740	0.01384	0.0107672
MSCI Islamic	2740	0.01432	0.0107119

Source: Computed based on data from *DataStream*.

The generally lower return and risk (standard deviation) seen for the Islamic indices relative to their conventional pairs is logical. Recall that a key consideration in *Shari'ah* stock screening is leverage. In the Dow Jones and the Malaysian SAC screening processes, a 33% threshold is used for debt. Though there are marginal differences, in all cases, *Shari'ah* screening eliminates firms with too much debt in their capital structure. This limit on leverage implies that Islamic portfolios will invariably have lower leverage relative to conventional portfolios. Debt/leverage, as we know, increases the volatility of returns, i.e., risk. High leverage is an advantage during up-market cycles but becomes a disadvantage during down cycles. In terms of portfolio theory, *ceterus paribus*, stocks or portfolios with high financial leverage will have higher betas. As is well documented, high beta stocks outperform in good times but underperform in bear markets. The often-seen empirical evidence of Islamic portfolios underperforming in good times but outperforming their conventional counterparts during down cycles can be attributed to this bias against debt. To better understand the periodic difference in comparative performance, we break the Dow Jones data into four different sub-periods, each of three years.

Figure 10.12 shows the relative performance of the Dow Jones indices over four different, three-year sub-periods. Notice the stark difference in relative performance in the third sub-period (2009–2012) relative to the earlier two. The third sub-period, which is the period following the breakout of the US subprime-induced global financial crisis, saw the Islamic index clearly outperforming the conventional one. The period 2001 to 2004 was a bullish period, so too was the period 2005 to 2008, the last part of which led into the crisis. During up-markets, the Islamic index clearly trails. The last sub-period window shows very mixed results. These analyses by time segments serve to illustrate the argument made earlier that the Islamic indices tend to do better during downturns.

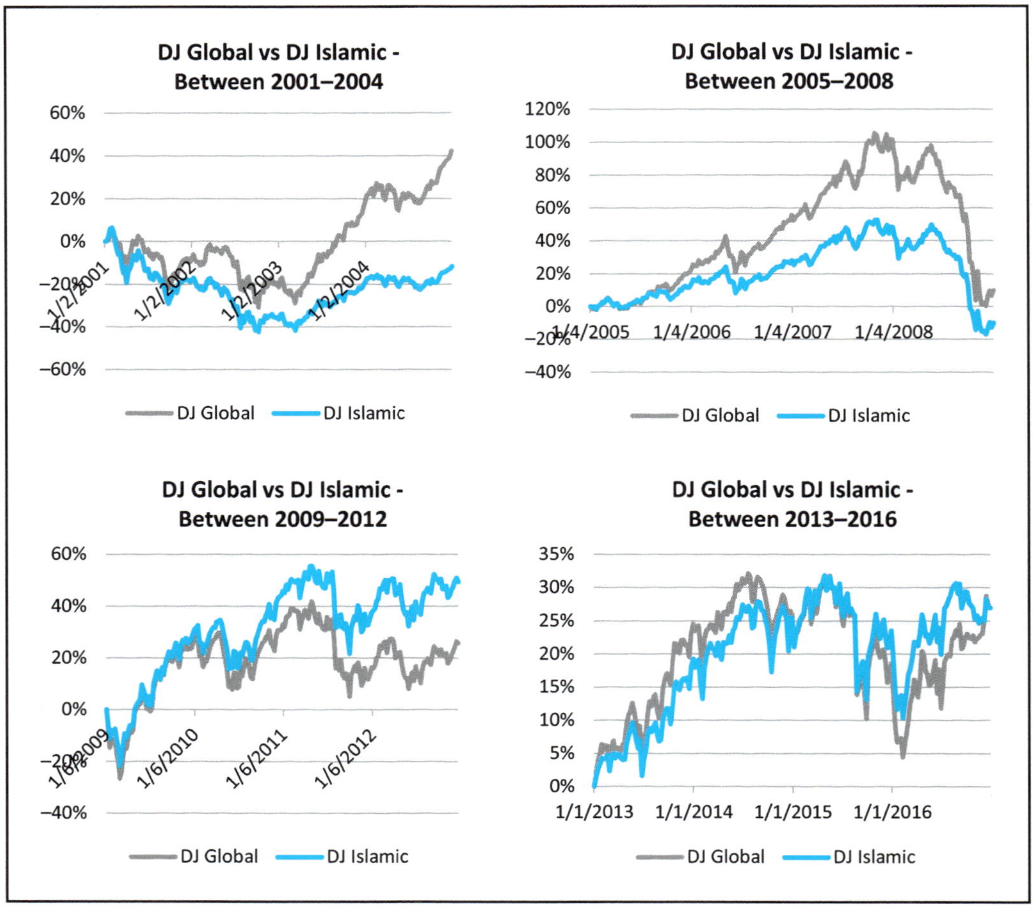

Figure 10.12. Daily Returns of DJ Global versus DJ Islamic Index by Sub-Periods.

Source: *DataStream*.

10.6 The Stock Exchanges of the Islamic World

In Chapter 2, we briefly discussed the state of stock markets in the Islamic world. While a stock market located in an Islamic country need not only have *Shari'ah*-compliant stocks, a large portion of their listed stocks and components ought to be *Shari'ah* compliant. Also, we saw in Chapter 2, the stock exchanges of Muslim countries are very small relative to developed markets. Aside from small market capitalization, these markets are plagued by problems of liquidity and high volatility. Table 10.4 and Figures 10.13a and 10.13b show the relative annual returns and volatility of returns for nine of the largest Muslim stock exchanges and the S&P 500 and the MSCI World Index. The 16-year period, 2001 to 2016, is examined. The MSCI World Index is a market capitalization weighted index of 21 developed markets. The S&P 500 is an index of US stocks.

Table 10.5. Mean and Standard Deviation of Returns for Stock Exchanges of the Islamic World.

	MSCI WORLD	S&P 500	Indonesia	Turkey	Malaysia	Saudi Arabia	Kuwait	Pakistan	Egypt	Oman
YEAR	*MSWRLD* (%)	*S&PCOMP* (%)	*JAKCOMP* (%)	*TRKISTB* (%)	*FBMKLCI* (%)	*TDWTASI* (%)	*KWKICGN* (%)	*PKSE100* (%)	*EGHFINC* (%)	*OMANMSM* (%)
2001	−13.74	−5.66	−23.79	−44.51	−29.06	13.30	13.11	−27.38	−47.45	−12.06
2002	−16.16	−11.77	4.89	29.09	−1.04	7.67	27.08	22.32	−22.15	−19.67
2003	−22.48	−24.56	−12.22	2.68	−7.31	5.56	22.85	33.96	13.20	23.20
2004	43.10	36.75	90.77	64.44	34.76	87.28	69.19	105.41	121.56	51.89

(Continued)

Table 10.5. (*Continued*)

	MSCI WORLD	S&P 500	Indonesia	Turkey	Malaysia	Saudi Arabia	Kuwait	Pakistan	Egypt	Oman
2005	10.15	5.80	42.35	48.40	2.76	87.18	10.43	71.17	167.37	21.79
2006	12.06	6.83	14.03	70.27	2.78	108.03	62.42	35.08	74.67	48.13
2007	13.98	8.11	42.79	−12.48	33.21	−55.20	−8.92	1.66	5.81	8.68
2008	−0.35	−1.36	55.34	10.74	11.28	20.85	43.89	32.01	50.80	79.02
2009	−49.88	−46.73	−53.09	−48.06	−35.30	−56.49	−62.00	−61.87	−64.65	−53.01
2010	50.94	50.25	98.29	106.88	42.68	45.82	30.25	68.62	76.15	37.57
2011	18.35	19.50	35.09	23.46	17.19	−7.56	−0.02	16.21	−11.62	−3.45
2012	−3.22	3.61	12.12	−4.15	4.68	20.91	−13.24	13.54	−3.71	−11.01
2013	7.81	10.85	22.15	32.89	4.18	−2.73	−1.19	41.88	6.71	4.10
2014	19.22	22.32	−3.13	−20.96	12.78	30.12	0.00	40.92	43.89	18.90
2015	6.26	13.49	19.29	36.21	−0.57	2.70	0.00	32.00	6.82	−7.50
2016	−12.32	−7.43	−13.16	−10.96	−8.66	−34.86	0.00	−6.95	−34.47	−18.19
Avg.	**3.98**	**5.00**	**20.73**	**17.75**	**5.27**	**17.04**	**12.12**	**26.16**	**23.93**	**10.53**
Std. Dev.	**0.2456**	**0.2284**	**0.3990**	**0.4223**	**0.2089**	**0.4755**	**0.3142**	**0.3946**	**0.6221**	**0.3288**

Source: *Thomson Reuters — DataStream.*

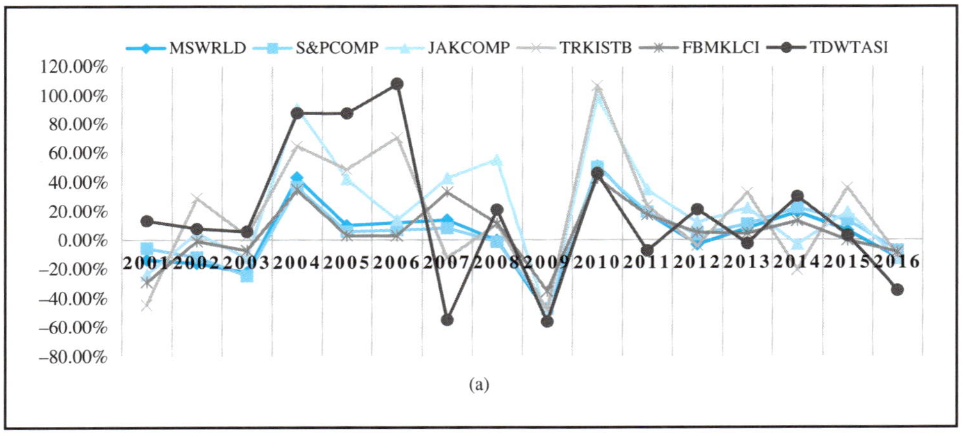

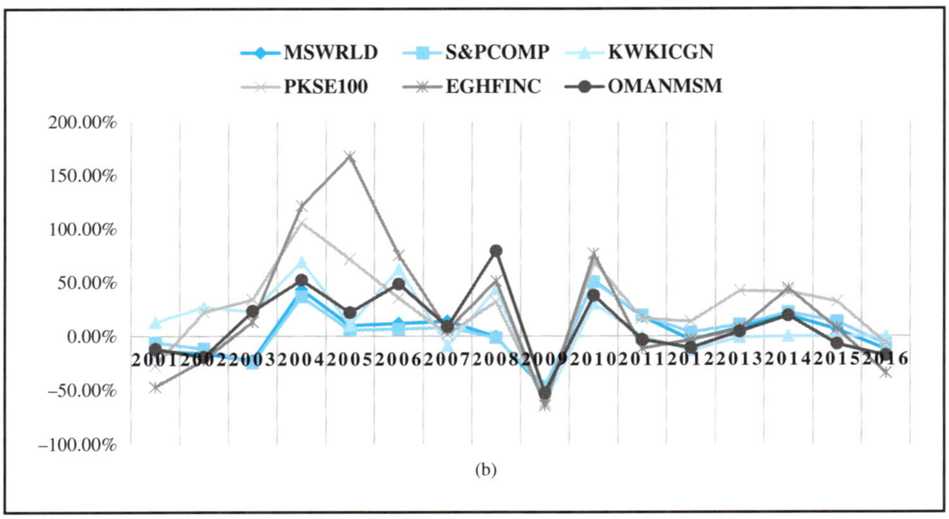

Figure 10.13. (a) and (b) Relative Annual Returns and Volatility of Returns for Nine of the Largest Muslim Stock Exchanges and the S&P 500 and the MSCI World Index

Source: Graphics based on data from *Thomson Reuters — DataStream.*

It is clear from Figures 10.13a and 10.13b that the Islamic stock exchanges have much more volatility of returns compared to the S&P 500 or the MSCI World Index over the 10-year period. This visual evidence is confirmed in the statistics shown in Table 10.3. The huge variation in returns between years is obvious. Pakistan, for instance, has returns ranging from 105% in 2004 to –61% in 2009. The stock markets of Egypt and Saudi Arabia also portray significant volatility in returns. Interestingly, with the exception of Malaysia, whose returns closely correlate with the S&P 500, all the Islamic stock exchanges have a mean return for the 16-year period, which is much higher than that of the S&P 500 or the MSCI World. However, their volatilities as measured by the standard deviation are also several folds higher. The required risk premiums for investing in such countries would certainly be higher, implying that the cost of equity capital would be higher for companies operating from these countries.

A key measure of a stock market's size is market capitalization, which is the sum total of the market capitalization of all listed stocks at a given time. The market capitalization of a stock on a given day is simply the closing price of the stock multiplied by the number of stocks the firm has outstanding. Table 10.5 shows the 10-year average market capitalization of select Muslim countries relative to the US and South Korea. It is obvious that the stock exchanges of Muslim countries are very small relative to developed countries. Even Malaysia, which has the largest market capitalization among the Muslim countries, is small relative to the US Market capitalization as a percentage of Gross Domestic Product (GDP) is often used to determine the relative importance of a stock market to the nation's economy. It can also be an indication of how important a source of corporate funding the equity market is. Figure 10.14 shows market capitalization as a percentage of GDP for selected Muslim countries and the US and South Korea. With the exception of Malaysia, which has market capitalization to GDP approximating 136% and clearly belongs with the developed markets, the other Muslim countries have smaller ratios. This is clear indication that equity markets do not play as important a role in Muslim countries as they do in developed ones. The banking sector probably plays a predominant role within the financial sectors of these Muslim countries. The infantile nature of equity markets in most Islamic countries is symptomatic of the overall underdevelopment of capital markets in Muslim countries.

Table 10.6. 10-year Average Market Capitalization (2006–2015, US$ Billions).

Country	Avg. Mkt. Cap. (US$ bils)
Egypt	78.92
Indonesia	296.51
Iran	102.5
Malaysia	365.3
Nigeria	53.8
Oman	28.7
Turkey	221.4
United Arab Emirates	134.7
South Korea	1,020.8
United States	19,318.4

Source: World Bank Database.

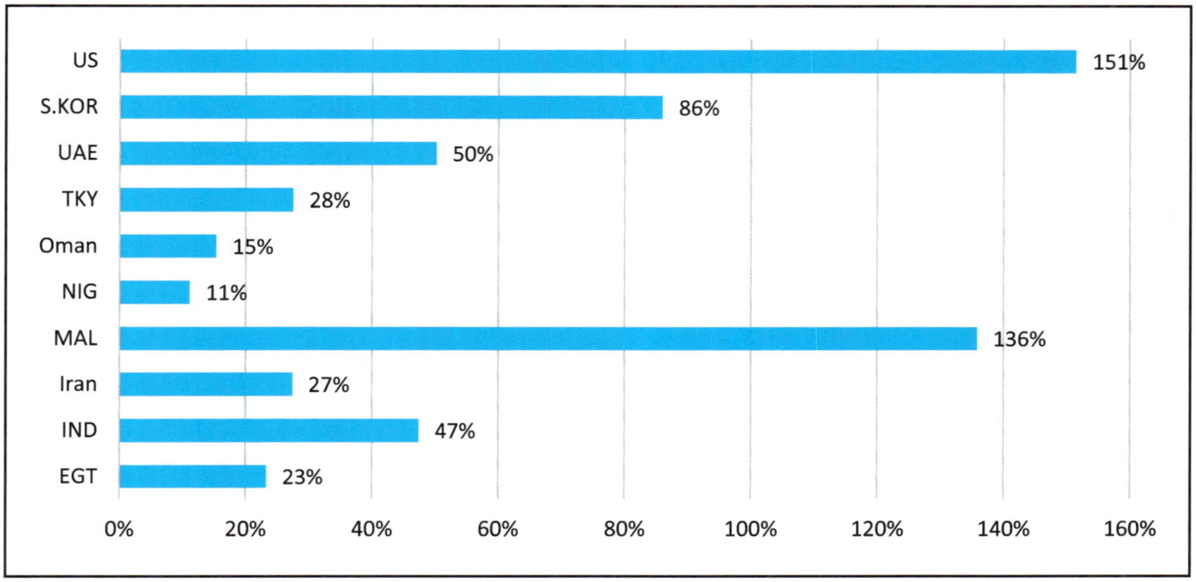

Figure 10.14. 10-year Average Market Capitalization to GDP (2006–2015).

Summary

Equity financing which resembles *mudarabah*-type financing is congruent to the *Shari'ah* requirement that risk and returns be shared. Even so, not all listed stocks can be deemed *Shari'ah* compliant. The need to identify *Shari'ah*-compliant stocks has led to the development of the *Shari'ah*-screening techniques. Aside from the Malaysian SAC, Dow Jones, *Financial Times*, and other financial information providers have developed *Shari'ah*-screening filters. There are some differences in the screening techniques. The Malaysian SAC includes mixed businesses, provided they fulfilled certain quantitative and qualitative thresholds. The capital structure of the firm is not considered directly but through interest costs or earnings. The Dow Jones filter, on the other hand, excludes mixed businesses and considers financial leverage. Like the conventional equities market, the Islamic equities market can and does, in the Malaysian context, include the several components found in conventional equity markets. Based on *Shari'ah*-compliant stocks, an Islamic equity market can have Islamic ETFs, Islamic REITS, Islamic Mutual Funds, Islamic Private Equity, and structured products. Though operationally the same, the Islamic version has its *Shari'ah* committee that oversees governance and *Shari'ah* compliance. Islamic Mutual Funds, Islamic REITS, and ETFs are functionally the same but are governed by *Shari'ah* requirements. Given *Shari'ah* requirements, these entities will have to avoid leverage, short positions, instruments that have *gharar*, etc. Despite these restrictions, Islamic Mutual Funds and REITs have experienced very rapid growth, much faster in many cases, than their conventional counterparts. Given the huge popularity of Islamic equity products, financial information providers have designed and introduced several Islamic indices. Today, just about every country or market has an Islamic index parallel to a conventional one. Examining the stock markets of Muslim countries, most are more volatile than the S&P 500. This increased volatility may simply be a reflection of both smaller size and a lower stage of development.

Questions and Problems

1. Evaluate an equity investment from the *Shari'ah* viewpoint.
2. If equity investment is acceptable from a *Shari'ah* viewpoint, what is the need for stock screening filters?
3. State and briefly explain some differences between the Dow Jones *Shari'ah* screening filter and that of the Malaysian SAC.
4. Some have argued that "tight" *Shari'ah* screening filters for stocks are desirable and it is better to err on the side of conservatism. What is the potential downside to this argument?
5. Explain the difference between the following:
   (a) Islamic ETF versus Conventional ETF
   (b) Islamic REIT versus Conventional REIT
6. What are some of the benefits of investing in stocks through a mutual fund? How different are the benefits of it to an Islamic Mutual Fund?
7. In most countries, where the conventional banking and finance predominates, the list of *Shari'ah*-compliant stocks grossly under represents the financial sector. The commodities sector, on the other hand, fills in the "slack" and is often weighted more than its "true" contribution to overall GDP. In view of this, discuss the circumstances under which a broad-based Islamic Portfolio (or Islamic Mutual Fund) could outperform or underperform a broad-based market index.
8. Briefly explain the popularity of Islamic REITS in Muslim countries. What accounts for their popularity?
9. A REIT does three key functions, (i) managing tenancy within its property, (ii) cash flows management, and (iii) ensuring appropriate insurance for its assets. Describe how an Islamic REIT undertakes these functions and how it might be different from that of a conventional REIT.
10. Private Equity Funds (PEFs) have been extremely popular among high-net-worth individuals in developed countries. Given *Shari'ah* requirements and prohibitions, briefly explain why Islamic Private Equity Funds have not been as popular in Muslim countries, even those with well-developed markets.
11. LEXIS REIT owns seven properties located in different parts of the country. On total asset value of RM125 million, it earns RM11.875 million in earnings before interest and tax, and net Profit is RM9.375 million. LEXIS REIT is required to pay 90% of its net profits as dividends. Assuming there are 62.5 million shares outstanding and the REIT is trading at RM2 per share;
    (a) Determine the dividend yield for the REIT.
    (b) If LEXIS can expect Net Profits to grow at 2.5% per year over the future, what is the appropriate value per share of the REIT if the required return is 8%.
    (c) What is the expected capital gains for the stock, is it typical for a REIT? Explain briefly.
12. How different is *mudarabah* from equity? To a firm seeking funding, in what way could *mudarabah* be more advantageous than issuing new equity?
13. (a) Explain why an ETF, including an Islamic ETF, may sell at a price lower than the value of the assets within. Why might an investor be interested in an instrument that sells at a discount to value?
    (b) How relevant is the Dividend Discount Model (DDM) to valuation of a *Shari'ah*-compliant stock? Discuss.
14. MCB a large property developer intends to issue a REIT. The total current value of rentals from the five properties that will be placed in the REIT is RM25 million per year. All five properties are office complexes. The REIT prospectus states that 90% of all rental revenue will be paid out as dividends.
    (a) If the required yield for office complex REITs is 7%, what amount can MCB expect to raise from the REIT?
    (b) What is the expected total value of the REIT if on average rentals are expected to grow 1.5% per year?
    (c) Explain why the capital gains yield from REITs cannot be high.
15. Several studies have shown that an Islamic Equity Index typically underperforms its conventional counterpart during bull cycles but outperforms during bear cycles. Given your understanding of how *Shari'ah* constituent stocks are screened and stock pricing explain why this is to be expected.

Bibiliography

Dow Jones & Company Inc. *Guide to the Dow Jones Islamic Market Index*.

Dow Jones & Company Inc. (2007). *Dow Jones Islamic Market Index Rulebook*.

Ernst & Young (2011). The Islamic Funds and Investment Report.

IOSCO (2005). Islamic Capital Markets: Fact Finding Report, The International Organization of Securities Commission.

Islamic Finance News (2009). September 25.2009

Khan, A. P. (2016). Essays on Equity Indices and Exchange Traded Funds: Islamic versus Conventional unpublished PhD Thesis, INCEIF.

Khan, A. P., I. B. Obiyathulla and A. M. Mohammed Masih (2015). *Performance and Trading Characteristics of Exchange Traded Funds: Developed vs Emerging Markets. Capital Markets Review*, Vol. 23, pp. 40–64 .

Khatkhatay and Nisar (2007). "*Shari'ah* Compliant Equity investments: An Assessment of Current Screening Norms." *Islamic Economic Studies*. Vol. 15, No.1, July.

Malaysian Islamic Capital Market, Quarterly Bulletin — several issues.

Sardehi, N. (2008). *Islamic Capital Markets — Developments and Challenges* (VDM Verlag Publishers, Germany).

Securities Commission (2001). The Capital Market Master Plan — Malaysia.

The Malaysian Reserve (2017). September 25.

World Bank Database

Websites

http://www.djindexes.com/mdsidx/downloads/imi_rulebook.pdf

www.sc.com.my/eng/html/icm/ICM-IOSCOFactfindingReport.pdf

http://www.mifc.com/index.php?ch=menu

http://www.zawya.com/middle-east/financial-markets

http://www.bursamalaysia.com

https://financial.thomsonreuters.com Thomson Reuters — DataStream

http://www.bloomberg.com

Websites of respective Muslim Country Stock Exchanges

Chapter 11

DERIVATIVE INSTRUMENTS: PRODUCTS AND APPLICATIONS

Topics in this Chapter

Chapter Objective

This chapter is designed to provide an introduction to derivative instruments, their trading systems, and applications. The four main derivative products, Forwards, Futures, Options, and Swaps, are described in detail and their uses are explained. On completing this chapter, you should have a good understanding of derivative instruments, their application in risk management, and their markets.

Key Terms			
amortizing swap	exercise price	interest rate swap (IRS)	put option
arbitrage	exercise style rate exchange	inverse floater	reference rate
arbitrageurs	financial engineering	long position	reset frequency
asymmetric information	fixed rate payer	market maker	risk
basis swap	floating rate payer	market yield	risk management
cash settlement	forwards	notional principal	short position
clearinghouse	forward-starting swap	novation principle	speculation
commodity swap	futures	options	spot price
counterparty risk	hedgers	over-the-counter (OTC)	strike price
equity swap	hedging	plain-vanilla swap	
exchange traded contracts (ETCs)	interest rate risk	portfolio insurance	

11.1 Introduction

Derivative instruments, in their current form, are relatively new instruments. Compared to financial assets such as stocks and bonds which have been exchange traded for more than a century, derivative instruments, especially financial derivatives, are very new instruments. For example, even the world's oldest exchange-traded financial derivative, interest rate futures, is hardly 30 years old. Many of the more exotic forms of derivatives are instruments that did not even exist a decade ago.

Despite being new, derivative instruments have turned out to be very popular. Trading volume in derivatives has shown impressive growth in recent years. Interestingly, the volumes of trading in several derivative contracts have outpaced that of the underlying assets on which they are based. Despite their obvious popularity, derivative instruments have been blamed for having precipitated several financial scandals which resulted in spectacular losses. Examples of these are Barings PLC–Sumitomo Corporation's losses (US$2.6 billion) on copper derivatives; Metallgesellchaft AG's (DM1.8 billion) losses on oil futures; and Orange County California's losses on interest rate derivatives.

The most recent derivatives-induced loss happened in 2005 with China Aviation Oil's (CAO) Singapore subsidiary reporting losses close to US$50 million. The losses were due to positions CAO had taken in Option contracts on oil derivatives.

All of these above losses have been widely reported. Given the size of the losses, they had attracted much attention. Since each of these scandals involved derivative instruments, a widespread misconception appears to have occurred with regard to derivative instruments in general. The misconception appears to be that there is something inherently risky about derivatives and that prudence would require that one avoids these instruments. As the reader works his way through this book, it would be clear that the common perception of derivatives is untrue. Derivatives are "powerful" financial instruments which, if improperly used, can cause serious problems. When used intelligently, derivatives can reduce risks and allow for all kinds of flexibility. Indeed, if one examines each of the abovementioned scandals in detail, it will be evident that in every case, the cause of the problem was not the use but the *misuse* of derivatives. In each case, the players involved had used derivatives to take huge speculative positions, almost all of which were irrational.

11.2 What Are Derivative Instruments?

Derivative instruments are essentially financial instruments that *derive* their value from the value of an underlying asset. As such, a derivative instrument has little value in and of itself. Its value is entirely dependent on the value of its underlying asset. For example, suppose I buy and hold a crude palm oil (CPO) futures contract, the value of this contract will fluctuate as the value or price of spot CPO rises and falls. Should the underlying asset, CPO in this case, rise in value, then the value of the CPO futures contract that I am holding as a buyer would also increase in value. Alternatively, should the spot price of CPO fall, then the value of my CPO futures contract would also fall. This happens because a derivative is a "claim" on the underlying asset at a predetermined price and at predetermined future period(s).

So, unlike spot market transactions, where assets are bought and sold for cash at prevailing spot prices for immediate delivery, derivative market transactions allow for future transactions at prices determined today. The term "derivative" denotes the fact that these instruments *derive* their value from elsewhere. Like many other capital market instruments, derivative instruments may be traded as exchange-traded contracts (ETCs) or over-the-counter (OTC). While an exchange-traded derivative is traded on a formal exchange, an OTC derivative is a customized bilateral contract between two parties. While prices are arrived at through market trading for ETC derivatives, prices for the OTC products are arrived at through negotiation among the parties.

Though the analysis and pricing of derivative instruments can be complicated and highly quantitative, the basic principles and logic of derivatives are relatively straightforward. Today, there is a broad spectrum of derivative instruments, many with very exotic names and highly specialized purposes. This chapter focuses on the four main derivative instruments, which are forwards, futures, options, and swaps.

11.3 Common Derivative Instruments

As mentioned above, forwards, futures, and options are probably the three most common derivative instruments. A fourth and an increasingly popular derivative is the swap contract. As derivative instruments, forwards, futures, options, and swaps derive their value from their underlying assets. However, key differences in some of their features lead to substantially different payoffs and therefore, in their purpose of use. We examine next the basic definition of each of these four derivatives.

- **A Forward Contract:** A forward contract can be defined as a contract between two parties agreeing to carry out a transaction at a future date but at a price determined today.
- **A Futures Contract:** A futures contract can be simply defined as a standardized and exchange-traded form of forward contract. As in a forward contract, a futures contract represents a formal agreement between two parties to carry out a transaction at a future date (contract maturity date) but at a price determined at contract initiation. Thus, from an operational viewpoint, forwards and futures are essentially the same. The difference being that futures are standardized and exchange traded.
- **An Option Contract:** An option contract provides the holder the right but not the obligation to buy or sell the underlying asset at a predetermined price. While a call option provides the right to buy, a put option would provide the right to sell.
- **A Swap Contract:** A swap can be defined as a transaction in which two parties simultaneously exchange cash flows based on a notional amount of the underlying asset. The rates at which the cash flows would be exchanged are determined based on a fixed rate for the fixed cash flow and on a reference measure; for example, it could be an interest rate like three-month KLIBOR) for the floating cash flow.

11.4 The Evolution of Derivative Instruments

Like other products, derivative instruments evolved as a result of product innovation. As is usually the case, the innovation was in response to increasingly complex needs. As business environments became increasingly sophisticated, new and better financial products were needed to manage changed needs. The requirement that every newly evolved product must provide increased benefits or "value-added" over existing products in order to survive applies equally to derivatives. Forward contracts, which are the simplest derivatives, were the first, followed by futures contracts, which had several advantages over forwards. The next phase of evolution involved options. Options provided the flexibility that forward and futures contracts could not. Swaps and a host of other exotic derivatives and structured products have followed this evolution, and now constitute a substantial portion of the overall market for derivatives.

The key utility that users could derive from derivative instruments is help with managing their risks. Risk management is indeed the *raison d'être* of derivatives. The original justification for derivatives was risk management. However, it is true that given the features of these instruments, they could just as easily be used for speculative and arbitrage purposes.

If the need to manage risks was the original need for derivatives, the need to manage increasingly sophisticated risks led to the evolution of these instruments. There were two driving forces behind the evolution: first was the shortcomings associated with certain derivatives instruments themselves; and second, the evolving nature of risks. The evolution process, however, did not result in the substitution of the existing instrument by the new; rather, the evolution has been complementary. That is, both the old and new instruments co-existed.

Risk management or hedging requires that we establish a position in a derivative instrument that will give us an exposure opposite to that of our underlying position. If we are long (holding) an underlying asset and therefore exposed to falling price of that asset, we hedge by taking a derivative position that will benefit when the asset's price falls, for example, by going short (sell or make delivery) a forward or futures contract on the asset. The idea of establishing an exposure that will offset our underlying exposure is the basic logic of hedging.

11.5 Forward Contracts

Chronologically, the first derivative instrument was probably the forward contract. Not surprisingly, forward contracts were also the simplest type of derivatives. In a forward contract, two parties undertake to complete a transaction at a future date but at a price determined today. The two parties could be a producer who promises to supply the product (underlying asset) and a consumer who needs the product at a future date. Clearly, both parties here are faced with risk, essentially price risk. While the producer would be fearful of a fall in the spot price between now and six months from now, the consumer would be susceptible to an increase in the spot price. Since both face risk but in the opposite direction, it would be logical for both parties to meet, negotiate, and agree on a price at which the transaction can be carried out at the future date. Once the terms have been formalized and documented, a forward contract would have been created. The benefit of such a forward contract is that the parties have eliminated *all* price risk. Both parties have "locked-in" their price and cost. Figure 11.1 shows the mechanics

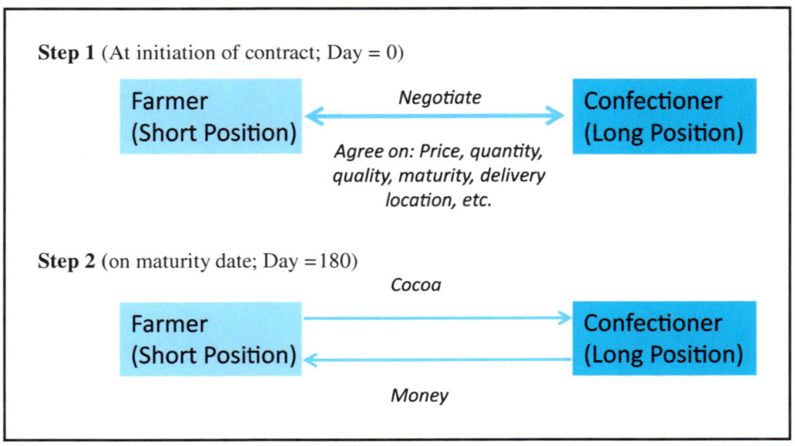

Figure 11.1. Mechanics of a Forward Contract.

of a forward contract between a cocoa farmer who will have cocoa available in six months and a confectioner who needs cocoa for his inventory in six months. Notice that both parties are now exposed to price risk. The farmer would be afraid of falling prices of cocoa, whereas the confectioner would be afraid of rising cocoa prices.

11.6 The Need for Futures Contracts

The next step in the evolution from forward contracts was futures contracts. Futures contracts were innovated to essentially manage risk. One would be tempted to ask why this contract was needed if forward contracts were sufficient for risk management purposes. As pointed out earlier, a newly innovated product will not survive unless it has some value-added over existing products. The fact that futures contracts have become increasingly popular and have huge trading volume is testimony to its benefits over forward contracts. The need for futures contracts came about given the problems associated with forward contracts.

The forward contract has a number of issues, including three main problems. The first may be classified as that of multiple coincidences. Here, the party to a forward contract would have to find a counterparty that not only has the opposite needs with respect to the underlying asset, but also with regard to timing and quantity. The counterparty must need the product in the right quantity at the right time. Thus, a number of factors will have to coincide before a forward contract can be drawn up. A second problem with the forward contract often lies in the way the forward price is arrived at. Typically, the forward price is arrived at through negotiation. Depending on the bargaining position, however, it may be possible that a forward price is forced upon the other party. This may either be due to urgency on the part on one party (e.g. perishable goods) or more commonly due to asymmetric information. A third and probably most important problem with forward contracts is counterparty risk. Counterparty risk refers to default risk of the counterparty in the contract. Though a forward contract is a legally binding arrangement, legal recourse is slow, time-consuming, and costly. Default risks in forward contracts arise not so much from "dishonest" counterparties but from increased incentive to default as a result of subsequent price movement. When spot prices rise substantially above the forward price, the seller has the incentive to default. The buyer would have the incentive to default if the opposite happens — i.e., spot price decreases.

As these shortcomings of the forward contract became apparent over time, a new instrument that would provide the risk management benefit of forward contracts while simultaneously overcoming its problems was needed. The resulting innovation was the futures contract. A futures contract is essentially a forward contract standardized with respect to contract size, maturity, product quality, place of delivery, etc. With standardization, it was possible to trade them on an exchange, which in turn increases liquidity and therefore reduces transaction costs. In addition, since all buyers and sellers transact through the exchange, the problem of multiple coincidence of wants is easily overcome. One would transact in the futures contract maturity closest to needed maturity and in as many contracts as needed to fit the underlying asset size.

With exchange trading, the second problem with forward contracts, that of being possibly locked into an *unfair* price, would not exist. This is because each party is a price-taker with the futures' price being that which prevails in the market at the time of contract initiation. As exchange quoted prices are arrived at by the interaction of many buyers and sellers, they would, by definition, be "fair" prices.

The problem of counterparty risk is overcome in futures contracts by means of the *novation principle*. The exchange acts as an intermediary, guaranteeing each trade by being the buyer to each seller and seller to each buyer. What this means is that each party transfers the counterparty risk of forwards on to the exchange in the case of futures contracts. This transfer of risk to the exchange by parties to the futures contract has to be managed by the exchange, which now bears the risk. The exchange minimizes the potential default risk by means of the *margining process* and by *daily marking to market*. The basic idea behind the margining and marking to market process is to reduce the incentive to default by requiring initial deposits (initial margins), recognizing losses as they occur, and requiring the party whose position is losing to pay up as the losses accrue (margin calls).

These margining and marking to market process have been refined and fine-tuned over the years by futures exchanges to such an extent that incidence of market cornering and systemic defaults have been reduced to negligible rates. Table 11.1 shows how changes in the spot price at maturity can lead to implied gains and losses to parties in a futures contract. It is this potential gain or loss that gives rise to the incentive to default. The margining and daily marking to market process, however, ensures that the parties pay up for the losses as they occur and therefore have no incentive to default at contract maturity.

Table 11.1. Payoff to Long and Short Positions.

		Implied Profit /Loss	
Spot Price at Maturity	**Futures Price**	**Farmer (Short)**	**Confectioner (Long)**
RM 70 per ton	RM100	+RM30	–RM30
RM120 per ton	RM100	–RM20	+RM20

11.7 The Need for Options

Though futures contracts have been able to overcome the problems associated with forward contracts, they were still inadequate in some respects to later-day business needs. In particular, there were two inadequacies that stimulated the search for further product innovation. The first is the fact that while futures contracts enabled easy hedging by locking in the price at which one could buy or sell, being locked-in also means that one would not benefit from subsequent favorable price movements. Would it not be wonderful to have an instrument that protects you from unfavorable price movements while, at the same time, enabling you to take advantage of favorable price movements? This is precisely what options do.

In essence, options have at least three important advantages over forwards and futures. First, option contracts provide the best of both worlds: downside protection and upside potential. Second, options are extremely flexible and can be combined in various ways to achieve different objectives and cash flows. Finally, as we will see later, there may be complicated business risk situations that cannot be handled with forwards and futures but can be easily handled with options.

Following the advent of options, a whole new area of finance known as ***financial engineering*** came about. Financial engineering revolves around the designing of risk management solutions to complex risks. Since derivatives, particularly options, are extremely flexible instruments, they form the building blocks of financial engineering.

11.8 Options: Key Features and Trade-offs

All exchange-traded options come in two basic forms: calls and puts. A call option *provides the holder the right but not the obligation to buy the underlying asset at a pre- determined price*. A put option, on the other hand, *provides the holder the right but not the obligation to sell the underlying asset at a predetermined price*. The predetermined price at which the transaction will be carried is known as the *exercise* price or *strike* price. Unlike futures and forwards, options require the payment of a premium on purchase. That is, one pays a premium to acquire a call or a put option.

Depending on whether the option is American or European style, this right might be exercised at different times. While a European-style option is only exercisable at maturity, an American option can be exercised at or any time before maturity. Given, this additional flexibility, an American option would be more valuable than a European option, assuming all other features are the same.

An option contract therefore should, at the very least, specify the following five features:

(i) The type of option, whether call or put;
(ii) The underlying asset;
(iii) The exercise price or strike price;
(iv) The maturity or expiration date; and
(v) The exercise style, whether American or European style.

While the long position (buyer) has a right but not the obligation to exercise, the short position (seller) is obliged to fulfil the buyer's wants should he choose to exercise. For example, if the buyer of a call option chooses to exercise, i.e., buy the underlying asset at the exercise price, the seller is obligated to provide him the underlying at that price. The opposite would hold for a put option. If the holder of the put chooses to exercise, i.e., choosing to sell the underlying at the exercise price, the seller of the put must stand ready to buy the underlying asset at the exercise price. Chart 11.1 summarizes this relationship.

Chart 11.1. Option Position and Rights/Obligations.

Position	Calls	Puts
Buyer (Long)	Has the right but not the obligation to buy underlying asset at exercise price.	Has the right but not the obligation to sell underlying asset at exercise price.
Seller (Short)	Is obliged to sell underlying at exercise price.	Is obliged to buy underlying at exercise price.

Note: When buyers of options choose to exercise, sellers face potential assignment. Assignment refers to the process by which notification is given to sellers that their obligation is due, that they must now sell if they had shorted call options or buy if they had shorted puts.

As will be evident, the fact that options provide a right but not an obligation to the holder gives tremendous advantage. This added flexibility is the source of value-added that options have over other financial instruments. A holder only needs to exercise if it will be profitable for him to do so. For example, let us say you buy a three-month American-style call option on Maybank's stock at an exercise price of RM20 per share. It means that you can exercise your option, i.e., "call it" at RM20 per share at any time before or on the maturity date in 90 days. Thus, you would only exercise the option if Maybank's stock goes higher than RM20. If the stock does not reach RM20 by the expiration day, the option would be unexercised. For this privilege, you pay to buy the option. This payment is the option premium. So, if you do not exercise because the underlying stock did not go higher than the exercise price, the premium paid is a loss to you and a profit to the seller of the option. Note that the maximum you can lose is the amount of the premium; however, the potential profit is technically unlimited.

While an unexercised option will become worthless after maturity, prior to maturity, the holder can either exercise it (if profitable to do so) or sell it in the secondary market. The price at which it can be sold would, of course, depend on the expectation of the underlying stock's price at maturity. It is normal that an option will pass through several owners before reaching maturity.

11.9 Payoff and Risk Profile of Option Positions

11.9.1 *A Long Call Position*

One way to appreciate the advantages of options is by examining the payoff attained by investing in an asset via options as opposed to investing directly in an asset, e.g., a stock. One could take a long position (buy and hold) in a stock and be subjected to the full impact of the change in value of the stock or invest in the stock via a call option and attain a more favorable risk profile. For example, suppose you are bullish on a stock but instead of buying (long) the stock, you decide to buy a call option on the stock with an exercise price of RM12 at a RM0.20 premium. What is the payoff to this long call position? The payoff profile to this long call position is shown in Figure 11.2.

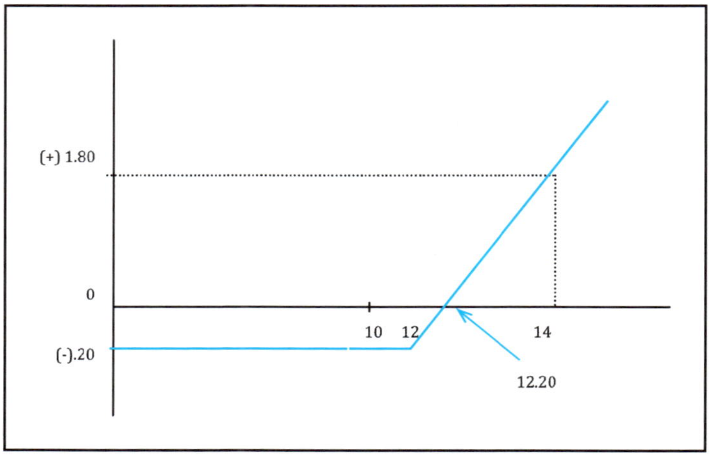

Figure 11.2. Long Call Position.

A long call strategy is certainly superior to that of a long stock position, in that the loss potential is now limited to the cost of the premium. At any stock price above RM12.20, the long call position breaks even. The breakeven point for calls is exercise price plus premium. The risk profile is essentially one of unlimited profit potential and limited loss potential. It is for this risk profile that options are said to provide the best of both worlds. They let you benefit from a potential upside rally in the underlying asset but limit your losses if prices move unfavorably.

11.9.2 *A Short Call Position*

The easiest way to understand the payoff profile for a short call position is to look at it as the "mirror opposite" of the long call position. Figure 11.3 shows the payoff profile to a short call with an exercise price of RM12 and a premium of RM0.20. It shows an unlimited loss potential if price rises very far above the strike price (naked option).

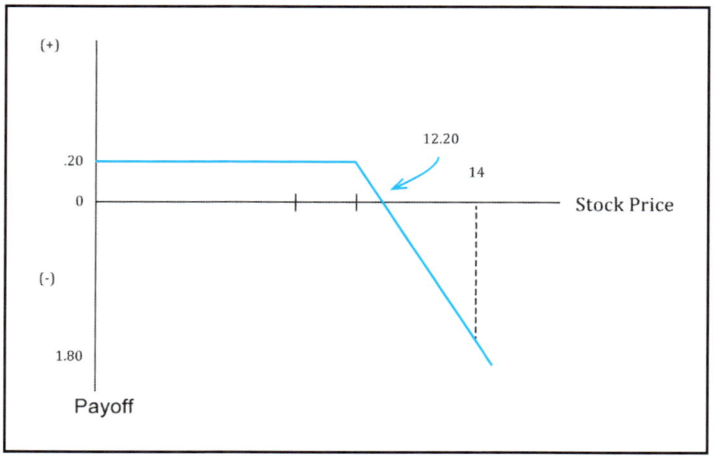

Figure 11.3. Short Call Position.

11.9.3. *Long and Short Put Positions*

You are bearish about a stock, but rather than short the stock, you buy a put with exercise price of RM12 at RM0.15 premium. What is the payoff to this strategy?

Compared to a short stock position, a long put position (see Figure 11.4) limits the loss potential. If your (bearish) expectation is correct and the underlying stock's price fall, you gain but should price move unfavorably (rise), then your potential loss is limited to the amount of the premium. The put breaks even at RM11.85. The breakeven point for puts is the exercise price minus put premium.

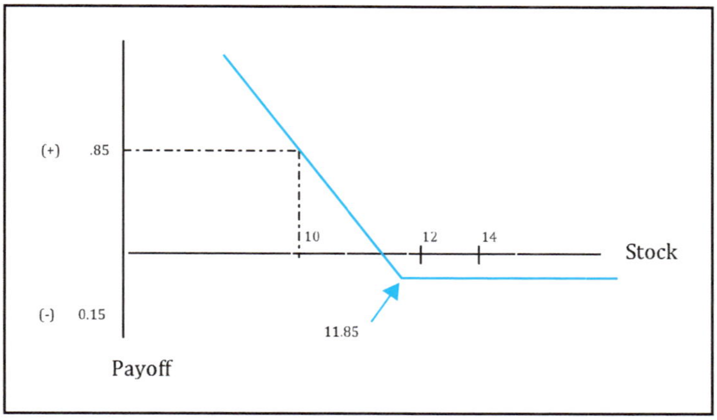

Figure 11.4. Long Put Position.

Again, as in the case of the short call, one could think of the payoff profile for a short put (see Figure 11.5) to be the exact opposite (mirror opposite) of that of the long put position. Note that losses could be unlimited for the put seller if prices fall far below the strike price (naked put).

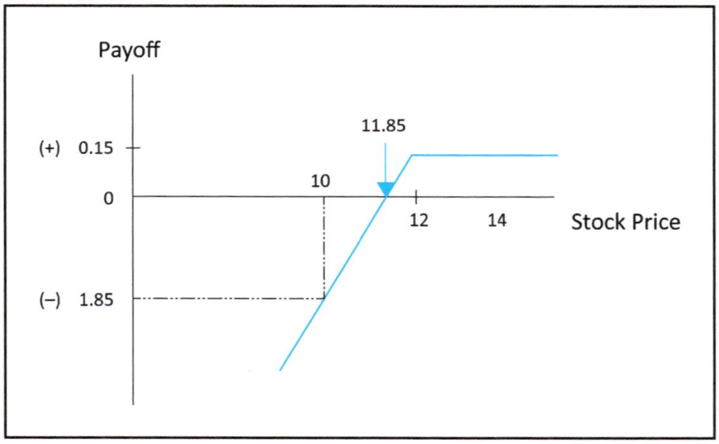

Figure 11.5. Short Put Position.

11.9.4 *Options versus Stock Positions*

To understand the differences in risk profile between positions in a stock as opposed to options, we examine their payoffs next. This would also enable the reader to appreciate the risk mitigation property of options. We begin with an examination of a long stock position (buying and holding a stock) as opposed to a long call position. This is followed by the short stock and long put positions.

11.9.4.1 *Long stock versus long call position*

Both the long stock and long call positions are appropriate if one had a bullish expectation. Between the two positions however, there are some differences. To see these differences, we examine the payoffs taken together. Table 11.2a shows the relative payoffs for a long stock and a long call position. The two positions are, respectively,

Table 11.2(a). Relative Payoff to Long Stock and Long Call.

Stock Price at Maturity	Payoff to Long Stock	Payoff to Long Call
9.50	(9.50)	(0.20)
10.00	(2.00)	(0.20)
10.50	(1.50)	(0.20)
11.00	(1.00)	(0.20)
11.50	(0.50)	(0.20)
12.00	0	(0.20)
12.20	0.20	0
12.50	0.50	0.30
13.00	1.00	0.80
13.50	1.50	1.30
14.00	2.00	1.80
14.50	2.50	2.30

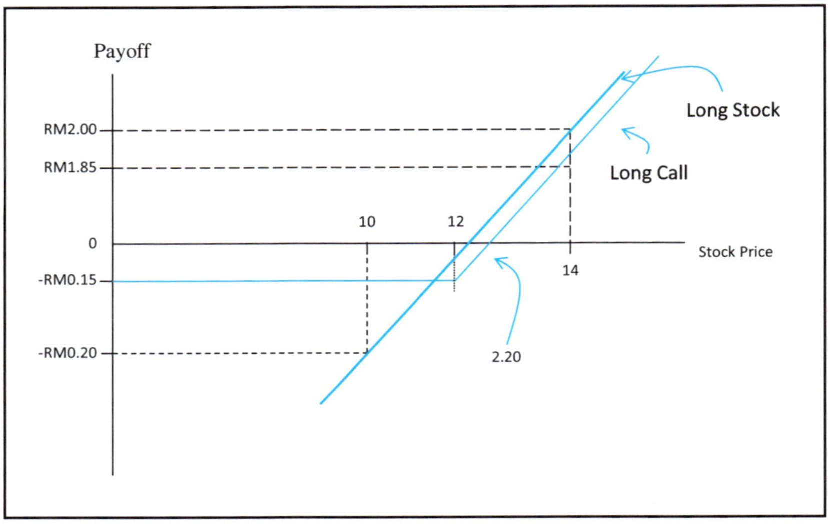

Figure 11.6a. Payoff to Long Stock and Long Call.

long stock at RM12 and long, RM12 Call @ 0.20. The first column shows a range of possible stock values at a given maturity date of the option. A stock obviously has no maturity date. The second and third columns show the resulting profits or losses for the stock position and the long call position.

Notice that if one plots the third column on a payoff diagram, the result will be exactly the call option payoff shown in Table 11.2. Figure 11.6(a) plots the three columns of Table 11.2 on to a payoff diagram.

Overall, there are three key differences to note. First, the long call position cuts off loses to a maximum of RM0.20, which is the premium. For a stock price below RM11.80, the stock position losses much more than the call position. Second, when prices rise, both positions make money, but the call position has a payoff that is always RM0.20 lower than that of the stock position. This difference, being the call premium incur for the option. The third difference is that, the long call position only makes money after the breakeven point is reached. The breakeven in this case is RM12.20 (Exercise price + Call premium). The option position is superior in that it enables one to participate in the upside rally of the stock, just as holding the stock would, but protects the downside by cutting off loses beyond RM0.20, in the event the stock declines in value.

(i) Short Stock versus Long Put position

Both the short stock and long put positions are consistent with a bearish expectation. Shorting a stock can be thought of as taking a position where one promises to deliver or sell the stock at a predetermined price on a future date. In this case, the predetermined date is the option maturity. Once again, to see the differences between the short stock and the long put positions, we examine the payoffs taken together. Table 11.2b shows the payoffs taken together. As earlier, the two positions are short stock at RM12.00 and Long, RM12.00 Put @ 0.15. Figure 11.6b shows the payoffs in terms of a diagram.

Table 11.2(b). Payoff to Long Put and Short Stock

Stock Price at Maturity	Payoff to Short Stock	Payoff to Long Put
9.50	2.50	2.35
10.00	2.00	1.85
10.50	1.50	1.35
11.00	1.00	0.85
11.50	0.50	0.35
11.85	0.15	0
12.00	0	(0.15)
12.50	(0.50)	(0.15)
13.00	(1.00)	(0.15)
13.50	(1.50)	(0.15)
14.00	(2.00)	(0.15)
14.50	(2.50)	(0.15)

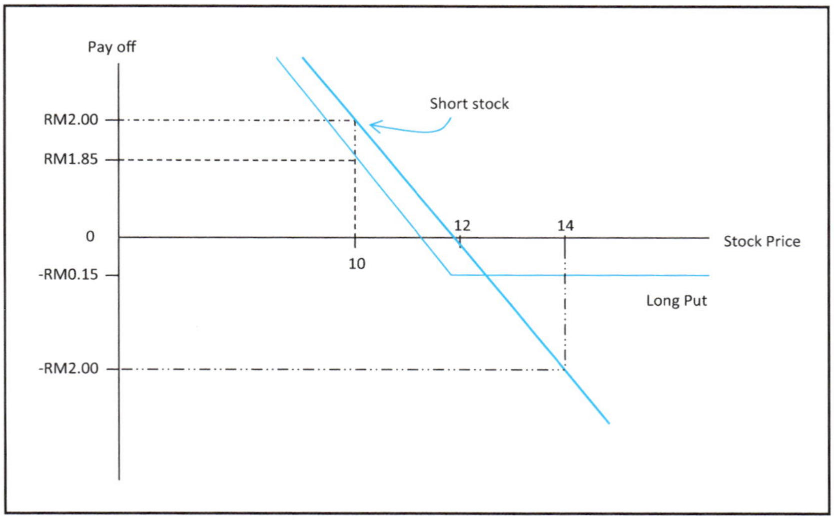

Figure 11.6b. Payoff to Short Stock versus Long Put Position.

Again, as in the previous case, we note the three key differences between option and stock positions. First, the long put position cuts off loses to a maximum RM0.15, which is the amount of the premium. The short stock position, however, has potentially unlimited losses. Second, when the underlying stock price falls, both positions gain; however, the profit from the long put position is always lower by RM0.15 relative to the stock position. The lower profit reflects the premium paid for the put. The final difference is that whereas the short stock begins to profit below RM12.00, the put position requires a further fall in the underlying stock to at least RM11.85 before it begins to make money, the RM11.85 price being the breakeven point for the put position (exercise price *minus* put premium).

(ii) Forward/Futures versus Option positions

Comparing the payoffs to a position in forwards/futures with that of options would provide results equivalent to that of the above stock versus option comparison. Earlier in the chapter, it was alluded that long stock and long forward/futures positions are equivalent in payoff terms as are the respective short positions. This arises from the fact that a forward or futures position is obligatory at maturity. For example, if one holds a long position in a forward or futures contract at maturity, the holder is *obliged* to purchase the underlying asset at the predetermined forward/futures price. If the underlying asset price is lower than the predetermined forward/futures price then an "implied" loss is made. On the other hand, if the underlying asset price is higher, an "implied" profit is made on the forward/futures position. As such, when viewed at maturity, the long forward/futures position has a payoff equivalent to that of the long stock position. A short forward/futures position and a short stock position have equivalent payoffs. Thus, comparing forward/futures positions with that of options would provide results equivalent to that of comparing stock and options positions.

Expectations and Option Positions

As we have seen from the above payoff diagrams, the payoff to positions at expiry or maturity of the options depends on the underlying asset's price performance. For example, the long call position makes money when the underlying asset moves up in price. On the other hand, the long put position makes money if the underlying asset's price falls. Thus, if one were to take naked[1] or speculative positions with options, the option strategy would clearly depend on the expectation of the underlying asset's performance.

Someone who is bullish about the underlying asset's performance would obviously choose a long call position. Such a position benefits if the expectation is correct. The long call position earns as much as long underlying (stock) position less the premium for prices above the exercise price. Someone who is bearish would exercise long put options. The long put position makes as much profit as the short underlying position but less the option premium for prices below the exercise price.

As expectations change, so do the option premiums. For example, if most investors are bullish about an underlying asset, few would want to write or sell calls on that asset. Since there will be many buyers but few sellers for the call, the premium rises in order to induce more sellers. The same logic applies when most investors are bearish about an underlying asset, the premiums on the put would rise (see Table 11.3).

Table 11.3. Expectations and Options Premiums

Expectation of Underlying	Demand for Option		Premium	
Asset Price	Calls	Puts	Calls	Puts
Bullish	Increase	Decrease	Increase	Decrease
Bearish	Decrease	Increase	Decrease	Increase

11.9.5 *The Pricing of Options*

The appropriate price or value of an option is essentially its correct premium. When options are traded, it is the premium that changes. There are several models available to price options. Among these are the Binomial, Trinomial, Lattice, Finite Difference, Monte Carlo models, and so on. However, the most common and possibly most user-friendly is the Black–Scholes Option Pricing Model (BSOPM). Today, most options traders use the Binomial Model for pricing American-style options and the BSOPM for European-style options. For their work on the BSOPM, its authors, Fisher Black and Myron Scholes, won the Nobel Prize for Economics in 1995. To determine a Call option's price or premium, the BSOPM requires five inputs. For example, in valuing a Call option on a stock, the five input variables would be:

(i) Current Stock price (S)
(ii) The exercise price (k)

[1]A naked or uncovered position is a single position with no offsetting positions.

(iii) Time to maturity (t)
(iv) Risk free interest rate (r)
(v) Estimate of the stock's price (σ, std. dev.)

The Black–Scholes option pricing model for a call option is as follows:

$$C = S.N(d_1) - Ke^{-rt}{\cdot}N(d_2)$$

$$d1 = \frac{\ln(S/K) + [r + (\sigma^2/2)]T}{\sigma\sqrt{T}}$$

$$d_2 = d_1 - \sigma\sqrt{T}$$

where

T = time to expiration (as % of year)
e^{rt} = exponential function of rf and T
$N(.)$ = cumulative standard normal distribution function
ln (S/K) = natural logarithm of S/K

Calculating option prices with the BSOPM is a three-step process. First, determine the values of d_1 and d_2 as shown above. Next, using the cumulative normal distribution table, find the values of $N(d_1)$ and $N(d_2)$. The third step would be to plug in the values of $N(d_1)$, $N(d_2)$ and the other variables into the model and solve. The example below illustrates the process (see Box 11.1).

Box 11.1. Illustration: Using the BSOPM to Determine the Value Call Option

ABAC Corporation's stock is currently selling for RM19.60. A 90-day call option on the stock with a RM20 exercise price is being offered to you. Suppose the stock price volatility is 40% and the risk-free interest rate is 8%. What should the call option's premium be?

Given the information above, the variables are as follows:

S_o = RM19.60
K = RM 20
t = 90 days (0.25 as percentage of year)
r = 8%
σ = 40%

Step 1: Calculate d_1 and d_2

$$d_1 = \frac{\ln(19.6/20) + (0.08 + (0.4^2/2))0.25}{0.4 \times (\sqrt{0.25})}$$

$d_1 = (0.0198)/0.20 = \mathbf{0.099}$

$d_2 = 0.099 - 0.20 = \mathbf{-0.101}$

Step 2: Determine $N(d_1)$ and $N(d_2)$ from table:

$N(d_1) = 0.5398$
$N(d_2) = 0.4602$

(*Continued*)

Box 11.1. ***(Continued)***

Step 3: Plug in values and solve

$$C = \text{RM}19.60\ (0.5398) - \text{RM}20^{*}\ e^{-0.08\times0.25*}\ (0.4602)$$
$$= \text{RM}10.58 - \text{RM}\ 19.60\ (0.4602)$$
$$= \text{RM}\ 10.58 - \text{RM}9.02$$
$$= \text{RM}1.56$$

The correct premium or fair value for the 90-day call option would be RM1.56.

For a given underlying stock, the same exercise price and maturity, it is obvious from the payoff diagrams above that the Put option has payoff opposite to that of the Call option. In other words, when the Call option is profitable to exercise, the Put would not be and vice versa. Thus, the BSOPM for valuing a Put option is essentially a rearrangement of the Call option equation above. The BSOPM for a valuing a Put option is as follows;

$$P = Ke - rt{\cdot}N(-d_2) - S{\cdot}N(-d_1)$$

Again, the same three steps would have to be followed. Intuitively, the minus signs before d_1 and d_2 can be attributed to the fact the Put has a negative slope (long position), whereas the long Call position has a positive slope. In other words, while the Call option gains when underlying stock price rises, the Put gains only when the underlying stock value falls.

11.10 Interest Rate Swaps

Interest rate swaps (IRSs) belong to a category of derivatives known as *swaps*. Swaps are customized bilateral transactions in which the parties agree to exchange cash flows at fixed periodic intervals, based on an underlying asset. Being customized, swaps are over-the-counter (OTC) instruments. Depending on the kind of underlying asset, there are different kinds of swaps. For example, a currency swap is one where parties exchange a cash flow in one currency for cash flows in another currency. A commodity swap is one where parties exchange cash flows based on either a commodities index or the total return of a commodity in exchange for a return based on a market yield. Equity swaps constitute an exchange of cash flows based on different equity indices. An interest rate swap (IRS), on the other hand, is a transaction in which the parties exchange cash flows based on two different interest rates.

In its most common form, a fixed-for-floating swap is where one party pays an amount based on a fixed interest rate whereas the other party pays in exchange, an amount based on a floating interest rate. The size of the payment is determined by multiplying the interest rate with the "notional principal". The notional principal is the principal amount on which interest payments are calculated. The notional principal remains unchanged over the maturity of the swap. Typically, in an IRS, cash flows are swapped at fixed predetermined intervals over the tenor of the agreement. The fixed intervals, known as reset periods, may be monthly, quarterly, semi-annually, etc., whereas the tenor or maturity of the swap may be five or 10 years. Figure 11.7 outlines the cash flows involved in a

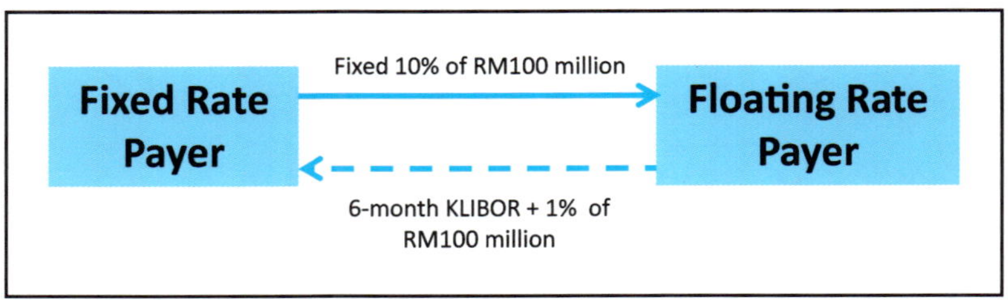

Figure 11.7. A Fixed-For-Floating Interest Rate Swap.

fixed-for-floating IRS of five-year maturity and RM100 million notional principal. If the reset frequency is six months, then a total of 10 cash flow swaps will occur for a swap of five-year maturity. The fixed-rate payer will pay an annualized 10% fixed rate while the floating-rate payer, will pay six-month KLIBOR + 1%.

The cash flow payment based on the interest rates will occur once every six months. Since the payments are to be made simultaneously, often the cash flows are netted such that only a single payment occurs. As to who pays whom, it would obviously depend on which rate is higher. If the floating rate, six-month KLIBOR + 1%, is higher than the fixed rate of 10%, the floating-rate payer pays the difference. If the floating rate is lower than 10%, then the fixed-rate payer pays the difference. To see how this works, we examine two scenarios (see Box 11.2): first, if the six-month KLIBOR is at 6% at reset period, and a second scenario, where the six-month KLIBOR is at 11.2%.

Box 11.2. Illustration: Payoffs to IRS at Maturity

Scenario 1: Six-month KLIBOR = 6%

The payment obligation for each party is as follows:
Fixed Rate Payer: [10% × RM100,000,000] /2 = RM 5,000,000
Floating Rate Payer: [(6% + 1%) × RM 100,000,000] /2 = RM3,500,000

Since the fixed rate payer's obligation is higher by RM1.5 million, he pays this amount. The netted cash flow will be:

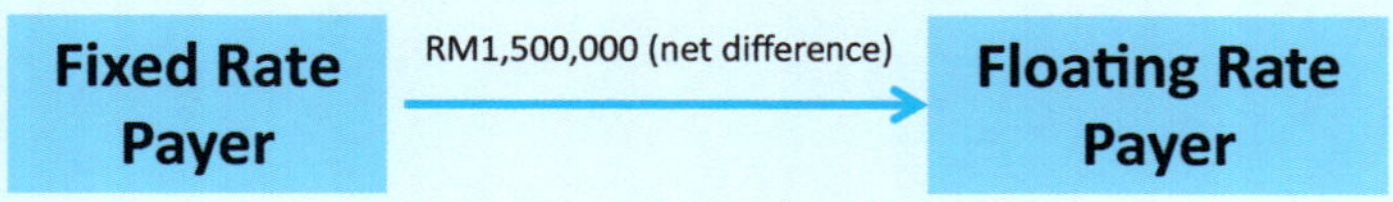

Scenario 2: Six-month KLIBOR = 11.2%

With changed floating interest rate, the payment obligation would now be:
Fixed Rate Payer: [10% × RM100,000,000] /2 = RM500,000
Floating Rate Payer: [11.2% + 1%) × RM100,000,000] /2 = RM6,100,000

Here, since the floating rate payer's obligation is higher, he has to pay the fixed rate pay the net amount of RM1,100,000. Now the cash flow will be:

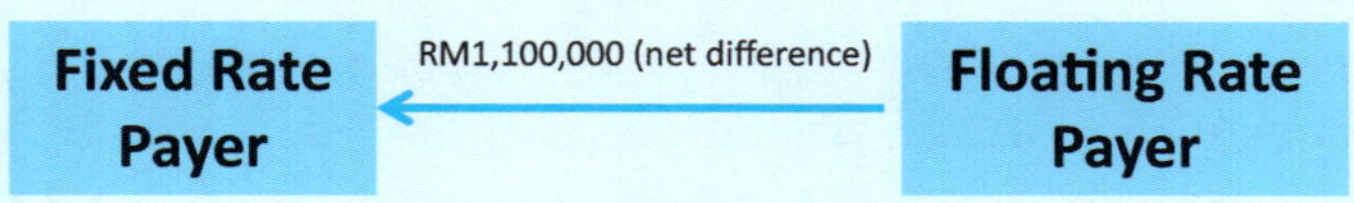

There are two factors to note from Box 11.2. First, the notional principal is never exchanged. Second, only the net difference is paid at the beginning of the reset period. Thus, at the beginning of any reset period, there will be a cash flow if the two rates are unequal. Since the fixed-rate payer's obligation is known upfront, it is changes in the floating interest rate that will determine the direction and quantum of payments (see Table 11.4).

Table 11.4. Swap Terminology.

Fixed Rate Payer	The counterparty in a swap agreement who pays based on a fixed interest rate.
Floating Rate Payer	The counterparty who pays based on a floating interest rate.
Reset Frequency	The time interval over which the floating rate is reviewed and reset.
Reference Rate	The market interest rate on which the floating rate payer's payment will be based typically an interbank rate like KLIBOR, LIBOR, T-bill rate, etc.
Notional Principal	The principal amount on which interest payment amounts are determined. Notional amount is never exchanged, only the interest amounts based on it.

Interest rate swaps grew out of parallel or back-to-back loans and currency swaps that multinational firms had used in the 1970s to access blocked funds or circumvent capital controls. Thus, the currency swap is the predecessor to IRS. Since its introduction in 1981, IRS has become extremely popular. Transacted volume, measured by total notional amount, exceeds US$50 trillion according to the International Swaps and Derivatives Association (ISDA). That IRS has become so popular in developed markets, despite being an OTC instrument, has to do with the initiatives of ISDA, which has streamlined and standardized much of the paperwork for IRS, making the process much more simplified and thereby incurring lower costs. Though the fixed-for-floating, or *plain-vanilla swap* as it is often known, is the most common form, there are other variants. *A basis swap* is one where both rates are floating and parties try to lock-in or profit from differences in swap spreads. *A forward-starting swap* enables parties to lock-in current favorable yields for financing issues that will be carried out at a future date. An *amortizing swap* is one where the notional principal reduces over time, while a swap with an *inverse floater* is one where the floating rate is negatively correlated with a benchmark reference interest rate. Finally, there are also swaps with embedded options. Being customized products, any structural form or variant is possible as long as it is mutually agreed by the two parties. Though an intermediary is not necessary, it is very common. Intermediaries are usually merchant or commercial banks. Insurance firms too are common intermediaries. Intermediaries play one of two roles, which are either as a *broker* or *market maker*. As a broker, an intermediary designs the swap and collects a fee. As a market maker, the intermediary becomes the counterparty. Thus, they are not intermediaries in the strict sense. As market makers, some banks stand ready to undertake and enter into a swap transaction.

11.11 The Main Players in Derivative Markets

As is the case with other financial markets, there are thousands of institutions and traders involved in derivative markets. However, they could all be classified into three broad categories, namely (i) *hedgers*, (ii) *arbitrageurs*, and (iii) *speculators*. If hedging is the *raison d'être* for derivative markets, then obviously hedgers would be major players. Hedgers use derivative markets to manage or reduce risk. They are typically businesses that use derivatives to offset exposures resulting from their business activities.

The second category of players — arbitrageurs — use derivatives to engage in arbitrage. Arbitrage is the process of trying to take advantage of price differences between markets. Arbitrageurs closely follow quoted prices of the same asset in different markets looking for price divergences. Should the prices be divergent enough to make profits, they would buy on the market with the lower price and sell on the market where the quoted price is higher. Since most financial markets are integrated by computer networks, arbitrage activity boils down to hitting the right keystrokes. As arbitrage opportunities can quickly disappear, quick action is needed. Thus, institutions (i.e., commercial banks, investment banks, currency dealers, etc.) that engage in arbitrage activities invest huge amounts of money in global computer networks and telecommunications equipment. Note that arbitrage opportunities also arise from distorted government policies that fix prices at a given level. For instance, near-zero interest rates in Japan led to the yen carry trade whereby arbitrageurs borrow in yen and lend in other currencies. Similarly, near-zero interest rates create arbitrage commodities in asset and commodity markets.

In addition to merely watching the prices of the same asset in different markets, arbitrageurs can also arbitrage between different product markets, for e.g., between the spot and futures markets or between futures and option markets or even between all three markets. It is in this type of arbitrage that sophisticated financial engineering techniques come into play.

The final categories of players are the speculators. Speculators, as the name suggests, merely speculate. They take positions in assets or markets *without* taking offsetting positions. For example, if they expect a certain asset to fall in value, they would short (sell) the asset. Should their expectation come true, they would make profits from having shorted the asset. On the other hand, should the price increase instead, they would make losses on their short position. Speculators therefore expose themselves to risk and hope to profit from taking on the risk.

Having described the activities of the three major categories of players, it would be pertinent to ask if these activities are useful from a societal viewpoint. Hedging is undoubtedly useful. Aside from enabling businesses to plan better, the reduction in fluctuation of their product prices can help reduce costs and thereby provide a tangible benefit to society. Consumers would benefit since producers, being able to hedge, would need to charge lower risk premiums. Societal benefits from arbitrage activity are much less direct. The benefits accrue from the proper realignment of prices. Arbitrageurs, by means of their activities, ensure that prices in the different markets (spot, futures, and options) do not diverge from each other. As product prices are perhaps the most important signal in market economies, proper price discovery has serious implications on resource allocation. Arbitrage activity enhances the price discovery process. For example, arbitrage between markets in different countries "internationalizes" product prices, which forces less efficient producers to enhance productivity in order to remain in business. Arbitrage also helps reduce the distortionary effects of government regulation or intervention.

Speculative activity tends to hurt more than help. The evils of speculative activities are well documented. While speculative activity is harmful, there are some benefits. First, speculative trading increases trading volume. This in turn provides two benefits: (i) the increased trading volume reduces transaction costs, thereby making it cheaper for genuine hedgers to hedge, and (ii) there is an increase in liquidity. As a result, markets become deeper and broader, thereby reducing execution risks. Finally, the fact that speculators are willing to take risks means that hedgers have someone to pass on their risks. Despite the benefits, it will be difficult to make a case in favor of speculation. Speculative activity can be disruptive, and regulators have often been unable to keep such activity under control. This has largely to do with the fact that it is a very fine line that separates hedging and arbitrage from speculation.

11.12 Commodity versus Financial Derivatives

Today, derivative contracts are available on several types of underlying assets. In developed markets, such as in the US, futures and options are available on several categories of assets. Among the underlying assets are agricultural commodities, metals, energy, currencies, stock indexes, etc. Table 11.5 shows examples of some of the underlying assets within each category:

Table 11.5. Underlying Assets, Derivative Category, and Type.

Category	Asset Type
Physicals	
• Agricultural Commodities	— Wheat, Soybean, Crude Palm Oil, Citrus, Coffee Beans, Corn, Rice, etc.
• Metals and Energy	— Gasoline, Gas Oil, Propane, etc. — Gold, Silver, Copper.
Financials	
• Foreign Currencies	— US$, ¥en, DM, Can $, Sfr, Eurodollars, Euros.
• Equity and Bond Futures	— T-bills, T-bonds. — KLIBOR futures, T-bill futures, etc. — Various Stock Indexes.

Broadly speaking, these underlying assets can be divided into two categories, namely *physicals* and *financials*. All commodity derivatives such as those on agricultural commodities, metals, energy, etc., which have a physical underlying asset, have what is known as actual or physical settlements. This means that, on maturity of the derivative, there is actual physical delivery of the underlying asset.

Unlike the commodity derivatives, which call for physical delivery at maturity, financial derivatives such as foreign currencies, stock indices, and interest rate derivatives have what is termed as *cash settlement*. Cash settlement means that the buyer does not receive the actual underlying asset but the monetary equivalent of the asset. Cash settlement happens either because the underlying asset does not exist in a tangible form (interest rate derivatives) or because physical settlement could be very cumbersome, for e.g., in the case of stock index futures. So, in the case of cash-settled contracts, the parties simply "take out" the money left in their margin accounts, profits and losses having been adjusted to these accounts.

11.13 Derivative Markets and the Role of the Clearinghouse

The clearinghouse is a vital ingredient of any well-functioning derivatives market. As the name suggests, a clearinghouse has the main objective of *clearing* trades. Simply put, clearing trades means identifying who has bought, who has sold, what amount, who needs to pay, who needs to deliver, to whom should delivery be to, etc. Though mundane, these are highly essential functions. Problems with any of these basic functions could seriously affect the integrity and credibility of the system and potentially lead to systemic risk.

A clearinghouse's functions can be broadly categorized into two basic areas: (i) record keeping and (ii) risk management. In its first function as record keeper, the clearinghouse registers all trades that take place on the exchange. When a customer does a trade, his broker has to clear the trade with the clearinghouse. The broker does it directly if the broker is a clearing member; otherwise, the broker clears through another broker who must be a clearing member. Thus, every transaction that takes place on an exchange ultimately gets channeled for registration with the clearinghouse. Aside from being able to record the positions taken by customers or traders, this activity forms the basis by which the clearinghouse is able to carry out its second function, risk management. There are two levels of risk that the clearinghouse has to manage. The first is the risk faced by clients or traders. Notice that when a customer takes a long or short position, he or she is faced with counterparty risk. That is, the risk that the other party to the transaction might default. By means of the *novation principle*, the clearinghouse imposes itself as the intermediary in every transaction done through the exchange and sent to it for registration. Basically, the clearinghouse substitutes itself as the buyer to seller and the seller to every buyer. This substitution by the clearinghouse is a key facility in enhancing liquidity since it enables buyers and sellers to enter and exit markets easily. Since the clearinghouse guarantees the transaction upon registration of the trade, customers eliminate their counterparty risk.

Now that the clearinghouse has guaranteed every transaction, it has to make sure that neither of the two parties to any derivatives transaction will default. It does this by means of the *margining* and *marking to market process*. The margining process will be discussed in detail in Chapter 12. Both the novation and margining processes are intended to ensure the integrity of transactions; the clearinghouse, however, has to further ensure the financial integrity of the intermediaries, i.e., the brokers, through whom customers trade. The clearinghouse does this by requiring and monitoring performance bonds from its clearing members. The clearing members would require such bonds from the non-clearing brokers who clear trades through them.

11.14 Applications: Using Derivatives to Manage Risk

Having seen how derivative instruments work, we now examine how these instruments can be used in managing risks. Recall from our discussion earlier that while derivatives can be used easily for arbitrage and speculative purposes, the *raison d'être* of these instruments is *risk management*. We had also discussed that one would use different derivative instruments to manage different types of risks. For example, to manage price risk associated with commodities, we would use commodity derivatives for exchange rate risk, currency derivatives, and so on. In this section, we examine three different types of risks and explore how three different categories of derivative instruments could be used in managing the risks. The three types of risks are: (i) equity risk, (ii) interest rate risk, and (iii) exchange rate or currency risk. We will use an option to manage equity risk, an interest rate swap for interest rate risk and a forward or futures contract to manage exchange rate risk.

Box 11.3. Spot, Futures, and Competitive Strategy

A *Bloomberg* report in April 2017 argues that OPEC's attempt to curtail US shale drillers by increasing output and thereby causing spot prices to fall has had no impact whatsoever on shale oil production, the reason being that the US shale oil producers had locked in their revenues by hedging with oil futures for the rest of the decade. The shale oil producers had undertaken anticipatory hedges by shorting oil futures contracts equivalent to their expected output levels. As such, OPEC's actions, which had caused spot prices to fall 14%, would have had no effect because the fall in spot prices would have been exactly offset by the gains in their short futures position. It appears that the shale oil producers had learned their lessons from the oil price rout of 2014–2016 to better manage their price risks. The real loser in this episode would be the OPEC members, whose attempt to use pricing to curtail the competition had failed. The price cut would have reduced their contribution margin and revenue but not their market share.

The entire episode points to a key fact about the use of derivative instruments such as forwards, futures, options, and swaps. Aside from hedging, these instruments can be a strategic competitive tool. For example, an importer who had taken a long (buy) call option position would have a huge competitive advantage against competitors if the currency in which the imported product is denominated appreciates against home currency. The option position enables him to undercut prices and gain market share against unhedged competitors. Similarly, an exporter who has shorted currency futures or bought currency puts would be able to gain market share at the expense of unhedged competitors by keeping foreign currency price the same even as the foreign depreciates. The gains from the derivative position offset the losses from the depreciating foreign currency. In the episode above, OPEC could not kill off a marginal competitor because that competitor had protected their revenue from falling spot prices. Revenue had been detached from spot prices through hedging. By way of such hedging, the US shale oil industry has changed the industry's dynamics. Though small, they need not live at the mercy of OPEC.

That derivatives can do all these is not obvious to many. For far too long now, a majority of *Shari'ah* scholars have brushed aside derivatives as mere tools of speculation. Such disdain not only exposes Islamic banking and finance to the vagaries of international financial markets but also prevents them from building barriers against many risks. Risk management, therefore, continues to be the soft underbelly of Islamic finance, this, despite the fact that the preservation of wealth is a key *Shari'ah* requirement. An obvious case in point is risk management at Islamic mutual funds. While conventional mutual funds have an array of derivative instruments like, Equity Index futures, Index Options, Single Stock Futures, Equity swaps, etc., with which to hedge short-term market fluctuations, an Islamic mutual fund manager has no equivalent *Shari'ah*-compliant instrument with which to hedge. Despite the availability of *Shari'ah*-compliant equity indices for at least a decade, the next logical step of a *Shari'ah*-compliant index futures or options has not happened. A key reason for this missing link is the fear that *Shari'ah* scholars have about their potential use for speculation. While there is no denying that speculation accounts for a substantial portion of derivative volume, prohibiting their use has serious costs. Given the kind of equity market volatility we have seen in recent times, the inability to hedge against such volatility is a serious handicap. In the absence of equity derivatives, the only way a fund manager can get protection against expected market turbulence is by liquidating his position fully or partially and then returning when the turbulence has passed. For a fund manager, this would be an extremely high transaction cost strategy. Worse, when all fund managers hit the exits at the same time, a self-fulfilling crisis occurs. Such collective action would serve to accentuate market fluctuations. The availability of derivatives would enable managers to ride out storms by insuring their portfolio values by hedging for the period of the expected turbulence. Thus, it should be no surprise that numerous academic studies have found equity markets to have become more stable, not less, post derivative introduction.

Source: Adapted from author's op-ed piece in *Derin Ekonomi*.

11.14.1 *Illustration: Managing Equity Risk Using Options*

Hedging a Long Stock Position (Portfolio Insurance)

The most obvious need for a hedge arises when one has a long stock or long underlying position. With a long stock position, one is exposed to downward movements in the stock's price. An increase in the stock's price is favorable. Thus, an investor with a long stock position would want to protect downside risks while keeping the upside profit potential as much as possible. In order to achieve this, the investor should combine the long stock position with an option position that would profit if the stock goes down in value. The idea is that, should the stock fall in value, the losses on the stock will be offset by the gains on the option position. On the other hand, should the stock rise in value, the option which would be out of the money would be left unexercised. Such a strategy gives the investor the best of both worlds; he is protected from price falls but keeps intact the upside profit potential.

In determining the appropriate option position, the investor begins by asking, what option position would make money if the underlying asset goes down in value? Recall from earlier that there are two option positions that would gain when the underlying asset goes down in value. These are the short call position and the long put position. Clearly, the short call position will only provide downside protection to the extent of the premium received. Furthermore, the short call will mean that the upside potential on the stock cannot be realized by the investor since a rise in the underlying stock price would mean that the purchaser of the call would exercise, and the investor, once assigned, will have to give up the stock at the exercise price of the call option he sold. Therefore, the logical hedge choice would be to use the long put position. This strategy of hedging stock positions with put options is a popular strategy. Portfolio managers quite routinely use this strategy to protect their portfolio of stocks from short-term fluctuations by going long index put options. Thus, this strategy is often commonly referred to as "Portfolio Insurance". We examine a numerical example of this strategy next.

Box 11.4. Illustration: A Portfolio Insurance Strategy

Suppose you had just gone long (purchased) one lot of Syarikat XYZ's stock at a price of RM15.00 each, for a total investment of RM15,000. You believe this stock has long-term potential but wish to protect yourself from any short-term downside movement in price. Suppose three-month at the money put options, with a strike price equal to RM15.00, on the XYZ stock are being quoted at RM0.15 each or RM150 per lot (RM0.15 × 1,000). The appropriate option strategy to hedge the long stock position would be:

Long 1 lot, 3 month, XYZ Put @ RM0.15.

Combined Position: • Long 1 lot, XYZ Stock @ RM15
• Long 1, three-month XYZ Put @ RM0.15

Table 11.6 shows the payoff to the long stock, long put, and the combined position for a given range of stock prices at option maturity in three months.

Table 11.6. Payoff to Hedged Long Stock Position.

Stock Price at Maturity	Value of long stock position	Profit/Loss to Long Put position @ 0.15	Value of combined position at maturity
8.00	8,000	6,850	14,850
12.00	12,000	2,850	14,850
15.00	15,000	(150)	14,850
18.00	18,000	(150)	17,850
20.00	20,000	(150)	19,850

(*Continued*)

Box 11.4. (*Continued*)

Notice that at prices below RM15.00, the long put becomes profitable and offsets the loss in the long stock position. For example, at a stock price of RM8.00, the long stock position is worth RM8,000, a loss of RM7,000 from the original stock value of RM15,000. However, this loss is almost fully offset by the gain from the put options. The profit of RM6,850 from the put is arrived at as follows:

Proceeds from Exercise of Puts	=	RM15,000
Less: Cost of Stock Delivered on Exercise	=	(RM 8,000)
Less: Premium Paid for Puts	=	(RM 150)
Profit from Puts		....
	=	RM 6,850
		======

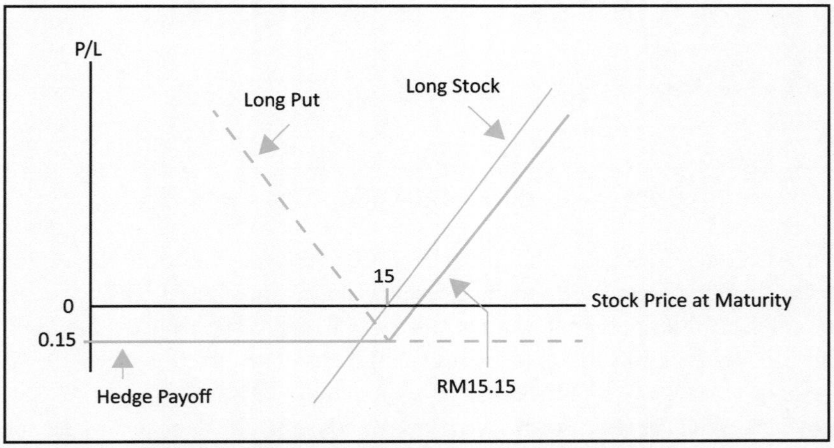

Figure 11.8. Payoff profile to portfolio insurance.

The dotted line in Figure 11.8 represents the payoff to the long stock position, the dashed line shows the payoff of the long put, while the bold line represents the payoff of the overall hedged position. (These lines, when multiplied by 1,000 for one lot of stocks, would represent Columns 2, 3 and 4, respectively, of Table 11.3).

Notice that the risk profile of the combined hedge position is identical to that of a call option, i.e., a RM15.00 Call @ 0.15 would have the same payoff profile. (*Note*: one could derive the call payoff by subtracting RM15,000 which is the current value of the one lot of stocks from Column (4) of Table 11.2).

11.14.2 *Managing Interest Rate Risks Using Interest Rate Swaps*

In understanding how an interest rate swap (IRS) can help in managing rate risks, we examine a situation where a company which has borrowed at floating interest rates and therefore needs protection against rising rates. By way of an IRS, the borrower should be able to "lock-in" a borrowing interest rate. The next illustration shows how this could be done (see Box 11.5).

Box 11.5. Illustration: Hedging against Rising Interest Rates

Suppose a borrower, Syarikat ABC, has a five-year RM10 million loan from Maybank. Maybank charges interest based on a six-month KLIBOR + 2%, payable semi-annually. Syarikat ABC obviously has interest rate exposure. The firm's funding costs will increase as the six-month KLIBOR rises. How can the firm hedge? Using a three-month KLIBOR futures contract

(*Continued*)

Box 11.5. (*Continued*)

would only partially solve matters. The futures contract would only lock-in rates over the next three months. While a rollover strategy can be used, the rates locked-in will be progressively high as spot interest rates rise. A second problem with using interest rate futures is that most of the distant maturity contracts would be inactive. Given these circumstances, the logical way for Syarikat ABC to manage the rate risk would be through an IRS. Syarikat ABC should enter the swap as the fixed-rate payer and floating-rate receiver. If the notional principal and reset frequency are structured to match the underlying position that it has with Maybank, then Syarikat ABC would have perfectly hedged its interest rate risk (see Figure 11.9).

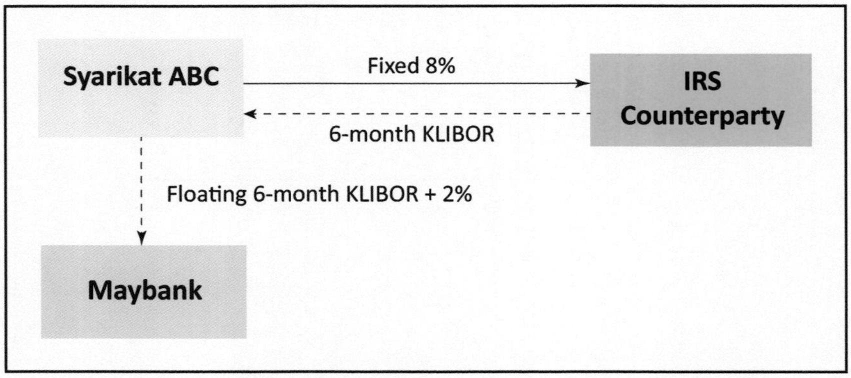

Figure 11.9. Hedging against rising rate with IRS.

In the IRS, Syarikat ABC pays an annualized fixed rate of 8% every six months on RM10 million notional.

In exchange, it receives a cash flow equivalent to the prevailing spot six-month KLIBOR rate on RM10 million notional.

Syarikat ABC protects itself from rising interest rates because its increased payments to Maybank will be offset by the increased payments it receives from the counterparty as interest rates rise. Since both the receivable from the counterparty and the payable to Maybank are referenced on a six-month KLIBOR, Syarikat ABC's inflows from the swap offset the outflow to Maybank. With the IRS, Syarikat ABC has effectively turned its floating rate payable into a fixed rate one, effectively a 10% annualized fixed rate loan. (8% to swap counterparty and 2% spread over KLIBOR to Maybank).

11.14.3 *Managing Foreign Exchange Risk with Currency Derivatives*

To see how currency derivatives could be used in managing currency risk, we work through an example of a Malaysian importer and exporter. For simplicity, we assume the foreign currency payable of the importer and the receivable amount of the exporter is the same. We will examine how these companies can use forwards, futures and options to hedge their exposure.

Box 11.6. Illustration: Managing Currency Risk Using Forward Contracts

Malaysian Importer: Cadbury Malaysia Berhad imported chocolates from Cadbury Schweppes UK. The invoice amount is £1 million and is payable in 90 days.

Malaysian Exporter IOI Corp. Bhd., a large Malaysian palm oil producer, exported a shipment of crude palm oil to Unilever UK. The invoice amount is £1 million, payable in 90 days.

In this example, both Malaysian companies have currency exposure. The importer, Cadbury Malaysia Berhad, who has to pay in foreign currency, would be afraid of the foreign currency appreciating against the Malaysian Ringgit. The exporter, IOI Corp. Bhd., which is to receive foreign currency payment, would be afraid of the foreign currency depreciating against the ringgit. If the risk is not hedged, the importer, Cadbury Malaysia, could lose due to currency

(*Continued*)

Box 11.6. ***(Continued)***

exchange if the British Pound appreciates against the Malaysian Ringgit. This is because an appreciating Pound would increase the Ringgit costs for Cadbury, while a depreciating Pound would reduce the Ringgit revenue for IOI Corp. Bhd.

Suppose today's quotation of the MYR/£ exchange rate is as follows:

Spot rate MYR/£: RM 6.90 per £

90 day forward rate: MYR/£: RM 7.10 per £

In using a forward contract, Cadbury Malaysia, which has to pay in pounds, would go "long" pounds and "short" ringgit. The counterparty would typically be a bank. Figure 11.10a shows the transaction or cash flow that would be exchanged on Day 90 (contract maturity).

On Day $t = 90$ (maturity date)

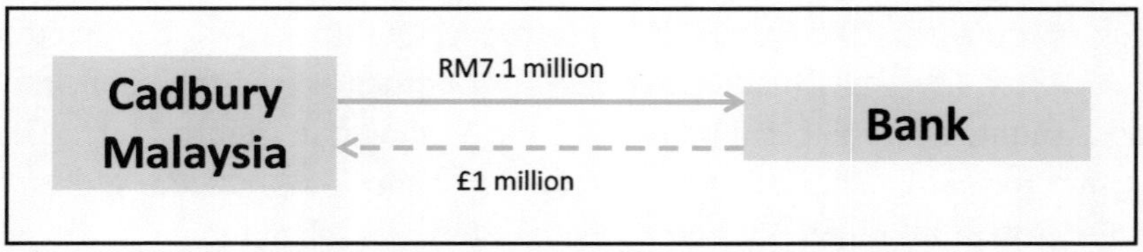

Figure 11.10. (**a**) Importer: Long £, Short MYR.

Though the exchange of currency takes place on Day 90, Cadbury Malaysia would be fully hedged against fluctuations of the £/MYR rate from the day it enters the forward contract. Once, the documentation of the contract is completed (on Day 0), Cadbury Malaysia would "lock-in" its ringgit cost of the imports, the ringgit cost being RM7.1 million, which is the payable amount due in pounds multiplied by the 90-day forward rate.

In the case of the exporter, IOI Corp. Bhd., the appropriate hedge strategy would be to short pounds in the forward contract (see Figure 11.10b). In this case, the cash flows on the maturity day would be as follows:

On Day $t = 90$, maturity day

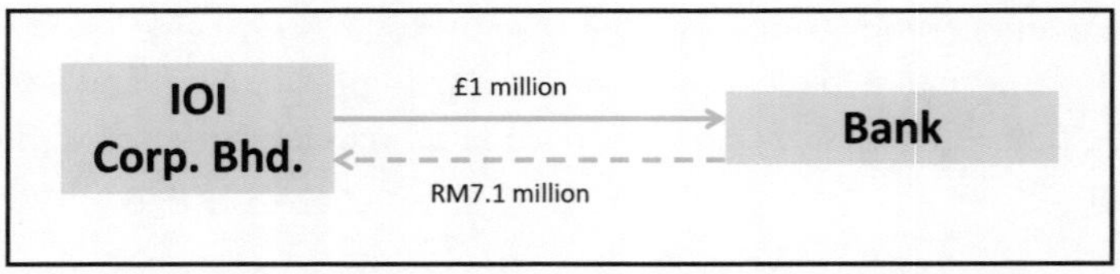

Figure 11.10. (**b**) Exporter: Short £, Long MYR.

In this case, IOI Corp. Bhd. gets to "lock-in" its ringgit revenue of RM7.1 million by going into the forward contract.

11.15 What Derivative to Use?

We have thus far examined the mechanics of forward, futures, options, and swap contracts. We have seen in detail how these instruments work to protect against risk and exposure. When faced with a choice of several available derivative instruments, one would have to decide which instrument to use. Typically, when we have an underlying exposure, we would need to use only one of the available instruments to hedge the exposure. So, how do we decide which is the best instrument? As with most things, the decision involves trade-offs and a number of considerations. Availability and ease of use would be a key consideration while transaction cost and liquidity of the instrument would be another. The "fit" between ones' needs and the standardized features of a contract is another. For example, while forwards may be cheap, one may not find a bank willing to be the counterparty if one does not have an established credit track record. While options are highly flexible and advantageous compared to forwards and futures, they are certainly more expensive. Finally, while OTC instruments such as forwards and swaps allow for customization, one would be faced with counterparty risk and issues of pricing when using them. So, in deciding on the appropriate instrument to use, we need to balance cost, convenience, and other issues.

11.16 Overview of Global Derivatives Trading

As with most other financial innovations, the introduction and trading of derivatives took place in the US, particularly in Chicago. Chicago, which is located in the mid-western grain belt, is well known for its commodities exchanges. Three of Chicago's exchanges, the Chicago Mercantile Exchange (CME), the Chicago Board of Trade (CBOT), and the Chicago Board Options Exchange (CBOE), are among the world's oldest and largest derivatives exchanges. Today, the trading of derivatives has spread globally, with derivative exchanges having taken root in Europe and Asia. In fact, some of the more recently established exchanges such as Eurex, a Swiss-German Exchange, have seen such tremendous growth in trading volume. Global trading of derivatives received a major boost when the Chicago Mercantile Exchange (CME) introduced Globex, a global electronic trading platform for derivatives. Globex (see Box 11.7) has made possible cross-border, round-the-clock trading in derivatives. The growth in global traded volume over the period 2001 to 2017, is shown in Figure 11.11. The very rapid growth seen from 2001 to 2008 came to a stop with the onset of the US subprime-induced, global financial crisis in 2008. Following a sharp drop, growth in traded volume appears to have stabilized.

Box 11.7. Derivatives Trading Goes Global via Globex

The derivatives market received a major boost in the early 1990s when Chicago Mercantile Exchange (CME) launched Globex in 1992. It was the first electronic trading platform for futures contracts. This electronic platform extended the accessibility of the exchange's products to market participants, regardless of their location. It was an innovation that revolutionized trading technology. Physical trading was conducted on trading floors, with trading "pits" designated for different derivative products or different maturities. Brokers or their representatives (known as Locals) executed customer orders by trading among themselves via a complex array of hand signals. While such physical trading brought a sense of excitement and urgency to trading, the system was fraught with human errors and other problems. Transaction costs too were higher relative to electronic trading. With globalization and evolving trading dynamics and strategies, Globex caught the fancy of investors, and a decade later, on October 19, 2004, the one billionth electronic transaction was recorded on Globex. Today, approximately 80% of the derivatives trade on CME is executed via Globex.

With the introduction of new classes of derivatives, CME's Globex expanded the horizon by including numerous other options and future contracts on underlyings as diverse as interest rates, equity indexes, foreign exchange, agricultural commodities, energy, metals, weather, real estate, and environmental commodities. Today, Globex has also expanded the derivatives market beyond national boundaries, with accessibility of over 100 countries to its derivative contracts. This has brought in liquidity, standardization, and a round-the-clock market for derivative market players. Though technology and economic logic would justify migration to fully electronic systems, entrenched interests have ensured that physical trading, through brokers, remains. As a result, products traded on Globex have evolved into three categories:

- Side-by-Side contracts trade for a portion of the day simultaneously with open outcry
- Electronic-Only contracts that trade only electronically
- After-Hours Electronic contracts that are traded electronically after the product stops trading via open outcry.

Malaysia's Bursa Malaysia stepped up as one of the pioneer emerging market countries to move its derivatives contracts, comprising commodity, financial, and equity futures to the Globex platform in September 2010. Following the move, foreign participation in Malaysian derivatives rose 57% in 2011, a sure sign of how global trading platforms can enhance liquidity in domestic markets.

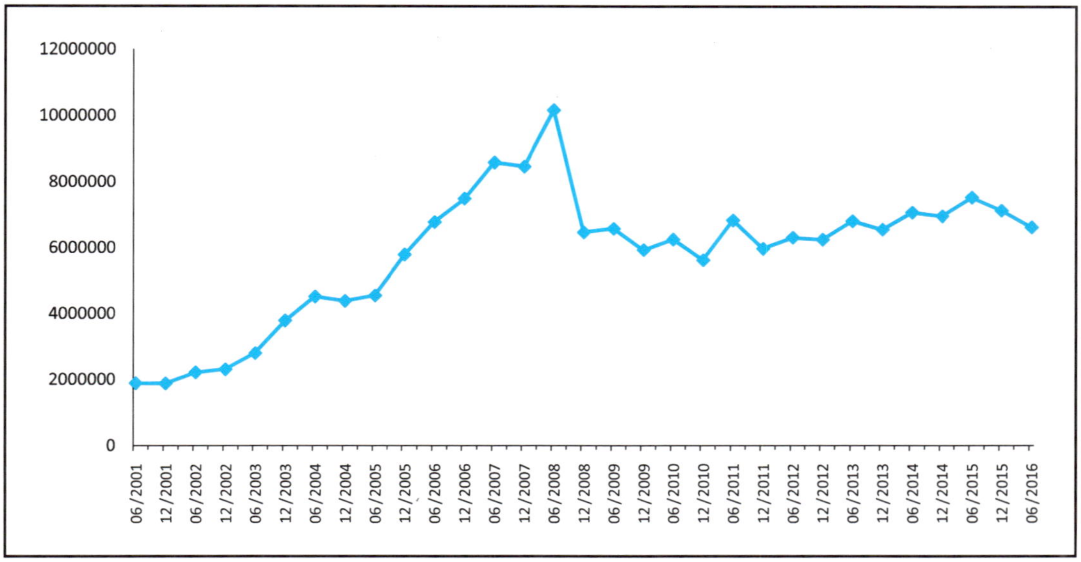

Figure 11.11. Growth in Total Value of Derivative Contracts Outstanding (June 2001–June 2016; US$ million).

Source: Bank of International Settlements.

When the growth is decomposed into financial versus non-financial derivatives (physicals), we see a sharp contrast. Financial or cash-settled derivatives have experienced much faster growth since the late 1990s. Today, a large portion of the total global traded volume of derivatives consists of trading in financials such as equity indices, equity derivatives such as Single Stock Futures, and equity options, interest rate derivatives, and currency derivatives. Interestingly, much of the growth in financial derivatives has come from the new markets of Asia. Figure 11.12 shows the decomposition of trading by underlying category for the six-month period from January to June 2016.

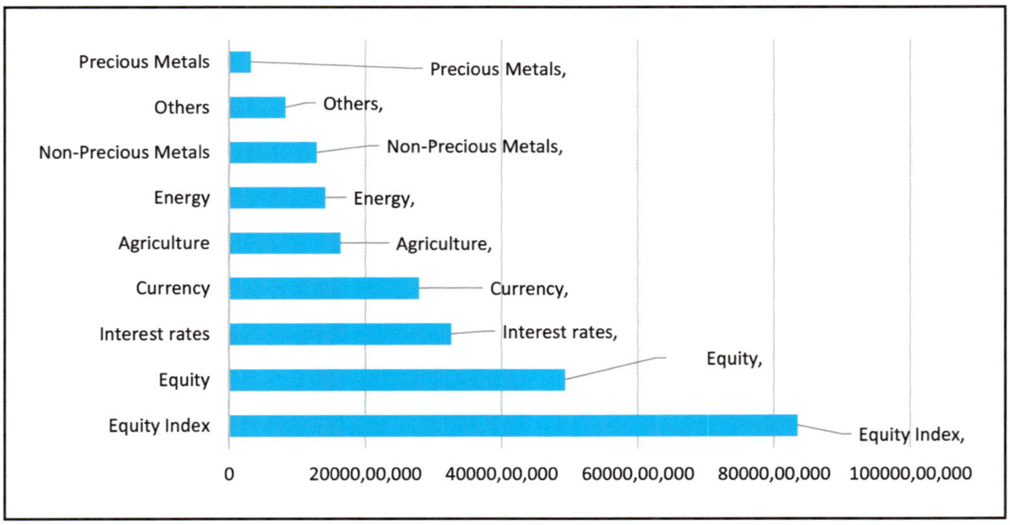

Figure 11.12. Global Futures and Options Traded Volumes by Category (January–September 2016) (Number of Contracts).

Source: Futures Industry Association.

Figure 11.13 shows a decomposition of the financials into its three key categories: equity, interest rate, and currency derivatives. Though interest rate derivatives were the more popular product in the 1990s, equity derivatives have overtaken them since the middle of 2000. From 2007 onwards, traded volume for equity derivatives was several-fold larger than that of interest rate derivatives, and the gap appears to be widening until 2011. Foreign exchange or currency derivatives appear to have caught up with interest rate derivative contracts. The lack of growth in interest rate derivatives is probably due to the current interest rate regime. Globally, interest rates are currently at historic lows. With very low interest rates and minimal likelihood of sharp rises anytime soon, the extent of interest rate risk is small. This probably explains the near-zero growth seen in interest rate derivatives.

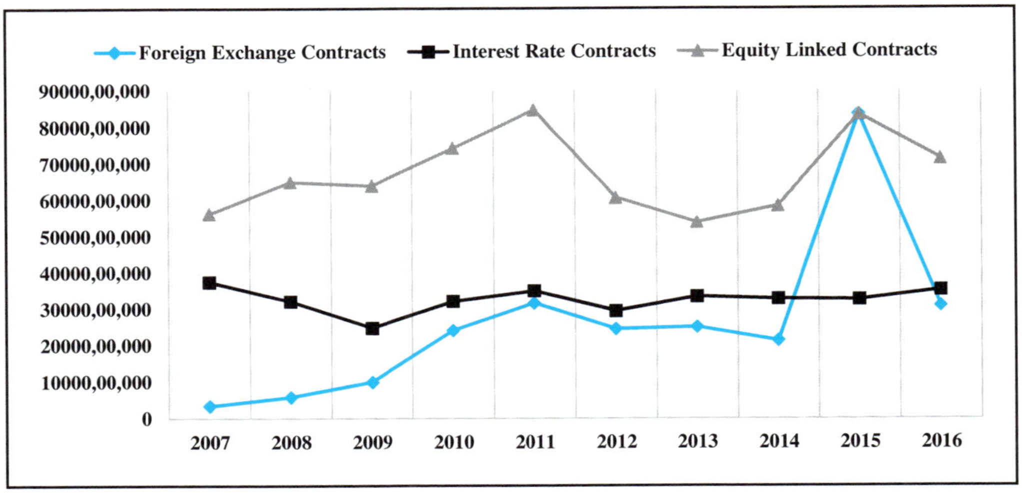

Figure 11.13. Trading Activity of Key Financial Derivatives. (2007–2016) (US$ million) (Based on the Number of Contracts Traded and/or Cleared at 81 Exchanges Worldwide).

Source: FIA Annual Survey Reports (2007–2016).

11.16.1 *Asia: The New Growth Area for Derivative Contracts*

Table 11.7 shows a sample of the world's derivatives exchanges ranked by traded volume. Though Malaysia was one of the earliest in Asia to have introduced derivative instruments, several Asia exchanges have now outperformed. In particular, exchanges in India, China, Korea, and Taiwan have all outperformed Malaysia in terms of trading activity. Even Thailand appears to have outdone Malaysia despite a much later entry into derivatives.

Table 11.7. Sample of Derivatives Exchanges Ranked by Traded Volume (2016).

Rank	Exchange	Traded Volume
1	CME Group	3,942,202,299
2	National Stock Exchange of India	2,119,462,820
3	Intercontinental Exchange	2,037,932,884
4	Moscow Exchange	1,950,145,218
5	Eurex	1,727,766,695
6	Shanghai Futures Exchange	1,680,711,841
7	Nasdaq	1,575,700,250
8	Dalian Commodity Exchange	1,537,479,768
9	BM&FBOVESPA	1,487,305,788
10	CBOE Holdings	1,184,553,418
11	Zhengzhou Commodity Exchange	901,297,047
12	Korea Exchange	692,990,540
16	Hong Kong Exchanges and Clearing	344,642,173

(*Continued*)

Table 11.7. (*Continued*)

Rank	Exchange	Traded Volume
17	Japan Exchange	337,537,333
21	Taiwan Futures Exchange	241,678,556
23	Singapore Exchange	172,421,585
26	Borsa Istanbul	107,253,507
27	Thailand Futures Exchange	69,576,164
28	London Stock Exchange Group	54,065,044
36	Dubai Gold and Commodities Exchange	19,669,786
37	China Financial Futures Exchange	18,335,855
39	Malaysia Derivatives Exchange	14,226,034
46	Pakistan Mercantile Exchange	3,481,167
48	Dubai Mercantile Exchange	1,949,658
51	Indonesia Commodity & Derivatives Exchange	558,409

Source: Futures Industry Association (http://www.futuresindustry.org).

Chicago's CME, which had earlier lost its top position, has now regained it. The National Stock Exchange of India has the second highest derivatives volume as at end 2016. The Intercontinental Exchange is a multinational exchange operating in several countries. Perhaps a reflection of China's economic prowess, several of China's exchanges appear in the list. Malaysia's Bursa Malaysia Derivatives now ranks 39th by traded volume. At the rate of growth seen lately among Asian exchanges, it is highly likely that the world's top derivative exchanges will soon be the Asian ones.

Box 11.8. Bursa Malaysia Derivatives Berhad: Origins and Evolution

Bursa Malaysia Derivatives Berhad (BMD) is currently Malaysia's only derivatives exchange. BMD is the result of the merger of two derivative exchanges, COMMEX (Commodity and Monetary Exchange of Malaysia) and KLOFFE (Kuala Lumpur Options and Financial Futures Exchange). Today, BMD trades a total of 13 derivative contracts. Of these, six are commodity derivatives, three are equity contracts, while the remaining four are interest rate derivatives. The contracts and categories are as follows:

1. Commodity Derivatives

- Crude Palm Oil Futures (FCPO)
- Crude Palm Kernel Oil Futures (FPKO)
- USD Crude Palm Oil Futures (FUPO)
- USD RBD Palm Olein Futures (FPOL)
- Options on Crude Palm Oil Futures (OCPO)
- Gold Futures (FGLD)

2. Equity Derivatives

- FTSE Bursa Malaysia KLCI Futures (FKLI)
- FTSE Bursa Malaysia KLCI Options (OKLI)
- Single Stock Futures (SSFs)

(*Continued*)

Box 11.8. (*Continued*)

3. Interest Rate Derivatives

- Three-Month Kuala Lumpur Interbank Offered Rate Futures (FKB3)
- Three-Year Malaysian Government Securities Futures (FMG3)
- Five-Year Malaysian Government Securities Futures (FMG5)
- 10-Year Malaysian Government Securities Futures Contract (FMGA)

Figure 11.14 shows the total monthly volume and month-end open interest across all derivative contracts of BMD over the 20-year period from 1997 to 2016. Overall, there appears to be healthy growth in volume, particularly since 2002. Most of this growth has come from the commodity contracts, especially the CPO futures contracts. Within equities, the most popular is the KLCI Index futures and among interest rate derivatives, the three-month KLIBOR futures. The CPO futures contract has consistently been the exchange's main derivative contract. As is evident from Figure 11.14, post-2007, the monthly volume appears to average approximately 250,000 contracts.

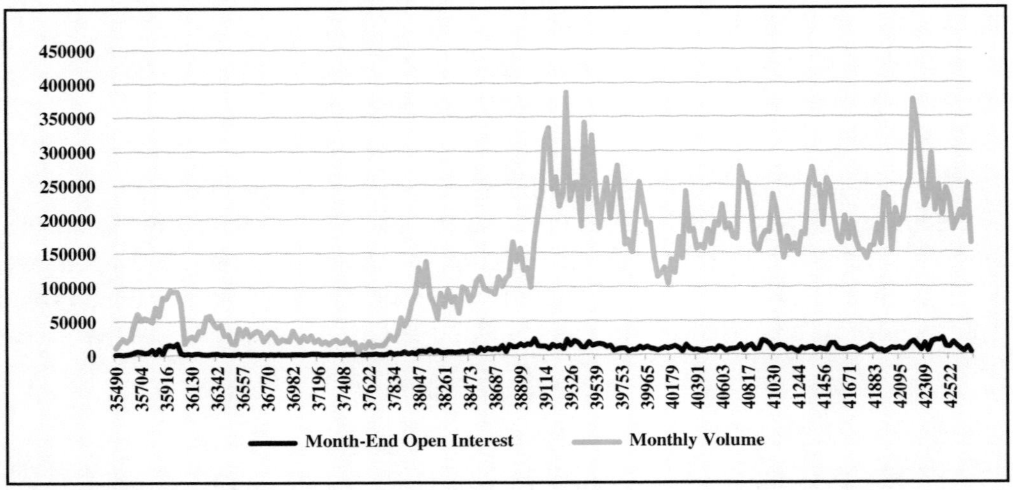

Figure 11.14. Trading Performance, Monthly Volume, and Open Interest (1997–2016).
Source: *Thomson Reuters Eikon*.

With the exception of the above three contracts — CPO futures, Stock Index Futures, and the three-month KLIBOR futures — some of the other contracts have had disappointing performances. The Index Options, the three-year and 10-year MGS futures and Crude Palm Kernel Oil futures contracts have shown poor performances. Several days of zero or inactive trading were a common feature of these contracts. While the three earlier mentioned contracts have seen renewed interest and a clear increase in activity, the latter contracts have yet to see a revival. Lack of familiarity with derivatives and investor education appear to be impediments. Both Bursa Malaysia and the Securities Commission have and will continue to invest heavily on investor education.

Summary

This chapter provides an introduction and an overview of derivative instruments. We examined the rationale for the evolution of derivatives and how the latter instruments were an improvement to existing ones. The key players in derivatives markets were also discussed. Hedgers use derivatives for risk management, speculators use derivatives to bet on price movements of the underlying asset, and arbitrageurs use derivatives to take advantage of pricing differentials.

The differences between commodity and financial derivatives were also examined. While commodity derivatives have tangible underlying assets and may have physical settlement, financial derivatives have, as underlying, financial assets and are cash-settled at maturity. We examined in detail the mechanics of how forwards, futures, options, and swaps function. The comparative advantage of each instrument and how they can be used in hedging or risk management was explored. The basic logic in hedging is to take a position opposite to that of our underlying position. Additionally, one would use a different category of derivative instruments to hedge different types of risks, for e.g., commodity price risk with commodity derivatives, currency risk with currency derivatives, interest rate risk with interest derivatives, and so on. Thus, the appropriate hedge strategy would depend on the type of risk and the nature of the exposure. We saw that while both an importer and an exporter may face the same type of risk, i.e., currency risk, the nature of their exposure may be different. The importer who has to pay in a foreign currency would fear an appreciation of the foreign currency, while an exporter who will receive the foreign currency would fear the opposite. Since the nature of their exposure is different, their hedge strategies would differ. The chapter also described how some instruments like forwards and futures enables us to "lock-in" a value whereas options enables us to establish a maximum (ceiling) on a cost and a minimum (floor) on a receivable. Finally, in deciding on the appropriate instrument to use, one would have to balance factors such as cost, convenience, counterparty risk, and other factors.

Questions and Problems

1. What is a derivative instrument? How is it different from stocks and bonds?
2. The evolution of derivative instruments has meant that each new derivative was an improvement on its predecessor. State the operational advantage(s) of (a) futures over forwards, and (b) options over futures or forwards.
3. Who are the key categories of players in derivative markets? Briefly describe the objective of each category of players.
4. (a) What benefit(s) do arbitrageurs bring to derivative markets?
   (b) How might the absence of speculators hurt hedgers?
   (c) What benefit(s) do speculators bring to derivative markets? In what way might some of their activity hurt markets?
5. Differentiate between commodity derivatives and financial derivatives. Does either category have any impact on its use for hedging, arbitrage or speculation?
6. State an advantage of cash settlement over physical settlement. Does the absence of physical delivery make financial derivatives any less suited for hedging, arbitrage, or speculation?
7. A corporate treasurer, who was long three-month futures contracts on British pound sterling for £400,000, subsequently goes short three-month pound forward contracts for £400,000. Assume the exchange rates in both cases are equal. What is his net position in British pounds?
8. If futures can be used for hedging, arbitrage, and speculation, what is the need for options?
9. Your company has just exported Crude Palm Oil to a Japanese customer. You will receive ¥30 million in 90 days. Do you have exposure? Suppose forwards, futures, and options were available on the currency, which would be the best instrument to hedge? Explain why.
10. Melaka Food Industries Bhd has requested a RM20 million, three-year loan from its bank, Maybank. Maybank, however, is willing to lend on a floating rate basis at three-month KLIBOR + 1.5%. Assume the loan will have to be serviced quarterly. The Chief Financial Officer (CFO) of Melaka Food Industries is worried having heard that interest rates are likely to rise over the foreseeable future. Advise the CFO on how he could use an IRS to hedge his company's interest rate exposure.
11. You hold a medium sized portfolio of money market instruments, T-bills, negotiable certificates of deposits (NCDs), short-term Cagamas bonds, and Malaysian Government Securities (MGS). As these instruments are highly interest-sensitive, you intend to hedge using derivative instruments. Assuming the following three interest derivatives are available, show how you would structure the hedge.
    (a) Interest Rate Futures
    (b) Interest Rate Options
    (c) Interest Rate Swaps
12. Your company will be receiving £3 million in 90 days from its British customer, As CFO, you know that you have at least three possible means of hedging the exposure: (i) using currency forwards, (ii) using currency futures, and (iii) currency options (where necessary, assume the contract size is £1 million).
    (a) Specify the position you would establish using each alternative.
    (b) If you had to choose one alternative, which would you choose? State the factors you would consider in making the choice.
13. Your company is expecting to receive 30 million Euros in three months (90 days) for a shipment you have just sent to your customer in France.
    A. Outline the appropriate hedge strategy using the following derivatives;
       (i) Forward
       (ii) Currency futures
       (iii) Currency Options
    B. What three key factors would you consider in deciding on the correct alternative?

14. (a) Briefly explain the likely impact on underlying stock market volatility if equity options and equity index futures are introduced.
    (b) Using an example, describe an exposure that can only be hedged appropriately with options.
    (c) Compare and contrast the purchase of Fire Insurance on property with that of a put option.
15. You own six lots of RHB Islamic stock. Each lot is 1,000 stocks. The stock is currently selling at RM13.00. While you are bullish about the long term prospects of the stock, you are worried about short-term volatility, specifically surrounding the impending merger discussion. You want to hedge your position over the next three months and lock-in the current value. You have the following information for traded options on the stock.
    - three-month RM13.00 Call @ 0.30
    - three-month RM13.00 Put @ 0.20

    State your hedge strategy, plot the payoff profile, and identify the resulting position. What is the maximum upside and downside to the strategy?

Bibliography

Brealey, R. A., S. C. Myers and F. Allen (2011). *Principles of Corporate Finance*, 10th Edition (McGraw Hill, NY, USA).
Bodie, Z., A. Kane and J. Marcus (2009). *Investments*, 8th Edition (McGraw Hill, NY, USA).
Derin Ekonomi — Turkish monthly Magazine on Economics & Finance.
Obiyathulla, I. B. (2017). *Financial Derivatives: Market and Applications in Malaysia*, 4th Edition (McGraw Hill).

Websites

Thomson Reuters- Eikon
Websites of respective Muslim Country Stock Exchanges
Websites of the various Stock exchanges
http://www.zawya.com/middle-east/financial-markets
http://www.futuresindustry.org
https://www.bis.org

Chapter 12

SHARI'AH-COMPLIANT DERIVATIVE INSTRUMENTS

Topics in this Chapter

Chapter Objective

This chapter is designed to provide an overview of Islamic financial instruments and contracts that have derivative-like features, and recently developed *Shari'ah*-compliant derivate instruments. It also discusses how these instruments could be used in risk management. On completing the chapter, you should have a good understanding of Islamic finance instruments with derivative-like features and an appreciation of the need for the recently developed *Shari'ah*-compliant derivative instrument

Key Terms		
call option	*gharar*	*maysir*
commodity *murabaha*	Islamic financial instruments	*salam*
embedded call	Islamic profit rate swap (IPRS)	settlement price
embedded put	*istijrar*	*sukuk* with embedded options
forward contract	*jahl*	*wa'ad*
futures contract	*joala*	

12.1 Introduction

In Malaysia and other Middle Eastern countries, the growth in Islamic banking, and in particular, the amount of funds under management of Islamic asset management and mutual funds, has been impressive. As outlined in earlier chapters, there have been several developments in the Malaysian financial sector that have provided the impetus to the growth of Islamic banking and finance. Among these have been the establishment of the Islamic Interbank Money Market (IIMM) and its instruments, the outstanding success with *sukuk*, the introduction of Islamic Indices, Islamic ETFs, and Islamic REITs. These developments, coupled with the fact that there has been a several-fold increase in funds managed under Islamic mutual funds and asset management companies, mean that Islamic finance invariably comes into contact with derivative instruments. Despite the huge strides made in Islamic banking and finance, derivative instruments, especially the use of financial derivatives, have remained a controversial issue. The issue is further clouded by the often-contradictory stand of Islamic jurists and scholars with regard to the acceptability of derivative instruments. Still, a number of Islamic financial instruments and contracts that have derivative-like features exist. These being the *bay' al-salam, istisna, joala*, and *istijrar* contracts. In addition to these, there are the recently developed Islamic Profit Rate Swaps, the *Shari'ah*-compliant derivative instruments that are based on *wa'ad* and *sukuk* with embedded options. Thus, the market and its practitioners have moved on with using derivative-like instruments out of necessity even though *Shari'ah* scholars are yet to reach a consensus on their acceptability.

12.2 Necessary Features of Islamic Financial Instruments

As laid out in Chapter 3, all Islamic financial instruments and transactions in general must meet a number of criteria in order to be considered *halal* (acceptable). At a primary level, all financial instruments and transactions must be free of at least the following five items:

(i) *riba* (usury);
(ii) *rishwah* (bribery/corruption);
(iii) *maysir* (elements of gambling);
(iv) *gharar* (unnecessary risk arising from unclear contracts or specifications); and
(v) *jahl* (ignorance — taking advantage of the counterparty's ignorance).

Riba, which literally translates to usury, is more commonly referred to as the charging of interest. *Riba* can be in different forms and is prohibited in all its forms. For example, *riba* can also occur when one gets a positive return without taking any risk. As for *gharar*, there appears to be no consensus to what *gharar* means. It has been taken to mean unnecessary risk, deception, or intentionally induced uncertainty. In the context of financial transactions, *gharar* could be thought of as looseness of the underlying contract such that one or both parties are uncertain about specifications and possible outcomes or alternatively, that the contract could be read in a number of ways such that one party could easily deceive (i.e., involve in deception with) the other party. *Maysir*, from a financial instrument viewpoint, would be one where the outcome is purely dependent on chance alone — as in gambling. Finally, *jahl* refers to ignorance. From a financial transaction viewpoint, it would be unacceptable for one party to gain in a transaction due to the other party's ignorance.

In addition to these requirements for financial instruments, *Shari'ah* has some basic conditions with regard to the sale of an asset (in this case, a real asset as opposed to financial assets). Since a derivative instrument is a financial asset dependent on the value of its underlying asset (real asset in most cases), the *Shari'ah* conditions for the validity of a sale would also be relevant to derivatives. Aside from the fact that the underlying asset must be *halal*, at least two other conditions have to be met: (i) the underlying asset or commodity must currently exist in its physical, sellable form, and (ii) the seller should have legal ownership of the asset in its final form. These conditions for the validity of a sale would obviously render impossible the trading of derivatives and their use in anticipatory hedging. However, *Shari'ah* provides exceptions to these conditions to enable deferred sale where needed.

12.3 Islamic Finance Instruments with Features of Derivative Instruments

A number of instruments and contracts exist in Islamic finance that could be considered a basis for derivative contracts within an Islamic framework. In this section, we examine two such contracts: (i) the *bay' al-salam* contract, and (ii) the *istijrar* contract. While the *bay' al-salam* contract has provisions and precedence, *istijrar* is a recent innovation practiced in Pakistan. Two other contracts, *istisna* and *joala*, which are related to the *bay' al-salam* contract, are also briefly examined.

12.3.1 *Bay' al-salam*

Bay' al-salam is essentially a transaction where two parties agree to carry out a sale or purchase of an underlying asset at a predetermined future date but at a price determined and *fully paid* for today. The seller agrees to deliver the asset in the agreed quantity and quality to the buyer at the predetermined future date. This is similar to a conventional forward contract, however, the big difference is that in a *salam* sale, the buyer pays the entire amount in *full at the time the contract is initiated*. The contract also stipulates that the payment must be in cash form. The idea behind such a 'pre-payment' requirement has to do with the fact that the objective in a *bay' al-salam* contract is to help needy farmers and small businesses with working capital financing. Since there is full prepayment, a *salam* sale is clearly beneficial to the seller. As such, the pre-determined price is normally *lower* than the prevailing spot price. This price behavior is certainly different from that of conventional futures and forward contracts where the futures price is typically higher than the spot price by the amount of the carrying cost. The lower *salam* price compared to spot is the "compensation" by the seller to the buyer for the privilege given him.

The *bay' al-salam* contract is subject to several conditions, of these the important ones are as follows:

(i) Full payment by buyer at the time of affecting sale.
(ii) The underlying asset must be standardizable, easily quantifiable, and of determinate quality.
(iii) The *salam* contract cannot be based on a uniquely identified underlying asset. This means the underlying commodity cannot be based on a commodity from a particular farm or field, etc. (By definition, such an underlying would not be standardizable).
(iv) Quantity, quality, maturity date, and place of delivery must be clearly enumerated in the *salam* agreement.
(v) The underlying asset or commodity must be available and traded in the markets throughout the period of contract.

Given our earlier description of futures contracts, it should be clear that current exchange-traded futures would conform to these conditions, with the exception of the first, which requires full advance payment by the buyer. However, given the customized nature of *bay' al-salam*, it would closely resemble forwards more rather than futures. Thus, some of the problems of forwards namely "multiple coincidence", potential for price squeeze, and counterparty risk can exist in the *salam* sale. Counterparty risk, however, would be one-sided. Since the buyer has fully paid the amount, it is only the buyer who faces the seller's default risk and not both ways as in forwards and futures. In order to overcome the potential for default on the part of the seller, *Shari'ah* allows the buyer to require security, which may be in the form of a guarantee or mortgage.

The *bay' al-salam* contract can also form the basis for the provision of working capital financing by Islamic financial institutions. Since financial institutions would not want possession of the underlying commodity, parallel contracts may be used. Though not all jurists are in agreement about its permissibility, the literature cites two venues for parallel *salam*.

The first is a parallel *salam* with the original seller, while the other is an offsetting transacting by the financial institution with a third party. In the first alternative, the financial institution, after entering into the original contract, gets into a parallel *salam* to sell the underlying commodity after a time lapse for the same maturity date to the original seller. The resale price would be higher and considered justifiable since there has been a time lapse. The difference between the two prices would constitute the bank's profit. However, the requirement is that both transactions should be independent of each other. The original transaction should not have been priced with the intention to do a subsequent parallel *salam*. Under the second alternative, the bank, which had gone into an original contract, enters into a contract promising to sell the commodity to a third party on the maturity date of the contract. Since this second transaction is not a *salam* contract, the bank would not receive advance payment.

12.3.2 *The Istisna and Joala Contracts*

In addition to *bay' al-salam*, there are two other contracts where a transaction is made on a "yet to exist" underlying asset. These are the *istisna'* and *joala* contracts. The *istisna* contract has, as its underlying, a product to be manufactured. Essentially, in *istisna*, a buyer deals with a manufacturer to manufacture a needed product to his specifications. The price for the product is agreed upon and fixed. While the agreement may be cancelled by either party before production begins, it cannot be cancelled unilaterally once the manufacturer begins production. Unlike the *salam* contract, the payment here is not made in advance. The time of delivery too is not fixed but negotiated. Like the *bay' al-salam*, a parallel contract is allowed in *istisna*. Thus, the *istisna'* contract may be used by Islamic banks for product financing.

The *joala* contract is essentially *istisna* but applicable for services as opposed to a manufactured product. Thus, for e.g., when a school wants to use the services of a tailor to make several hundred uniforms, the *joala* contract would be an appropriate arrangement. The conditions described for the *istisna* contract above apply in the case of *joala*.

12.3.3 *The Istijrar Contract*

The *istijrar* contract is a recently introduced Islamic financing instrument. Introduced in Pakistan, the contract has embedded options that could be triggered if the underlying asset's price exceeds certain bounds. The contract is complex in that it constitutes a combination of options, average prices, and *murabahah,* or cost plus financing. *Istijrar* involves two parties, a buyer, which could be a company seeking financing to purchase the underlying asset, and a financial institution.

A typical *istijrar* transaction could be the case of a company seeking short-term working capital to finance the purchase of a commodity. The company approaches a bank seeking working capital financing to purchase a needed raw material. The bank purchases the commodity at the current price (P_0) and resells it to the company for payment to be made at a mutually agreed upon date in the future — for e.g., in three months. The price at which settlement occurs on maturity is contingent on the underlying asset's price movement from t_0 to t_{90}. Where t_0 is the day the contract was initiated and t_{90} is Day 90, which would be the maturity day.

Unlike a *murabahah* contract, where the settlement price would simply be a predetermined price, P^*, where $P^* = P_0 (1 + r)$, with r being the bank's required rate of return, the price at which the *istijrar* is settled on maturity date could either be P^* or an average price (P) of the commodity between the period t_0 and t_{90}. As to which of the two prices will be used for settlement depends on how prices have behaved, and which party chooses to "fix" the settlement price. The embedded option is the right to choose to fix the price at which settlement will occur any time before contract maturity. At the initiation of the contract, both parties agree on the following two items: (i) in the predetermined *murabahah* price P^*, and (ii) an upper and lower bound around the P_0 (banks purchase price at t_0).

For better clarification, the different prices are shown below in a continuum. Prices increase as one goes to the right.

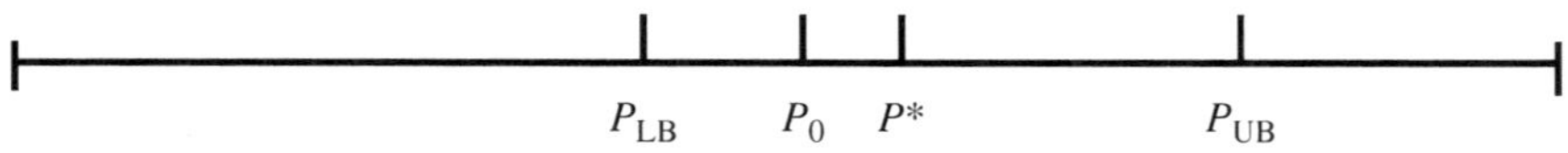

where P_0 = Price that bank pays to purchase the underlying commodity.
P^* = Murabahah price, $P^* = P_0\ (1 + r)$.
P_{LB} = The lower bound price.
P_{UB} = The upper bound price.

The settlement price (P_s) at t_{90} would be:
(i) $P_s = P$ if the underlying asset price remained within the bounds. or (ii) $P_s = P^*$ if the underlying asset exceeds the bounds and one of the parties chooses to exercise its option and use P^* as the price at which to settle at maturity.

For either party to exercise its option and thereby fix the settlement price at P^*, the spot price during the term of the contract must have exceeded the bounds at any time. As to which party would exercise would depend on the *direction* of the spot price movement. For example, if the spot price at any time breaks through the upper bound, the buyer would get worried. Whether he will exercise or not would depend on his expectations of the spot price over the remaining period of the contract. If he believes that the price is likely to keep increasing, thereby causing at which settlement will occur to be greater than P^*, it will be in his interest to "exercise" by fixing the settlement price now at P^*. He would then notify the bank that he is exercising his option and that the settlement would be P^*. Should spot prices be falling such that it breaks the *lower* bound, the seller, i.e., the bank, would have the option to fix the settlement price at P^*.

The settlement price is determined as follows:

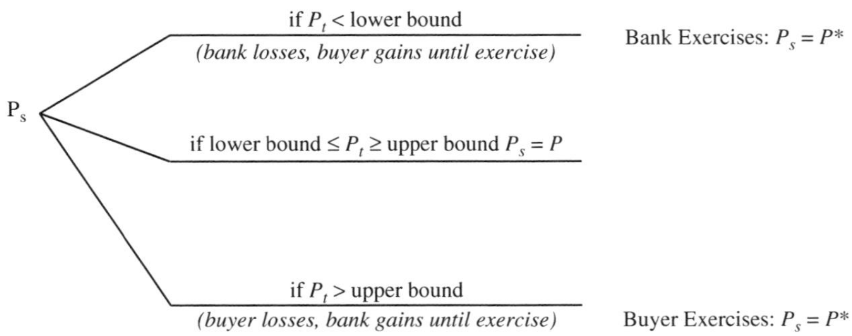

where Ps = Settlement Price at Maturity
P = Average price, P_{to} to P_{tqo}
P_t = Spot Price of underlying commodity on day t
P^* = The predetermined, cost-plus or *murabahah* price

Analyzing the *istijrar* contract in its entirety from an option's viewpoint is complicated since it has two different exercise styles rolled into one. Such an instrument would be unusual in conventional finance. Still, for our purpose here, the embedded options in the *istijrar* can simply be thought of as follows — the fact that the buyer gets to fix the buying price at P^* when the price goes higher implies that he has a *call option* at an exercise price of P^* while the bank a *put option* at the same exercise price.

What the *istijrar* contract attempts to do is to allow for the impact of price changes but to cap the benefits that accrue as a result. By definition, since price changes are allowed only within a band, the advantage to one party and the disadvantage to the other party are capped. The maximum potential gain or loss is limited. Such a contract fulfils the need to avoid a fixed return on a riskless asset which would be considered *riba* and also avoid *gharar,* in that both parties know, upfront, what P^* and the range of other possible prices would be between the upper and lower bounds.

Box 12.1. Derivatives and the Risk-Sharing Philosophy of Islamic Finance

Shari'ah requires the use of risk-sharing contracts as a means of avoiding *riba*. As we saw in Chapter 3, *ribawi* contracts typically require all business risks to be borne by the borrower while the lender receives a fixed return detached from the returns of the underlying business. In a risk-sharing contract, the parties to the transaction agree to share the potential upside and downside, i.e., the profits and losses are to be shared. Each party agrees to give up a portion of his potential profit in exchange for a reduction in his loss potential. This is beneficial since the sharing of returns means the sharing of risk.

Invariably, both parties come out better since the loss potential for both parties are now limited. One should be able to see the obvious similarity here between a risk-sharing contract and a hedging contract. In both cases, parties to the transaction get to limit their loss potential in exchange for giving up some of their profit potential. To see how a hedge transaction using a derivative contract could be similar to a risk-sharing contract, consider the following scenario.

Suppose, the cocoa farmer and confectioner in the example of the earlier chapter, use a 90-day forward contract on cocoa for 10 tons and the hedge price is RM10,000 per ton, then the payoffs to hedged and unhedged positions would be as follows:

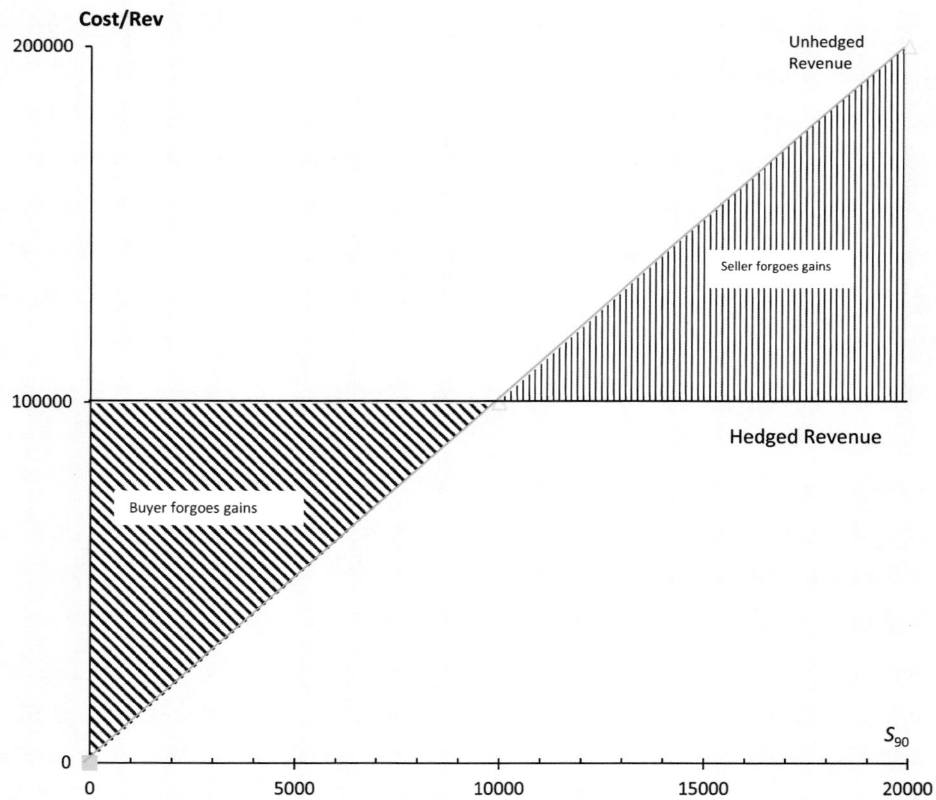

(Continued)

Box 12.1. (*Continued*)

In the diagram S_{90} is the spot price on Day 90. The unhedged revenue is the positively sloped line. It increases in value as the spot price increases. The hedged revenue, on the other hand, is a flat line at RM100,000, which is the total contract value (RM10,000 × 10 tons). To see the risk-sharing element, notice the two shaded areas. At any spot price below RM10,000, the buyer stands to gain had he not hedged. Similarly, at any spot price above RM10,000, the seller stands to gain had he not hedged. It should also be clear that in the region, where one party gains the other party to the transaction stands to lose. Thus, in a hedge transaction, one party agrees to forgo his potential gains in exchange for the other party agreeing to forgo his. In the above example, the confectioner agrees to forgo his gains if the price is below RM10,000. This translates into the farmer not making the losses otherwise. Similarly, the farmer forgoes his gains at prices above RM10,000, thereby avoiding "losses" to the confectioner in the form of higher cost. This is essentially, risk-sharing. Obviously, the parties to the hedge are not making sacrifices for altruistic reasons but because the sacrifice of potential profit leads to the avoidance of potential loss. Seen in this light, when used for hedging, derivatives can be considered a form of risk-sharing.

Source: Obiyathulla Ismath Bacha (2013), *Risk management, derivatives and shariah compliance.* AIP Conference proceedings. http://proceedings.aip.org/dbt/dbt.jsp?KEY=APCPCS&Volume=1522&Issue=1

12.4 The Islamic Profit Rate Swap

The Islamic Profit Rate Swap (IPRS) is a fairly new innovation by Islamic financial institutions (IFIs) to manage their duration gap defined as duration of assets exceeding that of liabilities and the resulting impact on their profits. Islamic banks, especially those in Malaysia, have large asset–liability duration mismatches. Banks, given the nature of their business, have inherent mismatches. The asset side of their balance sheet, which shows the financing that have been undertaken, would typically have a longer maturity (duration) than their liability side, which shows their deposits. Since banks typically take short-term deposits and lend them out for longer periods, the average duration of their assets (loans to customers) is usually longer than the average duration of their liabilities. As we saw in Chapter 5, duration is a measure of interest rate risk. Financial instruments with longer duration would fall more in value than those with shorter duration.

This implies that banks with large asset–liability duration gaps will see the value of their assets fall much more than the value of their liabilities when interest rates rise. This differential fall in value will mean that the bank's net worth will be reduced by the amount of the difference in values. For example, if rate-sensitive assets are higher than rate-sensitive liabilities by RM50 million, then the potential squeeze on net worth will come from this RM50 million. Conventional banks handle such risk in three common ways; first, by using adjustable rate mortgages or loans with floating interest rates. In Malaysia, conventional banks price housing loans as BLR + x percent, thus, as the Base Lending Rate (BLR) changes, the interest charged on the loan changes. The + x percent is a constant rate reflecting the risk premium.

The second method is by using interest rate derivatives, such as interest rate futures contracts, to hedge against rising interest rates; and lastly, by using interest rate swaps. An IRS is a customized transaction between two parties: one party pays a fixed interest rate based on a notional principal whereas the counterparty pays a floating interest rate based on the same notional principal. Conventional banks, in managing their interest rate risk, typically enter into an IRS as the fixed rate payer and floating rate receiver (see Chapter 9 for a detailed discussion of IRS).

The IPRS serves a similar function to IFIs. IFIs that need to protect themselves from interest rate increases can use the IPRS to hedge their profits and net worth. Though Islamic banks operate on an interest-free basis, keep in mind that most Islamic banks operate with dual banking systems. That is, Islamic banking operates side by side with conventional banks and within a larger conventional financial sector.

Furthermore, Islamic banking is not exclusive to Muslims but shares a common customer pool with conventional banks. This inevitably ties in Islamic banking with the rest of the financial system. Funds flow between Islamic and conventional banks in both directions. As a result of this, interest rate changes in the conventional sector translate into changes in the cost of funds with the Islamic banking system. Just as we saw in Chapter 4, how the Islamic Interbank Money Market is linked with the conventional money market with rates in both markets moving synchronously, the same linkage is present in the banking system. So, interest rate risk is a reality for Islamic banks operating within a dual banking system, which is why the IPRS is a relevant tool. Box 12.2 shows how the IPRS helps with managing profit rate risk.

Box 12.2. Illustration: An Islamic Profit Rate Swap

An Islamic bank has just assessed its exposure to potential rate changes. The bank's average duration of assets is five years while duration of liabilities is two years. This mismatch implies that if rates rise, the value of its assets will fall two and a half times more than that of its liabilities. This will obviously result in an impairment of its net worth if not hedged. Further analysis by the bank shows that its rate-sensitive assets are greater than rate-sensitive liabilities by RM120 million. As is typical for banks, this Islamic bank's income from assets is mostly at fixed profit rates while its cost funds are floating. How can the bank use an IPRS to protect itself?

Answer: The IFI can go into an IPRS as follows:
Stage 1:

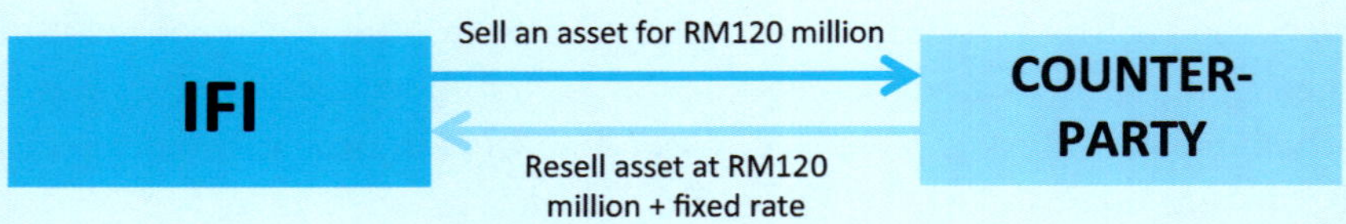

Stage 2:

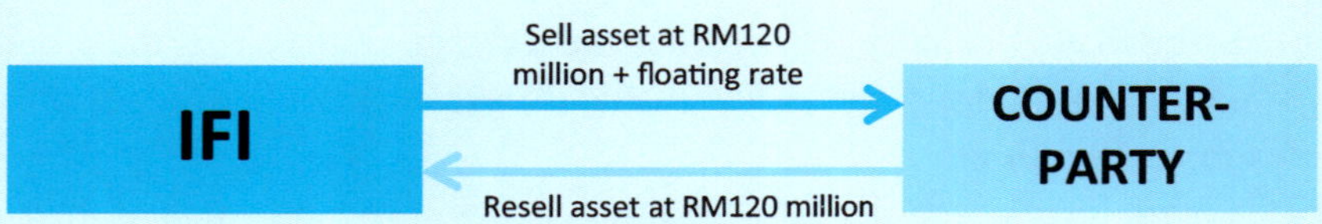

Note: There are typically two stages in the IPRS. Given the cash flow above, at the end of Stage 1, the IFI will have to pay the counter party the net cash flow which is a fixed profit rate. This fixed profit rate is a percentage of the notional value of RM120 million. Using the same logic, the result of Stage 2 will be a net cash flow payable by the counter party to the IFI, equivalent to a floating profit rate based on the same notional amount of RM120 million. The net of these cash flows can be shown as:

Resulting Cash flow combining Stages 1 and 2

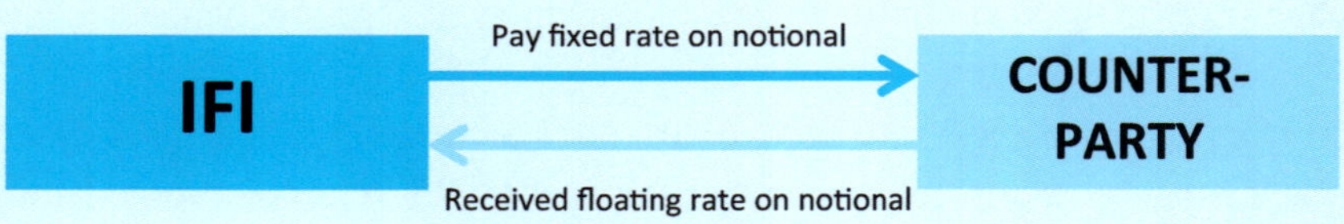

12.5 How is the IFI Hedged?

The following cash flows show how the IFI is hedged by means of the above IPRS. Since the IFI earns fixed, it uses the fixed proceeds on the IPRS. If rates rise, the increase in the IFI's cost of funds will be offset by the increased amounts it receives in the IPRS (see Figure 12.1).

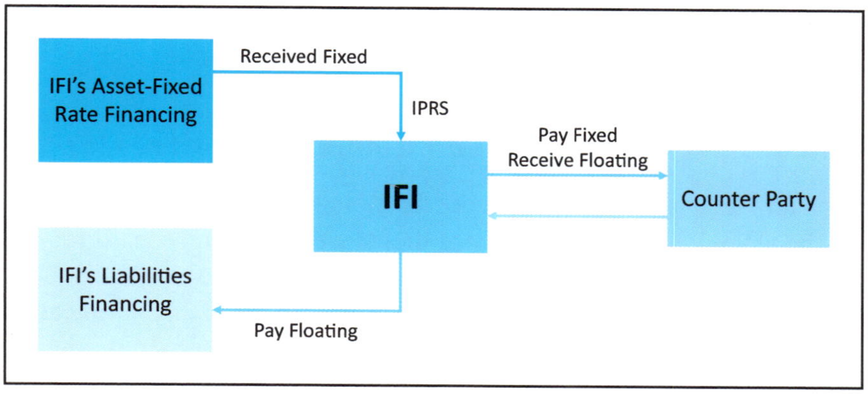

Figure 12.1. The IFI is Hedged by Means of an IPRS.

12.6 *Sukuk* with Embedded Options

As we know, *sukuk* are means by which businesses can raise non-equity, external financing in a *Shari'ah*-compliant way. In Chapter 6, we saw the advent of exotic *sukuk*. Exotic *sukuk* are *sukuk* with complex structures. This has been the result of wanting to have altered risk profiles, different cash flows profiles, or cash flow profiles dependent on outcomes (contingent payoffs). The need for such cash flows is often the result of wanting to avoid fixed returns and cash flows. Thus, we have seen of late, *sukuk* that would have payoffs attached to commodity prices, *sukuk* that are exchangeable at maturity to equity of the *mudarib* (KFC, Malaysia) or groups of stocks of other companies, held by the *mudarib* (Khazanah, Malaysia). There has also been *sukuk* with embedded options. The options could be call options on the underlying asset made available to the *mudarib* or put options on the asset made available to the SPV (trustees). Figure 12.2 replicates the *sukuk* structure with an embedded put option, shown in Chapter 7.

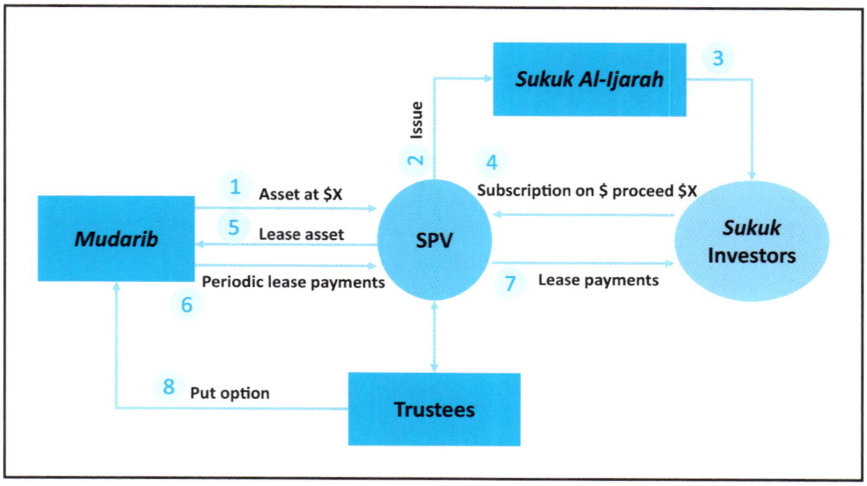

Figure 12.2. *Sukuk ijarah* to Finance a Sale-Lease Arrangement with an Embedded Put Option.

Here, the embedded put option enables the trustees, who act on behalf of the *sukuk*-holders, to exercise the put by selling the underlying asset to the issuers at the exercise price. Notice that the *sukuk*-holders will only want to exercise the put if it is in their favor, i.e., if they cannot find a third party willing to pay more. Thus, with the embedded put option, there is no "guarantee" of what the cash flow at maturity is, ahead of time. Embedding options in *sukuk* allow issuers to overcome the issue of fixity in cash flows, which has been a source of unease among *Shari'ah* scholars. In Chapter 6, we also saw several *sukuk* with embedded call options. The Khazanah exchangeable *sukuk* described in Chapter 6, are essentially *sukuk* with embedded call options.

12.7 Derivative Instruments — How *Shari'ah* Compliant Are They?

If there is one area of Islamic finance that is still deeply mired in controversy, it is probably the permissibility of derivative instruments. The validity and permissibility of these instruments appears to vary by scholar/jurist. Even where Islamic scholars have found them objectionable, their reasons for objection differ. There does not appear to be a consensus. Much of the work by Islamic scholars has been of a highly juridical nature. They examine derivatives within the narrow confines of contractual arrangements and thereby miss the broader picture of why instruments like futures and options are needed in modern business environments. The economic argument appears to have been lost. Not only is there no consensus, the approach to evaluating the instruments appears to differ among scholars. In the case of options, for e.g., some have examined their validity under the *fiqh* doctrine of *al-Khiyarat* or contractual stipulations, while others have drawn parallels between options and *bai-al-urbun*, *urbun* being a transaction in which a buyer places an initial good faith deposit with the seller. Should the buyer decide to go ahead with the transaction, the payment is adjusted for the initial deposit but is non-refundable if the buyer decides not to proceed with the transaction. A third view has been to examine options in the light of *gharar*, or uncertainty. In at least one other situation (Abu Sulayman, 1992), options have been viewed as totally detached from the underlying asset. When viewed solely as a promise to buy or sell an asset at a predetermined price within a stipulated period, *Shari'ah* scholars find nothing objectionable with options. However, it is in the trading of these promises and the charging of premiums that objections are raised. In the case of futures contracts, some *ulamas* have objected stating that deferred sale is not allowed, while others cite precedents to deferred sale such as *ba'i salam* but have objections to futures on other grounds, mostly that it encourages speculation.

Many *Shari'ah* scholars have provided their opinions on the validity or otherwise of exchange-traded derivatives. Since they are individual opinions, they are diverse and are often conflicting. As mentioned above, there is no consensus. While a definitive opinion, acceptable to all, may still be far off, there has been an obvious softening in the stance against derivative instruments, especially of over-the-counter instruments such as forwards and swaps. The negative stance of *fuqaha* against exchange-traded derivatives appears to be rooted in the suspicion that they could be used easily for speculative purposes. The following is a list of some of the opinions and commentary on the opinions.

12.7.1 *Views of Shari'ah Scholars on Exchange-Traded Derivative Instruments*

Opinions on Futures Contracts

(i) *Fatwa* of Imam Al-Haramaini Al-Jauwaini

- The trading of futures is *halal* if the practice is based on *darurah* and the needs or *hajaat* of the *ummah*.

(ii) Syariah Advisory Council (SAC) of Securities Commission, Malaysia

- Futures trading of commodities is approved as long as underlying asset is *halal*.
- Crude Palm Oil futures contracts are approved for trading.
- For Stock Index Futures (SIF) contract, the concept is approved. However, since the current FBM KLCI-based SIF has non-*halal* stocks, it is not approved.

Note: Thus, it implies that an SIF contract of a *halal* index would be acceptable.

(iii) Ustaz Ahmad Allam (Islamic Fiqh Academy, Jeddah, 1992)

- Stock Index Futures (SIF) trading is *haram*, since some of the underlying stocks are not *halal*.
- Until and unless the underlying asset or basket of securities in the SIF is all *halal*, SIF trading is not approved.

Note: This position appears consistent with that of the Shariah Advisory Council (SAC) of Malaysia's Securities Commission.

(iv) Mufti Taqi Usmani (Islamic Fiqh Academy, Jeddah)

Futures transactions not permissible for two reasons:

- According to the *Shari'ah*, sale or purchase cannot be affected for a future date.
- In most futures transactions, delivery or possession is not intended.

Note: While it is indeed true that the majority of futures contracts do not end up in delivery but are offset before maturity, the above position ignores the fact that there are many instances where even genuine hedgers have no intention of delivery but are hedging their inventory. Since they will be using the commodity held in inventory for production, they cannot deliver. Their objective in using the derivative contract is really to protect (lock-in) the value of their commodity assets held in inventory. For example, a jeweler may short gold futures contracts purely to preserve the value of his inventory of gold bars.

Opinions on Option Contracts

(i) Ahmad Muhayyuddin Hassan (1986)

Objects to option trading for two reasons:

- Maturity beyond three days as in *al-khiyarat* is not acceptable.
- The buyer gets more benefits than the seller — injustice.

Note: The first argument that maturity beyond three days is unacceptable is a literal imposition of a requirement for *urbun* contracts, which are really good-faith deposits and thus are contextually different. In contemporary business situations, being allowed to only hedge for three days has little utility or practical value.

The second argument that the buyer gets more benefits, and this therefore constitutes an injustice that ignores several issues. First, it ignores the fact that the buyer pays a premium which the seller receives. So, the benefits to the buyer do not come free. Second, being rational, the seller would not sell an option unless he is convinced the premium he receives is worth the risks he undertakes. Keep in mind that the option's premium changes as the riskiness associated with the underlying asset changes. In a rational world with knowledgeable players and transparent pricing, trades or products that are systematically biased cannot survive. The market for such a product will simply cease to exist.

(ii) Abu Sulayman (Islamic Fiqh Academy, Jeddah, 1992)

- Acceptable when viewed in the light of *bai-al-urbun* but considers options to have been detached and independent of the underlying asset, therefore unacceptable.

Note: The argument that exchange traded derivatives are detached from their underlying asset is wrong. A derivative, by definition, derives its value from that of the underlying asset. Furthermore, this argument ignores the fact that deviations in pricing between the traded derivative and underlying asset will lead to risk-free arbitrage. The presence of arbitrage will ensure the derivative moves in line and is never detached from its underlying.

(iii) Mufti Taqi Usmani (Islamic Fiqh Academy, Jeddah)

- Promises as part of a contract is acceptable in *Shari'ah*; however, the trading and charging of a premium for the promise is *not acceptable*.
- Yet, others have argued against options by invoking *maisir* or unearned gains, i.e., the profits from options may be unearned.

Note: The argument that profits from options are "unearned" ignores the fact that both parties to an option position take risks. The seller faces potentially large downside risks, the buyer, the potential loss of the premium he has paid. Thus, one could make the case that the profits earned arise from the risks undertaken.

(iv) El Gari (1993) and Yusuf Qaradawi

- El Gari argues in favor of call options based on the framework of *bai-al-urbun*.
- Yusuf Qaradawi argues that the ruling by Ibn Hanbal on *urbun* should be adapted to modern times, implying that the use of options could be justified on the basis of *urbun*.

(v) Hashim Kamali (International Islamic University Malaysia, 1998)

- Finds options acceptable.
- Invokes the *Hanbali* tradition, cites Hadiths of Barira (RA) and Habban Ibn Munqidh (RA).
- Also draws parallels with the *bai-al-urbun* in arguing that premiums are acceptable.
- Cites that contemporary scholars such as Yusuf al-Qaradawi and Mustafa al-Zarqa have authenticated *bai-al-urbun*.

(vi) *Shariah* Advisory Council (SAC) Securities Commission, Malaysia

- No formal opinion on options.
- However, the SAC has approved as *halal* the trading of warrants, as long as the underlying stock is designated as a *halal* stock.

Note: The fact that there are no equity options, only index options available currently has meant that there is no urgency. Index options are disallowed based on the argument that some of the stocks in the FBM KLCI are non-*halal*.

12.7.2 *Need for Harmonization*

The fractious nature of the debate and opinions is obvious. It appears that any number of objections could be made for a given derivative instrument. The object of juridical analysis appears to be a microexamination of each and every feature of a derivative instrument to see if it passes an often subjective religious filter. The overall economic benefits derived from their use and the societal benefits that could accrue do not seem to have been given due consideration. Aside from individual interpretation, the differing opinions among *madzhabs*/*imams* complicates the situation further. Thus, an option contract may be found objectionable for exactly opposite reasons. For example, when seen from the viewpoint of subject of sale (*mahal al-aqd*), the subject in options are rights/obligations, which some like Abu Sulayman (1992) find objectionable because rights/obligations are different (detached) from the underlying asset. When seen solely as conferring rights/obligations, options are deemed *independent* of their underlying asset. While the sale/purchase of assets is entirely acceptable, the transaction of abstract things such as rights and obligations are not recognized in the *Shari'ah*. On the other hand, if options as derivatives are considered attached to the underlying asset, then objections have been made on the problem of paired contractual obligations (*'aqdayn fi aqd*). The existence of paired contractual obligations invalidates both the option contract and the sale contract of the underlying asset. Thus, an option may be found objectionable if it is deemed to be independent of its underlying asset and again objectionable if it is dependent and therefore paired. The irony that an instrument could be prohibited based on two diametrically opposite viewpoints appears to have been lost. Furthermore, unlike other prohibitions where the default position is one of impermissibility, the default position where financial transactions are concerned, according to most *fuqaha*, is permissibility, unless there is clear evidence of *riba*, *maysir*, or *gharar*.

The above example illustrates the difficulty in arriving at any form of consensus. While some *madzhabs* like the *Hanbalis* have been broader in their acceptance, the *Shafi'* and *Hanafis* have been less so. For example, the *Hanbalis* are somewhat liberal when it comes to option of stipulation (*Khiyar-al-Shart*). They hold that stipulations that remove a hardship, fulfill a legitimate need, provide a benefit or convenience, or facilitate the smooth flow of commercial transactions, are generally valid as a matter of principle (Ibn Taymiyah).

12.8 *Shari'ah*-Compliant Instruments for Managing Exchange Rate Risk

Until recently, there were hardly any *Shari'ah*-compliant instruments for managing foreign exchange risk. The thinking among *Shari'ah* scholars with regard to foreign exchange risk had been to use "on-balance-sheet" techniques. On-balance-sheet techniques avoid the use of derivatives like forwards, futures, swaps, etc., which are "off-balance-sheet", but require changes in the way one does business. A simple on-balance-sheet technique would be to require a company to price all its foreign transactions in its home currency. For example, they should price all imports and exports in their home currency such that exchange rate risk is avoided. In doing so, the company is effectively passing on all exchange rate risk to its counterparty. While such a technique can mitigate exchange rate risk, it invariably hinders one's competitiveness. Unless a company has some monopolistic power, it may not be possible to price only in home currency.

Given the realities of exchange rate risk in a world with extensive cross-border transactions and the handicap that a restriction to on-balance-sheet techniques places, there has been allowances made to enable currency risk management (see Chapter 11 for a more comprehensive discussion). In response to these "relaxations", a number of IFIs in the Gulf States and in Malaysia have developed a number of *wa'ad*-based products for managing currency risk. A *wa'ad* is a unilateral promise by one party to another in exchange for a fee. There are three *wa'ad*-based products available for exchange rate risk management. These are (i) a *wa'ad*-based currency swap that uses bilateral commodity *murabaha* contracts; (ii) a *wa'ad*-based forward contract; and (iii) a *wa'ad*-based currency option contract. Given the complexity and the controversy surrounding organized commodity *murabahah*, the currency swap is not as popular while the latter two appear to be much more popular. Chapter 13 will provide a detail description of each of these contracts.

Box 12.3. Derivative Instruments, Risk Management, and *Shari'ah* Compliance

The acceptability of financial derivative instruments like forwards, futures, options, and swaps for *Shari'ah*-compliant businesses remains unresolved. As of now, there appears to be no consensus on whether Muslim businesses can use derivative instruments for their risk management needs. While the issue is still being debated and deliberated, risk management remains the soft underbelly of Islamic banking and finance. Still, there has been some progress. *Shari'ah* scholars have allowed the use of *wa'ad* (promise)-based contracts in the case of managing exchange rate risk. Today, *wa'ad*-based contracts that mimic currency forwards and currency options are available both in the Gulf and in Malaysia as *Shari'ah*-compliant ways of hedging exchange risk. The allowance for such an innovation came after years of debate and "pressure" on *Shari'ah* scholars in view of the obvious need for such instruments. The approval for the use of these instruments came with the requirement that the Islamic bank entering into these bilateral arrangements must ensure that the customer is using the derivative solely for hedging. The bank verifies this by requiring the customer who will become the counterparty to show documentary evidence of its underlying currency exposure. Even if this puts the onus on banks to ensure the derivatives are not misused for speculation, it is indeed a workable solution and has been well accepted. It is hard to imagine prohibition on the use of currency derivatives in a world with such volatile exchange rates.

(*Continued*)

Box 12.3. (*Continued*)

Much of the reluctance that *Shari'ah* scholars have with derivatives arises from the fear that they can easily be used for speculation. While this fear is real and well-placed, one needs to also consider the huge handicap placed on Muslim businesses from a blanket prohibition. Given the state of the world, businesses today face many complex risks. Often a risk is not visible until it hits. A classic case is that of contingent exposure, a common occurrence for companies involved in bidding for competitive international tenders. For example, when a company submits a bid to undertake a future foreign currency denominated transaction, and the outcome of the competitive bid will be known a month later, its foreign currency exposure is contingent upon its bid being selected. The bidding company does not know until a month later whether its bid has been accepted; yet, since the bid commits the firm to undertake a future transaction at a predetermined foreign currency amount, its currency exposure begins the very day it submits the bid. So, how does one hedge such exposure? The only way to hedge such contingent exposure is by way of currency options. In fact, derivatives evolved from forwards to futures and then to options precisely to enable the management of such complex risks.

Perhaps due to the continued suspicion surrounding derivatives, as of today, managers of Islamic Mutual Funds have little means to manage the equity risks they face other than through traditional methods of asset allocation. Since it is not possible reverse allocations overnight or within short periods, asset allocation strategies enable managers to make a call on medium- and long-term market moves, not short-term corrections. Whereas the conventional fund manager can ride out short-term market turbulence and sharp drops by hedging with equity index options or index futures contracts, there is no such avenue for the *Shari'ah*-compliant fund manager. These instruments can be executed very quickly and at much lower cost than asset allocation entails. There are two issues to note here. First, this inadequacy of Islamic mutual fund managers goes against the *Shari'ah* requirement for the preservation of wealth. Second, there are larger implications for the competitiveness of Islamic Mutual funds and indeed its long-term viability *vis-à-vis* conventional mutual funds. There is no reason why an accommodation cannot be made here as in the case of currency risk management with strict requirements for their use only in cases of hedging.

Finally, the lack of a coordinated stand on the use of derivatives has resulted in the stunted growth of risk management within Islamic finance. Despite the huge strides that Islamic banking and finance have made in the last decades, *Shari'ah*-compliant risk management has not kept pace. Inadequate risk management capability will be a serious drag on Islamic banking and finance as it moves from infancy to growth. There is an obvious need for a well-considered and enlightened stand on the use of derivatives for hedging.

Source: Author's op-ed piece in *Derin Ekonomi*, December 2015.

Summary

This chapter examines derivative instruments within the Islamic finance framework. The chapter began with an outline of the necessary features for financial instruments to be *Shari'ah* compliant. To be *Shari'ah* compliant, all financial instruments must be free from five elements namely *riba, rishwah, maysir, gharar*, and *jahl*. *Riba*, which is commonly equated to interest, must be avoided in all its forms. The objective of *Shariah* in requiring the avoidance of these elements is to ensure social justice and fair play to all parties in a transaction. A number of instruments and contracts exist in Islamic finance that could be considered a basis for derivative contracts within an Islamic framework. The *bay' al-salam* is a transaction where two parties agree to carry out a sale or purchase of an underlying asset at a predetermined future date but at a price negotiated and fully paid for today. While this is similar to conventional forward contracts, the key difference is in the timing of payment. In forward contracts, payment is made on maturity, whereas in the *salam* contracts, full payment is at the contract initiation. The logic of full upfront payment is based on the fact that the *salam* contract is intended to help needy farmers and small businesses with working capital financing. Given the customized nature of the contract, *salam* shares some of the problems associated with forward contracts. The *istisna* and *joala* are two other contracts where a transaction is made on a yet to exist underlying asset. The *istisna* has, as its underlying, a product to be manufactured. The *joala* is appropriate when contracting for services to be performed in the future.

The *istijrar* is a financing contract with embedded options that could be triggered if the underlying asset's price exceeds certain bounds. The embedded option is the right to choose to fix the price at which settlement will occur any time before contract maturity. *Sukuk* are another instrument with embedded options. Here, the embedded options enable the *sukuk*-holders to either buy the underlying asset (embedded call) or sell the underlying asset (embedded put) at predetermined prices. In doing so, the fixity of cash flows is avoided. The IPRS is a *Shari'ah*-compliant method by which an IFI can manage its profit rate risk and immunize its net worth. Just as a fixed or floating interest rate swap can help a conventional bank manage its duration gaps and interest rate exposure, an IPRS can do the same for an Islamic bank.

In the area of exchange rate risk management, there are a number of *wa'ad*-based contracts that are *Shari'ah* compliant variants of the conventional currency forward and currency option contracts.

Questions and Problems

1. What is the need for an IPRS? How is it different from an interest rate swap?
2. What is the rationale for embedding options within *sukuk*? In what way does it make sukuk more *Shari'ah* compliant?
3. Briefly describe how an Islamic Money Market Fund with a huge holding of short-term papers can protect itself from falling rates by way of an IPRS.
4. Describe some of the instruments available for a *Shari'ah*-compliant way of managing exchange rate risk.
5. Compare and contrast the *istijrar* contract with its closest conventional contract. What are the main similarities and differences?
6. Which conventional derivative contract does a *bay' al-salam* contract closely resemble? What are the similarities and differences? What common problems are applicable to both *bay' al-salam* and the conventional contract?
7. Differentiate between *bay' al-salam, istisna*, and *joala* contracts. What are the similarities and differences?
8. a. What is the rationale for full payment upfront by the long position in the *bay' al-salam* contract?
   b. How much in-built leverage is there in the *bay' al-salam*?
9. Evaluate the *bay' al-salam* contract in terms of its applicability for hedging, arbitrage, and speculation. Outline the possibilities and constraints of the contract for such applications.
10. Would it be possible for one to speculate on interest rate movements using the IPRS? Explain your answer.
11. As Head of Treasury Operations for a large *takaful* firm, you are considering how to hedge a RM100 million holding of a sovereign *sukuk*. The *ijarah*-based *sukuk* has three years left to maturity and pays a semi-annual *ijarah* payment referenced on KLIBOR. The *ijarah* payment is determined as six-month KLIBOR + 0.5%. You are worried that sharp reductions in KLIBOR over the next three years could reduce your returns. Your boss, the CFO, has asked you to fully hedge the position.
    (a) Identify a *Shari'ah*-compliant way by which you can hedge the position.
    (b) Plot the structure of the hedge, and show the cash flows and other needed details.
    (c) While you have hedged one risk, state the new risk that arises as a result of this hedge position.
12. You work for a large fund management house. One of its newest and most successful funds is "KLIMM", which is an Islamic Money Market fund. The fund has RM300 million invested in Islamic Money Market Instruments. Just like a mutual fund which would use unit holders' funds to invest in stocks, a money market fund invests in money market instruments and gives a return to its investors from the money market investments. Your boss has asked you to examine the interest rate exposure of KLIMM. The fund (KLIMM) pays investors a profit distribution every six months. Assuming your boss wants you to consider a three-year horizon and the total fund size is expected to be at RM300 million over that period,
    (a) Identify a *Shari'ah*-compliant way by which KLIMM can manage its profit exposure.
    (b) Structure the hedge and show the exact cash flows, periodic intervals, and other details.
    (c) Prove that KLIMM will be protected regardless of interest/profit rate movements (use a figure if necessary).
13. Bank Koperasi is an Islamic bank that provides financing mostly to government servants. It offers, housing, auto, appliances, and personal financing products to all levels of government servants. Given rapid growth in recent years, the bank had raised funding by way of placements in the Islamic Interbank Money Market (IIMM). It currently has approximately RM200 million of papers outstanding in IIMM on any given month. The bank is planning an equity issuance in two years that should reduce the bank's reliance on money market funds. Meanwhile, Mr Kamal, the CFO, is worried about the impact of rising interest rates on the cost of these funds.
    (a) Design an Islamic Profit Rate Swap (IPRS) that can help Bank Koperasi to cap its funding cost for the next two years. (Show cash flows and direction of flows.)

(b) Briefly explain how Bank Koperasi will be immune from a rise in rates.
(c) Assuming the cash flows in the IPRS above are exchanged once a year, what is the likely impact on the duration gap of Bank Koperasi? Explain.

14. Suppose the Government, in attempting to Islamize the derivative markets, prohibits the trading of CPO (Crude Palm Oil) futures and requires futures to be replaced by *bay' al-salam* contracts on CPO, what benefits/problems would you foresee for:
    (a) Hedgers
    (b) Speculators
    (c) The overall economy

Bibliography

Al-Suwailem, S. (2006). "Hedging in Islamic Finance," Occasional Paper No. 10, Islamic Development Bank, Jeddah.

Capital Market Products According to Islamic Jurisprudence. Securities Commission Malaysia, URL: https://ribh.files.wordpress.com/2007/08/capital-markets-products-according-to-islamic-jurisprudence.pdf.

Derin Ekonomi (2015). December.

Khan, T. and H. Ahmed (2001). "Risk Management — An Analysis of Issues in Islamic Financial Industry," Occasional Paper No. 5, Islamic Development Bank/Islamic Research and Training Institute, Jeddah.

Mohammad Hashim Kamali (2002), *Islamic Commercial Law: An analysis of Futures and Options*. Ilmiah Publishers (Kuala Lumpur, Malaysia).

Obiyathulla I. Bacha (2013), Risk Management, Derivatives and Shariah Compliance, American Institute of Physics, Conference Proceedings. AIP Conf. Proc. 1522, 17 (2013); doi: 10.1063/1.4801099. http://dx.doi.org/10.1063/1.4801099

Obiyathulla, I. B. (2017). *Financial Derivatives: Market and Applications in Malaysia*. 4th Edition (McGraw Hill, Malaysia).

Obaidullah, M. (1999). "Financial Options in Islamic Contracts: Potential Tools for Risk Management," *Journal of KAU Islamic Economics*, Vol. 11, pp. 3–26.

Resolutions of the Securities Commission Shariah Advisory Council — Securities Commission, Kuala Lumpur.

Websites

http://www.zawya.com/middle-east/financial-markets

Chapter 13

EXCHANGE RATES AND THE FOREIGN EXCHANGE MARKET

Topics in this Chapter

13.1. Introduction
13.2. What is an Exchange Rate?
13.3. Exchange Rate Risk
13.4. The Foreign Exchange Market
13.5. Foreign Exchange Market Players
13.6. Spot and Forward Markets
13.7. Bid-Ask Spreads
13.8. The Forward Market for Exchange Rates
13.9. Rates
13.10. Forward versus Spot Rates
13.11. Forward Market Players
13.12. Cross
13.13. Nominal versus Real Exchange Rates
13.14. *Shariah*-Compliant Techniques for Managing Currency Exposure

Chapter Objective

This chapter is designed to provide an overview of foreign exchange markets, its activities, and products. The chapter discusses what exchange rates are, how they are quoted, and how changes are measured. Exchange rate exposure and its management are examined in depth. The chapter concludes with an examination of *Shari'ah*-compliant techniques for managing currency exposure. On completing the chapter, you should have a good understanding of how foreign exchange markets work and of the *Shari'ah*-compliant alternatives now available.

Key Terms		
arbitrageurs	foreign exchange market	*salam*
ask price	forward market	*sarf*
Bank for International Settlements (BIS)	forward rate	short position

(*Continued*)

(*Continued*)

Key Terms		
bid price	hedgers	speculators
bid-ask spread	Islamic FX forward	spot market
carry trade	Islamic FX *wa'ad*	spot rate
cross rates	nominal exchange rate	terms of trade
currency exposure	premium	triangular currency arbitrage
exchange rate	Purchasing Power Parity (PPP)	*wa'ad*
foreign currency (FC)	real exchange rate	

13.1 Introduction

The foreign exchange (forex) market is an important part of any nation's capital market. Depending on how one looks at it, one could either consider the foreign exchange market as a component of the capital market or as a link between domestic capital markets with global capital markets. Either way, the forex market can be a key source of liquidity for a domestic capital market. Actions of participants in the forex can either increase liquidity in a domestic capital market through capital inflows or drain liquidity through capital outflows.

The proper functioning of a domestic capital market and its well-being can depend, to a large extent, on equilibrium in the foreign exchange market and the national currency's exchange rate (see Figure 13.1). So, what exactly are the exchange rate and the foreign exchange market?

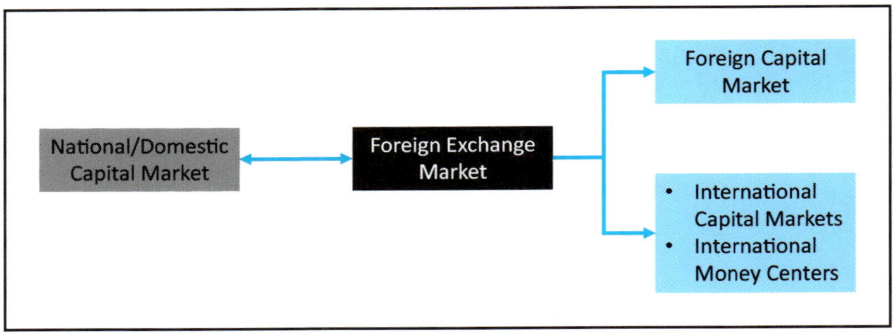

Figure 13.1. The Link Between Domestic and International Capital Markets.

13.2 What is an Exchange Rate?

An exchange rate can simply be defined as the price of a foreign currency in terms of a local currency. For example, when we say the MYR/USD exchange rate is RM3.56, it means that the price per US Dollar (USD) in terms of Malaysian Ringgit (MYR) is RM3.56. It costs RM3.56 to buy US$1. If exchange rates are simply prices, then just as prices change when demand, supply and other factors change, so do exchange rates. For example, if the demand for US$ by Malaysians increase, *ceteris paribus*, the US$ will increase in price against the Ringgit. We call such an increase an *appreciation*. In this case, since the US$ has increased in value against the Ringgit, we say the US$ has appreciated against the Ringgit. If the US$ has gone higher in price in Ringgit terms, it follows that the US$ price of the Ringgit must be lower. We call such reduction in value *depreciation*. Since an exchange rate is a quotation involving a pair of currencies, an appreciation of one must mean a depreciation of the other. However, unless the exchange rate is unitary, that is one to one, the percentage appreciation of one currency need not equal the percentage depreciation of the other. To understand this, let us work through an illustration.

Determining Percentage Appreciation/Depreciation of Currencies

- Suppose on the spot rate on January 2, 20XX is: USD/MYR Exchange Rate = RM3.42 per US$
- The exchange rate at year-end on December 31, 20XX is: USD/MYR Exchange Rate = RM3.20 per US$

Given the above spot exchange rates:

(i) Which currency has appreciated or depreciated?

(ii) What is the percentage appreciation or depreciation?

Based on the above rates, it is clear that the Malaysian Ringgit (MYR) has appreciated against the US$. This is because it costs less in December to buy a US$ as it did in January (i.e., RM3.20/US$ as opposed to RM3.42/US$). Since the Ringgit value of the US$ has fallen, we say that US$ has depreciated against the MYR.

- MYR has appreciated against USD.
- USD has depreciated against MYR.

Box 13.1. Illustration: What is the Percentage Appreciation/Depreciation?

Generally, the percentage appreciation and depreciation of a currency can be computed as follows:

$$\%\text{Appreciation} = \left[\frac{e_1 - e_0}{e_0}\right] \times 100 \qquad (13.1)$$

$$\left[\frac{\frac{1}{e_1} - \frac{1}{e_0}}{\frac{1}{e_0}}\right] \times 100 \Rightarrow \left[\frac{e_0 - e_1}{e_1}\right] \times 100 \qquad (13.2)$$

Where

e_1 = exchange rate in the new period

e_0 = exchange rate in the previous period

% Depreciation =

In using Equations 13.1 and 13.2 one has to be careful about the terms by which the exchange rate is quoted. Equation 13.1 would work if the exchange rates are entered as US$ value of MYR, however, we are given exchange rates as Ringgit (MYR) value of US$. To convert from the stated MYR value of US$ to US$ value of MYR is a simple process. One simply takes the reciprocal.

	MYR Value Of US$	*US$ Value Of MYR*
e_0	3.42	**1/3.42 = 0.2924**
e_1	3.20	**1/3.20 = 0.3125**

Thus, e_0 of 3.42 MYR per US$ is equivalent to 0.2924 US$ per MYR.

The percentage appreciation of MYR is determined using Eq. (13.1):

$$\left(\frac{e_1 - e_0}{e_0}\right) = 100 - \left(\frac{0.3125 - 0.2924}{0.2924}\right) \times 100 = 6.87\%$$

(Continued)

Box 13.1. (*Continued*)

Thus, MYR has appreciated 6.87% against the US$ over the one-year period.

The percentage depreciation of US$ is determined using Eq. (13.2):

$$\left(\frac{e_0 - e_1}{e_1}\right)\times 100 - \left(\frac{0.2924 - 0.3125}{0.3125}\right)\times 100 = -6.43\%$$

Percentage appreciation of MYR = 6.87%
Percentage depreciation of US$ = 6.43%

The exchange rate, therefore, is a price, and like other prices, it is influenced by demand and supply conditions. While exchange rates are a price, it is a very important price, in the sense that it has widespread impact on the overall economy. Just an incorrect price will distort a product's demand and supply equilibrium, a misaligned exchange rate, especially against currencies of key trading partners, and could impact a nation's competitiveness. This happens because an exchange rate dictates the *terms of trade* between any two countries. An undervalued or underpriced exchange rate increases a nation's competitiveness, whereas an overvalued exchange rate reduces competitiveness. These changes in competitiveness come hand in hand with other factors. For example, trying to gain competitiveness by deliberately undervaluing a currency may only work temporarily. Over a longer period, such undervaluation causes imported inflation and provides perverse incentives and a myriad of other problems, including dysfunctional industrial growth. The long-term consequences could be heavy.

13.3 Exchange Rate Risk

Having discussed changes in exchange rates, we now turn to the related issue of exchange rate risk. If exchange rates can change, the parties involved foreign currency transactions would be exposed to exchange rate risks. Exchange rate risks can simply be defined as the potential change in the value of assets, liabilities, revenues, and costs as a result of changes in the exchange rate. To understand how changes in exchange rates can cause changes in revenues, costs, assets, or liabilities, we go through the following illustration in Box 13.2:

Box 13.2. Illustration: Understanding Exchange Rate Risk

- **Changes in revenue due to exchange rate change**

A Malaysian exporter of sawn timber has just shipped 500 tons to his Japanese customer, the Marubeni Corporation. The exporter has priced the product of RM30 million and has, therefore, invoiced Marubeni Corp. for ¥300 million. This Yen amount was arrived at using the current spot rate of ¥10 per MYR. Marubeni has 90 days to pay the ¥300million. As is typical with most cross-border transactions, where at least one party would be faced with exchange rate exposure, the Malaysian exporter is exposed to exchange rate risk in this case. Marubeni Corp. of Japan has no currency exposure since they are paying in Yen, which is the home currency. The exposure, therefore, is for the Malaysian exporter who has a foreign currency receivable. This ¥300 million receivable is revenue for the Malaysian company.

Depending on what the spot rate between Yen and MYR is on Day 90, the ¥300 million received may have a value different from the expected RM30 million. If the Yen appreciates over the next 90 days, the proceeds in MYR could be

(*Continued*)

Box 13.2. (*Continued*)

higher than RM30 million. If, on the other hand, the Yen depreciates, proceeds could be lower. It is this uncertainty and the resulting implied "gain" or "loss" that is the exchange rate risk. We examine below the Ringgit (MYR) proceeds for three different spot rates on Day 90.

(i) Spot Rate on Day 90: Yen depreciates to ¥12 per MYR

$$\text{Proceeds in MYR} = \frac{¥300\text{mil}}{12.0} = 25 \text{ million}$$

Ringgit (MYR) proceeds = RM25 million

Thus, implied loss based on expected RM30 million.

= (RM25 million – RM30 million)
= (RM5 million)

The Malaysian exporter would have made an exchange loss of RM5 mil.

(ii) Spot Rate on Day 90: Yen unchanged at ¥10 per MYR

$$\text{Proceeds in MYR} = \frac{¥300 \text{ million}}{10} = \text{RM30 million}$$

Ringgit (MYR) proceeds = RM30 million.

Since the proceeds equal the expected RM30 mil, there will be no exchange gain or loss.

(iii) Spot Rate on Day 90: Yen appreciates to ¥8.5 per MYR

$$\text{Proceeds in MYR} = \frac{¥300 \text{ million}}{8.5} = \text{RM35.29 million}$$

Ringgit (MYR) proceeds = RM35.29 million.
Implied gain = (Actual proceeds – Expected proceeds)

= RM35.29 million – RM30 million
= RM5.29 million

With the appreciation of the Yen, the Malaysian exporter stands to gain RM5.29 million as a result.

What can we summarize from the above illustration?

For receivables or revenue denominated in Foreign Currency (FC):

FC appreciation against HC (Home Country) = Exchange gain
FC depreciation against HC (Home Country) = Exchange loss

(i) Changes in costs due to exchange rate change

A Malaysian distributor of electrical appliances has just confirmed the import of a range of flat screen HDTVs from Samsung of South Korea. Samsung will invoice the amount of Korean Won (KRW) 980 million for the goods. Payment will be due in 90 days. The current MYR/KRW rate is RM0.30 per 100 Won.

To examine the impact of a change in the MYR/KRW exchange rate on the Malaysia's company's Ringgit cost, we examine two scenarios. First, if the Won appreciates against the Ringgit, and second, if the Won depreciates against Ringgit.

(i) Spot Rate on Day 90: KRW appreciates to RM0.33 per 100 won

Cost in MYR = [(W980 mil. × 0.01) × 0.33] = RM3,234.000

(*Continued*)

Box 13.2. (*Continued*)

Based on the exchange rate on Day 0, of RM0.30 per 100 Won, the Ringgit cost would have been:

Cost in MYR = [(W980 mil. × 0.01) × 0.30] = RM2,940,000

Implied exchange loss due to higher Won
= Expected Cost – Actual Cost
= RM2,940,000 – RM3,234,000
= RM294,000

(ii) Spot Rate on Day 90: KRW depreciates to RM0.26 per 100 Won

Cost in MYR = [(W980 mil. × 0.01) × 0.26] = RM2,548,000

Based on Day 0, exchange rate of RM0.30 per 100 Won, the Malaysian importer makes an implied gain from the Won's depreciation. This exchange rate gain is:

Expected Cost – Actual Cost
= RM2,940,000 – RM2,548,000
= RM392,000

Summarizing from the above example:

For costs or payables denominated in a foreign currency (FC):

(ii) FC depreciation against HC (Home Country) = Exchange gain
(iii) FC appreciation against HC (Home Country) = Exchange loss

Again, the size of the gain or loss would depend on the extent of exchange rate change (see Table 13.1).

Table 13.1. Exchange Rate Change and Gains/Losses.

FC Denominated	Item	Impact if FC Appreciates Against HC	Impact if FC Depreciates Against HC
Exports	Revenue	+	–
Imports	Cost	–	+
Receivable	Asset	+	–
Payable	Liability	–	+

Exchange rate exposure arises the moment one enters into a foreign currency denominated transaction. Depending on one's position in the transaction and the direction of change in the exchange rate, an exchange rate-induced gain or loss is possible. This uncertainty is known as exchange rate risk. In Section 13.11, we examine some of the ways by which this exchange rate risk can be managed. Having discussed exchange rate movements and the potential consequences, we now turn to a discussion of the foreign exchange market, its evolution, and the key determinants of exchange rate change.

13.4 The Foreign Exchange Market

The foreign exchange market is by far the largest asset market where value is concerned. According to the Bank for International Settlements (BIS) which undertakes a triennial survey of global foreign exchange activity, the mean daily traded volume of currencies and exchange rate derivatives globally exceeds US$3.2 trillion. Adjusting for reduced volume on Sundays and weekends, the annual total volume of foreign exchange traded globally would be in the vicinity of US$800 trillion. Table 13.2 shows a statistical summary.

Table 13.2. Global Foreign Exchange Market Turnover. Daily Averages — 2001 Until April 2016 in Billions of US Dollars

	2001	2004	2007	2010	2013	2016
Spot transactions	386	631	1,005	1,489	2,047	1,652
Outright forwards	130	209	362	475	679	700
Foreign Exchange Swaps	656	954	1,714	1,759	2,240	2,378
Currency Swaps	7	21	31	43	54	82
Options and Other Products	60	119	212	207	337	254
Total	1,239	1,934	3,324	3,973	5,357	5,067

Source: BIS Triennial Survey 2016.

Figure 13.2 plots the average total daily volume over the years 1995 to 2016. The growth in traded volume is obvious. Over the 21-year period, the average total daily has nearly quadrupled. Growth appears most rapid over the last 10 years from 2007 to 2017. The average daily total volume has grown in excess of 20% year on year, a clear indication that the growth trend is still in place and not tapering. Aside from the massive total size, what makes the foreign exchange market impressive is the rapid growth rate.

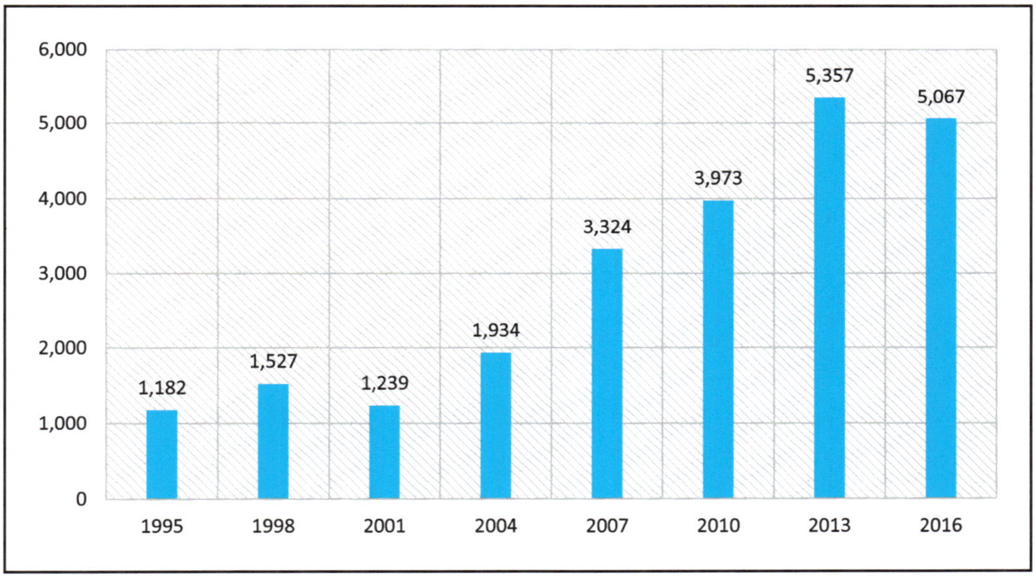

Figure 13.2. Growth in Average Daily Volume (1995–2016).

Critics of the foreign exchange market point at this very rapid growth in traded volume and the obvious disconnection with the growth in international trade to argue that the foreign exchange market is one fraught with speculators and speculative activity. The typical argument is that the traded volume of currencies is several folds larger than that of the total cross-border transactions in goods and services. While the BIS report acknowledges the increased presence of hedge funds and carry-trades, one has to keep in mind that a single import or export transaction can lead to a series of forex market transactions before it is "fully hedged". For example, an importer with a foreign exchange currency payable would, on entering forward contract with his bank, eliminate his currency exposure.

However, his bank which is the counterparty now has the risk. The bank will now go into another forward or other currency market contract with another counterparty to manage the risk. This "passing on" of exposure can go on a few more times until a counterparty with the exact opposite needs as the importer is found. Thus, genuine hedging needs can lead to a cumulative value of trade in the forex market, far larger than that of the underlying transaction.

Despite being the largest market in the world and possibly the deepest, the foreign exchange market is the least organized. Unlike other markets that trade in assets and have organized exchanges and registered brokers or players playing by well-defined rules, the foreign exchange market has more of these. There is no physical exchange and, as such, no single set of ground rules that becomes abiding on the players within. The foreign exchange market is really a global network of banks linked electronically. These banks and other large financial institutions trade among themselves, both for their own accounts and for their customers. It is this "wholesale" trading that dictates the rates of exchange among currencies. One can imagine a network that is pyramidal in shape with a small number of very large players at the top and numerous small players (commercial banks) at the base. As this computerized network is across borders, there is no single set of rules that apply to all players. Furthermore, in the absence of a centralized exchange, players are not necessarily registered. All of these enable anonymity. Thus, big trades could be done without revealing who the buyer or seller is. While this anonymity may be helpful for central banks, e.g., to hide their trades when intervening in exchange rate markets, it can be a disadvantage, e.g., when defending a currency during a speculative attack.

Despite these inconveniences, the foreign exchange market is highly efficient, especially in the context of informational efficiency. Given the computerized nature of the market, price changes are disseminated in real time and are available to all participants. Furthermore, given the size and depth, price manipulation is practically impossible, especially with regard to the major currencies. Geographically, the world's largest center for foreign exchange trading is London, United Kingdom. This is followed by New York (US), Switzerland, Japan, and then Hong Kong. As a sample, Table 13.3 shows the total foreign exchange turnover for the top nine countries, for the month of April 2010 on which the BIS Triennial Survey is based.

Table 13.3. Top Nine Countries by Foreign Exchange Turnover. (Total Turnover for April 2016; in US$ Billions and Percentage)

Country	Amount	% of Total Turnover
United Kingdom	2,406	36.94
United States	1,272	19.53
Singapore	517	7.94
Hong Kong SAR	437	6.71
Japan	399	6.13
France	181	2.78
Switzerland	156	2.39
Australia	121	1.86
Germany	116	1.78
Other Countries	909	13.95
Total	6,514	100

Source: Statistics Explorer (http://Stats.bis.org/statx/).

The pre-eminence of London is a carryover from history, where London acted as the "clearinghouse" for all transactions between countries within the British Colonial Empire. Where currencies are concerned, the US dollar is by far the most actively traded currency. The Euro is a distant second and accounts for less than half the traded volume of the US$. This is followed by the Japanese Yen, the Pound Sterling, and the Australian dollar. Table 13.4 lists the top 20 currencies based on the BIS 2016 Triennial Survey.

Table 13.4. Top 20 Currencies by Traded Volume.

Rank	Currency	Rank	Currency
1	U.S. dollar	11	Mexican Peso
2	Euro	12	Singapore Dollar
3	Japanese Yen	13	Hong Kong Dollar
4	Pound Sterling	14	Norwegian Krone
5	Australian Dollar	15	Korean Won
6	Canadian Dollar	16	Turkish Lira
7	Swiss Franc	17	Russian Ruble
8	Chinese Yuan	18	Indian Rupee
9	Swedish Krona	19	Brazilian Real
10	New Zealand Dollar	20	South African Rand

Source: BIS Triennial Central Bank Survey 2016.

Notice that the currencies of the two biggest Asian countries, the Indian Rupee and the Chinese Renminbi, are in 8th and 18th places, respectively. The Chinese Renminbi has had very impressive growth in traded volume, a reflection of China's increasing economic prowess. Given China's growth and dominance in trade, it is likely that the Renminbi could be within the top five currencies in the immediate future. South Korea, the other Asian manufacturing powerhouse, has the Won in 15th place.

Box 13.3. The Evolution of Exchange Rate Regimes

If one examines the current global system of exchange rate determination, one would see a mixed bag of subsystems. Some currencies are on fixed exchange rate regimes, others on some variant of floating rate system, and yet others on crawling pegs, regional currency agreements, and so on. Few, if any currencies, are truly on a free float, though the Australian, Canadian, and New Zealand dollars would come close. This hotchpotch of subsystems was not always the case.

At different times of modern history, the world, or at least a majority of the world's currencies, had been on common exchange rate regimes. Three such "recent" systems were: (i) The Classical Gold Standard (1821–1914), (ii) The Gold Exchange Standard (1925–1931), and (iii) The Bretton Woods System (1946–1971). The "non-system" that we have today has been in place since 1971, when the Bretton Woods System collapsed. You would notice from the dates attached to each regime that the collapse of one was followed by a period of "non-system" before a new regime was put in place. The collapse of an exchange rate regime and economic and political turbulence are closely related and often go together. The causal relationships are often both ways.

Broadly speaking, today's exchange rate arrangements can be categorized into three categories: (i) Fixed/pegged, (ii) Free Float, and (iii) Managed Float. Placing these three categories in a continuum, we would have fixed exchange rates at one end and free floats at the other. In between these two extremes would be a wide range of managed floats.

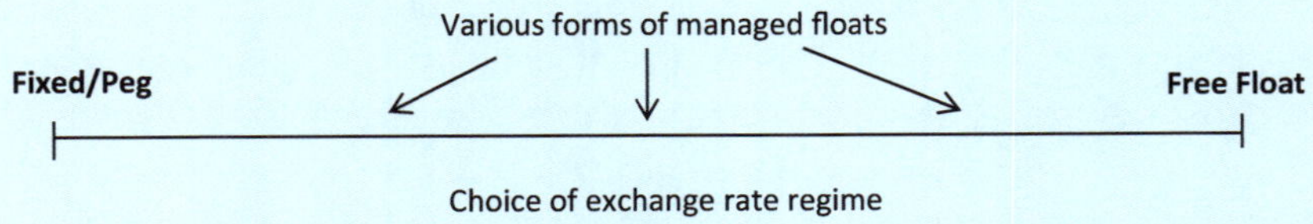

(*Continued*)

Box 13.3. (*Continued*)

A fixed exchange rate is one where a currency's exchange rate against another is fixed by government fiat. The most common way to do this is by way of "pegging" the domestic currency at a desired exchange to a major currency. Usually, the currency of the country's major trading partner or the currency in which most of the country's international trade is denominated in. The Gulf Cooperation Council (GCC) countries all have currencies "pegged" to the US$. Unlike Hong Kong, which has an officially announced peg to the US or Malaysia for a period following the Asian Financial Crisis of 1997–1998 (the Malaysian Ringgit was pegged to the US$ at RM3.80 per dollar from September 1998 to July 2005), many countries do not necessarily announce their "peg".

A freely floating exchange rate is one where the issuing government does not intervene at all but allows market forces to determine the exchange rate. Given the free float, the currency will adjust automatically to policy changes. This implies that a freely floating currency will never be substantially misaligned at any given time. Thus, the possibility of a speculative attacked on a freely floating currency is minimal. It is the misalignment of an exchange rate that causes a currency to be overvalued and thereby vulnerable to a speculative attack.

As with everything in economics, the choice of exchange rate regime involves trade-offs. The trade-offs can be shown as follows;

Exchange Rate	Key Advantage	Trade-Off
Fixed	Exchange rate stability (especially with pegged currency)	No domestic policy flexibility — especially monetary policy.
Free Float	Retain full policy flexibility	Exchange rate of home currency can be volatile.

A fixed exchange rate has the advantage of providing exchange rate stability, particularly against the currency to which it is pegged. However, the trade-off is that the government loses domestic monetary policy flexibility, i.e., it cannot conduct independent monetary policies. For a country with a fixed peg, domestic policies, especially monetary policies, must be in sync with that of the currency to which it is pegged. Thus, for example, Hong Kong, which has a fixed peg of the HK$ to the US$, has no domestic monetary policy to speak of. It needs to follow the policies of the US. Failure to do so could mean that the peg would not hold. Maintaining a "looser" monetary policy while holding on to the peg could mean "overvaluation" of the domestic currency, thereby making it vulnerable for a speculative attack. This was exactly what happened to Argentina's peso in January 2002. Despite having pegged the peso to the US$ in the late 1990s, the Argentinean government had adopted a much more expansionary monetary policy than required to maintain the peg. The result was an overvaluation of the peso and a speculative attack, causing a sharp devaluation and removal of peg.

As we saw above, exchange rate policies involve trade-offs. A managed float is essentially a "middle-of-the road" policy. In a way, it is an attempt at getting both a degree of policy flexibility and some exchange rate stability at the same time. Typically, under a managed float, the Central Bank will try to keep the exchange rate of its currency within some "band" or range against another currency or a group or basket of currencies. Each time the home currency depreciates below the lower bound, the central bank intervenes to bring it back up. Similar intervention happens if the home currency appreciates "too much".

What was unique about the Classical Gold Standard, the Gold Exchange Standard, and the Bretton Woods systems was that they were fixed exchange rate, gold parity systems. In essence, the exchange rate among currencies was fixed according to the gold parities or gold reserves backing the currency. Thus, reserves of gold determined how valuable or otherwise a currency was. Governments which were signatories to these arrangements were required to do everything within their means to ensure that the "pegged" exchange rate holds. The problem with such a system was that domestic money supply became dependent heavily on availability of gold reserves. For example, in order to increase domestic money supply, governments had to first increase their gold reserves. As a result, not only were governments unable to adopt countercyclical policies, exchange rate stability meant that external shocks were transmitted directly into the domestic economy. Furthermore, being a fixed exchange rate system, it was subject to speculative attacks every time there was a perceived misalignment. The fact that gold-backed system had collapsed three times in recent history is testimony to its brittleness.

13.5 Foreign Exchange Market Players

Given the oligopolistic nature of the foreign exchange market, a number of large money center banks dominate currency trading. These are large commercial banks located in the global money centers such as London, New York, Tokyo, Zurich, Hong Kong, and so on. In addition to these banks, there are foreign exchange dealers. These are institutions located in the money centers specializing in a few currencies. These dealers hold inventory and are always able to provide bid-ask quotes for the currencies they specialize in. The third largest players are the central banks. Central banks are active in foreign exchange markets, largely for the purpose of exchange rate management. As we will see later, central banks intervene in foreign exchange markets for the purpose of managing the exchange rate of their currency. They do this by buying or selling their home currency *vis-à-vis* a foreign currency. The fourth largest participants are probably the multinational corporations (MNCs). MNCs, by virtue of their business activities across borders, are big players in foreign exchange markets. To date, there has been another category of active participants in forex markets. These are hedge fund and other large fund managers. These players are interested in arbitraging in currencies between markets and in what is commonly known as the *carry trade*. The carry trade has more to do with arbitraging interest differentials rather than currencies. However, since it involves borrowing and lending in two different currencies, it accounts for a large chunk of the traded volume in some currencies. A key carry trade would be to borrow Japanese Yen in Japan, which has low interest rates, convert the Yen to, say Australian Dollar, and place the funds as deposits in Australia, which has higher interest rates. As long as the Yen does not appreciate against the Australian Dollar, such a carry trade would be profitable. Though such carry trades can be profitable at certain times, theoretically, this inefficiency ought to be arbitraged away. Also, notice that the carry trade involves extensive exchange rate risk. One is short Yen and long Australian Dollar in this instance.

While there are obviously numerous different types of players, they can all be categorized into three broad categories according to objective. These are hedgers, arbitrageurs, and speculators. *Hedgers* are essentially using the foreign exchange market to manage their risk. As we saw above, importers, with payables in foreign currency, and exporters, with receivables in foreign currency, face exchange rate exposure. To manage these exposures, hedgers would use the currency markets, particularly forward contracts. If hedgers use the currency markets to manage their exposure, arbitrageurs use them to take advantage of mispricing. Arbitrage is the activity of taking advantage of market mispricing. Since currencies are traded concurrently in several markets, *arbitrageurs* look for small deviations in the quote rates. Once they see a small deviation, they arbitrage by going "long the underpriced currency and short the overpriced one". In the case of intermarket arbitrage, they would buy in the market where the currency is underquoted and sell it in the market where it has the higher relative price. Such arbitrage, often known as *triangular currency arbitrage* because it involves three currencies, is popular and has been refined to such a fine art that these days such arbitrage is undertaken by computers preprogrammed to identify and undertake the arbitrage in real time. Such "program trading" implies that mispricing, if any, disappears very quickly.

The final category of players, *speculators*, use the currency markets to take positions based on their expectations. For example, they would go long (take a buy position) a currency they expect would appreciate and short currencies they expect to depreciate. Their profit or loss will depend on whether the currency moved in line with their expectations and on the size of their bets (position). Though speculators add little economic value, their activity increases trading volume and liquidity. This in turn reduces the transaction costs and reduces the liquidity risks for genuine hedgers. So, there may be indirect benefits to hedgers from the presence of speculators, aside from the fact that speculators would willingly take on the risk that hedgers want to transfer.

13.6 Spot and Forward Markets

Foreign exchange transactions can be categorized into two broad categories: spot transactions and forward transactions. As the name suggests, a spot transaction is for immediate delivery whereas a forward transaction is for delivery at a predetermined future date. Suppose one wants a foreign currency immediately, the appropriate price to pay would be his or her bank's quoted spot rate for the currency. When it comes to exchange rate quotation, most financial newspapers would show three categories of quotes. These are:

- Spot quotes
- Forward quotes
- Cross rates

As mentioned above, the spot quote gives the spot price of a foreign currency. Spot exchange rates come in two versions or terms, *American* terms and *European* terms. Both refer to the same exchange rate but from different viewpoints. When an exchange rate is quoted in American terms, it would be in the form of:

Home Currency price per unit foreign currency (HC per FC).
A quote in European terms on the other hand would be:
Foreign currency price per unit home currency (FC per HC).

For example, we see the MYR/US$ quote as follows:
RM3.24 per US$, this would obviously be an American term quote.

Alternatively, if the quote is:
US$0.3086 per MYR, this would be the European term quote.

In Malaysia, both the American and European terms are used in exchange rate quotations. Converting from one to another is easy; one simply takes the reciprocal. For example, in the above quotation, the taking reciprocal of the American term quote of MYR/US$ rate gives the European term equivalent.

$$\frac{1}{(3.2)^4} = 0.3086$$

Alternatively,

$$\frac{1}{0.3086} = 3.24$$

A point of caution is in order. Since each quotation term states the price in terms of a different currency, one has to mindful of needed changes when using Equations 13.1 and 13.2 earlier in the chapter, when computing percentage appreciation or depreciation.

13.7 Bid-Ask Spreads

In currency transactions, banks do not charge commissions. They profit from bid-ask spreads. The bid-ask spread, often denoted as b-a spread, refers to the difference between the prices at which the bank buys versus sells a foreign currency. Generally:

Bank buys at the = bid price
Bank sells at the = ask price

So, the bid-ask spread is essentially the difference between the buy and sell prices and would constitute the profit earned by the bank.

Box 13.4. Illustration: The Bid-Ask Spread

The following are spot rate quotations by Bank Negara Malaysia, on March 20, 2017

	Bid	Ask
1 US Dollar	4.4300	4.4350
1 Euro	4.7658	4.7729
100 Japanese Yen	3.9360	3.9419
1 Singapore Dollar	3.1672	3.1715
100 Indonesian Rupiah	0.0332	0.0333
100 Philippine Peso	8.8317	8.8444
100 Thai Baht	12.7559	12.7751

There are two things to note from the above quotations. First, the bidding price is lower than the asking, and second, the bid-ask spread is different for different currencies.

The bid-ask spread is often described as a percentage, which could be computed as:

$$\left(\frac{\text{Ask Price} - \text{Bid Price}}{\text{Ask Price}}\right) \times 100$$

Based on the above equation, the b-a spread percentage for the above seven currencies would be as follows:

1 US Dollar	0.11%
1 Euro	0.15%
100 Japanese Yen	0.15%
1 Singapore Dollar	0.14%
100 Indonesian Rupiah	0.30%
100 Philippine Peso	0.14%
100 Thai Baht	0.15%

Box 13.5. The Problem with Pegged Exchange Rates

In October 2016, Egypt, which had pegged its pound to the US$ at 8.8 per US$ was forced to float its currency. This forced de-peg, caused the pound to fall immediately to 13 per US$, effectively devaluing the pound by 32%. In the days that followed, the fall continued; the Egyptian pound has now depreciated some 50% against the US$. The consequences of this sudden deterioration in the nation's terms of trade are likely to be felt for some time to come. In an attempt to prevent further falls, the Egyptian Central bank raised domestic interest rates by 3%. It appears that even with Egyptian treasuries yielding 22%, the devaluation could not be avoided. For some developing countries, this cycle of peg, forced devaluation, crisis, and re-peg seem to be ongoing. Lessons do not seem to be learnt.

While Egypt is the latest Muslim nation to be in the throes of a currency crisis, it is by no means the only one. Turkey, Indonesia, and Malaysia have all seen their currencies slide over the last many months. Interestingly, the oil exporters of the Gulf, all of whom with the exception of Kuwait, have hard-pegged their currencies to the US$ have not experienced any devaluation despite oil having fallen more than 50%. Obviously, their currency reserves and

(*Continued*)

Box 13.5. (*Continued*)

economic fundamentals have not deteriorated to a point requiring devaluation. They may be well-advised to move to more flexible regimes now.

While one can always debate the efficacy of foreign exchange markets to correctly reflect a nation's fundamentals, the fact that four key Muslim nations have had to let their currencies slide is testimony to the extent of misalignments that can occur. Overvalued exchange rates invariably lead to depreciations, and pegged or quasi-pegged exchange rate regimes are usually at fault. The Egyptian pound, for example, was reportedly selling at 18.25 pounds per US$ when the official rate was 8.8. When the deviation between the official pegged rate and equilibrium rate is large, a black market forms for the US$ with the obvious result that there will be a shortage of US$ at the official rate. A two-tier market such as this gives rise to all sorts of perverse incentives, especially to exporters. With exporters under declaring their US$ earnings, the shortage worsens and the wedge between the official and black market rates widen further, setting the country up for a fall.

Pegged exchange rates have the main advantage of providing exchange rate stability for the home currency against the pegged currency; however, it comes with a number of disadvantages. First, is the fact that the nation choosing to peg loses domestic monetary policy flexibility. For a peg to hold over an extended period, the pegging country will have to follow lock step the monetary policies of the country it chooses to peg to. In the best case of a long holding peg, the HK$ to the US$, Hong Kong effectively has no independent monetary policy. Its monetary policies are simply those of Washington. While such subservience has enabled Honk Kong's peg to hold close to 30 years, the same was not the case for Argentina. Argentina, which chose to peg its peso to the US$) in 1991 had to give up and float its currency in 2001, barely 10 years later. In pegging the peso to the US$ at parity (1 peso for US$1), Argentina had already overvalued its currency. As the US$ rose subsequently, Argentina ran into serious current account deficits and the resultant increase in borrowing. Argentina had also increased domestic money supply way beyond that of the US, causing its peso to be grossly overvalued at the pegged rate.

A pegged exchange rate regime restricts a nation from independently changing its money supply, interest rates, and target inflation rates. Herein lies the problem. Domestic needs may require variations to money supply and/or interest rates. As these changes in monetary variables occur, the equilibrium exchange rate begins to deviate from the pegged exchange rate. Short-term deviations may not matter much but even a marginal 5% deviation over a period of several years compounds into serious misalignment in the pegged exchange rate. Since developing countries like Egypt would require more accommodative policies than the US, the equilibrium rate goes lower effectively causing the pegged rate to be overvalued. The problem is, such overvaluation sneaks up without notice. It typically begins to show up as current account deficits as the overvaluation makes imports cheaper and exports more expensive. With the loss of competitiveness, there is a slow draining of foreign reserves. Where the reserves are not much, a build-up of foreign currency debt results. More ominously, overvalued exchange rates erode and can kill off the domestic industrial base. Comparative advantage notwithstanding, it would be difficult to produce and compete globally from nations with grossly overvalued exchange rates.

Yet, exchange rates can be used advantageously to reach the exact opposite results. For example, the economic powerhouses of the Far East, Japan, Korea, Taiwan, and even China, had all pulled themselves up to developed status through deliberately undervaluing their currencies. Using exchange rates to build an industrial base and then grow exports has been a standard strategy of the Far East nations. For an undervaluation strategy to work, the domestic value-added must be significant, with the import content of exports miniscule.

The majority of Muslim nations appear to be on some form of fixed or quasi-peg regimes. Where export competitiveness is not the main thrust of policy, flexible exchange rates with broad intervention bands may be more logical as they avoid the huge misalignments possible with hard pegs. Ironically, it is with fixed exchange rate regimes that one sees speculative attacks. A fixed exchange rate offers speculators a one way option with little downside.

Source: Author's op-ed column in *Derin Ekonomi*, November 2016.

13.8 Cross Rates

Cross rates are simply an *implied* spot exchange rate, given two other spot rates. Cross rates are used extensively and are an integral part of the spot market in currencies. The use of cross rates arises from practical needs. One can imagine the amount of newspaper or hardcopy space that will be needed if the exchange rate of every currency against every other currency is to be quoted. Suppose there are 160 currencies available, if a currency is to be quoted against the other 159 currencies, the total number of quotations would be (n^{n-1}) in the millions. To avoid the resulting clutter, cross rates are used. As defined above, a cross rate is an implied exchange rate, given two spot rates. Thus, to compute a cross rate, we would need two spot exchange rates, one of which involves the currency for which need the rate. For example, suppose we want to know the Korean Won (KRW)–Malaysian Ringgit (MYR) spot rate. If a direct quote is unavailable, we could determine the implied if we knew the following spot rates:

(i) KRW/US$ spot; and
(ii) MYR/US$ spot

Since the US$ is the common denominator. We compute the implied MYR/KRW rate based on the other two.

Box 13.6. Illustration: Computing Cross Rates

Suppose you wish to compute the KRW/MYR cross rate. (*Note*: Standard notation used in Forex Markets, MYR for the Malaysian Ringgit; KRW for Korean Won.)

You observe the following two quotes:

1 US$ = 1,220 KRW
1 US$ = 3.20 MYR

Given these, what is the KRW/MYR cross rate?

$$\frac{\text{KRW Per \$}}{\text{KRW Per \$}} = \frac{1220}{3.20} = 381.25$$

We would like to cross rate as 381.25 KRW per MYR.

Alternatively, if we had computed the cross-rate as:

$$\frac{\text{KRW Per \$}}{\text{KRW Per \$}} = \frac{3.20}{1220} = 0.0026$$

This would be read as RM0.0026 per KRW. We would have arrived at the same result if we had taken the reciprocal of the earlier cross rate.

$$\frac{1}{381.25} = 0.0026$$

13.9 The Forward Market for Exchange Rates

Having discussed spot markets, we now turn to a discussion of the forward market in exchange rates. As defined earlier, a forward exchange rate is essentially an exchange rate at which currencies will be "swapped" at a predetermined future date and amount. The need for a forward market arises from the need to manage currency risk from foreign currency exposure. For example, as we saw earlier, an importer who needs to pay in foreign currency (FC) will fear an appreciation of the FC against the home currency (HC). Alternatively, an exporter with FC payable would be worried about an appreciation of the FC.

Businesses with such foreign currency exposure can forward contracts in the FC to hedge their exposure. Though forward contracts may not be available in all currencies, most actively traded currencies have forward contracts on them. Obviously, the major currencies like the US Dollar, Yen, Euro, Pound Sterling, Singapore Dollar, etc., have forward contracts easily available. The ability to hedge easily in these currencies is a key reason for denominating many transactions in these currencies.

Forward contracts have fixed future maturities. For example, most financial newspapers will show forward quotes on currencies for 30, 60, and 90 days. Typically, the major currencies have four quotes on any given day. The first quote would be the spot quote followed by three forward quotes of 30-, 60-, and 90-day tenors, respectively. A 30-day tenor simply means that the forward contract will be executed 30 days from today. Since a forward contract is a *customized agreement between two parties agreeing to carry out a transaction at a predetermined date but at a price agreed upon today*, it would be possible to negotiate for other tenors, for e.g., a forward contract that will expire say 42 days from today.

13.10 Forward versus Spot Rates

Forward exchange rates or forward prices are determined based on spot prices. Typically, forward prices are determined using what is known as a cost of carry model, which adjusts the spot price for known carrying costs. In the case of exchange rates, a forward exchange rate would be determined by taking the difference in prevailing interest rates of the two currencies for the tenor concerned. For example, if it is a 90-day forward rate, then the relevant interest rate would be the three-month rates in each currency. Since an asset's price depends on many factors, including expectations, a whole range of factors, from a nation's politics to economic performance, may affect a currency's forward rate. Given both known costs (interest differentials) and expectations, the forward rate could be higher or lower than the spot rate. When the forward rate is higher, it is said to be at a *premium*. When the forward rate is lower than the spot rate, the forward is said to be at a *discount*. Whether a forward rate is at a premium or discount has an important implication. When a currency's forward rate is at a premium, the implication is that the market expects that currency to appreciate over the future. Alternatively, if the forward rate is at a discount, the expectation would be that the currency will depreciate over the future:

$$F_t > S_0\text{; forward at premium;}$$

$$F_t < S_0\text{; forward at discount.}$$

13.11 Forward Market Players

As with most other derivative markets, forward markets are used by a wide array of players. Still, we can divide these players into three broad categories according to their motivation for use. These three categories would be (i) hedgers, (ii) arbitrageurs, and (iii) speculators.

Hedgers would use forward markets for the purpose of managing their exchange rate exposure. The illustration below shows how an exporter or importer can use the forward contract to manage their exposure. Arbitrageurs are players who try to profit from perceived mispricing. In the case of forwards, an arbitrageur will take a long (buy) position if he feels the forward rate is undervalued relative to the spot rate. If, on the other hand, the forward rate is deemed to be overvalued, the arbitrageur would take a short (sell) position in the forward while being long in the spot market. Arbitrageurs always have two simultaneous positions to take advantage of the mispricing between the two asset markets. The idea is to long (buy) the asset that is relatively undervalued and short the one that is overvalued. In the simple case of the forward and spot exchange rates, the basic arbitrage strategies would be as follows:

Arbitrage Strategy

If forward is overpriced:

- Short forward contract
- Long spot

If forward is underpriced:

- Long forward contract
- Short spot

It is worth noting that if the size of the long and short positions are equal, the arbitrageur has no net exposure. Yet, he makes profit from the mispricing. This is *pure arbitrage* or *riskless arbitrage*.

Speculators are basically players who take positions based on their expectations. Unlike hedgers and arbitrageurs, who always have two positions (long or short in forward spot), speculators often take a single position. That is, a speculator would long a forward contract if he thinks that currency is likely to appreciate against the other currency in the exchange rate quote. Alternatively, the speculator would take a short position in a forward if he thinks the currency would depreciate. The most basic speculative strategy can therefore be summarized as:

Currency Expected to	Strategy
Appreciate	⇧ Long position in forward contract
Depreciate	⬇ Short position in forward contract

Box 13.7. Illustration: Hedging Currency Risk with Currency Forwards

Syarikat Sawit, a large Malaysian Palm Oil producer, has just exported 200 tons of Crude Palm Oil (CPO) to their Japanese customer. As agreed, Syarikat Sawit has invoiced in Japanese Yen (JPY) with a credit term of three months (90 days). The invoice amount is ¥30 million.

If Syarikat Sawit does nothing, it will be exposed to fluctuations in JPY/MYR rate. If the Yen depreciates, Sawit's Ringgit proceeds will be lower; the opposite will be the case if Yen appreciates. Since Sawit has a Yen receivable, its worry will be about potential depreciation of the Yen. To avoid this, Syarikat Sawit could go into a 90-day Yen forward contract with its bank. Assume that Syarikat Sawit's banker Maybank's 90-day forward quote for Yen is ¥10 per MYR. Since Syarikat Sawit will receive Yen, it should take the short position in the forward contract.

Short position	=	sell or make delivery
Long position	=	buy or take delivery

So, Syarikat Sawit's correct strategy in the forward contract would be:

Short ¥30 million for 90 days @ ¥10 per MYR

(*Continued*)

Box 13.7. *(Continued)*

The chronology of events would be as follows. Today (Day 0), Syarikat Sawit calls Maybank and enters into the 90-day forward contract. No money changes hands at this point. Only the paperwork and documentation is completed. On Day 90, the transaction is executed.

Day 0

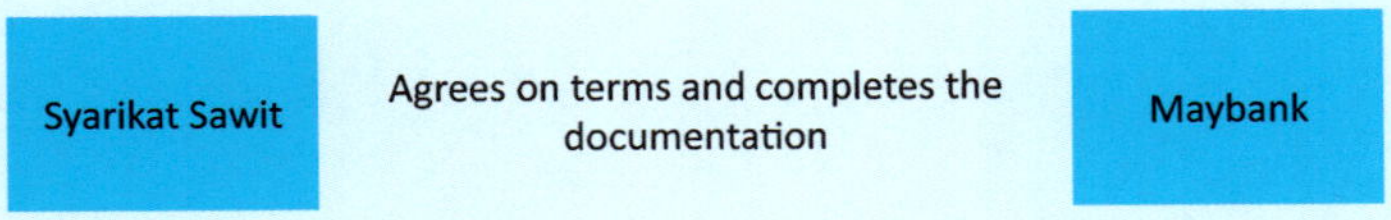

Day 90

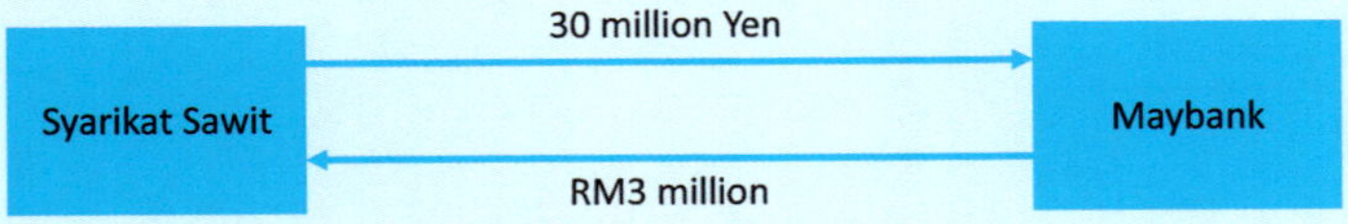

On Day 90, which is the maturity day of the forward contract, Syarikat Sawit passes on the ¥30 million it receives from its Japanese customer to Maybank. In exchange, Maybank gives Syarikat Sawit the Malaysian Ringgit as quoted in the forward rate. Since the forward rate was ¥10 per MYR, Syarikat Sawit receives RM3 million in exchange for the ¥30 million.

Notice that by way of the forward contract, Syarikat Sawit effectively "locks in" its ringgit revenue of RM10 million. Following the signing of the forward contract on Day 0, Syarikat Sawit has effectively eliminated its exposure to fluctuations in the JPY/MYR rate and locked in its ringgit revenue. This is how exchange rate risk is managed. Figure 13.3 shows the payoff profile for a hedged vs unhedged position.

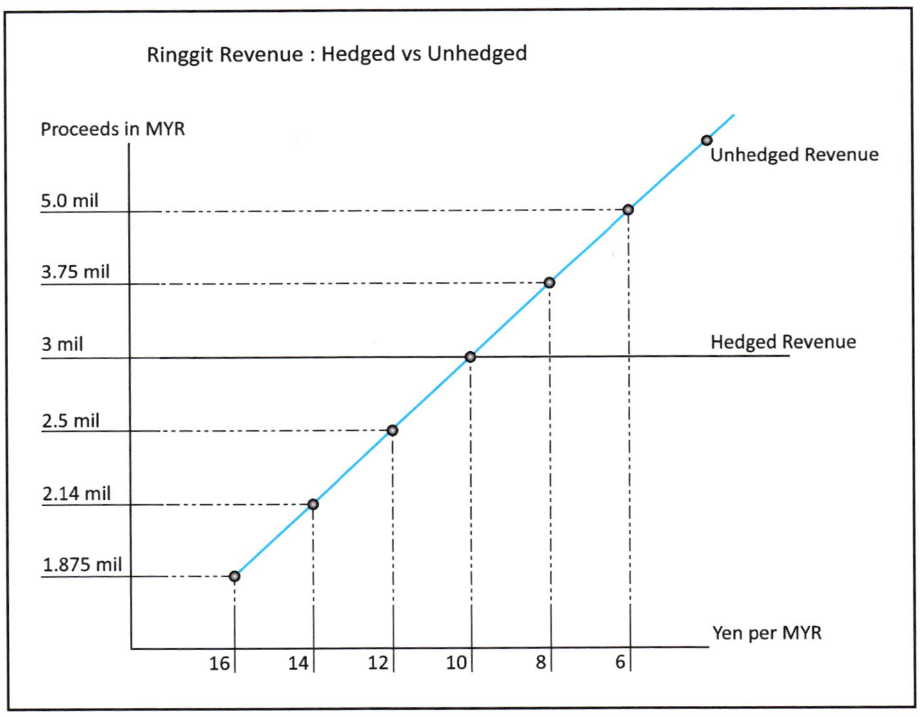

Figure 13.3: Payoff to Hedged and Unhedged Positions.

Just as the exporter in Figure 13.3 needed protection against depreciation of the Yen, a Malaysian importer who has to pay in Yen at a future date will have to worry about appreciation of the Yen. Suppose a Malaysian importer has to pay ¥10 million in, say 30 days, we could use the 30-day Yen forward contract to hedge his risk. Since he has to pay in Yen, he should take the long position in the forward. That is he needs to receive Yen at contract maturity. By entering into a 30-day forward contract for ¥10 million today, he will effectively lock in his ringgit cost. Otherwise, appreciation of the Yen over the next 30 days will lead to an increase in the ringgit cost.

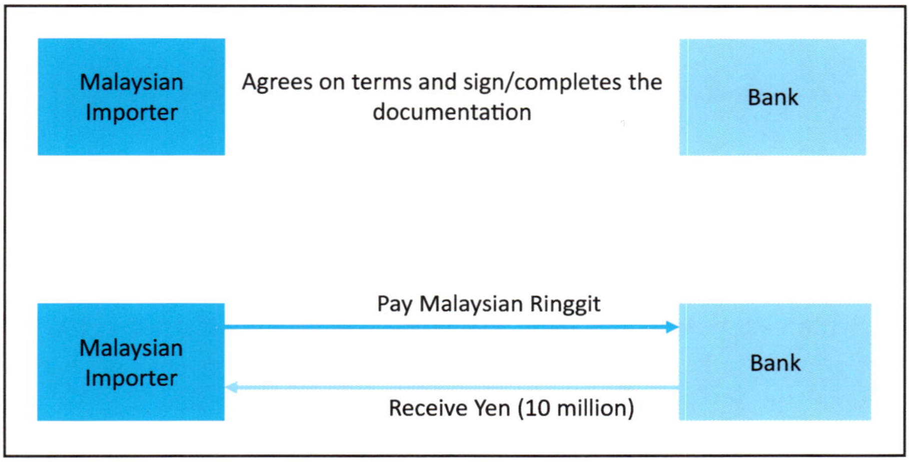

Box 13.8. Faced with a Depreciating Rupiah, Indonesia Tweaks its Interest Rates and Hedging Rules

In mid-August 2012, Bank Nasional, Indonesia's Central Bank, announced that it had raised the interbank money market rate by 25 basis points and further liberalized hedging rules for the rupiah. These announcements came following the announcement of a widening trade deficit for June 2012 and the further weakening of the rupiah as result. The rupiah had fallen 4.5% against the US$ over the first eight months of 2012. A trade deficit results when a country's imports exceed the value of its exports. Trade deficits are typically negative for a currency because the deficit will result in an "outflow" of reserves.

Depending on a country's macro-economic fundamentals, a trade deficit could either be a sign or weakness or strength. For example, if a given trade deficit was due to large imports of capital goods, it could be a sign of strength since the imported capital goods would increase future productive capacity, which in turn would likely increase future export capacity. Though trade deficits are rare for a large commodity exporter like Indonesia, they are common for rapidly developing countries. Where a trade deficit is recurrent or due to heavy importation of consumer goods, currency markets react negatively. In Indonesia's case, the trade deficit occurred amid strong economic growth. The country had reported a 6.4% GDP growth, an impressive performance. However, since the June trade deficit happened to be the third monthly trade deficit, currency markets appear to be weary of the rupiah — thus the central bank's policy response. Raising domestic interest rates helps to prevent further falls of the rupiah and temper domestic inflation. The rule change on hedging now enables the rupiah to be hedged for as short as one week where previously, the shortest hedge position was three months. The Indonesian Central Bank is obviously hoping that the ability to hedge short-term exposures would attract inflows and help shore up the rupiah.

Source: *The Star* (August 17, 2012); *The Jakarta Globe* (August 11, 2012).

13.12 Nominal versus Real Exchange Rates

Just as nominal and real prices can deviate in the presence of inflation, so too can exchange rates. Recall that a real price is the nominal price adjusted for inflation. If inflation is zero, then there is no difference between real and nominal prices. However, when inflation is positive, say 5%, then nominal prices will increase by 5%, whereas the real price is unchanged. This relationship can be shown as follows:

$$P_{\text{nom}} = P_{\text{real}}\,(1 + \text{inflation rate})$$

$$P_{\text{real}} = P_{\text{nom}}\,/(1 + \text{inflation rate})$$

As is evident from the above equations, the higher the rate of inflation, the larger the deviation between real and nominal prices. Furthermore, as long as the increase in the nominal price equals the inflation rate, the real price is left unchanged. The real price only changes if the change in the nominal price is not equal to the inflation rate. For example, if the nominal price increases by more than the rate of inflation, then the real price too has increased. An 8% increase in nominal price when inflation is 5% implies an increase in the real price by about 3%. On the other hand, if nominal prices go up by only 6% when inflation is 8%, real prices would have gone down by about 2%.

A multi-period version of the above equations can be written as:

$$Pt_{\text{nom.}} = P_{\text{real}}\ (1 + \text{inflation rate})t$$

$$P_{\text{real}} = Pt_{\text{nom}}\ /\ (1 + \text{inflation rate})t$$

Where exchange rates are concerned, the same logic applies. This logic is encapsulated within a parity or equilibrium condition within international finance, known as Purchasing Power Parity (PPP). According to PPP, a country with higher relative inflation should see its currency depreciate in relative terms. The percentage depreciation should equal the inflation differential. For example, if Thailand has 3% higher inflation than Malaysia, its currency, the Thai Baht, should depreciate 3% against the Malaysian Ringgit. If the currency depreciation equals the inflation differential, then PPP is said to hold. When PPP holds, the *real exchange rate is unchanged*. So, in the earlier example, when the Baht falls 3% against the Ringgit because Thailand has 3% higher inflation, the nominal exchange rate has depreciated 3%, but in real terms, the exchange rate is unchanged. An important implication of PPP is that, when the real exchange rate is unchanged, there is no change in a country's competitive position. It is only when there is a change in the real exchange rate that a country's competitive position is changed. For example, if the Thai Baht falls 7% against the MYR in the presence of 3% higher inflation in Thailand relative to Malaysia, then the Baht is *undervalued* in real terms against the MYR by about 4%. Such an undervaluation in real terms would make Thai exports more competitive against Malaysian exports in overseas markets. Alternatively, if the nominal depreciation of the Baht is only 1% against the MYR, then going by PPP, the Baht would be *overvalued* by about 2%. The Baht would be overvalued because it did not fall as much as it should have. Such an overvaluation in real terms would mean that Thai exports would be less competitive against Malaysian exports.

The key point to keep in mind is that nominal exchange rate changes do not necessarily lead to changes in competitiveness. What really matters is changes in the real exchange rate not nominal exchange rates.

13.13 *Shari'ah*-Compliant Techniques for Managing Currency Exposure

With the ascendance of Islamic banking and finance, there has been innovation with regard to structuring *Shari'ah*-compliant means to manage currency exposure. Until recently, the basic philosophy appears to have been to use "on-balance-sheet" techniques. That is, *fuqaha* would favor the use of on-balance-sheet techniques to manage foreign exchange risks. On-balance-sheet techniques avoid the use of derivatives like forwards, futures, swaps, etc., which are off-balance-sheet but require changes in the way one does business. A simple on-balance-sheet technique would be to require a company to price all its foreign transactions in its home currency, for e.g., price all imports and exports in home currency such that exchange rate risk is avoided. In doing so, the company is effectively passing on all exchange rate risks to its counterparty. While such a technique can mitigate exchange rate risks, it invariably hinders one's competitiveness. Unless a company has some monopolistic power, it may not be possible to price only in the home currency. Given the obvious difficulty that this philosophy places on Muslim businesses, there have been appeals to *fuqaha* to reconsider the prohibition of on/off-balance-sheet techniques (Chapra & Khan,

2000). Perhaps in response to these, there have been a number of developments that have made *Shari'ah*-compliant tools possible. The three key developments were:

(i) The convention of *fiqh* scholars at its Muktamar in Kuwait (1409H) recommended that forward and futures contracts be transacted based on Islamic nominate contracts such as *salam, sarf,* and *wa'ad.*
(ii) The OIC's Islamic Fiqh Academy pronounced that the *wa'ad* is obligatory and can stand in a court of law if it is made as a unilateral promise in a commercial transaction and if violation of the promise can cause one to incur liabilities or losses. (*Note*: In *Shari'ah, wa'ad* means promise may not be binding legally.)
(iii) BNM's *Shariah* Council, in its resolution of April 2005, pronounced that IFIs are allowed to enter forward currency transactions based on a unilateral binding promise.

It would be noted that in all three cases, the allowance is specifically for purposes of hedging only.

Box 13.9. *Shari'ah* Views on the Trading of Currencies

The legal definition of the currency exchange (*sarf*) contract is *the exchange of one monetary form for another in the same or different genera*, i.e., gold for gold coins, silver for silver, gold for silver, silver for gold, etc., whether it is in the form of jewelry or minted coins. Such trading is permitted since the Prophet (PBUH) permitted such exchange. However, in addition to the five basic conditions that an instrument must avoid *riba, gharar, maysir, rishwah*, and *jahl*, currency exchange contracts require the fulfilment of the following four additional conditions. These are:

(i) Mutual receipt prior to the contracting parties' parting;
(ii) Equality of quantities if monies of the same genus are traded;
(iii) Inapplicability of additional conditions (*syart*); and
(iv) Non-deferment.

The need for these conditions arises from the saying of the Prophet (PBUH): "Gold for gold, in equal amounts, hand to hand; and silver for silver, in equal amounts, hand to hand", as well as his (PBUH) saying: "Do not trade one of them absent (thus, deferred) for the other immediately delivered".

These were authenticated by major narrators with the exception of al-Bukhari on the authority of Ubadah Ibn al-Samit: "Gold for gold, silver to silver, wheat for wheat, barley for barley, dates for dates, and salt for salt, in equal amounts, hand to hand; and if the genera differ (in an exchange), then trade as you wish provided it is hand to hand" (*c.f.* Al-Hafiz, Al-Zayla, 1st edition, (hadith), Vol. 4, p. 4).

In response to the above stated developments, a number of IFIs in the Gulf States and in Malaysia have developed a number of *wa'ad*-based products for managing currency risk. We examine two generic versions of *wa'ad*-based products below.

(i) The Islamic FX Forward

The most popular *wa'ad*-based forex product is probably the Islamic FX forward. Known alternatively as the Islamic FX outright, FX Forward *wa'ad-I*, or by other names, it involves the use of a unilateral *wa'ad*. Under this arrangement, an IFI provides a unilateral promise (*wa'ad*) to a customer in return for a fee. Depending on the customer's needs, the *wa'ad* by the IFI could be either to buy or sell a currency in exchange for another at a predetermined price and future date. Depending on the IFI's product structure, there may be another unilateral *wa'ad* by the customer to the IFI. The customers' *wa'ad* would obviously be in the opposite direction that is promising to deliver or take delivery of the currency from the IFI at a pre-determined price or exchange rate.

By way of these *wa'ad* arrangements, a customer effectively "locks in" the exchange rate at which he will buy or sell a currency to the IFI. In essence, this *wa'ad* arrangement replicates a conventional forward contract.

Box 13.10. Illustration: Using Islamic Forward *Wa'ad* to Manage Currency Risk

A Malaysian importer has a Taiwan Dollar (TWD) 30 million payable to ACER Corp. for a shipment of notebook computers. Payment is due in 60 days. The Malaysian company is afraid of any appreciation of the TWD against the Ringgit. To hedge this risk, the Malaysian Company enters into an Islamic FX forward *wa'ad* contract as follows:

Step 1: t = Day 0; negotiate terms and finalize documentation

Step 2: t = Day 60

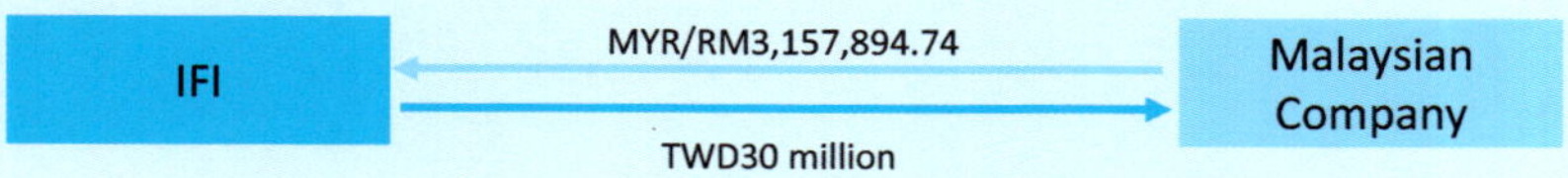

Assuming the IFI charges a fee of say RM2,500 for the unilateral promise it makes to the Malaysian Co., the importer would lock-in a MYR cost of:

30 million TWD @ 9.5 = RM3,157,894.74
+ Fee Charged = RM2,500.00
Hedged Cost = **RM3,160,394.74**

Notice that the hedged cost of RM3,160,394.74 to the Malaysian company is locked-in on Day 0. Thus, over the following 60 days, the Malaysian company is unaffected by any changes in the MYR/TWD rate.

(ii) The FX *wa'ad* (FX Option)

This is another *wa'ad*-based forex product offered by IFIs, notably by Calyon, the Islamic banking subsidiary of Credit Agricole. This *Shari'ah*-compliant product effectively replicates a conventional currency option. A customer intending to use this product will "buy" a promise from the IFI to either buy or sell one currency for another foreign currency, for a fee. In essence, the customer is buying the right to buy or sell a currency at a predetermined rate in essence for a fee. At a future maturity date, the customer can exercise this right. If a customer buys the right to sell a foreign currency under this *wa'ad* arrangement, he is effectively purchasing a put option on the currency in conventional terms. A *wa'ad* arrangement to buy a currency would constitute a long call position.

Notice that with *wa'ad* option, one is not "locking in" a cost as was the case with the *wa'ad* based forward. With the option, one establishes instead a maximum cost or a "ceiling" on the payable. To see why this is so, suppose the TWD depreciates against the Ringgit over the next 60 days, it may be better for the Malaysian company to not exercise the *wa'ad* option with the IFI, but instead purchase the TWD at a lower spot rate. Depending on how much the TWD depreciated, the cost of the shipment would be lower.

Box 13.11. Illustration: Using an FX *Wa'ad* Option to Hedge Currency Risk

Suppose the Malaysian company in the earlier example wants to use a *wa'ad*-based option rather than the *wa'ad* forward the arrangement. Cash flows would be as follows:

Step 1: *t* = Day 0

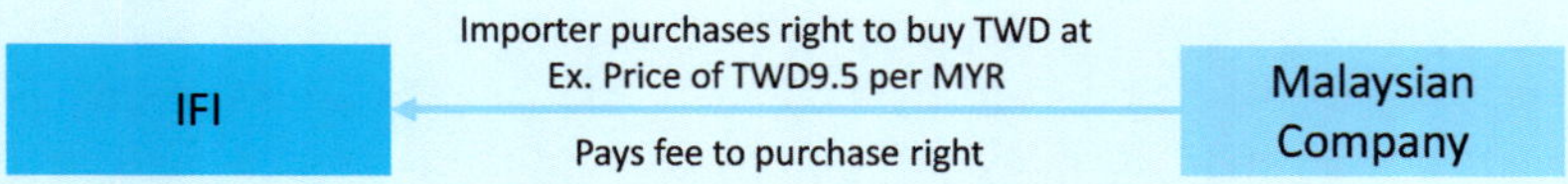

Step 2: *t* = Day 60; if the Malaysian company chooses to exercise.

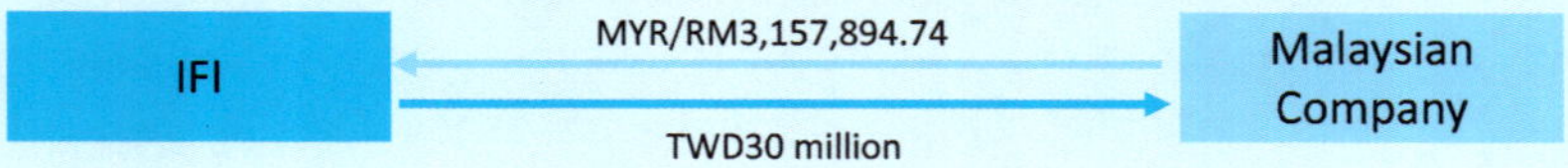

Here, the Malaysian company is effectively buying a 60-day call option on TWD30 million for a fee. This fee is very much like the premium for a call option. Suppose the IFI charges a fee of RM20,000 for the *wa'ad* option, then the Malaysian company is assured that its maximum cost on the shipment from Taiwan is:

Payment on Exercise = RM3,157,894.74
Fee (Premium) paid to IFI = RM20,000.00
Maximum Cost = RM3,177,894.74

For example, let us say the TWD depreciates against the Ringgit such that on Day 60, the rate is:

Spot rate on Day 60 = 12 TWD per MYR
Or = 0.0833 MYR per TWD

It is obvious that not exercising the *wa'ad* option would be better.

$$\frac{\text{TWD}\,30\,\text{million}}{12} = \text{RM}\,2,500,000$$

The cost of the TWD 30 million will be RM2.5 million if purchased in the spot market. The company's total cost will be RM2.502 million if the RM20,000 fee paid to the IFI earlier is included.

Thus, with the *wa'ad* option, the Malaysian company is buying itself insurance against appreciation of the TWD. While the forward protects against TWD appreciation but does not allow the company to take advantage of TWD depreciation, the option contract does. It is this flexibility of options that make it more attractive. Given that options allow one to hedge against unfavorable movements while also providing the opportunity to take advantage of favorable movements, their cost (premium) would be much higher. So, the fee paid to the IFI in the *wa'ad* forward would be much lower than that paid for the *wa'ad* option.

Box 13.12. Exchange Rates and the Policy Trade-offs

Being commodity producers, most Muslim countries have witnessed serious pressure on their currencies arising from a widespread fall in commodity prices. While none of the GCC currencies, all of which are pegged to the US$, appear at risk of devaluation, currencies of countries like Malaysia and Indonesia have come under intense pressure. One would have

(*Continued*)

Box 13.12. (*Continued*)

thought that the worst hit would be those dependent on one or a narrow group of commodities. Those with a manufacturing based ought to be impacted less. Yet, this is clearly not the case. The GCC countries that depend almost entirely on a single commodity export, oil, appear to have had much less pressure on their currencies than more diversified economies like Malaysia, which brings us to the interesting question of what exactly are exchange rates, exchange rate policy, and the trade-offs involved. Exchange rates are nothing but a price. The price of a foreign currency in terms of home currency and vice-versa. Since countries have a single unique currency for all their domestic transactions, the "price" of this currency is very important. A currency mispriced or misaligned over a period of time can have serious long-term consequences on a country. This "pricing" is often premised on the exchange rate policy. Exchange rate policy can vary over a spectrum, with fixed exchange rate or pegs at one end and free floats at the other, with different levels of managed floats in between. While several Islamic countries and the GCC in particular, have opted for fixed peg of their currencies to the US$, no Islamic country has a free float. Most Muslim countries, as is the case with the majority of nations, have some form of managed float. As with everything in economics, these policies involve choices and trade-offs, the key trade-off being between exchange rate volatility and monetary policy flexibility. A currency on a fixed peg would have no volatility against the currency it is pegged to; however, in exchange for currency stability, the country would have little domestic monetary policy independence. Taking the case of the GCC countries, their domestic money supply growth, and interest rates have to be in sync with that of the US. Deviations over any sustained period would put pressure on the peg. While a pegged rate that is undervalued can hold for some time, an overvalued rate can attract speculative attacks. This was exactly the case with Argentina. A currency pegged to the US$ can become overvalued if domestic money supply growth is faster than the US or if inflation rates are higher, causing real interest rates to be lower in relative terms. Thus, a decision to peg is not a one-off decision followed policy inertness. It requires careful maintenance, in particular, the ability to defend the peg with foreign reserves or raising domestic interest rates substantially if the need arises. As a rule, the more independent monetary policy is, the greater the chances of misalignment. The more subservient it is, the better the chances for synchronicity and continued alignment. Given these trade-offs, most countries opt to settle for a little of both, i.e., some exchange rate stability and some level of policy independence. Thus, the popularity of managed floats, which essentially means allowing the home currency to fluctuate within a band against one or more major currencies. Here, the trade-off is the size of the band. The broader the band, the more policy independence but also more currency volatility.

A policy of deliberately over or undervaluing one's currency, may be sensible over short periods. Overvalued exchange rates can help check domestic inflation and improve the welfare of citizens by making imports more affordable, but overtime can hamper export competitiveness. For example, Kuwait and Bahrain have pegged their currency to the US$ at a rate that is obviously expensive/overvalued *vis-à-vis* other currencies. This may make sense as their only export, oil, is denominated in US$, and being price-takers, export competitiveness is not an issue. On the other hand, their expensive currencies make luxury German automobiles, French biscuits, and Swiss chocolates very affordable for their citizens, thereby improving welfare. However, there is a cost; it will be very difficult for globally competitive industry or manufacturing to root at such exchange rates. So, if these countries are serious about diversifying their economies, they ought to take another serious look at their exchange rates.

Deliberately undervaluing a currency may be more sustainable over a longer period relative to overvaluation. Japan, South Korea, and China, more recently, are examples of countries that have used undervalued home currencies to pull themselves up the development chain. Undervaluing one's currency is effectively announcing to the rest of the world the willingness to do the same work, or sell the same products at a lower foreign currency price. Thus, it is no surprise that one's export competitiveness is enhanced. However, such a policy only works when the domestic value-added is high, i.e., the import content of exports is very low. In the post-war period, Japan grew by importing low-cost commodities in raw form and using these to produce for export, automobiles, electrical appliances, and electronics that were highly valued. Since the import content is very low, the higher import price due to undervaluation is easily absorbed. Malaysia, Indonesia, and similar countries that manufacture for export a small part of the value chain cannot use undervalued exchange rates to leap frog. The import content of exports is far too high to make such a policy successful. Whatever advantages one can derive from exchange rates is temporary at best. One cannot devalue one's way to prosperity nor peg one's currency to avoid depreciation.

Source: Author's op-ed column in *Derin Ekonomi*, August 2015.

Summary

The foreign exchange market plays a very important role within an economy. The forex market links domestic capital markets to foreign ones. Forex market activity is often a key determinant of liquidity within a capital market. An exchange rate is quite simply a price of one currency in terms of another. Much like the prices of other things, exchange rates reflect the forces of demand and supply.

Demand and supply for a currency may in turn be affected by a myriad of factors. Unless one begins with an exchange rate that is one to one, the percentage appreciation of a currency against another will not equal the percentage depreciation of the other. Spot exchange notes may be quoted in European or American terms. Spot rates may also be available as cross rates. A cross exchange rate is an implied exchange rate given two exchange rates. Firms with receivables in foreign currency (FC) would be afraid of FC depreciation against home currency. On the other hand, firms with FC payables would be afraid of FC appreciation against home currency. One can hedge or manage such exchange rate exposure by using currency derivatives such as forwards, futures, or options. Using forwards or futures one can "lock in" a home currency cost or revenue resulting from a FC payable or receivable. A key determinant of a currency's appreciation or depreciation is the nation's rate of inflation. Often, inflation works move exchange rates through changes in interest rates. According to PPP, currencies of countries with higher inflation should depreciate against currencies with lower relative inflation.

With the ascendance of Islamic banking and finance, *Shari'ah*-complaint techniques of currency risk management have been innovated. Most of these are structured products based on *wa'ad*. A *wa'ad* is a unilateral promise by one party to another. When used in commercial transactions, the *wa'ad* becomes legally binding. The chapter described and illustrated the use of two *Shari'ah*-compliant products. These were the Islamic FX forward, which replicates two conventional forward contracts, and the FX *wa'ad* (option). The *wa'ad*-based option enables a customer to buy or sell a foreign currency at a predetermined future date and price in exchange for a fee paid to the IFI. Operationally, the cash flows to this product would resemble that of currency call and put options.

Questions and Problems

1. The Ringgit went from RM3.60 at end 2009 to RM3.10 at end 2010 against the US$.
   (a) Which currency appreciated? Which depreciated?
   (b) Determine the percentage appreciation or depreciation of the Ringgit.
   (c) Determine the percentage appreciation or depreciation of the US$.
2. If the Saudi Riyal is 3.750 against the US$, what amount, in Riyal, would you get by exchanging US$3,000?
3. The Saudi Riyal is 3.750 per US$ while the Ringgit is 3.10 per US$.
   (a) Determine the cross rate between the Ringgit and the Riyal.
   (b) How much, in Riyal, would you get for RM100?
   (c) How much, in Ringgit, would you get for 2,000 Saudi Riyal?
4. Briefly explain the following:
   (a) What is meant by exchange rate risk?
   (b) Why do exchange rates change?
   (c) Define cross exchange rate.
   (d) What is forward exchange rate?
5. An importer with a £10 million payable in 60 days is looking into hedging his exposure. He has the following information:
   - MYR/£ spot rate = RM6.15/£.
   - MYR/£ 60 day forward rate = RM6.22/£

   (a) Based on the above quotes, what is the market's expectation about the Pound Sterling relative to the Malaysian Ringgit?
   (b) State the hedge strategy using forwards which the importer can protect himself.
   (c) What is the Ringgit amount that can be locked in if he uses the 60-day forward?
6. Use the information in Question 5 above:
   (a) What would be the importer's implied gain or loss if the spot rate on day 60 is RM6.36/£.
   (b) What is his implied gain or loss if the spot rate on day 60 is RM6.08/£.
7. Again, using the information in Question 5 above, show how:
   (a) The importer can use a *wa'ad*-based Islamic forward contract to hedge his exposure.
   (b) The importer can use a FX *wa'ad* option to hedge his exposure.
8. For each of the following events/items, state whether the impact is positive (+), negative (–) or no impact (0).
   (a) A Malaysian company has imported from Japan. The Yen appreciates against the Ringgit.__________
   (b) A Malaysian company has imported from Japan, what is the impact if theRinggit appreciates against the Yen. __________
   (c) A Malaysian company borrows in Euros from Deutsche Bank. The loan is repayable in six months. The Ringgit appreciates against the Euro. __________
   (d) If the loan in (c) above is repayable in one lump sum in five years from now and the Euro now appreciates against the Malaysian Ringgit. __________
   (e) A Malaysian mutual fund invests in an Australian ETF (Exchange traded fund). The Australian Dollar appreciates against the Malaysian Ringgit. __________
   (f) The ETF above rises in value while the Australian Dollar appreciates against the Ringgit. __________
   (g) The Australian ETF falls 20% while the Australian Dollar appreciates 20% against the Ringgit. __________
9. A Malaysian exporter has €10 million receivable in three months.
   (a) What is the exporter's risk, the Euro appreciating or depreciating? Explain.
   (b) Explain how the exporter can hedge the exchange rate risk.
   (c) Make a graphical projection showing the hedged versus unhedged proceeds to the exporter.

10. State the categories of players in the foreign exchange market.
    (a) What are their objectives?
    (b) Briefly state how a speculator could use a forward (or futures) contract to speculate on a currency's expected appreciation.
    (c) How would the speculator's strategy change if he wants to take advantage of a currency's expected depreciation?
11. Your company is a nationwide retailer of computers and electrical appliances, and routinely imports goods from several countries. You have just received a large shipment of computers and other equipment from Samsung of Korea. A payable of Won 800 million is due in 90 days. Your boss, the CFO, is conservative and insists that you hedge the position. The current quotes for the Ringgit/Won exchange rates are as follows:
    - Spot rate = 0.08 ringgit per Won
    - F_{30} days = 0.0785
    - F_{90} days = 0.0735
    - Fee for F_{90} forward @ 0.0735 = RM2,000 for 800 million Won.
    - Fee for F_{90} option @ 0.0735 = RM10,000 for 800 million Won.

    Assuming *wa'ad*-based currency forwards and options are available, outline the best means to hedge the position. Justify your answer and state the hedge strategy.
12. You work for a large Malaysia-based food products distributor. Your company supplies foodstuff and provisions in raw or processed form to the food and beverage (F&B) industry, both domestic and international. Your boss has asked you to submit a bid to supply a list of food items to a UAE-based restaurant chain which will cater food during a large international event to be held over three weeks in Dubai. As your firm will be competing with other international food suppliers, you are required to submit a bid in UAE dirhams. The closing date for submission is in two days. You have worked out the costing, and after discussing with your boss, it is decided that you will submit a bid for 40 million UAE Dirhams. The winning bidder will be announced in one month from closing date and will have another month to ship the need foodstuff to Dubai. Full payment of the winning bid in UAE Dirhams will be made at end of the third month. Given the highly competitive nature of the bid, you have priced it with very thin margins. You are worried that any unfavorable movement in the exchange rate could quickly erode your profits. You are seeking a *Shari'ah*-compliant way to hedge the currency risk.
    (a) Your bank offers both *wa'ad*-based forwards and currency options. Which of the two is the appropriate hedging instrument? Justify your answer
    (b) Given the following additional information, determine the hedged amount under your chosen alternative:
    - Spot MYR/Dirham = RM1.10 per dirham
    - 90 day *wa'ad* forward rate = RM1.12 per dirham
    - 60 day *wa'ad* forward rate = RM1.115 per dirham
    - 90 day *wa'ad* Call option strike rate = RM1.12 per dirham
    - 90 day *wa'ad* Put option strike rate = RM1.12 per dirham
    - Call premium RM 500 per 1 million dirham (strike price as above)
    - Put premium RM 335 per 1 million dirham (strike price as above).
13. Cycle & Carriage (C&C), a Malaysian importer and distributor of Mercedes Benz cars, has a €15 million payable to Daimler-Benz of Germany, in 60 days. Given the problems in Europe, there has been extreme volatility in the MYR /EURO exchange rate. You have been asked to advise C&C on how best to handle this exposure. C&C is open to use either FX forward *wa'ad* or FX Option *wa'ad* contracts, if necessary. You have the following information:
    - MYR/EURO Spot = RM4.05
    - MYR/EURO 30 day Forward = RM3.98
    - MYR/EURO 60 day Forward = RM3.82

- MYR/EURO 90 day Forward = RM3.74
- Quoted rate for 60 day forward *wa'ad* = RM3.825
- Fee for forward *wa'ad* = RM 5,000 flat rate
- Fee for 60 day RM3.825 exercise price *wa'ad* option = RM25,000

(a) If the *wa'ad* forward is used, state the exact strategy and MYR amount that can be locked in.
(b) If a *wa'ad* option is used, state the strategy, type of option and the MYR amount locked-in.
(c) Given the information in the case what is the best course of action? Justify.

14. A Malaysian exporter of rubber wood furniture will receive €30 million in 90 days from its French importer. Worried about currency fluctuation that could cause it losses, the Malaysian company wants to use either a *wa'ad*-based FX forward or option contract. Its bank quotes a 90-day forward rate of MYR 4.75 per Euro.
    Assuming the total transaction cost for the forward is RM2800 while that of the option is RM25,000.
    (a) Outline the appropriate strategy using *wa'ad* forward. Show the diagram and determine the MYR revenue locked-in.
    (b) Outline the appropriate strategy if the *wa'ad*-based option is used. Assume the exercise value is also MYR 4.75 per Euro. What is the MYR revenue for the Malaysian company from using the option?
    (c) Under what circumstances might it be sensible to use the option instead of forward?

Bibliography

Al-Suwailem, S. (2006). "Hedging in Islamic Finance," Occasional Paper No. 10, Islamic Development Bank, Jeddah.

Bank for International Settlements (2007). *BIS Quarterly Review*, December 2007.

Bank for International Settlements (2016). *BIS Triennial Survey*, April 2016.

Capital Market Issues According to Islamic Jurisprudence. Resolutions of the Securities.

Chapra, M. U. and T. Khan (2000), Regulation and Supervision of Islamic Banks.

Islamic Development Bank, Islamic Research and Training Institute, 2000.

Commission Shariah Advisory Council. Securities Commission, Kuala Lumpur.

Derin Ekonomi (2015). August.

Derin Ekonomi (2016). November.

Khan, T. and H. Ahmed (2001). "Risk Management — An Analysis of Issues in Islamic Financial Industry," Occasional Paper No. 5, Islamic Development Bank/Islamic Research and Training Institute, Jeddah.

Marina M. (2010). CIFP Professional Practice Paper [Unpublished Manuscript] INCEIF.

Obaidullah, M. (1999). "Financial Options in Islamic Contracts: Potential Tools for Risk Management," *Journal of KAU — Islamic Economics*, Vol. 11, pp. 3–26.

Obiyathulla, I. B. (2017). *Financial Derivatives: Market and Applications in Malaysia*, 4th Edition (McGraw Hill, Malaysia).

Shapiro, A. L. (2013). *Multinational Financial Management*, 10th Edition (John Wiley & Sons (Asia) Pte. Ltd, Singapore).

The Jakarta Globe (2012). August 11.

The Star (2012). August 17.

Websites

http://www.bnm.gov.my — Bank Negara Malaysia
http://www.mifc.com/index.php?ch=menuhttp://www.sc.gov.my
Websites of respective Muslim Country Stock Exchanges
http://www.zawya.com/middle-east/financial-markets
http://www.bursamalaysia.com — Bursa Malaysia
Websites of the various Stock exchanges

Chapter 14

CAPITAL MARKETS AND GOVERNMENT POLICY

Topics in this Chapter

Chapter Objective

This chapter is designed to introduce students to the role of government in promoting capital markets. On completing this chapter, you should have a good understanding of the risk-sharing mechanism and how it can help governments finance fiscal operations via capital markets. You should also be able to identify the policies that can be undertaken to promote capital markets for effective risk-sharing

Key Terms		
collective risk-sharing	macromarket instruments	public-private partnership
divisibility	non-exclusivity	risk-sharing
government policy and stock markets	public goods	
international risk-sharing	public policy	

14.1 Risk Sharing

Previous chapters have explained the workings of conventional and Islamic capital markets. The focus of discussion in these chapters has been the private sector. The takeaway from these chapters is the ways and means by which capital markets can be used by people to manage their risks. Chapter 1 described how Arrow and his colleagues had demonstrated that, given a set of assumptions, a decentralized economy — one in which government plays a minimal role — allocates risk to those who are best able to bear it. Markets were assigned this optimal allocation role using instruments whose pay-offs were contingent on the outcome of activities financed. Theoretically, this would represent the most desirable form of market capitalism; an economy in which risks were shared among the participants. It was explained, also in Chapter 1, that risk sharing is the operational essence of Islamic finance.

Experience has shown that market capitalism, left to itself, fails in actuality to manage certain types of risk, e.g., risk to the livelihood of people and catastrophic risks. This is a violation of one of the major assumptions of neoclassical model of Arrow and his colleagues, that of complete markets. Additionally, much of financial transactions in contemporary market capitalism relies on risk transfer or risk shifting rather than risk sharing. As a consequence, it becomes necessary for governments to step in and correct these "market failures".

14.1.1 *Collective Risk Sharing*

As mentioned in Chapter 1, people face two types of market risk: (1) *systematic* (aggregate risk, or undiversifiable risk) and (2) *unsystematic* (idiosyncratic risk, specific risk, residual risk, diversifiable risk). The first relates to risk that is posed by general economic conditions dependent on macroeconomic factors such as growth of the economy, fiscal and monetary policies, interest rates, and inflation. Such risks are undiversifiable and therefore uninsurable. However, sound macroeconomic policies that strengthen economic fundamentals, effective international policy coordination, and the stability of the domestic and financial system can mitigate such risks to a significant degree. Unsystematic risk (or idiosyncratic risk), on the other hand, relates to risks that are specific to individuals or firms, such as unforeseen shocks to household income or firm's profits. Such risks are diversifiable, and therefore, insurable. High correlation between consumption and an individual's employment income means that sickness, accidents, and lay-offs all pose idiosyncratic risks that can be mitigated through risk-sharing arrangements that reduce dependence on wages as the only source of income, thus weakening the correlation between income and consumption. In other words, through risk sharing, the individual "smooths" her/his consumption.

In a society, risk can be shared among its members and/or between its members and its state. Both in the industrial and developing economies, people find ways and means of sharing risks to their livelihood. In particular, they use coping mechanisms when faced with a reduction of their income relative to consumption. In more developed financial systems, the coping mechanism is investing in financial assets or in acquiring insurance to mitigate against personal risk. In developing countries with weak financial markets, people rely on informal insurance, borrowing or saving to cope with idiosyncratic risks. In such societies, theory suggests that perfect informal insurance is possible if communities pool their incomes to share risks.

Then, each member of the community could be assigned a level of consumption dependent on the aggregate level of income and not on that of the individual member. This arrangement would assure perfect risk sharing (Morduch, 1999a; 1999b) to mitigate idiosyncratic risk, so that a given household's income would not affect its level of consumption. However, empirical studies in India (Townsend, 1994, 1995; Revallion and Chaudhuri, 1997), Thailand (Townsend, 1995), China (Jalan and Revallion, 1997), Indonesia (Gertler and Gruber, 1997), Philippines (Fafchamps and Lund, 2003), and elsewhere indicate that perfect risk sharing through income pooling is not supported fully by data, although in a number of countries, it plays a crucially important role. Figure 14.1 shows risk as decomposed into systematic and unsystematic components.

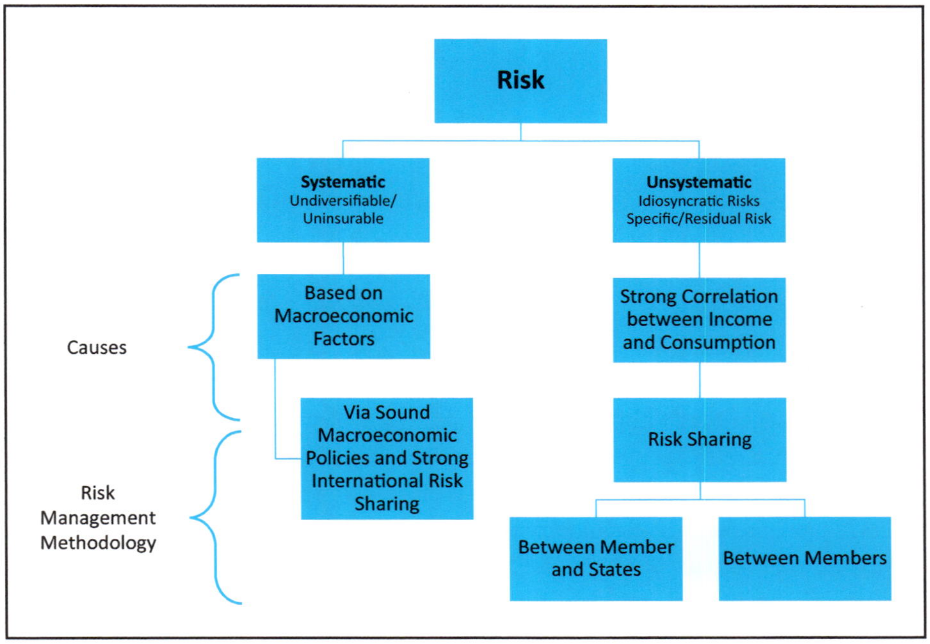

Figure 14.1. Risk and Its Components.

Generally, empirical studies suggest that, in low-income countries, saving, borrowing, the use of buffer stock, working longer hours or taking a second job, gift exchange, and private transfer of cash and clothing are mechanisms used in risk sharing (Kippins, 1997; Cox and Jimenz, 1998).

Analysts suggest that public policy and strengthened institutional framework in developing countries can go a long way in reducing risk. Better governance that can reduce damages to households due to mismanagement, achieving and sustaining economic and political stability, and financial sector development are examples of policy improvements. In terms of institutional framework, clear and secure property rights, contract enforcement, trust among people and between government and people, and other institutions can reduce risk and strengthen social solidarity, bring private and public interests into closer harmony and ensure coordination to achieve risk sharing.

Public policy could also help in mobilizing savings of poor household and thus reduce vulnerability to income shocks. Examples of Safe Save Program implemented among poor households in the slums of Dhaka, Bangladesh, and microfinance programs in Asia, Africa, and Latin America are cited as success programs of saving mobilization among poor households (Morduch, 1999a; 1999b; Bencivenga and Smith, 1991) suggest a strong relationship between deposit mobilization, strengthening of efficiency, and economic growth. Public policy to forge integration and support for saving mobilization in developing countries help risk mitigation sharing, thus building resilience in face of shocks.

Microfinance is considered as means of risk sharing. However, there are now empirical evidence suggesting that while microfinance in its original form helps reduce poverty in low-income countries by providing small, uncollateralized loans to poor borrowers, it does not allow businesses to grow beyond subsistence. Aside from high interest rates that reduce available resources, it is thought that the structure of typical microfinance contract has features such as peer monitoring and joint liability designed to reduce moral hazard risk that create tension between risk taking and risk pooling. The latter allows greater opportunity for informal risk sharing due to repeated interaction among the borrowers. Joint liability and peer monitoring — which are features common to most microfinance programs under which small groups of borrowers become responsible for one another's loan and all members are held responsible for consequences of one member's failure to repay the loan but do not reward other members in case of success — discourage risk taking and development of entrepreneurial impulses among borrowers (Thomas and Worral, 1997; Murduch, 1998; Chowdhury, 2005; Armendariz De Aghion and Morduch,

2005; Fischer, 2013). In addition to saving mobilization and encouraging more efficient microfinance, better access to the financial sector through developing microcredit and insurance markets in rural and poverty-stricken regions are promising ways and means by which public policy can assist development of risk sharing to allow households to cope with risk.

Systematic risks, such as exposure to financial crises in the last few decades have been forceful reminders of how various shocks can affect economies. The nature of shocks, availability of institutions that shape risk sharing within or outside each economy, and the resilience of the domestic economy determine how well it can cope with shocks. Serious dissatisfaction and the subsequent public protests highlight the fundamental question of how risk should be shared or allocated across a society ex-ante and what criteria should decide the outcome. As reviewed in Chapter 1, Arrow (1971) demonstrated that in a competitive market economy in which markets are complete and securities with state-contingent pay-offs are available, it would be pareto optimal for the economy if its members share risk according to each participant's ability to bear risk. In the absence of complete markets, which include all possible future contingencies, the efficiency of risk-sharing mechanisms will depend on the institutional structure, the degree and intensity of informational problems, and policies designed to render the economy resilient to shocks.

Generally, risk-sharing procedures and objectives are perceived to involve trade-offs between efficiency and fairness, therefore distributional impact of ways and means of risk sharing are considered important. These trade-offs are thought particularly acute in case of policies that are aimed at allocating the burden of adverse macroeconomic shocks within a society. For example, a society can ex-ante decide, on the basis of equity, efficiency, or both to allocate the burden of consequences of a shock to those who either benefit the most from or exacerbate the shocks by their behavior. Shocks may be so large and their consequences so serious that even if such a policy were accepted ex-ante, institutional consideration (e.g., limited liability) and political economy forces (powerful lobby) may prevent not only a fair and efficient distribution of costs ex-post but also the assignment of residual costs after the initial costs of the shocks have been socialized. It is difficult to conceive of any known criterion of fairness and/or efficiency in Western thought that could be satisfied by the outcome of resolution (non-resolution) of consequences of the 2007/2008 global financial crisis.

14.1.2 *International Risk Sharing*

The degree to which any economy can absorb shocks and how well it can cope with its consequences depend on risk-sharing mechanisms available internationally or domestically. One of the most important arguments advanced in favor of globalization was that of improved risk sharing that would bring people across the world closer to create a "global village". On theoretical ground, expecting much greater degree of risk sharing between and among economies — resulting from greater freedom of movement of resources, the advent of technological advances and information super highways, and advances in financial innovation — was not unrealistic. After all, these advances would have meant progress toward market completion — a condition of optimal risk sharing posited in Arrow's conception. Or, at least, progress could be expected toward design and widespread use of Arrow Securities, i.e., those whose pay-offs were contingent on the performance of the underlying asset, e.g., equity-based securities with close links to the real sector of the economy. Much of the progress in information technology and economic liberalization, however, led to development and innovation of risk-shifting and risk-transferring financial instruments, with increasingly more tenuous relations to the real sector to the point of near full decoupling of financial and real sector developments (see Chapter 1).

The perception that globalization has not improved international risk sharing, despite considerable potential welfare gains, is supported by a voluminous research (see, for example, Tesar, 1995; Van Wincoop, 1999; Lee and Shin, 2008; Imbs, 2006). This literature examines the relationship between each country's volatility in income or consumption with that of corresponding variables in the rest of the world (or the rest of the region). By and large, the empirical research concludes that there is very limited — compared to potential suggested by theory — international risk sharing, and that globalization has not contributed much to improve risk sharing globally. Indeed, even in one of the most economically vibrant regions of the world, the Asia-Pacific Rim, risk sharing among and between countries has not been significant (Kim *et al.*, 2003, 2006; Hall *et al.*, 1998; Kim and Sheen, 2004; Lee and Shin, 2008; Gaston and Khalid, 2010).

Given the poor state of development of international risk sharing, Shiller (1993, 2003–2005) has long suggested that much progress could be made in exploiting the considerable potential in international risk sharing through "macromarket instruments". These instruments can be developed within each country, then traded on the international capital markets, thus diversifying each country's exposure to macroeconomic and income shocks and allowing consumption smoothing by its citizens (see also Borenzstein and Mauro, 2002; 2004). Reasons given for failure of adoption of sovereign risk-sharing instruments are informational problems, issues relating to policy commitment and credibility, governance, international contract enforcement issues and, in general, moral hazard. In the absence of macromarket securities that could improve international risk sharing, it would be expected that international institutions mandated to help ensure global financial stability through risk sharing would have developed effective mechanisms to protect countries against severe shocks. Such has not been the case thus far. Perhaps improvements in governance and improved representations in international financial institutions could accelerate the strengthening of international risk sharing.

Given the slow pace of consideration given to macromarket instruments of risk sharing, sovereigns are left with attempts to develop institutions that mitigate or spread risks. These include developing policy credibility, reputation for fiscal prudence, low debt-to-GDP ratio, low fiscal deficits, monetary policy that leaves room for flexibility while highly credible with anchoring inflation expectations, macroprudential regulation, and structural policies that allow rapid adjustment in wages and prices. All these measures afford countries strong degree of resilience and capacity to absorb and cope with temporary shocks; at least this was demonstrated in the response of Asian emerging markets — that had learned well the lessons of 1997–1999 crises — to the 2007/2008 global financial crisis (Sheng, 2009).

Countries can also attempt to spread risk of exposure to shocks by developing strong equity markets open to foreign investors, limiting external borrowing to that denominated in domestic currency, accumulating substantial foreign reserves, and developing ways and means of investing them in foreign asset markets. Institutions such as sovereign wealth funds allow diversification of sources of income and trade openness, encouraging long-term foreign direct investment, and maintaining exchange rate flexibility. Countries, especially small open economies, can also form monetary unions. Membership in such unions can help strengthen resilience to a number of shocks. However, such gains come with a trade-off in loss of flexibility in policy-making (particularly monetary policy). This constraint may at times be unhelpful to countries facing shocks, as has been demonstrated by dire circumstances of a number of members of the European Monetary Union.

14.1.3 *Government and Risk Sharing*

Government is the ultimate risk manager in a society. In contemporary societies, risk management is the central role of government. The span of this function covers risks to international and domestic security to the risk of contagion from communicable diseases. This spectrum of government risk management policy could be considered as a series of responses to shortcomings on the part of the market and non-governmental sector to correct risk-related failures. Among government risk management responsibilities, a great many are responses to this kind of failures pervasive in a contemporary "free-market" economy.

As noted in Chapter 1, neoclassical theory suggests that, in a well-functioning free market economy — with complete contingent markets or with Arrow–Debreu securities — risk would be optimally shared among market participants according to their ability to bear risks. Such an economy would develop markets where all kinds of risks would be traded. In a society with such a well-functioning economy, the government would play a minimal role. In the absence of such an economy, however, risk-related failures can render economic relations and transactions dysfunctional. In contemporary "free market" economies, even in some of the richest, complete markets for risk in an Arrow–Debreu sense do not exist. For example, while a homeowner can buy insurance against the risk of fire damage to a residential dwelling, there is no available market to trade the risk of decline in home prices. Nor is there a market to trade risk to allow purchasing of protection against unforeseen shocks to income and livelihood. The fact that well-functioning markets for these risks, and a wider array of others, are unavailable signal that the collective well-being of societies is much less than its full potential.

14.1.4 *Government and Risk Bearing*

Understanding the distinction between risks that are specific to an individual consumer, household, or firm (idiosyncratic risks) and those that are highly correlated across all participants in the economy (systematic risk, aggregate risk) is crucial for risk management. Sometimes what is an idiosyncratic risk for an individual or a firm may be systematic risk for another. What would be an idiosyncratic risk to a major internationally active bank may become systematic for a small bank in a given locality in that country. For a firm operating in a local community as the only monopoly employer, its idiosyncratic risk will be systematic for the community. Various types of market failure make the private market for risk-bearing less than optimal.

In principle, government interventions could potentially increase market efficiency. In practice, however, there are cases where intervention in the form of insurance against risk raises the possibility of government (on behalf of the public) assuming risk of losses and private sector capturing the gains. Such is the case in the example of deposit guarantees in a fractional reserve banking system. It is thought that aside from the famous moral hazard problem and the "too big to fail" issue, there is also the distributional impact of such interventions. Deposit insurance, intended to reduce the risk of bank runs and protect the payment system, raises more questions about redistribution than its efficiency implications. It is argued that it is "the managers and stockholders of high-flying deposit institutions that force deposit insurers into funding their plays at subsidized interest rates, and politicians and government officials whose jobs are made more comfortable who gain the most from deposit insurance" (quoted in Wright, 1993).

In addition, it is argued that deposit insurance "favors large depositors (the old and/or the rich) over taxpayers to the extent that it increases yield on insured deposits. To the extent that it lowers the costs of loans, deposit insurance is presumably capitalized in the value of fixed and quasi-fixed assets financed, such as existing houses, land, other real estate, and other capital. Those who own such assets when government policies become more generous — generally citizens who are older and richer than the average taxpayer — profit from the shift. These are also the persons with the greatest political clout per capita. The government should be active in protecting the public. Governments set and enforce fire codes, teach fire safety, and prosecute arsons. They should perform similar functions in banking." However, by providing deposit insurance, "government has accomplished the equivalent of relaxing the fire codes by subsidizing insurance and encouraging people to play with matches" (Wright, 1993). These words were written 15 years before the onslaught of the global financial crisis.

In most economies, governments play a major role in bearing risk on behalf of their citizens. For example, governments provide social safety nets measures and insurance for a variety of financial transactions. The history of economic explanation for government's role in the economy spans more than a century as economists attempted to explain the justification of the role as being necessitated by the divergence between public and private interests. Some six decades ago, Arrow and Debreu (1954) focused on finding precise conditions under which public and private interests would converge as envisioned in a conception of Adam Smith's invisible hand conjecture. The result was an elegant proof that competitive markets would indeed have a stable equilibrium, provided some stringent conditions were met. It was clear, however, that even under the best of actual conditions, markets did not perform as envisioned either by Smith or Arrow–Debreu. Consideration of violations of the underlying conditions spawned a voluminous body of literature on the theory and empirics of market failure. This concept became the starting point of analytic reasoning that justifies government's intervention in the economy to protect the public interest (Stiglitz, 1993).

The reason that contemporary societies implement social safety nets, such as social security, healthcare, and public unemployment insurance programs, is that individual households face substantial risk over their lifespan, such as mortality risk, wage and other income-wide risks, and health risks. As private insurance markets do not provide perfect insurance against all risks, there is said to be a market failure and government intervention is called for to correct it. What has become clear in the wake of the global financial crisis is that, even in the most advanced industrial economies, the existing social safety nets have become incapable of coping with the adverse consequences of the crisis. Not only has the crisis shaken previous level of confidence in markets, nearly all analyses of its causes attribute it to market failure in one dimension or another. This has intensified calls for government's interventions to counter the adverse effects of the crisis on income and employment, to strengthen social safety nets, and to reform the financial sectors. The most important lesson of the crisis has been that people often carry too large a risk of exposure to massive shocks originating in events that are beyond their influence and control. Hence, attention has been focused on ways and means of expanding collective risk sharing.

14.1.5 *Collective Risk Sharing and Social Justice*

Here-to-fore, it has been assumed that government intervention, in the form of activities such as providing social safety nets, public goods, and deposit insurance, were solely for the purpose of addressing various kinds of market failure. While this is a crucial justification for intervention, there is an important dimension of government's role that has not attracted much attention. Much of these activities in provision of social safety net, from a minimal amount in some countries to substantial amounts in welfare states, is also about collective risk sharing. This dimension has been particularly neglected in the analysis of government provision of social insurance and services in which the sole focus has been on the issue of trade-off between equity and efficiency; the issue at the heart of state versus market debates.

Relatedly, in these debates, the focus on distortions caused by taxation to finance these activities neglect to consider what taxes are financing in a particular society. An important risk-sharing use of taxes is in the area of transfer payments or automatic stabilizers intended to provide a cushion to citizens' consumption should they be affected by adverse consequences of shocks. Automatic stabilizers work without any discretionary government decisions. For this reason alone, there is no automatic way these safety net measures can differentiate between temporary and permanent or persistent shocks. While the former tends to help stabilize the economy, the latter can create fragility in the fiscal positions of government in the medium or long term. This places an emphasis on the appropriate design, eligibility criteria, and focus on alternative ways and means of addressing consequences of more permanent shocks.

Some have argued that government risk-sharing schemes intended to mitigate the consequences of adverse shocks to income are akin to insurance and as such they raise the issue of moral hazard. Additionally, it is argued, they have adverse incentive effect in that they cause labor supply to be inefficiently low. The standard argument is that while more equity can be achieved through redistribution, using taxes and transfers, it comes at the cost of reduced efficiency because it will adversely affect the incentive to work. A number of studies (Andersen, 2008, 2010, 2011; Sinn, 1995, 1996) argue that this is too simplistic a view. Consider a simple example where the tax system imposes a proportional tax on income. The tax then is used to provide a lump-sum transfer. In this example, those earning high income are taxed to finance lump-sum transfer to low-income earners. This is an ex-post redistributive system, but ex-ante, it is income-risk reduction device to the potential recipients. This implies that a tax-redistribution, risk-sharing scheme has an insurance effect which runs counter to the incentive effect, raising the possibility that such scheme may lead to larger rather than smaller labor supply effect as the former may dominate the latter (Andersen, 2011).

One of the strongest risk-sharing programs of existing welfare-states is in the area of human capital through investment in free education financed by taxes. These programs allow the society as a whole to share the risk involved in educating its younger members. Investment in human capital through education is known to have two important characteristics. First, since human capital is an important driver of growth, there is substantial pay-off to the society in the medium to long term in terms of tax payment and higher productivity. Second, it is also known that this pay-off is at least as large as, if not larger than, investment in equity markets. Since in the absence of free education some households, if not most, will be resource-constrained to finance higher education, private financing may mean that the society's potential human capital is not utilized efficiently, leading to lower productivity, and thus, lower average income. Figure 14.2 encapsulates the risk sharing inherent in the relationship.

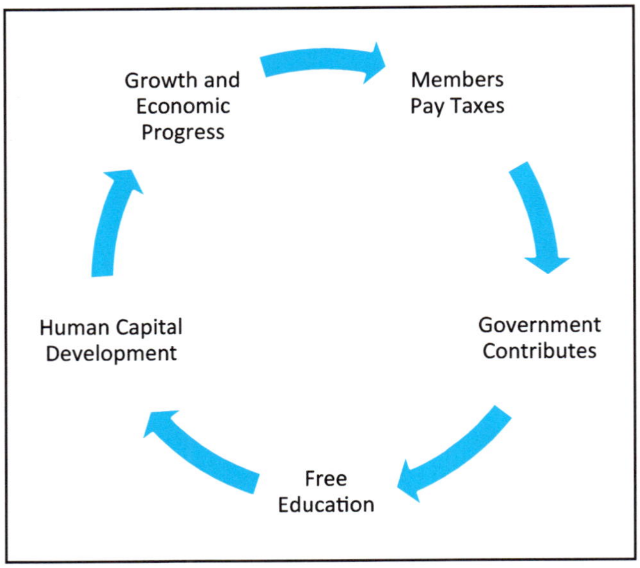

Figure 14.2. Risk Sharing: Taxes and Education.

14.1.6 *Risk Sharing and SME Financing*

Theoretical literature suggests that, in most economies, risk sharing's potential within, between, and among countries remains underexploited, leading to substantial loss of welfare. Much of the financial sectors' activities are interest rate-based, thus forcing financial transactions into credit–debtor relationship with its own peculiarities, requirements, and constraints. Hence, a large portion of productive activities remain finance-constrained; examples are small- and medium-sized enterprises (SMEs), the rural poor and non-banked communities everywhere, as well as individuals and very small firms in the informal economy. Largely due to the non-existence or incomplete availability of insurance, these segments of the economy are exposed to idiosyncratic and systematic risks. Microfinance was briefly discussed earlier. In the case of SMEs, financial constraint is one among a number of others — such as access to markets and regulations that, for the most part, are designed for incorporated businesses that have access to capital market and taxation codes. However, as long as the financial constraint is binding, resolving other issues, while important, would be of little help. The major source of finance for SMEs is the banking system that provides external funding for these firms (Levitsky, 1986; World Bank, 2010). Banks, however, prefer to deal with large transactions because of the high costs of risk appraisal, processing, and monitoring.

It is also argued that because SMEs do not provide sufficient information and their operations tend to be opaque, there is a risk of moral hazard due to information asymmetry, which leads banks to charge a high-risk premium (Beck, 2007). On the other hand, substantial benefits are claimed for encouraging relaxation of finance constraint for these firms. These include social benefits that accrue due to growth, entrepreneurship, private sector development, job creation, and improved income and wealth distribution (Beck 2007). A number of government policies and instruments have been used to create improved risk-sharing environment for SMEs. These measures have been targeted to the supply and demand side of the market as well as to the financial sector (for more details of these instruments of risk sharing, see Tan, 2009; WB, 2008; Beck *et al.*, 2006; World Bank, 2010; Duan *et al.*, 2009).

14.1.7 *Public–Private Partnership*

In the course of the last three decades, concerns have been raised regarding the ability of governments to deal with severe fiscal constraints. Additionally, concerns have also been expressed regarding the relative efficiency of governments to provide public services. Pressure has been exerted on governments to find alternative ways and means of delivering public services through sharing governance functions with the private sector. Outsourcing is one example where government's traditional functions of procurement, provision of public goods, and provision of services have been relegated to the private sector.

A risk-sharing instrument that has been popular with many governments over the last two decades has been Public–Private Partnerships (PPPs). This concept refers to a cooperative venture between governments and the private sector in which risks and returns are shared through a long-term contract according to which "the private sector becomes involved in financing, designing, constructing, owning or operating public facilities or services" (Hodge, 2004). In every one of these functions there are risks (Hambros Bank, 1995). The effectiveness of a given PPP depends much on the degree to which risks are shared. Case studies have demonstrated that in a number of projects throughout the world, risks have been shifted to one side, mostly to governments, or transferred rather than shared (see, for example, Ball *et al.*, 2003; Greve, 2003; Hodge, 2002; Berg *et al.*, 2000; Canadian Council for PPPs, 1997; Collins, 1998; Jacobson, 1998; Savoie, 1999). When there is no risk sharing and there are losses, the government bears the costs, but the gains accrue to the private sector. Provided that risk-sharing contracts are designed such that risks are allocated consistent with both market conditions and expectations and are transparent and flexible to allow both the government and private sector partners to deal with external shocks, PPPs have the potential to benefit the parties as well as the society at large. These benefits may well include efficiency gains, improved value for money, and greater fiscal space for the government. Figure 14.3 shows how risks can be shared by way of PPPs.

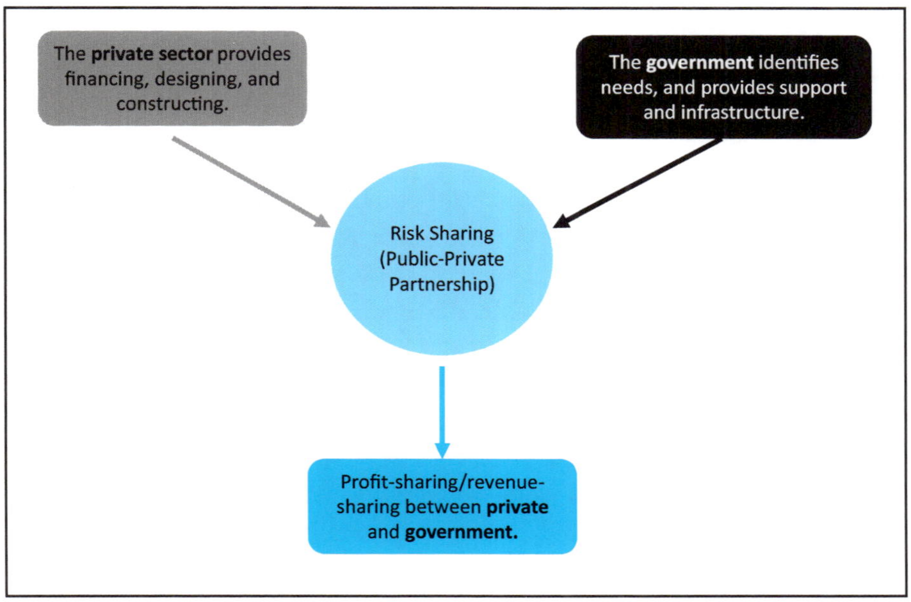

Figure 14.3. Risk Sharing Through Public–Private Partnerships.

14.2 Islamic Finance and Risk Sharing: Role of Public Policy

So far, this chapter has discussed risk sharing within the conventional environment of finance. The next few sections deal with the role of government in conducting public policy, particularly monetary and fiscal policy, in promoting risk sharing and, simultaneously, increasing the effectiveness of monetary policy while creating greater fiscal space and more stable macroeconomic environment (Askari and Mirakhor, 2014). As mentioned earlier, empirical evidence suggests that the vast potential opportunities for risk sharing existing within, between, and among countries remain unexploited, suggesting loss of human welfare as a result. Governments can do much to improve this situation. There are powers available to a government that private sector does not have. For one thing, in its capacity as the risk manager of the society and as its agent, it can promote risk sharing broadly by removing many of the barriers to its spread. It can reduce informational problems, such as moral hazard and adverse selection through its potentially vast investigative, monitoring, and enforcement capabilities. Through its power of implementation of civil and criminal penalties for non-compliance, a government can demand truthful disclosure of information from participants in the economy. It can force financial concerns that would attempt to appropriate gains and externalize losses, by shifting risks to others, to internalize them by imposing stiff liabilities or taxes.

Using its power to tax and control money supply, a government has the significant ability to make credible commitments on current and future financing issues. It can use its power to tax to create an incentive structure for intergenerational risk sharing whereby the proceeds from taxation of current income-earning generation is redistributed to reduce risks to human capital of the youth of current and future generations. Governments can also reform the incentive structure that provides strong incentive structure in favor of risk transfer in order to create a level playing field between risk sharing and risk transfer. Without government intervention, individuals are unable to diversify the risk to their most valuable asset: their human capital. The young have significant human capital but insufficient financial capital. For the old, on the other hand, the case is the opposite. As Merton (1983) suggested, a trade is possible between these generations, but laws prohibit trade in human capital (except through wage employment); therefore, the young cannot make credible commitment of their human capital through private contracts. There is no possibility for private contracts to commit future generations to current risk-sharing arrangements. This, in effect, represents another case of commitment failure. Using its powers of taxing and spending, unparalled monitoring and enforcing capabilities, and its control of money supply, the government can resolve these issues. No private entity can credibly commit not to default on an obligation as can the government.

14.2.1 *Macromarket Instruments*

One of the most promising instruments that would allow governments to improve risk sharing is the category of instruments called "macromarket" securities that can allow people to mitigate risks to their income and countries to enhance international risk sharing. These securities were proposed by Shiller (1993). While there are now ways and means available in many economies that allow protection against idiosyncratic and systematic risks, evidence suggests that much of individuals' incomes are still exposed to considerable risk. Even in rich economies, where a wide array of instruments of risk mitigation is available, the most important instrument of risk sharing being equity market instruments, significant portion (about 90% in the US) of "an average person's income is sensitive to sectoral, occupational, and geographic uncertainty" (Athanasoulis *et al.*, 1999). Moreover, these macromarket instruments could be used to hedge risks of a country's economy by investing in other nations' macromarket instruments. For example, in a macromarket for a given economy, an investor could buy a long-term claim on that economy's national income. Such an instrument would represent a claim, much like a share in a corporation. Prices of these instruments in the macromarkets would fluctuate as new information about national and international economic developments become available, similar to what happens when new information regarding corporate profits become available in equity markets (Athanasoulis *et al.*, 1999; Shiller, 1994, 2003; seen also Ismath Bacha *et al.*, 2015; Rizvi *et al.*, 2016).

These instruments can be effective means of improving inequalities of income within and among nations and allow faster international convergence. They would also facilitate intergenerational risk sharing. Such instruments issued by governments can also have the benefit of replacing government debt instruments that have adverse impact on income distribution because they mostly benefit already wealthy bond-holders (Folden, 2000).

Examples of such instruments are GDP-indexed bonds. These instruments have been around for some time (see Borensztein and Mauro, 2004; Shiller, 2005; Balkenhol, 2007; Ismath Bacha *et al.*, 2015; Rizvi *et al.*, 2016). The rates of these bonds are tied to the rate of growth of GDP of specific countries. The most recent development in this area has been the development of global GDP weighted bond indexes, as described in an *Institutional Investor* article. In May 2012, Barclays and Standish Mellon Asset Management Company announced an actively managed global bond strategy benchmarked to World GDP Index that weighs a nominal GDP-based combination of four countries (the US, Japan, the UK, and Canada) and six country blocks (Eurozone; Latin America; Emerging Europe; Middle East and Africa; other Europe, which consists of Greenland, Norway, Sweden, and Switzerland; and Australia and New Zealand). To reflect market opportunities, all government corporate and securitized bond offerings of US$500 million or more are issuance-weighted. Analysts believe that these instruments provide a better opportunity for risk diversification as emerging markets are present in this index with higher weight than in traditional bond indexes. Figure 14.4, which is derived from data provided in the *Institutional Investor* article, shows the distribution of weights by the selected countries and country blocs. As can be noted from the figure, China and India are left out of the index, presumably because their debt markets are not well developed. Also, note that emerging market has a weight of 20.9% in the new index as opposed to a weight of 8% in the traditional bond index.

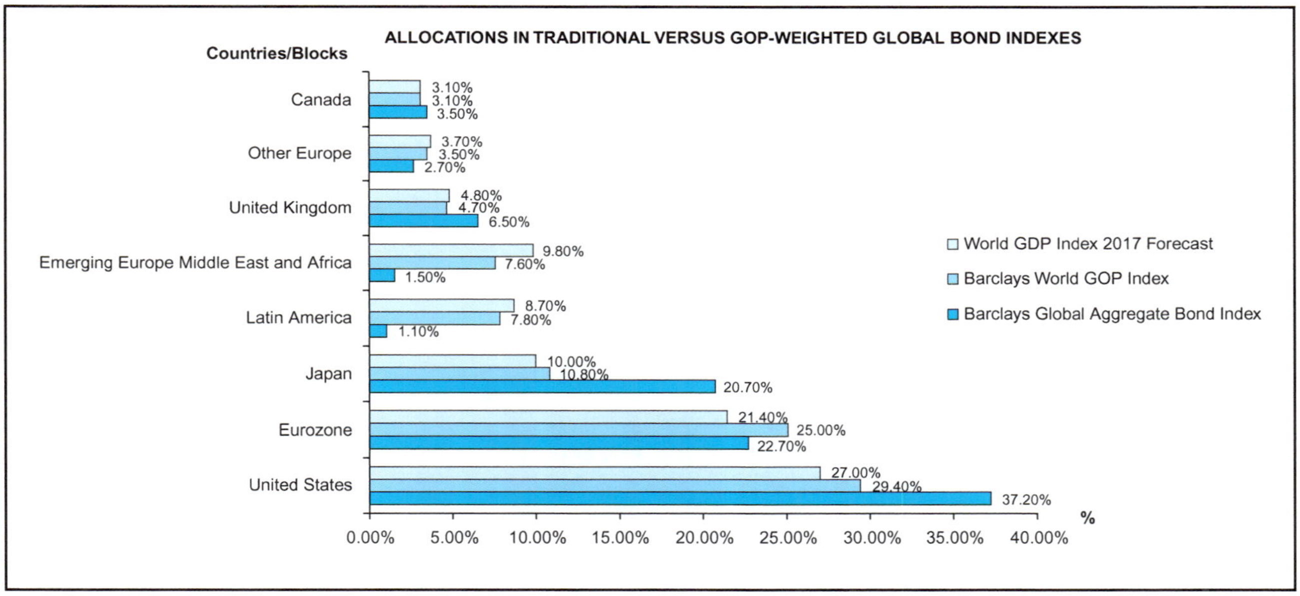

Figure 14.4. Traditional versus GDP — Weighted Bond Indexes.

Source: Based on article titled "Global Fund Managers Embrace GDP — Weighted Indexes." *Institutional Investor*, October 18, 2012.

The use of macromarket instrument in Islamic finance will be discussed in Section 14.2.2.

14.2.2 *Islamic Finance, Risk Sharing and the Stock Market*

A compelling case can be made that the first-best instrument if risk sharing is a stock market which is arguably the most sophisticated market-based risk-sharing mechanism. Developing an efficient stock market can effectively complement and supplement the existing and to-be-developed array of other Islamic finance instruments. It would provide the means for business and industry to raise long-term capital. A vibrant stock market would allow risk diversification necessary for management of aggregate and idiosyncratic risks. Such an active market would reduce the dominance of banks and debt financing, where risks become concentrated, creating system fragility (Sheng, 2009).

Idiosyncratic risks impact the liquidity of individuals and firms when they materialize. With an active stock market, individuals can buffer idiosyncratic liquidity shocks by selling equity shares they own on the stock market. Firms too can reduce their own idiosyncratic and liquidity risk through active participation in the stock market. As well, they can reduce risk to the rate of return to their own operation — such as productivity risk — by holding a well-diversified portfolio of shares of stocks. Thus, incentives are created for investment in more long-term, productive projects. Importantly, by actively participating in the stock market, individuals and firms can mitigate the risk of unnecessary and premature liquidation of their assets due to liquidity and productivity shocks (Smith, 1988; Pagano, 1993). Moreover, an active and vibrant stock market creates strong incentives for a higher degree of technological specialization through which the overall productivity of the economy is increased. This happens because without sufficiently strong risk sharing in the financial system through the stock market, firms avoid deeper specialization, fearing the risk from sectoral demand shocks (Saint-Paul, 1992). The reason stock markets are such effective tool of risk sharing is because each share represents a contingent residual equity claim.

14.2.3 *Government Role in Promoting Islamic Stock Market*

It can be argued that the actual operation of Islamic finance market differs from its ideal. In essence, there is a market failure; missing markets in equity sharing. Strong government policy action can create an incentive structure for the Islamic finance market to complete the spectrum of its instruments. The market has developed an array of short-term, liquid, and reasonably safe instruments which are considered *Shari'ah* compatible. This was not the case some 30 years ago. Then too, there was a missing market for Islamic instruments for which there was substantial demand. It took considerable commitment of resources and credibility on the part of governments, notably Malaysia, to organize this missing market to meet existing demand. Figure 14.5 depicts the key components of the Malaysian paradigm of government initiatives taken to develop the market for Islamic Finance.

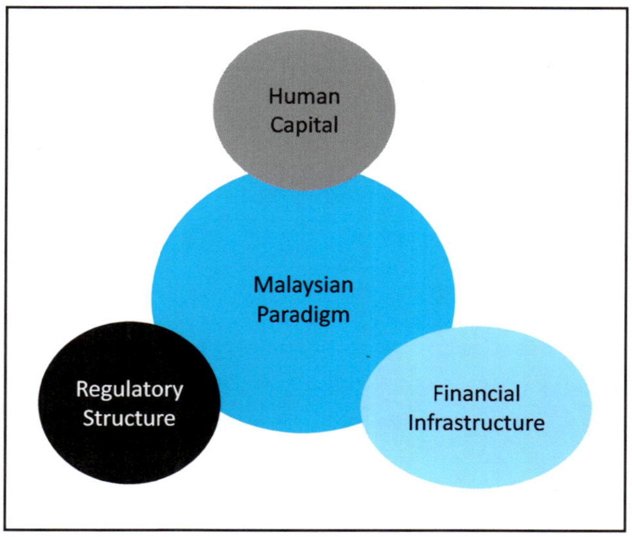

Figure 14.5. The Malaysian Paradigm to Developing Islamic Finance.

From a historical perspective, the late 1970s and early 1980s represent the beginning of the age of Muslim awakening. Perhaps, with the passage of time, private sector would have organized the missing market of Islamic finance on its own. However, it appears likely that progress may not have been as rapid as it has been with government intervention. Of the paradigms of government actions to create this market, by far the most successful has been the Malaysian Paradigm. Characteristics of this paradigm included not only the top-down push by the government but also other ingredients that had to be put in place for the venture's success. The most important of these ingredients were human capital, regulatory structure, and financial infrastructure to allow the emergence of Islamic banks. (One of the most important regulatory devices that created an effective impetus to the development of Islamic finance in Malaysia was the "no leakage rule". This rule required that the financial resources mobilized by the Islamic banking window had to be utilized in empowering financially Islamic contracts only).[1]

The success of the Malaysian paradigm in a relatively short span of three decades recommends it strongly as an appropriate framework for future progress. Specifically, this paradigm would suggest that the same kind of intense dedication and commitment could successfully generate the ways and means of pushing the agenda of Islamic finance forward in terms of developing medium-to-long-term instruments of risk sharing. This way, governments' commitment of resources and credibility could energize innovations and development of the needed instruments. In this context, one strategy would be for governments to develop the long-term, high-return, riskier end of the spectrum of instruments of risk sharing, i.e., stock market. This would create the needed incentive for the private sector to design and develop instruments in between the short-term, liquid end of the market on the one hand, and the stock market on the other. Figure 14.6 shows some of the key requirements for developing a well-functioning Islamic Finance sector.

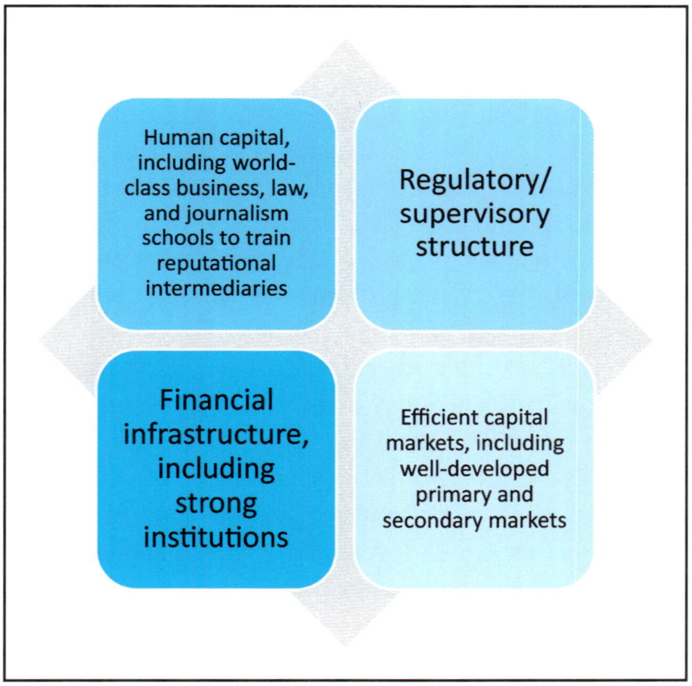

Figure 14.6. Key Requisites for Developing the Islamic Finance Sector.

14.2.4 *Advantages and Disadvantages of Stock Markets*

A large number of theoretical and empirical studies over the recent decades have focused on the investment–employment–growth benefits of stock markets (see the reference list in Askari *et al.*, 2012). When risk is spread among a large number of participants through an efficient stock market, closer coordination between the financial and real sector is promoted as well as better sharing of the benefits of economic growth and financial system stability. Risk transfer through debt instruments, in contrast, along with high leverage, weakens the link between the financial and real sector, thus posing a threat to financial sector stability. Especially as the growth of pure financial instruments, i.e., those with little connection to real assets, far outpaces the growth of the real sector activities, a phenomenon emerges called decoupling, whereby finance no longer is anchored in the real sector. The result is financial instability, leading to frequent bouts with crises (see Chapter 1).

As mentioned in Chapter 1, Reinhart and Rogoff (2009) demonstrated the high-frequency occurrences of crises in the history of the conventional system. Aside from the fact that all crises have been debt crises, all too often financial sector crises have required large government interventions and massive bailouts. Thus, while private financiers enjoy the gains of robust pure financial innovations that ultimately lead to decoupling, the society at large suffers the pain of saving the real sector from the vagaries of financial sector crises. This is what Sheng (2009) called, "privatizing the gain, socializing the pain".

Aside from the fact that, through risk sharing, stock markets (i.e., equity share markets focused on new investment, not speculation, as emphasized by Bogle, 2012) become an effective instrument of financing long-terms investment, they have an added benefit of being an instrument which individuals and firms can use to insure against liquidity and productivity shocks. As mentioned in Chapter 1, while some individual idiosyncratic risks can be mitigated through purchase of insurance policies, such as health, life, and accident, there are potentially a large number of unforeseen, therefore unpredictable, personal or family risks that are not as of yet insurable and for which no insurance policy can be purchased; e.g., risks to a person's livelihood. An individual can buffer against uninsurable risks by buying shares of stocks in good times and selling them when and if a liquidity shock is experienced. Similarly, stock markets can be used to diversify the risk of shock to asset returns. Firms too can use the stock market as a buffer against liquidity and productivity risks. These insurance functions of stock market create motivation and incentives for investing in projects that have higher returns (are more productive) but lower liquidity.

Empirical studies have demonstrated that countries with robust stock markets rely more on equity and long-term financing and less on banks and short-term debt. Firms place greater reliance on external capital than on internal funds. With a strong stock market, venture capitalists can recoup their capital investment in a project through initial public offerings, thus promoting faster rollover of venture capital to make it available more frequently to finance other productive real sector projects. Not only can individuals and firms benefit from the existence of a vibrant and robust stock market that provides risk-sharing opportunities, countries too can benefit from risk sharing with one another.

A large body of empirical research in recent years in the area of international risk sharing has demonstrated that there are gains to be made by countries when they trade in each other's securities. For example, a 2005 study shows the welfare gains to be made by the 10 East Asian countries through sharing risk among themselves and separately with the OECD. The study (Kim *et al.*, 2005) considered risk sharing in the case of these countries between 1970–2000 and found low levels of risk sharing among the countries themselves and between them and the OECD. Indonesia and Malaysia had the lowest level of risk sharing and therefore the largest potential welfare gains from improving the sharing of risk between them and other East Asian countries. The magnitude of gains was even higher through increased risk sharing with OECD. These results could be replicated in other areas and regions.

Question arises as to why is international risk sharing so low? This question is one researchers have been trying to answer in recent years, along with another related puzzle called the equity premium puzzle that has been attracting attention since it was first formulated in 1985 by two researchers, Mehra and Prescott (1985). It refers to a significant differential existing between stock market returns and the rate of interest paid on a safe bond (US Treasury bonds) over an extended period of time even after account has been taken of risk. Economic theory would assert that the differential should not exist. Capital should have left debt instruments and moved into equities until the rates equalized. Hence, the puzzle to be explained is why does this high differential continues to persist? Over the years, the study, originally using US data, has been replicated in a number of countries with the same results. The differential cannot be explained by the existing theory of behavior under risk. Researchers have used varieties of utility functions and risk characteristics, but the puzzle remains largely unexplained. Similarly, there have been attempts to explain the low international risk-sharing puzzle, but formal modeling has not been fruitful. It is suspected that reasons which explain low participation in domestic equity market, hence the emergence of the equity premium puzzle, are the same factors that could explain the low international risk-sharing puzzle. The prime candidate is low trust level and, a related factor, cost of entering the market.

Equity markets that are shallow also have limited participation. Empirical evidence (Guiso *et al.*, 2005; Erbas and Mirakhor, 2007) suggests one reason for low participation of population in stock market is the fact that people generally do not trust stock markets. Low level of trust, in turn, is explained by institutional factors and education. Moreover, high transaction costs — especially information and search costs as well as the high cost of contract enforcement — are crucial factors inhibiting stock market participation. These factors too stem from the institutional (rules of behavior) framework in the economy. Stiglitz (1989) suggests that disadvantages of equity finance stem from two informational problems:

(i) An adverse signaling effect, which leads good companies not to issue as much equity shares for fear that it may signal poor quality; and
(ii) An adverse incentive effect problem, which suggests that equity finance weakens the incentive for the entrepreneurs to exert their maximum effort for highest possible joint return.

This happens because once the project is financed, the entrepreneur knows that net returns have to be shared with the financier and therefore may not be motivated to work as hard as when the returns would not have to be shared. While the idea has intuitive appeal, empirical evidence does not support it.

Allen and Gale (2007), on the other hand, suggest a more plausible and empirically stronger reason why stock market participation is limited. They argue it is because of the costs involved. These include:

(i) information costs;
(ii) enforcement costs; and
(iii) costs due to weak governance structure of firms and markets.

Their analysis concludes that if these costs are prohibitively high, firms leave the equity market and resort to debt financing through banks (Allen and Gale, 2007, pp. 101–115). However, banks are highly leveraged institutions that borrow short (deposits) and lend long. This maturity mismatch creates potential for liquidity shocks and instability. And, perhaps to different degrees, even in the case of banks, there are information problems that lead to market failures such as credit rationing, which paralyze the opportunity for risky but potentially highly productive projects because they are rationed out of the market.

There are two conflicting views of the behavior of banks in financing of projects. Stiglitz (1989) suggests that to protect their financial resources, banks generally discourage risk taking. Therefore, there is an inherent agency conflict. The entrepreneur (agent) is interested in the high end of the risk-return distribution. The bank (principal), on the other hand, interested in safety, is concerned with the low end of the risk-return distribution. This, Stiglitz asserts, "has deleterious consequences for the economy". He further suggests that "from a social point of view equity has a distinct advantage: because risks are shared between the entrepreneur and the capital provider the firm will not cut back production as much as it would with debt financing if there is a downturn in the economy" (Stiglitz, 1989, p. 57). In contrast to Stiglitz's assertion that banks concentrate on the lower end of the risk-return distribution for safety reason, Hellwig (1998, p. 335) argues that there is an oft-neglected informational problem of banks he refers to as "negative incentive effects on the choice of risk inherent in the moral hazard of riskiness of the lend strategy of banks". This risk materialized dramatically in the period leading up to the recent financial crisis (see Askari *et al.*, 2012; Sheng, 2009).

14.2.5 *Creation of Vibrant, Robust Stock Market: The Role of Government*

Allen and Gale (2007) suggest that a successful, deep, and active stock market requires information, enforcement, and governance costs to be eliminated or at least minimized. Once this happens, the cost of entry into equity market becomes low and "there is full participation in the market. All investors enter the market, the average amount of liquidity in the market is high, and asset prices are not excessively high" (p. 115). As mentioned earlier, if the Islamic rules of market behavior — such as faithfulness to the terms and conditions of contracts, trust, and trustworthiness — are in place in a society, the informational problems and transaction costs, governance, and enforcement issues either would not exist or would be at low levels such as not to create deterrence to stock market entry.

There is, however, a paradigm gap between what Islam teaches and the actual behavior in the market. For this reason, actions governments take and the institutions they create to remedy the deficit in informational, enforcement, and governance behavior to reduce the cost of participation in stock markets have to be stronger and more comprehensive than that existing today. These policies, actions, and institutions should have the competence, efficiency, and enforcement capabilities to elicit the kind of behavior the results of which replicates or closely approximates those expected if market participants behaved in compliance with Islamic rules (see Box 14.1).

Box 14.1. Government Policies and the Institutions to Strengthen Capital Markets in Muslim Countries

(i) Policies to create a level playing field for equities to compete fairly with debt-based instruments; this means removing all legal, administrative, economic, financial, and regulatory biases that favor debt and place equity holding in a disadvantage;
(ii) Creating positive incentives for risk sharing via the stock market;
(iii) Investing in massive public education campaign to familiarize the population with the benefits of stock market participation; the kind of campaign that the Prime Minister Thatcher's Government ran in the U.K. which increased stock market participation substantially in a short span of time;
(iv) Investing in human capital to produce competent, well-educated, and trained reputational intermediaries — lawyers, accountants, financial journalists, and *Shari'ah* scholars — which means investing in the creation of world class business and law schools;
(v) Limiting short sales and leverage (including margin operations) of non-bank financial institutions and the credit-creation ability of banks through prudential rules that effectively cap the total credit the banking system can create;
(vi) Developing strong and dynamic regulatory and supervisory system for the stock exchanges that not only continuously monitor the behavior of markets and participants but stays a few steps ahead of those with penchant and motivation to use regulatory arbitrage to get around rules and regulations;
(vii) Finding ways and means of regulating and supervising reputational intermediaries or, at least, mandating that they become self-regulating to ensure minimization of false reporting or misreporting under threat of liability to market participants;
(viii) Ensuring completely transparent and accurate reporting of the day's trade by all exchanges;
(ix) Instituting legal requirements for the protection of the rights of minority shareholders.

Policies and actions presented in the Box 14.1 are not exhaustive by any means, but even this incomplete list will help reduce the cost of market participation, invest the market with credibility and reduce reliance on debt financing. It is worth noting that just one element of the above list, the legal protection of minority shareholders' rights, gives countries large stock market capitalization, larger minority shareholder participation in the stock market, more publicly listed forms relative to the total population, less concentrated ownership, higher dividend payout, and lower cost of capital. Black also believes that a country will have the potential of developing a vibrant stock market if it can assure minority shareholders of good information about the true value of businesses the listing companies are engaged in, and that there is sufficient legal, regulatory, and supervisory protection against company self-dealing transactions such as insider trading.

Lack of good information about a firm's true values and the existence of possibility of company self-dealing create the problems of moral hazard and adverse selection. Both problems can be addressed by legal rules and procedures as well as by existence of efficient and credible public and private institutions that monitor the stock market and companies listed on the stock exchange. These laws and institutions can assure investors of the honesty of dealings by firms and of the full transparency and accuracy of reporting and information. Extensive laws regarding financial disclosure and securities laws with strong sanctions in imposing risk of liability (to investors) on accountant, lawyers, firms' insiders, and investment bankers in retaliation for false reporting; fraudulent, misleading information; or faulty endorsements can be powerful tools to dissuade all concerned from the temptation of defrauding investors by false reporting and misleading information.

Requiring reputational intermediaries to be licensed by regulators, and revoking licenses or imposing heavy fines and initiating criminal proceeding against misbehavior weakens the incentive structure for abuse of reporting, endorsing, and information processes. Strong listing standards which stock exchanges enforce fully through imposition of heavy finds or even delisting of companies that violate disclosure rules would discourage false information from reaching investors. Existence of an active, dynamic, well-informed financial press can be valuable in creating a culture of disclosure. A strong, independent, and dynamic regulatory agency would be needed to monitor and supervise the stock market and behavior of its participants, and aggressively promote a culture of transparency by requiring prompt and accurate reporting on all trades in the market. Finally, it bears repeating that the government must invest considerable resources on development of world class business and law schools to ensure competent source of supply of human capital to reputational intermediaries.

While policies and institutions are crucial in reducing the cost of participation in stock markets and thus promoting widespread risk sharing, governments need to do more; they must lead by example. They could become active in markets for risk sharing. Generally, governments do share risks with their people. They share risks with individuals, firms, and corporations through tax and spending policies. They are silent partners. They also share risks of life of the poor and disadvantaged through social expenditure policies. They share the risk of the financial system through monetary policy and deposit guarantees. They could choose to finance part of their budget, at least development spending, through risk sharing and direct ownership of development projects with their citizens. This way they would reduce the debt burden on the budget. This reduction in government borrowing reduces the burden on monetary policy as well.

Governments undertake public goods projects because the characteristics of these goods — importantly, indivisibility and non-exclusivity — prohibit their production by the private sector and therefore are undertaken by governments. However, their social rate of return is substantial and much higher than private rates of return. A recent popular proposal suggests that these projects should be undertaken jointly with the private sector, hence the PPP label. The proposal has a number of problems: market distortion and information and governance problems being just some of these (see Choudhry and Mirakhor, 1997).

14.2.6 *Macromarket Instruments, Government Finance, and Risk Sharing*

Financing a portion of government's budget through the stock market has advantages, some of which are summarized here:

(i) It can energize stock market — provided that all preconditions, in terms of human capital, legal, administrative, and regulatory framework — are met and helps strengthen the credibility of the market.
(ii) It deepens and broadens the stock market.
(iii) It demonstrates that stock markets can be used as a tool of macroeconomic risk and financial management.
(iv) It reduces reliance of budget on borrowing, thus imparting greater stability to the budget and mitigates the risk of "sudden stops".
(v) It has positive distributional effect in that the financial resources that would normally go to service public debt can now be spread wider among the people as returns to the shares of government projects.
(vi) It enhances the potential for financing of larger portfolio of public goods projects without the fear of creating an undue burden on the budget.

(vii) It makes the task of monetary management simpler by limiting the amount of new money creation and limiting the number of objectives of monetary policy.
(viii) It promotes ownership of public goods by citizens; thus have a salutary effect on maintenance of public goods as it creates an ownership concern among the people, and to some extent mitigate "the tragedy of commons".
(ix) It has the potential of strengthening social solidarity.
(x) It also has the potential to promote better governance by involving citizens as shareholder–owners of public project.
(xi) It provides an excellent risk-sharing instrument for financing of long-term private sector investment.
(xii) It is also an effective instrument for firms and individuals to use to mitigate liquidity and productivity risks.
(xiii) By providing greater depth and breadth to the market and minimizing the cost of market participation, governments convert the stock market into an instrument of international risk sharing as other countries and their people can invest in the domestic stock market.
(xiv) It will change the basis of monetary expansion from credit to equity as economic expansion in the real sector maps onto the financial sector.
(xv) Finally financing part, or all, of the budget shortfalls through risk-sharing instruments leaves the next generation with means of wealth creation rather than a debt burden of financing the present generation's government deficits.

The design of risk-sharing instruments to be issued by governments is not difficult. These instruments can be traded in the secondary market if the shareholders experience a liquidity shock. Their rate of return can be structured as an index of return tied to the rate of return to the stock market. If the domestic stock market is not deep, then an index of regional and/or international stock market returns can be included. The argument is that since social rate of return to public goods are much higher than to privately produced goods and services, the investment in public goods should have a rate of return at least as high as the return to the stock market to promote efficient resource allocation.

Of course, since governments are usually less risky, the rate of return to government-issued shares has to be adjusted downward to take account of governments' risk premium. Depending on the country and the interest rate its government pays for borrowed money, it is unlikely that the rate of return it would pay to holders of equity shares it issues would be any higher than the rate interest after adjusting for the lower credit risk of governments. Even in the unlikely event that a few basis points higher has to be paid, the trade-off is worthwhile, considering the positive contributions the instrument would make to the economy and the society (see Choudhry and Mirakhor, 1997; Ul-Haque and Mirakhor, 1999; see also Bacha *et al.*, 2016).

14.2.7 *Future of Islamic Finance*

A healthy debate is in progress regarding the future of Islamic finance. The progress of Islamic finance over the last three decades is well recognized. As explained in Chapter 1, in the course of its evolution thus far, the market has developed an array of short-term, liquid, low-risk instruments. While instruments of liquidity are needed in the market, so are instruments of long-term investment. What is of concern is that very little or no effort is spent developing instruments that can serve the long-term, less liquid, higher-return investments that have greater potential for generating employment, income, and economic growth. There is a strong perception that Islamic finance is focusing on the development of relatively safe instruments with debt-like characteristics promising maximal return with minimal risk in the shortest possible time, which is what is thought to be driving Islamic finance. Currently, this is a major apprehension. Concentrating market energies on these types of instrument has possible detrimental effects. There is the possibility of repeatedly reinventing the same short-term, liquid, safe instruments with only a small difference in fine tuning, slicing, and dicing risk for purpose of product differentiation.

However, the critics of IFI as is currently operating must recognize some serious constraints under which the industry has to operate. First and foremost among these constraints is the general lack of a level playing field between interest rate-based debt financing and risk sharing, equity-based financing. In contemporary market capitalism, biases in favor of debt financing are a well-entrenched feature of the financial system. These biases permeate throughout the economy in incentive structure, legal and administration institutions, and in macroeconomic policies. Fiscal and monetary policies are conducted in all contemporary economies, including Muslim countries, on interest rate debt financing basis. Embedded within a fractional reserve banking system that accommodates high leverage, the fractional reserve system plus the incentive structure favoring interest rate mechanism create a major disadvantage. Among the reforms of the conventional system suggested post-2007/2008 crisis has been the elimination of the fractional reserve system (Kotlikoff, 2010; Benes and Kumhof, 2012; King, 2016).

The second constraint on contemporary IFI operations is the lack of *Shari'ah*-compliant, competitive, liquid, credible, long-term, and widely used hedging and liquidity management instruments. Government bonds serve this function in the conventional system. It may be argued that there are *sukuk* in the market that can be used for liquidity and hedging management. However, the *sukuk* that exist in the market are comparatively few, of large denomination, and not traded in secondary market as they are bought and held. In all Muslim countries, monetary and fiscal policies operate with interest rate-based bond issues; instruments that IFI cannot use legitimately for hedging and liquidity purposes. In effect, Muslim governments' macroeconomic policies strengthen interest rate mechanisms, and importantly these policies define adverse competitive conditions exogenously for IFI (Askari and Mirakhor, 2014).

The fourth constraint is imposed on IFI as it operates in international financial markets, as it must, by the legal environment. Lack of compatibility between *Shari'ah* rulings and the legal systems governing financial centers imposes a legal risk on the international operations of IFI. This constraint has been demonstrated in a number of legal cases in major financial centers involving IFI contracts. Finally, more rapid and dynamic expansion of IFI internationally has been hampered, as adverse political environment in some major international financial centers have imposed constraint on operations of IFI in these centers. These constrains are challenges that IFI has to overcome in order to maintain its momentum (Mirakhor and Haneef, 2012).

As discussed earlier, governments can do much more to alleviate some of the most important and urgent of these constraints. It is clear that the IFI, left to itself, does not have the incentive and/or the capacity to develop long-term, risk-sharing instruments. There is a perception that the demand-driven market values safety, and this is the reason why longer-term, riskier Islamic finance instruments are not being developed. While the market should have instruments to meet short-term, low-risk, and liquid trade financing demand, it would be unfortunate if the future evolution of Islamic finance focuses only on short-termism at the cost of neglecting investment needs of the real sector. While instruments developed so far emphasize safety, the recent 2007/2008 crisis in the conventional system as well as the turmoil in the *sukuk* market demonstrate that no one instrument is immune to risk and that it is unrealistic to perpetuate a myth that safety with high returns in financial markets is possible. There is always risk. The question is how to allocate it to those who are in the best position to bear it and how to build a system resilient to absorb shocks emanating from materialization of risk. The answer must surely lie in a system that provides full-spectrum menu of risk-sharing instruments.

A related concern is that by focusing solely on short-termism, there is the possibility of emergence of path dependency. Economic changes generally occur in increments. Growth of markets and capital formation are path-dependent. That is, later outcomes are partly a function of what has inspired in the earlier rounds of economic and financial exchange (Shen, 2009). Once path dependency sets in, change becomes difficult. At times, path dependency is exacerbated by insularity and silo mentality generated by a perception that all is well with established way of doing things therefore no change is required. There is a concern that such path dependency may well emerge that conveys a message that short-termism, safety, and liquidity (as well as apparent absence of *riba*) are all there is to Islamic finance. Clearly, this is not so. Islamic finance is more about risk spreading and risk sharing. For those who are able to participate in the financial sector, Islamic finance provides risk sharing through *mu'amalat*. For those unable, due to poverty, to utilize instruments of Islamic finance to mitigate risk, the financially able are commanded to share the risks of the less able through the redistributive instruments prescribed by Islam. As explained in Chapter 1, the financially more able are obligated to share the risks to the life of the poor not as an act of charity but as a duty of redeeming the right of the less able; a right that is a direct result of the property rights principles of Islam. Finally, inheritance laws are also means of risk sharing.

Arguably, the stock market is the first-best instrument of risk sharing. Developing an active and efficient stock market can promote international as well as domestic risk sharing, which render the economy and its financial system resilient to shocks. Moreover, it is suggested that the lack of available long-term equity instruments within the menu of Islamic finance instruments is akin to a market failure; creating a strong ground for government intervention. Additionally, the introduction of Islamic finance at the global level represents a remedy for the failure of financial markets to meet a strong demand for Islamic instruments. It took a top-down approach, government commitment, dedication, and investment of resources, particularly in the case of Malaysia, to correct this market failure. Once again, government intervention can remedy the current failure of the market to develop long-term, more risky, higher return equity instruments.

Some 65 years ago, Domar and Musgrave (1944, Chapter 1) argued that "if the government fully shared in gains and losses, it can actually encourage risky investment" (Stiglitz, 1989). This, a government can do by developing a stock market with characteristic of low-cost entry to ensure the widest possible participation by investors. In doing so, governments could also ensure that stock markets would have limitations on short selling and leverage operations by establishing market-based regulatory measures. Creating such a stock market would represent a leap forward by providing an effective instrument for domestic and international risk sharing and long-term equity investment. Government can enhance the credibility and appeal of the stock market by financing part of its budget through issuing equity shares that would be traded in the market (Askari *et al.*, 2012). It can also mount a public information campaign to educate the population regarding the risk-sharing characteristics of the stock market.[2] Islamic finance has developed instruments to serve the low end of the time-risk-return profile of its transactions menu. Such a stock market will serve the high end. The intermediate space of the menu can then be left for the private sector to complete.

One of the most appealing dimensions of the risk-sharing characteristics of Islamic finance is the legacy that current generations can leave future generations when and if a Muslim government adopts Islamic macroeconomic policies: no debt. Financing government's fiscal operations through interest rate-based debt and using the same instrument to conduct monetary policy has left the future generations of many countries in the world with a legacy of large debt burdens. This is risk shifting at its worst; present generations shift the risk of their overconsumption to the next generation.

When and if governments implement risk-sharing methods of financing their fiscal operations by issuing low-denomination, risk-sharing equity instruments so all people rather than only rich and high-net-worth individuals can participate in the fiscal operations of their government, the current generation leaves the next generation with a legacy of wealth rather than debt. This is in addition to the fact that through risk sharing method of financing fiscal operations, governments can have positive distributional impact as greater numbers of middle and lower income classes participate in the market for governments' risk sharing equity issuance. Moreover, this method of financing imparts powerful resilience, stability and, perhaps even antifragility impulse, to the economy (Askari *et al.*, 2012; Askari *et al.*, 2016; Rafi and Mirakhor, 2018).

Summary

This chapter focused on risk sharing methods of financing and it application in the conventional and the Islamic system. It has argued that conventional system has long been familiar with risk sharing. At a theoretical level, risk sharing is a fundamental concept of the classical and neoclassical economics. In practice, however, the utilization of risk sharing has been much more limited. This is due mostly to the fact that the entire operation of the conventional finance has been geared both practically as well as institutionally toward risk transfer. After all, the entire banking system at the center of the conventional system has been based on risk transfer. Regulatory and supervisory institutions of the system too have been geared to risk transfer. Frequent occurrences of financial crises have demonstrated how rapidly risk transfer switches to risk shifting in this system. Nevertheless, the chapter discussed examples of uses of risk-sharing methods in the conventional system. These include microfinance and private–public–partnership programs.

The chapter considered risk sharing as the essence of Islamic finance and focused on how such a system could be implemented comprehensively. It argued that, in its current format, the Islamic finance industry faces formidable challenges. These have to be met if the industry is to maintain its momentum as an alternative financing method. Some of these challenges can be characterized as being similar to market failure requiring government intervention. One such beneficial intervention would be for governments to implement policies that strengthen primary and secondary equity markets to allow growth of public trust in the operations of stock markets. It was argued stock markets are the first best instruments of risk sharing, provided that certain conditions are satisfied. The chapter summarized these conditions.

Another way governments can help the growth and dynamism of Islamic finance industry is to finance part or all of their operations through risk-sharing instruments that mobilize the financial resources of their own people. The chapter discussed how these instruments are to be designed and marketed. Overall, the chapter emphasized the beneficial aspects of risk sharing as opposed to risk transfer or risk shifting methods of financing activities. For risk sharing finance to succeed, strong capital markets are essential.

Questions and Problems

1. Explain the difference between systematic and idiosyncratic risks.
2. What are the problems of the original form of microfinance?
3. Explain how international risk sharing can be strengthened?
4. How can members of a society share risk amongst themselves?
5. How does public policy and strengthened institutional framework in developing countries contribute to reducing risk?
6. Can risk sharing contribute to social justice? How?
7. What role can a stock market play in a risk-sharing framework?
8. What are the key advantages and disadvantages of stock markets?
9. Does empirical proof support development of stock markets for economic growth?
10. Why is international risk sharing so low?
11. What role can governments play in creation of robust stock markets?
12. What are key benefits of financing a portion of government's budget though the stock market?
13. How can risk sharing help SMEs?
14. Explain the "ingredients" of the Malaysian Paradigm.

Bibliography

Allen, Franklin and Douglas Gale, 2007. Understanding Financial Crisis. Oxford: Oxford University Press.

Andersen, T. M. (2008). "The Scandianavian Welfare Model — Prospects and Challenges," *International Tax and Public Policy*, Special Issue, Vol. 15, pp. 45–66.

Andersen, T. M. (2010). "Income Taxation: Incentive vs. Insurance," Working Paper, School of Economics and Management, Aarhus University, Denmark.

Andersen, T. M. (2011). "Collective Risk Sharing: The Social Safety Net and Employment," School of Economics and Management, Aarhus University, Denmark, (oekonomi@econ.au.dk).

Armendariz de Aghion, B. and J. Murdoch (2005). *The Economics of Microfinance* (MIT Press, Cambridge).

Arrow, K. J. (1971). *Essays in the Theory of Risk-Bearing* (Markham Publishing Company, Chicago) pp. 1–229.

Arrow, K. J. and G. Debreu (1954). "The Existence of an Equilibrium for a Competitive Economy," *Econometrica*, Vol. XXII, pp. 265–290.

Askari, H. *et al.* (2012). *Risk Sharing in Finance: The Islamic Finance Alternative* (John Wiley and Sons, Singapore).

Askari, H. and A. Mirakhor (2014). "Risk Sharing, Public Policy and the Contribution of Islamic Finance," *PSL Quarterly*, Vol. 68, No. 271, pp. 345–379.

Athanasoulis, S. *et al.* (1999). "Macro Markets and Financial Security," *Federal Reserve Bank of New York Economic Policy Review*, Vol. 5, No. 1, pp. 21–39.

Bacha, O. I. *et al.* (2015). "Risk sharing in Corporate and Public Finance," PSL Quarterl Review, Vol. 68, No. 274, pp. 187–213.

Balkenhol, B. (2007). "Access to Finance — The Place of Risk-sharing Instruments," *Savings and Development*, Vol. 31, No. 1, pp. 69–78.

Ball, R. *et al.* (2003). "Risk Transfer and Value for Money in PFI Projects," *Public Management Review*, Vol. 5, No. 2, pp. 279–290.

Beck, T. (2007). "Financing Constraints of SMEs in Developing Countries: Evidence, Determinants and Solutions." World Bank.

Beck, T. *et al.* (2008). "Bank Financing for SMEs around the World: Drivers, Obstacles, Business Models, and Lending Practices," World Bank Policy Research Working Paper No. 4785.

Bencivenga, V. and B. D. Smith (1991). "Financial Intermediation and Indigenous Growth," *Review of Economic Studies*, Vol. 58, No. 2, pp. 195–209.

Benes, Jaromir and Michael Kumhoff (2012). The Chicago Plan Revisited. Working Paper, WP/12/202, International Monetary Fund, Washington DC.

Berg, S. *et al.* (eds.) (2000). *Private Initiatives in Infrastructure: Priorities, Incentives and Performance* (Institute of Development Economics, Tokyo).

Bogle, John C. (2012). The Clash of the Cultures: Investment vs. Speculation. New York: John Wiley.

Borensztein, E. and P. Mauro (2002). "Reviving the Case for GDP-Indexed Bonds," IMF Policy Discussion Paper (IMF, Washington, D.C.) (PDP/02/10).

Borensztein, E. and P. Mauro (2004). "The Case for GDP-indexed Bonds," *Economic Policy*, Vol. 19, No. 38, pp. 165–216.

Canadian Council for Public Private Partnerships (1996). Best Practice Guidelines.

Choudhry, N. N. and A. Mirakhor (1997). "Indirect Instruments of Monetary Control in an Islamic Financial System," *Islamic Economic Studies*, Vol. 4, No. 2.

Collins, S-O (1998). "In the Twilight Zone: A Survey of Public-Private Partnerships in Sweden," *Public Productivity and Management Review*, Vol. 21, No. 3, pp. 272–283.

Cox, D. and E. Jimenez (1998). "Risk Sharing and Private Transfers: What about Urban Household?" *Economic Development and Cultural Change*, Vol. 46, No. 3, pp. 621–637.

Domar, Evsey D. and Richard A. Musgrave (1944). "Proportional Income Taxation and Risk-Taking," The Quarterly Journal of Economics, Vol. 58. No. 3, pp. 388–422.

Duan, H. *et al.* (2009). "An Analysis of Causes for SMEs Financial Difficulty," *International Journal of Business and Management*, Vol. 4, No. 6.

Duval, R. *et al.* (2006). "Structural Policies and Resilience to Shocks," OECD Working Paper.

Erbas, N. and A. Mirakhor (2007). "The Equity Premium Puzzle, Ambiguity Aversion and Institutional Quality." IMF Working Paper, International Monetary Fund, Washington, DC.

Fafchamps, M. and S. Lund (2003). "Risk-Sharing Networks in Rural Philippines," *Journal of Development Economics*, Vol. 71, No. 2, pp. 261–287.

Fischer, G. (2013). "Contract Structure, Risk Sharing and Investment Choice," *Econometrica*, Vol. 81, No. 3, pp. 883–939.

Folden, M. (2000). "The Effectiveness of Government and Transfers as Insurance," SSE/EFI Working Paper Series in Economics and Finance No. 377.

Gaston, N. and A. Khalid (eds.) (2010). *Globalization and Economic Integration: Winners and Losers in the Asia-Pacific* (Edward Elgar, Cheltham, U.K.).

Gertler, P. J. and J. Gruber (1997). "Insuring Consumption Against Illness," NBER, Working Paper No. w6035.

Greve, C. (2003). "When Public-Private Partnerships Fail. The Extreme Case of NPM –Inspired Local Government of Forum in Denmark." Paper presented at the *EGPA Conference*, Oerias, Portugal, September 3–6.

Hall, V. *et al.* (1998). "Pacific Rim Business Cycle Analysis: Synchronization and Volatility," *New Zealand Economic Papers*, Vol. 32, No. 2, pp. 129–159.

Hambros Bank Ltd. (1995). *Risk Analysis for Public Private Partnerships* (Hambros Bank Ltd, London).

Hodge, G. A. (2002). "Who Steers the State When Governments Sign Public-Private Partnerships?" *The Journal of Contemporary Issues in Business and Government*, Vol. 8, No. 1.

Hodge, G. A. (2004). "Risks in Public-Private Partnerships: Shifting, Sharing or Shirking," *The Asia Pacific Journal of Public Administration*, Vol. 26, No. 2, pp. 155–179.

Imbs, J. (2006). "The Real Effects of Financial Integration," *Journal of International Economics*, Vol. 68, No. 2.

Jacobson, L. (1998). "Partnership Problems," *Government Executive*, Vol. 30, No. 5.

Jalan, J. and M. Revallion (1997). "Are Poor Less Well Insured? Evidence on Vulnerability to Income Risk in Rural China." Policy Research Working Paper 1863. World Bank, Development Research Group.

Kim, D. and J. Sheen (2004). "Risk Sharing within Australia and with New Zealand." Presented at *Australian Macroeconomic Workshop*, University House, Australian National University, Canberra, Australia.

Kim, S. *et al.* (2003). "Financial Integration and Consumption Risk-Sharing in East Asia," Working Paper 03-13, Korea Institute for International Economic Policy.

Kim, S. *et al.* (2005). "Regional Versus Global Risk Sharing in East Asia," *Asian Economic Papers*, Vol. 3, pp. 195–201.

Kim, S. *et al.* (2006). "Financial Integration and Consumption Risk Sharing in East Asia," *Japan and the World Economy*, Vol. 18, No. 2, pp. 143–157.

King, M. (2016). *The End of Alchemy: Money, Banking, and the Future of the Global Economy* (W. W. Norton, New York).

Kippins, A. B. (1997). *Producing Guanxi: Sentiments, Self, and Subculture in a North China Village* (Duke University Press, Durham, N.C.).

Kotlikoff, L. J. (2010). *Jimmy Stewart is Dead: Ending the World's Ongoing Financial Plague with Limited Purpose Banking* (Wiley, New York).

Lee, J. W. and K. Shin (2008). "Welfare Implication of International Financial Integration." Asian Development Working Paper Series on Regional Economic Integration No. 20.

Levitsky, J. (1986). "World Bank Lending to Small Enterprises: A Review." World Bank, Washington, D.C.

Mehra, R. and E. C. Prescott (1985). "The Equity Premium: A Puzzle," *Journal of Monetary Economics*, Vol. 15, pp. 145–161.

Merton, R. (1983). "On the Role of Social Security as a Means for Efficient Risk Sharing in an Economy Where Human Capital is not Tradable," in Z. Bodie and J. Shoven (eds.) *Financial Aspects of the United States Pension System* (University of Chicago Press, Chicago).

Morduch, J. (1998). "Does Microfinance Really Help the Poor? Evidence from Flagship Programs in Bangladesh." Hoover Institution, Stanford University, Stanford, California.

Morduch, J. (1999a). "Between the State and the Market: Can Informal Insurance Patch the Safety Net?" *The World Bank Research Observer*, Vol. 14, No. 2, pp. 187–207.

Morduch, J. (1999b). "The Microfinance Promise," *Journal of Economic Literature*, Vol. 37, pp. 1,564–1,614.

Othman, A., N. Mat Sari, S. O. Alhabshi and A. Mirakhor (2017). *Macroeconomic Policy and Islamic Finance in Malaysia* (Palgrave Macmillan, New York).

Pagano, M. (1993). "Financial Markets and Economic Growth," *European Economic Review*, Vol. 37, pp. 613–622.

Rafi, U. and A. Mirakhor (2018). *Antifragility of Islamic Finance: The Risk-Sharing Alternative* (Peter Lang, New York).

Reinhart, Carmen M. and Kenneth S. Rogoff (2009). This Time is Different: eight Centuries of Financial Folly. Princeton: Princeton University Press.

Revallion, M. and S. Chaudhuri (1997). "Risk and Insurance in Village India: Comment," *Econometrica*, Vol. 65, No. 1, pp. 171–184.

Rizvi, S. A. R., O. I. Bacha and A. Mirakhor (2016). *Public Finance and Islamic Capital Markets: Theory and Application* (Palgrave Macmillan, New York).

Saint-Paul, G. (1992). "Technological Choice, Financial Markets and Economic Development," *European Economic Review*, Vol. 36, No. 4, pp. 763–781.

Savoie, D. (1999). "Public-Private Partnerships: A Word of Caution," *Insight*, Vol. 4, No. 1.

Sheng, A. (2009). *From Asian Global Financial Crisis* (Cambridge University Press).

Shiller, R. (1993). *Macro Markets: Creating Institutions for Managing Society's Largest Economic Risks* (Oxford University Press, New York).

Shiller, R. (2004). "Radical Financial Innovation." Cowles Foundation Discussion Paper No. 1461. New Haven, Connecticut, 06520-8281.

Shiller, R. (2005). "In Favour of Growth-Linked Bonds," *The Indian Express*, March 10.

Shiller, R. (2003). *The New Financial Order: Risk in the 21st Century* (Princeton University Press, Princeton, New Jersey).

Sinn, H. W. (1995). "A Theory of the Welfare State," *Scandinavian Journal of Economics*, Vol. 97, pp. 495–526.

Sinn, H. W. (1996). "Social Insurance, Incentives and Risk Taking," *International Tax and Public Finance*, Vol. 3, No. 3, pp. 259–280.

Smith, S. C. (1988). "On the Incidence of Profit and Equity Sharing," *Journal of Economic Behavior and Organization*, Vol. 9, pp. 45–58.

Stiglitz, J. (1989). "Financial Markets and Development," *Oxford Review of Economic Policy*, Vol. 5, No. 4.

Stiglitz, J. (1993). "Perspectives on the Role of Government Risk-Bearing within the Financial Sector." in Government Risk-Bearing, *Proceedings of Federal Reserve Bank of Cleveland*, pp. 109–130.

Stiglitz, J. (1990). "Peer Monitoring and Credit Markets," *World Bank Economic Review*, Vol. 4, No. 3, pp. 351–366.

Tan, H. (2009). "Evaluating SME Support Program in Chile using Panel Firm Data," World Bank Policy Research Working Paper No. 5082.

Tesar, L. (1995). "Evaluating Gains from International Risk Sharing." *Carnegie Rochester Conference Series on Public Policy*, Vol. 42, pp. 95–143.

Thomas, J. and T. Worral (1997). "Informal Insurance Arrangements in Village Economies." Department of Economics Discussion Paper 97/08, University of California Berkeley.

Townsend, R. (1994). "Risk and Insurance in Village India," *Econometrica*, Vol. 62, pp. 539–592.

Townsend, R. (1995). "Financial System in the Northern Thai Villages," *Quarterly Journal of Economics*, Vol. 110, pp. 1,011–1,046.

Ul-Haque, N. and A. Mirakhor (1999). "The Design of Instruments for Government Finance in an Islamic Economy," *Islamic Economic Studies*, Vol. 6, No. 2, pp. 27–43.

Van Wincoop, E. (1999). "How Big are Potential Welfare Gains from International Risk Sharing?" *Journal of International Economics*, Vol. 47, February, pp. 109–235.

World Bank (2008). "Finance for all? Policies and Pitfalls in Expanding Access." World Bank Policy Research Report.

World Bank (2010). "Global Economic Prospects 2010: Crisis, Finance and Growth." Washington, D.C.

Wright, B. D. (1993). "Public Insurance of Private Risks: Theory and Evidence from Agriculture." in Government Risk-Bearing, *Proceedings of Federal Reserve Bank of Cleveland*, pp. 45–65.

Endnotes

1. For more detailed information on the progress of Islamic finance in Malaysia, see Othman *et al.* (2017).
2. It is crucial to emphasize that the type of stock market being advocated here is not the type that is operating today. It is a type in which shares of investment are traded not speculative transaction which now constitute the major portion of trades (Bogle, 2012).

Chapter 15

POTENTIAL ROLE OF CAPITAL MARKETS IN REDUCING INCOME AND WEALTH INEQUALITY

Topics in this Chapter

Chapter Objective

This concluding chapter examines the potential role of capital markets in addressing a key contemporary issue, that of rising inequality. While economies have been growing quite impressively, the income gap between the rich and the poor has also widened. It appears that much of the benefits of growth has accrued to a small portion while the majority of the population has seen little income growth. Such disparity is unacceptable, particularly from an Islamic viewpoint. As the chapter argues, a key factor contributing to this widening income disparity is the current reliance on debt and debt-based financing. The chapter examines, potential solutions, including risk sharing finance.

Key Terms		
Arrow-Debreu Model	financialization	redistribution
asset based redistribution	income gap	risk-sharing
bounded rationality	inequality	shared prosperity program
enforceability of contracts	political capture	tax transfer
equality efficiency trade-offs	property rights	Theory of Contracts

15.1 Introduction

Over the last decade, there has been growing evidence that, across the world, the gulf between the "haves" and "have nots", between the rich and the poor, is widening at an alarming rate. Data on inequality suggest that "the vast bulk of the benefits of modern economic progress has been going to a small number of people" (Blasi *et al.*, 2014, p. ix).[1] According to data released by the World Inequality Lab,[2] in 2016, the top 10% of income earners captured 37% of national income in Western Europe, 47% in the US, 55% in Brazil, 61% in the Middle East, and 63% in South Africa. Between 1990–2016, in the Middle East, the top 10% of income earners captured between 60%–66% of national income while the share of bottom 50% was less than 10%. Data also suggests that, in almost all economies, there has been a hollowing out of the middle class over the past few decades. It appears that the trajectory of inequality is for continuation of increased inequality. If so, the societies will begin to look "more like feudal societies where a small group of lords rule the economy" (Blasi *et al.*, 2014, p. ix). Aside from the consideration that large inequality in the face of widespread poverty and deprivation is morally objectionable, there is evidence that extreme inequality poses risk to governance, social cohesion, economic growth, and efforts at poverty alleviation.

Here-to-fore, societies have attempted to address inequality through tax transfer and, income redistribution policies. However, as data indicates, such policies have been unable to stop the increasing trajectory, much less stop and reverse the alarming trend. For this reason, recent debates have focused on alternatives that emphasize wealth redistribution. There is a close relationship between wealth and income distribution, especially in contemporary economies where the distribution of income has shifted in favor of wealth-holders and against the wage-earners. Data suggests that, as of 2016, "more than 70% of the world's adult owns under $10,000 in wealth. This 70.1% of the world holds only 3% of global wealth. The world's wealthiest individuals, those owning over $100,000 in assets, total only 8.6% of global population but own 85.6% of global wealth".[3] Based on this information, views have gained support among researchers that the problem of income inequality cannot be resolved without addressing the underlying problem of wealth inequality. Stiglitz (2015, 2017), for example, argues that negotiating new social contracts is crucial in order to reorient income and wealth distribution.

There are views that, given the present configuration of wealth–political power relationships in which the rich use their wealth to create laws and regulations that make it possible for them to increase their wealth and political power, it is not likely that the economically powerful would allow realignment of legislative, legal, and administrative institutions toward fairer and more just income and wealth distribution. Instead, such arguments hold that the solution, and possibly the only way to slow and eventually reverse the trend toward greater inequality is to increase the participation of citizens' share in asset acquisition. This would increase asset-holding and wealth-building which, in turn, expands income-earning capacity of the "have nots". This chapter will focus on these proposals and then consider Islamic solutions to the problem of inequality. The chapter begins with brief coverage of the position of the discipline of economics regarding inequality from mid-1950s to the present.

15.2 Mainstream Economics and Inequality

After decades of neglect (roughly from 1950s to about mid-1990s), the mainstream economics' attention to inequality has only recently intensified.[4] The popularity of research by Piketty (2014) and his associates has been one reason for intensification of global interest in the question of inequality. A question arises: why did mainstream economics neglect the question of income and wealth distribution? A compelling case can be made that the main reason for the neglect of inequality is the analytic framework of mainstream economics. Fundamental to this framework is the "model of man" as an acquisitive, intensely self-interested, non-cooperative, non-sympathetic individual with perfect foresight as well as the cognitive ability to choose among alternatives the one that served her/his self-interests the best. Such individuals participate in markets that are complete, i.e., every product and service has a market, by entering into complete contracts. The latter means that terms and conditions stipulated in contracts cover all contingencies. The framework is thought to be the stylized conception of the market economy envisioned by Classical economics. Mainstream economics taught that such an economy, with no state intervention,[5] had a social optimum; it was the job of economics to find that equilibrium for each society.

Between mid-1950s and mid-1970s, elegant theoretical models of such an economy were constructed and conditions for social optimum defined. The canonical model came to be known by the names of its most important intellectual contributors: the Arrow–Debreu–Hahn–McKenzi "competitive general equilibrium model".[6] Importantly, this model is thought by mainstream economics to be the analytic conception of Classical economics. However, the expectation of practical existence of the canonical model was deemed unrealistic due to the fundamental assumptions of complete markets and contracts of the canonical model. It has been argued that a first-best approximation of such an economy can exist practically provided that: (i) risk of the economy is shared among participants according to the ability of each participant to bear risk; and (ii) all securities in the capital market are "state contingent", meaning that the rates of return to these securities depend on the return to the underlying economic activity they represent. An example of such securities would be risk-sharing *sukuk* in Islamic capital markets.[7]

During the same period, two important postulates were advanced that, for all practical purposes, made consideration of distributional questions irrelevant to mainstream economics.[8] The first of these was the work of Kuznets (1955) on the relationship between economic development and inequality.[9] Based on a combination of empirical observations and theoretical construct, Kuznets postulated that, at the early stages of economic development, equality declines but as it proceeds, there will be a turning point and equality begins to improve. Two years later, Kaldor (1957) stylized its results into an economic growth model. One of the major assertions of this model was that the factor shares, those of labor and capital, remain constant throughout the process of development. This meant that the share of national income received by labor and capital remain constant overtime.[10] Twenty years later, Kuznets' postulate received major support from a young and bright economist, Montek Ahluwalia. Using a different methodology and cross-sectional data, Ahluwalia (1976) found empirical support for Kuznets U-curve. However, in the decades that followed, Kuznets' U-curve was severely challenged. Thereafter, a consensus emerged that no empirical support could be found for the inverse relationship between development and equality (Kanbur, 2012).

The second postulate posited as being responsible for mainstream economics' neglect of inequality is the "equality–efficiency trade-off" thesis. The idea comes from a paper by Okun (1975), in which a negative relationship between policies addressed to reducing inequality and efficiency was postulated. Astonishingly, for almost a decade and half, the idea went unchallenged without any attempt to find empirical support for the idea. When empirical studies confronted the idea, "the trade-off turned out to be more like a unicorn than hard science" (Bowles, 2012, p. 20). Not only empirical support for the idea was not forthcoming, research found that inequality had a negative impact on economic performance (Bowles *et al.*, 1990; Persson and Tabellini, 1994; Alesina and Rodrik, 1994).

15.3 Questioning the Axioms of the Mainstream Framework

Assault on the assumptions of mainstream economics started as early as the second half of the last century, with Herbert Simon's challenge of the model of man (Simon, 1947; 1957). Simon questioned the assumption that the economic man had perfect foresight with complete information that allowed that him to evaluate the choice of the best among alternatives. He argued that the cognitive capacity of humans is limited, information was costly, and future was unknown, and therefore uncertain. Under the assumptions of the framework, rational decision-making meant that the "economic man" had to know all the alternatives as well as the consequences of each alternative in order to choose the best among them. These, Simon said, were impossible conditions for humans to meet. Their rationality, he argued, is constrained by the availability of information, cognitive capacity, and time. These limitations impose a "bound" on human rationality. Hence, Simon argued, instead of perfect rationality, humans possess "bounded rationality" and in choosing among alternatives, their objectives have a threshold. They choose heuristic strategies to find the alternative that meets this threshold. Once satisfied with their choice, they stop searching. Hence, instead of searching for the alternative that "maximizes" their utility, they search for the one that "satisfies" them.[11]

The next element of the analytic framework of mainstream economics to come under scrutiny was the assumption of the economic man as non-cooperative, unsympathetic, self-interested being. Experimental economics showed that not only humans are cooperative, they are sympathetic, empathic (other-regarding) and engage in reciprocity (Bowles and Gintis, 2011). Moreover, behavioral experiments provided evidence that not only do humans share, even when amounts involved are high, they are willing to punish unfair behavior, even if it costs them to do so. Hence, humans display "inequality aversion" (Cameron, 1999; Abbink *et al.*, 1996; Fehr and Gaechter, 2000; Fong, 2001; 2007). Another set of assumptions of the analytic framework to be examined were complete markets and complete contracts. These assumptions meant that not only every product or service imaginable had a market of its own, every contract was entered into without costs and with the full willingness of the parties in transactions.

As early as 1931, John R. Commons had noted that transactions were the foundations of exchange and that these transactions were not costless. And in 1960, Ronald Coase called attention to "costs of market transaction". In the next three decades, a number of new fields developed in economics that had strong influence on and implications for the mainstream economics. Among these were the new fields of transactions economics (Williamson, 1981), information economics (Akerlof, 1970; Spence, 1973; Grossman and Stiglitz, 1980; see also Lofgren *et al.*, 2002), contract theory (Holstrom, 1979; Grossman and Hart, 1983; see also Hart and Holstrom, 1985); and game theory. The latter field had its beginning in 1944 with the publication of a book by John von Neumen and Oskar Morgnestern (*Theory of Games and Economic Behavior*, published by Princeton University Press). As a specific field of study, however, game theory economics, as a study of cooperative and conflictual human behavior in the market place, did not come into its own until the 1970s. Importantly, experimental research since then provide empirical evidence of the limitations of the assumptions of the "model of man" underlying mainstream economics. Information economics deals with the question of how information affects economic behavior. A specific question addressed in this field is on information asymmetries and their implications for the structure of transactions and design of contracts. Importantly, research in this field raised questions regarding the validity of assumptions of mainstream economics of costless transactions, perfect information, and complete contracts.

15.4 Theory of Contracts

This field is concerned with explaining the effects of the behavior of parties on the structure and design of contracts. Research in this field relate directly to two assumptions of mainstream economics: self-interest and complete contracts. Regarding the first assumption, contract theory suggests that when both parties to a contract are motivated by their own self-interests, there is very little incentive to enter into contracts that serve both parties. Indeed, under this assumption, some contracts become impossible. One such impossible contract is an interest rate-based debt contract. Under the self-interest assumption, there is no incentive for a debtor to repay such a debt. To make such impossible contract possible, economies have to create an incentive structure with positive and negative elements, such as tax incentives and punitive legal means, to enforce debt contracts.

Regarding the assumption of complete contracts, informational problems of principal–agent relations render contracts incomplete because the parties are unable to specify what the parties should do in future eventualities (Bolton and Dewatripont, 2004). Moreover, the assumption creates coordination problems, and the problem of organically aligning plans of the parties to a contract. For example, coordination problem exists in designing usual labor contracts since these contracts cannot include many factors, such as the level of required effort, honesty, and trust, that influence the actions of participants in an employment contract and impact their interest but cannot be covered by contracts. This is also the case with debt contracts. These contracts are enforceable only by a third party, governments exercising their coercive force, at high costs. In performing this function, governments, in effect, provide creditors with free insurance. Contract theory terms the conflict between the interests of the two parties to these contracts as principal–agent problems that lead to coordination failures and suboptimal result.

A major contention of the theory of contract is that principal–agent problems arise because the incentive structure of contracts is not efficient to elicit the kind of behavior from participants that can serve the interests of both parties to the contract. This idea gave birth to the field of incentive economics (Laffont, 2000), a discipline that searches for contract designs where both parties have sufficient incentives so that the contract can achieve efficient outcomes in terms of improving gains from exchange (as compared to contracts without an incentive structure). These types of contracts are referred to as "incentive-compatible contracts". Examples of such contracts are those in the labor and credit markets where agents become residual claimants, in effect becoming property rights owners (have "skin-in-the-game") and principals themselves. An example of the first type of contracts is one that allows labor to share in the profit of the firm (Weitzman, 1984). An example of incentive-compatible contracts in the credit markets is a risk-sharing contract where risks and rewards of contract are shared between parties (see Chapter 13). The major advantage of incentive-compatible contracts is that because agents become residual claimants, these contracts improve productivity. In effect, the incentive structure of these contracts elicits cooperation, coordination, truth telling, trust, hard work, and efficiency in resource use and management, factors that could not be written into pure principal–agent contracts and enforced. The arrangement modifies the governance structure of contracts, thus attenuating coordination problems which improve the efficiency of outcomes of economic undertakings. Contracts that are not incentive-compatible involve considerable transaction costs to design and enforce.

Incentive compatibility consideration is not limited to labor and capital markets, it can affect the macroeconomy as well as the whole society. In 1984, Weitzman showed how risk sharing arrangements can lead to economic stability and prosperity. In the last two decades of the 20th century, new institutional economics (NIE) achieved the status of a sub-discipline within economics. NIE contends that economic performance of countries depends much on their governance structures composed of rules governing economic behavior and their enforcement characteristics. These rules, according to NIE, determine the institutional "scaffolding" of the economy, usually contained in the countries' social contracts (North, 1990). Outcome of the workings of the social contract determines the distribution of income and wealth in the society. As mentioned earlier, Stiglitz (2015; 2017) asserted that the main reason for the massive inequality in the US is that the country's social contract has become impaired. The solution to inequality requires a new social contract that rewrites major rules (about 40, according to Stiglitz, 2015) contained in the institutional scaffolding of the economy and governing economic behavior. This idea is not limited in its application to the US only. It is especially relevant to countries in which inequality is even higher than the U.S., for e.g., the Middle Eastern countries and some in Asia, Africa, and Latin America, in which there is no workable social contract or one that is impaired considerably. In such societies, existing implicit or explicit social contracts have created poor governance structures that have, through time, become self-reinforcing.

Social groups that are privileged by poor governance have no incentive to allow reforms and changes in social contract that would provide for wider sharing of income and wealth. On the contrary, these groups have strong incentives to spend resources to maintain an inefficient and, more often than not, corrupt governance structure. Hence, there is strong inertia in countries with high inequality against fundamental changes, such as those suggested by Stiglitz, in social contracts. The inertia has created a feedback loop between increasingly poor governance and higher concentration of wealth. While hope for fundamental changes should be kept alive, search needs to continue for less radical but more effective solutions than those that have demonstrated their inability to stem the tide of massive inequality around the world.

15.5 How Did We Get Here?

There are a number of explanations concerning the massive inequality. As mentioned in Chapter 1, Keynes (and before him, Karl Marx) had argued that inequality is an inherent feature of market capitalism and suggested that government intervention, through its power of tax and spend, can mitigate forces of inequality. Piketty (2014) and others have shown that adoption of Keynesian policies, especially income redistribution, regulations of markets, and empowerment of labor unions, held back the march of inherent inequality of capitalism in many countries for about four decades. Deregulation policies of the 1980s and the 1990s "unchained" capitalism, resulting in the surge in income and wealth inequality. Stiglitz (2018) argues that globalization has accelerated the surge of inequality. However, it has become clear that there were a set of policies implemented during 1980s and 1990s across the world that left countries unprotected against globalization. These policies that were recommended by international financial institutions (IFIs) have become known as "liberalization policies" aimed at reducing the role of governments while increasing and strengthening the role of markets. An important element of these policies that had devastating consequences for poverty and income and wealth distribution was the weakening, and in some cases, the removal of social safety nets that had protected vulnerable groups for decades.

Theoretical and empirical bases of liberalization policies were laid during the 1980s and 1990s in parallel with the creation of fields of research in economics reviewed in previous sections of this chapter, but there were shifts of views on the policies needed to lead to prosperity. During the decades of 1950s to 1970s, the progress of countries was summarized in economic "development", and it was thought that the problem of "underdevelopment" was insufficiency of capital. Hence, emphasis was placed on mobilizing internal and external resources to accelerate investment and capital accumulation as the answer to "economic backwardness". Financial resources were not flowing to developing countries because the rates of interest (as the price for the use of financial resources) were suppressed. In the 1980s and 1990s, emphasis shifted to "getting-the-relative-prices-right". The idea was that the problem of "underdevelopment" was the distortions in relative prices that resulted in misallocation of resources.

It was argued that inefficiencies in allocation and use of resources were themselves results of wrong government policies, including government ownership of production facilities and widespread price and administrative subsidies to various sectors of the economy, government-directed sectoral allocation of banking credit, and constraints on internal and external trade as well as on money and capital markets. The most important distortion created as a result was that prices of resources deviated from their "true scarcity price", i.e., their opportunity costs. Policies recommended by the new thinking included reduction in the public sector's intervention in the economy, privatization of public enterprises, including in the education and health sectors, and removing all subsidies and constrains that impaired the free operation of the market. The collection of policies contained in the new thinking was referred to as "liberalization of the economy", which meant that the minimization of the role of government in the economy; allowing unrestrained working of all markets for resources, goods, and services; as well as the removal of constraints on external trade and financial and capital markets would allow prices of resources to converge to their opportunity costs. The theoretical foundation of "liberalization" policies was the general equilibrium competitive model, according to which a market economy with no government intervention will have a social optimum that will ensure equality of all relative prices.

An area which was subjected to aggressive liberalization policies was the financial sector. Initially, the recommendation to developing countries to liberalize their financial sector first and before other sectors was based on research by McKinnon (1973) and Shaw (1973) that argued there is massive distortion and misallocation of financial resources in developing countries due to directed lending and ceilings on interest rates. According to this view, there was, presumably, an equilibrium "market rate of interest" that cleared the market for financial resources. Government policies, such as directed lending and caps on interest rate, would "repress" the financial sector, force a deviation of actual interest rate from its market rate, and waste resources. The most important issue in relation to "financial repression" is the question of the benchmark compared to which one judges the financial sector to declare it repressed. That benchmark according to liberalization theory is the "market interest rate". However, in actuality, there is no such interest rate that comes about by the free interplay of forces of supply and demand. Interest rates that prevail in the market are determined by policies in countries that dominate international financial markets. It cannot be claimed that such rates are determined by either the true opportunity cost of financial resources or by any reasonable measure of the marginal productivity of these resources. The latter is a requirement of the free market, competitive general equilibrium model that lays at the foundation of liberalization policy recommendations.

It should be noted that all theories of interest rate determination are equilibrium theories of price determination as a result of interaction of forces of supply and demand, meaning that they are all ex-post theories.[12] Hence, these theories cannot explain the existence of fixed, predetermined rate of interest in an economy in which, ostensibly, market forces freely operate to equate prices of factors and products to their opportunity costs. The absurdity of the claim by the mainstream economics that a policy-determined rate of interest is "the market rate of interest", and thus represents the opportunity cost of financial resources, has never been as obvious as in the years following the financial crisis in which policy rates in a number of countries had been negative or zero. During the same period, the opportunity cost of financial resources, as measured by the rate of return to the real sector of the global economy, was estimated to have been at least 14% (see Bacha and Mirakhor, 2015). This significant deviation of the "market" rate of interest from its opportunity cost represents a sizable financial repression.[13]

During the decades of 1980s and early 1990s, the liberalization school generalized repression in the financial sector to all sectors to develop the idea of the need for policies in order to "get the prices right", especially in developing economies. Soon, the necessity of liberalization of developing economies became the central agenda of IFIs. The totality of these policies became known as the "Washington Consensus" (Williamson, 2004). To be sure, there were researchers who questioned both the underlying theory of the liberalization school and the idea of forcing developing countries to implement the liberalization policy advice of IFIs (see, for example, Diaz-Alejandro, 1985; Villanueva and Mirakhor, 1990; Akyuz, 1993). In the event, these objections were not taken seriously nor were the adverse results of the policies in countries where they had been implemented. These included increases in inequality, corruption and poverty, and deterioration of health and education. IFIs continued to push an even more aggressive model of liberalization, called the "big bang", according to which the entire economy was to be "liberalized" at once. Their best opportunity for implementation of such policies came in the 1990s with the fall of the Soviet Union and then the Asian Crisis. With a very few exceptions, Malaysia being one, a large number of countries accepted and implemented the policy recommendations of IFIs that resulted in instability and increased unemployment and poverty in the short and medium term and accelerated the increase in wealth and income inequality in the long run.

In the late 1990s and early 2000, policy debates extended liberalization ideas to the institutional scaffolding. Liberalization of economies by itself was no longer sufficient. Not only did economies have to be liberalized to "get-the-prices-right", policies were needed to "get-the-institutions-right". Policy recommendations focused on the reforms of the "rules of the game", including property rights, contract enforcement, and overall governance structure (Acemoglu and Johnson, 2005; Rodrik, 2000).

The shock of the financial crisis of 2007/2008 led to search for its underlying causes. Aside from technical reasons, attention was also focused on the general moral failure of financial institutions and other market players which, in their pursuit of greed, had betrayed their fiduciary responsibilities and had committed "economic crimes against humanity".[14] Hence, the policy recommendations' field widened to include advice to "get-the-values-right", meaning that aside from getting the prices and institutions right, there is a need for policy-makers to also keep paying attention to meta-economic values by designing their economic and financial policies in ways that preserve and develop values that relate to social, moral, and spiritual capital of the society. Research has demonstrated the damage that large inequality of income and wealth inflict on these values. Therefore, getting the distribution right through sharing of economic prosperity rather than allowing a small group to capture a lion's share of national income becomes an important objective of societies.

15.6 Destructive Effects of Inequality

Much has been said about the damages that high income and wealth inequality bring about. It erodes trust, damages social mobility for the present and future generations, increases social resentment, undermines effective governance, creates a "winner-takes-all" society, and leads to the breakdown of social solidarity (Kanbur and Stiglitz, 2015; Teuling, 2014). In effect, "inequality is a stealthy blade that is silently severing the social bond and simultaneously undermining social solidarity" (Rosanvallon, 2013). Moreover, inequality is "a cause of global imbalances, debt bubbles, and financial crises and undermines sustainable prosperity" (Dauderstat, 2014). Research has revealed that inequality undermines long-term growth prospects (Benabou, 1996; Kumhof and Rancier, 2010; Rajan, 2010; Cynamon and Fazzari, 2013). Piketty (2014) argued that not only inequality reduces long-term growth, but it also creates a situation whereby further growth reinforces further inequality. While research has shown that inequality constrains economic growth, it has also rejected the hypothesis of a trade-off between growth and equity (Ostry *et al.*, 2014). Moreover, research suggests that broad sharing of the fruits of economic growth supports long-term prosperity (Stiglitz, 2015).

Research by Piketty and his colleagues have revealed a paradox within mainstream economics. The data used in this research shows that overtime, the ratio of capital (wealth) to output has increased as has the rate of return to capital. However, the standard theory would suggest the opposite. That is, as stock of capital increases, the standard theory would expect that the rate of return to capital should decline. One explanation is that the rise in the rate of return to capital is rent, meaning that this is not return to productive capital; one that leads to real investment, increase in capital formation and productive capacity of the economy. Instead, it is return to financial capital that is not being employed in productive activities. Moreover, Piketty (2014) argues that much of the accumulated wealth is due to inheritance that, in recent years, has been allowed to be passed from one generation to next without being appropriately taxed or employed in productive activities. Instead, it was used in purchase of paper securities (representing existing debt securities or existing debt-based equity shares which do not help capital formation in the real sector). Moreover, in most countries, taxation of inheritance either does not exist or is very low. As accumulated wealth is inherited by the next generation, the problem of inequality is exacerbated as the pattern of income distribution is shaped by the distribution of inherited wealth. As OECD emphasizes, "higher inequality of incomes of parents tend to imply higher inequality of life chances of their children".

To achieve greater equality of opportunities without tackling increasing inequality in income will be very difficult (OECD, 2015; see also Kanbur and Stiglitz, 2015). Moreover, it appears that an inevitable consequence of high inequality is the wealthy in the society promoting a governance structure that leads to the capture of the state and its legislative and enforcement capabilities by them. Hence, the alliance of the wealthy and state institutions perpetuates and exacerbates inequality. This alliance damages and ossifies political processes and weakens the political system (Benabou and Tirole, 2006). The totality of the corrosive effects of inequality on the present and future societies is the reason Piketty argues for high income taxes (as much as 80%) as well as wealth and inheritance taxes in order to impose limits on rents collected by the wealthy on their unproductive capital.

In its 2011 report on inequality, OECD suggests that "Inequality raises political challenges because it breeds social resentment and generates political instability. It can also fuel populist, protectionist, and anti-globalization sentiments. People will no longer support open trade and free markets if they feel they are losing out while a small group of winners is getting richer and richer" (OECD, 2011, p. 40). Rosanvallon (2013, p. 4) asserts that "continued inequality in the extreme brings the society to the brink of breakdown and revolution". He reminds that it was the rampant inequality that gave rise to the demand for equality and became the "mother idea" and the "rallying cry" of the French Revolution. He sees similarities in the pathologies of the present inequality crisis and that of the first European inequality crisis initiated by the Industrial Revolution that reached its peak in the wake of the first globalization (1880–1900). The response to the first inequality crisis manifested itself in the form of nationalism, protectionism, and xenophobia. However, there is a paradox, Rosanvallon argues, that while surveys show discontent with the injustices of inequality in many societies, there is no concrete action to demand policies to address aggressively the problem of inequality. He asserts that "...a general sense that inequalities have grown 'too large' or even become 'scandalous' co-exists with tacit acceptance of many specific forms of inequality and with silent resistance to any practical steps to correct them. Widespread social discontent is thus associated with practical passivity in the face of generalized inequality" (p. 5).

15.7 What Can Be Done: Proposed Solutions

There are a number of solutions that have been advanced. A proposal by Stiglitz[15] was mentioned whereby societies (his focus is on the US, but his proposal is applicable to other countries) would need to renegotiate new social contracts which address directly questions of inequality and ensure that the fruits of prosperity are shared more equally to avoid emergence of a small group of wealthy individuals that capture a lion's share of countries' wealth while the greatest portion of population live in poverty and depravation. Another solution discussed above was that Piketty (2014), who proposed taxing income at high levels as well as taxing wealth and inheritance and redistributing to the rest of the population. These types of solution that focus on radical approaches to redistribution are referred to as "hard solutions". The challenge for these types of solutions is their political viability due to the phenomenon of "political capture".[16] As was mentioned above, the wealthy co-opt political processes and political institutions in order to perpetuate the distribution that favors them. Therefore, they do their utmost to perpetuate the present inequality. It is difficult to see what incentive structure could be devised in order to overcome the inertia against change, especially if existing political institutions and processes are to be involved, as expected to change laws to combat inequality. For this reason, a number of "soft solutions" have been proposed.[17] These solutions are termed "soft" because they do not challenge or require structural changes in, the existing political institutions or processes. Such proposals take the current distribution of income and wealth as given and focus on attenuating the income consequences of market operations by distributing results of additional growth more equally. One such "soft" solution is the program proposed by the World Bank.

15.7.1 *World Bank's Proposed Solution: Shared Prosperity Program*

Over the last few years, the World Bank has been advocating a set of policies whose implementation is to accelerate poverty alleviation as to the reduction of inequality gap. The program, referred to as "shared prosperity", aims at boosting the income levels of the bottom 40% of the population in member countries through more equal sharing of the economic growth. It should be noted that the "shared prosperity" program of the World Bank excludes income redistribution of income and wealth. According to the World Bank's Vice President for Poverty Reduction and Economic Management, "We are not suggesting that countries redistribute an economic pie of a certain size, or to take from the rich to give to the poor. Rather we are saying that if a country can grow the size of its pie, while at the same time share it in ways that boost the income of the bottom 40% of its population, then it is moving toward shared prosperity. So, the goal combines the notion of rising prosperity and equity".[18]

The statement of the World Bank Vice President implies that current income and wealth inequality has to be taken as given, meaning that the stock of inequality remains intact. The idea is that any additional growth should be shared more equally, especially with the bottom 40% of the population. According to this program, this should happen through public investment in health, education, infrastructure, financial inclusion, pro-poor transfers, and wage policies to reduce the impact of inequality. A question arises as to how different is this new program from that of the "trickled down" program of mainstream economics? World Bank's answer is that emphasis should be on policies that ensure that sharing of the fruits of growth is broad based; investments should be focused on job creation; economic opportunities should be broadened; and that the societies would need to commit to new social contracts that improve and equalize opportunities for all citizens. Given the earlier discussion that high inequality of income and wealth is directly related to the governance of societies that favor the wealthy and that the latter create an inertia against any change that improves income and wealth distribution, it is difficult to see what new incentives the World Bank's program offers this group to motivate them to either agree to a fairer distribution of the fruits of growth or, more importantly, allow a change in the social contract that favors more equal distribution. Moreover, as Piketty (2014) argues, wealth inequality leads to income inequality, which in turn leads to more wealth inequality. Thus, it would appear that without some income and wealth redistribution, there is low probability that the World Bank's program of shared prosperity would succeed in either promoting more equal distribution or making a significant dent in widespread poverty.

A related issue is the question of what constitutes "prosperity" and how to achieve "sharing". The root word of prosperity is the Latin word "prosperous," meaning progress in line with hopes and expectations. Currently, prosperity is taken to mean well-being manifested either as a state of "being" or "having". Over the last five decades, "having" has eroded the value of "being". Environmental, nutritional, social, economic, and political crises have brought home the idea that equating prosperity with high level of consumption, accumulation of material possession, and rising purchasing power need to be attenuated with the urgency of considering prosperity as a state of being. In this context, there are views that argue that reducing income inequality alone is not sufficient for prosperity in its latter meaning. For example, Sen (1992, p. xi) argues that we must "focus on our ability to achieve valuable functionings that make up our lives, and, more generally, our freedom to promote objectives that we have reason to value". Sen (1992, p. 5) defines "functionings" as ranging "from the most elementary ones, such as being well-nourished, avoiding escapable morbidity, and premature mortality, etc., to quite complex and sophisticated arrangements, such as having self-respect, being able to take part in the life of the community". To achieve the desired level of functioning, a person must have "capabilities", i.e., abilities, to function. A good society, Sen argues, is one which provides equality of capabilities as well as the equality of freedom to choose among alternative "capability set". This approach suggests that rather than focusing on equality of income and wealth, much attention should be paid to what people are able effectively to do and be.[19]

Rosanvallen (2013) looks beyond the present inequality, arguing that the stakes "are much larger. It is a whole era that is coming to an end: an era based on a certain conception of social justice...there is a collapse of a set of old ideas of justice and injustice" (2013, pp. 7, 9). Societies, he argues, must do a fundamental rethinking of equality "not merely as a measure of distribution of wealth" but as a rational concept "articulated in connection with three other notions: similarity, independence, and citizenship." (2013, p. 10). Similarity means that humans share some essential properties. Therefore, they are "alike", with remaining differences irrelevant to the relationship among them. Independence means considering members of the society equally as autonomous, i.e., without subordination and inequality in exchange. Finally, the third term, citizenship, suggests understanding equality as participation in "community membership and in civic activities".

15.7.2 *Targeting Wealth Inequality: Asset-based Redistribution*

Section 15.7.2 discussed proposals that look beyond inequality to fundamental societal changes whose consequences would be reduction in inequality. In this context, major proposals are those of Stiglitz that requires societies to renegotiate their social contract to reorient distribution toward more equality. Sen's proposal would focus attention on policies that would create opportunities to achieve capabilities of members of the society to be able to "function". This would require means that would guarantee life, nutritional, health, education, and security to function as involved members of the society. This proposal requires means of facilitating "having" as well as "being" to every citizen. Similarly, Rosanvallen argues that concern with inequality should go beyond income and wealth, and focus on ways and means needed to render each citizen an active and effective member of society and its civic activities. Aside from these proposals, most other direct solutions to inequality require income-based redistribution. In this context and as discussed above, Piketty proposes high-income taxation as well as taxation of wealth and inheritance, to be redistributed and transferred to the lower-income groups, as a solution to inequality. Aside from their political challenges, income-based redistribution proposals have well-known perverse incentive effects (see, for example, Bowles and Gintis, 1998). Theoretically, the arguments of these proposals hold that increasing the income of the poor through income distribution will stimulate aggregate demand that will then increase employment and income. However, empirical support for this claim is sparse (see, for example, Bowles and Boyer, 1995).

Perhaps the most important criticism of income-based redistribution proposals is that most of them leave the current wealth distribution mostly untouched and focus on taxing and transferring income. However, since in most societies use of resources are under the command of the wealthy, leaving current wealth concentration intact, means that the assets that constitute wealth receive the lion's share of rewards (rents) from market operations, as shown by research carried out by Piketty and his colleagues, thus, exacerbating income inequality rather than diminishing it. Moreover, by ignoring asset inequality, income-based redistribution proposals leave the underlying governance structure, as well as all inefficiencies associated with it at the microeconomic level such as coordination failure, intact. For a number of years, some economists have been proposing an asset-based redistribution (see, for example, Bowles and Gintis, 1995; Bowles, 2012; Blasi *et al.*, 2014). The major advantage of these proposals is that they do not involve radical, hard redistribution that challenge directly the political inertia in the system. Asset-based proposals' major claim is that income redistribution is productivity-dampening while asset-based distribution is productivity-enhancing. Whereas income redistribution leaves assets and wealth undisturbed, the asset-based approach redistributes assets and disregards income distribution. Because the asset-based approach increases productivity (see DeScioli *et al.*, 2017), it is thought that it would have a better chance of being implemented than the redistributive programs that do not.

What explains the claim that asset-based redistribution would be productivity-enhancing? The focus of these approaches is the governance structure: rules that govern and regulate the behavior of economic agents. Efficient governance possesses rules, constraints, and incentives that minimize or avoid coordination failures in economic activities. As we discussed earlier, coordination failures stem from independent plans and actions of individual agents that lead to less desirable outcomes, such as low productivity, that would otherwise be possible. The famous "the tragedy of the commons",[20] environmental degradation, and other cases of market failures such as unemployment are examples of coordination failures. Generally, governance structure of societies is expected to avoid the occurrence of coordination failures, and, if and when they do occur, to take action to correct them. In societies with high inequality, governments have no incentives to correct and attenuate coordination failures through public policy. As discussed earlier, the wealthy in these societies use enormous resources to manipulate the governance structure to set up laws and institutions that help them to perpetuate inequality but to allow them to accumulate more wealth. A weak government is preferred by the wealthy because a strong government can implement policies that enhance productivity by solving coordination problems that reduce inefficiencies that result from misallocation of resources by the wealthy. Since a governance structure determines allocation and uses of resources as well as the production of goods and services, the performance of an economy depends crucially on its governance structure. Inequality, therefore, constrains policies that can improve governance structure and enhance productivity and thereby the performance of the economy.

Concentrated asset ownership creates perverse incentives that reduce productivity. Asset-based redistribution approach proposes that focus should be placed on identifying dimensions of asset concentration that lead to these results and devise ways and means of reorienting these dimensions, such as ownership claims and the governance structure of contracts. Central to the solution is the broadening of asset ownership so that all participants in an economic contract, including labor, shareholders, entrepreneurs, and managers, can become residual claimants. Doing so would mean that coordination failures would be mitigated because it removes management — ownership-control (principal–agent problem) as a source of inefficiency since all participants in the contract would be shareholders and, therefore, principals, each sharing the risk of the activity. Such a change in the ownership and governance structure has positive incentive effects for reducing transactions costs, including information and monitoring costs that the usual vertical governance imposes on production. Aligning control with claims on the residual, meaning making each contract participants recipient of residual income, in effect, making each stakeholder owner. This attenuates coordination failure due to possession of private information since each stakeholder has incentive to share information with others in order to promote the good of all. Moreover, since each stakeholder has an incentive in promoting the efficiency in production, monitoring actions of participant become unnecessary thereby reducing costs of production since, as owners, all stakeholders become liable for the consequence of their actions.

One of the advocates of asset-based distribution is Bowles (2012),[21] who argues that highly unequal distribution of assets inhibits implementation of growth-enhancing governance structure for three reasons. First, asset-poor individuals cannot enter into contracts available to the wealthy. Asset-poor are often forced to accept fixed-price contracts that, from their perspective, are clearly suboptimal (for example fixed-wage and predetermined, fixed-rate loan contracts) rather than contracts with returns that are more in line with the scarcity value (opportunity costs) of their resources. Fixed-price contracts impose constraints on many dimensions of behavior that are highly productivity-enhancing, such as hard work, providing full information, promise keeping, trustworthiness, risk taking, solidarity, and cooperation. Because of measurement difficulties, it is often not possible to write contracts that include these dimensions. Even if it were possible to do so, monitoring them would be costly. Hence, these types of contracts lead often to coordination failure because they lack strong enough incentive structure to elicit maximum level of response from productivity-enhancing dimensions of behavior.

There are other inefficiencies of high asset concentration in terms of lost opportunities to would be entrepreneurs, innovators, and workers who could well increase output, employment, and income, but for being asset-poor are, according to evidence,[22] shut out of credit market (think small- and medium-size firms that are severely credit-constrained). Bowles (2012, p. 37) argues that "where contracts in financial markets are incomplete or are unenforceable, individuals lacking in wealth are either precluded from engaging in a class of contracts that are available to the wealthy, or enter into these contracts on unfavorable terms." The reason "why an individual's amount of wealth influences the kinds of contracts she can engage in is that only those with sufficient wealth can undertake projects on their own account, that is without borrowing. And, among those who borrow, those with more wealth borrow on better terms. This is because greater wealth on the part of the agent allows contracts which more closely align the objectives of the principal and agent. This is the case, for example, when the borrower has sufficient wealth to post collateral or put her own equity in a project, and therefore has greater incentive to supply effort, to adopt more prudent risk levels preferred by the leader (the principal), to reveal information to the principal, and to act in other ways that advance the principal's interest but that cannot be secured in a contract."

It is the contention of the asset-based redistribution that there is a class of contractual relationships (governance structure in economic exchange) that is incentive-compatible, enhances productivity, and generates higher levels of employment and income without creating or exacerbating income and wealth inequality. The chief characteristic of this class of contracts is that it reduces or eliminates the distinction between principal and agent in its governance structure since everyone participating in these contracts have "skin-in-the-game" (Rafi and Mirakhor, 2018). Asset-based redistribution, in effect, rewrites the property rights claim characteristic of vertical governance structure by allowing would-be agents to become principals, thereby creating a horizontal governance structure. This restructuring of governance structure creates space for would-be agents (or effectively silent principals, as is the norm in vertical governance structures where there is separation of management and control) to share in at least three crucial dimensions of property rights: (i) right to control access to assets; (ii) right to control disposition of assets (or their use); and (iii) right of claim to residual income from the use of assets. An example of this class of contracts is a joint partnership, where the ownership of an economic venture is shared between two or more partners. They share the property rights claim jointly and have joint claim on the residual income of the venture as well. These types of contracts are called "profit-sharing" or "profit-loss sharing" or "risk-sharing" contracts. As mentioned in Chapter 1, Weitzman (1984) proposed an incentive-compatible model of employment contracts in which labor would receive a base wage and share in the profit of the firm. While Weitzman's proposal allowed labor a share of the residual profit, it did not extend ownership or control claim to labor. While the asset-based redistribution proposals (Bowles, 2012; Kohler, 2015) make a compelling case for the superiority of the proposal as compared to income-based redistribution as a solution to the growing problem of inequality, it has not, as of yet, provided a detail blueprint of how to implement.[23] Section 15.8 focuses on risk sharing as propagated by Islamic finance as a solution to the inequality problem.

15.8 Inequality, Risk-Sharing Islamic Finance, and Capital Market

An Islamic approach to resolving the issues and problems of inequality and the asset-based redistribution proposal share common some features, especially the structural change in governance framework. There are also features that are different, most crucial being the fact that risk sharing does not just represent a class of contracts but is a fundamental organizing principle of an Islamic economy and its financial system. For such a system, capital markets become the core mechanism of allocation of financial resources because of the prohibition of the interest rate as the mechanism of allocation of financial resources. Hence, risk sharing Islamic finance severely curtails the operations of money markets since, by definition, money today is traded for more money in the future, which is also the basic definition of *al-riba* (but, also see Alaabed *et al.* (2016) on the performance of the present configuration of Islamic Banks). The other crucial characteristic of risk sharing Islamic finance is its requirement that returns to finance are determined by returns to the real sector of the economy. Hence the requirement of a close relationship between the financial sector and the real sector as contrasted with gradual separation between the two as a result of financialization and creation of a "paper economy." In an ideal Islamic capital market, where mechanisms such as short sales, margin buying, and trade in "paper securities" are absent, the only securities traded are those representing ownership claims to real (rather than purely financial paper claims) assets.

Before discussing the solution to inequality from an Islamic perspective, it is pertinent to ask whether and to what extent would inequality exist in an ideal Islamic economy?[24] To begin with, an analysis of the institutional structure (rules governing behavior of agents) of such an economy reveals hard constraints on the emergence of large income and wealth inequality. It is important to note that there is no insistence in the Qur'an or in the *Sunnah* on equality of income nor does one find prohibition against accumulation of wealth, provided that the wealth-holder has complied with all rules of behavior prescribed in the Qur'an. Among these rules are those that govern property rights, contracts, sharing, cooperation, consultation, interest rate-based debt contracts, market behavior, redistribution through charges imposed on income and wealth,[25] and inheritance (see Chapter 1). Crucially, the Qur'an prohibits accumulation of idle wealth and admonishes Muslims, directly and forcefully, to allow its circulation in productive activities (see Verses 34, 35: Chapter 9). Considering only three of these rules, prohibition on interest rate-based debt contracts, accumulation of idle wealth, and the laws of inheritance that break up even the legitimately acquired wealth at the time of the passing of the holder, it is not difficult to see how Islam mitigates wealth concentration. Additionally, rules governing market behavior, risk-sharing finance, contracts, cooperation, and redistribution that guarantees minimal but decent standard of living for all reinforce mitigation of emergence of high inequality. The operation of these rules leaves little doubt that the governance structure, whether at the societal macrolevel or at the level of firms, will have to be one of horizontal rather than vertical and authoritarian. Benefits of such governance structure have been mentioned above (Bowles, 2012).

The institutional scaffolding of such an economy, particularly the absence of interest rate-based debt contracts and the requirement of risk-sharing financial contracts, makes capital markets the central allocating mechanism of financial resources. Earlier chapters have shown how such capital markets can serve mobilization of financial resources through the use of risk sharing instruments and thereby increase employment, income, and balanced economic growth. Given the discussion presented in this section and other chapters of this book, the irony of ground-level facts that Muslim countries have one of the highest concentration of wealth, high incidence of poverty, and poor governance[26] could not be lost on anyone. It is a small wonder then that the uninformed will question the usefulness of Islam in managing contemporary societies. However, if and when Muslims themselves decide that the time has come to implement economic and social policies that reduce inequality and improve social justice, they will find the most enlightened and effective institutional scaffolding in their own heritage.

Summary

This chapter examined the potential role of capital markets in addressing a key contemporary issue: that of rising inequality. While economies have been growing quite impressively, the income gap between the rich and the poor has also widened. The chapter presented the arguments of economic thinkers for the cause of inequality. The thoughts of Kuznets, Stiglitz, Rosanvallon, and Piketty on the cause and possible solutions for inequality were discussed. It appears that much of the benefits of growth has accrued to a small portion while the majority of the population has seen little income growth. Such disparity is unacceptable, particularly from an Islamic viewpoint. The chapter makes the case that the key factor contributing to this widening income disparity is the current reliance on debt and debt-based financing. Accordingly, the risk sharing principles of Islamic Finance are presented as potential solution to rising inequality.

Questions and Problems

1. What conditions are needed for the existence of the Arrow–Debreu–Hahn–McKenzi "competitive general equilibrium model"?
2. What does Simon Kuznets postulate about the relationship between economic development and inequality?
3. Explain Herbert Simon's reservations about the "Economic Man"?
4. How essential is self-interest assumption to the theory of contracts?
5. Explain the "liberalization of the economy" and its implications.
6. Give some examples of the damages to society from income and wealth inequality.
7. What are the solutions proposed by Stiglitz on the issue of inequality?
8. What are the proposed solutions by Piketty?
9. What is the goal of the "shared prosperity" program?
10. List two differences between asset-based redistribution and income redistribution.
11. Discuss the solutions to inequality from an Islamic perspective.
12. In the asset-based redistribution proposal, what are the three crucial dimensions of property rights that would be agents could share?
13. Explain three reasons why Bowles argues that highly unequal distribution of assets inhibits implementation of growth-enhancing governance structure.
14. Explain the "tragedy of the commons".
15. What were the policies that led to the surge in income and wealth inequality?

Bibliography

Abbink, K., G. E. Bolton and F. F. Tang (1996). "Adaptive Learning versus Punishment in Ultimatum Bargaining." Discussion Paper No. B-381, Fridrich-Wohlms-Universtat Bonn, Rheinische.

Acemoglu, D. and S. Johnson (2005). "Unbundling Institution," *Journal of Political Economy*, Vol. 113, No. 5, pp. 949–995.

Ahluwalia, M. S. (1976). "Inequality, Poverty and Development," *Journal of Development Economics*, Vol. 3, No. 4, pp. 307–342.

Akerlof, G. (1970). "Market for Lemons: Quality Uncertainty and the Market Mechanism," *Quarterly Journal of Economics*, Vol. 8, No. 3, pp. 488–500.

Akyuz, Y. (1993). "Financial Liberalization: The Key Issues". UNCTAD, Discussion Papers, No. 56.

Alaabed, A., M. Masih and A. Mirakhor (2016). "Investigating Risk Shifting in Islamic Banks in the Dual Banking Systems of OIC Member Countries: An Application of Two-Stage Dynamic GMM," *Risk Management*, Vol. 18, No. 4, pp. 236–263.

Alesina, A. and D. Rodrik (1994). "Distributive Politics and Economic Growth," *Quarterly Journal of Economics*, Vol. 109, pp. 465–490.

Alverado, F., L. Chancel, T. Piketty, E. Saez and G. Zucman (2017). "Global Inequality Dynamics: New Findings from World Inequality Report," *American Economic Review*, Vol. 107, No. 5, pp. 404–409.

Bacha, O. I. and A. Mirakhor (2015). "A Risk-Sharing Banking Model." Paper presented at the *Inaugural Symposium on Islamic Economics and Finance*, Istanbul, Turkey, September 8–9.

Benabou, R. (1996). "Inequality and Growth," *NBER Macroeconomics Annual 1996*, Vol. 11, pp. 1–72.

Benabou, R. (2000). "Unequal Societies: Income Distribution and the Social Contract," *American Economic Review*, Vol. 53, pp. 641–973.

Benabou, R. and J. Tirole (2006). "Belief in a Just World and Redistributive Politics," *Quarterly Journal of Economics*, Vol. 121, No. 2, pp. 699–746.

Blasi, J. R., R. B. Freeman and D. L. Kruse (2014). *The Citizen's Shar: Reducing Inequality in the 21st Century* (Yale University Press, New Haven).

Bolton, P. and M. Dewatripont (2004). *Contract Theory* (MIT Press, Cambridge).

Bowles, S. and R. Boyer (1995). "Wages, Aggregate Demand and Employment in an Open Economy: A Theoretical and Empirical Investigation." In G. Epstein and H. Gintis (eds.), *Macroeconomic Policy after the Conservative Era: Research on Investment, Saving and Finance* (Cambridge University Press, New York). Chapter 5, pp. 236–264.

Bowles, S. and H. Gintis (1998). *Efficient Redistribution: New Rules for Markets, States and Communities* (Department of Economics, University of Massachusetts, Amherst).

Bowles, S. (2012). *The New Economics of Inequality and Redistribution* (Cambridge University Press, New York).

Bowles, S., D. M. Gordon and T. Weisskopf (1990). *After the Wasteland* (M. E. Sharp, Amrok, New York).

Bowles, S. and H. Gintis (2011). *A Cooperative Species: Human Reciprocity and Its Evolution*. (Princeton University Press, Princeton).

Cameron, L. A. (1999). "Raising Stakes in the Ultimatum Game: Experimental Evidence from Indonesia," *Economic Inquiry*, Vol. 37, No. 1, pp. 47–59.

Corning, P. (2011). *The Fair Society* (University of Chicago Press, Chicago).

Cynamon, B. Z. and S. M. Fazzari (2013). "Inequality and Household Financing During the Consumer Age." Working Paper No. 752, Levy Institute, Annandale-on-Hudson, New York.

Dauderstat, M. (2014). "Shared Prosperity in Emerging Economies: From Paradigm Shift to Reality Shaft." Working Paper, Friedrich Ebert Stiflung.

DeScioli, P., A. Shaw and A. W. Delton (2017). *Share the Wealth: Redistribution Can Increase Economic Efficiency.* Pdescioli.com/papers/descioli.shaw.delton.redistribution.pb.inpress.pdf.

Diaz-Alejandro, C. (1985). "Good-Bye Financial Repression, Hello Financial Crash," *Journal of Economic Development*, Vol. 19. No. 1–2, pp. 1–24.

Fehr, E. and S. Gaechter (2000). "Fairness and Retaliation: The Economics of Reciprocity," *Journal of Economic Perspectives*, Vol. 14, No. 3, pp. 159–181.

Fields, G. (2001). *Distribution and Development: A New Look at the Developing World* (Russel Sage Foundation, MIT Press, Cambridge).

Fong, C. (2001). "Social Preferences, Self-interest and the Demand for Redistribution," *Journal of Public Economics*, Vol. 82, No. 2, pp. 225–246.

Fong, C. (2007). "Evidence from an Experiment on Charity to Welfare Recipients: Reciprocity, Altruism and Empathic Responsiveness Hypothesis," *Economic Journal*, Vol. 117, No. 522, pp. 1,008–1,024.

Grossman, S. and J. E. Stiglitz (1980). "On the Impossibility of Informationally Efficient Markets," *American Economic Review*, Vol. 70, No. 3, pp. 393–408.

Grossman, S. and O. Hart (1983). "An Analysis of the Principal-Agent Problem," *Econometrica*, Vol. 51. No. 1, pp. 7–45.

Hart, Oliver and Bengt Holstrom (1985). Theory of Contracts. Paper presented at the World Congress of Econometric Society held in Cambridge, Massachussets.

Holmstrom, B. (1979). "Moral Hazard and Observability," *Bell Journal of Economics*, Vol. 10, No. 1, pp. 74–91.

Kaldor, N. (1957). "A Model of Economic Growth," *Economic Journal*, Vol. 67, No. 67, pp. 591–624.

Kanbur, R. (2012). "Does Kuznets Still Matter?" Cornell University Working Paper, 2012–2012-1, Ithaca, New York.

Kanbur, R. and J. E. Stiglitz (2015). "Wealth and Income Distribution: New Theories Needed for New Area," Vox: CPER, August 18.

Kohler, Pierre. (2015). "Distributive Policies for Sustainable Development: Looking at the Role of Assets and Equity." United Nations Department of Economics and Social Affairs Working Paper N0. 139. ST/ESA/2015/DWP/139.

Kumhof, M. and R. Rancier (2010). "Inequality, Leverage and Crises." Working Paper No. WP/10/268, International Monetary Fund, Washington, D.C.

Kuznets, S. (1955). "Economic Growth and Income Inequality," *American Economic Review*, Vol. 45, No. 1, pp. 1–28.

Laffont, J. J. (2000). *Incentives and Political Economy* (Oxford University Press, Oxford).

Lofgren, Karl-Gustaf, Torsten Persson and Jorgen W. Weibull (2002). "Markets with Asymmetric Information: The Contributions of George Akerlof, Michael Spence and Joseph Stiglitz," *Scandinavian Journal of Economics*, Vol. 104, No. 2, pp. 195–211.

McKinnon, L. I. (1973). *Money and Capital in Economic Development* (The Brookings Institution, Washington, D.C.).

North, D. (1990). *Institutions, Institutional Change, and Economic Performance* (Cambridge University Press, New York).

OECD (2011). *An Overview of Growing Income Inequalities in OECD Countries: Main Findings* (OECD Publications, Paris).

OECD (2015). *In it Together: Why Less Inequality Benefits All* (OECD, Paris).

Okun, A. (1975). *Equality and Efficiency: The Big Trade-Off* (Brookings Institution Press, Washington D.C.).

Ostry, J., A. Berg and C. Tsangarides (2014). "Redistribution, Inequality, and Sustainable Growth." VOX, Centre for Economic Policy Research (CEPR) Policy Portal, March 6.

Persson, T. and G. Tabellini (1994). "Is Inequality Bad for Growth?" *American Economic Review*, Vol. 48, pp. 600–621.

Piketty, T. (2014). *Capital in the Twenty-First Century* (Harvard University Press, Cambridge).

Rafi, U. and A. Mirakhor (2018). *Antifragility of Islamic Finance: The Risk-Sharing Alternative* (Peter Lang, New York).

Rodrik, D. (2000). "Institutions for High Quality Growth". NBER Working Paper Series No. 7540, Washington, D.C.

Rajan, R. G. (2010). *Fault Lines* (Princeton University Press, Princeton).

Rosanvallen, P. (2013). *The Society of Equals* (MIT Press, Cambridge).

Sen, A. (1973). *On Economic Inequality* (Clarendon Press, Oxford).

Sen, A. (1992). *Inequality Reexamined* (Harvard University Press, Cambridge).

Shaw, E. S. (1973). *Financial Deepening in Economic Development* (Oxford University Press, New York).

Spence. M. A. (1973). "Job Market Signaling," *Quarterly Journal of Economics*, Vol. 83, No. 3, pp. 355–377.

Simon, H. A. (1947). *Administrative Behavior*, First Edition (Macmillan, New York).

Simon, H. A. (1957). *Models of Man, Social, and Rational: Mathematical Essays on Rational Human Behavior in Social Setting* (John Wiley, New York).

Stiglitz, J. E. (1987). "The Causes and Consequences of Dependency of Quality on Price," *Journal of Economic Literature*, Vol. 25, No. 1, pp. 1–48.

Stiglitz, J. E. (2002). "Information and the Change in Paradigm in Economics," *American Economic Review*, Vol. 92, No. 3, pp. 460–501.

Stiglitz, J. E. (2012). *The Price of Inequality: How Today's Divided Society Endangers our Future* (W. W. Norton, New York).

Stiglitz, J. E. (2015). *Rewriting the Rules of the American Economy: An Agenda for Growth and Shared Prosperity* (Roosevelt Institute, New York).

Stiglitz, J. E. (2017). "Wealth and Income Inequality in the Twenty-First Century." Presented at the *18th Annual Meeting of the International Economic Association World Congress*, Santa Fe, Mexico, June 19–23, 2017.

Stiglitz, J. E. (2018). *Globalization and its Discontents Revisited* (W. W. Norton, New York).

Teuling, C. (2014). "Why Does Inequality Grow? Can We Do Something About It? VOX, CEPR's Policy Portal, June 15.

Villanueva, D. and A. Mirakhor (1990). "Strategies for Financial Reforms," *IMF Staff Papers*, Vol. 37, No. 3, pp. 509–536.

Weitzman, M. (1984). *The Share Economy* (Harvard University Press, Cambridge).

Weitzman, M. and D. Kruse (1990). "Profit Sharing and Productivity." In A. Blinder (ed.), *Paying for Productivity: A Look at Evidence* (Washington, D.C.: The Brookings Institution), pp. 95–142.

Williamson, J. (2004). "A Short History of Washington Consensus." Paper presented to the conference *Toward a New Global Governance*, Barcelona, Spain, September 24–25, 2004.

Willamson, O. E. (1981). "The Economics of Organization: The Transactions Cost Approach," *American Journal of Sociology*, Vol. 87, pp. 548–577.

Wilkinson, R. G. and K. E. Pickett (2009). "Income Inequality and Social Dysfunction," *Annual Review of Sociology*, Vol. 35, pp. 493–511.

Endnotes

1. The most common measure of inequality, which is the Gini coefficient, indicates the extent to which a society's distribution of income deviates from perfect inequality at zero. A Gini Coefficient of one represents perfect inequality, where all the nation's income accrues to one person.
2. Available at: wir2018.wid.world/files/download/wir2018.
3. Available at: https://inequality.org/facts/global-inequality)
4. At the margin of mainstream economics, to be sure, there have been scholars concerned with inequality. An example is Amartya Sen, who has been writing regarding inequality and poverty since the 1970s (see, for example, Sen, 1973; 1992). Worth mentioning are the various research and policy work of the World Bank on poverty and inequality. Socialist economics has always been concerned with inequality from its beginning to the present.
5. The assumption of "no government intervention" is derived directly from the mainstream economics' model of man which would make this intervention unnecessary for a market economy in which participants were assumed omnipotent and rational who knew what best served their self-interests.
6. For a brief discussion of the characteristics of this model, see Chapters 1 and 13.
7. See Chapter 13 and Bacha *et al.* (2016) for the design characteristics of such *sukuk.*
8. With the exception of discussions of welfare economics which held that those who were hurt by economic policies should be compensated. But even here, some held that such compensation is not necessary so long as these policies resulted in highest welfare for the collective society.
9. Represented by equality U-curve or inequality inverse U-curve.
10. A number of research work by Piketty, especially his famous book (2014), and others showed that this assertion was counterfactual.
11. Works of Simon have been credited with providing the impetus for the beginning of two new fields in economics: behavioral and cognitive economics.
12. This means that, just like the process of market determination of prices of all other goods and services in the market, interest rate, as the equilibrium price of financial resources, is determined after the demand and supply have interacted in the market and only after the market for financial resources is "cleared".
13. Compelling arguments have been made that the main cause of existence of this financial repression has been the official creation of central banking and the fractional banking system beginning in the U.K. in mid-1880s and adopted by all economies over the next 50 years. This system was challenged in the U.S. during the Great Depression by a group of economists, most of whom were faculty members of the economics department of the University of Chicago, but also included Fisher from Yale University. This group offered a plan for restructuring the banking system of the U.S. called the Chicago Plan. The issue was forgotten until the 1990s and especially after the financial crisis (see Chapters 1 and 13).
14. See Zuboff, S. (2009). "Wall Street's Economic Crimes against Humanity," *NewsWeek*, March.
15. See also his new book, Stiglitz, J. E. (2018). *Globalization and its Discontents Revisited* (W. W. Norton, New York).

16. See OXFAM (2014). "Working for the Few: Political Capture and Inequality". Available at: http://www.oxfam.org/sites/www.oxfam.org/files/bp-working-for-few-political-capture-economic-inequality-2014-en.pdf. See also, McKay, A. (2009). "Assets and Chronic Poverty: Background Paper," Chronic Poverty Research Centre, Working Paper No. 100, University of Sussex.
17. For an excellent coverage of this topic see Akin, T. (2017). "Wealth Inequality and Risk Sharing." PhD Dissertation, INCEIF, Kuala Lumpur, Malaysia.
18. Speech by Mr. Jaime Saaveda-Chanduvi, World Bank, Washington D.C., May 8, 2013.
19. For a list of requirements of human well-being, see Corning (2011), Chapter 5, pp. 87–111.
20. The tragedy of the commons occurs in case of resources, products, public goods whose ownership is held in common and not specifically assigned to particular individuals or groups. Each individual acting independently use such resources in accordance with their own self-interests behave against the common good. The concept was originally developed in relation to pastures that were commonly used by a group of herders. In 1968, Garret Hardin articulated the concept observing how cattlemen destroyed a common pastureland. See Garret Hardin, 1968. "The Tragedy of the Commons". *Science*, vol. 162, pp. 1,243–1,248.
21. For a detailed discussion, see Akin (2017).
22. See, for example, Holtz-Eakin, D., D. Joulfaian and H. S. Rosen (1994). "Sticking It Out: Entrepreneurial Survival and Liquidity Constraints," *Journal of Political Economy*, Vol. 102, No. 1, pp. 53–75; Guiso, L., T. Jappelli and D. Terlizzese (1996). "Income Risk, Borrowing Constraints, and Portfolio Choice," *American Economic Review*, Vol. 81, No. 1, pp. 158–172; Gross, D. and N. Souleles (2002). "Do Liquidity Constraints and Interest Rates Matter for Consumer Behavior? Evidence from Credit Card Data," *Quarterly Journal of Economics*, Vol. 117, No. 1, pp. 149–185; Banerjee, A. and E. Duflo (2010). "Giving Credit Where Credit Is Due," *Journal of Economic Perspective*, Vol. 24, pp. 61–79.
23. An interesting exception is a proposal by the Institute for the Future of Palo Alto, California. See Gorbis, M. Universal Basic Assets: Manifesto and Action Plan. Available at: www.iftf.org. Accessed October 23, 2018.
24. An ideal Islamic economy operates within and institutional framework elements of which are drawn from the Qur'an and Sunnah. For detailed discussion, see Mirakhor, A. and H. Askari (2018). *Ideal Islamic Economy: An Introduction* (Palgrave Macmillan, New York).
25. To see how fiscal policy (tax and transfer) works according to Islamic teachings, refer to Othman, A. *et al.* (2017). *Macroeconomic Policy and Islamic Finance in Malaysia* (Palgrave Macmillan, New York).
26. See Askari, H., H. M. Khan and L. Mydin (2017). *Reformation and Development in the Muslim World* (Palgrave Macmillan, New York).

INDEX